COLLAPSE OF THE BRONZE AGE

COLLAPSE OF THE BRONZE AGE

THE STORY OF GREECE, TROY, ISRAEL, EGYPT, AND THE PEOPLES OF THE SEA

Manuel Robbins

Authors Choice Press
San Jose New York Lincoln Shanghai

Collapse of the Bronze Age
The Story of Greece, Troy, Israel, Egypt, and the Peoples of the Sea

All Rights Reserved © 2001 by Manuel Robbins

No part of this book may be reproduced or transmitted in
any form or by any means, graphic, electronic, or mechanical,
including photocopying, recording, taping, or by any
information storage or retrieval system, without the
permission in writing from the publisher.

Authors Choice Press
an imprint of iUniverse, Inc.

For information address:
iUniverse, Inc.
5220 S. 16th St., Suite 200
Lincoln, NE 68512
www.iuniverse.com

ISBN: 0-595-13664-8

Printed in the United States of America

Contents

Preface vii
Acknowledgments xi
1 Introduction 1
2 Battle at Kadesh 22
3 Hittites Build an Empire 33
4 Homer and the War at Troy 62
5 Evidence of Troy 85
6 Collapse of the Mycenaean World 108
7 What Happened in Greece 130
8 Sea Peoples Attack Egypt 146
9 Invaders and the Hittite Evidence 169
10 Collapse of the Hittite Empire 191
11 Cyprus, Destruction and Renewal 204
12 Sea Peoples and Cyprus 220
13 Israel and Canaan 240
14 Origin of the People of Israel 261
15 Last Attack of the Sea Peoples 278
16 Homeland of the Invaders 297
17 Origin of the Philistines 315
18 Aftermath 337
Appendix 347
Quotations and Illustrations 357
Bibliography and References 363
Index 409

Preface

The Bronze Age was a time of remarkable cultural and material accomplishment. The great pyramids, the skillful sculpture and imposing temples of Egypt, the palaces of Greece with rich and colorful frescos, the temples of Babylonia reaching skyward, the small arts of every description were but a part of the material manifestations of this, the first era of civilization. Trade linked lands from Greece through Anatolia (present-day Turkey), Syria, Mesopotamia, Canaan, and Egypt in a network of mutual benefit. In the decades around 1250 BC, the Bronze Age world was stable, secure, sure of itself.

Then in a time close to 1200 BC, a series of remarkable events began. These events changed forever the landscape of civilized nations. Greek civilization was severely damaged, and then descended into an ultimate collapse. Hittite power in Anatolia was destroyed, and the once mighty Hittites were never again to appear on the world stage. Life in Cyprus and the Syrian coast was severely disrupted as cities were abandoned or destroyed. The coasts of Egypt and Canaan were assaulted and the Nile mouth invaded. Egypt survived, but sank into a profound decline. When these events had worked to completion, a new chapter in history had opened.

Hardly anything of the past is more mysterious than the circumstances that brought the Bronze Age to this end. For more than a century, scholars have attempted to understand what happened in those times. Hard evidence is meager, though theories are plentiful. The most dramatic and far-reaching of these theories is that invaders from northern or central Europe—barbarians as some have called them—driven southward by forces the nature of which can only be guessed, swept across Greece causing extensive destruction. According to this theory, they entered Anatolia and then proceeded down the Syrian coast, pillaging and burning, and finally throwing their barbarian might against Egypt. Some scholars picture this as a great population movement involving whole peoples, and they speak with assurance about "the great migrations."

In a less wide-ranging variant of the theory, Greece and the Hittite lands were attacked by barbarians from the north, but the destruction in Cyprus, Syria, and Egypt were due to others, to desperate people pushed forward by the European invaders. Whatever the cause, the evidence of destruction is widespread.

At the time of the disturbances, a mysterious group of people appeared, the Peoples of the Sea. Their ships dominated the waters off the coasts of Syria. They were present in Cyprus. Their assaults on Egypt are described and vividly pictured on monuments in Egypt which bear the only extended texts dealing with these great disturbances. Some historians believe that the Peoples of the Sea were the vanguard of the assumed migration from Europe, and hold them responsible for the catastrophes that ended the age. Much about the Sea Peoples is lost in the obscurity of time, but what is certain is that one group of the Peoples of the Sea settled on the coast of Canaan. We know them as the Philistines.

Until the discoveries of modern archaeology, these dramatic events were hardly known. Only two occurrences of those remote and turbulent times had been retained in the cultural memory of the modern world. These were the Trojan War and the Exodus, immortalized in the two greatest literary works of the distant past, *Iliad* and the Bible. But even these works are silent concerning the larger historical context in which these events took place.

In spite of widely believed theories, much remains uncertain. Were there really great invasions or migrations that damaged or destroyed civilizations at the end of the Bronze Age, as many scholars believe? What is the evidence of destruction? Who were the Peoples of the Sea and from where did they come? Was there a Trojan War, as nearly all ancient Greeks believed, and did ancient Israel originate as a result of an Exodus from Egypt? These are among the most fascinating and controversial questions that relate to the close of the Bronze Age.

The problem of evidence of those remote times is formidable. As one scholar (*Barnett, 1975*) has noted: "If we wish to obtain a picture of this period of sudden decline and collapse, we have to be content to pick our way through a bewildering tangle of evidence, much of it highly fragmentary, much of it highly conjectural and insecure."

By far the best evidence is provided by surviving Bronze Age texts. Some few informative texts have been found engraved on monuments in Egypt and on clay tablets in the ruins of several ancient cities. Unfortunately, what remains from those times is uneven in coverage, and it is not possible to obtain from them a comprehensive and connected story. Worse, for the crucial years around 1200 BC, surviving texts are very few. In most of the lands affected by the great disruptions, no contemporary texts at all have been found.

When there is insufficient text, it is necessary to depend on the mute evidence produced by archaeological excavation, the evidence of the spade. But such evidence requires interpretation, and that is where serious problems may arise. The archaeologist excavates and finds remains dating to the very end of the Bronze Age. Tumbled walls are found, and charred wood and broken pottery. Are these evidence of purposeful destruction? What was the date of the destruction? Who were the destroyers? Unfortunately, interpretation of evidence is not a science. Conclusions may differ, even among experts who study the same evidence. Further, when the excavation evidence is considered together with text evidence–if any such text evidence exists—even greater controversy may arise.

In these circumstances, it is surprising to find that much of the writing about this period tends to excessive certainties. The many shifts of scholarly opinion and interpretation over the years–hardly justified by any new evidence—demonstrates that much of what passes for history of the end of the Bronze Age are structures built on shifting sands. In view of this, it is the intention in this book to describe, so far as it is possible, the events of those times and to examine the evidence anew.

The plan of this book is essentially as follows. The first chapter briefly introduces the reader to Bronze Age civilization, chronology, and the important ethnic groupings of that time, as will be helpful for the later chapters. Following is a discussion of the Battle of Kadesh. That serves to introduce the Hittites and the Egyptians, and several other peoples of the period. The Battle of Kadesh, which led to an enduring peace near the end of the Bronze Age, serves as a political and social backdrop of the final disintegration. A following chapter is devoted to the Hittites and also introduces the peoples of western Anatolia who will play a role in later discussions. Among those peoples are the Trojans. In view of the importance of the story of the Trojan War in the culture of Western civilization, Homers tales are examined at length in order to locate the Trojan War in a historic context.

With that foundation, the further destructions in those times are reviewed. The collapse of Greek civilization, the destruction and abandonment in Cyprus, the vanishing of the Hittites, and the destruction of Ugarit are examined. The Peoples of the Sea are introduced and their attacks on Egypt investigated.

It was in the circumstances of those times that the Exodus from Egypt may have occurred and that Israel began to be defined as a people in Canaan. In view of the central role that the Bible has in Western civilization, the origin of the Israelites and the beginnings of Israel are considered in detail.

The book moves toward a conclusion with the description of the final attack of the Peoples of the Sea on Egypt. Through this attack, the Philistines emerge for the first time in history, and it was then that they and Israel were set on the road to a destined collision. The origin of the Sea Peoples, and the Philistines in particular, are the subject of great interest and vigorous debate. The problem is taken up anew, and new conclusions are presented concerning their origin. A final chapter deals with the aftermath of the crisis years.

Style

The majority of readers do not require footnotes or in-text references and are put off by them. For that reason, footnotes are omitted and references are held to a minimum. For students and others who wish to delve further, an extensive list of references is provided at the end of the book with keys that indicate the relevant content.

Conventional spellings of Greek, Egyptian, and Biblical names are used. However, there are no established conventions for Bronze Age Anatolian names (people and places). Here, the simplest spelling is usually employed, and "*s*" is used in place of "*sh*" where it is uncertain which sound the ancient texts really intended. Names from the "Amarna letters" come predominantly from Syria and Canaan, and again, there are no standardized spellings. Here, spellings from a work by Moran are used (Moran 1992, see references). The works of Homer are frequently mentioned here. With constant repetition, the definite article begins to be wearing. It is unnecessary and is omitted. Thus, references here are to *Iliad,* and not repeatedly to *the Iliad.* That omission is in accord with the usage of M. Hadas, Jay Professor of Greek at Columbia University (Hadas, 1950).

Acknowledgments

A number of scholars have helped me by supplying needed information, or by reading and reviewing drafts of chapters. I extend thanks to all listed below. Responsibility for this text, however, is entirely mine, and none listed below can be held accountable for any fault that may be found with this work.

I wish to acknowledge, with gratitude: Professor Mike Baillie, Queens University, Belfast; Richard Beal, Oriental Institute University of Chicago; Birgit Brandau; Annie Caubert, the Louve; Professor Getzel Cohen, University of Cincinnati; K. L. Gage, CDC-Division of Vector-borne Infectious Diseases; Professor Allan Gilbert, Fordham University; Professor Oliver Gurney of Oxford; Professor Sigrid Jalkotzy, Universitat Salzburg; Barbara Kling; Professor Dietrich Koppenhofer, Eberhard-Karls-University; Professor Peter Kuniholm, Cornell University; Carter Lupton, Milwaukee Public Museum; Sturt Manning, University of Reading; Professor Amihai Mazar, Hebrew University; Professor Kyle McCarter, Johns Hopkins University; Professor Machteld Mellink, Bryn Mawr College; William Moran; Amit Romano, Haifa University; Professor Brian Rose, University of Cincinnati; Professor G. Kenneth Sams, University of North Carolina; Professor Alan Schulman; Professor Shelley Wachsmann, Institute of Nautical Archaeology, University of Texas.

Special thanks are extended to Elizabeth Townsend for providing the art work which illustrates the citadel of Troy, and to Patricia McCart-Malloy, who provided certain original drawings. Detailed sources for art and quotations will be found before the bibliography.

Thanks are also extended to my wife, Renee Robbins; to Elaine Robbins, copy editor of the text; to Helen Brumbaugh of the Cherry Hill Library and to the library systems of the University of Pennsylvania and Bryn Mawr College.

1
INTRODUCTION

The events that will be described took place in a remote time: the Bronze Age and its immediate aftermath. It was a period which may be unfamiliar to some readers, and may therefore be difficult to place on a "mental map." When was that period? Where did those events take place and who were the peoples involved?

The term "Bronze Age" came into use in the nineteenth century. Scandinavian archaeologists observed in their excavations that the earliest implements found were fashioned of stone, those of a later time of bronze, and still later of iron. From these observations they proposed the terms Stone Age, Bronze Age and Iron Age, the so-called Three Age System. These archaeologists may have been inspired in part by the early Greek poet Hesiod and his concept of ages. Hesiod writes:

> First, all the deathless gods who dwell on Olympos made a golden race of mortal men....and they lived like gods without sorrow....Then those who dwell on Olympos made a second generation which was of silver and less noble by far....Zeus the Father made a third generation of mortal men, a brazen race... in no way equal to the silver age but terrible and strong....Their armour was of bronze, their houses were of bronze, and bronze were their implements. These were destroyed by their own hands and passed to the dank house of chill Hades....And again, Zeus made yet another generation....For now truly is a race of iron, and men never rest from labor and sorrow by day and from perishing by night. (Hesiod)

Hesiod was concerned with the moral degeneration of mankind, but the sequence in his metaphor is a reasonably accurate representation of the order in which metals came into use. Gold was the first metal worked by man, since it could be found in metallic form and did not require chemical separation from its ores. Copper, not mentioned by Hesiod, was probably second, closely followed by lead and silver. But it was bronze which gave the name to the Age. Bronze is an alloy of copper with arsenic or more commonly with tin.

How the alloying process was discovered is a mystery, but tin-bronze proved to be easy to cast in various forms. As the Bronze Age progressed, bronze was pressed into more uses—knife blades, axes, arrowheads, spear points, swords, armor, caldrons and cooking ware, statuary, and a variety of everyday hardware. Finally, iron came into use.

Though the development of bronze was important, the real significance of the term Bronze Age is that civilization first blossomed in that period from seeds set earlier, in the Neolithic or Late Stone Age. It was in the Neolithic that agriculture began, the greatest discovery or invention of mankind. Agriculture fixed man in one place for a season or longer, and with food in excess of need, for part of the time at least, time and energy could be given to the development of crafts. Stone was worked with increasing skill, resulting in implements which, in some cases, were of exquisite craftsmanship and beauty. Animals were domesticated, and wool began to be used in the weaving of fabrics. Even beautiful pottery was made during the Neolithic period. While it was not the golden age of Hesiod, to some degree the Neolithic was a period of freedom from constant want.

How civilization should be defined, and how it developed from a Neolithic foundation are matters in dispute. It was not a matter of refined manners and high sensibilities, but of the development of certain social and economic structures. It was typified by an increased stratification of society and the emergence of powerful elites—kings, military leaders, leading priests, among others—who had managed to gain control of much of the wealth. That wealth was primarily in the form of agricultural surpluses, the capital of those earliest times.

Organization by these elites of agricultural production, particularly of wheat and barley, resulted in greater yield and greater wealth. Much of this wealth was directed to the support of secondary producers, those who made luxuries of increasing refinement and artistry, valued by the elites as tokens of prestige and marks of social status. Compensated from the increasing wealth, craftspeople were able to further develop and refine techniques and skills, and they became nearly full time specialists—the potter, the weaver, the bronze smith, for example.

Activity and power were substantially concentrated in major population centers. It was in the cities, primarily, that wealth was increasingly directed toward monumental construction of palace and temple. The palace was a symbol of royal power, the temple a symbol of divine appointment of kings, and assurance of divine protection for the community.

In Egypt, developments proceeded somewhat differently, with less initial emphasis on cities and more on great monuments, of which the Pyramids were the ultimate and unrivaled expression. In Greece, at the farthest edge of the civilized world, developments also proceeded somewhat differently. Belief did not require elaborate temples; offerings were made at outdoor shrines or residential chapels.

Writing, the use of symbols to render grammatical structures, began at about 3200 BC in Mesopotamia. It seems to have appeared in Egypt at about the same time or only slightly later. The art of writing spread through the civilized world and was in the hands of a new specialist—the scribe—employed not only by palace or temple, but by anyone who could afford the scribe's fee.

Increasing population and increasing number of towns and cities were other results of continuing agricultural development. Wars frequently erupted, essentially over control of resources, water rights, arable land, man-and women-power, minerals, and access to ports and trade routes and their revenues. The quest for power and control led to conquest of one city or one land by another, at first resulting in limited and short-lived empires, but ultimately of empires of increasing scope and duration.

Trade was a dominant factor in the Bronze Age. Raw materials that moved in trade included foodstuffs, oil, spices, precious metals, copper, tin, bronze, ivory, gemstone, glass, resins and timber. Processed products included bronze weapons, carved ivory, seal stones, perfume, wine, pottery, jewelry, cups and bowls in gold or silver, fabrics, and finished clothing. In time, capital was expressed in terms of precious metals, primarily silver. Toward the end of the Bronze Age the use of scales and standard weights for measuring out precious metals facilitated trade.

Traders plied great distances between the civilized regions over established sea and land routes. Highways and byways connected far-flung cities, large and small. Some time in the Bronze Age, the trade network may have extended to Spain, England, the Baltic Coast, central Africa, Arabia, and India. By relay, what was produced in one land might reach the most distant country; and civilized Greece, Cyprus, Crete, Anatolia, Syria, Canaan, Egypt, and Mesopotamia might benefit. Wide-ranging trade is illustrated by the discovery of a fine bracelet of silver in Abydos, Egypt, well south along the Nile. By isotope analysis, it has been proved that the silver came from the Laurion mines near Athens, Greece. The date was about 2000 BC.

Much international trade, requiring as it often did substantial capitalization, international agreements, and military escorts, was directed from the royal palaces. It was largely a kingly prerogative. However, something resembling a middle class probably arose as a result of this intense activity. It might have included certain craftsmen, merchants and soldiers. But this middle class and the elites together were but a small fraction of the population. The great majority of men and women continued to labor on the land, and the supposed benefits of civilization hardly reached them, and they frequently lived at a level little different from their ancestors in the Neolithic period.

World View

Though records of the Bronze Age are scarce, enough survive to tell something of the way the peoples of the time saw the world. In spite of geographic dispersion, ethnic diversity, and the several thousand year span of the Bronze Age, there seems to have been a degree of uniformity in certain core beliefs.

Perhaps most surprising from the viewpoint of today is the intensity with which these ancient peoples believed in the gods. There was no other concept, no alternative view, by which one could account for the occurrences of nature and even many human events. Whether it was disaster or favor, large event or small, the gods were involved. They were everywhere. Prayers and offerings were a constant necessity, offered to the gods from the king or the most humble person. Even personal names reflected deep belief. Many personal names of the Bronze Age were theophoric, meaning that they bore the name of a god or they referred to a god. Thus, the Egyptian king-name *Ra*messes means "*Ra* [the sun god] has made him."

Gods were sometimes thought to have wide dominion, but more often, particularly among settled peoples, gods or goddesses tended to be seen as local, rooted in one spot. A forest or river might have a divinity who had jurisdiction there, whose power was localized there, and who might need to be dealt with as one approached that feature. Each city had a primary god, or a few gods, who were considered to be resident there, who ruled there, and whose supernatural power was largely effective only there. A traveler from one city to another would leave the power of one god and enter the region of power of another. Thus, the existence of an unlimited number of gods was thought nothing strange, and it was acknowledged that foreigners had gods of their own.

In time, the view developed that the gods related to one another in some sort of rational way. They communicated with one another. They lived in a social or political order, not unlike arrangements among mortals. It began to be seen that the gods formed a family with a powerful father with wife and children. Or one was king of the gods and others were subordinate deities. With conquest and empire, logic dictated that the gods of the conquering land ruled over the gods of conquered cities or lands.

Kings were to some extent deified, and that was certainly true in Egypt, where the king was considered a son of a god and a god himself. Homer's hero-kings were descended from gods through distant ancestors, while the hero Achilles was descended directly from a goddess. It is possible that here, as perhaps elsewhere, Homer reflects Bronze Age concepts.

These views were sustained by deep belief, and substantial wealth and energy were dedicated to the construction of temples—the gods' house—and to the supporting priesthood. Temples in Mesopotamia and Anatolia are largely in ruins, but the temples of Egypt have survived relatively intact, and display a vast and sumptuous construction. In

Egypt, at least, temple estates included extensive landholdings and serfs or slaves to work them. Temples were centers of economic as well as religious activity, maintaining their own agriculture and industries and engaging in redistribution and trade.

Legal systems existed, with support of the gods, and many records survive of contracts, deeds, trials and court findings. There were international treaties, and these required the gods of both sides as witnesses. A lengthy list of their names was appended to treaties, and treaty copies might be placed in the temple so that the gods would be mindful of them. A king recognized the severe risk of divine retribution if treaties were violated, and treaties seemed to have been well respected. Hittites believed that disasters followed from transgressions against the gods. A great plague among the Hittites was traced to the violation of an international treaty which had been witnessed by the gods. Egyptians believed that the gods established the world in a just and stable order, ever unchanging, yet threatened by destructive chaos and discord. Such chaos and discord accompanied the less than civilized peoples who surrounded and pressed in upon Egypt. Under the direction of the gods, the kings of Egypt were sometimes required to suppress those peoples by war, and in such wars the outcome was foreordained. Egyptian kings were always victorious. These particular beliefs probably were held in other lands and are but a fraction of the total religious viewpoint of the ancient world.

The duties of kings were various, including the close management of daily affairs, judicial actions, trade activities, and diplomacy. The king's power was not absolute, at least in Mesopotamia and Anatolia, where kings shared some degree of power with a council of leading men. The same may have been true in Egypt. Egyptian king Ramesses II consulted his leading men in the aftermath of the Battle of Kadesh, and that may mask a larger role which councils of senior elites played in Egyptian rule. Ultimate decisions among the Hittites were referred to the *pankus*, which seems to have been an assembly of the chief fighting men. Homer speaks of the war council of the Greeks who advised the king, and that may reflect Bronze Age practices. With these councils or assemblies, a wise king would need to engage in what today would be called politics. They would need to be consulted and conciliated.

Incorporated foreign peoples also needed to be conciliated and kept quiescent, and that too was best dealt with by good politics or diplomacy. The Hittite king traveled a circuit of shrines of the gods of incorporated peoples, and participated in their religious festivals. Hittite records show that the life of kings was demanding, requiring much travel and constant attention, and that is likely to have been true for many kings of the Bronze Age.

Central to the role of the king was that of war leader in the field, and chief priest at home. The king was appointed to his office by the gods. Hence he had a superior access to them. Through leadership in war and access to the gods, he ensured the security and well being of the people. The king was to establish justice and to protect the weak—an ideal striven for but probably seldom fully achieved. Another Ramesses, the third of that name, could say with pride that under his rule, a woman could walk anywhere she wanted with without fear of molestation. From Mesopotamia, king Ur-Nammu had it written that he established justice in the land and eliminated evil and strife. Hammurapi oversaw a great codification of the laws and claimed that he had established truth and justice in the land and furthered the well being of the people.

The family of the king was not exempt from responsibilities. Sons held leadership positions in the army. Hittite queen Pudu-Hepa was an active participant in political and diplomatic affairs throughout a long life. Egypt had at least two female "kings"—wives or daughters of Pharaohs. Diplomatic marriages were the norm, and among Hittites and Hurrians, and probably others, daughters were married off to create bonds of vassal loyalty or reinforce international treaties.

By the Late Bronze Age, experience of civilization was already over two thousand years old. Ideology, religion and political and social institutions had evolved and weathered challenges and seemed to have provided solutions to the problems of life and society. Bronze Age civilization was, to a large extent, a mature and successful system.

Time Scale

The following table will allow the events described in the balance of the book to be placed in a time perspective.

Writings dealing with ancient history or archaeology need to refer to BC dates. Some readers find these difficult at first since they seem to run in reverse, as is evident in the table. Thus, the year 4000 BC is five hundred years earlier than the year 3500 BC and the year 1570 BC is seventy years earlier than 1500 BC. Such dates are evident in the year-dates of kings, for example that of Egyptian king Tut (1334-1325 BC). Tut ascended the throne in 1334 BC and died nine years later in 1325 BC. From the perspective of the year AD 2000, Tut came to the throne 2000 + 1334 = 3334 years ago. Similarly, per the table, agriculture began approximately 8000 BC or about ten thousand years ago, and the great pyramids of Egypt were begun about 4,560 years ago.

NEOLITIC PERIOD

    Early agriculture in Near East,
    animal domestication   8000 BC

BRONZE AGE

Early temples, early irrigation works in Mesopotamia	4000 BC
Early cities in Mesopotamia	3500 BC
Cuneiform writing in Mesopotamia, hieroglyphics in Egypt	3200 BC
Early histories, king-lists in Mesopotamia,	3100 BC
Scorpion and Narmer, first known Egyptian kings	3100 BC
First City of Troy (Troy I)	3000 BC
Khufu Pyramid, first great pyramid in Giza, Egypt	2560 BC
Royal cemetery of Ur	2500 BC
Sargon, king in Akkad, and early empire	2300 BC
First dynasty in Babylon	1900 BC
Beginning of Troy Sixth City (Troy VI)	1800 BC
Assyrian merchant colony in Hittite region of Anatolia	1800 BC
Pitkhana and Anitta, first known Hittite kings	1800 BC

Beginning of Hyksos rule in lower Egypt	1650 BC

Late Bronze Age Begins

Evidence of Hyksos rule in Egypt	1570 BC
First evidence of Mycenaeans in Greece	1550 BC
Beginning of Hurrian kingdom of Mitanni	1500 BC
Egyptian king Thotmose III campaigns north in Canaan and Syria	1460 BC
Hittite king Suppiluliuma campaigns south through Syria to Canaan	1344 BC
Battle of Kadesh	1274 BC

[Beginning several decades after Kadesh, a period of disturbances and destructions: Exodus; Trojan War; Greek palaces, Cyprus, and Canaan cites destroyed; Hittites vanish; Sea Peoples appear; Dates in following chapters]

IRON AGE

David, king in Israel	1000 BC
Homer, *Iliad* and *Odyssey* composed	800 BC
Alphabetic writing in Greece	800 BC
Evidence of the earliest book of the Bible	630 BC

Beginning of Babylonian captivity	586 BC
Persians conquer Asia, Egypt	525 BC
Second Temple dedicated in Jerusalem	515 BC
Classical Period of Greece Begins	500 BC
Alexander conquers Egypt, Asia	326 BC

Certain dates here and elsewhere in this book are precise, meaning that they happened in some specific year, even though that year may not be known accurately. King-dates and dates of battles fall into that category. Except for Scorpion, Narmer, Pitkhana and Anitta, kings of an almost legendary time, king-dates given in the following chapters are probably accurate to within a few years.

No precise year can be assigned to most other entries in the table, however, in part because they represent ongoing processes or transitions rather than specific events. The beginning of writing, to take one example, falls into this category. "Neolithic period," which was the last phase of the Stone Age, also falls into this category, as do the terms Bronze Age and Late Bronze Age, which is the last subdivision of the Bronze Age, and the Iron Age.

Nothing magical happened at just those transitions. It is not as if the Stone Age or Neolithic closed and the Bronze Age opened, as in a play in which the curtain closes on one act or one scene and then opens again to reveal another. Much went on as before, but the increasing manufacture and use of bronze was a symptom of the increasing pace of civilization. The discovery or invention of bronze did not create civilization, but in the East it contributed to the accelerating development of civilization. It required intensification of trade in order to obtain the needed metals, copper and tin. In contrast, Europe north of Greece had its own Bronze Age in which much skilled bronze work was produced, but this region did not enter a stage that can be termed civilization.

Similarly, no sudden shift in the use of metals characterized the end of the Bronze Age and beginning of the Iron Age. Some small amount of iron had been made in the Bronze Age. As the Iron Age began, hardly any more iron was in use than earlier, and bronze continued to be made and widely used. Now, however, a curtain did close in a way, and opened again to show a new scene—one in which society and the political structure had been transformed in various degrees. The elites were particularly affected by the change. It was not iron which brought about these circumstances. It seems, rather, the highly disturbed circumstances at the end of the Bronze Age brought about the increasing use of iron. Trade routes over which tin was brought to the civilized centers were disrupted, and iron was pressed into service. Once the techniques of manufacture of iron and its products were mastered, iron slowly but steadily replaced bronze in utilitarian applications.

At the end of the table is the term "Classical period." It refers to the renewal of high culture in Greece after an extended deep and severe regression that followed the end of the Bronze Age. It was in the Classical period that the Parthenon was built, the great playwrights, sculptors, and philosophers of Greece flourished, and historians, including Herodotus and Thucydides, lived. It was a time of extensive scholarship and prolific writing, much of which has survived.

With the conquests of Alexander, a new term is usually applied, the "Hellenistic period." In this book, one simple term is needed to describe all of the period of revived learning and writing in the Greek world. As no such convenient term exists, "Classical period" is stretched to cover the need. As the term will be used here, it represents the time period of ancient writers who lived a few decades before 500 BC and extends forward to include writers who lived in the Hellenistic Period and later in the time of Roman domination.

Ethnic Landscape

In the Late Bronze Age, civilized states existed in a vast arc from Greece in the northwest to Egypt in the southeast. Figure 1-1 shows the location of these and other lands and the regional names which are used here. Other maps following supplement this map. Most names will be familiar, except possibly Anatolia, which is the name by which Turkey is known when referring to ancient times, before the Turkish people arrived in that land. It is also called Asia Minor, but Anatolia is the preferred term, even among Turkish scholars. Mesopotamia is the region that lies between and near the Tigris and Euphrates Rivers and corresponds, approximately, to present-day Iraq. It was a land of many independent cities and rulers, but toward the middle and end of the Bronze Age, the city of Babylon began to dominate the cities of southern Mesopotamia and Assyria much of the northern region.

Geographic names used here mostly refer to cities, or regions, rather than nations. With the possible exception of Egypt, which had a uniform culture and continuous ideology and united rule for many centuries, the concept of "nation" was hardly understood in ancient times. For example, there was no nation of Syria as there is today. As used here, "Syria" refers to a region. The basic political unit in this region, as in much of the Bronze Age world, was the city-state, a small political entity perhaps a few tens of miles in length and breadth. It might contain one central city surrounded by supporting towns and villages. The king resided in that city, and there too were the temple, the central market, the scribes, and many of the craftsmen.

Frequently enough, through the shifting fortunes of politics and war, these small city-states were incorporated into a larger political structure, and the "little kings" of such city-states would then be subordinate to a Great King. The little kings had become vassals, or perhaps subordinate allies. However, the larger unit, the area over which the Great King ruled, was no nation in the modern sense. People did not identify with the larger entity. They did not see themselves as citizens of the larger region. Their "nation" was the clan, or the town, or at most the city-state from which they came and they recognized no wider loyalty. Ask a person from Syria, for example, what his country was, and he might reply Alalakh, or Ugarit, cities of the region.

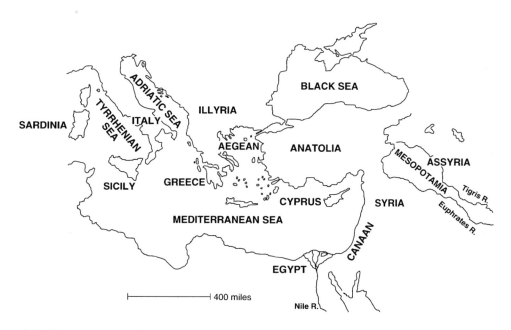

Figure 1-1. Names commonly used when referring to lands or regions of the Bronze Age.

Who were the various peoples of the Bronze Age with which this book is concerned? It is natural to wonder about race, but little is known of that matter. Murals in the palaces of Crete and Greece show those peoples to be black-haired. Men, who presumably spend time out of doors, are shown with ruddy or tanned complexions. Women are shown with white complexions. Egyptian artists recorded the appearance of various groups that Egypt encountered. Distinctions in appearance among these groups are sometimes evident in hair style or dress style. These are not racial but cultural matters. Semites, Hittites, and Egyptians are illustrated similarly in that they have black hair and men tan complexions. Women, if they are illustrated at all, are shown with white complexions, or tan if of lower social strata. Some Libyans are shown with blue eyes and red hair. Black Africans are also illustrated.

That is nearly as far as the idea of race can be carried so far as knowledge of these ancient peoples is concerned. As race is a biological concept, and as the ancients are not available for current biological examination (though a few bones and a few mummies exist), the race of these peoples in any narrowly defined sense is and will most likely remain unknown. In any case, as early as the origins of these ancient peoples can be discerned through the fog which covers the past, they are already quite mixed.

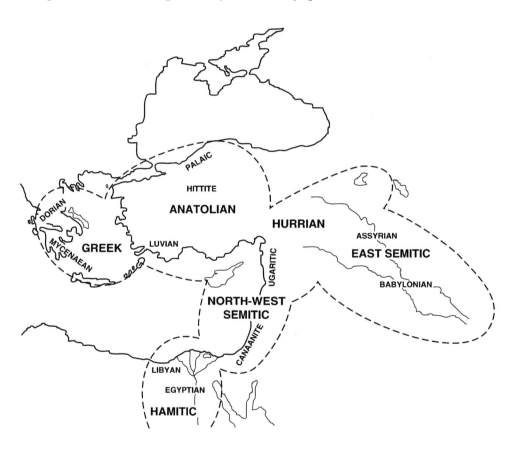

Figure 1-2. Ethnic regions of the Late Bronze Age based on linguistic or historical data. Boundaries are somewhat uncertain.

In place of the concept of race, ethnicity must be considered. Unlike race, which usually refers to more or less fixed genetically derived traits, ethnicity refers to culture, to belief and behavior learned at mother's knee, in the family and community. Ethnic characteristics include religious beliefs, songs and stories, legends, theories of origin, manners and standards of behavior, customs in dress, preferences or taboos in food, and much else. To the extent that these are identical among people in a community, and different from corresponding elements in some neighboring group, the community will recognize their own unity and their distinctiveness. In turn, they are also seen as distinct by their neighbors. With distinction recognized in both directions, the community is a distinct ethnic group.

Of all of the characteristics related to ethnicity, language is the most important. As with other elements of ethnicity, language is not uniquely tied to race. Unlike the song of birds, specific languages are not genetically programmed and peoples of diverse origins have often come to use the same language. Conversely, people of identical origin have come to adopt different languages. Yet it is language by which the ancients are best identified, since substantial evidence of the language of many Bronze Age peoples survives in ancient texts or geographic names. Thus, language, and to a lesser extent geography or place, are the most important means by which to identify these ancient peoples.

In a region along or close to the east coast of the Mediterranean Sea, from southeastern Anatolia to the eastern part of the Nile delta, a family of languages known as North West Semitic was spoken, Figure 1-2. How close these languages were to one another, and whether people from the north and south extremes of this region could understand one another, is a matter which linguists have not decided. Ancient Canaanite, Ugaritic, Aramean, Moabite, Edomite and Hebrew were part of this language group, as was the later Phoenician, a branch of Canaanite. It is likely that many linguistic regions in ancient times contained small groups that spoke some foreign tongue. People who retained a Hurrian language may have lived in the region in which North West Semitic languages were dominant. Even if Hurrian speech had died out, Hurrian names were still in use there toward the end of the Bronze Age.

Similar pockets of "alien" ethnicity no doubt existed in many places during the Bronze Age. Isolation created by geographic features allowed this survival. To some extent also, low population density in the Bronze Age insulated some groups from contact with surrounding populations and from assimilation. Low population density, a feature of those early times, is somewhat difficult to picture today. It is estimated that the entire population of the Near East toward the end of the Neolithic may have been only a hundred thousand people. In the Bronze Age, Sargon of Akkad (see preceding table) conquered his limited world and created an empire with an army of only about five thousand men. Apparently, that was all that he could effectively muster, and all that he needed. When the Hittites and Egyptians clashed at Kadesh, as will be described in the next chapter, their entire armies, including all reserves and vassal contingents, were hardly larger than single infantry divisions of the twentieth century.

Most "cities" of the Bronze Age would be seen as no more than small towns by modern eyes. It is estimated that as late as the Classical period, the population of Europe was no more than twenty million. Such low populations in the Bronze Age rendered lands permeable to invaders. There was insufficient population to block an invader, who might sweep across substantial distances and encounter only a few isolated hamlets. Only in southern Mesopotamia was there a relatively high population density during much of the Bronze Age.

In southern Mesopotamia, in the earliest part of the Bronze Age, there was an ethnic group known as Sumerians. They are credited with the earliest writing and the development of the earliest civilization. The script which they invented and employed is known as cuneiform, and it was later adopted by many peoples throughout the Near East and Anatolia. Sumerian speech was unrelated to any other language, ancient or modern. For that reason, a relationship of the Sumerians to any other peoples cannot be recognized. In later centuries, diverse peoples arrived in Mesopotamia. By the Late Bronze Age, East Semitic languages had already been long dominant in the region. In southern Mesopotamia, that language was Babylonian, also called Akkadian. In the north along the Tigris River, the related Assyrian language was used. Akkadian texts, written in the cuneiform script, contain the earliest known representations of a Semitic language.

Eastern Semitic and North West Semitic languages had common roots, though people of the western and eastern regions probably could not understand one another except through study. It is a natural view to associate race with language. Possibly, the original speakers of an earliest Semitic language were, in some remote time, a unified group of fairly narrow biological variability, whose descendents spread into the regions in which North West Semitic and East Semitic were later spoken. The supposed Semitic homeland is thought to have been the desert, or perhaps the Mediterranean coast. Such matters are speculative and complicated by the fact that speech and race need not track one another.

Mesopotamia illustrates better than other regions the distinction between race and ethnicity. In the mountains to the north and east of Mesopotamia lived various peoples, barbarians of diverse speech and origins. History records frequent invasions of such peoples into Mesopotamia. Once they had established themselves in and around the cities of Mesopotamia, in many cases they adopted Semitic speech and customs and in that way became Semites.

People of Egyptian speech lived along the Nile River and the Nile Delta. They were the major group but not the only group in residence. It is certain that peoples of Semitic speech lived in part of the eastern delta in the Late Bronze Age and probably even earlier. Political control did not follow speech, and those Semitic groups were, most of the time, under the rule of the Egyptian king.

Libyans, peoples living to the west of Egypt, are noted in Egyptian records as early as 1900 BC. The ancient Egyptian language is thought to be related to the ancient Libyan language, of which modern Berber may be a descendant. Ancient Egyptian speech also shares linguistic features in vocabulary and grammar with Semitic speech, and a possible early common origin of Semitic and Egyptian peoples has been considered, but cannot be proved.

"Mycenaean" is the term given by archaeologists to the culture, civilization, and people of the Late Bronze Age in Greece. The name comes from Mycenae, the Bronze Age city in Greece whose citadel Heinrich Schliemann excavated in 1876, and in which he found remarkable treasures. Homer told of Mycenae as the city of Agamemnon, leader of the Achaeans who attacked Troy, and so the term Mycenaean has been given to the entire Late Bronze Age Greek civilization.

It had long been assumed that the Mycenaeans, the Achaeans of Homer, were ethnically Greek. But how could one be certain? Until the 1950s, there was no proof, and there were those who had doubts. Limited examples of Mycenaean writing on clay tablets, in a script called Linear B, had been recovered in the ruins of Mycenae, Pylos, Thebes, and from Knossos in Crete, cities of the Late Bronze Age. The writing baffled scholars, but in the 1950s, using systematic code-breaking methods, Michael Ventris was able to assign sound values to the elements of the script. The language proved to be a very early form of Greek. That demonstrated that those Late Bronze Age cities were occupied by speakers of the Greek language. Archaeological evidence in certain of those mainland cities showed that a continuum of culture went back at least to 1550 BC, so that the presence of Greek-speaking people in Greece can be assumed to extend back to at least that date.

Mycenaean culture owed much in every art and craft to the culture of Crete just to the south. Linear B was a modification of the earlier Linear A script that was used in Crete, where a remarkable and creative civilization had developed in the middle of the Bronze Age. Texts in Linear A have been recovered from Cretan archaeological sites, and while the sound values of many of the symbols in this script have been worked out, the underlying language remains unknown. In part for that reason, the ethnic relationship of these people to any other remains an enigma awaiting some new discovery. However, by about 1450 BC, Greeks began an occupation in Crete, and Crete was substantially "Mycenaeanized."

Where did the Greek people originate? That is one of the delicious controversies which have occupied the time of scholars for over a century. The problem is intimately related to another problem, the origin of the so-called Indo-European family of languages.

It has probably always been obvious to those with a linguistic bent that the Irish and Welch languages were related to one another, constituting with a few other languages a Celtic language group, or that English, Dutch, German, and the Scandinavian languages formed another such family, or that the Romance languages were related to one another. Effort would also show a Slavic family of related languages. Gathering extensive word lists from various languages, in 1767 James Parsons showed that these linguistic families, and Greek also, were fundamentally related to one another. He showed also that Persian and Bengali, an important language of India, were related to one another and, very surprisingly, to those language families of Europe. The basic relationship was affirmed by William Jones, an English scholar assigned as a judge to India. In his leisure time, he studied Sanskrit, the ancient written form of the Indian language. In a talk delivered in 1796, he confirmed the intimate connection of Sanskrit with ancient Greek and Latin, and to the Germanic and Celtic families also. The relationship goes deep, and extends even to words in which the pronunciation is now no longer similar in the various languages, and to grammatical constructions.

This extensive group of languages is commonly referred to as "Indo-European." "Indo" refers to the Indian member of the relationship, and indicates the vast geographic region of the Old World in which these languages are or were spoken.

Scholars sought an explanation of the origin of this linguistic relationship. The easiest and most obvious explanation is that these languages are later branches of a single ancient language which must have existed in some remote time in the past, spoken by one people living in one region. From that region, wherever it may have been, migrations carried the language into all of the regions of Europe and Asia in which its later descendants are known. The search for the original homeland has produced many candidates: northern Germany, the Balkans, the central steppe of Asia, the north coast of the Black Sea, among others.

Today scholars are less sure of that simple explanation, requiring as it does mass migration. They show how a language may spread by diffusion, or by the influence of a small group of elites coming from outside, and that large population movements are not necessarily required. That much is evident from the Romance languages—Portuguese, Spanish, French, Italian, Romanian—which are all derived from Latin. No one believes that a massive invasion of Romans occupied France. Rather, vernacular Latin was adopted by peoples in France who were originally speakers of Celtic or Germanic languages.

The question of the homeland or "origin" of the original Indo-Europeans, if it ever existed, is still in a state of great uncertainty.

Greek is an Indo-European language. No one has ever seriously supposed that Greece was the original homeland of Indo-European speech. Therefore, Greek speech in some very early form must have entered from outside. There are a series of place-names in Greece, very ancient in origin, which seem to be pre-Greek. That suggests that speakers of some language other than Greek lived there originally, and it is to them that these names are due. It might be reasonable to conclude that people of Greek speech arrived and merged with them, or conquered them. That view is supported by the fact that much of the ancient Greek vocabulary consisted of non-Greek words primarily pertaining to plants or animals native to Greece, names of which invaders would not have in their own vocabulary.

The language which the assumed invaders brought would not have been Greek in any recognizable sense. It would have been some no longer existent variety of the Indo-European speech which over time, influenced by the earlier native language, became the recognizably Greek language of the Mycenaean Linear B tablets. "When did the Greeks come?" can at most mean "When did those who introduced this proto-Greek language come?" There is some evidence of widespread destruction in Greece around 2000 BC, and the presence of certain new pottery, and it is assumed that these marked the arrival of those who brought the proto-Greek speech. Since the assumed homeland of Indo-European speech was to the north, it is supposed that it was from the north that the newcomers came. So runs the most popular view. Of course, if the proto-Greek language entered the mainland by linguistic diffusion, then there were no invaders. The answer is lost in the obscurity of time.

Hittites were, politically and militarily, one of the most important peoples of the Late Bronze Age, the dominant people in Anatolia. The home of the Hittites was within a loop of the Halys River, on a broad plateau surrounded by mountains. Earliest existing notice of the Hittites is contained in the records of an Assyrian merchant colony (see table) at Kultepe in Anatolia where, presumably, the Assyrians were trading for metals. A few towns, possibly Hittite, were also mentioned in those Assyrian records, as were nearly legendary kings Pitkhana and Anitta.

After the Bronze Age, the Hittites were forgotten and they were completely unrecognized again until the twentieth century. They had vanished, and with that disappeared knowledge of them, a gap of over three thousand years. The works of Homer, which deal with Troy, a city of Anatolia, demonstrate no knowledge of Hittites. The Bible mentions Hittites several times, but these are likely not the Hittites of central Anatolia referred to here.

In the nineteenth century, ruins were noted near the Turkish village of Boghazkoy east of Ankara, and excavations began there in 1906. With amazing good luck, archives were almost immediately found, containing over ten thousand records of the Hittites, written in the cuneiform script borrowed from the Babylonians. This was the site of the Hittite capital, Hattusa. Translations of Hittite writing came forth rapidly, and translation work continues even now. Hittite texts provide an unrivaled amount of information, allowing an outline of Hittite history to be constructed. These texts furnish insights into inner thoughts of individuals which do not appear again in ancient texts until the writing of the Bible.

Early in the process of translation came the recognition that the Hittite language was a member of the Indo-European language family. Verb forms followed the Indo-European pattern, and shows good parallels with Greek, Latin, and other Indo-European languages, as did some vocabulary. One sentence which was examined early in an attempt at translation was *"NINDA-an e-iz-za-at-te-ni wa-a-tar-ma e-ku-ut-teni."* NINDA was an already known cuneiform word meaning "bread," and it was guessed that the sentence had to do with eating. There was also the word *e-iz-za-at-te-ni*, suspiciously similar to the German "essen," eat. Then there was *wa-a-tar-ma*, which might refer to water. Indeed, those proved to be correct assumptions. The translation is "Now you eat bread; water, however, you drink." What is quite amazing is that Hittite contained these words, words with clear relationship to those still used in European languages, a remarkable demonstration of linguistic conservation. It is all the more remarkable, since Hittite is the most linguistically remote of known Indo-European languages, suggesting a separation of Hittite from all the other Indo-European languages at a very early date, perhaps five thousand years ago. Hittite records provide the earliest known writing of any Indo-European language, earlier than Greek Linear B, earlier than the Vedas of India.

Outlying from the Hittite heartland on the plateau, other related languages were spoken, Palaic to the north, and Luvian to the west and south. The kinship of these Anatolian languages—Palaic, Luvian, Hittite—is clear to linguists, but it is doubtful that they were so close that those who spoke one could directly understand the other without study.

Inevitably, the question of the origin of the Hittites and speakers of Palaic and Luvian arises. On the commonly held assumption that language matches peoples, some early movement into Anatolia of peoples bearing the Indo-European language is sought. On the basis of rather weak evidence, that movement is assumed to have taken place in about 2000 BC or earlier, and is further assumed to have come from the west, since the east was assumed to be blocked by peoples of Caucasian speech.

As is indicated by the discovery of Hurrian names in a number of Bronze Age records, people of Hurrian speech or descent lived in the mountains of eastern Anatolia, near the headwaters of the Tigris and Euphrates, and in Syria. At one time, kings with Hurrian names ruled as far south as Canaan. A king of Jerusalem bore a Hurrian name, as did several other kings in that region. Like the Hittites, the Hurrians were unknown until recent times, though it is possible that the term "Horite" of the Bible refers to them. In the Late Bronze Age, Hurrians organized one or several states of some power and influence, of which the most important was Mitanni.

Hurrian influence on the Hittites was strong, especially in religion, and Hittite kings of the Late Bronze Age may have been of Hurrian descent. That influence is shown by a number of Hittite royal names, some of which will be mentioned in the text, including that of a king with the personal name Urhi-*Tesub* and queen Pudu-*Hepa*, where Tesub and Hepa (Hepat) are Hurrian god-names. Hurrian names of both kings and commoners continued in use in eastern Anatolia and northern Syria for a substantial time, well after the destruction of Hurrian political power.

The Hurrian language is completely unrelated to the large Indo-European or Semitic families of languages spoken to their west and south. The kinship of Hurrian is thought to be with the so-called Caucasian languages that may have descendants in the Caucasus region today.

Very strange among the Hurrians is the presence of Indian names. Indian gods known from the Veda, the most ancient written documents of India appear, include Mitra, Indra, Varuna, and the Nasatya twins. King-names of Indian type, including that of Tushratta (who will be mentioned in later chapters), and other names as far south as Canaan. In the Hittite archive, a Hurrian horse training manual was found, and the instructions are clearly in Indian, including words for numbers recognizable from several modern Indo-European languages. These Indian names and words are the earliest existing record of the Indo-Iranian branch of the Indo-European language family.

The origin of the Hurrians is unknown, and there is no compelling reason to think that they were not living in the mountains of eastern Anatolia as early as the Neolithic. As for the Indians, it seems likely that at some time, a group of warriors of Indian ethnicity merged with certain Hurrian groups and became dominant among them. Their role in horse raising is associated with a supposed Indo-European early domestication of the horse which, some scholars maintain, became closely associated with various early Indo-European warrior elements. The Indians introduced a word to the region, *Mariannu,* which was used in later years as far south as Egypt to refer to chariot warriors or a warrior caste.

The Political Landscape

The events and situations described in the following chapters developed within the historical circumstances of the times. It is particularly difficult to describe those circumstances that relate to Greece, since nothing is really known of the history of Greece in the Bronze Age. Much must be inferred from archaeological evidence.

The Shaft Graves of Mycenae reflect a time near the beginning of Mycenaean culture. In the graves, the remains of kings have been found, interred among an assortment of riches and with many bronze weapons. Homer's *Iliad*, which seems to reflect a time at the end of the Mycenaean period, tells of a war and warriors. Thus, it appears that the Mycenaean Greeks long had a warrior orientation, and other archaeological discoveries in mainland Greece support that view. But it is now also known that these people were energetic traders as well. Greek pottery of the Mycenaean period has been found in the Aegean islands, Anatolia, Cyprus, Syria, Canaan, Jordan, and Egypt. To the west, it has been found in southern Italy. Judging by pottery remains, Greek overseas trade was particularly intensive and successful in the years between 1400 and 1230 BC. Since most items of trade are perishable, there is little remaining evidence of other materials which the Greeks traded, but textiles and aromatic oils are likely to have been among those things.

There is some evidence of Greek colonization overseas. Did trade follow the flag? Did the Greeks attempt to secure raw materials or open new markets at the point of the sword? There is no clear answer. It is known that Greeks obtained control of the Cretan capital of Knossos in about 1450 BC, and thereafter took over the extensive Cretan seaborne trade network. It is also known that by about 1300 BC, and perhaps earlier, Greeks had carved out enclaves on the west coast of Anatolia, where they encountered the Hittites. The story of the Trojan War tells of the Greek siege of Troy, a city on the northwest coast of Anatolia, and some suspect that there was a Greek economic motive behind all the fine talk of rescuing Helen from the Trojans. There is a suspicion also that the Greeks maintained a trading enclave on Cyprus, and possibly in Ugarit on the Syrian coast. It is sufficient to say that the Greeks, like others of the Bronze Age, were opportunistic, expanding into territories that could be won at an acceptable cost.

In Anatolia, it may have been the early Hittite king Anitta who terminated the Assyrian trade colony, and who first began to assert Hittite imperial ambitions. In the years following his reign, Hittites consolidated control of cities and agricultural lands on the Anatolian plateau. By the time of King Hattusili I, near 1600 BC, a Hittite army was already moving through the mountain passes to the south, attempting to gain control of northern Syria. In Syria were ancient and cultured cities made wealthy through location on the caravan routes connecting the Mediterranean coast with Mesopotamia. Then, in an audacious move, Hattusili's son, Mursili I, led an army in a daring raid on Babylon far to the south and sacked it, though he did not hold it.

Hittite political stability was not firm in those early days of Hittite power. On his return home, Mursili was assassinated. Hittite control in Anatolia crumbled, and the Hittites pulled back to a limited area around their capital, Hattusa. In following generations, Hittite energies were largely devoted to reestablishing control in central Anatolia itself, but a desire for wider domination was not quenched. When they were not opposing Hurrians or Egyptians, Hittites looked westward. In that direction, Hittite ambitions required control of Arzawa, a land of Luwian-speaking people with substantial ambitions of their own.

In the wake of the Hittite pullback from northern Syria, The Hurrians began to consolidate various principalities into a powerful state known as Mitanni, with its capital on the upper Euphrates River. Mitannian control extended from the northern reaches of the Tigris River westward across northern and central Syria to the Mediterranean coast. Mitanni held the Assyrians as vassals. So long as Mitanni existed as a strong power, the Assyrians were not a significant factor in the region as they would be in following years.

Egypt had been united since the time of semi-legendary king Narmer, and perhaps even earlier. Egyptian civilization had developed remarkably. The building of the pyramids was already long in the past when, in the dynasty of King Wegaf (1782-1778 BC), political unity began to crumble. Several independent states formed in the Nile delta. Kings bearing Semitic names took control of the eastern delta and a substantial distance up the Nile. These were the Hyksos, of whom history speaks. That situation lasted about a century when an Egyptian named Ahmose (1570-1546 BC) began a counterattack, and the Hyksos rulers were expelled from Egypt. That brought the Egyptian army to the northeastern part of the delta, to the doorstep of Canaan. Subsequently, a series of Egyptian kings lead military campaigns to the north. Egyptian king Thotmose III (1504-1450 BC), a brilliant military commander, advanced through Canaan into Syria. Kadesh, a strategically important stronghold, was taken by the Egyptians. In an audacious move, which would match the thrust of Mursili into Babylon years before, Thotmose struck north to the city of Kargamish on the Euphrates in eastern Anatolia. As he advanced, he encountered the growing Hurrian presence already mentioned.

In following years, the Hittites, Hurrians, and Egyptians continued to vie for control of Syria. Now it was one who dominated, now it was another. With the advance of Hittite king Suppuluiuma (1344-1322 BC) into southern Syria, to the edge of Egyptian-controlled Canaan, a direct clash between Egypt and the Hittites became inevitable.

2
BATTLE AT KADESH

With the reign of Akhenaton (1350-1334 BC), Egypt entered a very strange period. This king, a deep mystic, had discovered or rediscovered the god of the sun. In a land in which a multitude of gods had been worshiped for over 1500 years, he insisted on the worship of this one god only. To firmly establish the new belief, he abandoned the Egyptian capital at Thebes and its entrenched Amon priesthood and built a new capital at a site near the present-day village of El-Amarna.

The name which the king chose, Akhen*aton*, was based on the god's image, the sun-disc, the *Aton*. His family changed their names to incorporate that term, and those in his royal court who wanted to curry favor did likewise. Fanatic supporters of Akhenaton and his god attacked the old shrines, chipping out or painting over the names of the old gods. Sun worship was pushed to extremes. It is said that even a foreign ambassador was required to stand in the harsh Egyptian sun for hours, waiting for an audience with the king. There are few records of the reaction of the conservative elements and the still powerful Amon priesthood to all of this. They must have resisted the new heresy, openly or secretly. It is easy to imagine the chaos and conflict which Akhenaton's reforms produced in a society which believed that things were intended to remain ever the same. The attention of the powerful and the influential in Egypt turned inward, consumed by the struggle between the old and the new.

At that time, Egypt controlled an extensive territory in Canaan and southern Syria. As Egyptians focused on internal matters, attention to that region waned. Thus, there was little organized Egyptian opposition when Hittite king Suppiluliuma and his army thrust southward into Syria. In Syria, there were a number of small kingdoms that paid tribute to Mitanni or Egypt under compulsion of arms, but their kings were weather vanes, quick to swing in the direction of the prevailing wind. One after another, these little kings took the Hittite vassal oath. Farther south, beyond the Hittite reach, some kings in Canaan took advantage of events and loosened the Egyptian noose, enjoying an illusory independence.

Following Akhenaton, Smenkhare ruled a scant two years and was followed by Tutankhamon (King Tut), who reversed the religious reforms. The very name of Akhenaton was removed from monuments in a burst of fury against all that he had done. Later kings whose backgrounds were military strove to restore Egyptian dominance in Syria and Canaan and none was more energetic in this than Seti I (1291–1279 BC). Seti strengthened Egyptian control in Canaan and sent an Egyptian force north, to Amurru, where Benteshina was king, Figure 2-1. The appearance of that force at his doorstep surprised and frightened Benteshina. He was under oath as a Hittite vassal and the presence of an Egyptian army placed him in a difficult position. Under pressure from the Egyptians, Benteshina renounced his allegiance to Muwatalli, the Hittite king. He wrote to Muwatalli, explaining how he had little choice under the circumstances. The Hittites must understand Benteshina's difficult position. One had to bow to realities. Far off in Hattusa, the Hittite capital, Muwatalli (1295–1271 BC) and his advisers drew their own conclusions and began preparations for war.

Seti was succeeded by his son, Ramesses (1279–1212 BC), the second of that name. The reign of Ramesses II was to be one of the most illustrious in Egyptian history. Ramesses was well equipped to rule. Earlier, Seti had placed Ramesses by his side as co-ruler, enabling Ramesses to develop skills of leadership under the watchful eye of his father.

Ramesses Marches North

While a prince, Ramesses had accompanied Seti in the military campaigns in the north. When he became king, Ramesses took measures to ensure army loyalty and support, for he had ambitious military plans of his own. He intended to accomplish in Syria what his father had not, and win even greater glory. Ramesses refined his plans and organized, and by the fourth year of his rule, he was ready. In the spring of 1274 BC, Ramesses put his plans into operation. The Egyptians would, once again, go north.

A vast military assemblage was in camp at Kantir, the royal residence in the northeastern part of the Nile Delta. Four armies assembled there, drawn from different regions of Egypt and each named for the primary god of the region. The army of Amon from Thebes was there, Pre from Heliopolis, Ptah from the Memphis region, and Sutekh from the eastern delta. As in a modern army, each was composed of organized units and contained several combat arms. There were infantry units that used the bow, and other units which used the curved Egyptian scimitar. There were chariot forces, with each chariot manned by a driver and a bowman. There were officers, planners, and logistic specialists. This was a professional army, and its ranks were reinforced with reserves. In addition, auxiliaries from vassal states would join along the line of march. There were also aliens, including the Sherdan, in the Egyptian forces.

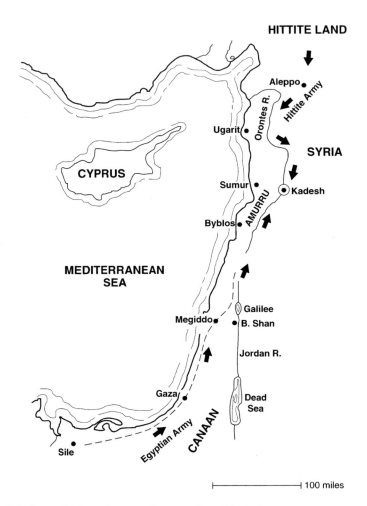

Figure 2-1. The Hittite and Egyptian armies march to Kadesh.

Sherdan were foreign adventurers, and in Ramesses' second year, they had attacked Egypt from the sea and were defeated and many captured. As they were fierce fighters, the Sherdan were given a choice. Either work the farmlands of Pharaoh as slaves, or accept land, food, and clothing from the Pharaoh and, in return, fight for Pharaoh. The decision was an easy one, and the Sherdan were used as elite infantry troops.

The march north was planned in detail, and each unit assigned its position. Logistics were arranged, and each vassal king along the line of march knew what food and drink he would be required to supply. Camp locations were planned, and the march coordinated so that even detached units would join the main force at a prearranged place and time. Strategic intelligence was gathered by commanders of forward garrisons and vassal kings.

The army set out, following the great trunk road which was ancient even then, and which went along the Canaan coast close by the ancient cities of Gaza, Ashkelon, and Ashdod. Farther along, the highway turned inland and the army followed toward the fortress at Megiddo. Conferences were held with Egyptian and vassal commanders from Megiddo and Beth Shan. The army continued northward along the western shore of the Sea of Galilee, past Dan and further northward along the River Jordan.

The Jordan originates in the Bekaa, a valley between north-south mountain ranges. High in the valley, the Orontes River also originates, and runs north until it finally reaches the Mediterranean Sea. The Egyptians proceeded into the Bekaa, their objective the fortress-city of Kadesh on the Orontes, at the north end of the valley. Kadesh (Qids) was a Hittite vassal city.

That a decisive battle would have to be fought with the Egyptians had been decided by the Hittites some time before. The defection, under Egyptian pressure, of Benteshina a few years before could not be tolerated. With a much smaller population than Egypt, Hittites depended on a network of vassal states and the military forces which they supplied, and Benteshina's defection was ominous. The vassal states in Syria must not be lost.

In Hattusa, preparations were made, everything was done which could be done to set things in order, to ensure that there would be no distractions. New treaties were arranged with the vassal states of western Anatolia. Among the treaty stipulations was one requiring the vassals to provide military support in case of war with Egypt. That support would be needed in the coming battle. To the north of Hatti, there were the Kaska tribes. These had been temporarily pacified, in part by hiring many as mercenary units in the Hittite army.

With preparations made, the Hittite forces came down through the Taurus Mountains and into Syria. Little is known of the organization of the Hittite forces, but frequent wars in Anatolia kept the Hittites militarily proficient. Massive chariot forces, mobility, rapid deployment of infantry and night attacks, were favored Hittite elements of war, and would be employed if possible once the enemy was met.

There are no known Hittite accounts of the battle. The battle is known entirely from Egyptian records. These are preserved at several major temples and monuments in Egypt, in hieroglyphic text and large-scale sculptural reliefs, and in a few fragmentary papyrus scrolls. They tell that Ramesses and his armies continued north and reached the headwaters of the Orontes River. The army of Amon was in the lead, followed at some distance by the army of Pre, and farther down the road by the army of Ptah. Army Sutekh was well to the rear. As they marched along the east bank of the river with Kadesh only a few miles ahead, two Shasu (Bedouin) appeared. These were brought before Ramesses, who interrogated them. They had been with the "Wretched Fallen One of Hatti," they said, who has held his forces far back in Aleppo, afraid to approach Kadesh out of fear of

Pharaoh. Fallen One of Hatti, or Wretched Fallen One of Hatti, are two endearing terms the Egyptians used when referring to the king of the Hittites.

Aleppo was more than 100 miles to the north. The Hittite army did not threaten. Flushed with confidence, Ramesses and a few of his household troops mounted their chariots and dashed ahead, crossed to the west side of the Orontes at a river ford about seven miles south of Kadesh and pulled up on a plain northwest of the city. Here, they waited for Army Amon to come up. Amon arrived and began to set up camp. In addition to the usual facilities of a military camp, the Pharaoh's pavilion and those of the princes and other dignitaries were set up. While the camp bustled with preparation, scouts brought in two Hittites with disturbing news. The two had been captured and were introduced into the Presence. "Where is he, the Fallen one of Hatti?" asked Ramesses. "I have heard that he is in the land of Aleppo to the north…." After persuasion was applied, the captives revealed the truth. The entire Hittite army was camped just out of sight, hidden behind the city of Kadesh. Egyptian intelligence had been deceived. Ramesses had been tricked.

As this news was being digested, events were happening back along the road. The army of Pre had crossed at the river ford and was marching toward the camp when suddenly, out of nowhere, a huge Hittite chariot force struck them in the flank. Totally surprised, caught in road-march formation and unprepared for a fight, the men of Army Pre panicked. They scattered like flushed quail, many racing for the Pharaoh's camp. Hittite chariotry followed in hot pursuit. Bursting into the camp, the Hittites created a new panic. With that, the army of Amon broke and men fled in all directions creating further chaos. Egyptian inscriptions describe the situation. Of the Hittite forces, they said:

> They covered mountains and valleys and they were like the locust by reason of their multitude. He [the Hittite king] left no silver in his land, he stripped it of all its possessions and gave them to all the foreign countries in order to bring them with him to fight.

The Egyptian text tells that it was only through the superhuman valor of Pharaoh that the day was saved.

> His Majesty started forth at a gallop, and entered into the host of the Fallen Ones of Hatti, being alone by himself and none other with him. So then His Majesty went to look about him and he found 2,500 chariots hemming him in on his other side, consisting of all the champions of the Fallen Ones of Hatti and many foreign countries which were with them…

The text continues:

> His Majesty being powerful, his heart stout, none could stand before him. All his territory was ablaze with fire, and he burned every foreign country with his hot

breath, his eyes savage when he saw them, and his might flared up like fire against them. He took no note of millions of foreigners, he regarded them as chaff. Then His Majesty entered into the host of the Hatti enemies....and His Majesty killed the entire host of the Wretched Fallen One of Hatti, together with his great chiefs and all his brothers, as well as all the chiefs of all the countries who had come with him, their infantry and their chariotry being fallen upon their faces, one upon another, and His Majesty slaughtered and slew them in their places, they sprawling before his horses and His Majesty being alone, none other with him. (*Kadesh*)

Thus, in Egyptian records, it is written that Ramesses defeated the Hittites, and did so single-handedly. This sort of vast overstatement, typical of what is found on the monuments of other Egyptian kings, makes it difficult to know what really happened. From information in the inscriptions, it is learned that a detachment of Egyptian special troops had been in Amurru and had been expected to come into camp that day. Possibly, they came upon the scene of battle just as the troops of Amon were fleeing the camp, and possibly they reversed the tide of battle. The scattered soldiers of Amon and Pre drifted back, rallied, and in repeated counterattacks, drove off the Hittite chariot force which may have been distracted in looting. Shortly after, Ptah came up in time to see the damage. Army Sutekh came up well after the action was over. There were probably significant casualties on both sides. Amon and Pre were seriously shaken by the action. A very angry Ramesses held a field court marshal, and there seems to have been capital punishment for cowardice among both troops and officers.

Among the Hittite forces, the infantry had seen no action and was still fresh. But the chariotry had taken serious casualties, particularly among the officers. Yet it is certain that not all of the Hittite chiefs and the king's brothers had been killed as Ramesses claimed. King Muwatalli lived, and a brother of Muwatalli succeeded in due time to the kingship of the Hittites, taking the throne name Hattusili.

The following morning, Muwatalli sent a message to Ramesses offering a truce. Ramesses consulted with his officers, and it was decided that a truce would be no breach of honor since all the world was aware of Pharoah's god-like invincibility. And so the war was over. Ramesses and the army returned home, banners in the wind, prisoners trailing in handcuffs, wagons of booty gathered along the way. At home in Egypt, a great victory was proclaimed.

The Hittites, so far as is known, spoke little of this event, except to note that "Muwatalli took the field against the king of Egypt and the country of Amurru and....defeated the king of Egypt and the country of Amurru." It is interesting to note that the Egyptians went home, but the Hittites stayed. They retained Kadesh and other Syrian possessions. In short order, they pushed still farther south as far as Damascus. The battle was a draw, in which the Hittites were left on the field and in control.

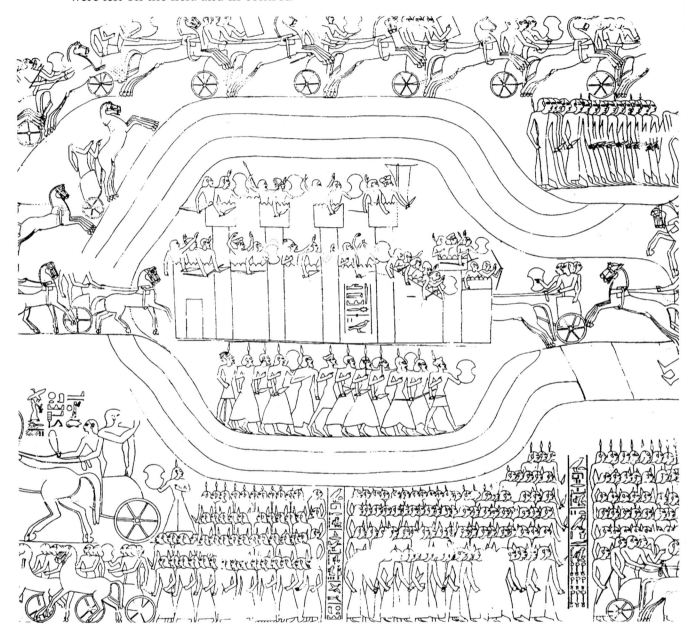

Figure 2-2. In the center, the citadel of Kadesh surrounded by the Orontes River and a tributary. Hittite allies are on the battlements and in front of the fortress. The Hittite army is across the river, above and below. The battle is off to the right and is not shown here. From a relief at Luxor temple, Egypt.

Egyptian records provide some information about the size of the two armies at Kadesh. One places the Hittite force at seventeen thousand infantry and chariot and the Egyptian army at twenty thousand. These numbers may seem small considering that the Hittite and Egypt empires were superpowers of that time. But in view of the very much smaller population in the world in that time, and in consideration of difficulties in supplying large forces in the field, these numbers are realistic, and perhaps even exaggerated.

Temple Scenes

Ramesses publicized his "victory" in monuments all over Egypt. At Luxor there are the remains of a remarkable temple with sculptures in relief illustrating the story of Kadesh. Long before Ramesses, Egypt had mastered the techniques required to execute such large scale illustrations, and the Kadesh sculpture at Luxor is a masterpiece of composition and clarity. The problem that the designer faced was to represent the complex and tumultuous events of Kadesh, including Ramesses' supreme heroism and victory. It was necessary to show each of the groups who participated in the battle in such a way that the onlooker would instantly recognize each. While hieroglyphic text accompanied the panorama and explained it, the designers knew that many onlookers would be illiterate, and others would not have the patience to read the inscribed text. The illustration had to tell the story. The designers and sculptors succeeded well, figure 2-2. In the left center, the viewer sees the fortress of Kadesh, with battlements and towers. Around Kadesh, the streams of the Orontes flow. On the battlements warriors excitedly wave their weapons. Just outside the fortress others are assembled, armed and ready. They are armed with bows, spears, short-swords. These warriors are part of the Hittite forces. Distinct nationalities are evident. Hittites can be recognized by their hairstyle. From the ears forward, the head is shaved bare. From the ears back, the hair flows thick and straight down the back. Shasu are recognized by their strange hair-wrap, Syrians by their long hair, beards and robes, and other nationalities by long braided hair, or a beret. Presumably, the Egyptian viewers recognized representations of these different nationalities.

In the right center (omitted from Figure 2-2) is Ramesses in his chariot, facing Kadesh. He is superhuman in size, towering over ordinary mortals. His horses rear as he draws his bow full back, aiming at the enemy. His draw of the huge bow is effortless, languid, his appearance perfect and god-like.

Across the bottom at the left, the Hittite infantry is drawn up, rank upon rank, armed with spears and short-swords. Forward of them is the Hittite chariotry, charging toward the right and surging around Ramesses. The chariots each carry two fighters and a charioteer.

Across the top of the illustration, other Hittite chariot formations are charging forward, also surging around Pharaoh. Several nationalities are evident among the Hittite chariotry.

On the far left is a figure of larger than ordinary size, yet much smaller than Ramesses. He is well back from the action, though looking toward it, but his chariot is faced away from the action as if a quick escape is contemplated. This is how the Egyptians present Muwatalli, the Hittite king.

In the center of the composition, between the illustrations of Kadesh and Ramesses, is a scene of chaotic battle. Hittite chariots and horses are overturned. Bodies, all of them Hittite or Hittite allies, are tumbling through air, upside down, prone on the ground, or in the river. Many are impaled with arrows, apparently from Pharaoh's effortless bow, for no other Egyptian archers are shown in action. It is a massive slaughter. Some of the Hittite chariotry escapes the field of combat, fleeing into the shelter of the fortress of Kadesh.

In the upper left, orderly ranks of Egyptian infantry are marching toward the scene of battle. This is the detachment coming in from Amurru. It is the story in pictures as Ramesses wanted it told. The enemies' ranks are vast. Ramesses defeats them single-handedly. He is god-like. The gods protect Pharaoh and protect Egypt, a theme seen in other Egyptian illustrations from other times. God-like, larger than life, Pharaoh smites the enemy. They are crushed beneath his feet or under the wheels of his chariot. In most such illustrations, the enemy are not shown in neat ranks as are the Hittites at Kadesh. Usually, they are shown as a disordered mob. Illustrated this way, they represent the forces of disorder and chaos, and the gods of Egypt and Pharaoh keep the forces of disorder away from Egypt.

After Kadesh, Ramesses II returned to Egypt and lived a long life. He filled Egypt with monuments: temples, inscriptions, massive statues dedicated to his own immortal glory. Egyptian kings each had several names, and one of the names of Ramesses was User-maatre-setepenre, as it may have been pronounced. The English poet Percy Bysshe Shelly used this name in the form in which it was handed down from Classical times: "Ozymandias." In his poem of that name, he wrote of a recent traveler who came upon the remains of a fallen statue of Ramesses in the Egyptian desert. On the base, there is an inscription:

> My name is Ozymandias, king of kings;
> Look on my works, ye Mighty, and despair!
> Nothing beside remains. Round the decay
> Of that colossal wreck, boundless and bare
> The lone and level sands stretch far away.

So far as is known, Hittite kings set up no great monuments to themselves.

National Groups at Kadesh

With Pharaoh at Kadesh were the Sherdan. The most striking thing about them as shown in the illustrations are their helmets. In shape it is much like those worn by modern armies. Following the head contour across the top and down to the brow, it came down to cover the ears and then the upper neck. Mounted at the top of the helmet is a ball on a stalk. More will be said of Sherdan in a later chapter.

Figure 2-3. An Egyptian attempt to portray Hittite allies or vassals. By their conventionalized appearance, most are from Syria, including Kadesh. Fourth from left is a Hittite, while the first, sixth, ninth, and twelfth are Shasu.

On the Hittite side, sixteen different national groups are named in the Egyptian inscription. There are contingents from Syria, Kargamish, Ugarit, Aleppo, and of course Kadesh. The Anatolian states or peoples in support of the Hittites, either as mercenaries or in conformity with their vassal obligations, included Arzawa, Dardany, Lukka, Masa, Kaska. Names as shown represent the most likely reading of the Egyptian hieroglyphics. In Egyptian hieroglyphic writing only consonants are represented; vowels were understood by the Egyptian reader based on familiarity and the context of use. Modern translators are left guessing. As an example, the name "Sherdan" is spelled Sh-R-D-N in the Egyptian hieroglyphic text. Does this represent Sherden, Sherdan, Shardan, Shardana? Each has been proposed by scholars. In addition, hieroglyphics use the same symbol to represent both the "l" sound and the "r" sound. Thus, there appears in Egyptian hieroglyphic the name L-K or perhaps R-K. And what are the vowels in this name? As it turns out, scholars are agreed in taking this name to represent Lukka as shown in the list above, the Lukka people. The problem of the intended sound in hieroglyphic writing is a particularly serious one where ethnic names are concerned, since it is important to be able to match the pronunciation of the name as the Egyptians heard it to names written in a different language, in a different place. Names of some of the Sea Peoples are affected, and the problem leads to uncertainty of their identity and origin.

3
Hittites Build an Empire

After the Battle of Kadesh, Hittite influence and control extended westward to the Aegean Sea, eastward to the Euphrates river, and southward in Syria nearly to the border of Canaan. In this vast territory were assorted kingdoms pledged to the Hittites. The Hittite king was responsible for their foreign relations, extracted tribute from them, defended them, and called upon their armies in time of need, so it is accurate to refer to a Hittite empire. It was, so far as is known, the most extensive empire of the Late Bronze Age. Military contingents from these vassal states and certain subordinated tribes appeared with the Hittites at Kadesh. The Hittite king drained away all of his silver to hire them, Ramesses said, to which there was a degree of truth. Hittite policy was to pay vassal troops once they reported to the Hittites for duty.

Extensive as was this empire, and powerful as was the Hittite army, the empire was not entirely stable or secure. Not everyone accepted Hittite rule serenely, particularly in Anatolia itself, and Hittite history reflects a continuing effort to control troublesome neighbors. In the mountains to the north of the Hittite heartland were the Kaska tribes, who seemed to have had an enduring and inexplicable hostility to the Hittites. Hattusa, the Hittite capital, was located dangerously close to Kaska country. Once, and perhaps more than once, Kaska raiders succeeded in entering Hattusa and putting the city to the torch. Counterattacking Hittite armies might burn Kaska villages but find few Kaska, most of whom would vanish into the inaccessible mountains. Thus, the Hittites could never deliver the decisive blow which would defeat the Kaska once and for all.

In southwestern Anatolia, in the mountains and along the Mediterranean coast, were the Lukka people. Like the Kaska, Lukka were largely village dwellers. Their cities were small and few and the Lukka were, in part for that reason, resistant to complete domination by the Hittites. Hattusa was safely distant from Lukka country, however, and occasional Lukka uprisings were more of an annoyance than a threat.

In contrast to these groups, which were usually poorly organized, the country of Arzawa was a formidable rival of the Hittites. For a time around 1350 BC, Arzawa controlled Seha

River Land and Wilusa and other states in western Anatolia, forming what was in effect an Arzawan empire.

Arzawa, Seha River Land, Wilusa, and other nearby states were completely unknown to historians until the Hittite texts were translated in the early 1900s, though the name Arzawa had been found earlier in an Egyptian record. It was evident that these lands were important in the history of Anatolia in the Late Bronze Age, but their geographic locations were far from clear. Unfortunately, no map has ever been found in the Hittite ruins. There is no reason to think that the Hittites used maps. Hittite texts furnish no location, provide no compass direction, give no distances. As a result, the political geography of Anatolia as it existed in Hittite times has been somewhat of a mystery.

Clues have been found, however, in certain Hittite texts. Hittite kings attended religious festivals as part of their duties, and the texts report the circuit of cities through which they traveled. These provide information on the geographic relationship of one city to another. Records of military campaigns list cities through which Hittite armies passed, or near which they camped or fought, and sometimes the number of days' march between cities is given. Rivers were crossed, and sometimes it is possible to guess which rivers these were. A march that might terminate near the sea, a military campaign near the sea—all of these data provide clues which are useful to geographers. Further clues are available in the names of cities mentioned in the Hittite records. With slight changes in sound, some names continued to be used almost a thousand years after the end of the Bronze Age, and their locations are known from the writings of Classical period geographers.

This information forms a jigsaw puzzle, one in which pieces are missing but in which the existing pieces must fit together in some logical way. Here experts differ, proposing a number of differing solutions, with a variety of conflicting maps. For use here, the geography developed by John Garstang and O. R. Gurney is followed, with modifications. Their work, summarized in *Geography of the Hittite Empire* (1959), has been attacked by critics as questionable so far as locations in northern and eastern Anatolia are concerned, but appears to remain reasonable in the west. They locate Arzawa near the Aegean coast, with the Seha River Land just north along the coast. Wilusa is further north on the coast but stretching substantially inland. The Lukka, as already noted, lived on or near the southwest coast, Figure 3-1.

Garstang and Gurney place Arzawa where Lydia was located in the Classical period. Lydia is known to have had rich and extensive farmlands in the broad valley of the Maeander River. Those same fertile lands probably supported a large population in the Bronze Age, which would likely have been a source of the economic and military strength of Arzawa. Mysia of the Classical period was likely the successor to the Seha River Land. Phrygia occupied much of what was Wilusa, and also additional territory inland to the east. Classical Lycia corresponds approximately to the territory of the Lukka of Hittite times.

Figure 3-1. Western Anatolia and northwest Syria, 1250-1200 BC. Names in parentheses are post Bronze Age.

In addition to these, Hittite records mention certain cities in the west. Apasas, as the Hittites called it, is likely to have continued to exist into the Classical period when it was known to the Greeks as Ephesos (Ephesus). The name Ephesos is likely a Greek adaptation of the earlier Bronze Age name, Apasas, or of some name in the Luvian language similar to Apasas but closer in sound to the Greek. Milawata, also called Millawanda, was almost certainly Miletus of Classical times. The Hittites knew of Troy. Hittite records also refer to Lazpas, and this is thought to be the island which the Greeks called Lesbos.

Rebellion in the West

In the great arc of states which extended from Greece to Egypt, and which included most of the civilized world of the Bronze Age, there is no region of which less is known than western Anatolia. But without reckoning with western Anatolia, the situation that existed at the end of the Bronze Age cannot be completely understood. Though most of the history of the region is lost, vanquished by time, it is certain that these lands with their fertile valleys, relatively large populations, and extensive coasts must have had a strong influence on much of the rest of the Bronze Age world. Here lived vigorous and ambitious peoples, able to stand against the Hittites on many occasions. At one time, an Arzawa army penetrated into Hittite country and may even have entered Hattusa itself. Under one of her kings, Tarhunda-Radu, Arzawa exchanged diplomatic correspondence with Egypt, thus attaining status as an international power.

The royal courts of these western countries were literate, for not only did they exchange correspondence with other countries, but participated in written treaties. What the arts and the literature of these populous and presumably civilized lands might have been is unknown. Their capitals, except for Troy, have not been found. For that reason, it is profoundly disappointing in some ways that excavations at Troy have yielded little Bronze Age art and no archives. Archaeologists have reached Bronze Age levels at Miletus, but exposures are not yet extensive. The precise location of the site of Apasas, the Arzawan capital, though no doubt near Ephesus, is not yet known.

Obviously, the discovery of the archives of these western cities or states could be overwhelming in importance. Until such a time, almost all of the history of these lands must be inferred from the Hittite records. Fortunate though it is that the Hittite archives with their thousands of records have been found, it must be recognized that the records necessarily tell of the situation in western Anatolia from the Hittite viewpoint. Events seen almost entirely through Hittite eyes and written about primarily by them can seriously distort historic interpretation.

The Hittite perspective of the western lands seems to have been that they were breeding grounds of instability and at times sources of active threat. On several occasions, Hittite armies marched westward and imposed friendly kings who were required to sign Hittite vassal treaties and take the vassal's oath. While the demands imposed on vassals by the Hittites were often surprisingly light, the Westerners sometimes saw the Hittites as oppressors, and the story in the West is one of occasional rebellion against Hittite domination. Revolts were particularly likely to occur when the Hittite army was engaged elsewhere, or when the government in Hattusa itself was in turmoil for one reason or another.

The motivation for such uprisings was, in part, the ambition of local kings or men who would be kings. But the frequency of uprisings suggests other factors, something akin to nationalism. Westerners and Hittites spoke closely related languages, and it is likely that their social organization and beliefs were similar. However, similar does not mean identical, and those who had ambitions or grievances would have found ways to exaggerate the differences. Further, people who may have been of Hurrian ancestry had succeeded to the throne in Hattusa and brought with them alien Hurrian gods and Hurrian beliefs. These foreign beliefs probably flowed westward with the Hittite armies and, if made an issue by local firebrands, may have added to resentment of the Hittites. Certainly the requirement to hand over tribute to far-off Hattusa was also a source of resentment.

The Hittite records tell of the West largely in terms of strong opponents who troubled the Hittites. The earliest known of these men was Madduwatta.

Madduwatta Wins a Kingdom

The events to be described occurred during the reigns of King Tudhaliya II (1390-1370 BC) and his son Arnuwanda I (1370-1355 BC). Tudhaliya carried out an aggressive military campaign in western Anatolia, defeating Arzawa, and smashing an anti-Hittite alliance called the Assuwa league. Possibly Greeks were involved, since certain evidence may indicate their presence in western Anatolia at that time. A fine sword of Mycenaean manufacture was discovered just outside the walls of Hattusa and may have been a war prize taken from Greeks during that campaign. On it is inscribed:

> As Tudhaliya the Great King shattered the Assuwa-County he dedicated these swords to the Storm-God, his Lord.

The other swords that this inscription mentions have not been found. His campaign in the west finished, Tudhaliya withdrew and returned to Hattusa. No doubt he thought that the west had been pacified. It is against this background that Madduwatta arose.

Scribes of King Arnuwanda prepared a tablet, written in cuneiform, about three thousand words in translation, which summarizes what is now known about the Madduwatta affair. The text is referred to today as the Indictment of Madduwatta, or the Misdeeds of Madduwatta, since it takes the form of an accusatory presentment.

Madduwatta is surely one of the most interesting characters of which ancient history provides some record. Of Madduwatta's beginnings, nothing is known. He entered the picture as a very minor Hittite vassal with some small territory in the west. Somehow, for a reason not explained in the Indictment, he ran afoul of Attarissiyas, a warlord whose base of operations was probably in the southwestern corner of Anatolia, in the area marked as "Lukka" on the map, or possibly in Millawanda. Attarissiyas attacked Madduwatta, who fled for his life, taking with him his wife, children, and a few loyal supporters. His troubles reached the ear of his lord, the Hittite king. Possibly, Madduwatta appeared at the court at Hattusa and explained his situation. The king found him a new vassal territory near Mount Zippasla, safely removed from his previous fiefdom. In return for his new fief, Madduwatta took the customary vassal's oath with its standard provisions. Among these were the stipulations that he would stay within the frontiers assigned to him, report rumors of rebellion, deliver back fugitives, and fight the king's enemies when requested to do so. In addition, he was particularly directed to treat Arzawa as an enemy.

There is no doubt that Madduwatta owed his life to the Hittites. King Arnuwanda did not hesitate to remind Madduwatta of what Tudhaliya, the king's father, had done.

> Attarissiyas the Ahhiyan drove you out of your land and pursued you and attempted to kill you. You fled to the father of My Majesty [the Hittite king referring to himself] who saved you from death and drove off Attarissiyas. ...You and your women, children, troops, chariot warriors, were sheltered by the father of My Majesty. He gave you seed, beer, malt, wine, bread, cheese, everything in abundance. ...The father of My Majesty preserved you, Madduwatta, together with your women, children, and troops when you were hungry, and saved you from the sword of Attarissiyas. For otherwise, the dogs would have devoured you. If you had escaped Attarissiyas, you would have died of hunger. (*Aid to the Hittites*)

The next that is heard of Madduwatta is that he has launched an attack on Arzawa. Whether this was done at the instigation of Hattusa or was entirely at his own initiative is unclear, but he suffered a severe defeat. Again, a Hittite force came to his rescue and he was restored to his rule in Zippasla. Hardly had he time to recover when his old enemy, Attarissiyas, appeared before Zippasla with an army of a hundred chariots and perhaps a thousand foot soldiers. Once again, Madduwatta ran for his life. A Hittite army under general Kisnapili was sent and defeated Attarissiyas. Madduwatta was set back on his throne.

It is apparently at this point that Madduwatta begins to consider his situation. Subsequent events show that Madduwatta had reached certain conclusions and made some fateful decisions.

General Kisnapili with his second in command, Partahulla, was dispatched by the Hittite king to Lukka territory. Here they were to deal with Dalawa and Hinduwa, two towns which were giving the Hittites trouble, perhaps by withholding tribute payments. What follows is best told in words from the Indictment.

> Madduwatta wrote to Kisnapili: "I'll attack Dalawa, and meanwhile you attack Hinduwa. In that way you will be able to defeat Hinduwa." So Kisnapili led his troops to Hinduwa for battle. But Madduwatta did not lead his troops to Dalawa. Instead, he sent a message to Dalawa saying: "The Hittites are marching on Hinduwa. Waylay them and attack them. Dalawa sent her troops out on the road and they ambushed our troops and captured them." They killed Kisnapili and Partahulla. And it was Madduwatta who incited them. Then Madduwatta enticed Dalawa away from allegiance to Hatti, placed Dalawa under oath to himself, and henceforth their tribute went to him. (*Geography*)

It appears that Madduwatta was on a path in which no treachery or deceit was too extravagant. He made a treaty with King Kupanta-Runta of Arzawa which, according to his oath, he was to regard as an enemy land. Kupanta-Runta had been an old foe of the

Hittites. When the Hittites inquired, Madduwatta had an explanation. He had a scheme. His treaty with Kupanta was really a ruse. Madduwatta agreed to it to put Kupanta off his guard. He would offer his daughter in marriage to Kupanta, and when Kupanta came to Madduwatta's house, he would be taken prisoner. "Do you agree?" he asks of the Hittite king. It may have been at this time that the Hittite king observed that "I have entered very deeply into the soul of Madduwatta." What he finds there is not recorded.

A new scheme was proposed. If the Hittite king would grant Madduwatta fief lands on the Siyanta River (apparently the upper Meander River), Madduwatta would stand as a sentinel against the Arzawans. The Indictment must omit other information, because the next thing which is reported is that Madduwatta has taken control of the kingdom of Arzawa!

To the Hittites, Madduwatta now proposed a joint attack on Hapalla, a small western kingdom in rebellion against Hatti. Madduwatta would get the spoils, the Hittites would regain control of Hapalla. Madduwatta led the Hittite army into a trap, and took Hapalla for himself.

In view of Madduwatta's treacherous behavior in the past, it is hard to understand how the Hittites could have been so gullible. By diplomacy, guile, or force, Madduwatta took control of a number of the nearby kingdoms which owed allegiance to Hattusa. They were pledged to him and paid tribute to him. A powerful coalition lead by Madduwatta was assembled with Arzawa at the center.

Finally, the Hittites had enough. An army was sent, and marched along the lower, or southern, route which lead from Hattusa to the West. The route passed through Pittassa. Madduwatta stirred up a rebellion in Pittassa that effectively blocked the Hittite advance. Rather than pressing forward, the Hittites abandoned their military operation and turned to diplomacy. An ambassador, Mulliyara, was sent to Madduwatta. Mulliyara spoke the words of the Hittite king and complained of the encroachments on Hittite-controlled territory. Madduwatta was also harboring a Hittite fugitive by the name of Niwall. "Turn Niwall over to me," the ambassador demanded. In a reply, breathtaking in its audacity, Madduwatta replies, "Niwall is not with me. He is staying with my son, and I can't be expected to be responsible for my sons' guests!"

Madduwatta was happy to receive delegations from the Hittites, to apply soothing words, and to constantly assure them of his loyalty to the Hittite king.

The last recorded activity of Madduwatta has to do with the land of Alasia. Scholars have not fully agreed about Alasia (see Chapter 11), but the preponderance of the evidence indicates that it was the island of Cyprus, or perhaps a portion of Cyprus. In another astonishing turnabout, agile Madduwatta joined with his former enemy, Attarissiyas. Together with the mysterious "man of Piggaya," they led a raid on Alasia, taking prisoners away with them. Arnuwanda, the Hittite king, was outraged and informed Madduwatta that Alasia was a Hittite protectorate. The king demanded an explanation and a return of prisoners. Madduwatta never lacked an excuse.

> When Attarissiyas and the man of Piggaya raided Alashia, I joined them. Neither Your Majesty nor your father ever said to me "Alashia is mine! Recognize it as such!" Now if Your Majesty wants the captives from Alashia returned, I will return them to him.

To which the king replied:

> Since Attarissiyas and the man of Piggaya are independent of My Majesty while you are a subject of My Majesty, why did you join them? (*Geography*)

Thus ends the tale of Madduwatta, so far as it is known. Not every line of the Indictment can be read clearly. The last two lines have been translated, enigmatically as: "Now I will squeal like a pig and then die (Page, 1963)." The significance of this is unknown.

Special attention should be given to two factors in the record of Madduwatta. The first is that Attarissiyas is referred to as "the man of Ahhiya." In later years, the word Ahhiya is given in the alternative form "Ahhiyawa." A great deal of scholarly attention has been given to this name. A fuller discussion appears at the end of this chapter, but in summary, the terms Ahhiya or Ahhiyawa appears to refer to the territory of the Mycenaean Greeks. This warlord Attarissiyas was in all likelihood a Greek operating on Anatolian soil. On that assumption, the Indictment of Madduwatta contains the earliest known reference to a Greek on Anatolian soil. It is, in fact, the earliest reference presently known to a Greek anywhere.

The second factor to be noted is the raid on Alasia (Cyprus) from Anatolian soil, very likely launched from the Lukka coast. This is a harbinger of events to come, events which would have their significance in history.

The Kaska Attack

How could Madduwatta, this once minor Hittite vassal turned renegade, get away with such affronts to Hittite power? It is particularly mysterious in view of the answer that Arnuwanda returned to the Madduwatta's message concerning Alasia. In this, the king says "…you are a subject of My Majesty…" Did Arnuwanda really consider Madduwatta to be a more or less faithful subject? Is it possible that many of his activities were carried out at the behest of the leadership in Hattusa? If this is so, then enemies of Madduwatta at the Hittite court may have intrigued to undermine him, resulting in the Indictment. Within present knowledge, it is impossible to say. However, it is likely that there is a quite different explanation for the failure of the Hittites to respond forcefully to what appears to be a clear pattern of treachery and deceit by Madduwatta. The Kaska had launched an attack into the heart of the Hittite realm.

In the century following 1450 BC, there were two or possibly three kings with the throne name Tudhaliya. Hittite records do not always distinguish between them and, as a result, it is not always clear to which king an ancient record refers. It is likely, however, that it was in the reign of Tudhaliya II and his son Arnuwanda I, the above mentioned kings, that the Kaska staged one of their most devastating attacks. So serious was the assault that Hittite attention could well have been drawn away from affairs in the West where Madduwatta was gnawing away at Hittite rule.

North of Hattusa and close to Kaska country, and thus especially vulnerable, were a number of old Hittite cities. These the Kaska wrested away. The impact of the loss of these cities was incalculable. They were not only key strongholds of the northern defense, but some were also holy cities containing the shrines of the most ancient and revered Hittite gods. Important among these were the cities of Nerik and Hakpis. That the situation was desperate is shown by Hittite prayers which have been found and translated. The following is directed to the god Zithariya, and through him to the other gods.

> The Kaskeans have begun the war. They boast of their power and strength. They make light of you, O gods! See! Zithariya is appealing to all of you gods; he brings his complaints before you. So pass judgment on his case all you gods! Let it be of great concern to all the gods!
>
> In fact the sanctuaries have been taken away not from Zithariya alone, they have been taken away from all of you; the Sun-goddess of Arinna, the Storm-god of Nerik, from Telepinus and from all the other gods.
>
> See! Zithariya is bringing his case before all of you. Take your own case to heart! Judge your own case as you pass judgment on the case of Zithariya!
>
> Blot out the Kaskean country O gods! Let every single god take thought of the place where he is worshipped and win it back!

(There is a gap in the record here, where it is probably urged that the Kaska gods be invited to a talk.)

> O gods of the Kaskean country! We have summoned you before this assembly. Come, eat and drink! Now hear the accusation which we bring against you! The gods of the Hatti land have done nothing against you! But you, the gods of the Kaska country began war. You drove out the Hatti gods and took over their realm for yourselves. The Kaskean people also began war. From the Hittites you took away their cities and drove them out of their fields and vineyards.

> The gods of Hatti and the Hatti people call for bloody revenge. The vengeance of the Hatti gods and the Hatti people will be wrought on you, the gods of the Kaskean country and the Kaskean people! (*ANET*)

In this prayer, it is interesting to note that the gods take sides in a war among men. Though they take sides, the gods are able to discuss their differences amicably. This situation foreshadows what will appear later in *Iliad*, the great work of the poet Homer. In *Iliad*, some of the gods support Troy and others aid the Greeks. But the gods still talk civilly among themselves while the deadly battle rages among men.

The Kaska problem continued. Arnuwanda and his queen, Asmunikal, offered a prayer in which they regret the loss of the northern cult city of Nerik and remind the gods of Nerik how well they have taken care of them in the past. This was, presumably, in contrast to the treatment the gods received at the hands of the barbarian Kaska. The gods of Nerik were assured that all of their worship will be maintained even though their images must be moved to Hakpis, a northern city still under Hittite control.

It is evident that the Hittites were hard-pressed. They needed more than the power of their armies to repulse the Kaska. In the time of the next Hittite king, it appears that the capital at Hattusa was invaded and burned. Arzawa took advantage of the situation and invaded the Hittite heartland. For a time, Arzawa was the dominant power in Anatolia. The king of Egypt wrote to the king of Arzawa: "I have heard that everything is finished and that the land of Hattusa has gone to pieces!" This is the low tide of Hittite rule.

Empire in the Southeast

Pressure from invading Kaska continued. Hattusa was abandoned and the government was transferred eastward to Samuha. Then, in a series of brilliant military campaigns while yet a prince, Suppiluliuma led Hittite armies westward, retook Hattusa, and advanced into Arzawa territory. As king, Suppiluliuma (1344-1322 BC) was able to deal with problems which had arisen far away in the southeast. There, the Hurrian state of Mitanni had grown powerful and threatened Hittite interests. Suppiluliuma lead his army in a direct attack on Mitanni but was repulsed. He reorganized, strengthened his forces, and returned. In a march through the mountains, striking Mitanni from the north rather than the east as before, he took the Mitannian capital of Wassukkanni by surprise. The report of this campaign is extensive, but the following provides the sense of it.

> I, My Majesty, Suppiluliumas, the Great King, the King of Hatti land, the Valiant, the favorite of the Storm-god....reached Wassukkanni. The inhabitants of the provincial center Suta together with cattle, sheep, horses, together with their possessions and their deportees I brought to the Hatti land. Tusratta the king had

departed. He did not meet me in battle. I turned around and recrossed the Euphrates. I vanquished the country of Halba [Aleppo] and Mukish....Because of Tusratta's presumptuousness, I raided all the countries in a single year and conquered them for the Hatti land. (*Deeds*)

Mitanni was never again an independent state. The Hittites propped up a new ruler friendly to them on the throne of Mitanni. Assyria, until then a vassal of Mitanni, wiggled free and began to assert itself.

Archaeologists have looked for the site of Wassukkanni, the Hurrian capital, but it has never been found. The archives of Wassukkanni could provide a treasure of information about events of these times, particularly those that are not fully understood from the Hittite records.

Suppiluliuma was not finished. Hittite forces rolled southeast, sweeping through Syria and close to Damascus and, in a subsequent attack, captured Kargamish an important fortress city on the Euphrates. When these campaigns were completed, Ugarit, Kadesh, and Amurru had become Hittite vassal states, and in Kargamish Suppiluliuma installed a son as king. This would be the beginning of a long line of Hittite kings in Kargamish through which the Great King in Hattusa controlled much of eastern Anatolia and northern Syria.

Figure 3-2. A Hittite, from a relief at Karnak temple. Many Egyptian relief sculptures and paintings meticulously illustrate the peoples with whom Egypt had contact.

While Suppiluliuma was at Kargamish, an unusual episode occurred which had to do with events in Egypt. Pharaoh Tutankhamon had died and was entombed in regal splendor. The tomb of King Tut, as he is called, is well known since it was rediscovered by Howard Carter at the west bank at Luxor, Egypt. In the forechamber of the tomb were chariots and weapons, gold-inlaid furniture, chests of jewelry. Of special interest is a representation of the king and his queen, Ankhesenamun, rendered in vivid color on a chair of gold. A picture of the king hunting also shows the queen. The inner chamber was entered and it was evident that it had been undisturbed since the day it was sealed. It contained even more spectacular finds, and on the mummy of the king was an exquisite mask of gold which covered head and shoulders.

Tut had died young, and Queen Ankhesenamun attempted to rule in his stead. She had no son to be heir to the throne, and no doubt she was pressed by ambitious suitors who thought they might gain the throne through her. Suppiluliuma received a strange message from Queen Ankhesenamun.

> My husband died and I have no son. They say you have many sons. If you would give me one of your sons, he would become my husband. I could never take a servant [subject] of mine and make him my husband!

When he heard this, Suppiluliuma called his leading men into council. "In all my years, I never heard such a thing!" They discussed the situation and decided to send the king's trusted deputy, Hattusa-Ziti, to Egypt to determine if this message was genuine. "Bring accurate information back to me," said the king. In due course, Hattusa-Ziti returned accompanied by the queen's representative with another message from the queen.

> Why did you say "they may be deceiving me?" If I had a son would I write to a foreign country in a manner which is shameful to my country and myself? My husband died. I have no son. Should I make one of my servants my husband? I have written to no other country about this, only to you! (*Deeds*)

Presumably, Ankhesenamun thought that if only she had a son through this Hittite prince, a legitimate heir to the throne, she might retain power as regent until he reached maturity. Her judgment of the situation could not have been more wrong. Suppiluliuma sent a son to Egypt, the young prince Zannanza. But he never arrived at the Egyptian court. Somewhere in Egyptian-controlled territory, Zannanza was waylaid and assassinated. There is no reason to doubt that the assassination was arranged by powerful Egyptians who were hostile to the idea that a foreigner should become king, especially a Hittite! Had this marriage taken place, the two most powerful states of the era would have united and much in history would have turned out differently.

However, it was time to turn attention once again to the West, where Arzawa was still powerful. Suppiluliuma reestablished Hittite influence and arranged vassal treaties with several small kingdoms around Arzawa. Apparently, some sort of treaty was established with Arzawa itself and its king Uhha-Ziti.

War prisoners from Suppiluliuma's retaliatory attack on Egyptian territory had been brought back to Hatti, and with them came a dreadful epidemic. Many died, including King Suppiluliuma himself. His son succeeded him, and within the year he too died in the epidemic. This contagion continued to rage for a number of years. A younger son of Suppiluliuma, Mursili II, took the throne.

Suppiluliuma left behind an empire. Successors struggled to preserve it.

Uhha-Ziti and Ahhiyawa

Mursili II (1321-1298 BC) was a true son of his father, an aggressive and brilliant military commander. In the first two years of his reign, he directed his attention to the north in a series of punitive raids against the Kaska. It is evident from succeeding events that this was but the first step in a strategic plan. First, the Kaska would be pacified, so far as possible, thus stabilizing the northern frontier. Internal rivalries among the Kaska would be exploited, and some Kaska would be taken into service as mercenaries. The Southeast was already stable under the watchful eye of the king's brother, who ruled from Kargamish. Full attention could now be given to the West, where there was unfinished business.

The king of Millawanda on the Aegean coast was bound to the Hittites by a vassal treaty. In Arzawa, King Uhha-Ziti began to feel threatened by a ring of Hittite vassal states with which he was increasingly surrounded. He responded by subverting Millawanda, drawing it away from allegiance to the Hittites. Ahhiyawa, the Mycenaean Greeks, were involved, secretly supporting the defection of Millawanda. Mursili could not allow Millawanda to renounce a vassal treaty. The West was bound to the Hittites by such treaties rather than by the presence of occupying Hittite troops, and if Millawanda was allowed to slip away, others might quickly follow. The West would again become an unstable and dangerous quagmire.

Mursili, still engaged with the Kaska, sent an army westward under two senior commanders, Gulla and Mala-Ziti. They attacked and entered Millawanda, inflicting significant damage. Archaeologists have found evidence of substantial destruction at the site of Miletus (Millawanda) datable to about this time which may have been due to this Hittite attack. Allegiance to the Hittite king was restored, presumably by placing a new puppet on the throne in Millawanda. Then the Hittite army returned home.

In the view of Mursili, more was required. Mursili had probably planned a showdown with Arzawa from the beginning. By the end of his third year of rule, a large Hittite army was on the move. It was joined en route by the army of Kargamish, brought up from the southeast by the king's brother. At the River Astarpa, well east of the heart of Arzawa country, an Arzawan army attempted to block the Hittite advance. The Arzawans, under the command of Piyama-Inara, the eldest son of Uhha-Ziti, were brushed aside by the advancing Hittites.

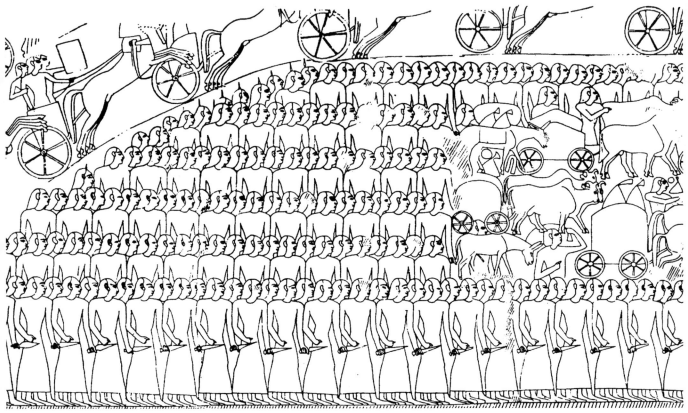

Figure 3-3. The Hittite army. Illustration shows infantry, chariotry, and logistical support in the center right.

Moving west quickly, elements of the Hittite army attempted to enter a Lukka fortress town which they had reason to think would be friendly due to a vassal treaty. They were shocked to find resistance. After a skirmish, some of these Lukka fled to Uhha-Ziti and asked him for protection. Mursili demanded that these fugitives be returned to him, and it is likely that there was a fugitive treaty between Arzawa and Hatti which obligated Uhha-Ziti to do so. Uhha-Ziti, by now an old and presumably wise king, unaccountably refused. "They came voluntarily" he said of the fugitives "and I will not turn them over." Nothing would anger the Hittites more than violation of the terms of a treaty since they took treaty obligations seriously. Perhaps Uhha-Ziti took this stand as a matter of principle. More likely Uhha-Ziti, giving thought to his own alliances with the Seha River Land and others, could not afford to be faced down. This was welcome news to Mursili. He now had a pretext for an all-out attack on Arzawa.

The decision to not return the Lukka fugitives was fatal for Uhha-Ziti and his house. To Uhha-Ziti Mursili wrote:

> My subjects who sought refuge with you have not returned to me. So now to arms! My Lord the Storm-god will decide the justice of our dispute. (*Geography*)

This was a formal declaration of war, and it is interesting that people of more than three thousand years ago were concerned to follow diplomatic protocol.

A strange sight appeared in the sky. A brilliant object proceeded from the rear of the Hittite army and moved westward across the sky toward the Apasas on the Aegean coast. It was in Apasas that Uhha-Ziti had his residence. Word soon reached the Hittites that the strange object crashed into Apasas, causing damage and confusion and wounding Uhha-Ziti in the knee. To the Hittites, this was the "thunderbolt" of the Storm-god and it was a sure sign, confirming to them the justice of their cause. This spectacular occurrence in the sky may have been a meteor. Possibly, it did land in or near Apasas (Ephesus) as the Hittites were told. Turning to a time about fourteen hundred years later, Acts 19:35 reports that the Ephesians venerated a holy object sent to them from heaven in the distant past, conceivably the meteoric stone which afflicted Uhha-Ziti during the reign of Mursili.

Uhha-Ziti looked at the damage in Apasas. Believing as did the Hittites in the intervention of the gods in the affairs of men, learning of the great strength of the approaching Hittite army, he drew the necessary conclusions. He and his family and others slipped out of the city and sought refuge over the sea, probably with the king of Ahhiyawa or under his protection.

Rather than return home for the winter as was the custom, the Hittite army camped in western bases. From these, they attacked as soon as weather conditions allowed. In the fourth year of Mursili, they cleared out remaining resistance at outlying fortresses. Tens of thousands of prisoners were taken and sent back to Hatti to work farmlands. A younger son of Uhha-Ziti organized resistance, but it was futile. Eventually, he emulated his father and fled to Ahhiyawa protection. The war was over. Arzawa, so far as is can be told from Hittite records, was never again an independent political entity, though the region continued to be referred to by that name.

Uhha-Ziti, like Madduwatta before him, is portrayed in the Hittite records as a troublemaker. Only the Hittite side of the story is known, however. It would be remarkable if some day the Arzawa archives were to be found and the story told from the Arzawan viewpoint. It is evident that significant national groups existed in western Anatolia, determined to plot their own course, determined to throw off the Hittite yoke.

After Uhha-Ziti a new political arrangement was established in the West. Wilusa, somewhat remote on the northwest coast, had remained loyal to the Hittites and was not affected. In Seha River Land and Mira, countries that had been aligned with Arzawa, new kings were appointed and placed under a vassal oath. It is likely that the Arzawan heartland was in part divided and allocated to these neighboring states. With this arrangement, the Hittites attempted to reassert control in the West.

The situation in Mira illustrates the unstable situation which affected the region. Before the war, Masuiluwa, the rightful king of Mira, was ousted by his brothers and sought protection at the Hittite court at Hattusa. In time he married a daughter of King Mursili. In the wake of the Hittite conquest of the West, Masuiluwa was reestablished on the throne of Mira and he took the usual vassal oath. It appears that he had every reason to be grateful to the Hittites, but in subsequent years he revolted against them. He was deposed and replaced. Ahhiyawa may have meddled and encouraged this disloyalty.

Mursili and his successors were mindful that Ahhiyawa was behind much of the trouble in the West. Ahhiyawa, the land of the Mycenaean Greeks, appeared to have backed Millawanda in her attempted secession, and may have emboldened Uhha-Ziti in his defiance of the Hittites, and subverted Masuiluwa also. Ahhiyawa would remain a factor with which the Hittites would need to reckon.

In his final years Mursili was very sick. Gods were borrowed from Lazpas and Ahhiyawa in an attempt to effect a cure. This probably refers to idols from the island of Lesbos and probably the Greek-occupied islands or shores. Presumably, the Hittite gods had not proved to be effective. The correct way to address these borrowed gods was not known. However, the Hittite priests were working on the problem and various incantations and prayers were tried. Before a formula could be found, Mursili died and was succeeded by Muwatalli.

Muwatalli II (1295-1271 BC) is the Hittite king of the Battle of Kadesh. In the years before that battle, Muwatalli was engaged in the West in a new attempt to impose friendly kings and achieve the stability which the Hittites thought they had established with the defeat of Arzawa. Muwatalli imposed new vassal treaties, including one with Alaksandus, king of Wilusa. This attention to the West and these new treaties were part of the preparation for the clash with Egypt that Muwatalli saw as inevitable.

These vassal treaties had a nearly standard form. They begin with the titles attached to the king, in this case: "Thus says My Majesty Muwatalli, the Great King, King of Hatti, beloved of the Storm-god, the son of Mursili, the Great King, the Valiant." Then a preamble stated the past relationship between the subject state and previous Hittite kings.

Treaty terms are then set forth. Typically, these include the obligation of vassal kings to return Hittite fugitives, and to report rumors of rebellion in nearby vassal states. There are also obligations of military support. The vassal must bring infantry and chariotry in support of Hittite military operations in his vicinity and in support of other nearby vassal kings. Further, the vassal king must provide military contingents in case the Hittite king comes into conflict with any of the other Great Kings, however distant. The kingdoms of Egypt, Babylonia, and Assyria are specifically mentioned. This clause explains the many vassal contingents that came with King Muwatalli to Kadesh. Treaties were witnessed by a very long list of gods of both Hatti and the vassal state, and their names were all included in the treaties. Treaty documents were placed in the temples of Hattusa, where the gods whose names were invoked could watch that the treaties were honored, or note whom it was that violated them.

These treaties were not one-sided. Loyalty to the Hittite king was rewarded by loyalty to the vassal. If the vassal king were attacked, the Hittite army would come to his defense, and so long as he adhered to the treaty, the Hittites would assure the throne to the vassal king and his descendants forever. The treaty with King Alaksandus of Wilusa states:

> If you keep well to these words then the thousand gods which I My Majesty, the Labarnas Muwatalli, the Great King have convoked, those of Hatti and Wilusa, shall protect you, your wife, your sons and grandsons, your towns, vineyard, field and meadow, your cattle and sheep. At the hand of My Majesty enjoy prosperity and a ripe old age. (*Geography*)

There is some evidence that during the reign of Muwatalli, some sort of arrangement or treaty was made with the king of Ahhiyawa, in which Ahhiyawan sovereignty over Millawanda was recognized, in return for an end to Ahhiyawan interference in western affairs. This would allow Muwatalli to concentrate on the coming conflict with Egypt, the climax of which was the Battle of Kadesh.

A Coup Brings Hattusili to Power

A few years after Kadesh, Muwatalli died. He had no son of his primary wife. In these circumstances, Hittite law directed that the eldest son of a secondary wife should succeed to the throne, and so Urhi-Tesub became king. He took the throne name Mursili III. His was to be a short reign (1271–1264 BC), due to a conflict with his influential and ambitious uncle, Hattusili, the brother of King Muwatalli.

Hattusili prepared a remarkable and lengthy document which has been recovered from the ruins of Hattusa. In this document, he justified his overthrow of Urhi-Tesub, the rightful king. While King Muwatalli ruled, Hattusili explained, there were those at court who were envious of the favors which the king bestowed on him and stirred up false accusations against him. Fortunately his protecting goddess, Sausga, watched over him. "If it was a plot of an enemy, if it was a plot of an opponent at law, if it was a plot of the palace,

My lady Sausga protected me." Muwatalli, the king, entrusted major military campaigns to his brother, and with the help of Sausga, Hattusili was always victorious. But these victories, according to Hattusili, only increased jealousies at court.

Earlier, King Muwatalli had moved the government of the Hittite empire from Hattusa to Tarhuntassa in the south in order to reduce vulnerability to attack from the Kaska. Anticipation of the inevitable war with Egypt played a role in the move, and the more southerly location would also place the government closer to the scene of action. At this sign of apparent weakness, the Kaska raised an insurrection. Hattusili, then a prince, was sent to the northern country to subdue the Kaska and restore order. According to Hattusili:

> Enemy horses were 800 chariot teams while it was impossible to count their infantry. My brother Muwatalli gave me 120 teams of horses, but as to infantry, not even a single man was with me. My lady Sausga marched before me and with my own resources I conquered the enemy.

As a reward for this victory Hattusili was given control of the North and was named king of the northern city of Hakpis. Hittite peasants who had fled before the Kaska advance were resettled. Normal life was restored.

When King Muwatalli marched south to Kadesh, Hattusili accompanied him together with the northern army. Once the Egyptian campaign was over, Hattusili headed home, but on his way he stopped at the southern city of Lawazantiya, where he made offerings to the goddess. This goddess was in the care of a local priest, and as matters worked out, Hattusili married the priest's daughter. This was Pudu-Hepa, who would be one of the most interesting and influential women of which ancient records provide a glimpse. "And we founded a family and the goddess gave us the love of husband and wife, and we got us sons and daughters."

When Muwatalli died, Hattusili was instrumental in placing his nephew Urhi-Tesub on the throne, or so he says. For a while, Hattusili continued to prosper. But then

> Urhi-Tesub observed the kindness of the goddess to me, he envied me, and he brought ill will upon me. He took away all my subjects,....and the depopulated areas I had settled again, all those too he took away from me. Only Hakpis, however …he did not take away.

Hattusili said that he endured this humiliation for seven years.

> But he [Urhi-Tesub] at the command of a god and the suggestion of man tried to destroy me. He took Hakpis and Nerik away from me. And I did not submit any longer….I sent him a declaration of war….Come! Let Sausga of Samuha and the Storm-god of Nerik decide the case!

There is little doubt that Hattusili had friends among the veterans of the army of the North, and of nobles who had grievances. Many had little respect for Urhi-Tesub whom they looked upon as illegitimate since he was the son of a secondary wife.

> To whatever nobles Urhi-Tesub banished, My lady Sausga appeared in a dream saying "…you are summoned in your strength, for I, Sausga, have turned all the lands of Hatti to the side of Hattusili." (*Chrestomathy*)

Pudu-Hepa, the wife of Hattusili, was probably able to ensure support from Lawazantiya, where her father was priest. Even some Kaska groups supported Hattusili. The result was inevitable. Urhi-Tesub was deposed, and Hattusili became king (1264–1239 BC). In exile, Urhi-Tesub attempted to foment trouble, even scheming with the Babylonians and Egyptians in an attempt to regain the throne.

Kurunta, a younger brother of Urhi-Tesub, supported Hattusili in the showdown. Hattusili rewarded him. From the sparsely occupied lands south of the Halys River, Hattusili marked out a kingdom around the city of Tarhuntassa for Kurunta and for his descendants. More than a reward to Kurunta was behind this. The road that connected Hattusa with the Mediterranean port of Ura passed through this land. Very likely, Kurunta was required to build population and strengthen defenses in this strategic region.

The records that survive and tell this story are those of the winner in the conflict between Hattusili and Urhi-Tesub, and it is likely that they are one-sided. There was, no doubt, an Urhi-Tesub side of the story which has not been recovered, if it was ever written. Hattusili proved to be an effective king, but it is very likely that his seizure of the throne created an enduring division of loyalties in Hittite society the effects of which, though not immediately visible, were to be felt in future years.

The Peace of Kadesh

Following the Battle of Kadesh, and some skirmishes along the borders, it became clear to the Egyptians that they were not going to reverse the results of Kadesh. The Hittites would not be pushed back. Ramesses was prepared to accept the fact. What the Egyptians needed now was stability along the border, and assurances that the Hittites under the new king would not push farther south. They were open to diplomatic overtures from the Hittites. The Hittites too needed a respite. There were problems in western Anatolia again. And in the East, Assyria was asserting itself dangerously. Since the conquest by Suppiluliuma, a remnant of Mitanni had been maintained as a buffer between Hittite territories and Assyria. Assyrian king Adad-Nirari I seized that remnant and incorporated it into his realm, showing contempt for Hittite interests there. Assyria now abutted Hittite territory, and Assyrian aggressive intent was worrisome.

In the protocol of those times, the term "Great King" was largely reserved for those who ruled over other kings, and Great Kings were entitled to call one another "Brother." In recent memory, no Assyrian king merited that recognition. Now Adad-Nirari wrote to Hattusili and asked that he be addressed as a Great King and Brother. To this insolent presumption of an upstart, Hattusili returned a sarcastic reply, and told Adad-Nirari not to write to him again about Great King and Brother. The Hittites knew that attention now needed to be given to the threat from Assyria.

Thus, great good sense and practical need finally brought Egypt and the Hittites together in the form of a peace pact now called the Treaty of Kadesh. Though the treaty was signed sixteen years after the Battle of Kadesh, it was in part a response to the new reality established by the battle. The Hittites may have suggested the idea, and from their experience in treaties, provided much of the language and content. It is certain that a good deal of diplomatic contact led up to the signing—in the form of the impress of the seals of the kings. Even Pudu-Hepa was a signatory. The treaty renounced aggression of one party against the other forever; promised military aid to the other should either party be attacked from abroad; ensured recognition of legitimate succession to the throne and in the case of usurpation, promised military aid to restore the rightful claimant; provided for extradition of fugitives; and bound future kings to observe the treaty.

Figure 3-4. Part of the Treaty of Kadesh. Written in cuneiform, this damaged tablet was found in the ruins of Hattusa. An Egyptian copy, written in hieroglyphics, appears on a wall at Karnak temple in Egypt.

The text of this treaty has long been known from an inscription on the wall of the Karnak temple in Luxor, Egypt. Then, early in the first excavations at the site of the Hittite capital of Hattusa, a most remarkable discovery was made: a Hittite copy of this same treaty. It is written in cuneiform on a clay tablet, and parts are missing Figure 3-4, but the text is in remarkable agreement with the Egyptian. This is not the Hittite master copy, however, which was inscribed on a silver tablet which has never been found. A Hittite copy in clay is displayed in a museum in Topkapi Saray, Istanbul.

Figure 3-5. Hattusili (right) introduces his daughter to Ramesses (left) on the eve of their marriage. She was given the Egyptian name Maatornefrure. From a relief on the portico of Abu Simbel in Egypt.

In the years that followed, the Peace of Kadesh was scrupulously maintained by both sides. Some time after the treaty, a marriage was arranged between Ramesses and a daughter of Hattusili. The untiring Pudu-Hepa was deeply involved in the marriage arrangements, and she wrote frequently to Ramesses about the details. An Egyptian record describes the reception of the bride:

> The daughter of the Great Prince of Hatti marched to Egypt, while the infantry, chariotry, and officials of his majesty accompanied her, mingling with the infantry and chariotry of Hatti….all the people of Hatti mingling with those of Egypt. They

ate and drank together, being of one heart like brothers, for peace and brotherhood were between them…

Ramesses seemed to have welcomed the new bride enthusiastically, and after the marriage, she quietly disappeared into the harem.

Piyama-Radu Looks for Empire

Most of what is known of the Piyama-Radu affair comes from a Hittite document known as the Tawagalawa Letter, given that name when a preliminary translation led to an incorrect conclusion that Tawagalawa was the primary subject of discussion. Tawagalawa was a brother of the king of Ahhiyawa and had spent time in Anatolia as a guest of the Hittites. New readings of the text, however, show clearly that Piyama-Radu was the subject. The activities of that remarkable character troubled the reigns of Mursili III (Urhi-Tesub) and Hattusili, and may have begun as early as the reign of Muwatalli. Piyama-Radu is yet another of those men who sought to defy Hittite control and establish an independent power in western Anatolia.

From his base in Millawanda, Piyama-Radu stirred up trouble in the Lukka region, in Seha River Land, and far up the coast in Wilusa, all of which were pledged to the Hittites. Since Millawanda was under Ahhiyawan control, Piyama-Radu must have had the backing of the Mycenaean Greeks. As there were supposed to be friendly relations between the rulers of Ahhiyawa and Hatti, it seems that the Greeks were playing both sides. The Hittites needed quiet in the West, particularly during the Egyptian and Kaska troubles, and wanted no problems with Ahhiyawa. For as long as it could, Hatti maintained the diplomatic fiction that the king of Ahhiyawa knew nothing of the activities of Piyama-Radu.

In time, his patience exhausted, Hattusili and the Hittite army marched west. While en route, Hattusili received a surprising message from Piyama-Radu. "Take me into vassalage. Send me the crown prince and he will conduct me to Your Majesty." Hattusili sent a representative of his own choosing saying, "Go, set him beside you in the chariot and bring him here!" Off went the king's representative to Piyama-Radu, but there had been a breakdown in communications. "My representative" complained Hattusili "was snubbed and humiliated by Piyama-Radu." Word came back from Piyama-Radu. "Give me a kingdom here on the spot! If not, I will not come!" This breach of civility was brought to the attention of the king in Ahhiyawa, as were various other complaints.

> He [Piyama-Radu] is continually raiding my land, but whenever I prevented him from doing that, he comes back to your territory. Are you now, my Brother, favorably disposed to this conduct?....The fact that Piyama-Radu is making repeated attacks on this land, does my Brother know this or does he not know it?

> But when my Brother's messenger arrived at my headquarters, he brought me no greetings and no present, but said "He has written to Atpas [governor in Millawanda] saying put Piyama-Radu at the disposal of the king of Hatti."

The Hittites marched to Millawanda to collect Piyama-Radu and—surprise!—he was no longer there. He had fled, taking ship to Ahhiyawa. Did the king of Ahhiyawa really expect Piyama-Radu to be turned over to the Hittites by Atpas? Atpas was the son-in-law of Piyama-Radu.

Piyama-Radu should come to him, wrote Hattusili to the king of Ahhiyawa.

> Piyama-Radu will be safe....Give Piyama-Radu a message. "Come, make an appeal to me, and I will set you on the road to promotion....If you are satisfied, let it be so, if you are not, then one of my men will bring you back, just as you came, to Ahhiyawa." (*Geography*)

A close relative of the queen would remain behind in Ahhiyawa until the matter was resolved, as a guarantee of safe conduct for Piyama-Radu. Finally, Hattusili offered an apology. Hattusili had used harsh words in an earlier communication to the king of Ahhiyawa, but at the time, Hattusili was young and impulsive. And hard words were returned. Now, they should put all this behind them.

The records say no more about Piyama-Radu, and this may indicate that he was, in the end, turned over to the Hittites.

Piyama-Radu had come close to wrenching the West from Hittite control, to establishing a new western empire, in effect a new Arzawa. It would have stretched from Wilusa in the north to the Lukka lands in the south, and included the old Arzawan homeland, Seha River, and other kingdoms as well. It would have looked westward to Ahhiyawa for alliance, rather than eastward to Hatti. With Ahhiyawan support, the threat of a new invigorated Arzawa could have been serious. In response, Hattusili applied military force, risking his relations with Ahhiyawa in order to repress the Piyama-Radu threat.

The whole affair indicates that diplomatically "correct" relations existed between Hatti and Ahhiyawa, yet at the same time, Ahhiyawa was willing to gamble in order to establish itself and its influence more firmly in Anatolia. It is obvious that there existed a longstanding and close political connection between leaders of Ahhiyawa (Greeks) and native western Anatolians.

With the end of the Piyama-Radu matter, some semblance of stability had returned to the western region. Masturi was set up as king in Seha River Land. He is one upon whom Hattusili could count, since he had married into the family of Hattusili. The bride, Massanuzzi, may have been of advancing age, and the marriage produces no children. The miracles of Egyptian medicine were well known, and a request was sent to Ramesses. Could Pharaoh send a physician would treat Massanuzzi so that she can bear a child? She is, after all, perhaps only fifty years old. Ramesses replies that he knows the lady well, and she is sixty if she is a day. The problem is beyond the skills of Egyptian science, he says, but a physician will be sent anyhow. In the absence of a male child, there could be trouble in the succession, and in the time of Hattusili's son, trouble emerges.

The archival records of the Hittites become sparse and fragmented for the later reign of Hattusili, and more so during the reign of his successors. Possibly, cuneiform was giving way to the form of writing sometimes called Hieroglyphic Hittite or Hieroglyphic Luwian. Moist clay is the ideal medium for cuneiform with its short straight lines easily impressed with a stylus, and records on baked clay preserve well. Hieroglyphic Hittite requires figure drawing for which clay is less suitable. A medium which will take ink, such as papyrus, is more suitable and may have been used. Such media are perishable, however. If official record keeping was moving to hieroglyphic (or even cuneiform done with ink), such records would not survive to the present. Whatever the reason for the dearth of records, the later years of Hattusili are not easy to follow. From the fragmentary evidence, it appears that there was further rebellion in the West. These problems, whatever they were, were inherited by his successor, Tudhaliya IV.

In the reign of Tudhaliya IV (1239–1209 BC) there was a continuation of the usual problems: trouble from the Kaska, disorder and revolt in the West, threatening developments from the direction of Assyria. Moving quickly, Tudhaliya launched a major attack into the Lukka lands and set matters straight temporarily. In Seha River Land, the lack of a legitimate successor caused a problem that Tudhaliya attended to. One Tarhunda-Radu ruled there now and revolted against the Hittites. A Hittite force was dispatched, Tarhunda-Radu was rounded up, and he with the booty, which included five hundred chariot teams and many prisoners, were sent back to Hatti. A tablet, not fully understood, has been recovered, apparently connected with this event, though it may derive from the time of the earlier king Tudhaliya. In it, leaders in Seha River say that they relied upon the support of the king of Ahhiyawa, but that support was withdrawn. What was the support that Ahhiyawa promised? It may well have been direct military intervention against the Hittites, for little else could be "relied upon," and little else could have helped Seha River Land toward independence. The implication is that Achaean Greek forces, and possibly the Mycenaean king himself, were active in Anatolia. If that is so, then relations between Ahhiyawa and Hatti were in a serious decline. The Hittites installed a new king in Seha River Land, and with his help, Hittites took control of Millawanda. A memo, probably to the new king in Seha River Land, tells that they jointly redefined the borders of Millawanda.

Another tablet, possibly addressed to the king of Seha River Land, asks for someone named Walmu, and asks also for documents which authenticate his legitimacy. According to the Hittite plan, Walmu would be installed as the king of Wilusa. Walmu would be a joint vassal of the Hittites and of Seha River. This joint vassal relationship seems to have been a new thing, and suggests an increasing role for the Seha River kingdom in the West. This increasing reliance of the Hittites on Seha River Land may have been a result of distractions in the Southeast, where the Hittites were at war with Assyria.

Records of historic interest are fewer now, and fragmentary. Tudhaliya was followed by the short-lived Arnuwanda III, and with finality, Suppiluliuma II. (More will be said of this Suppiluliuma in Chapter 9 and 10.) The curtain is closing on the Hittite Empire. This note about Walmu is the last of any consequence in the known Hittite records that mention Wilusa.

Ahhiyawa

Nothing is known of the name by which the people whom we now call Greeks called themselves or their land in the Late Bronze Age. Nothing significant as been learned on this matter from the Linear B tablets, the only surviving writing of the Greeks from that period. It is certain, however, that they did not refer to themselves as Greek. The terms "Greek" and "Greece" came from the Romans at a much later time. Greek writers of the Classical period knew themselves as "Hellenes."

The oldest surviving references on the matter appear in *Iliad* and *Odyssey*, the two great works of Homer. Homer, who lived well after the Bronze Age but well before the Classical period, presumably used ancient sources. In *Iliad* and *Odyssey*, those whom we now call Greeks are referred to as Danaans and even less frequently as Argives. But by far the most commonly used term for the Greeks is Achaeans or Achaians. Thus, *Iliad* begins:

> Sing, goddess, the anger of Peleus' son Achilles
> and its devastation, which put pains thousandfold upon the Achaians,
> hurled in their multitudes to the house of Hades strong
> souls of heroes, but gave their bodies to the delicate feasting
> of dogs, of all birds, and the will of Zeus was accomplished….
>
> (*Iliad* Book 1)

The English spelling Achaians or Achaeans is a representation of the Greek. The "*ch*" may have been pronounced as in Ba*ch*. As for the land from which they came, *Iliad* occasionally mentioned Akhaia. The "*w*" sound dropped out of use in the Greek language not long before the time of Homer, and it is supposed that, before Homer, the term was probably pronounced as * "Akhiawa" or something similar. (The * indicates that the word is derived on the basis of linguistic theory and that there is no surviving example of its use to confirm it.)

In 1924, only a few years after the beginning of the decipherment of Hittite, the Swiss scholar Emil Forrer made a remarkable pronouncement. He had found Greeks of *Iliad* mentioned in the Hittite texts. Forrer claimed that the word "Ahhiyawa" of the Hittite documents refers to the Achaeans of *Iliad* and *Odyssey*.

Hostility on the part of linguistic scholars to this was immediate and intense. There was no way, they said, to go from Greek "Akhaia" or even "Akhiawa" to Hittite "Ahhiyawa" under the linguistic rules which they believed to apply to the ancient Greek and Hittite languages. Many theoretical intermediate words were then proposed which would, hopefully, bridge the gap. These included *Akhhaiwoi, *Akhaiwiya, *Akhaiwa, *Akhaiwia. None proved satisfactory to all of the scholarly community. The Greek and the Hittite endings could not be made to match according to the linguistic rules. Far worse, the Hittite "*hh*" sound could not have come from the Greek "*ch*" ("*kh*") sound. One scholar proposed that both the Greek and the Hittite come from a yet older form, *Akhawyos, and proposes a subsequent evolution of both languages which would in time give the known Greek and Hittite terms.

The present state of things is that the equation Akhaia = [?] = Ahhiyawa (where [?] indicates one or several theoretical intermediate words) cannot be proved. Neither can it be disproved. Stated differently, it cannot be confirmed on the basis of present linguistic knowledge that the Hittites were referring to the Achaean Greeks when they wrote of Ahhiyawa. The linguists, with regret, turn the problem over to the historians and archaeologists.

It is small wonder that the there were difficulties for the linguists. The words Akhaia and probably also Akhiawa are terms which may date from a time close to that of Homer, approximately 800 BC. How the Greeks of the Bronze Age pronounced it is somewhat uncertain. It is difficult to prove the relationship of this word, first recorded after 800 BC, to the word Ahhiyawa, which appeared in Hittite records earlier than 1300 BC—a separation of over 500 years. A further problem is that, no matter how Bronze Age Greeks may have pronounced the term, there is no reason to believe that the Hittites heard it and pronounced it in quite the same way. It is likely the Hittites first heard the word not from Mycenaean Greeks directly, but from the inhabitants of the Luvian-speaking west coast. These Luvians would have altered the pronunciation somewhat in accordance with their own speech habits, and the Hittites would change the pronunciation further. Hittite records are in cuneiform, which must also introduce subtle sound shifts since no writing system can record sounds perfectly. The terms Akhaia and Ahhiyawa are separated by so much time, distance, and language that, though they may be related, there can be no proof. However, the historical records of the Hittites and archaeological evidence provide a strong circumstantial case that Ahhiyawa does refer to the territory of the Achaeans, that is, the Mycenaean Greeks.

In a Hittite tablet written by the scribes of King Tudhaliya IV, the king of Ahhiyawa is referred to as a Great King. After it was written, the title was scratched through and partly erased. It seems likely that the title was correct, but that the erasure resulted from some breakdown of relations between these countries. In the Tawagalawa Letter, Hittite king Hattusili refers to the king of Ahhiyawa as "my Brother." This is a term by which Great Kings address other kings of equal rank, or at the very least those who are independent, and not subordinate to another king. That probably means that the king of Ahhiyawa rules a powerful country, one of international stature. In a Hittite directive to the vassal king of far off Amurru, that king is instructed to block Ahhiyawa goods from passing to Assyria. Such goods could only arrive in Amurru by ship.

Ahhiyawa was to the west of the Hittites, that much is certain. Thus, Ahhiyawa is located westward, has a powerful king of internationally recognized stature, and has a merchant fleet which carries a substantial trade over great distances. Where to the west of Anatolia can a king be found who merits the address "my Brother" and the title "Great King" and who has a wide-ranging maritime capability? Only one land of that time known to archaeology or to history could merit that description, and that is Mycenaean Greece.

In the Tawagalawa Letter, Hattusili explains the Piyama-Radu problem to the king of Ahhiyawa. Everything about the content of this letter indicates that the king of Ahhiyawa controls Millawanda and its inhabitants, yet he is removed from Millawanda and its everyday happenings. This suggests that the king of Ahhiyawa rules from some significant distance, and that is consistent with a Mycenaean king ruling from the Greek mainland. A Greek king living in Rhodes would be another possibility.

Despite the great irritation which the people of Ahhiyawa frequently induced in the Hittites, there is no certain record of a direct military confrontation between them. It is true that Hittite king Tudhaliya II obtained Mycenaean swords while campaigning in the West, but the circumstances are not really known. Might they have come to western Anatolia in trade, or perhaps in the hands of mercenaries? It is also true that a Hittite army attacked Attarissiyas, a "Man of Ahhiya," a Greek, in order to save Madduwatta. Attarissiyas was an adventurer who may have been operating at his own initiative, with a few Greek comrades, leading warriors of Anatolian origin.

In the Tawagalawa Letter, King Hattusili raises some serious accusations against the king of Ahhiyawa, but he never raises his voice. He is polite to a fault, addressing the king of Ahhiyawa in an almost fawning manner. He apologizes for earlier strong language. Evidently, in dealing with Ahhiyawa the Hittite king must use diplomacy, not military force.

The fact that the Hittites and the Ahhiyawans never came into direct conflict but must deal through diplomacy suggests that the heart of the Ahhiyawan territory was inaccessible to Hittite military forces. These considerations are fully consistent with the view that Ahhiyawa itself is overseas, and is Mycenaean Greece.

Mursili pursued Uhha-Ziti, who escaped by ship to Ahhiyawa or Ahhiyawan territory using the port of Apasas (Ephesus). Similarly Hattusili tried to seize Piyama-Radu but he escaped by ship to Ahhiyawa territory from the port of Millawanda (Miletus.) That these fugitives took to the sea could indicate (but does not prove) that they were fleeing to the Greek mainland, or to a friendly Ahhiyawan island offshore, possibly Rhodes.

The presence of Greeks on the west coast of Anatolia is supported by archaeological evidence. Mycenaean remains have been found at several places on the western Anatolian coast, including Colophon, Ephesus, Miletus, Iasos, Musgebi. At Colophon and at Miletus, chamber tombs of the Mycenaean type have been found, and this means that Greeks lived there and died there. In Miletus, Mycenaean evidence from about 1400 BC forward is particularly strong, and includes, in addition to chamber tombs, Mycenaean pottery and weapons. New research is underway at Miletus and additional Bronze Age discoveries are anticipated.

Just off the western shore of Anatolia, there is evidence of a Mycenaean presence on the islands of Kos, Chios, and some indications on Samos. On the island of Rhodes, a large number of Mycenaean chamber tombs and settlements have been found. The definite presence of Mycenaean Greeks along the west coast and offshore islands fits well with the view that the term Ahhiyawa refers to them, or their land, and that it was they who helped Uhha-Ziti and Piyama-Radu.

That Greeks living in Anatolia, or islands off shore, were in communication with the Greek mainland is certain. The Greek mainland may seem remote. It is, however, less than two hundred an fifty miles from the port of the major Greek mainland city of Mycenae to Miletus over the most likely sea route. In contrast, it is over six hundred miles from Hattusa to Miletus over the route which Hittite armies were likely to have used. The Greek mainland, Rhodes and the lesser islands, Miletus, and possibly other enclaves on the Anatolian coast may have formed one Mycenaean Greek community, spread out but in close touch. It is likely that the Hittites saw the Mycenaean enclaves in Anatolia, the Mycenaean islands, and the Greek mainland as one ethnic entity, equivalent to the concept "the Greeks." When they referred to the interference in Anatolian affairs by Ahhiyawa, they were referring to "Greek" interference, without the pressing need, at least so far as documented writing is concerned, to distinguish the exact geographical source. "Ahhiyawa" would in some cases refer to the mainland, in other cases to one of the Anatolian offshore or on shore Greek enclaves.

It is true that it has not been proved that Ahhiyawa was Mycenaean Greece, but such things are not often susceptible to proof. The circumstantial evidence, however, appears to strongly support this conclusion, and supports no other. This preponderance of the evidence permits the acceptance here that the Ahhiyawans are the Achaeans, the Mycenaean Greeks.

Homer does not mention the Greeks of Anatolia, which is strange, since it is evident that Greeks had been active along the west coast of Anatolia for some time.

4
HOMER AND THE WAR AT TROY

The Trojan War is a shadowy affair historically speaking, known of primarily through *Iliad* and *Odyssey*. *Iliad* and *Odyssey* are the earliest existing works of European literature, and in the view of many, they are indisputably the greatest. Among early works which survive, only the Bible is comparable in its eloquence, lofty style, and influence on generations which followed. For the Greeks of the Classical period, for the Romans, *Iliad* and *Odyssey* were revered as treasuries of ancient truth. They were guides to history, right behavior, and religious belief. For them, the Trojan War was the great remembered event of the distant past, and the fixed point of reference for all else of a remote and dimly remembered time. That *Iliad* reported actual history was rarely doubted by these ancients. Even today, the influence of *Iliad* is so powerful that archaeologists and historians continue to refer to Agamemnon, Nestor, Priam, and their families as if they were real persons, which they may have been. They speak easily of the ruins at Pylos in Greece as Nestor's palace and the ruins at Mycenae as the site of Agamemnon's royal capital. The Late Bronze Age civilization of Greece is now called Mycenaean because the *Iliad* tells that Mycenae was the city of King Agamemnon, leader of the Greeks at Troy.

Greeks of the Classical period held that both *Iliad* and *Odyssey* were the works of one man, Homer. In these works, Homer tells of a great war which lasted ten years and to which much of the warrior manpower of Greece was committed. He tells also of social disruptions at home and wanderings abroad that were consequences of the war. Though no date was given, scholars of the Classical period calculated a date, and that date places the Trojan War toward the end of the Bronze Age. But *Iliad* and *Odyssey* are storyteller's work and not history. *Iliad* describes the war vividly, and *Odyssey* recalls it, but was there such a war of Greeks against Troy?

Archaeological excavations at Troy cover a span of over a century, but the archives or records of Troy have not been found. No clear and certain report is known of the Trojan War written close to the time of the event. All that is known today of the Trojan War comes from *Iliad* and *Odyssey* and a few related works, and those were first put into writing centuries after. For the present, it will be assumed that there was a Trojan War which provided a historic basis for the works of Homer, and that it took place at some time close to 1200 BC, the end of the Bronze Age. Whether those assumptions are valid or not will be explored.

The Greek text of *Iliad*, which is the basis of modern translations, dates to only about five hundred years ago, AD 1488. Only fragments of an earlier date exist. How has *Iliad* been maintained since ancient times? How likely is it that the present text preserves a true memory of a war more than three thousand years ago? Is it possible that there was an unbroken chain of transmission from such remote times to the present?

Oral Transmission and Preservation

In Greece of the Bronze Age, storytelling was no doubt a well-developed art requiring special skills. In villages and towns, there were likely to have been those who were recognized for that skill, and those of special ability would have been known and honored in a large region and invited to the palace to tell their stories. These were told in rhythmic cadence and were thus poetry, nearly a chant, sung to the tune of a few notes of a lyre.

Through these poet-singers of Bronze Age Greece, tales were maintained from generation to generation. Plot, poetic structure, even whole lines and stanzas were often preserved close to the form in which they had been handed down. But the poet-singer could not only recite, he could innovate. The training which his art provided gave him the means to do so. He might add his own color and poetic flourishes and he might also change the story from time to time according to need. A picture is given in *Odyssey*, which tells of the singer Demodocus, who has been called to entertain the king and guests. The king speaks:

> I say to you young men, alike to you sceptered kings.
> Come to my fair dwelling
> that we may entertain our guest within its halls.
> Let none refuse.
> And summon also Demodocus, the inspired singer, for the
> Muse has given him skill surpassing in song.
> ....
> The herald came, leading the matchless singer,
> whom the Muse loved greatly, giving him both good and ill.
> For she had bereft him of sight, but given him sweet song.
> Pontonoos set out for him a silver-studded chair

> amid the feasters against a tall pillar.
> The herald hung his clear-voiced lyre on a peg
> above his head, and showed him how to take it with his hands,
>   And set beside him a fine table, and on it a basket and a goblet
> filled with wine, so that he might drink as the spirit moved him.
>
> ....
>
> The Muse inspired him to sing the great deeds of men.
>
> (*Odyssey Book* 8)

Stories sung by the poet-singer might be a re-creation each time, yet in part drawing from memory according to timeless oral tradition. Demodocus could not read—he was blind—but it is nearly certain that none of the sighted poet-singers could read.

A form of writing, Linear B as it is called, existed in the Late Bronze Age in Greece, in Mycenaean times. It had been adapted from an earlier Minoan (Cretan) script developed to express a non-Greek language and was not well matched to the needs of the Greek language, nor to the poetic meter in which *Iliad* and *Odyssey* were sung. There is no evidence that Linear B was used to record poetry or song. So far as present evidence shows, Linear B was a tool only of the accountant and the palace bureaucrat in the time of the great palaces of the Mycenaean kings.

The practical and mundane world with which Linear B records dealt never intruded into the great hall of the king during the time that a poet-singer was singing his tales for the entertainment of the king and guests. It may be that no one saw the possibilities in Linear B for recording the legends and stories, or saw the slightest purpose in doing so. All existing evidence suggests that in the Late Bronze Age and the early Iron Age, stories of Troy were not maintained or preserved in written form.

In the time of Homer, hundreds of years after the Bronze Age, writing hardly existed in most of the Greek world. So far as is known, Linear B had vanished at the end of the Bronze Age as Mycenaean society began a decline and then a collapse. According to legend, Dorians, a primitive and uncultured lot it is assumed, infiltrated the Peloponnese in southern Greece (Figure 6-1). Mycenaean refugees fled decay and the rising Dorian tide. They set sail, many of them, for a new life along the shores or islands of western and southern Anatolia and Cyprus. In their journey, they were able to take with them only a few material things. But they brought with them their language, customs, beliefs, and stories. The palaces were gone, never to be rebuilt, but the stories of old were valued more than ever before as a link with the golden past. All was preserved in memory and by oral tradition.

Later and better preserved history illustrates the maintenance of oral tradition. There was the migration in AD 870-930 of Scandinavians to the new life in Iceland. Of those times it is noted that:

> At the outset the Icelanders had no written literature, but in poems and stories they nevertheless preserved the memory of events that had taken place long ago, not only in their own country but also in neighboring lands, especially Norway, where most of the first settlers originated. It is not without parallel for settlers in a new land to retain the memory of ancient lore better than their kinsmen who stay home. (*Icelandic Sagas*)

The new Mycenaean settlements were established primarily where there was a Greek presence in older and better days, frequently in or near a coastal town or city where a few Mycenaean craftsmen or traders lived, or in which trade had produced close contacts between the Greek and the resident non-Greek population. In other cases, scouts may have been sent out in the previous sailing season. They would seek suitable harbors and land that could support a grain crop, grapevines, and olive trees. Each settlement drew a population from a different Mycenaean city. In each, stories were cherished which were particular to the cities and territories of the old life. These stories, however distorted, preserved memories of that previous life.

Strangely, life in the new lands to which the Mycenaeans traveled produced few memorable legends. In fact, there may have been little to sing about. The new life was harsh, lacking the prosperity, creativity, and exuberance that characterized the old Mycenaean world. Hesiod, a poet who is thought to have lived only slightly after Homer, described the hard times that lingered long after the collapse of the Mycenaean world. He refers to a fifth age and a fifth race of man, one that had fallen away from the golden age. "For now is a race of iron, and men never rest from labor and sorrow by day and from perishing by night; and the gods shall lay sore troubles upon them." Hesiod went on to describe his time, in which men dishonor their parents in old age, ignore oaths, favor strength over justice. Judges were corrupted by bribes, poverty beset the land. It is not of the age of Homer and Hesiod that the great stories tell, but of an earlier, brighter age, the Bronze Age.

Generation to Generation

Homer, whom tradition holds to be the composer of *Iliad* and *Odyssey*, was born in the Greek world of the Anatolian west coast or the islands offshore. Of this the Greeks of the Classical period were sure. Scholars of the present day are less certain that both *Iliad* and *Odyssey* are the work of one man; and some maintain that two different composers were involved. Whether this is so may never be known. In the absence of convincing proof to the contrary, it is simplest to assume, as did the ancients, that there was but one composer for both works.

The Greek historian Herodotus (484–420 BC) said "Homer...lived but four hundred years before my time, as I believe." On this unsupported statement and little more, it is thought that Homer lived close to 800 BC. A time up to a hundred years earlier or later could be equally well argued from the limited evidence available. There is a tradition that Homer was blind, presumably because the singer Demodocus was so described. Tradition has the island of Chios as Homer's birthplace. Others of the settlement cities of the Anatolian shores claimed him. That is the total of knowledge concerning him.

In a time close to the period in which Homer lived, the Phoenician alphabet was beginning to be adapted to the Greek language, thus filling the void left by the end of Linear B hundreds of years earlier. The reestablishment of literacy must have been a slow process. Decades may have been required. It is not known for certain, but it is very likely that Homer and most of his contemporaries were nonliterate, even at a time when the new writing system was gaining acceptance in the Greek-speaking world. His was the calling of the poet-singer and, as of old, he required no written text nor is it likely that he could have produced one. If there was no writing from the end of the Bronze Age, how had the tale of a war at Troy been maintained until the time of Homer? It is the belief of most scholars that the elements of what would become *Iliad* and *Odyssey* were transmitted from the past to Homer's time by oral means, from one poet-singer to the next, from the earlier to the later, forming a chain of transmission from the distant past. That much has gained strong support as a result of the investigations in the 1930's by the American scholar Milman Parry.

Parry knew that fully one-third of the approximately sixteen thousand lines of *Iliad* are repeats. The only need that such repeats might serve is that they ease the task of the singer as he sings the tale. They are of no use in a written story. Such repeated phrases or stanzas provide a rest since they may be recited with little conscious attention, nearly automatically, allowing the poet-singer to organize in his mind the following lines, which could to some extent be a fresh creation. Maintaining a near-hypnotic rhythm, reciting stock phrases, in his mind assembling new fresh rhythmic phrases, he re-creates the tale.

As Parry observed, the name of a character may be joined to a descriptive attribute, for example "glorious Hector" and "Hector of the shining helm." These standardized expressions provide two alternative ways of completing the meter in a poetic line, depending on the meter of words which directly precede or follow. Such standard combinations, the singer held in memory. The singer would also draw upon extended descriptions of events or places, all in standardized poetic phrasing. There were stock descriptions of the clash of battle, or of the convocation of an assembly—all useful devices in oral storytelling.

Parry saw these things in *Iliad* and *Odyssey*, and recognized in them definite evidence that the poems had originally been created and transmitted by oral means. But the oral poet-singers of Greece were long dead and his conclusions were difficult to prove. When Parry learned that in the remote villages of Bosnia there were still active poet-singers, he went there to study their methods. What he found was a revelation to the world of Homeric scholarship.

Parry's research provides a direct picture of the operation of oral poetry, its methods, and its astonishing capabilities. The poet-singers of the Bosnian villages sang of the glorious age of the past which, in largely Muslim Bosnia, was the time of the Ottoman Empire. The Ottoman Empire, centered in Turkey, had receded from Bosnia centuries earlier but left its mark on Bosnian culture. While the Christian Serb neighbors of the Muslim Bosnians also had their poet-singers, the art was better preserved among the Muslims. Singers began to learn as children, listening to experienced singers, picking up stories and poetic expressions, and then as young men, trying their skills in the coffee houses. By degrees, their abilities grew. Parry found that some were more capable than others. One, Avdo Mededovic', was particularly outstanding, and it is from the performances of Avdo that much was learned.

Of particular interest was the length of a tale which could be retained and re-created by the singer. *Iliad* contains 15,693 lines in the Greek text and *Odyssey* 12,160 lines and it may seem impossible that such long works could have been preserved for generations without writing. According to Albert Lord, Parry's assistant and successor:

> When Parry was working with the most talented Yugoslav singer in our experience, Avdo Mededovic' in Bijelo Polje, he tried the following experiment. Avdo had been singing and dictating [to a recording machine] for several weeks; he had shown his worth and was aware that we valued him highly. Another singer came to us, Mumin Vlahovljak from Plevlje. He seemed to be a good singer, and had in his repertory a song that Parry discovered Avdo had never heard before. Without telling Avdo that he would be asked to sing the song himself when Mumin had finished it, Parry set Mumin to singing, but he made sure that Avdo was in the room listening. When the song came to an end, Avdo was asked his opinion of it and whether he could now sing it himself. He replied that it was a good song and that Mumin had song it well, but that he thought that he might sing it better. Avdo began and as he sang, the song lengthened, the ornamentation and richness accumulated, and the touches of character, touches that distinguished Avdo from other singers, imparted a depth of feeling that had been missing in Mumin's version. (*Singer*)

A subsequent analysis of the recordings showed that Avdo had preserved almost unchanged the themes of Mumin and much of his language as well. Those who remember how difficult it was to remember and recite before the school class a poem of a dozen or so lines may be amazed by this prodigious feat.

Avdo has given to Parry a song called "The Wedding of Smailagic' Meho." Sung from memory, re-creating themes and verses using the skills of a lifetime, this work totaled 12,000 lines—a length comparable to that of *Odyssey*.

From another singer, Demail Zogic, Parry recorded a much-loved song, "The Rescue of the Children of Ali-Bey," and recorded it in 1934 and again in 1951. The songs were performed, of course, from memory. The extended story of Ali-Bey was virtually the same, even to its words, when told seventeen years later which shows the stability which a poet-singer can maintain in his tale. That Avdo could listen, casually, to the recitation by Mumin of a song of thousands of lines, and then repeat the story, theme for theme and often word for word while adding his own color and poetic expression, is testimony to the ability of poet-singers to pass on intact both the story and the poetic language in which the story is told. The same talents can be ascribed to the Homeric poet-singers.

It is also clear that the singer can and does make at least slight changes. His memory is not necessarily at fault. Rather, it is that he does not accept that there is one "correct" version of a story, and he will alter themes and language if he feels that the result is better. He has stock phrases at the ready, meter is automatic to him, and he has the creative skill by which to easily accomplish this.

It cannot be assumed, however, that the oral poets method assures preservation of a tale over many generations in all of its essential historical elements. An illustration that a story based on historical events can change with retelling comes from times more recent than those of Homer. The Icelandic *Poetic Eddas*, put into writing about AD 1270, preserve a story which probably first gained currency on an oral basis. The story is called *Atlakvida*. In this tale, Atli, king of the Huns, covets the gold of King Gunnarr of Burgundy. Atli invites Gunnarr to a feast, seeking to wheedle out of him the location of the gold. In the course of events, Atli kills Gunnarr. Atli's wife, who happens to be Gunnarr's sister, seeks revenge. She kills Atli while he is drunk and asleep.

A longer and more complicated version of the story, the *Nibelunglied*, comes from Germany and was in written form by about AD 1200. Brunhilde is romantically involved with Sigfried but marries Gunther. Sigfried marries Krimhild, sister of Gunther. In the course of events, Gunther kills Sigfried. In time, Krimhild remarries, this time to Etzel, king of the Huns. Seeking revenge for the death of Sigfried, she provokes the brother of Etzel to slaughter the Burgundians, and in the fighting, the Burgundians kill Etzel but all of the Burgundians have also been killed.

These two stories have their origin in historic events: the invasion of Europe by the Huns and their slaughter of the Burgundians in AD 437. Atli in the Icelandic version, and Etzel in the German version have their historic counterpart in Attila, king of the Huns. He died at the hands of a woman in AD 454. There was a Gundaharius, a contemporary of Attila, upon whom Gunnarr and Gunther were based. Brunhilde has an actual counterpart in Brunechildis, a queen of the Franks of about AD 567, or possibly in Brunhilde, a Visigoth queen of a generation later. Thus, the Icelandic and German stories preserve memory of certain historic events of centuries earlier. But it is evident that details of the stories differ significantly in the two versions, so that one or both stories have changed with time. It is also noteworthy that Attila, Gundaharius, and Brunechildis were real people. In these tales, they have been brought together even though Brunechildis lived about a century later than Attila.

Poet-singers live with contradictory motives. They are preservers of knowledge of the past and want to give a true account. But they are also entertainers. If they fail to hold an audience, the stories will die and the past will be forgotten. And so, over time, the more dramatic deeds are selected; events are increasingly dramatized with the telling. Events that are due to "affairs of state," are explained on the basis of purely personal motives—love, hate, revenge—for such motives make a more compelling story. Characters from different times may be brought together indiscriminately.

There is no reason to doubt that among the Homeric poets-singers the same factors were in operation. Though details of past events have been forgotten over the generations, though changes have been made in the story, the poet-singers are sure that the Muse guides them in each telling, and they believe that their words are god-inspired, authentic. The Muse is invoked at the very beginning of *Iliad*, "Sing, goddess, the anger of Peleus' son Achilles…" and in *Odyssey* "Sing in me Muse, and through me tell the story of that man skilled in all ways…." And so, as it was transmitted from generation to generation, the story of the war at Troy underwent alterations of a kind which no one can now surely identify. It is certain that with the passage of time, from the Mycenaean period in the Bronze Age to the time of Homer, the transmission resulted in some loss of authentic fact and historic accuracy.

Composition of *Iliad* and *Odyssey*

It is known that there were compositions dealing with the Trojan War other than *Iliad* and *Odyssey*, and these are now lost except for summaries. These works told of the circumstances leading to the War, and went beyond *Odyssey* in telling of the aftermath of the War. Together with *Iliad* and *Odyssey*, they are referred to as the Trojan Cycle, or the Homeric Cycle, though few, even in the Classical period, believed that Homer composed all of them. Usually, they are thought to be late compositions, filling in around the stories of Homer, but there is no certainty of this. They could have been the work of Homer's contemporaries, or even predecessors, for Homer did not operate in a cultural vacuum.

Whether or not these other compositions already existed in the time of Homer, it is certain that he received much that was already formed. What then was Homer's contribution? What is the source of his towering reputation among the later Greeks, and Romans also?

No doubt Homer listened to the tales of Troy as sung by one or even several poet-singers in the time of his youth. Listening, absorbing, imitating, this was the means by which poet-singers first developed their skill. It is likely that stories which would be later be *Iliad* and *Odyssey* came down to Homer's time as unlinked segments, contradictory, and lacking in development of character and motive. Homer may have selected from among the themes and already composed material passed to him, reorganized and enlarged them, removed many contradictions, and brought forth a carefully structured and coherent story. Likely, some sections of song that he received from the past were of the highest poetic quality and could be taken whole. He would certainly have added his own imagery where he thought that the old could be improved, and dialog where it would help to better delineate the character of those in the story. The result was a new creation, a new work, and one in which the other poet-singers, his contemporaries, recognized greatness and granted to him without interference.

That Shakespeare based his work on old chronicles but immeasurably improved upon them, and that Bach reworked earlier musical themes, creating works of enduring greatness, provides a loose analogy for what Homer accomplished.

How Homer lived and practiced his craft is unknown. The ways of a singer of recent times may reflect the life of Homer. Living around AD 1800 in Ireland, O'Carolan was blind, and a bard. With the aid of a helper, he wandered from one wealthy mansion to another. He would stay a few weeks at each and, to the accompaniment of his harp, sing his immortal songs. Homer too may have lived as such a wandering poet-singer.

It may have been that, in Homer's time, the old stories were slipping away and the newer generation was taken by new beliefs emanating from Anatolia, Asia. The tale of Troy, which spoke of the unity and strength of Greeks assembled in a common endeavor, would have been a welcomed theme. Under these circumstances, a reworked and reinvigorated new story of Troy would have burst upon the Greek-speaking world as a marvel, and later generations would credit Homer as the author.

At some time in the distant past *Iliad* and *Odyssey* were put into writing, using the alphabetic script derived from the Phoenicians, which was to become the writing system of Greece from that time forward. Writing made it possible to stabilize and preserve the tale of Troy, and this must have been the primary motive in undertaking this difficult task. It is possible that *Iliad* and *Odyssey* began to be committed to writing as early as the time of Homer. Writing was probably too recent an innovation for Homer to have mastered, and a skill not needed in his craft. Possibly his sons or grandsons were able to read and write and it is with them that a written text of *Iliad* and *Odyssey* may have begun.

There are other possibilities. There was a group on the island of Chios who referred to themselves as the Sons of Homer, or Descendants of Homer, though the name does not necessarily imply an actual blood relationship. It is known that for generations they sang the tales of Homer. Perhaps it was they who undertook the writing task. However it was accomplished, it must have occupied a substantial span of time. It could not have been easy. The earliest writers could not have had the speed and proficiency of modern stenographers, and it must have been difficult for a poet-singer to slow the pace of his story with its demands for sustained cadence in order to accommodate the needs of the scribe.

It was said in later times that *Iliad* and *Odyssey* were put in writing by order of Pisistratus (561–527 BC), a leader in Athens centuries after Homer's time. Such a project would have done much for Pisistratus who had an interest in building up his own reputation in Athens. It did not hurt his purpose that *Iliad* and *Odyssey* told of King Nestor, whom Pisistratus claimed as a distant ancestor.

If the Pisistratus project took place, it may not have been the first, but an attempt to consolidate various existing texts with the objective of providing a standardized and authentic version. Athenian playwrights of the Classical period took many of their plots from *Iliad*, and at that time they were able to refer to a written text. Written versions certainly existed in Classical times, since the study of the works of Homer was the essential core of an education, particularly in Athens. Alexander the Great, when he embarked on his conquest of Asia, carried a text of *Iliad* in a silver box, and consulted it often, no doubt to gain inspiration from Achilles whose invincible deeds and pathological carnage he admired and so closely imitated.

It is known that Greek scholars in Alexandria, Egypt, in the period after Alexander, worked to maintain an authentic written text of *Iliad* and *Odyssey*, and worked to identify and remove what they considered to be spurious or late additions to the story. With the destruction of the western Roman Empire, the trail of the written text is lost. Byzantium preserved Greek culture until finally it was overrun by a Turkish army in AD 1453, and it may be that the texts of *Iliad* and *Odyssey* were preserved there and were reintroduced to Europe by Crusaders returning from the East.

The Bronze Age Remembered

Odyssey tells of the destruction of Troy, but it is largely taken up with the adventures of Odysseus. *Iliad* deals with the War itself. Is *Iliad* correct in its testimony of a Trojan War? Does it preserve authentic memories of the Bronze Age, and thus of a conflict of Greeks at Troy? *Iliad* contains inconsistencies, as all who are familiar with it know. Over the course of the story, the deaths of several hundred combatants are described, some in gruesome detail, and these contribute to the atmosphere of reality that pervades much of *Iliad*. It is a convincing war story, never surpassed in its portrait of the carnage of war. But in the telling, a number of fighters have been killed off more than once. No matter. To the rapt listeners, such would hardly be noticed. There are more serious inconsistencies, however. For example, the Catalog of Ships, as it is now called, forms the core of Book 2. Here are called out the Greek cities that sent men, their numbers, and the names of their kings and chiefs. The Catalog of Ships does not key perfectly with the balance of the *Iliad*, however. War leaders are named in the Catalog who do not appear in the rest of the story, and other leaders appear in the balance of the story who are never mentioned in the Catalog.

An important event of the *Iliad* involves a delegation sent to Achilles by Agamemnon. Agamemnon had wronged Achilles, and Achilles withdrew from combat. Without Achilles as their champion, the Greeks face defeat. It was necessary for Agamemnon to make amends, to make things well with Achilles with lavish gifts and promises for the future—all to draw him back into the war. Yet at a later point, the story proceeds as if the offer was never made. Apparently, two versions of the story had been combined, one with and the other without the offer to Achilles, and the inconsistency had not been removed.

Inconsistencies are evidence that *Iliad* cannot be an exact report of the past since two versions cannot both be right. Such evidence is really not needed, since the process of oral transmission over generations cannot preserve the past perfect and intact. While it is evident that the poet-singers had the remarkable ability to preserve even a long story, and to pass it from generation to generation, it is equally true that changes must seep in. The poet-singer remodeled his tales to enhance audience interest. Memories of certain things were allowed to fade away, things that were not important to the poet-singer or his audience but which might have been immensely significant to the historian of today. Possibly, through drift of content over generations, all factual moorings have been left behind. In that case, the Trojan War itself may be fictitious. The Roman playwright Lucian (whose audience apparently believed in reincarnation) has one of the characters in a comedy ask another, "Tell me about Troy, did it happen as Homer says?" He is answered, "Where did Homer get his information? At the time of the War he was a Camel in Bactria."

Scholarly opinion has its cycles, its fashions, and the current tendency is to attack the historicity of *Iliad*. The approach is to show that some of the social or economic content derives not from the Bronze Age but from a time close to that of Homer. Therefore, all of *Iliad* is suspect. That is a rather strange contention, difficult to prove, since no one really knows when Homer lived, where he lived, and what the social and economic situation in his time and place might have been. Those are matters of guesswork. Those who believe that *Iliad* preserves authentic memories of the Bronze Age do not deny some of the content may reflect a later time, but maintain that much of the Bronze Age remains. A few examples will illustrate.

Pandarus, a foremost fighter on the Trojan side, removes an arrow from his quiver and brings it to his bow:

> Squeezing the nock and string together, drawing
> the gut back to his nipple, iron head to the handgrip
> till he flexed the great weapon back in a half circle curve-
> the bow sprang! the string sang out, arrow shot away
> razor sharp and raging to whip through Argive ranks! (*Iliad* Book 4)

Iron was a widely used metal in the time of Homer, but some critics seem to assume that it was unknown in the Bronze Age. As *Iliad* speaks here of iron, the passage must have entered *Iliad* at a time well after the Bronze Age. And from this and other examples, it is an easy step to assume that much and perhaps all in *Iliad* is post Bronze Age. It is now recognized, however, that the Hittites and other Anatolians possessed iron in the Late Bronze Age and even earlier, though it was not widely used. Pharaoh Amenhotep III (1386–1349 BC) had a gift of two iron daggers and ten javelins with iron tips from King Tushratta of Mitanni. This was the same Tushratta who later was chased from his throne by Hittite king Suppiluliuma. In the tomb of the boy king Tutankhamon (1334–1325 BC) a marvelous knife was found with gold handle, quartz pommel, and glistening iron blade, no doubt a gift from an Anatolian king. A letter from Hittite king Hattusili (1264–1239 BC) to the king of Assyria states:

> As for the good iron which you wrote me about, good iron…in my seal-house is not available. That it is a bad time for producing iron, I have written. But they will produce good iron. So far, they will not have finished. When they will have finished, I shall send it to you. Today now I have an iron dagger blade sent on its way to you. (*Kizzuwatna*)

Pandarus is a Trojan ally and his homeland is not far from that of the Hittites. What would be more natural than that he would possess a few iron weapons, the latest in military technology, obtained from the Hittites as a gift or as booty captured in any of the many battles which occurred on the western fringe of the Hittite land?

In another passage, Achilles sets out prizes for the games in honor of his fallen friend Patroclus:

> [He] brought from his ships
> the trophies for the contests: cauldrons and tripods,

> stallions, mules and cattle with massive heads,
> women sashed and lovely, and gleaming gray iron. (*Iliad* Book 23)

Iron was rare and precious, worthy to be a prize. The women were captives, and it is likely that most of the prizes which Achilles set out were captured from Trojans or their allies, mostly Anatolians, who might be expected to possess iron. The Pandarus passage in *Iliad* makes clear that iron was known but was rare and that accords remarkably well with the situation at the end of the Late Bronze Age. That *Iliad* places a rare iron weapon, an iron arrowhead, in the hands not of a Greek but an Anatolian, supports the accurate recall of the Bronze Age in *Iliad*. The passage about prizes goes on to state that the winner of the contest might give the iron to one of his farmers for a plow-blade, which suggests a lower value on iron, typical of a later time, the Iron Age. This illustrates well how *Iliad* mixes memories of Bronze Age times with those of later times.

The use of the war chariot provides another example. *Iliad* describes the chariot as, in effect, a taxicab used to transport warriors to the place of battle where they dismount and fight on foot. Critics have maintained that this is evidence that Homer, or the generations of poet-singers leading to Homer, had lost memory of how chariots were employed in Bronze Age warfare. Due to ignorance, say the critics, the poet-singers changed the role of the chariot, giving it this taxi duty. Where are the rousing chariot charges, the attacks with lance and bow from the careening chariot, as seems to be known from the Bronze Age?

Military necessity may answer the question. The Trojans would have denied Greek chariots freedom of movement on the battlefield. Massed chariots were simply too dangerous. When properly employed, they provided surprise, shock, and concentration of force, much as does armor in our own time, and a chariot attack was capable of turning the tide of battle. The Trojans would have prevented unhampered use of chariotry by means of defensive ditches, earth barriers, and field obstructions such as sharpened stakes, skillfully deployed in the battle zones. *Iliad* tells that the Greeks put up just such defenses when they feared a Trojan attack on their own camp and beached ships. They threw up an earthwork and

> against the fortress, just outside the wall,
> the men dug an enormous trench, broad and deep,
> and drove sharp stakes to guard it (*Iliad* Book 7)

With chariot charges denied to them, the Greeks would have little use of chariots except as taxis. They had already brought their chariots ashore. These might as well be employed in some useful way. The warrior aristocracy of the Greek world were probably unused to traveling very far afoot in any case. That chariots served only to carry men to battle appears to be fully in accord of what was to be expected in this war.

Archaeologists might want to look for remains of these Trojan defenses, or the similar Greek defenses, but Homer has anticipated them. He tells that the evidence will not be found. It has washed away.

> All that flow from the crests of Ida down to breaking surf…
> The channels of all those rivers—Apollo swung them round
> into one mouth and nine days hurled their flood against the wall
> and Zeus came raining down, cloudburst powering cloudburst
> the faster to wash that rampart out to open sea.
> The earth-shaker himself, trident locked in his grip,
> led the way, rocking loose, sweeping up in his breakers
> all the bastion's strong supports of logs and stones…
> He made all smooth along the rip of Hellespont
> and piled the endless beaches deep in sand again…(*Iliad Book 12*)

Figure 4-1. Hittite war chariots at Kadesh, each with a three-man crew.

The use of chariots as "taxis" is not to be disparaged. It appears to have been an accepted part of Bronze Age offensive operations. The panic created in the Egyptian forces at Kadesh by the Hittite chariotry can be recalled. Egyptian illustrations of this battle show that, in addition to the driver and a fighting man, Hittite chariots carried a third man, Figure 4-1. It is unlikely that he would fight from the chariot where there hardly would have been room to handle lance or bow. Almost certainly, the third man was to fight dismounted. He would be rapidly brought to some vital place on the battlefield and dropped off for combat. By this means, skilled warriors could be quickly concentrated at a point of enemy weakness, an employment of chariotry which the military commander of the Bronze Age could not possibly have ignored. This is, of course, very nearly the action described in *Iliad*.

Iliad tells of cremation of those who died in battle. The funeral rites of Patroclus and Hector, culminating in great funeral pyres, are vividly described. On the other hand, almost all available archaeological evidence from Late Bronze Age sites in Greece shows burial or tomb interment rather than cremation. In later times, in the Iron Age, cremation was a frequent practice in the Greek world. For this reason, critics maintain, the description of cremation in *Iliad* comes from those later times.

However, the conditions which war imposes suggests that *Iliad* gives a valid report from Bronze Age times. The heroic dead, fallen at Troy, could not be shipped home for burial. Distances were too great, and the seas were too dangerous for sailing except in certain months. Yet the dead could not be buried in the plains of Troy, in hostile soil, the habitat of foreign gods. *Iliad* tells of the furious battle fought between Achilles and the river-god Scamander. His river flowed by Troy, and Scamander was angered by the slaughter which Achilles has wrought on Scamander's people, the Trojans. The people of the Bronze Age believed in the existence of gods or spirits of local places, loyal to those who had long brought offerings to them. Greek comrades could not be interred in such soil, infested with gods or spirits with Trojan loyalties. It was important for the dead to be in home soil inhabited by familiar gods. At home were the elaborate tombs which archaeologists have noted, and which appeared to be so important to the Mycenaeans. At home, the presence of the dead would validate the families' roots in local soil. At home, sons and grandsons could carry out the required rites. Given the difficulty of shipping home the dead, cremation on the plains of Troy would make every sense. It was the only available recourse in time of war. The cremated remains could be shipped home when sailing was possible. In *Iliad*, Nestor advises Agamemnon:

> at dawn you must call a halt to the fighting by Achaeans,
> form your units, bring on wagons, gather up the dead
> and wheel the corpses back with mules and oxen. Then
> at a decent distance from the ships, we burn the bodies,
> so every soldier here can carry back the bones
> to a dead man's sons when he sails home again. (*Iliad* Book 7)

Far from being an insertion from a later day as has sometimes been claimed, the description of cremation in *Iliad* may well be a striking confirmation of a measure necessitated by an overseas war, a war at Troy.

Fiery funeral pyres of two heroes mark dramatic turning points in *Iliad*. The first is for Patroclus, dear friend of Achilles. At the completion of the funeral and its ceremonies, invincible Achilles returns to the conflict. With his return, Troy is doomed. The second is for Hector. With the death of that great champion of Troy, the doom of Troy is sealed. The Hittite scholar Oliver Gurney has pointed out the remarkable similarity of these funerals as described in *Iliad* and a funeral rite described in a Hittite tablet (Gurney, 1990). The tablet is partly damaged and the text does not rise to the poetic quality of *Iliad*, but the comparison is revealing. Where the damaged text can be first read, the cremation has already taken place and the text continues:

> On the second day as soon as it is light the women go to the pyre to collect the bones; they extinguish the fire with ten jugs of beer ten of wine… (*The Hittites*)

From the funeral of Patroclus as described in *Iliad*:

> **At that hour the morning stars come rising up**
> to herald a new day on earth, and riding in its wake
> the Dawn flings out her golden robe across the sea,
> and the funeral fires sank low, and the flames died down.
> And the winds swung round and headed home again,
> over the Thracian sea, and the heaving swells moaned.
> And at last Achilles, turning away from the corpse-fire,
> sank down exhausted. Sweet sleep overwhelmed him.
> But Agamemnon's followers grouped together now
> as they approached Achilles
> the din and trampling of their feet awoke him.
> He sat up with a start and made his wishes known:
> Atrides-chief of Achaea's united forces—
> first put out the fires with glistening wine,
> wherever the flames still burn in all their fury…(*Iliad Book 23*)

From the Hittite text:

> A silver jar of half a mina and twenty shekels weight is filled with fine oil.
> They take up the bones…and put them into the fine oil in the silver jar, then they take them out of the fine oil and lay them on a linen….Now when they have finished collecting the bones, they wrap them up together with the linen cloth…and place them on a chair, but if a woman, they place them on a stool. (*The Hittites*)

From the funeral of Patroclus again:

> Then let us collect the bones of Menoetius' son Patroclus,...
> Then let us place his bones in a golden urn,
> sealed tight and dry with a double fold of fat. (*Iliad* Book 23)

The rite for Hector differed slightly:

> Then they collected the white bones of Hector—
> all his brothers, his friends-in-arms, mourning,
> and warm tears came streaming down their cheeks.
> They placed the bones they found in a golden chest,
> shrouding them round and round in soft purple clothes. (*Iliad* Book 24)

The Hittite rite continues with a note about the funeral feast. Animal sacrifices finish the Hittite ceremony.

> Two oxen and two lots of nine sheep have been brought....One ox and nine sheep they sacrifice to the Sun-goddess...one ox and nine sheep they sacrifice to the soul of the deceased... (*The Hittites*)

In *Iliad*, animals are sacrificed on the pyre. From the funeral of Patroclus:

> ...droves of fat sheep and shambling crook-horned cattle
> they led before the pyre ...

Dogs and horses are added, and sacrificed captives of Troy. All are dedicated to Patroclus. The funeral rites for Patroclus and Hector described in *Iliad* seems to reflect a memory of Bronze Age funeral rites of Anatolia, though there are differences of some detail.

Iliad and *Odyssey* provide a picture of adventurers, ruthless in battle, driven by pride of descent and concern with personal honor, yet ever alert to opportunities for booty and prizes of war. When in the 1950s Linear B writing began to be deciphered, a totally different picture of the Mycenaeans emerged. The contents of the Linear B tablets clearly showed that the Mycenaean palaces were centers of intensive economic activity. Palace personnel managed economic affairs through extensive control of materials and labor. Tablets record chariot wheels still usable, those needing repair, allotments of raw materials to craftsmen, agricultural products owed to the palace, allocations of land, even the names of individual cattle. Nothing escaped the attention of the intrusive palace administrators. No detail was too small, provided that it related to the economic interests of the palace.

This picture of the Mycenaean ruling class and their materialism is so different from that heroic image portrayed in *Iliad* and *Odyssey* that questions were raised. How could *Iliad* or *Odyssey* ignore such matters? Was this not evidence that the epics were composed in a much later time, a time when the palaces no longer existed?

There may be another explanation, however. The poet-singers of the Late Bronze Age, who probably first sang the tales which were later to become *Iliad* and *Odyssey*, lived in the real world. They could see the economic activity of the farms and the towns, the flow of goods to and from the palaces, the loading and unloading of trade goods in the harbors. They knew the craftsmen, the workers, the weavers, and they probably knew of the unceasing accounting activities of the palace scribes. But the stories which they sung were, from the beginning, romances. They were tales of far-off adventures and bold men. They were tales of knights and single combat. There was no need and no place in the songs for the workings of the local economy.

In the Middle Ages of Europe, similar romances were told. Who would expect to hear in tales of Arthur or Roland a discussion of the number of hams in the smokehouse, the number of cheeses due to the palace from the farms, the number of sheep which were to be sheared? The poet-singers did not "forget" life in the palaces. Such stuff as recorded in the Linear B tablets was simply alien to their purpose. In any case, the Trojan War took place on a distant shore, far from the Mycenaean palaces and their economic concerns. *Odyssey* does to some extent discuss life in the palaces, and much of what is in the Linear B tablets is evident in veiled form. Under control of the palace, it is evident from *Odyssey*, were herds of swine, flocks of goats, cattle, cultivated lands, women working at weaving on a production basis. The presence of smiths, carpenters, masons, and numerous other craftsmen can be inferred. Much that is revealed in the Linear B tablets could have been guessed from what is said in *Odyssey*, except the remarkable intrusiveness into daily life of palace officials. In *Odyssey,* a palace-centered economy is evident, even though the busy scribes are not mentioned.

There is ample evidence of memory of the Bronze Age in *Iliad*. Even the language preserves several Bronze Age features. Most of the *Iliad* is in the Ionian dialect which probably developed after the migrations to the islands and shores of Anatolia. However, some of the words in *Iliad* are in the ancient Mycenaean dialect which disappeared from everyday speech well before the time of Homer. How did Homer know of these words? What is the origin of the poetic lines that incorporated them? It appears that words and even whole lines from the earliest oral poetry had been preserved by the poet-singers, particularly in those cases where equivalent words in the contemporary Ionian dialect would not fit the poetic meter. Thus, the language of *Iliad* and *Odyssey* preserves evidence of the origin of the tales in the Bronze Age, and that suggests a retained memory of events of the Bronze Age.

Things are remembered of a more material nature, things which seem to have existed only in the Bronze Age. Tower shields are mentioned. These are body-length shields of rectangular shape. Figure of Eight shields are also mentioned. These too are body-length shields, given the name because of their shape, rounded at top and bottom and pinched in at the sides. Both were used by lightly armed combatants operating without benefit of armor. Bronze Age wall paintings from the palaces and engravings on gemstones show such shields, just as *Iliad* describes them. Then, there is the Boar's Tusk helmet.

> Meriones gave Odysseus bow, quiver and sword
> and over his head he set a helmet made of leather.
> Inside it was crisscrossed taut with many thongs,
> outside the gleaming teeth of a white-tusked boar
> ran round and round in rows stitched neat and tight–
> a master craftsman's work… (*Iliad Book 10*)

In the remains of the Bronze Age, archaeologists have found wall paintings and gem and ivory carvings illustrating just such helmets. Remarkably, actual remains of a boar's tusk helmet have been discovered. The match to the description of the helmet in *Iliad* is amazing. The tall shield and the boar's tusk helmet were already obsolete in the period in which the Trojan War probably occurred, which demonstrates that *Iliad* contains elements from various times of the Bronze Age, and not just of its close.

Among the components of body armor, greaves or shin-guards are mentioned in *Iliad*. Their use was apparently unknown in the time of the later poet-singers and of Homer. But the use of greaves in the Late Bronze Age is certain. They are illustrated on the Warrior Vase, Figure 7-1, that was found in the ruins of Mycenae and which dates from near the end of the Bronze Age. In a tomb in Cyprus, remains of greaves have been found also dating to the end of the Bronze Age. Here, *Iliad* recalls a component of armor, seemingly no longer in use in what is taken to be Homer's time.

Repeatedly, *Iliad* mentions the "clang" or "clatter" of body armor.

> For in his back even as he was turning
> the spear fixed between the shoulders and was driven
> on through the chest beyond it.
> He fell thunderously and his armor clattered upon him. (*Iliad Book* 5)

Critics have supposed that there was no such armor among the Mycenaeans. The Warrior Vase shows body protection which consists of a vest upon which appear to be small metal plates. From these, a clattering or clanging sound is not to be expected. Thus, it was a revelation when segmented body armor, much like that used by the knights of the Middle Ages, was discovered at Dendra, near Mycenae. The armor was of the Bronze Age. There is no doubt of the clatter and clang which would be produced when a fighter wearing such armor crashed to the ground.

In *Iliad*, a feast is set out, and on the table is a cup that belongs to King Nestor:

> And there in the midst
> The grand glowing cup the old king brought from home,
> Studded with golden nails, fitted with handles,
> Four all told and two doves perched on each,
> Heads bending to drink and made of solid gold
> And twin supports ran down to form the base. (*Iliad* Book 11)

Figure 4-2. A golden cup, restored, found by Schliemann in the ruins of Mycenae. Note supports running down to the base, nails (rivets), birds drinking. Except for the number of handles, the cup matches well the description of Nestor's cup.

This is the kind of vivid description which the poets-singers loved and would want to preserve. In the Bronze Age remains of Mycenae, a cup was found which has often been compared to Nestor's cup. It is of gold, with a gold foot, stem, and bowl. On opposite sides, two gold handles extend from the lip at the top down to the foot. The handles are attached by rivets or nails. On top of each handle are doves of gold with wings outspread. They face inward as if drinking from the cup. This cup is likely only one of many similar gold cups of its time, others of which may have had four handles.

It is possible, of course, that remains of body shields, or boar's tusk helmets, or cups such as Nestor's survived into much later times as heirlooms, or that artistic representations survived, serving as inspiration for late poet-singers. It is more likely, however, that these items were preserved in poetic memory, lines and stanzas brought to the new lands of the Greek diaspora.

That conclusion is supported by the Catalog of Ships. The Catalog of Ships is found in the second book of *Iliad*. In it, some 170 towns or cities are described together with the number of ships and men and the names of the leaders which each furnished to the War. Archaeologists have found in Greece the remains of a number of these towns or cities. Of the 170 of the Catalog, at least forty had ceased to exist or were otherwise unknown in Classical times. Probably these towns no longer existed in Homer's time either. Many were abandoned, either during the collapse or within a few generations after the collapse of Bronze Age society. It is unrealistic to believe that the Catalog of Ships had been assembled in or close to the time of Homer.

The Catalog of Ships was the work of poet-singers at a time which was close enough to the Bronze Age that towns and cities of the mainland were still fresh in memory. Yet it was sufficiently removed from the time of the Trojan War that the romantic conception could be maintained that all of Greece participated in the War.

The sole purpose for which the catalog could have been composed is in relation to a war at Troy. Without a continuing memory of conflict at Troy, the catalog would have served no purpose.

Since so much of authentic memory of the Bronze Age seems to be preserved in *Iliad*, it is likely that at least some of the specific elements of the story are also an authentic memory. But which elements are they?

Something can be learned by comparison with tales told in later ages. In the tales of Attila mentioned earlier, persons were brought together who lived in different times and places, but an actual war of the Huns and Burgundians was remembered. At the battle of Kosovo which took place in AD 1389, the Osmanli Turks defeated the forces of Serbia. Bosnian Christian poet-singers told of it, but they brought into the story persons killed years earlier, and made a traitor of one who was not. Still, the story preserved knowledge of a real war and its outcome. A Turkish version remembers the battle but tells that the Turks faced 500,000 Serbian infantry lead by 500 princes supported by 300,000 knights in armor mounted on fine horses. This version was recorded by a Turkish historian from tales told by peasants only a few decades after the battle, which shows how quickly an orally preserved tale can take flight from reality. But here also, the actuality of the battle or war was remembered. The Song of Roland tells of the withdrawal of Charlemagne's army from Spain which took place in AD 778. In the tale, there is a great battle in the pass of Roncesvalles in the Pyrenees in which the rear guard of Charlemagne's retreating army under the command of Roland is annihilated by a Muslim army. The defeat is due to treachery, and there is an arch villain. The Muslim forces are described as overwhelming in number and include an army brought from Egypt by the Emir of Babylon. In fact, Charlemagne was in Spain at the request of a friend, the Muslim Emir of Saragossa, and it was not Muslims who attacked the rear guard but a small group of Basques in response to the pillaging of the withdrawing army. There was an actual Roland in that army, but the attack on the rear guard was not due to Muslims, treachery, or a villain.

There are common elements in these orally preserved tales. People of different periods are brought together, and others may be invented. The scope of battle is enlarged, sometimes greatly. But usually, the main heroic characters are correctly recalled, and the fact that there was a battle or war is correctly remembered.

Memory begins to loose contact with reality after about three generations. Those who participated in the event, typically a battle or war, are no longer alive to correct the story when it is recounted by grandson or great grandson. In recent times, 1830, a local conqueror, Ibrahim Pasha, passed with his army through Cilicia in southern Turkey. There, he cleared a road for his guns to pass and hardly anything more. A later visitor to the area noted that the local people attribute the construction of every bridge, every old building to Ibrahim Pasha. In almost all the visitor heard about Ibrahim Pasha there was hardly anything which was not exaggerated. It was only two or three generations earlier that Ibrahim Pasha had passed by.

Much of this applies to *Iliad*. Certainly, many elements of the story are fictional, including the conversations and conflicts among the gods, conversations on the battlefield, conversations in the privacy of the palace between Hector and his wife, and no doubt much else. Many of the heroes and their deeds likely are of some other time, some other battle or war, waged in some other place, brought into *Iliad* by the strange attractive power of the growing epic. The Greek poet-singers had a treasure of remembered stories of conflict from various times and places. These were a rich source of names, incidents of battle, and the color of war and were probably incorporated into *Iliad* to enrich the story.

The size and duration of the Trojan War may also have been magnified by the poetic imagination. But some of the leaders, the heroes, are likely to be correctly remembered. That there was a war, or at least one or more battles involving Greeks at Troy, is also likely to be true.

From the vantage point which our time provides, *Iliad* should be recognized as war fiction, the most powerful and convincing war fiction yet composed. That is not a disparagement. Good war fiction builds invented elements atop a foundation of an actual war and, in good war fiction, the main aspects of the war are authentically told. Yet, with so much of *Iliad* likely to be fictitious, what is the assurance that there was a battle or war of Greeks against Troy at all? Support must be looked for outside *Iliad*, in the circumstances of the Late Bronze Age, and in the archaeological evidence, next.

5
EVIDENCE OF TROY

Did the Trojan War occur in the Late Bronze Age, as assumed in the previous chapter, or later, in the Iron Age? That the Trojan War occurred well before the time of Homer is certain, but *Iliad* and *Odyssey* give no date of it, and there are no contemporary reports of it. It is an old problem. Greek learned men of the Classical period considered it, and a way was found to calculate the date. Tradition told that after the Trojan War a new people, the Dorians, swept into Greece. According to one tradition, the Dorian occupation was completed two generations after the fall of Troy. Dorians replaced Mycenaean kings on the thrones of Greece, including the throne of Sparta.

In Classical times, there were lists of Spartan kings that were thought to go back to the first Dorian king of Sparta. If the period of rule of each of these kings were known, the time of the beginning of Dorian occupation could be calculated. From that, the date of the Trojan War might be closely estimated. But the lengths of their rule were not known. It had to be estimated, on the basis of the average length of rule as known from more recent kings. Investigation showed that there were, on the average, three kingly reigns per century, or 33 1/3 years per king, and this was thought to be accurate enough when taken over a sufficiently long list of kings. Some would reign for a longer time, others a shorter time, but the reign would average 33 1/3 years. On such a basis, or perhaps on some other basis not now known, the ancient scholars made their calculations, with results as shown below.

Scholar	Date of the War
Phanias of Eresus	1126 BC
Callimachus	1127 BC
Ephorus of Kyme	1135 BC
Sosibius	1171 BC
Eratosthenes	1183 BC
Ctesias	1183 BC
Timaius	1193 BC

Thrasyllus	1194 BC
Dicaiarchus	1212 BC
Cleitarchus	1234 BC
Herodotus	1250 BC
Douris of Samos	1334 BC

These results differ from one another to some extent because of differences in the assumptions made, including the time which may have passed between the Trojan War and the seating of the first Dorian kings in Sparta, the number of kings in the king list, and the duration of each rule.

Modern historians have checked the assumed average length of rule against the known periods of the kings of England from AD 1066 to 1461 and found 30 1/2 years as the average. The dates for Stuart and Hanoverian kings from AD 1603 to 1936 yields 30 1/4 years. These numbers are very close to the Greek estimate. Still, some historians are skeptical of the ancient calculations, questioning whether the earliest Dorian kings of Sparta could have been known in the Classical period. There was no writing in Greece in the time of those early kings. Could knowledge of the line of kings be retained by oral transmission over hundreds of years? There is no answer to this and other challenges to the calculations of the ancients, but it is remarkable that it is precisely within the span of years indicated that archaeologists and historians believe they find evidence for a Trojan War, or at least of destruction at Troy.

An exact date remains elusive. If some day the date of the fall of Troy is determined with certainty, a posthumous prize should be awarded to the ancient sage whose calculation was closest.

Legends may also supply a clue regarding the date. Greek legends refer to certain events which took place years before the Trojan War. But of the time period that followed the War, they mention only one or two more generations. The sons of the Trojan War heroes are mentioned, and then the legends fade. The sons may have been of the last generation before the palace and king-centered society of the Mycenaean world completely disintegrated. No exact time can be placed on that disintegration, except that it probably occurred somewhere in the span 1200–1100 BC as will be discussed in following chapters. On that basis, the Trojan War must have occurred in the generations before 1100 BC.

The intrigue and murder in the palace of Agamemnon following the Trojan War as reported in *Odyssey*, the wanderings of the heroic veterans of the War—these events seem to reflect the turbulent conditions of the 1200–1100 BC period. That too suggests a time in the generations before 1100 BC. Here, the Trojan War will be looked for in that approximate time or a bit earlier.

Homer and the Hittite Archives

When in the 1950s Michael Ventris found the key to the decipherment of Greek Linear B writing, hope was high that the Linear B texts would say something about the Trojan War. A number of tablets with Linear B text had been found at Pylos, traditionally the city of King Nestor, well known from both *Iliad* and *Odyssey*. The Pylos tablets were written around 1200 BC. But expectations were dashed. The tablets contained hardly anything but the dullest of business records and a few local military dispositions.

At the archaeological site of Troy, no trace of records has been found, a matter of great disappointment. Surely kings of Troy maintained archives in which to preserve copies of diplomatic correspondence and treaties. Perhaps the important records of Troy were kept on some perishable material. The archives of Troy would be a find of outstanding importance for which an archaeologist might trade all of "Priam's gold" discovered by Schliemann at Troy!

In contrast to the Greek tablets, the Hittite tablets were astonishing in the detail which they supplied. In 1924, only a few years after Hittite texts first began to yield their secrets, the Swiss scholar Emil Forrer reported that he had found in those texts clear references to places and personalities known from *Iliad*.

In a play by Christopher Marlowe, Faust asks about Helen of Troy. "Was this the face that launch'd a thousand ships, and burnt the topless towers of Ilium?" In this way is the destruction of Troy remembered in western art and literature. "Ilium" is the Latinized version of the Greek "Ilios," which is the basis of the name *Iliad*. Not Troy but Ilios is the term most often used in the Greek language text when referring to the great fortress-city. The Greek text uses word forms of the Classical period, but language and pronunciation change over the course of time. Centuries before the Classical period, in the era of Homer or his predecessors, the pronunciation was "Wilios." Some time after, but before the Classical period in Greece, the "*w*" sound disappeared from Ionian and Athenian speech, resulting in the later pronunciation "Ilios."

Forrer's surprising announcement was that Wilusa of the Hittite texts was Wilios of *Iliad*. Wilusa, it will be recalled from Chapter 3, was the land mentioned as a western country friendly to the Hittites. More will be said of Forrer's claim at the end of this chapter, but it is accepted here that Forrer was right. Wilusa is the Troy of *Iliad*.

Forrer found another connection between Wilusa and the Trojan War. In the Hittite records, he believed that he had found Alexandros, prince of Troy. Forrer had before him a copy of a vassal treaty, the "Alaksandus Treaty" as it is called, between the Hittites and Wilusa. The name of the king of Wilusa is given. His name is Alaksandus. *Iliad* tells that it was Alexandros (Alexander in English) whose affair with Helen brought about the terrible war. (Paris is his less frequently used name.) Many linguists and historians accept that the name Alaksandus is the same as the Greek Alexandros. But why does a king of Wilusa have a Greek name? It is one of the mysteries which result from insufficient knowledge of those times.

According to the preamble of the treaty, this Alaksandus was not the natural heir to the throne of Wilusa but had been adopted by the previous king, Kukunnis, at the insistence of the Hittite king. It is likely that Kukunnis had no sons—a serious matter in ancient times, and a particularly serious matter in a royal family. A problem of succession would almost certainly arise, leading to instability and possibly war. The Hittites abhorred instability. Where there was no son, adoption was the accepted remedy in the ancient world. Possibly, a Greek had attached himself to the Hittite court and made a reputation as a warrior in the Hittite service. Such a person would be a fine candidate as a "son" to king Kukunnis of Wilusa. His loyalty to the Hittites could be taken for granted. Perhaps the adoption was forced on the king of Wilusa. By such means, a Greek name may have come to the throne of Wilusa.

There are, of course, other possibilities. Alaksandus could be an Anatolian name. "Alexandros" (in its feminine form) is known from the earliest records of the Greek language, the Linear B tablets from Knossos in Crete. The records date to somewhat before 1400 BC. At that time in Crete there was a substantial Luvian-speaking population, and the name on the Linear B tablet could refer not to a Greek but to a resident of Luvian background. Luvian was the language of western Anatolia and Alaksandus might have been a perfectly proper Anatolian name. In Crete, perhaps, the name entered the Greek language. There, the Anatolian name Alaksandus, which would be meaningless as it stood in Greek, would have been changed to something of very closely similar sound which gave the name meaning to Greeks. Alexandros in Greek means "repeller of men," a fighting name fit for a king or prince. Such assimilations are common in the transfer of names between speakers of different languages.

Alaksandus of Wilusa is unlikely to be Alexandros of *Iliad*, however. While the date of the Trojan War is not known, the treaty with Wilusa may have preceded the War by decades or generations. Alaksandus of Wilusa is a king, while Alexandros of *Iliad* is a prince, the son of King Priam. It is not a serious difficulty. Royal names repeat in following generations. Alexandros of the Trojan War could be a second or third generation descendent of the Alaksandus of the Wilusa treaty. Or, there may have been but one Alaksandus, taken by the poet-singers from a somewhat earlier time and placed in the story of Troy and the time of the Trojan War. It will be recalled that in the tale of the Nibelungs, leading persons were placed together though it is now known that they lived generations apart. All of this is in perfect accord with the methods of the storytellers and the workings of oral tradition.

Hittite records strongly indicate that Wilusa was located where there are the remains of a city believed by archaeologists to have been Troy. An Alaksandus is documented as a member of royalty in Wilusa at a time close to that of the Trojan War. His name is remarkably like that of the Trojan prince whose missteps, according to *Iliad*, precipitated the War. A group who seem to be the Dardanians, Trojans of *Iliad*, appear in the Egyptian records of about that time. These are evidence that there was a Troy, an Ilios, a city-state of the Late Bronze Age. They support the view that the story of the Trojan War could have been drawn from an authentic background in the Bronze Age.

Hittite Reports of War

Since the Hittite records mention Ilios, Troy, and Alexandros, is it possible that the records also mention the Trojan War? That is, of course, a question of exceptional interest. The Alaksandus Treaty binds Wilusa and Hatti together in a bond of mutual military support. As is usual in the Hittite treaties with vassals, King Alaksandus is required to fulfill certain obligations, but as long as he does so faithfully the Hittites will help to defend Wilusa and support the king and his heirs forever. This strong alliance indicates that the Hittites would take seriously any attack on Wilusa. If an attack by Greeks on Wilusa took place during the period in which Hittites still ruled in Anatolia, the attack would have been recorded by the Hittites. Some note of it may exist in surviving records.

The clay tablets found at Hattusa in central Anatolia have been in the ground more than three thousand years. Time and weather have damaged them. They can be likened to memos on paper in a file cabinet which, in some disaster, have been scattered about and buried. Now, ages later, stacks of memos are dug up, but many of the pages have come apart and are now in fragments. Or the second and third pages are recovered more or less intact, but the first and last pages are missing. Due to the absence of these pages it is not possible to know the name of the person to whom the memo is addressed, the name of the memo writer, or the date. And in all cases, some of the words or portions of words are blurred or missing. This represents the situation of the clay tablets from Hattusa, and most other sites for that matter. Scholars have struggled with this problem, and much damaged text has been restored. Among the results, a number of records have been found which mention Wilusa, and a very few mention Wilusa in conjunction with Ahhiyawa. Those are the records of particular interest, and they hint at two different situations which might reflect the Trojan War as seen from the Hittite vantage point.

During the reign of the Hittite king Muwatalli (1295–1271 BC) or his successor Urhi-Tesub (1271-1264 BC), a letter was received from Manapa-Tarhunda, king of the Seha River Land. This vassal king had been confirmed in his position many years before by the Hittites. The letter brings disturbing news (illegible or missing text is indicated by brackets).

> I am your servant, Manapa-Tarhunda. I trust that with you and yours all is well. [....] came and brought Hittite troops. [....] went to attack the land of Wilusa. As for me, things are not well. I'm very sick and the sickness has prostrated me. Piyama-Radu has humiliated me. He has appointed Atpas over me, and has attacked Lazpas. Men who belong to me joined him as did your men also. (*Geography*)

Atpas is the son-in-law of Piyama-Radu, and he is governor or agent of the Achaean Greeks in Millawanda. He probably owes his position to the influence of his father-in-law, Piyama-Radu. It appears that Piyama-Radu has gained control of the Seha River Land and has installed Atpas as his front man, placing him over the rightful king, Manapa-Tarhunda.

According to the letter, there has been an attack on Wilusa (Troy). Hittite troops are on the move. While it is not explicitly stated, the proximity of the two sentences strongly suggests that this troop movement is related to an attack on Wilusa. It is possible that the Hittites are responding to a treaty obligation and moving troops to the defense of Wilusa. This seems particularly likely as Piyama-Radu, whom the Hittites despise, is involved. His attempts at empire-building are well known. The letter states that Piyama-Radu had attacked Lazpas (Lesbos), a likely stepping-stone to an attack on Wilusa (see Figure 3-1).

What is ominous in this is the de facto alliance which existed between the Achaeans and Piyama-Radu. Piyama-Radu runs to the Achaeans for protection when necessary. And, as an experienced intriguer, he might well have drawn the Achaeans into an unwise military adventure in Anatolia. While neither the Manapa-Tarhunda letter nor other Hittite records mention the Achaeans in connection with the attack on Wilusa, the Achaeans may have been involved in the attack. Perhaps troops were put ashore by the Achaeans, those of Piyama-Radu with their own, first at Lazpas then at Wilusa. Greeks had long been in Millawanda (Miletus) and Chios was a stepping stone to the north. Archaeological evidence shows that Greeks were settled on the island of Chios by approximately 1220 BC and may have even have arrived there a few decades earlier. The next stepping stone north would have been Lazpas. To the north beyond was Wilusa (Troy).

Further evidence of Greek involvement comes from the Tawagalawa Letter. Urhi-Tesub was succeeded on the throne by Hattusili. Piyama-Radu still lived, but he had fallen from his former heights. He had taken refuge in the territory of the Achaean king. The king of the Hittites wants assurance from the Achaeans that there will be no further trouble from Piyama-Radu. The Hittite king asks the Achaean king to speak with Piyama-Radu and say to him:

> The king of Hatti and I, in the matter of Wilusa over which we were at enmity, he has convinced me and we have made friends;...a war would not be right for us.

It is clear that the Achaeans and the Hittites had been on the verge of war over Wilusa. What could the circumstances have been? There are several possibilities; the Achaeans posed a threat to Wilusa, or were already at war with Wilusa, or had burned it. Diplomacy resolved the matter. Talks were held and direct conflict had been averted. And this outcome is to be explained to Piyama-Radu who, presumably, will be angry and disheartened by this turn of events.

If the circumstances were such that Wilusa was already under attack, then this may be the Trojan War of story and legend. The Manapa-Tarhunda Letter which appears to tell of an attack by Piyama-Radu on Wilusa cannot be dated narrowly and might correspond to the reign of Muwatalli, Urhi-Tesub, or possibly Hattusili, and thus in the time frame 1295-1260 BC. As will be seen, this may correlate with the destruction of the Trojan city referred to by archaeologists as Troy VI.

There is a story, not found in *Iliad*, which may relate to these events. *Cypria*, one of the Homeric Cycle of stories was mentioned in an earlier chapter. *Cypria* tells that the Greek army that embarked for Troy made a mistake in navigation. Instead of Troy, the army landed at Teuthrania, a number of miles south of the desired land fall. Here, thinking they were at Troy, the Greeks fought an inconclusive battle and in the process wounded a Teuthranian warrior named Telephus. After recognizing the error, the Greeks returned to their original port of Aulis in Greece to reorganize. Then, in a second attempt, they successfully landed at Troy.

The country which *Cypria* calls Teuthrania is located, it seems, in the place which the Hittites refer to as Seha River Land. The name Telephus appears to be a good Anatolian name of the Bronze Age, similar to the Anatolian name Telipinus. Here, in Greek legend, may be a reflection of the events described earlier, in which Seha River Land was attacked and King Manapa-Tarhunda forced to a temporary humiliation, followed by an attack on Troy. In Greek legend, the role of Piyama-Radu and his troops would not need to be emphasized, and memory of them might quickly fade away so that all attention could be given to the Greek role in the war with Troy.

That the Piyama-Radu affair may have provided the basis of the Trojan War legend is suggested by the circumstances just described. But the Trojan War of legend might reflect other historical circumstances. A few decades after the Piyama-Radu matter, Hittite and Greek interests clashed again. These later events, poorly documented in existing records, might also possibly represent the circumstances of the Trojan War legend.

At that time, Hittite king Tudhaliya was at war with Assyria. A letter has been found from this Hittite king to a vassal king in Amurru (Figure 2-1) which directs him to stop any Ahhiyawa goods from going to Assyria. While this intends a war embargo on Assyria, it also seems to suggest a certain hostility to the Achaean Greeks. From the Hittite archives, there is a document from this period in which the king of Ahhiyawa is referred to as a

"Great King," but that flattering title was then scratched out, and that too may indicate that there was a renewed hostility to the Achaeans. Another letter found in the archives tells that the Hittite king has participated in revising the boundary or reduced the territory of Millawanda, the main Greek enclave in Anatolia. That could have produced a breach between the Hittites and Greeks. It is at least possible that the Greeks had chosen that time to assault Troy, at a time when good relations with Hattusa no longer mattered and when the Hittites needed to direct their attention fully to the east, to Assyria. Hittite support to the Trojans would, under these circumstances, have been largely symbolic, perhaps a few troops and a flurry of diplomatic correspondence.

It is hardly evidence of a Trojan War, but only of a situation in which it may have taken place. The period would have been early in the reign of Tudhaliya, who ruled from 1239 to 1209 BC. If this is the time of the Trojan War, it might correlate with the destruction of Troy VIIa, to be discussed below.

At this point, it is useful to look at the archaeological site of Troy. Two incidences of destruction have been found by archaeologists in the citadel of Troy, and these may correlate with the two situations just discussed.

Troy, the City of Priam

Hissarlik hill in northwestern Anatolia, the site which Heinrich Schliemann excavated, is almost certainly the location of Troy of *Iliad*. A great city of the Bronze Age stood there. After the Bronze Age, according to the archaeological evidence, the site was occupied only thinly or intermittently. But there was sufficient continuity of occupation that it could be identified as Troy to a visiting Persian king centuries later, and still later to Alexander the Great.

That Hissarlik hill was the location of ancient Troy is consistent with the fact that Troy of *Iliad*, *Odyssey*, and *Cypria* was near a seacoast and that the Greeks assembled at Aulis, which is on a Greek shore opposite the northwest Anatolian coast. Hissarlik hill is a short distance inland from the coast. Archaeological investigation shows that on Hissarlik hill there was, so far as is known, the only great fortress-city of the Bronze Age along the entire western coast of Anatolia. Local geography around Hissarlik hill corresponds reasonably well with that described in *Iliad*. It is a fair conclusion that the ruin on Hissarlik hill is that of ancient Troy, whose memory is imperishable thanks to Homer, the man from Chios, an island off the Anatolian coast.

Hissarlik—the name is Turkish—is a mound of rock about 95 feet high. From the top there is an excellent view toward the west over the plain of the river Scamander, and beyond to the Aegean Sea. The Scamander flows north and expands into a marsh before reaching the sea near the Dardanelles, Figure 5-1. In ancient times, this marsh was a shallow bay that came near to the walls of Troy. Several miles to the southwest of Hissarlik, now shielded from direct view by a ridge of hills, is what is now called Besik Bay, where evidence has been found of a port and trading station of the Late Bronze Age. Here surely was a port of Troy. Remains of Greek pottery have been found there.

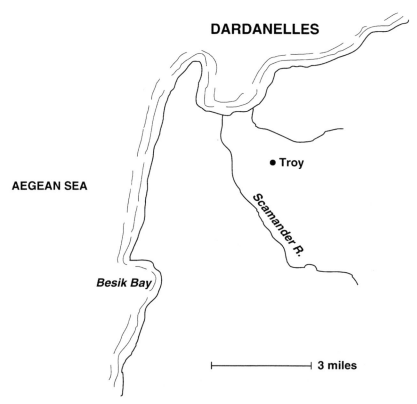

Figure 5-1. The site of Troy on Hissarlik hill, and bays where ships might land. Shore lines have changed since the Bronze Age and the bay to the north no longer exists.

On Hissarlik hill, years of excavation have left a battle field appearance. There are trenches, excavated walls from various periods, sections of restoration. Schliemann's excavations, begun in 1870, involving as they did deep trenching and a hasty search for the city of King Priam, caused significant damage to the site and to the archaeological record. This was certainly not his intention. His work was done at a time when archaeology had not yet shed the outlook of the treasure hunt. It was well before the meticulous excavation and recording methods of modern archaeology were firmly established. In any case, the site was much more complex than he could have anticipated, and he had dug well below the level of Priam's Troy, the Troy of *Iliad*, before the error was recognized. But recognize it he did, and he invited the architect W. Dorpfeld to conduct a more systematic examination of the site. Dorpfeld worked from 1893 to 1895 and established an orderly baseline for all later archaeological work at Troy. Even with Dorpfeld's systematic excavation work, many questions were left unanswered—those which might cast light on the Trojan War.

Carl Blegen of the University of Cincinnati and his team carried out work at Troy from 1932 to 1938. Excavating in what little ground was undisturbed by earlier excavations, the Cincinnati team proceeded with meticulous care in order to salvage and record evidence that remained; and it is upon their work primarily that much of the modern discussion of the history of Troy and the Trojan War depends. In recent years, Bronze Age Troy is under investigation again, by an archaeological team under the direction of Manfred Korfmann of Eberhard-Karls University in Tubingen.

Figure 5-2. An artist's reconstruction of the citadel of Troy VI as it would have appeared from the south, based on archaeological evidence. Troy VII was substantially similar. The outer town, not shown here, would have been in the foreground.

The site of Troy may have been occupied as far back as 3000 BC. Evidence indicates that there was on the hill at that time a small walled settlement. This settlement, given the designation Troy I by archaeologists, was expanded and the dwellings within the walls were remodeled in subsequent years, with the major changes given the designations Troy II, III, and so forth. It is Troy VI and VII which are of greatest importance for Trojan War research. Troy VI dates from approximately 1800 BC to some time after 1300 BC. At the heart of Troy VI was the citadel, Figure 5-2, a formidable fortress with thick defensive walls forming a circuit of oval shape about seven hundred feet across. These walls were constructed of large blocks of limestone laid with one horizontal course offset from the next, which gave a high degree of stability to the wall. Along the top, there was a breastwork of brick, which further increased the height. On the inside of the wall near the top, there were probably wooden platforms which would be used by archers if the fortress were under attack.

At its eastern section, walls overlapped with a space between forming an entrance passageway about six feet wide. This was, presumably, the main entrance to the fortress in time of war. Nearby was a tower of massive construction. The overlapping walls and tower formed a formidable defensive complex. Not only could defenders launch arrows down from the tower, but the double wall would forced attackers, bearing their shields on their right arms, to expose their left sides to a rain of missiles from defenders on the inner wall. Other towers jutted from the wall at strategic points, providing additional defensive capabilities. One of the towers sheltered a well and cistern, without which a protracted siege could not be withstood. What was undoubtedly the main peacetime gateway was in the south wall. This gateway was about 10 feet wide, and from it an avenue swept upward within the citadel, probably toward the palace.

The southwest section of wall was substantially less formidable: lower and narrower than the other sections and displaced inward from them. It is clear that this section was of an earlier period of construction. There seems to have been an effort underway to replace these weak sections with the newer, thicker, and higher walls. The replacement project was never completed. Within the citadel, few structures remain after the demolition carried out in Classical times by Greek and Roman engineers to make room for an Athena temple and a Roman theater, but Bronze Age foundations exist which are taken to be those of houses. The palace of the king is assumed to have been at the north or high end of the citadel but no remains of it have been found.

Outside of the citadel on the south side, there was a Bronze Age town, and here archaeological work is still in its infancy. Only limited traces of this town have been found thus far, and what might be the most interesting parts may lie below an area containing later Roman period construction. Evidence has been found of a surrounding defensive ditch or moat, and a palisade or wooden wall. About a third of a mile south of the citadel, a cemetery has been found, and here there are urns containing the remains of cremations. Cremation was the Trojan method of dealing with the dead, a disappointment to archaeologists, who prefer tombs or burials where items interred with the dead can provide information on dates, culture, and social conditions.

Almost all references to archaeological findings at Troy to date, including references to Troy VI and VII, pertain to the citadel and what was found within it, since little else had been investigated until recently. That provides only an incomplete picture of Troy which in the future must be supplemented by what will be learned from investigations in the outer town.

Destruction of the Sixth City

That Troy came to a fiery and destructive end at the hand of the Greeks is in keeping with lore that Greeks of the Classical period knew since childhood. *The Sack of Ilios*, one of the stories of the Trojan Cycle, tells the tale vividly—and a horrible one it is. Hector is dead, killed by Achilles. Troy is defeated. The Trojan women are sacrificed or enslaved. Andromache, the wife of Hector, is carried off as a prize of war. Her baby son, the son of Hector, is hurled down from the walls and killed. Troy is sent up in flames.

In contrast, *Cypria*, *Iliad*, and *Odyssey* say little about the end of Troy. *Iliad* only forecasts it. On Olympus the goddess Hera says:

> …Time and again we have sworn oaths
> …never to drive the fatal day away from the Trojans,
> not even when all Troy burns in ramping flames
> when the waring sons of Achaea burn her down!

In Troy VI, the Sixth City, at the eastern side of the citadel where the walls overlap to form an entrance passageway, excavation shows that the tops of the inner wall of the passage had collapsed inward. Within the citadel a house near that part of the wall collapsed outward toward the wall. Blocks from the house and wall intermingle in the space between them. Another house within the citadel and south of the first had also collapsed. Just inside of the South Gate another building had collapsed. Charcoal and ash associated with the collapse indicates fire. Based on the evidence of Greek pottery found in these ruins, the destruction is dated, somewhat uncertainly, in the span between 1300 and 1250 BC.

Many archaeologists and scholars with special interest in Troy are convinced that this destruction was the work of man, the result of a major attack by hostile forces, perhaps the evidence of the Greek attack on Troy. It is likely, however, that neither the Greeks nor anyone else could have done this damage. Due to the overlap, the inner wall is unapproachable by a battering ram which would lack space in which to operate. Nor, in the still standing sections of wall, is there any sign of scarring or bruising which battering would produce. And why would an enemy expend the effort? Why not attack at the weak southwest wall, the section that was never improved when the other walls were made stronger? In *Iliad*, Andromache tells Hector:

> Draw your armies up where the wild fig tree stands, there, where the city lies most open to assault, the walls are lower, easily overrun. Three times they have tried that point, hoping to storm Troy.... (*Iliad* Book 6)

There is no convincing evidence that this destruction was man-made. Evidence of an assault might include, in addition to signs of forced entry through the gate or wall: remains of abandoned or broken weapons, armor, shields; skeletons in disarray by the walls or in the streets, doorways, or dwellings; unhealed wound marks on the skeletons, or perhaps an arrowhead found within the confines of a skeleton; signs of widespread fire. Of these things, there is only the tumbled walls and some trace of fire. After the destruction, the citadel was restored and reoccupied. There would have been a cleanup which might have removed such evidence, but it is obvious that the cleanup wasn't thorough. In places, the restorers simply filled and rebuilt over the rubble of the destruction, which is why archaeologists were able to find the remains of tumbled walls and fragments of pottery.

If not the result of enemy attack, what caused the destruction? Blegen and his team of archaeologists believed that the destruction visited on the Sixth City was the result of a severe earthquake. Western Anatolia is one of the most seismically active regions of the world. All of the present evidence from Troy VI is consistent with earthquake, though there is not sufficient evidence to prove that it occurred.

Even if the destruction was caused by an earthquake, there could have been a connection with the Trojan War. Word of the destruction of the walls of Troy would have spread rapidly and would soon be known in every port of the Aegean. The Greeks may have decided that this was the time to strike, and strike they did, according to this view. But a Greek expeditionary force as massive as that described in *Iliad* could not be assembled in a day. Probably a year would be needed to prepare, and by then the damage to the walls could have been repaired. However, if the assault which may have been the basis of the Trojan War of legend was much more modest in scale than maintained in *Iliad*, it might have been mounted quickly.

There is another legend among the Greeks that might relate to a quick, opportunistic strike at Troy. It is related in *Iliad*, where it is placed perhaps one or two generations before the Trojan War. Speaking of Heracles, *Iliad* relates:

> He once sailed for Laomedon's blooded horses
> with just six ships and smaller crews than yours, true
> but he razed the walls of Troy.... (*Iliad* Book 5)

This story requires explanation, and it is provided by Apollodorus, a later-day Greek collector of legends. Laomedon is a king of Troy, the father of Priam. He contracted (can it be believed?) with the god Poseidon to build the strong walls of the citadel of Troy. Poseidon completed the task, but Laomedon refused to give him the horses that were to be his pay. Poseidon sent a sea monster to trouble Troy. Heracles, a legendary semi-superman and constant meddler in other people's affairs, killed the monster. He too was to be paid by Laomedon, but again Laomedon welshed. Heracles threatened Troy. In due time he gathered a force of fifty noblemen and set sail for Troy in eighteen ships (this number differs from that given in *Iliad*) of fifty oars each and conquered the city.

In his role as a god of land as well as sea, a major manifestation of Poseidon is earthquake. In *Iliad* Poseidon is the Earthshaker. An attack by Heracles may be a remembrance, a very dim one to be sure, of an earthquake at Troy which triggered an attack by Greeks.

If it was the destruction in the Sixth City of Troy which is evidence of the Trojan War, that conflict may be known from the Hittite archives, the letter from Manapa-Tarhunda mentioned earlier. The dates of the letter and of the destruction of Troy VI match reasonably well.

The Seventh City Is Destroyed

The reconstructed citadel is referred to by archaeologists as Troy VIIa. Ethnically, the occupants were the same as of old, and the way of life was much the same as earlier. At some time in the life of the reconstructed citadel, changes took place in the use of space. In the past, buildings stood well away from the citadel wall. Now, a series of dwellings were built right against the wall and large food storage jars were set into the floor, buried to their rims. Tightly packed dwellings and food storage suggest preparation for war, an expectation of a long siege. Did the king and the privileged people who lived in the citadel turn dwellings into food storage facilities? Or did refugees come within the walls, necessitating the close housing and stored food? Would the king allow refugees into the citadel, crowding the already limited space? The evidence provides few answers, but it seems that the political leadership or economic circumstances had changed significantly in some way, and the citadel could no longer be kept entirely for use by the elite. The circumstances could be those discussed in Chapter 3, in which the Hittites called for Walmu, whom the Hittite king wished to place on the throne of Troy.

Whatever the problems were, they were soon to be overshadowed by a second destruction. The destruction of the Troy VIIa citadel came at a time estimated by Blegen and his team as not more than one hundred years, and perhaps as few as fifty years, after the destruction of Troy VI. Both destructions may have occurred in one person's lifetime.

Most of the evidence of the Troy VIIa destruction is gone, the effect of time and human activity, but what remains—a mass of stones, bricks, burned and blackened debris—shows that the citadel was almost wholly destroyed by fire. In the remains of one house, archaeologists found fragments of a human skull with additional skull fragments scattered outside. Pieces of another skull were uncovered in another street. A human jaw bone with burnt matter was found in a house just outside the eastern wall of the citadel. On a hill beyond the citadel wall a skeleton was found by Blegen, thought to be of Troy VIIa date, the skull crushed and the jaw broken away, but most of the bones were still together yet lying in a way unlike what would be expected in a burial.

After the destruction of Troy VIIa, the citadel was again reoccupied, and this occupation is referred to as Troy VIIb. Very little is known of the lower town of Troy during the course of these events.

The presence in the destruction debris of Troy VIIa of extensive fire and scattered and damaged bones certainly suggests conflict. Given the limits on what can be expected to remain at a site so old, this seems to be evidence of an attack by a hostile enemy, brutal fighting within the citadel, and finally, the city put to the torch. The stories which men like Homer told were fashioned around some hard core of truth. Perhaps this is the destruction told in legends of the Greeks. In view of the possibility that this destruction is the basis of the war celebrated in *Iliad*, the date becomes important.

Dating for those times depends on pottery styles. Mycenaean pottery was widely admired and used not only in Greek cities, but in the coastal cities of Anatolia, Cyprus, Syria, Canaan, and even Egypt. The graceful shape and decoration made this pottery a desired luxury item. Designs changed rather slowly over the years, and archaeologists have been able to relate the progression of styles to relative and absolute dates at which the pottery was produced and used. The major stylistic periods of interest are termed Late Helladic IIIA, IIIB, and IIIC. (These designations are discussed in the next chapter. They have nothing to do with the designations, such as Troy VI and VII, assigned to Trojan remains.) At a certain time, perhaps around 1330 BC, the styles designated IIIB came into existence and began to replace IIIA. Similarly, sometime slightly after 1200 BC, the IIIC styles began to replace those of IIIB.

In the wreckage associated with the Troy VIIa, several hundred fragments of pottery were found, most of which are of Trojan design, but a number of the fragments are in the Mycenaean Greek style. Professor Blegen and those on his excavation team studied these fragments and concluded that there are none later than IIIB. Others, equally expert, look at the same material and believe that they see at least some that are early IIIC. There is no agreement. The problem is mostly that the fragments are small and reveal, at best, only small parts of the original overall pottery shape and decoration. What little is left is fairly general in appearance; they have a "could be anything" look. If the pottery is really IIIB, the destruction occurred at a time which cannot be pinned down much more narrowly than approximately 1330–1200 BC or slightly after. If the destruction occurred toward the end of this period, it might relate not only to the Walmu kingship but to tensions with Ahhiyawa in the time of Hittite king Tudhaliya IV (1239–1209 BC). If, on the other hand, early IIIC pottery is really present in the Troy VIIa remains, a time as late as 1165 BC could be indicated.

A Trojan War which might have occurred after 1200 BC will not be reflected in the Hittite records. After the reign of King Hattusili (1264–1239 BC), Hittite records become fewer. The Hittite grip on affairs in the West slackened, and the frequency of treaties and correspondence relating to the West was reduced. In terms of the realities of power politics, the period after about 1220 BC would present opportunities for an attack on Troy with some assurance that there would be no interference from the Hittites. After about 1190 BC, that assurance would be absolute. The time after 1220 BC was one of decreasing stability in the entire region, and a major attack on Troy would be consistent with the conditions of those times.

Some scholars believe that the Trojan War could not have taken place in this period since the situation on the Greek mainland had deteriorated. The kings of Greece would have been in no position for a concerted overseas adventure, it is supposed. However, epic story grows greatly with the telling. The historic attack of Greeks on Troy, or perhaps several different and unrelated attacks, may have been very modest in size. The great scope of the effort involving the whole Greek people (as told in the Catalog of Ships) may not have been a reality but a creative addition of the poet-singers. In any case, trouble at home is not necessarily a bar to an overseas war, and in fact may produce such a war, as will be discussed in Chapter 7.

Epic and Evidence—Has the War Been Found?

The epic tale of Troy that we have from Homer and from the other composers of the "Trojan Cycle" tell of the fiery destruction of the city. Archaeologists have produced evidence of damage to the Sixth City of Troy, and severe destruction to the Seventh City. It is usually assumed that one or the other of these is the basis of the Greek epic and is the historic counterpart of the Trojan War of *Iliad*. And so it may be. Yet no tablet has been found in the ruins which says "we are besieged by men of Ahhiyawa" and no arrowhead inscribed with a Greek name has been discovered in the remains of Troy. Archaeology cannot confirm that either destruction was at the hand of Greeks, and there are several reasons to be cautious about the identity of the destroyers.

Archaeologists know that a great many cities of the Bronze Age were attacked and burned, some more than once. The strong walls of most Bronze Age cities demonstrate a continuing concern with defense against potential enemies. Troy had been walled for hundreds of years, and the walls were occasionally strengthened, and those extensive construction activities could not have been undertaken solely with a possible attack from Greeks in mind. Over the years, there may have been many threats to Troy, a number of foiled attacks, and various attackers. The end of the Bronze Age was a particularly unstable and dangerous time, with many cities damaged or destroyed, from Greece to the borders of Egypt. Destructions in Troy of which archaeologists find evidence could have been at the hands of others, not necessarily the Greeks.

If the Greeks conquered Troy, it is strange that they did not occupy the land, with its rich and productive soil. And just offshore, there were teeming fisheries which could be exploited from Troy. Nowhere in *Iliad* or *Odyssey* is there an indication that Greeks occupied Troy or the lands which surround it, and there is no archaeological evidence of any Greek occupation in the citadel, the town, or the surrounding land in that period. The situation is consistent with a Greek attack on Troy, perhaps, but not with a Greek conquest of Troy.

Greeks may have attacked Troy but not conquered it. The poet-singers could have taken the deeds of Greeks on the Anatolian coast over years, including some at Troy, together with deeds of others, and woven them into the epic tale of Troy. The burning of Troy may be due to others. In *Iliad*, Homer shows a strange reticence to describe the destruction of Troy, as if that destruction was not a sure thing, or more likely not surely Greek.

There is a puzzling tale in the second book of *Iliad*. At the time in which the tale is set, the war has gone on nine years without resolution. On Olympus, Athena and Hera press Zeus to make a decision in favor of the Greeks. Others among the gods support the Trojans. Zeus put them all off, postponing a final decision. But at this moment, he wants to force the idle Greeks back into battle. Accordingly, he sends Dream to Agamemnon, leader of the Greeks:

> Go, murderous Dream, to the fast Achaean ships,
> and once you reach Agamemnon's shelter rouse him,
> order him, word-for-word exactly as I command.
> Tell Atrides to arm his long-haired Achaeans,
> to attack at once, full force,
> now he can take the broad streets of Troy,
> the immortal gods who hold Olympus clash no more,
> Hera's appeals have brought them round and all agree:
> griefs are about to crush the men of Troy. (*Iliad* Book 2)

"Atrides," the son of Atreus, is Agamemnon. As for his instructions from Zeus, nothing could be clearer. The Greeks are to arm and attack immediately, full force. Zeus himself has ordered it. Zeus himself has promised victory, and he has told Agamemnon exactly what to do. What is the result? Instead of obeying the king of the gods, Agamemnon tells his leaders that he intends to "test" the troops. He assembles the army and delivers a talk in which he says:

> Zeus is a harsh, cruel god. He vowed to me long ago
> ….that I should never embark for home
> till I brought the walls of Ilios crashing down.
> ……
> And now nine years of almighty Zeus have marched by,
> our ship timbers rot and the cables snap and fray
> and across the sea our wives and helpless children
> wait in the halls, wait for our return….And we?
> Our work drags on, unfinished as always, hopeless
> the labor of war that brought us here to Troy.
> So come, follow my orders. All obey me now.
> Cut and run! Sail home to the fatherland we love!
> We'll never take the broad streets of Troy. (*Iliad* Book 2)

There probably has never been a speech such as this by a commander endeavoring to motivate his troops, to rouse them to attack. Zeus never ordered such a speech! What did the men do? They ran for the ships!

The presence of this speech in the second book of *Iliad* is difficult to understand, and it is likely that the later poet-singers and Homer did not understand it either. Homer gives this speech what is at best a lame justification. Is it possible that this speech is a fragment remaining from a much earlier version of the story of Troy, from a time before *Iliad* took final form, a lost ending of an earlier *Iliad* in which the war ended not in victory but in stalemate? Is it closer to the historic truth than is the version in *Iliad*, *Odyssey*, *Cypria*, *The Sack of Ilios*? Certainly it is possible.

Was There a Trojan War?

There may be doubt of a Greek conquest or destruction, but there is no reason to doubt that the story of the Trojan War was inspired by historic events. On the plausible assumption that Ahhiyawa refers to the land of the Greeks, there is ample testimony in Hittite texts to Greek activities on the west coast of Anatolia over a period measured in centuries. They are noted as early as the time of Tudhaliya II around 1380 BC when

Attarissiyas was raiding about. They are noted again in the records of later Hittite kings. Known Hittite records probably reflect only a fraction of Greek activities on the west coast of Anatolia. While there is no firm evidence of it, it is entirely believable that Greeks were involved in an attack, or various attacks at different times, on Troy and other cities of the coast of Anatolia. Such attacks would have been known to the poet-singers, who would have passed the story or stories from one generation to the next. Conflict, whether large or small, would provide the solid nucleus around which legend and epic would crystallize. The size and scope would grow with the telling, and characters and incidents would be added as the story developed.

After the Bronze Age, Troy was hardly an important locality, hardly sufficient to be fought over, hardly to be remembered in Greek epic. Thus, when battles and heroes of the Trojan War are described in *Iliad*, they reflect encounters in the Bronze Age. If the Bronze Age is remembered at all in *Iliad*, then logically the essential core of *Iliad*, a battle or war of Greeks at Troy, is an authentic memory. Whether Greeks were able to enter the citadel and do damage is uncertain, but many archaeologists believe that the destruction in the Seventh City was due to them. One may accept or reject that view.

Scholars have proposed a number of causes or motives for the Trojan War. In the absence of indisputable records of events and dates, and sure knowledge of the specific circumstances in Greece and Anatolia, it is impossible to speak meaningfully about the cause. Under these circumstances, it might be best to leave the explanation to the ancients, whose account has a certain charm.

Concerning the cause of the War, the ancients had few doubts. The poet-singers told clearly that the conflict started among the gods. *Iliad* testifies that Athena, Hera, and Poseidon:

> ....clung to their deathless hate of sacred Troy,
> Priam and Priam's people, just as they had at first
> when Paris in all his madness launched the war.
> He offended Athena and Hera-both goddesses.

Listeners knew the full story. Zeus finds man overbearing, and thinks of war to reduce the race of heroes. Opportunity develops as a result of a wedding party to which the gods had been invited. Due to some oversight, the goddess Strife had been left off the invitation list. She is furious and is determined to disrupt the affair. She appears at the feast and rolls a golden apple among the goddesses. On it is inscribed "to the fairest." Athena, Hera, and Aphrodite each reach for it, sure that it is meant for them. The matter needs to be resolved. Who is well known to have an eye for feminine beauty? Paris, prince of Troy! He is asked to judge. Paris, flattered at being chosen as the judge, fails to see the unparalleled danger involved. Each of the goddesses secretly attempts to bribe him. Aphrodite offers the love of Helen, queen of Sparta, and Paris decides in favor of Aphrodite. Strife is now in full play.

The resulting hatred of Paris by both Athena and Hera is translated into hatred of his country, Troy. Aphrodite and her brother Apollo support Troy. Zeus supports war, but has not yet resolved its outcome. On the mortal plane, only mortal manifestations of this are seen. Paris is a guest of King Menelaus of Sparta. In the king's absence, Helen is taken (or elopes) and accompanies Paris to Troy.

The Helen story may have been believed in ancient times and may even have been true. The present tendency, however, is to dismiss it as myth. And even if there was such an occurrence, from the modern viewpoint it would be too slight to bring on war. However, it should not be entirely dismissed. The Greeks would have seen the Helen affair as a question of principle and honor, and a principle or high cause has brought about many a war. Here was an outrage. Paris—a foreigner—treated as an honored guest at the palace of King Menelaus, returned hospitality with treachery by taking Helen and the king's treasure also. In the ancient world, hospitality was mandated by the gods, and in Greece by Zeus himself. The guest had reciprocal obligations. What Paris did was an assault on the moral order. It would have been seen as an unforgivable insult by the other royal houses of Greece. *Iliad* describes the "arrogance" of the Trojans. It might have been enough to stir Greece to war, or to provide a moral justification for a war undertaken for other motives.

Was Wilusa Troy and Who Are The Trojans?

Emil Forrer was a genius with a talent for drawing controversy. So it was with his assertion that Wilusa was Wilios, and thus Troy. Immediately, a storm of scholarly controversy arose over this as with others of Forrer's claims. The linguistic correspondence of the names Wilios and Wilusa was not right, said the linguists. Or, perhaps it was right, providing that the original pronunciation in the Bronze Age was *Wilusia, or perhaps *Wiluwa. To the Greeks Wilusia or Wiluwa would, in time, become Wilios and then Ilios and then under Roman influence Ilium, while to the Hittites of the Bronze Age it was Wilusa. As with the debate over "Ahhiyawa," (Chapter 3), the problem could not be solved by linguistic arguments. Perhaps the Hittite records would help.

Evidence which places Wilusa on the north-west coast of Anatolia, the location of Troy, comes from a letter from King Manapa-Tarhunda of Seha River Land. In that letter, Lazpas and Wilusa are mentioned as targets of nearly simultaneous invasions. Lazpas is thought to be the island known in Greek as Lesbos, just off the northwest coast of Anatolia. Wilusa must therefore be nearby, on the northwest coast.

In the time of Hittite king Tudhaliya I (1460–1440 BC) or Tudhaliya II (1390–1370 BC), there was a confederation of states in western Anatolia which fought against the Hittites. A Hittite tablet has been found which lists countries of the confederation. They are presented in geographical order, starting at the south and ending in the north. Together at the bottom of the list, and therefore located in the northwest, are the names Wilusa and Taruisa. This too places Wilusa on the northwest coast of Anatolia.

The discerning eye of Forrer perused this list. Wilusa and Taruisa had caught his attention. Here at last in the Hittite records was not only Ilios but explicit mention of Troy, according to Forrer, given in the Hittite language as "Taruisa," an astonishing discovery! True, Wilusa and Taruisa, though listed next one another, here seem to be separate countries. Yet in *Iliad*, Ilios and Troy are one and the same. There may be ways to account for this discrepancy. The Hittite list was composed perhaps two hundred years before the Trojan War and at that time, Wilusa and Taruisa may have been separate but neighboring countries which later merged. It is also possible that these were distinct but allied kingdoms at the time of the Trojan War, but that the distinction was lost as tales of Troy were passed from generation to generation after the Bronze Age.

Evidence of the location of Wilusa in northwestern Anatolia supports Forrer's contention, and little opposes it. Linguistic and geographic arguments agree with one another. But who were the Trojans?

The Greeks had knowledge of a multitude of peoples and wondered about their origins. Explanations were not lacking and commonly took the form of a genealogy in which a founding ancestor gave his name to the city and to the people. As an example, *Iliad* accounts for the Trojans in this way.

> First of all, Zeus who gathers the clouds had a son, Dardanos who founded Dardania, since there was no sacred Ilion…Dardanos in turn had a son, the king, Erichthonios…Erichthonios had a son, Tros, who was lord of the Trojans and to Tros in turn there were born three sons unfaulted…Ilos, Assarakos and godlike Ganymedes…Ilos was given a son, the blameless Laomedon, and Laomedon had…Priam. (*Iliad, Book 20*)

In this way, several things are "explained." The close kinship of the Dardanians and the Trojans is evident. Troy was ruled by Dardanians, those mentioned by the Egyptians as among the Hittite forces at Kadesh. Ilos is probably to be read as the name Ilios. "Blameless Laomedon" is blamed elsewhere in *Iliad* for his failure to pay Poseidon for the construction of the great walls of Troy. And Priam is the unfortunate king who witnesses the end of Troy.

There is, of course, no truth to this account, which covers only six generations. Archaeological evidence shows that Troy had been occupied by one people from perhaps 1800 BC to the time of the destruction of Troy VIIa, and indeed for several generations more. The Trojans of the Trojan War were thus not latecomers. They were long in possession of their land. But who were they? To what people were they related and what language did they speak? It is apparent that the Trojans were related to the Dardanians, but this tells little, since nothing is known about the Dardanians.

At Troy, in an archaeological stratum corresponding to the beginning of Troy VI, what is called Gray Minyan ware was found. This pottery is steel-gray in color with a diffuse surface shine. Shapes are robust, yet attractive. Bones of horses were also found. The horse is thought be a marker of the presence of early Indo-European-speaking peoples. These finds are interpreted to mean that at about 2000 BC or slightly later, an Indo-European-speaking people arrived and occupied Troy and Gray Minyan was introduced by them.

Interestingly, similar Gray Minyan ware was found in northeastern Greece and is given a similar date. This has been thought to mark the first entry into Greece of people bringing with them the earliest form of Greek speech. Presumably, this pottery was introduced into Greece by the same people who brought it to Troy. By that measure, the Trojans were Greeks. *Iliad* could certainly be understood to support that view. Greeks and Trojans speak easily with one another. In *Iliad,* most Trojan personal names are Greek. *Iliad* states that among Trojan allies there are some of barbarous tongue, meaning that they did not speak Greek. As the Trojans are not said to be of barbarous speech, the implication is that they spoke Greek.

The Trojans were Greek, one might conclude. Except that it may not be true. Among archaeologists, it is now questionable whether Gray Minyan pottery is an indicator of the arrival of a new people. It may have developed locally on one side of the Dardanelles or the other. The design and the manufacturing technique may then have spread by diffusion.

Whether or not the Trojans spoke Greek, the poet-singers would present the situation as if they did. Greek and Trojan must be able to understand one another. Alexandros (Paris) has been a guest of Menelaus in Greece. Menelaus and Odysseus negotiated with the Trojan royalty over the return of Helen. Warriors of both sides talk to one another. In the most moving scene of the story, King Priam begs Achilles to release the body of Hector. *Iliad* could not be told unless the Greeks and Trojans could converse, and the story leads one to believe that it was done in Greek. It is obvious that all of this is a storyteller's requirement and need not represent a historic truth. Small countries such as Greece and Troy, located near other peoples who speak other tongues, tend to have many people fluent in those neighboring languages. In the Tawagalawa Letter, the Hittite king reports that a Greek rode in the same chariot as he. Surely, they talked with one another. But that does not mean that they were born to the same language.

Other possibilities need to be considered. Here, the Luvian language is a prime candidate. Luvian was the language spoken by most Anatolian peoples south and west of the Hittite core territory. It was probably the language of Arzawa and of the Seha River Land. According to C. Watkins (1986), Priamos (Priam) is a Greek rendition of Piyama-Muwas. Piyama-Muwas is a Luvian name, similar to the name Piyama-Radu. The name

Paris too may be Luvian, the Greek rendition of Pari-Zitis. The ending -Zitis, it may be remembered, appears in the name of that foe of the Hittites, Uhha-Zitis. Thus, the names Priam and Paris may simply be the best that Greeks could do with two difficult Luvian names. A bronze seal has recently been found in a late Troy VII context. On the seal are "Hittite" hieroglyphics which are really a representation of a Luvian dialect. The text indicates that the original seal owner was a scribe, a literate man, literate in Luvian. If this was an original Trojan object and not an import, it might demonstrate that, some years after the destructions, inhabitants of Troy spoke Luwian.

A final candidate, and a particularly interesting one is Etruscan. Virgil's poem, the *Aeneid* is based on a legend that Rome was founded by survivors from Troy, but Rome has a partly Etruscan early population. Is there a connection between the Hittite name Taruwisa and the name Etruscan? Little is known of the origin of the Etruscans, and if they are Trojans the mystery only increases.

6
COLLAPSE OF THE MYCENAEAN WORLD

Beginning in about 1200 BC, the civilized lands of the Bronze Age appear to have been struck by a series of catastrophes. It is certain that the mainland of Greece was very severely affected, but details are uncertain and the circumstances obscure. The history of Greece at the end of Late Bronze Age is completely unknown. The Linear B texts of Greece are not informative, and it appears that Greece alone among the major civilized regions produced no written correspondence, treaties, poetry, myth, religious texts, legal matter, or historical reports. The name of not one Greek king of the Bronze Age is known from any contemporary Greek record, and if the literate Hittites or Egyptians or others mentioned Greek kings by name, no record of it survives.

There is only the mute evidence of the spade. From such evidence, the collapse of Mycenaean Greek material civilization is evident, and from that may be inferred the collapse of the economy and society, but the course of events or the order of events cannot be reconstructed. And though there was destruction or abandonment of cities, towns, and villages in much of Greece, it has not possible to establish if these were more or less simultaneous, or if they occurred over many decades. How are these explained? The theory of a foreign invasion, a barbarian onslaught, has taken root and is supported by many, but whether it best explains events is the subject of this and the next chapter.

The most extensive body of information about events has come from what are taken to be the capital cities of Greek kings: Athens, Mycenae, Tiryns, Thebes, Iolkos, Orchomenos, and Pylos, (see Figure 6-1). Archaeological work has produced particularly interesting results at Pylos which, according to *Iliad*, was the city of King Nestor, and at Mycenae, which *Iliad* tells was the royal seat of King Agamemnon.

On the west coast of the Peloponnese, on an elevation within sight of the sea near the present-day town of Ano Englianos, is the site of what is thought to be ancient Pylos. Remains of a number of buildings have been excavated here, including the palace complex. Close within the entrance of the palace complex was an archive room. It was here that a treasure trove of Linear B records was recovered. Farther inside was an open court, and to the right of the court there was a small megaron or palace, the Queen's Megaron as it is sometimes called. In spite of the name, as in most rooms found in excavations, the original purpose or use is unknown and archaeologists assign names based on convenience or guesswork. The floor of this megaron was richly decorated in geometric patterns, and in the center of the floor was a small circular hearth.

Figure 6-1. The Greek world at the end of the Late Bronze Age included Greeks in Crete and the west coast of Anatolia.

Also opening on the court was the King's Megaron. Central to the palace complex, this megaron consisted of a porch, a vestibule, and a great hall. Build close to the floor in the center of the hall was an immense circular hearth and, above it, a suspended chimney.

Symmetrically arranged around the hearth were tall pillars which probably supported upper balconies which overlooked the hall. At one side was what is taken to be the king's throne. Behind the throne, there were two griffins painted on the wall, large and brilliantly colored, possibly heraldic symbols of the Pylian ruling family. There were other murals in bright colors, a religious procession, warriors, and a lyre player seated on a rock. Along the walls were friezes in geometric patterns and vivid color. As in the Queen's Megaron, the floor in the main megaron was divided into square sections, richly painted in abstract designs or geometric designs.

This megaron was, it is believed, the center of social and political activity of the king. Here, presumably, the leading men of the king's retinue were feasted and guests entertained. It is possible to imagine that it was here that poet-singers, ancestors in their calling to Homer, strummed the lyre and sang their tales. *Odyssey* provides a vivid description of such activities in the description of Demodocus, Chapter 4.

Attached to the hall were a number of rooms serving various purposes, primarily storage. In one of these rooms were found the remains of close to three thousand kylixes—graceful stemmed drinking vessels—and this could only have been the stock of a pottery manufacturing enterprise. It is evidence that the palace was directly involved in manufacturing and trade, much as were palaces or temples in other lands. The palace complex was a center of wealth and luxury and industrial enterprise.

Figure 6-2. An artist's reconstruction of the citadel of Mycenae as it would have appeared from the west, based on archaeological evidence.

At Mycenae, the palace complex had many of the same features as that at Pylos. Differences were in part due to differences in the nature of the site. The palace and a number of other buildings were built on a hilltop and were enclosed by a great defensive wall, Figure 6-2. It was a seemingly impregnable fortress or citadel, roughly triangular in plan, close to a thousand feet across.

Entrance to the citadel was by means of an ascending roadway which ran along the outside of the wall and which lead upward through the magnificent Lion Gate. Here, two massive rectangular stone pillars supported a huge stone lintel that formed the top of the gate. The pillars and lintel, which one may suspect was richly decorated in ornate bronze, framed the large doors. Above the lintel, there were two lions sculpted in deep relief, facing one another, rampant, with paws resting on a platform. Their heads, now missing, may have been covered in gold. The entire entrance-way was a stage whose purpose was to dramatize the power and wealth of the kings of Mycenae.

Directly inside the gate was the Grave Circle enclosing the Shaft Graves in which the pioneer archaeologist Heinrich Schliemann found treasures. This gravesite marked the resting place of kings from earliest Mycenaean times. Past the Grave Circle, a roadway continued up to the Great Court. The floor of the Great Court was divided into squares decorated in colorful geometric patterns as at Pylos. Opening on the court was the megaron of the king. In the megaron, there was a great hearth in the center and around it four great columns, as at Pylos.

There were other buildings within the citadel. One group, now called the House of Columns, contains a number of rooms, one of which is a small megaron which may been the home of another member of the king's family. A group of buildings next to the Grave Circle include what archaeologists have named the Granary, Ramp House, Warrior Vase House, South House, and Tsountas' House, this last named after one of the earlier archaeologists who worked at the site. Warrior Vase House derives its name from the remains of a vase which was found there by Schliemann. On this vase is the best depiction of Mycenaean soldiers armed for war, Figure 7-1.

The vase, found in fragments, has been restored and stands about 14 inches high. The soldiers, identically dressed and armed, depart for war. Behind them a woman waves good by. The soldiers carry spears to which are attached what are probably knapsacks containing rations. On the back of the vase other warriors are shown, wearing similar dress but with a different headgear.

Just outside of the citadel were other buildings and the great tombs, the most magnificent of which is the Treasury of Atreus, as it was called by Schliemann, after the father of Agamemnon and Menelaus. Of carefully cut stone and massive construction, this great structure was the largest domed building in the world for over a thousand years, until the Pantheon was built in Rome.

Pylos and Mycenae are representative of the centers of the Mycenaean kings. The palace complex contained private dwellings, public areas, shrines, archives, offices, and storage space for the products of light industries. Trade and the amassing of wealth seem to have been the major concern of the kings. The Linear B tablets from Pylos show the existence of a planned economy centered on the palace, and the same was no doubt true of other palaces. It was from the palace that much economic life of the kingdom was managed. Raw materials were allocated to craftsmen, production quotas were set, personnel were assigned to duties, and food was distributed in payment. It seems as though nothing escaped the attention of the palace bureaucrats. From the Mycenaean palace at Knossos, Crete, a tablet records even the names of individual oxen: Whitefoot, Dapple, Dusty, and Noisy.

Because a good deal of archaeological work has concentrated on the citadels and palaces of kings, descriptions of the Mycenaean world tend to emphasize the situation of royalty, and by implication, of the wealthy and land-owning strata of society. But it is obvious that there were also accountants, sculptors, goldsmiths, ivory carvers, carpenters, masons, furniture makers, bronze workers, armorers, potters, gem-cutters, chariot makers, horse tamers, leather workers, dyers, weavers, tailors, perfumers, olive oil producers, wine makers, bakers, poet-singers, and probably doctors and priests. Near Athens, miners and smelter workers labored at the Laurion mines to extract silver. There were fishermen, and a large number in towns and villages who worked at food production.

Very likely, land was held by the principal men-at-arms, pledged in loyalty to the king. In addition to managing their lands, they presumably spent their time in training in the arts of war and in sport, while their lands were worked by serfs, and slaves purchased or captured in war. In the midst of this centrally planned economy, there may also have been freemen working at crafts, trade, or farming, on their own initiative and at their own risk. As with most of the economic and social situation in Mycenaean Greece, little is known for certain and much must be inferred.

The remains of large quantities of Mycenaean pottery have been found in Rhodes, Cyprus, Syria, which is evidence of extensive trade links between Greece and those regions. Mycenaean pottery has also been found in Egypt, southern Italy, and Sicily. Objects of silver and lead from the Laurion mines have been found in Crete, the Aegean islands, and as far away as El Amarna in Egypt. Hittite, Syrian, Canaanite, and Egyptian objects have been found in Greece. It is likely that the Mycenaeans were at the center of sea-based trade network in the Mediterranean and Aegean Seas, and also of a land-based network which extended into northern Europe. In the comparatively peaceful and stable times before the catastrophes, trade, particularly across the sea, may have made a major contribution to the Mycenaean economy, a source of wealth for the elite strata of society and a livelihood for numerous craftsmen.

In 1960, underwater archaeological research began to probe an ancient shipwreck off Cape Gelidonya on the southern coast of Lycia in Anatolia (Turkey), and her cargo illustrates aspects of the sea trade. The merchant ship, plying the coasts of the Mediterranean in about 1200 BC, was in the metals trade. In the wreckage, divers found a good deal of scrap metal: knives, axe heads, picks and other discarded tools of bronze—material which could be fed into the bronze-casters' crucible. The ship was also hauling a large number of "ox-hide" ingots of copper, given this name because the shape of the ingots is that of a spread-out hide. One of the two great copper production centers of the Mediterranean was in Cyprus, a short distance to the east of the location of the wreck. It is apparent that the ship had taken on cargo in Cyprus and was heading westward, possibly to Greece. Ships heading westward stood in close to the southern shore of Anatolia in order to gain the advantage of the steady westward current which flowed there. But that coast was rocky and hazardous, one of the ship graveyards that made early sailing perilous, and on this coast were the Lukka pirates.

An even more vivid illustration of the sea trade was provided by another wreck found off Ulu Burun not far from Cape Gelidonya. The ship went down perhaps one hundred years earlier than the Gelidonya ship. An amazing variety of goods was carried in trade. Cargo included six tons of copper ox-hide ingots. It is possible that this huge load made the ship unmanageable in a storm which may have lead to her sinking. The rich cargo of these ships provide an idea of the variety of material traded in the ports of the Mediterranean toward the end of the Bronze Age.

Kingship in Greece

Greece is mentioned occasionally by the Hittites (Ahhiyawa), and perhaps only once by the Egyptians. Given the difficulty in the interpretation of archaeological remains and the lack of useful records, scholars have tried to find history in the Greek legends, including stories of the Trojan War. But what is historical or at least partly historical, and what is fictional? It is a judgment matter, in which different scholars reach different conclusions.

According to *Iliad*, Agamemnon was king of Mycenae at the time of the Trojan War. He may also have been king of all of Greece, a king over kings. Some passages in *Iliad* seem to support this. Among the Greeks assembled before Troy were Odysseus, Menelaus, Nestor, Diomedes, Idomeneus. These were kings in their own right. But it is obvious that Agamemnon rules over them. He alone is titled "King of Men." It is to him alone that Zeus has passed the scepter of kingship, and therefore he rules by divine right. Referring to Achilles' dispute with Agamemnon, the hot-headed Achilles is warned not to:

> …think to match your strength with the king, since never equal with the rest is the portion of honor of the sceptered king to whom Zeus gives magnificence. (*Iliad* Book1)

It is obvious that all recognize Agamemnon's leadership.

A strange reverence was given to those early kings who had been interred in marshal splendor in the Shaft Graves at Mycenae. They were memorialized centuries later when a monumental circle of stones was built around the site of the graves, and an extension of the great wall brought the Grave Circle within the protection of the citadel. That labor cannot be attributed to sentimentality alone. This attention in later centuries suggests that the later kings in Mycenae saw in those first kings a symbol of their own legitimacy, and perhaps of an anciently established priority of rule in Greece.

Certain other archaeological evidence might suggest single leadership, one supreme king ruling over lesser kings. It is noted, for example, that there was remarkable cultural uniformity among the Greek kingdoms. Frescoes in such diverse palaces as those at Pylos, Mycenae, Tiryns, and Thebes were remarkably similarity, in some cases, near identical. The language found in the Linear B tablets at Pylos and faraway Thebes is identical, suggesting that there was a single Mycenaean dialect spoken in the various kingdoms. A unified road, bridge, and culvert system seems to have existed over much of the Peloponnese. The pottery over several centuries which Greeks produced and traded across the Aegean and Mediterranean maintained a remarkable design uniformity despite the fact that there may have been several widely separated centers of manufacture. A strong centralized control may have been responsible for such uniformity.

It is also noteworthy that, at one point, the king of the Hittites seemed to think that there was a supreme king in Ahhiyawa. The Hittite king referred to a Great King in Ahhiyawa. Great King was a term usually reserved for a king over other kings. If there was one king over all of Greece, he would be the king of Mycenae, most likely, just as *Iliad* says, since archaeological evidence seems to show that Mycenae was the richest of the Bronze Age centers in Greece.

However, archaeology cannot confirm that conclusion. *Iliad* and other works of the Homeric Cycle furnish uncertain history, and they contradict as well a support the "single king" theory. Various kings are summoned to the War, but Agamemnon must send emissaries to convince them to obey the call. One king buys his way out of service. Odysseus and Achilles, each of kingdoms far distant from Mycenae, and presumably for that reason less subject to pressure from Agamemnon, are initially able to escape the call. There are passages in *Iliad* in which one or another king states that his commitment to the war is not due to any natural obedience to Agamemnon. It is, rather, because each has given his word to see the war to a conclusion. These are the actions of men who consider themselves independent, at least to some degree.

The powers of Agamemnon as portrayed in *Iliad* may be wartime powers only, granted him as necessary for the execution of a war on a foreign shore. Yet the complex relationship between the king of Mycenae and the other kings as described in *Iliad* might also reflect the situation during peacetime. It is possible that the king of Mycenae was, at least in principle, a supreme king in Greece, deriving power from some very ancient right. But his supremacy may have been more formal than actual. In wartime his powers would have been greatest, since leadership in war was a fundamental obligation of kingship. During peacetime, the various subordinate kings probably exercised a degree of independence. The situation probably changed with the circumstances and would not have been the same under each king of Mycenae over approximately four centuries of Mycenaean civilization. A strong king in Mycenae might bring other kings to heel. With a weak king at the center, the subordinate kings would be virtually independent.

Walled citadels, palaces decorated with vivid and colorful frescoes, decorated pottery, weapons, engraved gems, gold jewelry and richly carved ivory bespeak a rich and powerful leadership. Exploitation of the land, international trade, perhaps some opportunistic raiding, provided wealth. As the end approached, unforeseen no doubt, there is evidence of a drop in prosperity. Gem carving, gold work, and ivory work fall off in quality and quantity. Still, the palaces and palace-centered political and economic system remained intact. It was a necessity, developed over centuries.

Unfortunately, the Greek kingdoms with their highly centralized economies, whether under one king or several, were vulnerable to "decapitation," the destruction of leadership at the top, and with it the potential collapse of economic activities. Under the impact of causes not fully understood, the end came. Evidence shows that defenses were strengthened, palaces were destroyed, towns were abandoned, people were dislocated, population numbers collapsed. The economy was disrupted, made a partial recovery, and finally entered into a rapid decline. Mycenaean civilization tottered and collapsed. Greece plunged into an extended Dark Age. How is it to be accounted for? Destruction by invaders is but one possible explanation. Internal war between Greek kingdoms, or strife within the kingdoms, may have played a leading roll. And major disruption of the agricultural system and a resulting national collapse cannot be ruled out. These possibilities will be considered in the next chapter, but first the evidence will be reviewed.

Pottery Dating

To be able to interpret the evidence, it is important to know when events occurred. Without dates, or at least the order of events, the situation that befell Greece cannot be reconstructed. The Mycenaeans undoubtedly had a calendar, and some Mycenaean month names are known from the Linear B records. But there is no evidence of a means to record years. Nothing written on pottery or any other artifact which archaeologists have recovered in Greece provides a year date. Greek pottery styles provide the only broadly applicable link to dates, and these dates are only approximate. That dating method is crucial in the interpretation of the evidence, and a further description is required.

Specialists have noted that the shapes and painted decorations of Greek Late Bronze Age (Mycenaean) pottery changed over the years of production and use. They have established the order in which various styles—shape and decoration—came into or fell out of favor, and that provides a framework for a pottery dating sequence. The concept which is involved can be described in the following way. Imagine that there is a long shelf against the wall. Imagine also that specimens of the very earliest Mycenaean pottery have been placed on the far left end of the shelf. Several different pieces will be grouped there, representing various shapes and painted decorations current at that time. Moving rightward along the shelf, slightly later pottery specimens are displayed. This is continued along the shelf, ending with the last known Mycenaean pottery at the far right.

Pottery experts note major changes in style at certain points in this progression. Imagine that they place tags at these points of the shelf. By this means they divide the shelf, divide the styles, labeling the first section along the shelf as Late Helladic I, an intermediate section as Late Helladic II, the last section of the shelf as Late Helladic III. (The term "Late Helladic" refers to the Mycenaean period in Greece.) Only Late Helladic III is important for the present discussion.

Late Helladic III styles are further dividable into three substyles known as Late Helladic IIIA, Late Helladic IIIB, and Late Helladic IIIC. Of greatest interest here are IIIB and IIIC. As difficult as it may seem to anyone who has examined Mycenaean pottery casually and noted the seeming similarity of the designs of the various periods, pottery specialists discern certain style breaks within IIIB and also with less difficulty in IIIC. Thus, a finely divided sequence of pottery designs and styles are recognized. For time periods of interest here, the styles are divided and named as follows:

Pottery Style	Substyle	
Late Helladic IIIB	Late Helladic IIIB Early	(also called IIIB1)
	Late Helladic IIIB Late	(also called IIIB2)
Late Helladic IIIC	Late Helladic IIIC Early	
	Late Helladic IIIC Middle	
	Late Helladic IIIC Late	

An archaeologist might discover a tomb and, with luck, the tomb would not have been looted in ancient times. Mycenaean pottery might be found in the tomb. The archaeologist might take one such pottery specimen and compare it to pottery on the shelf. Based on a near match of pottery shape and painted decoration, the archaeologist might determine that the pottery from the tomb is from the IIIB Early period (the term "Late Helladic" can now be abbreviated as "LH," or even dropped). From another tomb, a pottery specimen might be found to be IIIC Middle, which suggests that the second tomb or its contents is later than the first. Such dates are referred to as relative dates.

That is, in essence, the primary means by which archaeological findings in Bronze Age Greece are given relative dates. In practice, there is no "shelf" but catalogs with illustrations of styles of the various periods. When a year or a narrow range of years can be assigned, it is called an absolute date. The absolute dates of Egyptian kings of the Late Bronze Age are known to within a few years. Occasionally, Mycenaean pottery has been found together with an Egyptian object bearing the name of an Egyptian king. That correlation of a specimen of Mycenaean pottery with a datable Egyptian object provides a narrow range of absolute dates for that pottery and that pottery style. By that means, certain parts of the pottery "shelf" have been dated. The remainder are dated on the basis of a best estimate.

The uncertainties inherent in this process can be imagined. The linkages to known Egyptian dates are seldom direct or exact, as two examples will show.

First, in the ruins of Ugarit (Figure 2–1) a clay tablet was found with a message from Beya, a high official in the administration of Egyptian queen Twosert. She ruled briefly on the death of her husband, Seti II. Beya's time in office may have ended about 1185 BC. The tablet was found with remains of LH IIIB Late pottery and none of IIIC style. This indicates that IIIB pottery may still have been in use as late as 1185 BC. Second, in Jordan, there was a shrine to Twosert. In that shrine, there was a stirrup jar in the IIIB style. It is assumed that the pottery was placed in the Twosert shrine during her period of rule, 1193–1185 BC. That too suggests that IIIB pottery still may have been in use as late as 1185 BC.

Beya's letter and the Twosert jar are the last evidence of the use of pottery of IIIB Late style. Thus, the end of LH IIIB Late is put at about 1185 BC. Other evidence supports this date, or at least a date close to it, but all the evidence is circumstantial.

By similar means, or by best estimates, absolute dates have been supplied to the chain of Mycenaean pottery, from beginning to end. For the periods of importance here, the dates are approximately:

Pottery Style	Substyle	Absolute Date
Late Helladic IIIB	IIIB Early	1330–1230 BC
	IIIB Late	1230–1185 BC
Late Helladic IIIC	IIIC Early	1190–1165 BC
	IIIC Middle	1165–1100 BC
	IIIC Late	1100–1065 BC

The chart shows that the styles of phase IIIB did not end until 1185 BC, several years after IIIC had begun in about 1190 BC.

The uncertainties inherent in this method are now clearer. The pottery found with Beya's letter and the Twosert stirrup jar may have been manufactured years earlier. In that case, Late Helladic IIIB may have ended years before the presently accepted date. Further, since Mycenaean pottery was in production at a large number of centers on the mainland and overseas, there is no guarantee that each center changed from one style to the next at the same time. In fact, it is certain that they didn't. For those and other reasons, the end of IIIB or the beginning of IIIC may be in error by a decade or two, earlier or later.

The scheme in the table above, with its precise years, gives the impression of scientific accuracy, which unfortunately it does not merit. In particular, dates of the subdivisions of IIIC are not based on any sound Egyptian correlations and are no more than expert guesses.

Archaeologists' attempts to employ this dating method meet further challenges. He or she finds only one or a few broken fragments of pottery. These may not be enough to reveal pottery shape, and may contain only a small portion of the original painted design. In these circumstances, the pottery fragments may not supply enough information. They could be matched, perhaps equally well, to pottery of IIIB or IIIC. The excavator might change his or her mind about the date as he or she continues to find more pottery fragments. And when the excavator shows the pottery fragments to fellow archaeologists, they will frequently disagree about the date. This has happened, as mentioned in Chapter

5, in the attempt to date the destruction of the city of Troy VIIa by means of Mycenaean pottery fragments found in the ruins.

As if these difficulties were not enough, there are more. It is usually difficult to be sure that a pottery fragment found in the earth, close or next to evidence of construction or destruction, is really contemporary with that evidence. That is what the archaeologist wishes to find, datable pottery in direct association with evidence, and sometimes he or she is guided by the wish rather than the fact. In view of these difficulties, it may be wondered why the pottery method is used for dating. The answer is that, for Bronze Age Greece, there is nothing else. Experiments in the use of Carbon-14 dating have been disappointing—providing widely divergent dates for a given period in Late Bronze Age Greece. And in any case, most excavations do not yield organic matter as required for C-14 dating. Tree ring dating is not yet directly applicable to Bronze Age Greece. In spite of scientific advances in dating, for the time period in which catastrophe struck Greece, dates must be obtained from pottery. However, the uncertainties inherent in pottery dating should be noted.

Evidence of Preparedness, Evidence of Destruction

The Palaces

It is primarily the evidence of destruction in the urban centers of Bronze Age Greece which has given shape to the barbarian invasion theory, and which has influenced other theories as well. Not all of the centers or cities experienced destruction. Athens survived, and seemed to have remembered that survival in later legends, yet even in Athens there is evidence that the city made preparations against the threat of a dangerous assault.

The Acropolis in Athens was the site of a typical Mycenaean citadel with a palace and structures relating to palace activity. Still visible today on the Acropolis are remains of the Bronze Age wall of the citadel. Archaeologists have found evidence that the walls were strengthened and a defensive bastion added in order to better protect the main gate. At close to the same time, within the citadel, a shaft was driven down through 120 feet of rock in order to reach water. A wooden stairway was fitted along the inside of this shaft. Likely, such specialized excavation work was done by experienced miners brought in from the silver mines of Laurion nearby. Earlier, water was obtained from a well outside the wall. However, to be able to withstand a long siege, a source of water accessible from within the walls was indispensable. Such preparations appear to show a concern of a possible attack, the need to withstand a long siege.

Archaeologists surmise that the construction of the well took place during pottery phase IIIB Late or possibly IIIC Early. (Pottery design phases are often used as stand-ins for absolute dates.). The well was used for only a few years or a few decades, after which the wooden steps gave way and were not repaired. Presumably the threat to Athens, if any, had passed. There is no evidence of destruction, no evidence of an attack on the citadel, and this is entirely in accord with the belief of later Athenians that Athens was never conquered, never abandoned. It appears to have remained occupied throughout LH IIIB and IIIC.

The remains of ancient Mycenae have been the flagship site for Bronze Age archaeological investigations in Greece. The interpretation of findings from Mycenae have tended to shape or influence conclusions reached at other sites. If the destruction at Mycenae is given a certain pottery date, a certain cause, the evidence at other Bronze Age sites is sometimes interpreted in a way which is consistent with that date and that cause. Unfortunately, both date and cause at Mycenae are uncertain. It is, for example, uncertain if there was one episode of significant destruction or several. The description below assumes two significant closely spaced destructions, which is the most common interpretation, but whether damage in certain buildings is to be assigned to the first or the second destruction remains a problem.

The first destruction occurred at the end of IIIB Early, and thus perhaps about 1230 BC. Within the citadel, Ramp House was severely damaged. Other damage was particularly strong among buildings outside the citadel. To the south of the citadel along the road from the Lion Gate, there were a group of attached stone houses. One, House of Shields, is given that name since an ivory carving in the form of a shield was recovered from the ruins. A Linear B tablet was also found, and vases carved of precious stone. House of Shields was destroyed by fire. Attached is the House of the Oil Merchant. Archaeologists found remains of a number of large pottery jars which once held oil, traces of which still remain. In this case, the name bestowed by archaeologists may convey the ancient function of the building, because this was surely a center of oil storage and distribution. Here were found finely carved ivory and the remains of walls which had been covered with decorative paintings, indications of the wealth or the elite status of owner. Here also, tablets inscribed in Linear B were found which dealt with oil and spices, and which recorded the names of bakers. Fire destroyed this building, a violent conflagration fed by the oil. Attached to this was West House which was caught up in the fire. Attached also was the House of Sphinxes, so named because of beautiful ivory carving of a sphinx which was found. Walls collapsed and a fire followed. Further south along the road was another cluster of houses. In Panagia I House, there is evidence of collapsed walls and chimney but no evidence of fire. Found also is evidence of a woman killed in the destruction, crushed under the collapsed walls. Panagia II also has shattered walls.

To the north of the citadel is Plaka House. In Plaka House, the walls collapsed and three adults and a child were crushed beneath.

Following this episode of destruction new building took place. It seems also that improvements were made to the defenses of the citadel. Access was developed to an underground spring which was just beyond the great wall, and that access was enclosed by a new extension of the wall, thus making water available from within the defensive perimeter. It is estimated that this work was done near the end of IIIB Late and was thus nearly contemporaneous with similar work at Athens, though again that is somewhat of a guess.

At nearby Tiryns, there also was destruction that may have been simultaneous with that at Mycenae. Subsequently, the elevation upon which the palace was located was strengthened and the massive defensive walls extended, and access to water from within the walls arranged.

The cause of these destructions in Mycenae and Tiryns has been debated. The action of barbarians has long been suspected. One archaeologist observed that the necks of the oil jars in the House of the Oil Merchant had been broken off, purposely he believed, so that the oil would feed the fire. However, today many scholars attribute the damage to earthquake. Certainly this region is, and presumably was, a seismically active area. Mycenae and Tiryns are sufficiently close that they could have been affected by the same earthquake. The fallen walls at Plaka House with the remains of people crushed beneath strongly suggests earthquake. Still, strengthened walls and ensured water supplies at Athens, Mycenae, and Tiryns are not the appropriate response to earthquake, but to expected attack. Why were these measures taken?

This was not the end of damage at Mycenae. What is usually taken to be a separate and more severe period of destruction has been dated to the end of IIIB Late, and thus about 1185 BC. Within the citadel, the palace complex was destroyed in a violent fire. A cluster of buildings south of the Grave Circle were heavily damaged but not burned. The Walls of Southwest House were toppled with some indications of fire, and plaster came raining down from the walls. Remnants of fresco painting were found with images of "Figure of Eight" shields, and of a lady in fancy dress. Human remains were also found, someone crushed by the falling walls. In South House also, walls collapsed. In the Cult Center, walls were damaged. The House of Idols burned down. Following this, Mycenae continued to be occupied into IIIC but with little evidence of rebuilding. This destruction in Mycenae is now attributed to another earthquake. The evidence is, however, not overwhelming. Many structures, including the vulnerable Lion Gate, show no shift in alignment.

Twenty miles south of Mycenae, the citadel of Tiryns was severely damaged in a great fire, at about the time of the destruction in the Mycenae citadel it is thought. Evidence of ground shift and of the remains of a woman trapped under the remains of fallen walls points to earthquake. A few miles east of Tiryns, Midea was severely damaged at the end of IIIB Late, an event again attributed to earthquake.

At Thebes, there is some evidence of a great fire and destruction in IIIB Late. At Iolkos, the palace was burned, possibly in IIIC. Little is known of the fate of the palace at Orchomenos. Near Orchomenos, on a high point in Lake Copais, was the fortress of Gla. Gla was part of the defenses of Orchomenos. Signs of fire have been found there, associated with late IIIB or possibly IIIC pottery.

No palace has been found near Sparta. Since the valley contains the remains of many late Bronze Age villages, there were probably kings in residence. Menelaus of *Iliad* and *Odyssey* could have been one of those kings. A building at this site, which excavators call the Menelaion—named for Menelaus—was destroyed in a fire.

On the west coast of the Peloponnese, the palace at Pylos and its associated buildings were consumed in a terrible fire, never again to be occupied. Dating the destruction has presented problems. Pylos was excavated under the direction of Carl Blegen, who also excavated at Troy. In the ruins at Pylos, Blegen and his team found pottery of a very early style, which suggests a very early date for the destruction. It now appears, however, that the pottery makers of Pylos were manufacturing antiques, and that has led to confusion in dating the end of Pylos. Finally, the excavators settled on the view that at the time of destruction, IIIB style pottery dominated but IIIC style was beginning to just phase in. This would place the destruction at about 1190 to 1180 BC and thus at about the time of the destruction in Mycenae. In view of the contradictory pottery evidence, no great faith can be placed in that date, however.

Near Pylos, at Mouriatadha, there was a defensive wall and a megaron or palace, also a tholos tomb such as favored by the powerful. Occupation here seems to have outlasted occupation at Pylos by several generations, further evidence that, as with Athens, some centers survived through those destructive times.

Testimony of the Pylos Tablets

With the translation of the Linear B tablets, a large number of which were found at Pylos, a very interesting light has been cast on the situation which prevailed at Pylos at the time of the destruction. These tablets contain records of short-term interest, written by scribing on the surface of moist clay which was then simply set out to dry. The unbaked clay could be recycled once the records were no longer needed. Information of long-term importance was, presumably, written on an ancient equivalent of paper or on hide. As fate would have it, the long-term records perished in the flames. The clay tablets, intended for short-term use, were baked hard in the great fire and survive to this day.

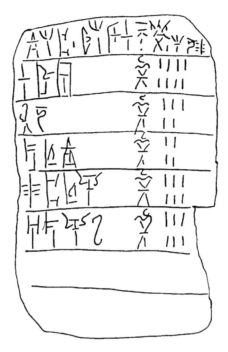

Figure 6-3. A Linear B record from Pylos lists the name of towns (left) and the number of men each is to make available for assignment to military duties (right).

Written in a very ancient form of Greek, Linear B has been a challenge for linguistic scholars, who do not always agree on translations. Thus, not everyone agrees in every respect with the translation and interpretation of the Pylos tablets made by the scholar L. R. Palmer. Palmer believed that he had identified in the Pylos tablets records of defensive preparations made in anticipation of an attack, the attack in which Pylos was destroyed (Palmer, 1963). In one tablet, there is a record of bronze gathered from sacred precincts and turned over to a bronze smith in order to make arrowheads and spear points. Another tablet begins "how the watchers are guarding the coastal regions...." This is followed by the name of a man who is believed to be a military commander, the location of his duty station, and the names of men assigned to him. The list continues with other military units identified in the same way. They are assigned to watch duties at designated watch stations. It appears that these watch stations were located at various points near Pylos, around the peninsula to the south and along the shores of the Gulf of Messenia, south of Pylos. Yet other tablets discuss the assignment of "rowers" who are dispatched to destinations which seem to fill gaps in the pattern of watch stations. About six hundred men are involved in this activity. Another tablet appears to describe the concentration of women and children in two rear assembly points, presumably for their protection.

Whether or not these various tablets address the same situation is uncertain, yet as all such records were short term, they must have been compiled closely spaced in time. Together, they speak of a situation of high tension and anxiety, a situation of high military alert. These dispositions appear to be directed to an attack expected from the sea, from the south. The watch screen, extending as it did over a long coast, must have been thin. It could not be expected to repel a determined attacker concentrating at one point. Shortly after the tablets were prepared, Pylos was burned to the ground.

These are representative of the evidence from what were, in Mycenaean times, the great centers of power. There is evidence of defensive preparations. There were destructions affecting the palaces and citadels at the end of IIIB Early and more, apparently, in LH IIIB Late or IIIC Early. Not all palaces or citadels were affected, and for those that were, it is not certain that all were affected at the same time or close to the same time.

The Isthmus Wall

As Figure 6-1 shows, the Peloponnese is almost an island, connected with the rest of the Greek mainland by a narrow isthmus. Archaeologists have found the remains of what may have been a defensive wall built partway across the isthmus. What remains of this construction consists of rough-cut stones in two parallel rows. The space between the rows was filled with earth and rubble and the composite wall is about twelve feet wide. On the north-facing side are the remains of what might have been towers. At Troy and Hattusa, defensive towers were built on the outside, facing the direction of the threat, and so it may have been at this wall. Pottery found next to the wall construction consists of small fragments of IIIB Late or the beginning of IIIC—the same period, it seems, as the strengthening of the citadels. The direction taken by the surviving segment of wall is not quite in accord with the idea that it is part of a wall which reached across the isthmus. In spite of this, the wall is usually interpreted as an attempt to prevent a massive invasion from the north.

The Countryside

It is largely in the palaces and citadels that archaeologists hope to find archives or other evidence which may reveal something of history, or items of great artistic merit. However, as in other regions, most of the population of Greece lived in the countryside. In the Late

Bronze Age, nearly every fertile valley of Greece contained clusters of towns and villages. Many of these sites have been discovered and mapped through ground surveys in which archaeologists walk the countryside checking for signs of ancient occupation. Due to the limited funds available for archaeological work, only a small fraction of these sites has been excavated. What has been learned is often limited to what can be seen on the surface, bits of pottery or building foundations. From the pottery, something can be learned of the period in which the town or village thrived.

Largely by these means, close to 500 settlement sites in mainland Greece have been found dating to the IIIB period. Pottery evidence from these sites shows something very remarkable. Almost half of the sites do not continue into IIIC. Has important evidence of continued occupation been missed? It is possible in some cases, but probably not enough to change the overall picture. A major disaster had occurred in the countryside.

The loss of so many towns and villages in the countryside must have affected the food supply in a very serious way, and in turn, this must have had an effect on the entire Mycenaean society. The population of mainland Greece in the IIIB period may have been a half million and perhaps as high as one million. The end of nearly half the settlements means that a major drop or shift in population had taken place. Evidence suggests some gain in population in some few regions, along the southwest coast of the Gulf of Corinth and the nearby island of Cephallenia, and on the east coast of Attica, the region in which Athens is located, and in nearby Boeotia. But these can hardly account for the overall removal or disappearance of close to half the population, hundreds of thousands of people.

In most cases, the pottery has not been dated so carefully that it is known when in IIIB the abandonments occurred, nor is it known for certain that they occurred at close to the same time in all places. Available evidence allows the possibility that a slow deterioration in the countryside could have started in mid-IIIB, with progressive abandonments of settlements continuing into the early part of IIIC.

Whatever the precise date, or dates, it is clear that something was amiss in Greece, something which went beyond the destruction of palaces or citadels. In those centers, the bold and self-confident building programs of the past had noticeably slowed. Pylos was not rebuilt. Palaces at Orchomenos and Iolkos disappeared and were not replaced. Some reconstruction took place at Mycenae and Tiryns during IIIC, but after another generation or two, no further construction took place. The use of the elaborate tholos tombs, of which the Treasury of Atreus is a magnificent example, faded away. The fine crafts were no longer pursued. Writing apparently ceased, and did not appear again in Greece for hundreds of years, and then in a different form.

Pottery production in Mycenae had a short reblossoming of creativity in IIIC Middle, after which it became tasteless and the execution unskilled. Mycenaeans migrated out of the mainland in increasing numbers, many heading for the islands to the south and east. And the great epic poems fall silent concerning anything past a generation or two after the Trojan War.

All of this indicates that the Mycenaean world of the mainland received some blow, or series of blows, toward the end of IIIB, which left it wounded, from which it survived for a time until a final deterioration set in.

Barbarians

As noted earlier, an invasion has been widely believed to account for these catastrophes. That Mycenae and Tiryns were, it now seems, severely damaged by earthquake and not human action, does not necessarily contradict that belief. The earthquake may have broken the political strength of Mycenae and Tiryns, opening the way to invasion. Barbarians, as they have been called, hearing of the damage (news would be carried over the trade routes) might have considered it as an invitation and an opportunity. Still, the invasion theory suffered from lack of direct evidence. But in the late 1960s and early 70s, attention of archaeologists was directed to certain evidence which was already before them but which they had ignored.

The evidence consisted of pottery of a kind completely different from Mycenaean pottery. Examples have been found at several localities in Greece, usually as a few fragments, but sometimes enough has been found to allow a reconstruction of an entire piece. This pottery began to appear in IIIB Late and increased in IIIC. There seems to be no evidence of this pottery at an earlier time in Greece. Unlike Mycenaean pottery, it is handmade, meaning that it was formed without the aid of the potter's wheel. It is usually crude in appearance and without painted decoration. Favored are open shapes such as cups or deep bowls. The surface is often burnished or crudely polished and decorated with marks pressed into the clay. These consist either of dimples pressed with the fingertip around the top rim, or vertical or slightly tilted grooves close together around the rim, or grooves in a band encircling the pottery just below the rim. Such pottery has been given several names: Coarse Ware, Handmade Ware, or Barbarian Ware. Here, the term "Coarse Ware" will be used when referring to the pottery described above.

Pottery fragments of this kind have been found in a wash or gully near the Menelaion at Sparta and at a nearby hill. The Menelaion destruction is dated to IIIB Late, and the Coarse Ware pottery is later and is dated to IIIC. Similar fragments of Coarse Ware were found in Mycenae, in an earth layer next to South House. This layer is above the IIIB Late level, which dates these fragments to IIIC. This conclusion is supported by the presence of IIIC Mycenaean pottery fragments along with the Coarse Ware. Coarse Ware was also found in the remains of Tiryns in a IIIB context.

Substantially similar pottery has been found elsewhere. It has been found in a range of shapes at Korakou and Aigeira in the northern Peloponnese, dated to early IIIC. There was no destruction associated with that pottery find. In Lefkandi in Euboea, an island just off the eastern coast of the mainland, such pottery was found, again without an associated destruction. It is also known from Athens, and the Perati cemetery near Athens, where no destruction has been detected. A similar pottery has been found in Troy VIIb, in Italy, Cyprus, and several other places, all with appearance of the Course Ware described above.

Perhaps the alternative term, "Barbarian Ware," is an appropriate one after all, since the ultimate origin of the pottery seems to have been in Europe, "barbarian" country. Europe, as the term is used here, refers not to the present boundaries, but to the region north of Mycenaean civilization, and between the Rhine and the Deniester Rivers. The dwellers of this vast territory were barbarians in the sense that their society and economy were organized on a much simpler level than were those of Mycenaean Greece and the Near East, less evolved in arts and technology, and without writing.

In Moravia, a number of sites have yielded pottery very similar to the Coarse Ware of Greece. To the east, in Hungary, very similar pottery has been found. So similar are some Hungarian specimens to those found in Greece that it might be assumed that the same hand made both. Farther eastward, similar pottery has been found in the Ukraine, and has been reported from the Black Sea coast of Romania. Closer to Greece, such pottery has been found in Italy, near Trenit in Albania, and near Vardarofta in Macedonia in northern Greece. It has also been found at several archaeological sites near the very ancient Greek oracular shrine at Dodona in northwest Greece.

Certain Hungarian finds have been dated to the equivalent of the Middle Bronze Age of Greece, and other somewhat similar pottery goes back to the Neolithic period. It is believed to be as early as 1700 BC at Dodona. Thus, the pottery style had ancient roots in Europe. As it was not known in Mycenaean Greece until much later, the movement of the pottery or its makers was, logically, from Europe to Greece rather than from Greece to Europe. The importance of the pottery lies in the possibility, as has been suggested by some scholars, that it represents evidence that European invaders were present in Greece at a time close to the period of troubles. They might have been the cause of the troubles.

In the time period of IIIB Late, a new sword design appeared in Greece, Crete, and the Syria-Canaan coast. Swords were used in Greece for centuries, but they were narrow and long weapons, designed primarily for the thrust rather than the slashing attack. These new swords, however, were wide and robust, with sharp edges, a firmly attached hilt, and center of gravity well forward allowing a slashing attack to be made with greater confidence and effectiveness. The origin of this sword is Europe where it was used long before its appearance in Greece. Examples have been found in Hungary, Germany, the eastern coast of the Adriatic Sea, and Italy on the western coast. Broadly, these localities overlap those from which Coarse Ware was at home. These swords, originating as they do in the barbarian world, could be additional evidence of barbarians in Greece. However, as will be shown next, there are other ways to account for the appearance of Coarse Ware pottery and slashing swords in Greece.

7

WHAT HAPPENED IN GREECE

Archaeological evidence of the end of the Bronze Age in Greece is sufficiently scanty, and contradictory, that various reconstructions of events are possible. Three generations or more of archaeologists and historians have believed in an onslaught by invaders from the north. The current view, however, is that Mycenae, Tiryns, and Midea were devastated by an earthquake, not by hostile action. That view may weaken the case for a barbarian invasion but it does not necessarily eliminate it. The earthquake theory also has weaknesses. It doesn't explain the collapse of so many major and minor centers, or the hundreds of rural settlements that disappeared. Nor does it explain the elaborate defensive measures that were taken. Conflict must be counted as part of the explanation, but it may not have been the result of invasion.

Had there been an invasion, a Mycenaean society that was economically strong and united in purpose should have been able to weather the assault. There were in the land all those fighting kings and men at arms, legend leads one to believe. Archaeology attests to the strongly walled citadels. If many population centers were destroyed by an invasion, an invasion which was able to displace or kill many hundreds of thousands of the Greek population, it must have been one of either very great destructive power or of overwhelming numbers of invaders.

Invasions are a constant factor in history, and there is no shortage of examples. The Mongol leader Timur (Tamerlane) attacked Persia and India in AD 1397. Before withdrawing, his hordes left appalling destruction with wholesale murder and burning. In Persia, he indulged his passion for brutality by piling up seventy thousand heads and in India by massacring one hundred thousand prisoners before destroying Delhi.

In the time of Caesar, Germanic tribes approached the Rhine from the northeast and overran or displaced the resident Celtic population. Later, they exerted irresistible pressure against Gaul west of the Rhine. They succeeded in crossing the Rhine with their families and settled in territory that was nominally under Roman control. They were not particularly destructive in the territories they entered. Their desire was to settle and reap the benefits of the existing system of agriculture and management that the Romans instituted.

Whether it was a slashing attack which cut its way into Greece in the manner of Timur, or a slower, more massive movement of peoples that forced its way into Greece in a manner similar to the Germanic movement, an invasion might have left evidence behind. Is there such evidence—a path of destruction, perhaps, or of a substantial foreign presence?

The Peloponnese is the most thoroughly investigated region of Bronze Age Greece, and it is there that evidence should be sought. Mycenae, Tiryns, and Pylos are only a few of the sites in the Peloponnese that experienced severe destruction. There is but one entrance to the Peloponnese by land, and that is through the isthmus. The Mycenaeans of the Peloponnese may have recognized that vulnerability, and the wall across the isthmus may have been a defensive measure.

Through ground surveys, archaeologists have mapped the location of towns and villages of Greece in LH IIIB, the pre-destruction period, including those near the isthmus. They have also mapped locations of towns and villages of LH IIIC, the post-destruction period. A strange thing is apparent when the maps are compared. There were clusters of towns or villages along the isthmus in IIIB. There were still many in IIIC, even on the north side of the wall, the exposed side. The change in the number of sites is no greater than in any other part of Greece. That does not seem consistent with the arrival at the isthmus of a large destructive horde poring through the funnel of the isthmus, overrunning the wall, pillaging and burning. It appears that no pattern of destruction exists on the isthmus to suggest that invaders entered the Peloponnese by that approach.

Did the invaders flank the isthmus wall and enter the Peloponnese by crossing the Gulf of Corinth? There is a narrow point in the gulf that might be crossed easily. Yet it was on the south shore, near those narrows of the gulf, that there was surprisingly little destruction. In fact, there were more towns in IIIC than earlier, and apparently an increased population. There is no clear evidence of an invasion of the Peloponnese across the Gulf of Corinth. That leaves the sea approach.

Many of the cities with their palaces and citadels were close to the sea coast, or within a day's march, and would therefore be vulnerable to attackers from the sea. However, if barbarians came by sea, it is unlikely that there could have been many of them. *Iliad* claims that a very large Greek army was transported by ship to Troy, but the epic probably exaggerates the number very greatly. In any case, Greece was a maritime power with a large fleet at her disposal. The various European peoples who lived near the extensive shoreline of the Adriatic Sea had their ships, beyond doubt. But there is no reason to think that any had so large a fleet as did the Greeks. Nor is there evidence of any large state or power commanding a large population located to the north of Bronze Age Greece. And if the number of invaders who came by sea was not large, it is hard to see why an assembled Greek army could not defeat them on Greek soil.

Admittedly, attackers coming from the sea might strike quickly, loot and destroy, and then quickly withdraw. Viking-like raids could strike different palaces or citadels in different years, and produce substantial damage. Such a raid may have been the fate of Pylos. Yet the Pylos tablets reflect no concern about a threat from the north, from the direction of the Adriatic Sea, the natural route which northern attackers would take. Pylos appeared to have looked for an attack from the south.

If the ships of the raiders made their way along the east coast of Greece and came upon Pylos from the south, it is difficult to see why they did not raid Athens first. Iolkos on the east coast also appears to have weathered the storm. Many towns and villages near the east coast continued to be occupied, while many sites deep inland disappeared.

There is nothing in the pattern of destruction which suggests that Greece experienced a significant penetration by land or sea. That places the burden of proof on evidence of a foreign presence in Greece.

European swords found in Greece might be evidence of the presence of aliens. The swords might have arrived in the hands of invaders. However, there is no evidence that these swords were associated with destruction. It is therefore likely that the swords reached Greece along trade routes. Greek trade touched along both coasts of the Adriatic, including various points in Italy and the shore opposite. Hungary, though inland, could be the source of these swords. From the Baltic Sea area in the north, an amber route once passed through Hungary and then to the Adriatic Sea. It is along this route that amber reached Greece, and swords could easily have joined the trade goods moving south.

To the military man in Greece, these swords would have been esteemed as prestige items since they were beautifully made, and might have been subjects for study of the latest in military technology. And perhaps they might have been useful in warfare. It is even possible that these swords were manufactured in Greece in imitation of northern models. Such swords were copied by bronze smiths in Ugarit on the Syrian coast perhaps as early as 1300 BC. What a Syrian smith might copy, a Greek smith might also copy. While the design of the swords owes its origin to the north, the presence of the swords in Greece does not necessarily imply that they came in the hands of northern invaders.

Coarse Ware in Greece represents a more perplexing problem. It is crude, unpainted and, frankly, too ugly to be anything for which a Mycenaean would trade, unless some kind of "barbarian chic" had become popular among the fashionable elements of Mycenaean society. Nor is the pottery likely to have entered Greece as containers for some northern delicacy. Coarse Ware included large bowls which might serve as food containers, assuming leather covers were used. But Coarse Ware found in Greece also included cups, too small to be usable as shipping containers. In any case, it is certain that at least some of this ware was manufactured in Greece. It is hard to believe that Greeks, who had access to the world's most beautiful wheel-turned pottery, would suddenly begin to make crude pottery in the barbarian style. It is in the small or remote villages of Greece that people of the lowest economic level would live and who might be expected to make their own pottery. Yet Coarse Ware is not reported from such sites.

With such information as is available, the conclusion is inescapable. It was not Greeks who made this pottery, nor was it imported. It was made in Greece by outsiders, who brought this pottery design tradition with them.

Here is the proof, it might seem, of a barbarian invasion, except that there are several reasons other than invasion that might account for the presence of foreigners and foreign pottery in Greece. It is no secret that the economy of the ancient world depended on slaves who labored in mines, fields, factories, and in the palaces. The same trade routes that might have brought swords from Europe might have brought slaves as well. Or, perhaps a result of increasing Greek activities on the Aegean, Anatolian, or Black Sea coasts, reflected in the story of the Trojan War, new sources of slaves were found. Once in Greece, thrown on their own resources for domestic pottery, these slaves might have made what they needed, just as they would have in their homeland.

Those were restless and insecure times in Greece, and a king might do well to strengthen his hand. It is possible that kings had invited barbarians to Greece as mercenaries. They, or their wives if they came along, might make such pottery in their camps as the need arose.

The circumstances in which this pottery has been found seems to be largely or entirely peaceful, with no clear association with destruction. It is sound evidence of an alien presence, but not of alien destroyers or of foreign occupiers.

Historians have known that invading peoples, even if they have come in large numbers, and come to stay, do not necessarily leave hard evidence of their presence. The Vikings (Normans) who settled in western France left almost no archaeological evidence of their presence as a distinctive people. Generations later, the Normans under William invaded and occupied England. Again, there is little or no archaeological evidence of their arrival in England, and later Norman features in palace and cathedral architecture is no more than might be expected from the natural flow of fashion from France to England. The Norman presence is known only from historic records and from certain non-archaeological remains. If there were nothing of those, nothing would be known of a Norman invasion and occupation of England.

In the Classical period, in 278 BC, Celts from Europe were invited into Anatolia by a king who needed help. They came, twenty thousand of them, and they settled. In short order, they overran much of the Anatolian plateau. The Romans knew them as Galatians. Of hard, clear evidence of their presence, archaeologists have found nothing. Shortly before AD 600, Slavs invaded Greece in large numbers and came to stay. Again, there is little or no archaeological evidence that would show that they had arrived and settled.

If barbarians invaded Greece at the end of the Bronze Age, how would that fact be recognized? They might leave no archaeological trace. There are no historical records from that time to tell of them.

In fact, as the example of the Normans, Celts, and Slavs may show, invaders can and often do leave a significant trace, though not an archaeological one. That trace is language. The Normans in France introduced Scandinavian place names into France. The French language that the Normans brought from France to England entered the language of England and is evident to this day. Many personal names in England continue to reflect a French origin more than nine hundred years after the invasion. Among the Celts in Anatolia, a Celtic dialect continued to be spoken after AD 300, as much as six hundred years after the Celts arrived. Celtic political institutions, similar to those that were part of their tradition in Europe, also continued in Anatolia. The Slavs introduced many Slavic place names in Greece. One of these is Sclavoforo, "Village of Slavs," near the site of ancient Pylos.

An invasion of Greece sufficiently large as to severely damage Mycenaean civilization should be expected to leave something of the invader's culture, at least language. Yet no alien language was known to the Greek scholars of the Classical period who were deeply interested in ethnic matters. That absence weighs heavily against any invasion theory.

Greeks of the Classical period inherited from their past a large body of legend, much of it concerning invasions, migrations, and wars. They considered these, collectively, as their earliest history. There is nothing in them that can be construed as a memory of an overwhelming invasion by aliens from the distant north, from well outside of the Greek world. That too weighs against the invasion theory.

In summary, there is little or no evidence of an alien entry or an alien presence in the Peloponnese. That absence of evidence probably speaks for other parts of Greece as well. There is no evidence that a foreign language established itself in Greece. It appears that there is virtually nothing which supports the theory that barbarians surged down from Europe and attacked Greece, destroying widely, settling, and in the process fatally injuring Mycenaean civilization.

Some who continue to support the theory say that the barbarians came suddenly and as suddenly withdrew, perhaps, as did Timur centuries later in Persia and India. Thus, invaders would leave no cultural trace, not even language. Or if they came to stay, they were swift to abandon their native language and native ways and quick to became culturally Greek, indistinguishable from native Greeks.

These suggestions show that the barbarian invasion theory is infinitely flexible. It can be reshaped to meet any or all objections. But a theory that flexible has but limited utility. Still, it cannot be altogether dismissed, though it is not quite as widely accepted as it once was.

The Dorians and the Return of the Sons of Heracles

Though there is no archaeological evidence of invasion, poets and historians of the Classical period spoke of an invader, a destroyer, a people who came and occupied much of the Mycenaean Peloponnese. Those were the Dorians. The legend of the arrival of the Dorians consists of two curiously intertwined strands. The first concerns the Heraclids, a term that means "Sons of Heracles" or "Descendants of Heracles." Heracles was a figure of the shadowy times before the Trojan War, and the story begins in those times. According to legend, the Heraclids were expelled from the Peloponnese and conspired to make a comeback. They were, so far as can be told, genuine Mycenaeans. The second strand concerns the Dorians, a different group most likely. They are Greeks of the backlands, non-Mycenaean in that they were little touched by the development of Mycenaean civilization to the south and east of them.

Tyrtaeus (650 BC), a Spartan poet, furnishes the earliest surviving information on the subject. More information was later furnished by the two great historians of Greece—Herodotus and Thucydides. It seems evident from what these historians report that at some very early time, the Heraclids and the Dorians, though so different from one other in culture and background, either joined forces or their separate legends became joined. By the time of Tyrtaeus, Heraclids and Dorians were synonymous.

In the Classical period, Dorian, a distinct dialect of Greek, was spoken in most of the Peloponnese. To Spartans and others of the Classical period who considered themselves Dorian, the Heraclid side of the story was flattering. It gave them a ready-made Mycenaean pedigree and, as "returners," a legitimacy as rulers in the Peloponnese. Late versions of the Heraclid-Dorian story were given by Diodorus (30 BC) and a century later by Apollodorus. Apollodorus tells that the invaders came in the time of Agamemnon's grandson. There are inconsistencies and contradictions, as in most ancient legends. After the decay of Mycenaean civilization, knowledge was preserved and transmitted to future generations by oral means. Inevitably, errors crept in. In the Classical period, when tales of the Dorians began to be gathered, they were already a patchwork. Different Dorian Greek communities might have their own locally invented versions. Story collectors and historians of Classical times did what they could to weed out errors and to make accounts consistent, but they seemed to have used little more than the resources of their own imaginations. As a result of these subjective processes, applied to stories already altered by generations of oral transmission, it is difficult to know what is history and what is invention.

This "invasion" might have been a process, perhaps an extended one, in which the Dorians advanced by degrees, by infiltration and by battle when necessary. Through a migration and war, the Dorians came to possess the Peloponnese. It is even possible that they began to arrive in small numbers, perhaps as mercenaries, as early as the days of Mycenaean strength, during LH IIIB. Legend tells that the Dorians attempted an early migration into the Peloponnese. The attempt failed. Most likely it was only when the Mycenaeans were weakened by other causes that the Dorians finally entered the Peloponnese in large numbers. Other peoples may also have infiltrated in small groups, some too insignificant to merit a separate legend, lumped together in Greek memory under the name "Dorian."

It is important to note that Dorians were no northern European barbarians coming from afar. They were Greeks, speakers of a Greek dialect, and the distance which they traveled in their migration was small. Coarse Ware found in Mycenaean sites may be theirs. Similar pottery has been found in Dodona to the north-west of Mycenaean Greece, the region which some believe to have been the early home of the Dorians.

As frequently happens when few hard facts are available, experts will disagree. At present, some scholars hold that there was no invasion or infiltration of Dorians. Certainly, a mass of archaeological evidence at one time thought to mark the Dorian presence in Greece—burial customs, pottery design, extensive iron use—are now recognized to have no relationship to Dorians. The best evidence of the arrival of Dorians in the Peloponnese is language: the displacement of the Mycenaean dialect by the Dorian dialect. While there could be other explanations for the presence of the Dorian dialect in the Peloponnese, the simplest is an invasion by Dorian-speaking peoples, as legend tells.

Neither northern barbarians or Dorians likely caused the disintegration of Mycenaean civilization. Dorians took advantage of it. They entered a region already weakened and partly abandoned. An earlier crisis in Greece must have paved the way. Since the crisis does not appear to have been caused from outside, a cause internal to Mycenaean Greece is most likely.

Crisis and Collapse

The great appeal of barbarian invasion theories is that one cause can be used to explain complex events. However, there is no reason to believe, nor does the evidence require, that the collapse of Mycenaean civilization was produced by a single cause. Had there been but one cause, whether war or natural catastrophe, a society which was otherwise healthy could be expected to have recovered. The Mycenaean civilization of the mainland did not. It was wounded, recovered for a time and only to a degree, and then slid into oblivion. It is a common observation that trouble comes in twos or threes, and it has happened that a multiplicity of troubles occur at nearly the same time. History provides examples of the convergence of uncommon events. In the year AD 1347, Plague raged in Cyprus. Then a devastating earthquake struck, destroying cities. It was followed by a damaging tidal wave that surged over much of the island, entirely destroying olive groves and the fishing fleet upon which the economy depended.

It is reasonable to expect that there were several contributing factors in the collapse of Bronze Age Greece. Which of these factors were operative, the order of their appearance, their interaction with one another, can only be guessed. Those factors are internal wars, as is consistent with all known Greek history; famine as may easily follow overexploitation of the land or a bad turn of climate; deadly plague which may accompany famine; decapitation which removes the top elements of leadership; systematic collapse in which the leading people of the society and the structure of society are unable to adjust to the magnitude of the adversity.

Strife

Iliad provides a picture of Greek kings united for war under Agamemnon, but such unity, if it ever existed, may not have outlasted the War and may not have been the usual situation in Greece. Greek legends deriving from the Bronze Age are filled with conflicts between kings, dynasties, and clans. Proetos overthrows the king of Argos and takes power with the help of a Lycian army. The "Seven" of Greek legend attack Thebes, fail, and their sons later succeed in sacking the great Mycenaean city. The father of Achilles destroys the city of Iolkos. Heraclids attacked Mycenae, attempting to regain power. The breach between the two chieftains, Achilles and Agamemnon, is the basis of *Iliad*. The intrigues, the conflicts, are endless. The entire known history of Greece to the time of Alexander is filled with conflicts of city against city. That dismal and tragic pattern in Greek history may have begun in the Bronze Age.

The improvements to the defenses of the citadels of Athens, Mycenae, and Tiryns were improvements to already existing fortifications. These earlier fortifications show an earlier expectation of trouble, and the concern may have been the aggressiveness of neighbors, not distant enemies.

It is precisely in hard times that the kings may have been most aggressive, thinking to make good their own economic losses by seizing the wealth of others. History tells that during bad times in medieval Europe, kings attacked neighboring or distant kingdoms in the hope of seizing their wealth. Scholars have worried about the apparent date of the Trojan War which, on the basis of some evidence, may have occurred at the time of disturbances in Greece. How could Greeks turn to a foreign adventure with such troubles at home? The Trojan War, if there was such, may have been waged to seize wealth in a futile attempt to stabilize a Greek kingdom close to economic collapse. It would have differed from a war of Greek against Greek only in the distance of the Trojan city. Internal turmoil would not necessarily prevent an overseas adventure. In medieval Europe, the First Crusade was launched during a period of troubles and strife. Among its purposes was to divert to foreign shores warrior and other elements made unruly by bad times.

Figure 7-1. The Warrior Vase, found by Schliemann at Mycenae, with the clearest representation of Greek fighting men of the end of the Bronze Age. Another group of warriors appears on the back of the vase.

Whatever the cause of the troubles in Greece, the palaces in Greece would have been targets. For kings, the palaces of other kings would have contained tempting wealth. For peasants, palaces would contain hoarded grain, and were the seats of oppressors who made incessant demands of their labor. Linear B tablets clearly show that industrial production was under close control of the Palace, and it is likely that much farm production was also closely managed from the Palace. Distribution of seed, time of planting, allocation of farm labor, harvesting—all might have been subject to Palace management. A society which is that centralized is particularly vulnerable to the impact of decapitation, the destruction of the palace leadership. Destruction of leadership would result in disruption of food production. If such disruptions were widespread and prolonged, there would have been further food shortages which would worsen a deteriorating situation.

Palace and field were tied together in one economy. It is certain that if some calamity were to strike at food production directly, it would affect the Palace. The Palace counted on food surpluses to maintain the large numbers who were not food producers. These included the household military, mercenaries, craftsman, palace bureaucrats, and many others in that complex society. Trade would be affected, since some farm products such as olive oil and wine were produced directly for trade, and other foodstuffs supported those who produced tradable goods.

Of the two directions in which trouble might flow, that from the farm to the Palace could be by far the more serious. If the Palace and its management system collapsed, the peasantry could find a means to survive. They had the most important capability of all, the ability to produce food. But a catastrophe that struck at food production directly—a natural calamity such as a prolonged drought—would cripple the peasantry and Palace alike. Stored grain would soon give out. Purchase of grain from abroad could not begin to meet the need. If the crisis were prolonged, Mycenaean society would have collapsed.

Famine and Pestilence

Some evidence indicates a more or less steady population growth in Bronze Age Greece from the Late Helladic II period into Late Helladic III. Food production undoubtedly increased in step with increased population. At first, this would not present a problem. There was a limited amount of good land with deep water-holding soils, and all that needed to be done was to clear the forest and place the land under cultivation.

However, as population continued to increase, many had no choice but to move to areas with poorer soils, perhaps stony or thin. Mountain sides would yield some crops if they were terraced and if mountain streams were controlled with dams. Marshy land could be drained and planted. Such newly opened lands would be marginal producers, requiring great labor, and returning poor yields for the labor and the seed invested. As population continued to increase and with it the need for food, land would be pressed harder, forced to yield more. This could be accomplished for a time by reducing the fallow, the rest period that land needed in order to regain fertility.

One thing is obvious: the short fallow lands and the marginal lands were particularly vulnerable to natural disasters because they were not very productive to begin with. A prolonged period of drenching rain might exceed the water control measures of reclaimed marshes, and would wash out mountain terraces and dams. A prolonged drought would create widespread problems, affecting the yield of good lands, but more severely the marginal lands, knocking them out of production. If this were to happen, famine might quickly result since the new lands were brought under cultivation in response to the food needs of the larger population. Even those on good lands would be affected if the drought were prolonged. Though they would have attempted to store away one or two years of grain and dried fruit in anticipation of crop failure, those measures would finally fail.

It would be natural if people left their withered lands, abandoned their villages, and moved to the larger towns seeking opportunity. Or, they might wander the land, rootless, a potential social menace. If the problem were prolonged, birth rate and infant survival would be affected and population would drop, causing additional abandonment of villages.

These problems would not immediately affect the powerful. The king and men-at-arms, some of whom were landholders, would continue to eat since they had the power of the sword to compel food for their tables. However, food surpluses were not there which had supported the many who were not food producers and upon whom the Palace depended. Social unrest might affect skilled craftsmen and peasants alike, possibly leading to class warfare or clashes between kingdoms. It would have been a good time for potters or other craftsmen to slip away to look for opportunities abroad.

Climate scientists seek evidence of such a drought in the Late Bronze Age in Greece. They do not find it, and possibly do not expect to find it. Soil or lake bottom sediments corresponding to that remote period have been studied and pollen analyses carried in a search for significant changes in plant growth. Unfortunately, the effect of ancient human activity, such as forest clearing, masks the effect which drought might produce in the pollen record. Other approaches to an understanding of ancient climate are underway, of which the most promising is the study of growth patterns in ancient tree specimens. That has not yet been productive thus far for the climate of Late Bronze Age Greece.

Climatologists have examined modern weather patterns in Greece. A weather pattern was found which existed for a few days in Greece in the winter of 1955 in which the central Peloponnese had less than normal rainfall while the coast of the Peloponnese and the region around Athens had normal rainfall. From this, they conclude that such a pattern is possible, might have occurred in ancient times, and might drive population out of the central Peloponnese and to the coasts and over to Athens. That argument seems unconvincing, however, and entirely too neat in the way it is made to account for the exact population displacements noted earlier. Above all, it is hard to believe that such a specific pattern of weather, seen only for a few days in modern Greece, could have existed in ancient Greece in just that one special way, and remain fixed and unchanging for the several years required to force people to move.

Whether or not that pattern existed, it is certain that drought and famine are no rarities. Famine has occurred repeatedly in ancient times and since, affecting various parts of the world and taking a terrible toll. Widespread famine, possibly resulting from drought, if continued long enough would account for much of what is known of the collapse in Greece at the end of the Bronze Age. To make matters worse, drought and famine could have been followed by a terrible scourge, the Plague.

Of all of the periodically occurring catastrophes which nature can produce, none is more horrible or destructive than the Plague. No other natural event has the power to devastate a population, dissolve the bonds of society, and frustrate recovery. It is certainly possible that it was Plague which dealt the blow to the Mycenaean world. Bubonic Plague and its twin, Pneumonic Plague, are caused by the same bacterium, transmitted to man primarily by the bite of a flea that ordinarily lives on rodents. When it is not afflicting human populations, the plague bacillus remains alive in wild rodent populations. Presumably, these rodents are largely immune to the effects of the disease. Plague still smolders in ground squirrels in the western United States, and in desert, forest, and mountain rodents in many places in the world. When unusual conditions bring these rodents into contact with domestic rats or directly with man, Plague may spring to the human population.

Wet years, for example, might expand the yield of the wild crops, such as acorns, upon which wild rodents depend, thus allowing a population explosion. A following drought would send the desperate creatures into the habitats of man in search of food, thus creating the conditions for transmission of Plague to humans. The clearing of mountainsides and forests for new farms would also offer the opportunity for man and infected rodents to meet.

Experiments in rats show that as few as three bacteria are enough to cause infection, and the coughing and spitting are a fertile source of contagion. Some people recover, and afterward are immune, and some have the disease only in a mild form. Most die, horribly. It is the contagiousness, rapid spread, unstoppability, horrible symptoms, and killing power which so frightened and defeated communities where Plague struck.

No sound texts from the Bronze or Early Iron Age are available which describe the impact of Plague. Some idea of Plague is provided by the records of a later age, however. An epidemic of Plague began in Egypt in AD 542 and quickly passed to Constantinople, killing ten thousand in a day. It entered Italy in AD 543 and caused huge mortality. Flashing again in 565, it left sections of Italy so depopulated as to be an easy target for Lombard invaders. It returned in the years 571 and 590 and then spread over the entire Roman world.

A clearer picture is available from the Late Middle Ages. The Black Death, as the Plague of that period was called, started on the north coast of the Black Sea. From there, in AD 1347, it was carried by ship to Genoa. It raged in Sienna from April to October, and in that time an estimated eighty thousand people died. In Florence an estimated fifty thousand to one hundred thousand died. The relatively small size of cities in those times places these numbers in a deadly prospective. The Black Death reached Spain and France, and it is recorded that thirty thousand died in Arles. By the summer of 1349, Plague had entered Belgium and Holland. In Tournay, it was twenty five thousand dead. To prevent panic, the city fathers forbade the ringing of church bells for the dead—the ringing was incessant—and forbade also the wearing of black at funerals.

Plague spread to England, Germany, and other countries, creating similar havoc. It is stated that it killed as many as a hundred thousand in Vienna in the year 1349. From the combination of famine and Plague, it is estimated that many regions of Europe lost three quarters of their population. In all of Europe, one third or more perished.

In many parts of Europe, there had been severe famine for several years before Plague struck. Plague seems to follow upon famine in many cases, either through decline of the health of the people, or to the proximity of man and rodent caused by drought.

Social effects were severe. Rich and poor were carried off by the epidemic without distinction. Country and city were affected. The rich who had country houses fled to the country, and many more country folk fled to the city. Towns were abandoned. Doctors and others who aided the sick were themselves infected and died. People became too frightened to aid the sick, even those in their own families. The dead were buried in mass graves—open pits outside of the towns and cities.

People grew fatalistic and gave themselves over to carousing and lawlessness. Brigands pillaged the countryside. Domestic animals died of the Plague. Wild animals roamed in abandoned farms and villages. Modern evidence indicates that a village may have remained infectious even after it was abandoned. If people were to return, they might then become infected, so that life would not return again to the village. The village was cursed. Plague raged in the East also. Peasants fled the land, leaving it largely abandoned, and filled the cities of Cairo and Damascus. Food production collapsed, thus worsening the famine.

Most devastating to recovery was the fact that Plague would seemingly pass, allowing a brief recovery, only to return again and again in following decades until it mysteriously disappeared, not to return for centuries.

In the absence of useful records directly from the Bronze Age, perhaps later Greek legend recalls something of an epidemic. The Dorians invaded the Peloponnese and captured the cities. Then an epidemic struck and the Dorians abandoned the Peloponnese. *Iliad* begins with an episode of epidemic, apparently Plague. Agamemnon took Chryses captive, intending to keep her as a prize of war. Her father, a priest of the god Apollo, came to the Greek camp and begged Agamemnon to release his daughter. Rather than doing so, Agamemnon chased the priest off with threats and insults. The priest moved off a safe distance and sent up a prayer:

> Hear me Apollo! God of the silver bow
> who strides the walls of Chryse and Cilla sacrosanct
> lord in power of Tenedos—Smintheus, god of plague!

> If ever I roofed a shrine to please your heart,
> ever burned the long rich bones of bulls and goats
> on your holy altar, now, now bring my prayer to pass.
> Pay the Danaans back—your arrows for my tears!
> His prayer went up and Phoebus Apollo heard him.
> Down he strode from Olympus' peaks, storming in his heart
> with his bow and hooded quiver slung across his shoulders.
> The arrows clanged at his back as the god quaked with rage,
> the god himself on the march and down he came like night.
> Over against the ships he dropped to a knee, let fly a shaft
> and a terrifying clash rang out from the great silver bow.
> First he went for the mules and circling dogs but then,
> launching a piercing shaft at the men themselves,
> cut them down in droves—
> and the corpse-fires burned on, night and day, no end in sight. (*Iliad*, Book 2)

The arrows of Apollo are the mythological expression of death by disease. That it was Bubonic Plague is suggested by the fact that animals as well as men were affected. Further, Apollo is called upon is in his role as "Apollo Smintheus," in effect "Apollo God of Mice," from which it might seem that the ancients recognized the role which rodents play in bringing Plague. In poetic and mythological clothing, this passage from *Iliad* suggests that Plague was in the camp of the Greeks. Can these legends bear truth?

Support for the possibility that it was Plague—or more likely the combination of famine and Plague—which was in part responsible for the devastation of Mycenaean civilization is provided by a comparison of what happened in Bronze Age Greece with the effects of the Black Death in the Middle Ages. In Greece, the rural population apparently collapsed. Towns and villages were abandoned and not reoccupied. Based on the reduction in the numbers of towns and villages, forty percent or more of the population disappeared in Greece, perhaps as many as four hundred thousand people. Most have to be accounted as deaths, though some population fled to certain cities. Considering the small capacity of most ships of that time, there is no reasonable possibility of an overseas emigration of that magnitude.

Where is the evidence for such numbers of dead, the remains of the many tens or hundreds of thousands? Any theory (other than that of mass migration) must consider the problem of graves. Archaeologists have not seen them, and yet the collapse of population in Greece is certain. Again, the lessons of Plague in medieval Europe may be useful. Out of great fear of the contagion and the numbers of new dead each day, those who died of Plague were not interred in sacred ground, in established cemeteries, but in hastily dug mass graves well outside of the cities. In Greece, masses who might have died of Plague would have been buried well away from recognized cemeteries, in locations not investigated by archaeologists. In any case, unprotected remains would probably not last in Greek soil after more than three thousand years.

One may well imagine that the life of the Mycenaean palaces was severely disrupted, with destruction in some cases. There were periods of recovery and then again collapse. This can be compared to the aftermath of the Black Death in the Middle Ages in Europe. One historian states of that time (Bautier, 1971):

> There were deadly famines, causing villages to be abandoned by the thousand, many of them permanently from Castile to Prussia, and from the Scottish border to the Greek Peninsula. Cultivated land which had been won from the waste and woodland reverted to fallow and pasture....The countryside was continually overrun by bands of adventurers, who ruined the farms and plundered the houses, forcing the inhabitants to seek refuge...industries declined or disappeared, commercial horizons in the east were lowered. (*Economic Development*)

That the results were due not to Plague alone but also to the earlier overexploitation of the land in response to increased population is suggested by another historian (Hay, 1953).

> It is, however, tolerably certain that in most of Western Europe the steady expansion of population and of agricultural production had halted....The reason for this may well be the over-exploitation of the new land....This land was marginal and its productivity not easily maintained...Scarcity thus became endemic, and when widespread famine followed by plague arrived, this merely intensified the contraction...Only in certain rural areas...does there seem to have been any steady rise in population....Elsewhere there is a decline revealing shrinking farms, empty villages, roads and paths overgrown and deserted...Lords struggled to maintain their position...by foreign adventure and civil war...(*Medieval Centuries*)

Based on what is known, it appears that the circumstances of decline and collapse in Greece match quite well the known result of famine and Plague of the Middle Ages in Europe. Plague is nothing new in the world and must have existed in the Bronze Age and famine is a recurrent event in history. That famine and Plague can occur together is certain, one causing the other, one increasing the impact of the other. They attack society from within, severely injuring the economy and damaging social order. Spasms of Plague and famine may occur over decades until Plague disappears as mysteriously as it came, and this pattern defeats attempts at recovery.

Famine, pestilence, strife, a disruption of trade, some or all of these may have dealt a serious blow to the economy and to society of Bronze Age Greece. Social and economic reverses are hard to manage. In military operations, an orderly retreat is much harder to manage than an advance, and can easily turn into a rout. Societies are able to manage a social and economic advance as prosperity and opportunity increase, as may have happened in Greece in the years before approximately 1250 BC. Production would have increased, workers and craftsmen would have been added, more ships are built, managers and record keepers employed, and individuals at all social levels would have adjusted quickly to increased prosperity and wealth. If a long term decline were to set in, however, society would have been less able to cope. No one wants to give up security, power, or position. In Greece, the palace bureaucrats would not dismiss themselves, princes would not willingly give up incomes, and mercenaries and craftsmen would not willingly give up employment. The entire way of functioning in that society, based as it was on intensive management from the Palace, was not easy to undo, not easy to simplify in response to leaner times. All of these factors would have placed Greece on the threshold of social instability. Conflict in which the lead elements in society perished (decapitation) might have been fatal to recovery.

It is easy to imagine that Greek society fell apart. Unruly mobs probably roamed the countryside, and warrior bands looked to satisfy their own needs. Perhaps Hesiod understood the cause of the ancient collapse. He said of the people of Greece at the end of the Bronze Age, "these were destroyed by their own hands and passed to the dank house of chill Hades…."

8
SEA PEOPLES ATTACK EGYPT

The term "Sea Peoples" is a modern one, given to various seaborne invaders and raiders who troubled the lands along the eastern Mediterranean near the close of the Bronze Age. Who these people were, where they came from, no one knows for certain. They were reported during the time of Ramesses II (1279–1212 BC). In the early years of his reign one group, the Sherden, came in their ships and attacked Egypt. Enough Sherden were captured to allow Ramesses to form an elite infantry unit from among them, and that unit was with him at Kadesh. Egypt might not have recognized it at the time, but the sea, which until then provided a barrier to invasion, had become a highway over which sea rovers could strike without warning.

Two generations after the Sherden invasion, Sea Peoples would again assault Egypt. They would not attack alone, but in company with Libyans, peoples who lived to the west of Egypt.

This attack came in the time of Merneptah, the thirteenth son of Ramesses II. His legitimate older brothers ranked above Merneptah in order of succession. Merneptah saw little real hope of ever succeeding to the throne of Egypt. Rather than idling at the royal court with its plots and harem intrigues, he took up a career in the priesthood and the army. In the army, he gained the friendship and loyalty of future army leaders, and learned the art of military organization and rapid mobilization, experience that later would prove to be invaluable. Campaign experience in Canaan also added to his military capabilities.

Ramesses ruled for a remarkable sixty-seven years. Older brothers died before Merneptah and, unlikely as the prospect may have seemed, when Ramesses died, Merneptah became king in Egypt (1212–1202 BC).

The Attack and Its Outcome

The Nile begins its course in the high country of East Africa. It flows north through the ancient land of Nubia and continues northward through desert country. It passes the ancient Egyptian capital at Thebes which includes Luxor, the Valley of the Kings, and Karnak. It continues northward, Figure 8-1, past another capital at Memphis. A few miles north of Memphis, near ancient Heliopolis and present-day Cairo, the river divides into several lesser streams that fan out to the northwest, north, and northeast before reaching the Mediterranean Sea. This is the Nile Delta. The lush and well-watered lands of the Delta were the main bread-basket of Egypt and held most of the population.

It was probably from Memphis that Merneptah departed to the south, to Thebes, to attend to religious obligations and to oversee an inventory of temple treasures. Pharaoh was, in effect, the chief priest of Egypt, but day-to-day operations were in the hands of a large temple priesthood. Over the years, the temples had been made rich and their priests powerful through royal gifts of land, cattle, and the spoils of war. Merneptah's inventory probably had to do with keeping the priesthood in check. Since Merneptah had worked in the highest levels of the priesthood, he was in an excellent position to insure that nothing was hidden from his accountants.

While this was taking place, in the summer of his fifth year of his rule, word came to Merneptah that Egypt had been invaded. The invaders included Libu and Meshwesh, Libyan peoples. Libyans had invaded Egypt in the time of Merneptah's grandfather, Seti, and had been repulsed. Merneptah's father also had conflicts with them. To control their movements, Ramesses had established a series of forts along the coast extending far to the west of the Delta. This time, and more worrisome, the Libyans were accompanied by strangers from over the sea.

Much of what happened is learned from texts inscribed on the wall of the great temple at Karnak. These inscriptions were written vertically, starting high on the wall and proceeding downward. As many of the topmost blocks have disappeared, substantial parts of the text are missing, and some remaining words are illegible. As a result, it is necessary to fill voids in the text with the most likely meaning. Part of the reconstructed text tells that:

> The wretched fallen chief of Libya, Meryey the son of Dedy, has fallen upon the west country with his bowmen. He has brought with him Sherdan, Shekelesh, Akwash, Luka, and Tursha, and the best warriors of his country. (*Egyptian Ancient Records*)

The identity and origin of the Sherdan, Shekelesh, Akwash, Luka, and Tursha, collectively referred to as Sea Peoples, will be considered later. Alien in appearance, seemingly countless in number, these Sea Peoples must have filled the Egyptians with dread.

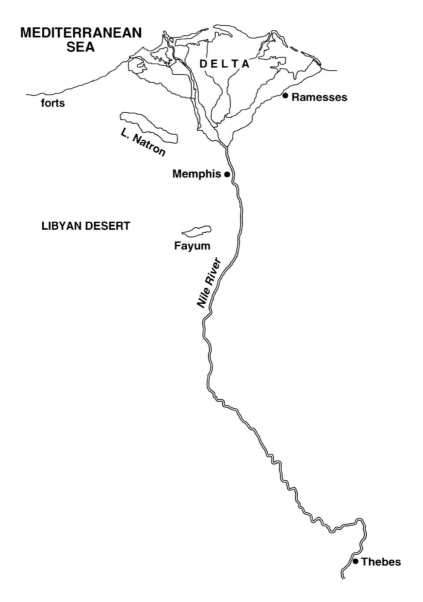

Figure 8-1. The Nile and Nile Delta. The straight-line distance from the Mediterranean Sea to Thebes is slightly over 400 miles. Egyptian control extended farther south, to Nubia.

It appears that the Libyan horde had thrust east along the coast, or perhaps farther inland and parallel to the coast, and had managed to slip past the Egyptian forts that

Ramesses had established. This was more than an invasion. It was a migration, driven by desperation, and included wives, children, cattle, and such furnishings as semi-nomadic Libyans might have. They came from a land where it had always been difficult to scratch out a living. They looked with longing toward the lush, well-watered lands of the Delta. This horde advanced into the western delta and then moved southward along the western branch of the Nile. They camped, it appears, near Lake Natron, and from there, some of their raiders attacked southwestward, overwhelming the western oasis of Bahriyah and cutting off Egyptian contact with other oases further southward. Others may have crossed to the east side of the Nile north of Memphis. That move, if sufficiently powerful, would have cut Egypt in half, isolating the Delta from all of the southern part of Egypt.

It may have been about this time that news was brought to Merneptah that a revolt had begun against Egyptian rule in the south, in Nubia. From Nubia, Egypt obtained soldiers, slaves, elephant ivory. Above all, there was gold. The mines of Nubia were a source of gold for Egypt, and this gold was sought by other countries who obtained it in trade.

No doubt, Merneptah saw a conspiracy. Meryey, the chief of the Libu, was behind this. The Libyans with their Sea Peoples would attack in the north, and the Nubians would rise at the same time in the south, presenting Egypt with a two-front war.

A decision had to be made. It was the Libyans and their dangerous allies who were the immediate threat to Egypt. Still Merneptah hesitated. Then Merneptah had a dream. It was as if a huge statue of the god Ptah were standing before him. The god extended a scimitar to him and said, "Take thou this. Banish thou the faint heart from thee." Merneptah called for mobilization of the army. As the Karnak inscription tells:

> It happened that when Merneptah rose to the throne of Horus, he was appointed to preserve the folk, he has arisen to protect the people of Egypt. The choicest bowmen were mustered, his chariotry was brought up from every direction, his scouts were assembled. His infantry marched forth, the heavy armed troops arrived, beautiful in appearance, leading the bowmen against every land. (*Egyptian Ancient Records*)

Mobilization took a fortnight, and by late March or April the opposing armies met at "the Horns of the Earth," probably referring to some terrain feature. It was a clash of archers and swordsmen. Strong Egyptian chariot forces were involved. The inscription continues:

> Every man of the foe was soaked in their blood. There was none that escaped among them. The bowmen of his majesty spent six hours of destruction among them. They were delivered to the sword. As they fought, the wretched chief of Libya halted, his heart seized with fear. He pulled back, knelt, unbuckled his sandals his bow, and his quiver and dropped them. Terror gripped his limbs. They slew those around him and of his possessions, his equipment, his silver, his gold,

his vessels of bronze, the furniture of his wife, his throne, his bows, his arrows, all of his things which he had brought from his land consisting of oxen, goats, asses, they were brought to the palace together with the captives.

(*Egyptian Ancient Records*)

Meryey fled, with Egyptians in pursuit. He managed to escape along with some others. The Karnak inscription further states:

> The commandant of the Fortress of the West sent a report to the Court saying 'The fallen Meryey has come, fleeing because of his cowardice, and he passed by me in safety by favor of night. The boasts which he uttered have come to naught. All that his mouth said has returned upon his own head. It is not known if he is alive or dead, but if alive, he will not command again, as he is now considered an enemy by his own troops. They have put another in his place from among his brothers, another who would fight him if he sees him. All the chiefs are disgusted.
>
> ….
>
> Their chief is like a dog, a man of boasting, without courage…

As for the Libyans left behind in Egypt, "The families of Libya are scattered upon the dikes like mice" and Pharaoh is "seizing among them like a hawk." Their camp with its leather tents was burned to the ground.

Thus closes Merneptah's account of the battle with the Libyans and Sea Peoples. There remain only the prisoners, the dead, and the spoils to count. Among the spoils are several thousand copper swords, referred to as swords of the Meshwesh.

The Karnak inscription includes the usual adulation of the Pharaoh and the usual propaganda as appears in the victory monuments of many Egyptian kings. Courtiers acclaim him. The people laud him. The gods watch over Egypt and act through the Pharaoh. They empower him. With their aid and direction, Pharaoh protects Egypt from her enemies, from chaos and disorder. Pharaoh is invincible in battle. He has no partial victories, only full and complete victories. Often, he utterly eradicates all of the enemy and no descendants are possible for them. Those whom he does not kill, does not crunch beneath the wheels of his chariot, beg for mercy: "Give us the breath of our nostrils" they cry. And they are sent into Egypt as slaves, or if fighters, are enlisted as special troops for Egypt.

The Sea Peoples Brigades

Inscriptions at Karnak, and on a granite monument found at Athribis in the southern Delta give casualty figures suffered by the Libyan coalition. From these, it is possible to form an idea of the size of the Sea Peoples force which, with the Libyans, attempted to conquer Egypt.

Assessment of the number of enemy casualties was a military necessity in ancient as in modern times. Reports could be gathered from troops as they return to camp. How many did you kill, or seriously wound, or see killed or wounded? Are you sure? But such reports are notoriously unreliable. In the furor, fright, and fatigue of battle, it is difficult for the soldier to know and recall, and he tends to overestimate. If there is a reward offered based on the number of enemy killed, the totals may be wildly inflated.

Some objective method of assessment is necessary. The Egyptians had such a method. One hand of each of the enemy dead was severed and brought into camp and the hands were counted. That was the practice if the enemy was circumcised. Most Egyptians were circumcised, as Egyptians had been from remote antiquity. However, if the dead enemy was not circumcised, then the phallus was cut off and brought in instead of the hand—a final circumcision indeed! In the mortuary temple of Ramesses III, a successor to Merneptah, a relief sculpture dealing with an entirely unrelated battle shows a pile of severed hands and separately a pile of severed phalli. Standing over each pile is a scribe with pad and pen, recording the count. It is, however, uncertain that the Egyptians always made this neat distinction between the circumcised and uncircumcised.

Inscriptions record the count according to the ethnic or tribal identity of the dead, and this could not possibly be done by scribes looking at hands and phalli alone. It is doubtful that the Egyptian troops, most of whom were uneducated peasants, had ever heard of a Luka, a Shekelesh, an Akwash, or a Tursha, and were able to distinguish between them. Likely, captured enemy were escorted back to the battlefield and asked to point out their dead. Some sort of count would have been made and coordinated with hand and phallus counts. These numbers were recorded with an unusual precision. For example, the Karnak inscription records 222 Shekelesh and 742 Tursha dead. Such exactitude suggests an attempt at an honest count and an honest report, since invented numbers would tend to be both rounded off and larger. The Athribis numbers are different, but not by a great amount.

Numbers are clear for the most part, but some of the accompanying texts are less so. Certain words are worn away or missing, and readings are therefore somewhat uncertain. It is difficult to distinguish subtotals from totals and to know if they are tallies of the dead alone or if they include the number captured as well.

The American Egyptologist Charles Breasted, whose translation's published in 1906 are still valued today, suggests that a total of 6,359 Libyans and 2,370 Sea Peoples were killed. However, he acknowledges that a reading that yields a much higher number is possible. Assuming that about an equal number managed to escape, slipping with Meryey past the Egyptian forts by night, the total of Libyans who fought would be about 12,000 and of Sea

Peoples almost 5,000, for a total of 17,000. It would have been a large fighting force for those times. When years earlier Ramesses II marched out against the Hittites, bringing with him the imperial army of Egypt, his army in the field totaled about 20,000. For the Libyans, a migrating horde whose numbers could not have been huge, these numbers must have included every man or boy capable of drawing the bow.

For the Sea Peoples, an army of 5,000 was also a sizable one, and it would be interesting to know how a force of this size came to this distant land.

The Conspiracy

The Sea Peoples came from the north according to the Karnak inscription. As will be shown, the home of most or all of them may have been in western or southern Anatolia. The circumstances of their arrival in Egypt are a mystery. This possibility is the simplest. Libyans entered the Delta and were marauding there for some time. Hearing of it in their distant lands, various elements who are called Sea Peoples decided that there was a golden opportunity which could not be missed. With the Libyans disrupting Egypt and distracting the Egyptian army, the Sea Peoples might gain a footing of their own in the rich lands of Egypt. Harbors of the north became busy as men prepared, and soon black ships appeared on the horizon and beached on the shores of the Egyptian Delta.

Events are unlikely to have unfolded that way. It is doubtful that Merneptah, an old soldier himself, would have allowed the Libyans to invade and loot and pillage in the Delta unmolested for such a long time that word of it would reach the outside world, encouraging foreign adventurers and allowing them time to organize and invade. Further, a direct invasion would meet formidable difficulties. The stories tell that the sailing of the Greek fleet for Troy and the landing on Trojan shores was a highly coordinated operation. In contrast, there is no evidence which would suggest that the Sea Peoples and their ships assembled at one port, arrived under the command of one leader, or were in any way militarily coordinated. In these circumstances, various ships would have made landfall at different points on the shores of Egypt over many days, vulnerable to attack from the local population.

Even an organized and coordinated assault on Egyptian shores would have been hazardous, as can be seen from recent history. In the summer of 1798, Napoleon mounted an invasion of Egypt. A fleet of four hundred transports carrying thirty five thousand troops set sail from French and Italian ports. It refitted and regrouped in Malta. Departing Malta in early July, the invasion fleet arrived at Egypt and in a coordinated landing came ashore west of Alexandria. The troops were inexperienced in landing operations and many could not swim. Though sick, thirsty, and starving, they somehow made it ashore during a stiff gale. No one had thought to supply them with canteens. That they were able somehow to land and quickly capture Alexandria saved them, for in Alexandria there was replenishment. Then they marched south for Cairo near ancient Memphis. According to the historian J. C. Herold:

> The troops had been told that they would find villages, food, and water; instead they found only desert, ruined hovels, mirages, sandstorms, and cisterns filled in by the Bedouins. At one well thirty men were trampled to death in a stampede for a few drops of brackish water. Stragglers were mutilated and killed by the ever-present Bedouins. Scores of men lost their wits and shot themselves. In vain did Generals Desaix, and Jean Louis Reynier, who commanded the vanguard divisions, plead with Bonaparte for rations, medicine, and draft animals; all he sent them was reams of his proclamation to the Egyptians. (*Napoleon*)

There is little reason to think that Sea Peoples, beaching on the Delta and marching inland, would have faired better.

The Karnak inscriptions seem clear on this point. There is no word of a direct assault on Egypt from the sea. The inscriptions tell that the Libyans were responsible for the presence of the Sea Peoples. When the Sea Peoples first become evident to the Egyptians, they were already part of Meryey's army.

How and where did Libyans and Sea Peoples come together? The presence of such a large force of Sea Peoples could not have been an accident, but the result of a plan. Libyans and Northerners had probably been in contact for some time. Along the coast west of the Delta, there is a town now called Marsa Matruh. In a lagoon offshore, there is a small island, Bates Island. Here, archaeologists have found the remains of buildings of the Late Bronze Age together with Late Bronze Age pottery from Cyprus, Crete, and Syria. Clearly, mariners from the north had been here, and used it as a trading station. There is evidence of metalworking, possibly the casting of metals as weapons to be traded to the Libyans. The many copper or bronze swords captured by Merneptah, referred to as "swords of the Meshwesh" come to mind. The peak of activity on this island seems to have been in the 1300s BC, but excavators say that this outpost may still have been active as late as the 1200s. When Ramesses extended the line of Egyptian forts toward this area, it may have dampened interest in the use of this island by foreigners, but perhaps it did not eliminate it. Here, or at some similar coastal trading post not yet discovered, would be a natural meeting place of Libyans and Sea Peoples.

It is in such a place the conspiracy may have been hatched. It could be assumed that Meryey and Sea Peoples' chiefs saw an opportunity and formed a plan. In due course, ships under sail and oar arrived over a period of weeks—a formidable armada. The ships would beach and the men come ashore in Libyan territory, or in thinly defended Egyptian territory where the Libyans could protect the landing and provide support. Thus aided, a formidable force could be assembled.

The plan may have seemed so sound that the Sea People leaders thought there was a good chance of success, even against the strength of Egypt. There would be strong Libyan forces stiffened by the skilled fighting men that the Sea Peoples would bring. Merneptah would be away from the capital on an annual administrative and religious round. A diversion in Nubia would distract the Egyptian army. All this would allow the Libyans and Sea Peoples to strike at the apex of the Delta and to cut Egypt in half and destroy Pharaonic power. It would have been a brilliant strategic concept.

What would induce the Sea Peoples to join Meryey in this risky venture? It was not for pay. The Libyans were impoverished, and a few gold trinkets taken by the Egyptians from Meryey's tent does not change the picture. It was starvation, it is clear, which forced the Libyans to scheme against Egypt.

> They spent their time going about the land, fighting, to fill their bodies daily. They came to the land of Egypt, to seek the necessities of their mouths. (*Egyptian Ancient Records*)

That may also describe the situation of the Sea Peoples, since there may have been famine in their northern homelands.

Whatever the motive of the Libyans and the Sea Peoples, the audacious venture failed. In coming years, the Libyans would appear again. They were far from finished, though Merneptah may have thought otherwise. Nor would it be the last of the sea raiders. The Sea Peoples would return.

Origin of the Attackers

Though the Egyptians probably knew of the homeland of the Sea Peoples, the information has since been lost. As a result, the origin of the various Sea People groups has been the subject of extensive study and debate for over a century. It has been characterized by historians as one of the great unsolved problems of ancient history.

There is hardly anything more than their names by which to determine their homeland and ethnic identity or affiliation. A clue may lie in the form of some of the Sea People names, those that end in "-*sh*" or "-*sha*." The vowel ending is uncertain since Egyptian writing does not give the vowel explicitly. Scholars have debated the significance of this ending. It may be assumed that the Egyptians heard the names directly from Sea Peoples captives, and that the -*sh* or -*sha* endings reflect the names as the Sea Peoples pronounced them. These particular endings have geographical significance. They relate to known place names. A *-sh* or *-sha* ending was common in Bronze Age place-names in Anatolia, and to a lesser degree in northern Syria.

The *-sha* ending seems to be equivalent to another place name ending, the *-ossos* type ending, known from many places in the ancient world. Examples from Crete are Kn*ossos* and Amn*isos*, both mentioned in *Odyssey*. Evidence of the equivalence of *-sha* and *-ossos* is provided by hieroglyphic writing on a monument of Egyptian king Amenhotep III (1386–1349 BC). This inscription records the names of a number of foreign cities. One such city is thought to have been pronounced Kunusha in Egyptian and a second would be Amnisha. These are believed to be the Egyptian rendering of the names Knossos and Amnisos. Thus

>Kunusha=Knossos
>Amnisha=Amnisos

From this, it appears that "*-sha*" = "*-ossos*." Throughout Anatolia and especially on the west coast, and also in Greece and Crete, many ancient city names end in *-osos*, *-ossos*, *-assos*, or *-issos*. Though some of these cities may have been established late in history, their names appear to maintain a very ancient tradition in these regions. In summary, the homes of the Sea Peoples might be looked for where the "*sha*" or "*ossos*" name ending is prevalent—Anatolia, Syria, Greece, and Crete.

Ancient place names from these regions can be examined to determine if any match the Sea People names. There are difficulties, of course. Vowels in the Sea Peoples names must be guessed. For that reason, the consonant structure of the name is the best basis for a match. Admittedly, a name with two or three consonants does not narrow matters greatly. For example, several ancient localities can be matched to the consonant sequence T-R-S or T-R-Sh. The Tursha, for example, have already been mentioned. It is also certain that the names of many ancient lands and cities are no longer known and are lost from examination.

In view of the fact that these Sea People names could each be matched to perhaps several different towns, cities, or regions, it is necessary to reach out to geographical linkages or historical probabilities. While Egyptian texts do not say that the several Sea Peoples groups were related, it seems likely that most of those who joined in the war against Merneptah came from regions close to one another. How else could these people come together in a joint effort? Why else would they come together unless by shared circumstances, possibly political dissolution, social breakdown, famine or some other situation in their homelands? How else could they trust one another enough to fight side-by-side, unless they spoke the same language and shared the same beliefs, customs, and religious rituals?

That much seems reasonable. Since the Luka are certainly from Anatolia, it is reasonable to expect that most of the other Sea Peoples are also from Anatolia. The origin of the Luka

The Lukka

A reference to the Lukka appears in a letter found in the Egyptian archive at Tel Amarna and dating about 1350–1334 BC. In the letter it is noted that the Egyptians accused the king of Cyprus of supporting a Lukka raid on Egypt, a suggestion which the king strongly rejects. This is perhaps the earliest known record of an attack on Egypt by a people later recognized as among the Sea Peoples.

Lukka may have been mentioned substantially earlier. In Byblos on the coast of Syria, a small obelisk has been found containing an inscription. It appears to mention "Kukun, the son of the Lukkan." Kukun is Anatolian name, substantially the same as that of the father of Alaksandus (discussed in Chapter 5). As Kukun was an Anatolian, so must have been his father, the Lukkan. This obelisk has been dated to around 2000 BC.

The Egyptian records of the Battle of Kadesh list the contingents that took the field under the banner of Muwatalli, king of the Hittites. One of those contingents was the Lukka. Since the Luka or Lukka came south with the Hittite army, their homeland must lie somewhere in the region close to or under the control of the Hittites. A Hittite tablet from the time of Tudhaliya II (1390–1370 BC) contains a list of places on the west coast of Anatolia. Though the characters are partly illegible, the list seems to begin with the name *Lukk*, which is taken to refer to Lukka lands. If that has been correctly read, it suggests that the Lukka lived near the southwest coast of Anatolia.

The conflicts of the Hittites with the western country, Arzawa, drew Hittite armies westward on several occasions. Hittite records show that during the reign of the Hittite king Mursili, Lukka men sought refuge with Uhha-Ziti, the king of Arzawa. His failure to return these men to Hittite control when requested to do so precipitated a war which ended badly for him. Years later, another Hittite king marched against Piyama-Radu of Arzawa because Piyama-Radu had been raiding Lukka lands. It is apparent from these references that the Lukka were located somewhere not far from Arzawa. This also places the homeland of Lukka somewhere in southwestern Anatolia.

In *Iliad*, an Anatolian people called Lycians, *Lukioi* in Greek, are prominent allies of Troy. The Greeks of the Classical period knew them. They were inhabitants of a region which they called Lycia (pronounced *Lukia*) which was in the southwestern corner of Anatolia. The language of Lycia of the Classical period was a later development of Luvian as has been established from city names and personal names found on tombs in Lycia of the Classical period. That the Lycians (Lukioi) were descendants of the Lukka of the Bronze Age is very likely.

Archaeologists have looked, but have not found much in the way of Bronze Age remains in Lycia, and for this reason some have come to believe that Lycia was unpopulated in that period. They might look harder. Though Lycia is mountainous, it has many broad valleys that today contain fertile farms. The soils were just as fertile in the Bronze Age, and it is inconceivable that it did not support a large population at that time. Tudhaliya IV wrote to Ramesses II to report his successful raid against the Lukka, naming cities that he attacked. The names of those cities can be identified with known cities of Lycia of the Classical period, which demonstrates that Lycia was populated in the Late Bronze Age and constituted at least part of the Lukka territory.

The name "Lukka" is thought to be related to the word "Luvian," the name of their language, which is not surprising, since the name of a people and the name of their language are usually related. In Hittite times, the Luvian language was spoken in Arzawa, as is known from the names of Arzawa kings. In the Classical period, the Arzawa region was known to the Greeks as Lydia (pronounced Ludia), and this also suggests that the people of this region continued to speak Luvian into the Classical period. In the Bronze Age, Luvian was most likely spoken well to the east of Lycia a well. This is shown by a tablet found in the port city of Ugarit on the Syrian coast. The tablet lists names of various merchants of Ura, a port city on the southeast coast of Anatolia. Many of the names are Luvian.

Thus, there was a broad band of Luvian-speaking people along the western (Aegean) and southern (Mediterranean) coast of Anatolia. Further, there is an inland region to the northeast of Lycia which in the Classical period had the name Lycaonia. This name, like the name Lycia, may indicate the presence of speakers of the Luvian language. Hittite records imply that the northeast bound of the Lukka territory was in Lycaonia. Between Lycia and Lycaonia, there is Pisidia, and the Pisidians may have been Luvian speakers.

If by the term "Lukka," the Hittites were referring to any of those who spoke Luvian, then a wide region in Anatolia is indicated. It is likely, however, that the Hittites thought of Luvian-speaking people of Arzawa as Arzawans, and similarly for other politically organized groups of the region. Those whom they called Lukka appear to be people of unaffiliated villages and towns, probably in Lycia, Pisidia, or Lycaonia, or all of these together.

The Lukka were people of southwest Anatolia. From almost any location in the Lukka region, a man could march down to the sea in a few days at most, and from there take to the sea in piratical raids on wealthy lands such as Egypt. Alone of all of the Sea Peoples, the home region of the Lukka is known with reasonable certainty.

The Akwash

Scholars generally accept that the name "*Akwash*" or "*Akwasha*" is the Egyptian equivalent of *Achaean* of Homer and of *Ahhiyawa*, of the Hittite texts, except that Akwash is a group or ethnic name while Ahhiyawa is a place name. If that is valid, the Bronze Age Greeks are to be recognized as one of the Sea Peoples. According to the best reading of the numbers inscribed at Karnak, there were 1,213 Akwash casualties, and they were the largest group among the Sea Peoples, the core of this Sea Peoples force.

When E. Forrer proposed that the people of Ahhiyawa were the Achaeans of Homer's *Iliad* and *Odyssey*, linguists reacted with indignation and denial. The names could not be equivalent, they said. For decades, the debate raged, ending only with exhaustion of the issue. Everything that could be said had been said. Strangely, the idea that the Egyptian Achwash are Achaeans has been accepted with a large measure of composure, perhaps resignation, by scholars. Such easy acceptance is somewhat odd, considering that another pronunciation of the Egyptian hieroglyphic yields "Ekwesh" rather then "Akwash" or "Akwasha," and then the match with Achaean (or the theoretical "Akhaiwa" or similar term) is fainter.

Further, the Karnak inscriptions clearly imply that the Akwash or Ekwesh were circumcised. Hardly anyone thinks that the Greeks of the Bronze Age were circumcised, but of course, no one really knows. The easy acquiescence on the part of scholars to the view that Greeks were among the attackers probably derives from their familiarity with *Odyssey*. This tale is told by Odysseus as he returns from the Trojan War:

> …I had been home no more
> Than a month, enjoying my family and wealthy estate,
> When the spirit urged me to fit out some ships and set sail
> For Egypt, along with my godlike comrades. Nine ships
> In all were readied, and quickly the great crew gathered,
> For six days I furnished the food for my loyal companions,
> That they to the gods might sacrifice and prepare a feast
> For themselves. On the seventh day we boarded our ships
> And sailed from broad Crete, with the North Wind blowing fresh
> And so fair that we ran on before it as if we were headed
> Down stream. Not a ship was harmed and we sat there
> Safe and sound while the wind and the men at the helms
> Kept us straight on our course.
>   On the fifth day, we came to the great
> Egyptian river and there in that fair-flowing stream

> We moored our ships. Then I told my trusty companions
> To stay by the ships and guard them, and I sent some scouts
> To high vantage points to get the lay of the land.
> But the crews gave in to their wanton violence, and carried
> Away by their strength they began to pillage and plunder
> The fine Egyptian farms. They abducted the women
> and children and murdered the men. But their cries were heard
> In the city, and at dawn the whole plain was full of foot soldiers
> And chariots and the flashing of bronze. Then Zeus, the hurler
> Of lightning, filled my men with ignoble panic,
> And such were the dangers that pressed from all sides, that not
> One man had the courage to stay where he was and fight.
> Thus, with keen bronze, their men cut us down by the dozen,
> And they led up others to their city as slaves…(*Odyssey Book. 14*)

It is not known if this preserves a memory of the invasion of Egypt during the reign of Merneptah, or of other raids on Egypt by Greeks of the Bronze Age or even later.

It is certainly possible that the Akwash were Greeks, but which Greeks? Not only were there Greeks on the mainland, but also in Crete and on the Anatolian coast and the island of Rhodes just offshore. In their enclaves on the Anatolian coast, Greeks were neighbors of the Lukka, and they might have allied with Lukka in various ventures. Legends preserved by the Greeks remember close contacts with the Lukka or Lycians. A Lycian army restores the king of Tiryns on the Greek mainland to his rightful throne. Giants from Lycia build the massive walls of Tiryns. Best known is the story of Bellerophon, told in *Iliad*. He is sent from Tiryns to the king of Lycia. The kings of Tiryns and Lycia are related by marriage. As for the age of these stories, the citadel at Tiryns ceased to be occupied shortly after the end of the Bronze Age, and *Iliad* says that Bellerophon was of a time before the Trojan War. These tales are of the Bronze Age.

It is believable that Greeks from the Anatolian coast could have been caught up with their Lukka neighbors in events, whatever they may have been, which impelled them to sail for the coast of Libya or Egypt.

The Shekelesh

In Egyptian hieroglyphics, this group is represented as Sh-K-L-Sh or, since it is not known if the "l" or "r" sound is intended by the third symbol, possibly Sh-K-R-Sh. This last spelling is, for some reason, discounted by Egyptologists. "*Shekelesh*" or "*Shakalasha*" are the usual assumptions for vowel placement and vocalization (pronunciation). However, many years ago the gifted historian Gaston Maspero read the name slightly differently, as "*Shagalasha*," and there is probably no basis for dismissing his reading. That name immediately suggested something to him. High in the mountains of southern Anatolia, and not more than a few days trek from the sea, is the ancient city of Sagalassos, Figure 8-3. Here is the desired match of endings: Anatolian -*ossos* for Egyptian -*sha*.

The "-*assos*" ending is very ancient in Anatolia, and the name Sagalassos in some form may also be very ancient. Indeed, there is archaeological evidence that there was occupation in that locality before 2000 BC, and occupation is certain in the area in the Late Bronze Age. At that time, well before the city of Sagalassos existed, the name Sagalassos may have referred to villages of the region. In the Bronze Age, this was Lukka territory or at least adjacent to it, and the Shekelesh or Shagalasha may have been a tribe of the Lukka.

There is no reason why the Sagalassians of the Bronze Age could not or would not march down to the sea in a time of economic difficulties at home, and there join their Lukka brethren in the risky business of piracy. Piracy usually raises a picture of ships overtaken, boarded, treasure seized, victims held for ransom. In fact, the most devastating actions of pirates have been raids on defenseless coastal towns. Occasionally, pirates have been land fighters where the chance of gain was great. Such may have been the manner in which the men of Sagalassos found themselves in Egypt, if in fact they were the Sh-K-L-Sh, but that remains uncertain.

The Tursha

These people are named in the hieroglyphics as the T-R-Sh. *Tursha* or *Teresh* are the two favored vocalizations. Several possibilities exist which may identify these people as Anatolians, though admittedly, no absolutely convincing case can be made for any of them.

First to be considered are the Trojans and Troy. Troy appears in a Hittite record as "Taruisa" or perhaps "Taruisha," Chapter 5. (Hittite writing did not distinguish "*s*" from "*sh*.") It is a reasonable assumption that the people of Taruisa called themselves by some name close to this. Stripped of vowels so that it can be compared to the stripped Egyptian spelling, it would be T-R-S, or T-R-Sh. If the conflict now called the Trojan War had already taken place before this attack on Egypt—and this is an uncertain matter—many Trojan refugees could be expected, and some would attempt to survive by living by their wits and their swords. Agapenor, according to a legend of the Greeks, departed from Troy with a number of Trojan prisoners, was blown off-course to Cyprus, and later established a settlement in Libya. The legend of Teukros also had Trojans on the move into the Mediterranean as occupiers.

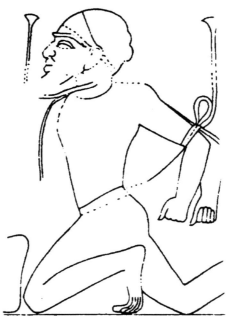

Figure 8-2. A "Tursha of the Sea" as he is called, shown as a captive. From Medinet Habu.

Second are the *Tyrsenians*, mentioned in two works of about 700 BC. In a poem known as *Hymn to Dionysus*, which tradition attributes to Homer, there appears the line "Presently there came swiftly over the sparkling sea Tyrsenian pirates on a well decked ship…" This name, "Tyrsenian" is the English rendering of the Greek "*Tursenoi*." In *Theogony*, a work by the poet Hesiod, these people are mentioned again. Those are the oldest references. A few hundred years later, the Classical period historians Herodotus and Thucydides mention them under the name "Tyrrhenians." The two different spellings arise from two different Greek dialects. Herodotus places these people in Lydia. Thucydides remarks that they were known to live on the island of Lesbos, offshore from Lydia. Lydia is the Classical period name for the land which in the Bronze Age was Arzawa, and possibly part of Seha River Land.

Tyrsenians are thus Anatolians, if the reports of the two historians are to be believed. However, the ancient historian Xanthus, himself a Lydian, reports nothing about Tyrsenians. Further, they are not mentioned in surviving Hittite records from the Bronze

Age, at least not by that name. However, these are not overwhelming evidence against the possibility that such people lived near the west coast of Anatolia in the Bronze Age.

It is these Tyrsenians, or their ancestors of the Bronze Age, who have been sometimes acclaimed as the Tursha who attacked Egypt. The main justification is the name. In the name Tursenoi, the "-*enoi*" is thought to be an ending which serves as an ethnic designator. "Turse" is thus the core of the name, and stripped of vowels it is T-R-S. That the Tyrsenians were pirates in the Classical period suggests that their Bronze Age ancestors may also have been sea-raiders.

Figure 8-3. Sites of destruction or survival, and of possible Sea Peoples' origin.

The third possibility shifts the geographic focus to the southeast coast of Anatolia. In a Hittite record containing a list of cities which contributed certain religious offerings, the names "Kummanni, Zunnahara, Adaniya, Tarsa…" appear together. These last two are with little doubt the cities of Adana and Tarsus, and thus it is certain that the city of Tarsus was in existence in the Bronze Age. If the Egyptians were to ask a man of Tarsus where he came from, he might point in a northerly direction and answer "from Tarsa," or "Tarsha," or "Tarssas." This answer would be written down by the Egyptians as T-R-S or T-R-Sh. Tarsus is close to the coast, and in later times an important port, Figure 9-2. Its people took easily to the sea. Tarsus is but a few hundred miles by ship from the coasts of the

Lukka—not a great distance even in those times—and there were probably frequent contact between these peoples.

Close by Tarsus is Adana, and from Adana, a later group of Sea Peoples was to sail forth. That the people of Adana could take to the sea as raiders makes it likely that their close neighbors of Tarsus would do the same.

Merneptah Points to Anatolia

The Karnak inscriptions provide an interesting note or clue on the origin of these Sea Peoples. Much of the inscription is damaged, and in the following exerpt, [.....] indicates illegible or missing words.

> They come to the land of Egypt to seek the necessities of their mouths; their desire is [.....] my bringing them like netted fish on their bellies. Their chief is like a dog, a man of boasting, without courage; he does not abide [.....] bringing to an end the Pedetishew whom I caused to bring grain in ships to keep alive the land of Kheta. (*Egyptian Ancient Records*)

"Kheta" is the Egyptian rendering of the name "Hatti," the land of the Hittites. It is not known who the "Pedetishew" were, but apparently they are involved in shipping. Here, Merneptah states that the Hittites are in a famine. The Egyptians are keeping Kheta alive, it seems, by sending grain. Now, for some reason—and the reason most likely is associated with the presence of the Sea Peoples among the Libyans—someone has brought the relief shipments to an end. Most likely it was Merneptah. For some reason, Merneptah seems to be blaming the Hittites!

It is unlikely that Hittites were in the Libyan forces that attacked Egypt or they would have been mentioned. It is inconceivable that the Hittite king backed or instigated the Sea Peoples' attack on Egypt. The Hittites, one may be sure, had more than enough worries close to home. Risking a diplomatic incident with Egypt, with whom they had long been at peace, is impossible to imagine. That peace was established years before, between Ramesses II and King Hattusili, after they had time to reflect on the lessons of the Battle of Kadesh. A "summit" meeting had taken place between these two kings, to affirm the peace. A daughter of Hattusili was married to Ramesses. It was a true peace, it lasted, and it benefited both sides.

The reason that Merneptah blamed the Hittites can most reasonably be understood in the following way. Merneptah believed that the Sea Peoples came from Anatolia. Presumably, he would have had some good reason for that belief. The lands of western and southern Anatolia were part of a Hittite empire. At least, that was the Hittite view of things and that view would be accepted by the Egyptians. Egypt would expect not only that the

Hittites would not attack them, but also that no people under Hittite control would be allowed to do so. Merneptah may not have known, or cared, that Hittite control in the West was an increasingly uncertain matter. Theirs was the responsibility for maintaining order in Anatolia. King Tudhaliya IV had led his armies into Lukka and reset matters in Millawanda and Seha River Land. The need for those actions indicated that all was not well, not truly under control. That there may have been a widespread famine in the west is a definite possibility, and such a situation could lead to social disintegration. Many in Anatolia would feel impelled to leave, to take a wild gamble rather than face the certainty of starvation. This may be the background for the attack on Egypt.

In a monument called the Merneptah Stela or the Israel Stela (Chapter 13), an extended text praises Merneptah and his deeds, particularly those of the Libyan War. One line seems to relate to a connection between Anatolia and the Sea Peoples attack. In free translation, it is "Libya is desolated and the Hittite world is at peace." As the whole monument is given to praise of Merneptah, he seems to be taking credit for peace in the Hittite world. By a stretch of the Egyptian imagination, the defeat of the Sea Peoples in Egypt might have been seen as sapping the military strength of those who were revolting against the Hittites in western or southern Anatolia.

As shown above, each of the Sea Peoples can be related to some region of Anatolia. Over three thousand years have passed since their time, most of the evidence is forever gone, and admittedly the case made for each is not overwhelmingly strong. But it becomes more persuasive when it is seen that not just one but most, perhaps all, can be accounted for as a people of the Anatolian soil. That Merneptah pointed his finger at the Hittites, and that the Lukka are assuredly from Anatolia, are good reasons to believe that this generation of Sea Peoples came from Anatolia.

That some of the Sea People homelands mentioned are inland does not mean that men would hesitate to go down to the sea. It is likely that for years men left the mountain valleys with their limited resources to take up the life of the sea. It may have been a tradition in many upland villages. Seamanship may have been second nature to those who were otherwise farmers. In the last century, in New England, in the days of sail, a steady stream of men from rural farms and villages, some many miles inland, took their chances with the sea.

Western Anatolians of the coast were probably occasional sailors or fishermen. They probably traded on an informal basis with the many settlements on the shores of the Aegean and Mediterranean. Swooping down on some coastal city in a piratical raid was also likely part of their tradition. Experience at sea, visits to other ports where one heard of great gain to be made in Egypt, a taste for piracy—all of these would have been perfect preparation.

There are over one thousand miles of coastline in western Anatolia, with many hidden coves and harbors. If determined men were to push off from these secret places, bound for Libya or Egypt, what local king could stop them?

Who Are the Libyans?

Judging by the invective heaped upon them and pictorial space allocated to them on Egyptian monuments, no people were more detested by Egyptians than the Libyans. Sweeping out of arid lands to the west, attacking, marauding, and fading into the desert waste, they were, after a time, an almost constant menace. The Nile Delta and valley were densely populated, but immediately to the west was a no-man's-land where Libyans roamed freely. Egyptian western borders were long, porous, essentially indefensible.

It is only from Egyptian records that the Libyans of the Bronze Age are known, and the information available concerning them is scanty. They are evident in Egyptian records as far back as 1900 BC. They are mentioned by Egyptian kings Amenhotep III (1386–1350 BC) and Akhenaton (1350–1334 BC), and are more extensively mentioned by Ramesses II, Merneptah, and Ramesses III. There were several Libyan groups of which two are particularly significant, the Meshwesh and the Libu. The Greeks were familiar with the Libu, or at least the name, from which the name Libya comes. "Libyans," as the term is used here, refers to various western groups—Libu, Meshwesh, and others.

The homeland of these Libyans was somewhere to the west of the Delta. The most likely home region for at least some of them is what in the time of the Roman empire was called Cyrenaica, near the location of the present-day city of Benghasi. Here, the environment is less severe than elsewhere, and there is grazing for the goats and sheep which were the mainstay of the life of the Libyans. As pastoralists, they might often have gone to Egypt to sell their herds. That would have brought them to the Delta or the upper Nile. Some Libyans had worked in Egypt, in menial jobs and in the army, and the experience opened the eyes to the wealth of the land. Army experience taught them contemporary military skills. They took this knowledge with them when they returned home.

Drought is a recurring theme in the ancient world. The need to relieve the effects of drought and famine, and the ambitions of Libyan leaders stimulated by what many of them had seen in Egypt, were probably behind the Libyan assaults.

Scenes of combat with Libyans are shown in sculptural reliefs on the walls of several Egyptian temples. Whether the king was Seti I, Ramesses II, or Ramesses III (Merneptah left no illustrations), the visual message is the same: terrible defeat for the Libyans. They are cut down by Pharaoh's arrows, crushed beneath the wheels of his chariot, run through by the swords of his soldiers. Hands or phalli are cut off and heaped up. If he is still alive, the Libyan is dragged before the statues of the Egyptian gods. His fate can be imagined.

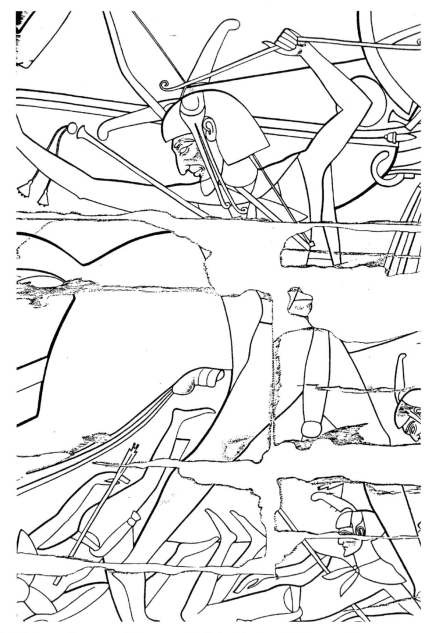

Figure 8-4. A Libyan, from a relief on a wall of the Medinet Habu temple.

From these sculptural reliefs and from ceramic tiles from the Medinet Habu temple which show them, the appearance of Libyans is unmistakable, and remarkably uniform,

Figure 8-4. The well-trimmed beard begins along the lower edge of the jaw and runs down to the chin and terminates in a short point. A mustache runs down along the cheeks and merges with the beard. Hair is thick and straight and sweeps smoothly over the back of the head behind the ear and down. It is cut straight across at mid-neck. A braided or curled lock starts at the top of the head and drops down in front of the ear to shoulder level. It is difficult to tell from the reliefs, which present only one side of the figure, but there is probably a lock on both sides.

Some Libyans are shown with one or two feathers tied in the hair. Over one shoulder a robe is tied, and this robe drapes under the opposite shoulder and drops down along that side of the body to the ankle. An illustrated tile shows such a robe in color. It is richly decorated with scalloped forms and colorful blossom patterns. A cape is tied around the neck and hangs over the back and is also decorated. The arms are bare and tattooed, and sometimes the legs are tattooed also.

Many Libyans wore a kilt as a basic covering. The kilt was a patterned fabric wrapped tight around the hip that fell to about knee level. Alternatively, the Libyan may wore a phallus sheath. This was a sock-like affair fixed to a belt and descending down the front. It is not certain, but those who wore the phallus sheath may have been Meshwesh.

On certain sculptural reliefs, some of the original painted color still remains. From the color, it is evident that Libu were fair-skinned, blue-eyed, and blond or redheaded. Because of this supposed "European" look, it has been suggested that these people were invaders of European origin. Whatever their origin, such people may have been in the region since the distant past. A daughter of Pharaoh Khufu (2500 BC) is pictured with fair skin and blond hair, which may indicate that such traits were long present in the region.

In total, the Libyan looked like no one else illustrated in ancient art. It is thought that the Berbers of the present day are their descendants.

As fighters, the Libyans were not entirely a chaotic mob. There was some degree of organization in their fighting force. There were specialists in various weapons and a there were a limited number of chariots. The bow was one of their weapons. Though it may seem primitive, the bow is lethal within its range against an enemy who was not armored, or only partially armored. The most surprising weapon in Libyan hands was the sword, and the most surprising thing about it was its length. The blade was dagger-shaped, with two straight edges running directly from the hilt to the point. Based on illustrations of the sculptural reliefs, the length was more than the distance from shoulder to the tip of outstretched fingers—perhaps 30 inches. This shape and this length was characteristic of so-called thrusting swords in use for centuries in Crete and Greece, and it is reasonable that the swords were made for the Libyan trade by specialists from one of those countries, perhaps on Bates Island. While this sword was employed as a rapier—a thrusting weapon—it could also be deadly in a slashing attack against those not wearing good armor. The Egyptians had nothing quite like it. They used the short curved scimitar.

These long swords of the Libyans gave them an advantage. Their more numerous chariots gave the Egyptians a bigger advantage. In the end, superior Egyptian chariots, numbers, and training probably made the difference and gave Egypt the victory.

9
INVADERS AND THE HITTITE EVIDENCE

The end of Hittite power came with surprising suddenness. Suppiluliuma II (1205–? BC) is the last known king in Hattusa. The date of his death is unknown. In contrast to the extensive records that the Hittites produced earlier, the collapse and the years following are enveloped in complete silence. Kings of other lands no longer mention the great Hittite power which once ruled from the Anatolian plateau. Only the Egyptians noted the end, a terse notice in an inscription on the wall of the mortuary temple of Ramesses III at Medinet Habu. Thus, the situation which prevailed, and the circumstances which marked the end of Hittite control over a vast empire are a deep mystery.

From their base on the Anatolian plateau, Hittite kings had ruled for centuries, practicing deft diplomacy or leading forth powerful armies. Hittites marched to the west, to the Aegean Sea, and overthrew Arzawa as an independent power. They placed handpicked kings on the thrones of the western Anatolian states. In the East, Hittite armies met and overwhelmed the Hurrian land of Mitanni, rolled over the small states of Syria, and matched arms with Egypt at Kadesh. For a time, they may have directly controlled Cyprus. Following Kadesh, there were only two major land powers, Egypt and Hatti. These were the superpowers of those times. Now there was only Egypt, and Egypt would soon sink into a strange decline.

Archaeologists have unearthed stark evidence of the end of the Hittites. The city of Hattusa itself provides the clearest example. According to Kurt Bittel, the archaeologist in charge of excavations at Hattusa for many years, "…clear signs of disaster have been found everywhere in the royal citadel. Not a single building was spared and the surface of streets and open squares was found covered with thick layers of charred wood and mud brick reddened by fire" (Bittel, 1983). It is difficult to imagine what enemy could have penetrated into this city and its citadel, defended as it was by what must have been the strongest defensive walls of any city of the Bronze Age. But the end was complete. No Hittite king rebuilt. There is no sign of Hittite reoccupation of Hattusa after this destruction, and the site may have been unoccupied for generations, perhaps centuries, after.

Other Hittite cities of the plateau appear to have met the same fate. Alaca Hoyuk about 15 miles north of Hattusa, Figure 9-1, was built up as a bulwark against the Kaska. It came to an end in a fiery catastrophe. To the east at Masat are the remains of another Hittite fortress-city, another bulwark against the Kaska. Here, the Hittite palace shows every evidence of a disastrous fire. South of Hattusa, in the remains of a city at Fraktin, there is evidence of a catastrophic fire. To the southwest of Hattusa, at Karaoglan near the present-day city of Ankara, are remains of a Hittite city that also underwent a terrible destruction. Bittel believes that these events occurred at about the same time and are related.

It appears that many cities in central Anatolia which were not destroyed were simply abandoned. The name Karaoglan, for example, is Turkish. The original Hittite name is not known. In Anatolia, in places away from the Hittite heartland, the names of several Bronze Age cities continued in use into the Classical period, when they were recorded by Greek and Roman geographers. That these names from the Bronze Age survived indicates that there was continuous occupation. There were always people present who would pass the original name on to the next generation of occupants, or the next conquerors. But few Bronze Age city names survived on the Anatolian plateau, indicating that their abandonment was lengthy and complete.

Not all Hittite cities were affected by these catastrophic events, however. In the west, certain Hittite cities show no evident destruction. South of the Hittite heartland on the Anatolian plateau was Tarhuntassa, established as a subkingdom for Kurunta by King Hattusili III (1264–1239 BC). Cities of Tarhuntassa appear to have survived. Whatever it was that struck the Hittite heartland apparently spared Tarhuntassa. The eastern city of Karahoyuk also survived. Farther east was the Hittite sub-kingdom of Kargamish. The city of Kargamish had been conquered by Suppiluliuma I (1344–1322 BC), who placed one of his sons on the throne. Kargamish and many of its subordinate cities survived, including Milid (Malatya) and Aleppo (Halab). But Ugarit on the Syrian coast met its end, and there is evidence of fire at Tarsus and Mersin on the Anatolian south coast.

Thus, the Hittite empire which Suppiluliuma I established had come completely apart, destroyed at its center. The oldest segment, the Hatti land, the core of empire, was gone, leaving the remaining parts disjointed, isolated, without strength or leadership.

Date of the Hittite Collapse

The Hittites did not, of course, report their own demise, or publish their own obituary. The exact date and circumstances of the end of Hittite imperial power are unknown. The time of the end can be bracketed, however, with the help of texts found by archaeologists in the ruins of Ugarit, augmented by temple inscriptions in Egypt.

In Ugarit, archaeologists have found extensive archives, with documents written in cuneiform on clay tablets. These included file copies of incoming and outgoing correspondence. Many are damaged and the texts are only partly readable. None contains dates. Many lack the name of the sender or the addressee. One of these tablets records a letter sent to Ugarit by Beya, a high official in Egypt. His term in office in Egypt is datable within narrow bounds, between 1193 and 1185 BC. Thus, the end of Ugarit could not have been earlier than the earliest date of Beya in office, 1193 BC. It may well have been later.

Another letter in the Ugarit archives provides a time link between the collapse of the Hittites and the end of Ugarit. Among the most remarkable of Ugarit tablets were several found in an oven, or kiln, where they had been placed for baking to render them permanent. The palace official who placed them in the oven never recovered them. The catastrophe which destroyed Ugarit intervened. These tablets mark the very last days of Ugarit. One tablet, though seriously damaged and not fully legible, appears to be a letter from a Hittite king to Ammurapi, king of Ugarit. If this Hittite king was the Great King in Hattusa and not the king in Kargamish (Ammurapi was subordinate to both), then the Great King of the Hittites was still ruling at the time of the fall of Ugarit. With that assumption, it appears that the Hittite king was still in power in 1193 BC, and perhaps for some years later. More will be said of the fate of Ugarit at the end of this chapter.

Next, there is the Egyptian inscription of Ramesses III mentioned earlier. On the wall of his temple at Medinet Habu, the end of the Hittites was reported. Since there is no other textual information reporting the end, historians tend to accept the word of Ramesses. The Hittite empire had expired by the time that the inscription was made. The temple at Medinet Habu may have been completed by 1165 BC and the texts for the temple walls could have been open to new information or to changes until perhaps 1170 BC. Thus, from circumstantial evidence, it appears that the Hittite empire collapsed at some time after 1193 BC but before 1170 BC.

At a time when the Hittites were beset by enemies on all sides, a brilliant and successful leader, Suppiluliuma I (1344–1322 BC), marched his armies to the west and to the southeast. He resoundingly defeated Hatti's enemies, and in the process established the Hittite empire. It is likely that the last king, Suppiluliuma II, chose his throne name with a purpose. He would emulate the great Suppiluliuma I. That statement would only have meaning if Hatti was beset by serious troubles such that a saving leader was required. Suppiluliuma II did deal with many enemies. But in the end, he failed. The empire that began with the first Suppiluliuma came to an end under the second.

A Search for the Enemy

There are few solid clues that can explain the end of the Hittites. In spite of this, and perhaps because of it, certain theories have been developed which are sometimes presented as established and undeniable fact. Many writings dealing with the history of those times speak of the "migrations," or the "great migrations." The direct agent of the Hittite destruction is often held to be one particular people of the migrations, the Phrygians. According to this "Phrygian Theory" as it may be called, Phrygians crossed from Europe to Anatolia, perhaps near Troy, and thrust themselves into the heartland of the Hittites. That there was any such a great migration from Europe is very far from certain. The Greek component of the broader migration theory, in which it is supposed that northern invaders destroyed Mycenaean civilization, is not supported by direct evidence. The Sea Peoples, who are often said to be part of the migration, and who were presumably cohorts of the invading Phrygians, were likely not Europeans at all. Still, in view of the widespread acceptance of the Phrygian Theory, it is useful to examine the evidence of invaders.

Phrygians

With the end of Hittite records, there is no further information concerning the western Anatolian states. No more is heard and nothing is known of the fate of the kingdoms of Arzawa, Seha River, Wilusa. Centuries later, Greeks adopted and adapted Phoenician alphabetic script to the Greek language. *Iliad* and *Odyssey* were committed to writing. In *Iliad*, Phrygians are mentioned. They were allies of Troy during the Trojan War, according to *Iliad*, and their home was along the Sangarius River to the east of Troy. Priam, king of Troy, was married to a Phrygian princess. He relates that in his youth he fought alongside the Phrygians:

> Years ago I visited Phrygia rife with vineyards
> saw the Phrygian men with their swarming horses there-
> multitudes-the armies of Otreus, Mygdon like a god,
> encamped that time along the Sangarius River banks.
> And I took my stand among them, comrade-in-arms… (*Iliad* Book 3)

Greeks of later years knew of the Phrygians and their capital at Gordion, a city by the Sangarius. Gordion was the stuff of legend, a rich city, and the home of King Midas, he of the Golden Touch.

The site of Gordion has been intensively excavated, and perhaps the most striking find is the so-called Tomb of Midas, a buried chamber lined in depth with wood beams and meant to resist the ages. A good deal of pottery was also found during the Gordion excavation, pitchers and bowls and pottery in goat or bird shapes. Much of the pottery is richly and skillfully painted in checkerboard and other patterns, or with animal figures. Intricately fashioned metal pitchers and bowls were found. These were treasures for a king. In addition, there were less elaborate ceramics for humbler use. All of these objects are considered to be Phrygian. Other Phrygian sites have been excavated near Ankara, Bogazkoy, Masat, and Fraktin, all locations of onetime Hittite cities.

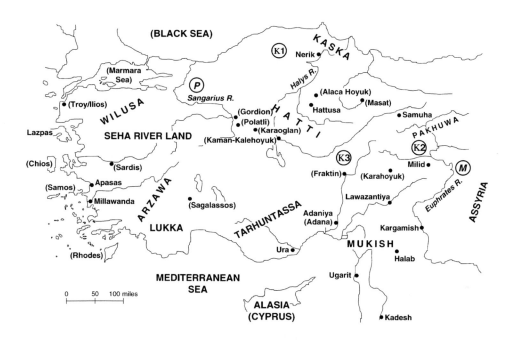

Figure 9-1. Positions of Phrygians, Kaska, and Mushki in various historical records.

Since Greek legend tells that the Phrygians were migrants or invaders from Europe, and Greeks also reported that they were spread over much of inner Anatolia, there can be little wonder that modern scholars point an accusing finger at the Phrygians. Their arrival marks the end of the Hittites.

How sound is this Phrygian Theory? In part, it depends on the time of arrival of the Phrygians in Anatolia. It needs to be shown that Phrygians arrived in Anatolia and were present in or near the Hittite homeland close to the time that the Hittite world collapsed, shortly before 1170 BC. There is a problem here. None of the elaborate tombs, colorful pottery, and skilled metalwork found in Gordion or those other sites with evidence of Phrygians, have been shown to be any earlier than about 800 BC. Obviously, that date is too late by almost four hundred years.

Excavations at Gordion have reached deeper and hence earlier levels. In those early levels, there is evidence of an earlier pottery. Shapes are recognizably Phrygian, like the pottery of the period after 800 BC. This earlier pottery appears suddenly in the archaeological strata, indicating a newly arrived people, and it is reasonable to believe that they were the ancestors of the Phrygians. Excavators believe that the pottery, and the people who made it, came to Gordion about 1000 BC. That date seems to be too late by almost two hundred years to account for the end of the Hittites.

Support for the Phrygian Theory has been sought in the records of the Assyrians—in reports of battles with a people called "Mushki."

Assyria had been quiet on the international scene for a number of years following the assassination of Assyrian king Tukulti-Ninurta (1244–1208 BC), but now a new king, Tiglath-Pileser I (1116–1093 BC), was on the move. He saw a tempting opportunity to assert Assyrian power and authority along the northern Euphrates where the Hittites once ruled. With his armies, he marched to the region marked **M** on Figure 9-1, his purpose to punish the Mushki. Tiglath-Pileser wanted to be sure that future generations appreciated his martial valor and ferocity, and he had inscribed:

> In the beginning of my reign, twenty thousand men of the land of Mushki and their five kings, who for fifty years had held the lands of Alzi and Purukuzzi [small regions near the upper Euphrates River whose location is only approximately known], which in the past had paid tribute and tax unto my lord Assur [the primary Assyrian god]— and no king had vanquished them in battle—in their own strength they had trusted and came down and seized the land of Kutmuhi. With the help of my lord Assur I gathered my chariots and my troops. I looked not behind me. Mount Kutmuhi, a difficult region, I traversed. With their twenty thousand warriors and their five kings I fought in the land of Kutmuhi and I defeated them. The corpses of their warriors I hurled down in the destructive battle like the Storm-god. Their blood I caused to flow in the valleys and on the high places of the mountains. I cut off their heads and outside their cities like heaps of grain I piled them up. Their spoil, their goods, and their possessions, in countless number I brought out. I carried off six thousand men, the remainder of their troops, who had fled from before my weapons and embraced my feet, I counted them as inhabitants of my land. (*Ancient Records of Assyria*)

Some historians believe, rightly or wrongly, that the Mushki (or Muski) that Tiglath-Pileser defeated were Phrygians. If that is so, it would place Phrygians at **M** around 1165 BC. If they came out of Europe, they may have been in the West, at **P**, even earlier, perhaps at the time of the destructions of Hittite cities. Substantial numbers of them may then have migrated across Anatolia, and in their movement from west to east, **P** to **M**, they may have overrun the Hittites and the Hittite capital of Hattusa.

One reason for the belief that Mushki were Phrygians is the supposed resemblance of the name "*Muski*" to "*Musoi*." These Musoi (Mysians) were a people known from *Iliad*, dwellers close to the Phrygians in the West, near Troy. From that proximity, it is but a step to assume that the Musoi were a branch or tribe of the Phrygians. The name of the later legendary king of the Phrygians, "Midas," he of the Golden Touch, is used to further buttress that assumption. As late as 700 BC, more than three hundred years after their encounter with Tiglath-Pileser I, there were still Mushki in the East. They joined an alliance against the Assyrians and, in what seems a repeat of earlier history, an Assyrian king attacked them. The name of the Mushki king whom the Assyrians attacked was Mita.

Are Mita and Midas one and the same? The time periods of Mita and Midas coincide well enough, and the difference in spelling does not stand in the way. Is it possible that this king ruled one people known as Phrygians in the West and Mushki in the East? Again, some historians assume so, and this assumption is taken to support the view that the Mushki of the time of Tiglath-Pileser were Phrygians.

This complex web of evidence, assumptions, and conjectures is aimed at demonstrating the complicity of the Phygians in the overthrow of the Hittites, primarily by demonstrating that they were at the right place at the right time. The evidence, however, is substantially weaker than might appear.

In the area where Tiglath-Pileser I attacked the Mushki, archaeological research produces evidence of the sudden appearance of many new villages in the Late Bronze Age, and in those villages a new type of pottery. This may be evidence of the Mushki and their recent arrival in the region. But the pottery is completely unlike any Phrygian pottery. In fact, the home of this pottery is in the Caucasus mountains to the northeast, and not in the West where the Phrygians lived. This newly settled people came from the Caucasus, it seems, not Europe.

As for the name Mita, it is certain that it was not introduced to the East by invading Phrygians. A Hittite record from the reign of King Arnuwanda I (1370–1355 BC) tells of a king of Pakhuwa. That king displeased the Hittites by marrying the daughter of an enemy. The Hittites leveled accusations against him. The name of this king was Mita. Pakhuwa, his homeland, was in the East close to the region where some years later Tiglath-Pileser attacked the Mushki. Mita of Pakhuwa lived close to two hundred years before the end of the Hittites, and thus it is certain that the name "Mita" was already at home in eastern Anatolia long before the end of the Hittites. If the name Mita does not come from the Phrygians, then there remains little or nothing to suggest that the Mushki were Phrygians, and little or nothing to demonstrate that the Phrygians had overrun Anatolia in the time of the Hittites.

The close similarity of the names Midas and Mita may be explained differently. Sometime in the years after 1000 BC, quite possibly a Mita dynasty among the Mushki in the east may have established itself over the Phrygians who were not far to the west of Mushki territory. The Greeks would have called a king Mita by the name Midas.

Before the Phrygians

The Phrygians arrived too late to influence the fate of the Hittites. However, there is evidence of a still earlier people who settled in Gordion. Deep Bronze Age levels at Gordion yield typical Hittite pottery. But in a layer directly above, and therefore later than the Hittites but earlier than the Phrygians, there is something distinctive. It is a coarse pottery which is roughly made without use of the potter's wheel. Excavators at Gordion refer to this pottery as "Handmade Ware." It is gray and decorated with rows of incisions along the rim, or with rows of depressions created by pressing the still wet clay with the fingertip. In all of these characteristics, the pottery is different from Hittite and Phrygian pottery and is similar to the mysterious "Coarse Ware" of Greece, Chapter 6. The presence of this Handmade Ware suggests the arrival of a new people, taking up residence along side the previous Hittite population, or more likely coming after them.

At Kaman-Kalehoyuk southeast of Ankara, a Japanese team which is excavating the ruins found similar pottery, apparently of similar date. In the remains of the VIIb city at Troy, very similar pottery was found alongside traditional Trojan pottery. Carl Blegen, the excavator at Troy, estimates that whoever brought this coarse pottery to Troy came one or two generations after the renewal of the city following the destruction of Troy VIIa. Like Coarse Ware of Greece, Handmade Ware of Anatolia may derive ultimately from Europe north or east of Greece. Applying an educated guess, excavators at Gordion place the pottery in the period 1100–1000 BC.

That date is understood to be the period in which the users of this pottery spread into western Anatolia. That would be too late to affect the fate of the Hittites. Very little Handmade Ware has been found thus far in Gordion in any case, which suggests that the users were not a very numerous people. They are unlikely to have constituted the great horde that might have overwhelmed the Hittites, and there is no archaeological evidence of their pottery or their presence in Hattusa at the time of the destruction or directly after. At Gordion, Kaman-Kalehoyuk and Troy, there is no evidence of destruction associated with the beginning of this pottery, which may mean that the arrival was a peaceful one. The presence of Handmade Ware in Gordion, Kaman, and Troy, and similar pottery in Greece is fascinating and unexplained, but one thing is clear: the people who made and used the pottery were not the destroyers of the Hittites.

Kaska

There was a people long resident in northern Anatolia who had the will and capacity to wreak havoc in the Hittite homeland: the Kaska. Kaska raids must have unnerved many a Hittite king. During the reigns of either Tudhaliya II (1390–1370 BC) or Tudhaliya III (1355–1344 BC)—records do not make clear which king it was—Kaska entered and burned Hattusa. At that time, Hattusa was not yet surrounded by the seemingly invincible double walls that it had later. During the reign of Arnuwanda I (1370–1355 BC), Kaska overran Hittite lands in the north of Hattusa and they stayed there for years. The Hittites offered prayers. Would the gods punish these Kaska? King Mursili (1331–1295 BC) also fought them.

It was for good reason that Muwatalli II (1295–1271 BC), in preparation for the coming conflict with Egypt, moved the capital to the south, out of the reach of the Kaska. Hattusa was left with only a garrison and a few elements of local government. Sensing weakness, Kaska again attacked and occupied Hittite lands north of Hattusa, driving Hittite refugees before them. The king's able younger brother, the future king Hattusili, was sent to restore order and reestablish a Hittite population in the region. Tudhaliya IV (1239–1209 BC) declared the Kaska land to be enemy territory. The Kaska were a continuing problem for the Hittites.

Tiglath-Pileser was the aggressive Assyrian king mentioned earlier, who lived shortly after the fall of the Hittite Empire. He attacked Milid, a city still under the control of Kargamish. He reported:

> I took my valiant warriors who wage relentless war to the finish and marched against the land of Mildish [Milid] with its haughty and insubmissive people ....I was as bold as a lion and advanced triumphantly over the summits of the steep mountains. I overwhelmed the land of Mildish so it was like a heap of ruins after a flood. I beat down their warriors in the midst of battle like a gust of wind. Their spoil, property, and goods I carried off. All their cities I burned with fire. I took hostages, and tribute and taxes I laid upon them.

Tiglath-Pileser then encountered the Kaska. "Hatti," as he employed the term, now referred to Kargamish and its subordinate territories and cities.

> Through my own valor, and because Assur, the lord, had put into my hand a mighty weapon which subdues the insubmissive, and commanded me to extend the frontiers of his land, four thousand Kaski and Urumi, soldiers of the land of Hatti, who were in revolt, and had seized the cities of the land of Shubarti [near the upper Euphrates] cities subject to Assur my lord. They heard of my coming against the land of Shubarti, the brilliance of my valor overwhelmed them. They were

afraid to fight and so they embraced my feet. These men together with their chariots and yolked teams I seized and counted them as inhabitants of my land.

(Ancient Records of Assyria)

The location of the battle (<u>K2</u> of Figure 9-1) was near the Turkish city of Elazig. In records of many centuries later, the Assyrians report that a Kaska group was settled at <u>K3</u>, near the Turkish city of Kayseri. It appears that it was from these facts that Kurt Bittel came to a conclusion. Writing of the Kaska he said:

> From the Pontic [Black Sea] area they repeatedly raided the Hittite lands, at least once even capturing the capital, and probably also played a role in the final fall of Hattusha. If we now in the 8th century BC, find them so far advanced to the south, all the way from the Halys bend in the west to the upper Euphrates to the east-in an area which had always been the immediate objective of their southward ambitions—we may reasonably interpret this as a result of their successful collaboration in the destruction of Hatti. *(Archaologische Situation)*

The southern locations to which Bittel refers are, presumably, <u>K2</u> and <u>K3</u>. Here Bittel uses "Hatti" to mean the Hittite homeland, the region around Hattusa. He formulates what can be called the "Kaska Theory" to account for the end of the Hittites.

This claim merits a closer look. The implication of Bittel's comment is that the Kaska attacked Hattusa and other Hittite cities, overran them, and proceeded south and southeast to lands from which they had been previously blocked by the presence of the Hittites. In map terms, this means that the Kaska, starting from their home region, <u>K1</u>, advanced to <u>K2</u> and <u>K3</u> by overrunning the Hittites. Based as it is on geographical logic, this theory is a near duplicate of the Phrygian Theory.

There are other ways, however, to understand the presence of Kaska in those last two localities. In a time shortly before Hittite King Suppiluliuma I (1344–1322 BC), Hittite control on the Anatolian plateau had fallen apart. Kaska overran the Hittite capital of Hattusa and settled at <u>K3</u>. From his base in Samuha, Suppiluliuma counterattacked and regained all of the lost lands and more, defeating the Kaska in the process. It is not known what happened to those Kaska. Hittite policy was to conciliate Kaska wherever possible. If they were willing to accept a treaty of subservience, the Hittites might well have left those Kaska where they were. If that happened, by the time of Tiglath-Pileser, Kaska would have long been settled south of the Halys River. It is certain that there were some Kaska who were loyal to the Hittites and who were in the Hittite forces at Kadesh. It was perhaps these Kaska.

After the collapse of Hittite power, the king of Kargamish would have every incentive to hold together and defend what he would deem to be one of the last bastions of Hittite civilization. He still controlled Milid. He might have employed Kaska and others in its defense, Kaska who were already settled close by, and who presumably were an established part of his domain. Tiglath-Pileser refers to "four thousand Kaska and Urumi, soldiers of the land of Hatti," which seems to confirm that the Kaska were in the military forces of Kargamish. Similarly, those Kaska whom a later Assyrian king encountered at **K3** may have been descendants of Kaska settled in those regions, well before the Hittite collapse.

In summary, the presence of Kaska south of the Hittite homeland is no proof that the Kaska overran and destroyed the Hittites. The absence of acceptable proof is regrettable, because it is likely that Kaska had a hand in the destruction. Many of the destroyed cities are close to the Kaska homeland in the north and the Hittites were always vulnerable to Kaska attacks.

Years earlier, when lands had been overrun and the capital at Hattusa burned by Kaska marauders, the Hittites resisted and recovered. A time could have come, however, when the Hittites were so weakened, due to circumstances yet to be identified, that they might no longer recover from a major Kaska attack.

The Westerners

For centuries, certain leaders in western Anatolia attempted to throw off Hittite domination, or actively opposed the Hittites. An Arzawa army threatened Hattusa itself once, and perhaps more than once. The names of those defiant leaders—Madduwatta, Uhha-Ziti, and Piyama-Radu—can be recalled. Thus, it is possible that a Western army swept eastward and destroyed Hattusa and Hittite power. A serious weakness among the Hittites may have been detected and which may have become widely known, and may have been an invitation for an attack. There was such a weakness or vulnerability, as will be discussed in the next chapter.

With the cessation of Hittite records, there is silence concerning events in the West. Archaeology also is silent, or nearly so. Hittite sites at Gordion and Polatli, located between the west coast and Hattusa, show no evidence of destruction. However, as noted earlier, Hittite Karaoglan was destroyed. The greatest destruction was in Hattusa and cities nearby. The pattern of destruction does not suggest an attack launched out of Arzawa or another western state, but does not disprove it either.

If rebellious Arzawans or other forces from the West put an end to the Hittites, finally accomplishing what their ancestors had attempted for centuries, Arzawa should have stood forth as the new dominant state in Anatolia. And yet, after the fall of Hattusa, nothing more is ever heard of Arzawa, or for that matter Seha River Land and most other states of the West. The oblivion is perfect and complete. No later Egyptian or Assyrian records acknowledge these states. No legends tell of them. In the lands that were Troy, Arzawa, and Seha, *Iliad* speaks of the Phrygians and Mysians, and later Greeks write of yet other peoples. The Greeks appear to have no memory of an Arzawa, or a Seha River land, and

Troy is remembered only through Homer and other works of the Trojan Cycle. In all likelihood, those western monarchies of the Bronze Age did not long survive the Hittites, and may have preceded the Hittites into oblivion.

It seems unlikely, then, that organized land forces from western states destroyed the Hittites. It is likely that those states were engulfed in this same mysterious collapse which lead to the end of the Hittites in central Anatolia.

War with the Sea Peoples

As discussed in the previous chapter, some or all of the Sea Peoples who participated with the Libyans against Merneptah came from western Anatolia. In the midst of what may have been a spreading collapse in Anatolia, the West may have become a breeding ground of piratical adventurers. Taking to the sea, harassing the sea lanes, raiding towns and cities along the coasts, these western people may have contributed to the end of their traditional foes in Hattusa.

On the walls of the Egyptian temple at Medinet Habu, and inscription says of the Sea Peoples:

> No land could stand before their arms, from Hatti, Kode, Kargamish, Yereth, Alashia on.

Many lands to the north are swept up into this one phrase: the Hittites, Cilicia, Kargamish, Arzawa, and Cyprus. There was chaos in the countries north of Egypt. That much seems certain. Reports and rumors came to Pharaoh. The sea lanes were blocked. Contact with Arzawa, southern Anatolia, and Ugarit was lost. Cyprus was in turmoil. Hatti, the bulwark, the rock of stability in the north, was no more. Cities were in flames. New stories of sea raiders may have come to Egypt daily and every destruction, real or imagined, would have been thought to be due to the Sea Peoples. The Egyptian scribes who prepared the texts for Medinet Habu accepted such reports and built upon them, enlarged them in broadest terms. They were less concerned with accuracy than with impression of an almost cosmic discord.

Thus, the inscription says that the Sea Peoples destroyed Kargamish, the Hittite regional capital in the East. Yet archaeological investigation shows no such destruction. Ugarit, a major trade partner of Egypt, was destroyed. Yet the inscription fails to mention it. Still, there is no reason to doubt that Sea Peoples created havoc and brought destruction to the Syrian-Anatolian coast and possibly inland as well. It seems certain that Cilicia, Mukish, Ugarit, and probably Cyprus were struck by them, all lands affiliated with the Hittites.

The Battle for Cilicia

From a homeland near the west and southwest coast, some Sea Peoples probably sailed eastward along the south coast of Anatolia. There is some reason to believe that others of the Sea Peoples may have come from Cilicia or nearby, or regions farther to the east (see Chapters 16 and 17). They may have established bases in western Cilicia, the inhospitable and rocky coast opposite Cyprus, Figure 9-2. Little archaeological work has been done in western Cilicia, and there are few known traces of Bronze Age settlements. It may seem an unwelcoming place, even to sea raiders. Yet the largest pirate enterprise in history, which took place in Roman times, was mounted from bases in just this region. From these bases, pirates radiated outward, established secondary bases everywhere in the Mediterranean, and they effectively took control of the Mediterranean Sea away from Rome. Even Caesar was captured by these pirates and held for ransom. Only through the remarkable energy and talent for organization for which it was famous was Rome able to finally overcome them, mounting a major coordinated land and sea attack on pirate bases over the whole Mediterranean coast.

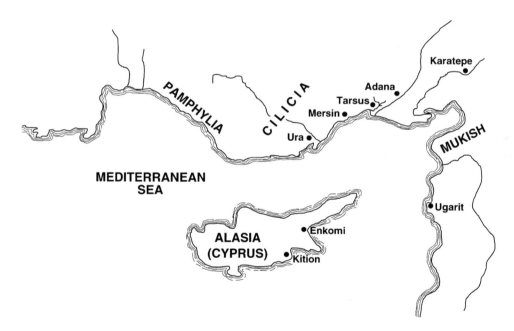

Figure 9-2. The rocky coast of Pamphylia, and the Cilician coast with its cities.

Direct evidence of the presence or settlement of Sea Peoples in Cilicia is, admittedly, not great even though in the Medinet Habu inscription above, "Kode" is mentioned. Kode is the Egyptian term for Cilicia. Remains of a good deal of Mycenaean-style pottery of various periods has been found in Cilicia. Some of the pottery was locally made, and it is sometimes thought that it might indicate the arrival of Greek elements, perhaps as invaders. Native Anatolians would make up the largest part of such an invading group, presumably, but it is hard to know what evidence of them to look for. Most of western Anatolia has not been excavated to Bronze Age levels and little is known of the characteristic pottery used by most of the people of the West. Much of what is known of it suggests that it was often plain and unpainted, and might not be recognized by archaeologists if found in Cilicia.

Tarsus of the Bronze Age was an important city of the eastern Cilicia. Hittites appeared to have ruled there, directly or indirectly. Archaeologists who excavated ancient Tarsus, under the direction of Hetty Goldman of Bryn Mawr College, found a large temple of Hittite design, Hittite pottery, and several Hittite seal impressions in clay. One seal impression was of that remarkable and energetic woman, Pudu-Hepa, wife of king Hattusili.

A vast burning destroyed ancient Tarsus, and this was followed by new occupation shortly after. Mycenaean pottery was found in the ruins of burned buildings. The pottery might have provided a date of the destruction, but the layers in which the pottery was found had been so disturbed that dating would not have been reliable. The most that can be said is that the destruction took place after the Pudu-Hepa seal was in place. She maintained official responsibilities even after her husband died, carrying on a public life into the reign of her son. It would be a guess, but her seal may date to about 1240–1230 BC. The destruction would have been later than that date, but how much later it is not possible to say. Goldman believes that the Sea Peoples were responsible for the destruction of the city and she notes that this time was "a peculiarly disturbed period, with wandering bands of robbers and pirates known to have haunted the eastern basin of the Mediterranean."

The Tursha, one of the contingents that joined the Libyans against Merneptah, were likely to have been men of Tarsus in eastern Cilicia. In a burst of Sea Peoples activity a generation later, men of the nearby city of Adana appear to have been deeply involved (Chapter 16). If men of Tarsus and Adana had joined the Sea Peoples in their raids, then it is clear that the Hittites had lost control of Cilicia, most likely even before the end of the Hittite Empire. Fire, which reduced Tarsus to ruin, might have been set during an internal struggle or revolt against Hittite rule. Admittedly, much of this is speculative. It is regrettable that not one ancient record has ever been found which would clarify events in Cilicia at the end of the Bronze Age, when the Sea Peoples were on the seas and the Hittites disappeared. There is, however, an interesting legend relating to Cilicia: the legend of Mopsus.

Most legends, including those of the Greeks, are the mere shadows of past events, events lost to history. They may have begun with actual events, reports of which, in the course of transmission from generation to generation, have lost touch in varying degrees with reality. Facts fade with time, and are replaced in stages by all sorts of invented matter. Another phenomenon is time-drift. The Greeks assigned many tales from the distant past to the Trojan War period or its direct aftermath since their knowledge of the past included no other time marker, no other milestone.

While keeping this in mind, it remains a curious fact that the Mopsus story bears a remarkable resemblance to events which occurred at the time of the Sea Peoples. The story is reported in a variety of forms from Greek or Roman authors who lived at various times. The earliest telling is closest in time to presumed actual events and, for that reason, probably closer to the truth. According to an early version of the Mopsus story, Calchas is the official "seer" of the Greek army at Troy. At war's end, he and other veterans make their way down the Anatolian coast and arrive at Claros near Colophon. Here, Calchas encounters a local seer, Mopsus. There is a challenge to see who is the better diviner. A series of tests are set up. Calchas looses, and (in one version) dies on the spot of shame. Mopsus takes charge of Calchas' group, and they proceed first to Pamphylia on the south coast, and then further to Cilicia. In Pamphylia and Cilicia, they establish settlements.

In support of the legend, Classical period writers relate that there were towns in Cilicia named for Mopsus. One was Mopsou-hestia on the Ceyhan River. The name means Mopsus' Hearth or Mopsus' Home. The second was Mopsou-krene, meaning Mopsus Spring. In what remains of Perge, an ancient city near the south coast of Anatolia, there are pillar bases which can be seen today and which are inscribed with the names of important city fathers, including the founders. One name is Calchas (who didn't die in Claros apparently) and another is Mopsus.

The ethnicity of Mopsus is uncertain. Greeks of the Classical period seem to make him one of their own. He came from Claros in what was Arzawa in the Bronze Age, and the earliest references to the legend come from the Greeks living in western Anatolia. They may have learned of Mopsus from their Anatolian neighbors, and Mopsus may have been an Anatolian.

The earliest record of that name appears in a strange place, the Indictment of Madduwatta, written at some time between 1390 and 1355 BC. The text is too damaged to know why this person is mentioned, but he is likely not the Mopsus of the legend but an earlier individual of the same name. The appearance of the name in an old Hittite text dealing with western Anatolian affairs suggests that the name is native to western Anatolia. However, a Greek, Attarissiyas, is mentioned in the same Indictment of Madduwatta, so it is possible that this Mopsus was a Greek. In the form Mo-ko-so, this name is recorded in a Linear B tablet from Knossos in Crete, and that too may suggest that the name is Greek. Yet it is known that there was a Luvian-speaking group living in Crete so that, again, the matter is uncertain.

The legends surrounding Mopsus has been refreshed by a remarkable discovery. In 1946, a Turkish-German archaeological team investigated a site with the present-day name Karatepe. Karatepe is north of Adana in a wild and remote part of the Taurus Mountains overlooking the Ceyhan River. There, these archaeologists discovered a remarkable "bilingual," an inscription in two languages, both telling the same story. One language was Phoenician, a West Semitic language close to Ugaritic. The other was in what is called Hieroglyphic Hittite but which is really a variety of Luvian. These inscriptions, dated to approximately 800-700 BC, were placed there by Azitawadda, a governor of the region. Translators quickly set to work. They were startled to find that Azitawadda claimed to be a descendant of Mopsus. The name is given as "Mopsus" in the Phoenician text, "Moxos" in the corresponding Luvian text (like the Mo-ko-so above). This discovery strongly suggests that Mopsus was a real person, and that he was associated with Cilicia.

The significance of the Mopsus story is that it reports a movement of a mix of Anatolians and Greeks from western Anatolia into Cilicia (and later, south to Canaan). Possibly, these were Sea Peoples. The legend is consistent with what is known of the relationship of Greeks and Anatolians among whom they lived. The history of western Anatolia, from Madduwatta and Attarissiyas to Piyama-Radu, testifies to the ease with which Greeks and western Anatolians could work together toward common objectives.

The Battle at Sea

The Sea Peoples raided along the coasts. It would be no surprise if they also engaged in battle at sea. A certain tablet was found in the ruins of the Hittite capital, Hattusa. The top of the tablet is missing, and missing with it are a number of lines of text which might have made the contents clearer. The text is by the last Hittite king, Suppiluliuma II, and it is the last known report from a king of the Hittite Empire. It deals with a monument which the king had set up in honor of his father, Tudhaliya IV. First, it tells that his father defeated Cyprus (Alasia or Alashia) and established or reestablished Hittite control there. Then, the text describes a sea battle:

> I mobilized and I, Suppiluliuma, the Great King, immediately crossed the sea. The ships of Alashia met me in the sea three times for battle, and I smote them; and I seized the ships and set fire to them in the sea. But when I arrived on dry land, the enemy from Alashia came in multitude against me for battles…. (*Cyprus Reconsidered*)

It is possible that these sea battles took place when Tudhaliya ruled. At that time, Suppiluliuma may have led a naval force for his father. However, Hans Gutterbock of the University of Chicago, a leading Hittite authority, strongly argues that the events happened when Suppiluliuma was king (Gutterbock, 1967). At that time, Cyprus was, presumably, a loyal vassal or ally of the Hittites. Why, then, would Cyprus ships attack the Hittites? It would make sense if certain Cypriote cities had risen against Hittite domination. It would make even more sense if the "ships of Alashia" to which Suppiluliuma referred were those of the Sea Peoples. The text might refer to alien ships based in Cyprus rather than ships belonging to the king or kings of Cyprus.

This sea battle is the only known naval engagement in Hittite history. The Hittites won, which demonstrates that the Sea Peoples, if it was they who engaged the Hittites, were not always victorious. But Sea Peoples were persistent, and they had their victories.

Battle in Mukish

Mukish seems to have been a target of a Sea Peoples invasion, indicated by the contents of two tablets which were found in the remains of the central archive of Ugarit. Since they were found close to one another (presumably they were originally filed near one another on the same shelf) they may relate to the same event, near the time of the end of Ugarit. The tablets are severely damaged, and only a few phrases can be understood.

The first is from Ewir-Sharruma, an Ugarit military commander. He writes to the mother of the king of Ugarit, the king being elsewhere:

> …and behold, the enemy who is in Mukish [….] to Mount Amanus [….] behold, the enemy destroyed [….] the enemies oppress me, but I will not leave my wife and children…. (*RS 16-402*)

Ewir-Sharruma also reports that he has two thousand horses entrusted to him by the king and is awaiting instructions. The second message is possibly from the King of Ugarit to his mother:

> If the Hittites mount, I will send a message to you, and if they don't, I will certainly send a message. My mother, don't be afraid and don't put worries in your heart. (*RS 16-379*)

Mukish, which was located near the mouth of the Orontes River, belonged to Ugarit and was an important grain-producing region. It is clear that there has been a battle in Mukish near Mount Amanus. The horses would be sufficient to equip several hundred chariots on the basis of two horses per chariot plus reserve teams. That would be a very strong chariot force. It is apparent that Ewir-Sharruma was facing a formidable enemy who has destroyed something of importance, a town or perhaps an Ugarit military formation. In the second message, the enigmatic "if the Hittites mount" may refer to the expected arrival of the Hittite army or, if already present, to their willingness to mount their chariots, to engage the enemy. Since the Hittite army is expected, or is already in the battle, it is clear that this is no local skirmish. It is a battle of imperial importance. The sender of the second message is clearly worried about the situation since he so emphatically assures his mother that there is no cause for worry.

Were the Sea Peoples the unnamed enemy? Were they now bold enough and strong enough to engage an Ugarit force in a pitched battle on land? Experience in raids against Ugarit and perhaps other coastal cities—cities of the soft life—may have convinced the Sea Peoples that an Ugarit military force was nothing to be feared. If a Hittite army was present, that might be another matter.

If Sea Peoples risked a major land battle, it would indicate that something significant was involved. If famine was disrupting society in Anatolia, the attack on Mukish would be understandable. It would have been a desperate attempt to seize productive grain-lands. Due to insufficient archaeological work in the region, it is difficult to judge whether the Sea Peoples were present and were able to seize and settle in Mukish.

Attack on Ugarit

Ugarit was a prosperous and successful mercantile city-state. Her people, who bore Hurrian and West Semitic names, were creative, industrious, and cultured. Her wealth must have been the stuff of legend, and the palace complex of Ugarit is one of the largest yet discovered in the ancient Near East. Written tablets have been found in the remains not only of palaces but private homes, indicating widespread literacy among a cultivated elite. Craftsmen of Ugarit were proficient in bronze work, gold and silver, in ivory carving, and in all the usual crafts of an important Bronze Age city.

Situated on the terminus of an overland trade route which connected Alalakh, Aleppo, Kargamish, and ultimately Assyria and Babylonia, Ugarit was an emporium for goods moving to and from distant points by land or sea. Ugarit ships called at Cyprus. To the south, they sailed to Sidon, Beirut, and Egypt. To the northwest, there was the port of Ura, the entrance for goods destined for the Hittite heartland, and Ugarit ships may have gone on to Crete and Greece.

Ugarit traded in a wide range of commodities which were important at that time: copper, tin ore, metallic tin, silver, gold, raw and worked ivory, work in bronze. In the remains of Ugarit, a magnificent sword has been found, the work of Ugarit bronze smiths, inscribed with the name of Egyptian king Merneptah. This may have been a trial fabrication for a sword intended as a gift for the Pharaoh. Above all, Ugarit traded in grain of Egypt and Mukish. For the grain trade, Ugarit employed ships of several hundred tons capacity, astonishing for those times. Such ships would have been larger than those in the fleet of Columbus in his first voyage across the Atlantic.

Now the end of the great city was approaching, foreshadowed in the records. These records, incomplete and damaged though they are, tell the story. Though undated, they are very likely to fall in the period between the combined Libyan and Sea People attack on Merneptah, 1208 BC, and the destruction of Ugarit shortly after 1193 BC. Because there are no dates in these records, the order in which the events occurred is uncertain, but that given here is probable.

On one tablet is a message from the king at Kargamish to the Grand Viser of Ugarit. Someone of the name Lunadushu had been living with the Sea Peoples, either as a captive or a spy. Now he is safely back in Ugarit and the king of Kargamish has learned of it. This message is a directive to Ugarit to send Lunadushu to Kargamish so that he can be closely interrogated about these sea raiders, the "Shikala who live on ships" and the land of "Shikila." On completion of the interview, Lunadushu will be safely returned to Ugarit.

In this message, "Shikala" was written in syllabic characters as "Shi-ka-la-iu-u." "Shikala" is only one of several possible pronunciations. Among others are "Sikalayu," and "Shikalayu." The name of these sea raiders seems to be the Hittite equivalent of the Egyptian "Shekelesh." And if not the Shekelesh, than these are another Sea Peoples group with a similar name, the *Sikils*, to be discussed in Chapter 16.

This message leaves no doubt that Sea Peoples were on the waters near Ugarit. But why such interest on the part of remote Kargamish? It can only mean that these Sea Peoples were creating problems for broader Hittite interests and not just those of Ugarit. The Hittites were a land power and knew how to deal with a troublesome group on land, but the Sea Peoples were another matter. They are elusive, they live on ships. If this letter to Ugarit dates to a time shortly after the attack on Merneptah, it may indicate that the Hittites were gathering intelligence in preparation for a massive strike against those Sea Peoples' bases which were within their reach. Would not Merneptah demand that the Hittites take such action?

Another message is a response to an earlier one from Ugarit. That earlier letter has not been found, but it must have been a plea from Ugarit for help. The response is addressed to Ammurapi, king of Ugarit, and begins with the usual flowery and extravagant salutation as was proper in those times. Then it continues:

> You say that you have seen the boats of the enemy at sea....Be strong!...Move your chariots and troops within the walls of the city...The enemy is very strong. (*RSL 1*)

It isn't certain who sent this message. The king of Cyprus would be in a good position to know that "the enemy is very strong." It is clear enough that these kings are frightened of the sea raiders, and have reason to be.

Another message is from Ugarit to Cyprus. The opening suggests that it may have been intended to be read out by a herald, likely a tradition from earlier times. "Say to my father the king of Alasia…'Thus says your son the king of Ugarit'" using an expression not necessarily of family relationship but of respect. Then there is the salutation, typical of letters of that period:

> At the feet of my father I fall. May there be peace with my father, your house, your wives, your troops, to all who belong to my father, great peace….

The text continues:

> May my father know that the enemy ships came. My cities were burned and evil things were done in my country. Does my father know that my troops are stationed in the Hittite land and my ships in Lukka country? Thus, the country is abandoned to itself. May my father know this. Seven ships of the enemy have come here and did us much damage. Be on the lookout for other enemy ships and send me warning. (*RS 20.238*)

The Sea Peoples had struck Ugarit. Seven ships might carry one or two hundred fighting men. By surprising a sleeping city located no more than a mile from the sea, that number could do great damage. With the laxness which is age-old in the East, sentries may not have been at their posts, or may have been asleep and no alarm given until the raiders had crashed through the city gates. Ugarit troops were far away with the Hittites. The attackers caused havoc in the city.

Why were Ugarit troops with the Hittite army, and the fleet in Lukka waters? It has been suggested that the Ugarit fleet was attempting to block the sea passage between southwest Anatolia and the island of Rhodes against a Sea Peoples' advance down the coast. However, it is doubtful that navies of that period could carry out open-water operations of that sort. It is more likely that the Ugarit fleet was carrying out an assignment against Sea Peoples' bases on the Lukka coast, possibly in coordination with Hittite attacks from the landward side. Cyprus, a Hittite vassal or protectorate, may also have contributed naval forces. History demonstrates that combined land-sea operations produce the best results against pirate bases, but if that was the objective, it was not fully successful. More Sea Peoples attacks were to come.

It has been 3,200 years since the end of Ugarit. Tablets have suffered the effects of time and many preserve only fragmentary messages. One such is a message to the king of Ugarit from Eshuwara, Grand Visir of Cyprus. There is a salutation, but a terse one. The message states:

> Concerning the matter of the enemy, your people, and your ships, and of the about face of your people, do not complain to me. Twenty enemy ships slipped away into the mountain region and were not stopped and we don't know where they have gone. I am writing you to inform you. Truly, may you know this. (*RS 20.18*)

Cyprus ships may have had an assignment against raider bases along the southern coast of Anatolia. Assigned a station next to the Ugarit fleet, they may have been in position to witness the incompetent performance of the Ugarit navy.

Other interpretations of this damaged text have been proposed, including one in which Ugarit seamen turned over twenty of their ships to the enemy. That Eshuwara of Cyprus is involved shows that Cyprus was caught up in the war against the Sea Peoples, which is no surprise. The coasts of Cyprus were even more vulnerable than those of Ugarit, and the sea raiders may have already seized bases along the Cyprus coast.

The Last Day of Ugarit

The tablets recovered from the oven are surely of the last days or even the final hours before the destruction of Ugarit. In a message, King Pgn (vowels are not given), who may have been a king of Cyprus, thanks the king of Ugarit for a food shipment, and writes about equipping a ship and strengthening something. From Ydn, whoever he may have been, there is urgent advice; equip 150 ships. This certainly cannot relate to peaceful maritime activities: only a dire threat would require the readying of so many ships.

The evidence shows that the end of Ugarit was attended by widespread destruction and fire. Was the destruction due to an attack by the Sea Peoples? It is an example of the ambiguity of archaeological evidence.

Claude Schaeffer, who for many years led archaeological excavations at Ugarit, at first thought of the Sea Peoples as the destroyers. Later, he came to believe that the city was destroyed in a violent earthquake (Schaeffer, 1983). What else could bring down such massive walls and cause fires so hot that bricks fused and limestone building blocks were roasted to lime? No skeletons were found, which to Schaeffer meant that foreshocks warned the inhabitants of a coming earthquake, allowing them to escape. Personal valuables were found buried under floors. Bronze and gold statuettes of the gods El and Baal were hidden away. Again, to Schaeffer, this was an indication that the inhabitants had enough warning to escape with the intention of returning. Above all there had been, so far as Schaeffer could see, no sign of military assault. Ugarit was vulnerable to earthquake. A century and a half earlier, Ugarit had been shattered. At that time, Abi-Milku, king of Tyre on the south coast, reported the situation to Egypt. "The city and the king have been annihilated by fire, half of it has been burned, and the other half is no longer there." But after that disaster, Ugarit recovered.

The results of later excavations at Ugarit have led to a different conclusion. Arrowheads were found. Excavators are certain that these were not from arrows kept in an Ugarit armory or any other weapons store. As archaeologist Marguerite Yon reports, "Violent fighting seems to have taken place throughout the city; the presence of numerous arrowheads dispersed throughout the destroyed or abandoned ruins (and not in orderly deposits as if they had been stockpiled weapons) provides evidence of this" (Yon, 1989). In one area of houses, 25 arrowheads were found, and in another housing area, at least 30 arrowheads. The conclusion is inescapable, according to recent excavators. The city was the victim of violent attack.

Ugarit, one of the greatest and most cultivated and prosperous cities of the Late Bronze Age, was never rebuilt. The economic conditions needed to sustain the city may have vanished. Caravan routes to Kargamish and Assyria may have been seriously disrupted by the Arameans, who were already on the move in the backlands, and the sea trade was disrupted by Sea Peoples. Some of the elite of Ugarit may have emigrated, but to where? To Cyprus, perhaps. Thus the great city ended, never to be rebuilt, providing one of the great mysteries which accompany those times.

From all of the surviving records, fragmentary and incomplete though they are, it is clear that Sea Peoples were ranging freely in the seas along the Anatolian, Cypriote, and Syrian coasts. They raided at will. Hittites gathered intelligence about them, about "Shikila who live on ships," to name but one group. There was a sea battle in which the Hittites were victors. There were landings in which the outcomes are uncertain, except that it is certain that Ugarit was destroyed.

In a few short decades, social and political dissolution had replaced stability throughout most of the Hittite realm. Hittite political power was broken. The kingdoms of western Anatolia may have met the same fate. Ugarit was gone and Cyprus was in turmoil. The irruption of the Sea Peoples into the seas and the coastlands of the eastern Mediterranean may not have been a cause but a symptom of social and political dissolution.

10
COLLAPSE OF THE HITTITE EMPIRE

An invasion or mass migration from Europe does not explain the collapse of the powerful Hittite empire, nor the depopulation of their land. Phrygians, who were late comers, did not destroy the Hittites. Nor did the makers of Handmade Ware. They too came late. Nor is there evidence that points to the Kaska, though they may have overrun a Hittite homeland which had already been nearly abandoned. The hostility of Arzawa and other western principalities is well documented, but there is no evidence that links them to the destruction of the Hittites. Arzawa too may have been engulfed in the catastrophe that ended the Bronze Age in Anatolia. The Sea Peoples, on the other hand, are certainly evident in the record as raiders of the southern flanks of the Hittite empire. Whether these were Shekelesh, Lukka, Akawasha, or combinations of such peoples, they wreaked devastation along the coast.

The direct effects of such raids could not have been felt far inland, however. In a later age, Vikings entered the rivers of France and created terror and destruction even as far as Paris. In southern Anatolia, there are no wide rivers along which raiders might advance in their ships. No overland assault northward into the interior of Anatolia by an overwhelming force of Sea Peoples, one capable of meeting and defeating the power of the Hittite empire in their full strength, is realistic. But an invading force might take a Hittite force by surprise, perhaps near the mountain passes close to the coast, and do damage.

The indirect effects of Sea People raids, however, could have been serious. Coastal states which were part of the Hittite empire may have lost faith in the ability of the Hittites to protect them. If the Hittites had solved the food transport problem, (to be discussed shortly), Sea Peoples might have harried the sea lanes along which grain moved. Confidence in the Hittite king may have been further shaken, even among the Hittites. But these were no more than contributing factors, requiring a further search for the cause of the collapse of the Hittites

The Enemy Within

Were the Hittites overthrown in a decisive battle against an overwhelmingly strong enemy? A search of the evidence for such an enemy or such a battle does not produce them. The search may be misdirected and futile. It may be necessary to look elsewhere, to other causes. The end of nations or empires need not be due to dramatic events, to invading hordes or conquering armies. Collapse of a society or polity may owe more to internal factors than to external ones. Perhaps the Hittites were experiencing such serious internal strains that a wind from any quarter might bowl them over, a push might topple them from power. A search for serious strains in Hittite society shows them to have been present. Disunity, political disintegration, and hunger were the enemy, it is proposed here, and some final military confrontation would merely ensure the end. For such an end, no enemy could claim glory.

Virtually all that is known of Hittite history had been assembled from surviving Hittite records. Starting with Tudhaliya IV, these records are fewer, and they are almost nonexistent for the time of his descendants Arnuwanda III and Suppiluliuma II. From the limited information available, something can be seen which indicates a breakdown in cohesion within the empire.

It may have started with the coup in which Hattusili (1264–1239 BC) seized the throne and Urhi-Tesub was deposed, Chapter 3. The top stratum of Hittite society was largely composed of close and distant relations of the royal family: princes, cousins once or twice removed, uncles, and others tied to the royal family through marriage. These would have constituted a wealthy, landowning aristocracy and which held key positions in regional government, the army, and the priesthood. Collectively, they held substantial power.

It was such people whom Hattusili attempted to bring to his side in preparation for his coup. Historic experience suggests that there may have been many in this stratum of Hittite society who did not favor the coup, who saw Hattusili as a usurper, without legitimate right to the throne. Conservatives might have deplored the assault on established law which the coup represented, and formed a "loyalist" clique looking toward a restoration of Urhi-Tesub or his descendants. They might not have expressed themselves openly so long as Hattusili and his heirs ruled successfully. But they could have been a potential disloyal element, waiting for this branch of the royal family to make a misstep. Thus the seeds of disunity may have been planted.

The astute Hattusili appears to have recognized the threat. He dealt with it by building up Kurunta, brother of Urhi-Tesub. For Kurunta, he carved out a kingdom in southern Anatolia, Tarhuntassa, as a reward for his support. Perhaps he made promises to Kurunta before the coup. That move may have succeeded in mollifying the Urhi-Tesub loyalist faction, but might not have reduced the degree of skepticism concerning Hattusili.

For the concession to Kurunta, Hattusili paid a high price. In the ruins of Hattusa, archaeologists have found an impression of a seal belonging to Kurunta, and on this he claims the title "Great King." This title is equivalent to the modern term "emperor." In past Hittite history, it was born only by the king in Hattusa. Was Kurunta asserting a claim to the throne? He was a son of the Great King Muwatalli, and his claim might have been legitimate. Were there now two Great Kings ruling in Anatolia? Or was Great King an empty title that Hattusili awarded to Kurunta as a bribe, in effect a big medal that Hattusili pinned on Kurunta's chest to flatter him, to quiet him? Whatever the reason, it could not help but increase the fissures in the ruling stratum of Hittite society. Hattusili supporters would view the Great King title as legitimizing Kurunta and his descendants, a dilution of royal central authority, and an admission of weakness.

Tudhaliya IV (1239–1209 BC), the son of Hattusili, fought a major battle against the Assyrians and was resoundingly defeated. As a result, the Hittites lost control of the copper mines at Ergani. Tudhaliya blamed the defeat on a vassal king who failed to bring up his army for battle at the appointed time. That a vassal could shirk his obligations in this way suggests a weakness on the part of Tudhaliya. In the ancient world, leadership in war was a central responsibility of kings, and success a justification for kingship. Never in the remembered past had Assyria humbled Hittite arms. This stinging defeat, and the fact that it was never avenged, must have seriously affected the way in which the powerful within the empire viewed Tudhaliya. It would have provided an additional reason to doubt the Hattusili-Tudhaliya line of kings, and this would further increase factionalism. Tudhaliya waged successful campaigns in the West, it is true. As compensation for the loss of the Ergani mines, he may have put Cyprus and its copper mines under firm though indirect Hittite control. But these successes may not have undone the damage.

It was also during the reign of Tudhaliya that a new political arrangement was made for Wilusa. Some western state, possibly Seha River Land (the tablets are too damaged to be sure) was recognized as jointly responsible with the Hittites for Wilusa. This seems to represent a delegation, a withdrawal of direct Hittite authority and responsibility in the West. It indicates an inability of the Hittites to continue to project power in the vital western region.

It was toward the end of Tudhaliya's reign, or perhaps during that of his short-lived successor Arnuwanda, that Sea Peoples attacked Merneptah's Egypt. As discussed earlier, these Sea Peoples may have originated in western Anatolia. As a great power and a treaty partner of Egypt, the Hittites were expected to maintain order and stability in their part of the world. That the Hittites failed to successfully exert control in western Anatolia seems to mark a decline in Hittite power, and a decline in Hittite prestige on the international scene. Merneptah probably sent a strongly worded protest to Hattusa about this Sea

Peoples matter. Such a communication would soon be known among the leading people in the Hittite empire, and would be an embarrassment to the Hittite king.

A fragmentary Hittite record of the time of King Suppiluliuma II (1205–? BC) indicates that Hattusa was forced to send her army into Tarhuntassa. No reason for this can be determined from the existing record. Was it civil war, insurrection, treasonous actions by Kurunta? Or did Hattusa send an army to aid the king of Tarhuntassa against a foreign attack? Whichever it was, it indicates a breakdown in security dangerously close to home.

It is useful to look again to Ugarit. For the small states of the Syria-Canaan region, political survival depended on knowing which way the wind was blowing. The king of Ugarit and his ministers needed to be alert to subtle shifts in the international power balance and needed to make adjustments accordingly. Was Assyria in ascendancy? Or Egypt? Should Ugarit begin to distance itself from Hattusa? The response of Ugarit to international affairs might reveal something concerning the situation in Hattusa.

A message found in an Ugarit archive reveals that the king of Assyria wrote to the king of Ugarit about the serious defeat which Assyria inflicted on the Hittites. The story didn't need telling. From the battlefield, the news would have traveled with the speed of the wind. The message was intended as a hint that Ugarit should begin to think about a shift of allegiance. Other texts indicate that Ugarit sought closer ties with Egypt. Kargamish chastised Ugarit for failing to forward taxes to the imperial treasury in Hattusa. Kargamish scolded the Ugarit king for failing a military inspection: his chariot forces and his ships were in a poor state of readiness. Further, Kargamish ships were birthed at Ugarit and the Ugarit king had failed to properly maintain them. And Kargamish accuses Ugarit of failing to dispatch troops to a trouble spot per Hittite orders.

Though Ugarit sent troops and ships to support the Hittites in what seems to be an anti-Sea Peoples campaign, the above messages indicate that an attempt was made by the leaders in Ugarit to back away from Hattusa, and it must be assumed that Ugarit saw with clear eyes a serious decline of Hittite power.

Hunger Strikes the Hittite Land

In the same period, an enemy stalked the land—one that Hittite kings could not defeat though they tried. The enemy was famine. No records say what happened in Greece in those times, but archaeological findings appear to match closely the known effects of famine, or famine and perhaps plague. From that match, famine and plague in Bronze Age Greece can be inferred. In the case of the Hittite land, there is less need to draw inferences. Hittite records tell of hunger. Some of the messages are from Hattusa, others from Ugarit. Some are reasonably complete and legible, while others are fragments from which only a few lines or a few words can be understood. They show that there were periods of severe hunger in Hatti during the reigns of King Hattusili and his descendants down to the last, Suppiluliuma—a span of three generations.

Found in the Hattusa archives is a message from Ramesses II concerning the shipment of grain to Hatti. Whether this was an emergency shipment or a routine shipment cannot be told from the message. Another Hattusa document is a file copy of a message from Queen Pudu-Hepa to Ramesses II concerning arrangements for the marriage of her daughter, the daughter of Hattusili, to Ramesses. In it, Pudu-Hepa expresses a concern for quick delivery of a dowry of cattle, sheep, and chattel-men to Egypt and also states that "there is no grain in my land." Were these two concerns related? Would the timely arrival of the dowry in Egypt remove impediments to the shipment of grain from Egypt? Another message indicates that a Hittite prince had been sent to Egypt to oversee grain shipments, and in Egypt, Merneptah notes that he has been sending grain to "keep alive" the land of Hatti.

There are other messages which cannot be dated exactly, but which scholars are reasonably sure come from this period. A message found in Ugarit from a Hittite king tells of increasing hunger. Scholars debate about the message's recipient. Some think it is to a son of Merneptah, or to the king of Ugarit, or possibly again, to a Hittite prince on a trade mission in Egypt, or Ugarit. Whoever the intended recipient may have been, there is a note of desperation:

> My son, concerning what you have written me, that one hundred ships [or, according to another reading, "the grain ships"] have arrived. Why have you [....] Do you not know, my son, that in my land I am enduring famine? Now, my son, send it and we will unload it in Ura or Lashti. We will unload it in whichever port you send it. (*Bo 2810*)

For the location of Ura, see Map 9-1. Lashti is unidentified.

From the Ugarit archives, a message from the Hittite king deals with grain shipments. It requests that the king of Ugarit provide ships and men to deliver two thousand measures of grain from the Mukish grainlands to the port of Ura. "It is a matter of life or death." The two thousand measures have been calculated to equal five hundred tons. The message states that the shipment can be handled by two ships, which indicates the huge capacity of Ugarit grain ships.

A fragment of a message to the king of Ugarit has the phrase "...and the shipment of food which you sent to the Sun, your lord, although there was no food in your realm...." From the archive in the palace of the queen of Ugarit, a message has been found thought to have been intended for a Hittite representative in Ugarit. In it appears the enigmatic "Since there is famine in your house we will starve to death." and "The living soul of your country you will see no longer."

The tablets found in the oven in Ugarit have been mentioned. One of these contained a message (RS-18.38) to the king of Ugarit (Figure 10-1). It is very damaged, which is regrettable because it appears to deal with the catastrophe that affected both Ugarit and Hatti. Due to the very poor condition of the text, readings are especially uncertain. In one reading, it is "the enemy advances, send what is available…." From this, it is not clear if it is food or military support which is requested, or both.

Figure 10-1. Found in the remains of Ugarit, dating to the last days, a transcription of a message in cuneiform (RS-18.38) from the king of the Hittites sounds a note of desperation.

Taken together, these messages and message fragments clearly speak of famine which is affecting the Hittite realm. Climatologists say that world climate has not changed significantly for the last 8,000 years. That means that conditions in present-day Turkey may illustrate circumstances in Hatti 3,200 years ago. What is known from Turkey in modern times makes it certain that famine would have afflicted the Hittites with great severity.

A series of maps have been published showing the location of moist and arid areas in Turkey in recent years, from 1928 through 1946. For the region in which the Hittite homeland had been located, there was widespread drought in 13 of those 19 years. Only in three years was the Hatti region nearly free of drought. In one cluster of seven consecutive years, 1928 through 1934, only one year was not significantly arid.

The result is shown by what happened to grain yields. Data are not available for precisely the area in which Hatti was located, but results of harvests from nearby regions are informative. For the drought year 1932, in the Konya region each planted acre was able to produce only one third the amount of wheat as in the moist year of 1931. For the Eskisehir region, there was a similar plunge in the yield per acre. Total wheat yield for these two regions dropped even more than these numbers indicate, to one quarter of that of 1931, because farmers, seeing poor conditions, did not plant in all the available acreage. Thus, fewer acres were planted and each planted acre yielded poorly.

The consequence of drought in Turkey is strikingly shown by another example. In 1874, drought struck the province of Ankara, adjacent to what was the ancient Hittite homeland. Of 52,000 people, it is reported that 20,000 died and 7,000 fled. It is easy to imagine the poor condition of those who remained. As for the animals, 81 percent of cattle and 97 percent of the sheep died. Another report states that in the three provinces of Kastamonu, Ankara, and Kayseri, 100,000 people and 100,000 head of livestock died (Kuniholm, 1990). Famine in central Anatolia was no new thing. A writer who lived near AD 400 called a food crisis in the region of Kayseri "the most terrible in the memory of man."

Ancient Hatti must have been a marginal land so far as agriculture is concerned, a land living on the edge of cultivability. Hatti was not Egypt, with its abundant water and large grain surpluses. There is no Nile in Anatolia. The Halys, the great river of Anatolia, flows through many deep gorges from which water could not be conducted by canals. Good years might produce only slight surpluses in Hatti which might be traded or set aside for emergencies. Though the city of Hattusa had a number of large grain silos, no great reserves could be built up. A drop in the crop yield to one quarter, as happened in 1932, would be a total catastrophe since, under ancient conditions, about one quarter of the full yield needed to be set aside as seed for the next year. A terrible decision would need to be made. Should one save the seed-corn for the next planting, or eat the seed now to fend off starvation?

A closer look at the drought maps for the years 1928-1934 shows the possible extent of the disaster in the Hittite world. If the pattern of aridity in the Bronze Age was like that of the 1930s, Tarhuntassa would have been in drought (Figure 10-2b). The affliction would have extended far to the west, putting Arzawa, Seha River Land, Wilusa, and part of the

Lukka territory in drought. Hunger would force people to seek survival as best they might, and the phenomenon of the Sea Peoples may thus in part be explained. To the east, Kargamish and nearby areas would also be affected. Much of the Kaska homeland would have had adequate rainfall, as would some of the Lukka region, no doubt a strange and terrible injustice from the Hittite viewpoint.

In a modern country, the effect of drought can be reduced through the delivery of food from other regions or even other countries. In more primitive conditions, famine is not easily dealt with because of a far less capable transportation system. Still, one may be certain that Hittite kings did not sit by idly watching their people starve. Urgent measures were taken, or tried, as the letters to and from Egypt and Ugarit show.

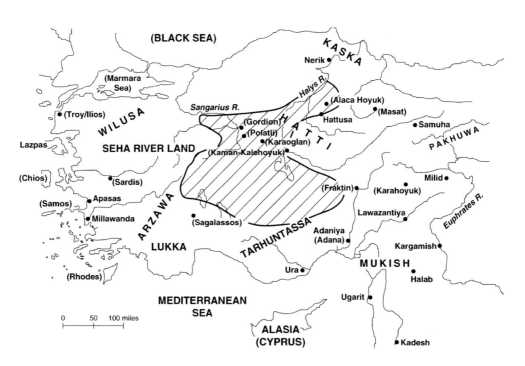

Figure 10-2a. Drought map of Turkey in the moderate drought year 1935, superimposed on a map of Anatolia in the Late Bronze Age. Shaded regions are in drought.

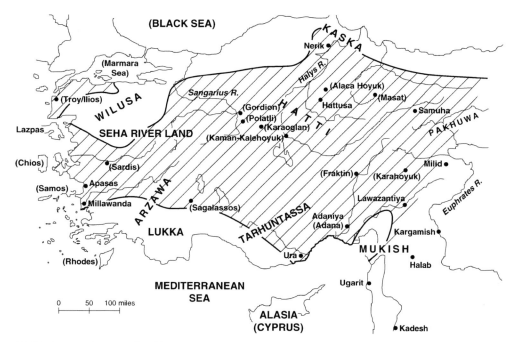

Figure 10-2b. Drought map for Turkey in the severe drought year 1932, superimposed on a map of Anatolia in the Late Bronze Age. Shaded regions are in drought.

Calculations reveal the great difficulty involved if grain imports were to relieve Hatti. To illustrate, a few assumptions need to be made. These are that the Hatti heartland had 50,000 people who were afflicted by the drought; and that 2,000 calories (kilocalories) per person per day needed to be supplied from outside the region. It is also assumed that two pounds of grain, to be used as bread or porridge, would supply the 2,000 calories and also minimal protein needs. Thus, 100,000 pounds or 50 tons of grain each day would need to be found somewhere. That somewhere could not be Tarhuntassa or other neighboring regions since they also would have been starving.

Thus, there was a need to import from more distant grain-growing regions, Ugarit and Egypt. If it is true that Ugarit grain ships had a capacity of 250 tons (as has been concluded from the translation of a message noted earlier), then one grain ship arriving at the port of Ura, every five days for the duration of the drought, would be needed. Too little is known about the Hittite economy to say how these huge importations would have been paid for.

The problem was not yet solved, however. It had hardly begun. Moving grain in large ships was easy and efficient, but then there was the problem of transportation overland. The straight line distance from Ura to Hattusa was about 260 miles, but the actual distance traveled was much longer. Assuming that the route from Ura went west through the mountain pass in the Taurus Mountains and then north through the cities of Tarhuntassa to Hattusa, a realistic distance of 335 miles might be involved.

A team of two oxen could pull a wagon with half a ton of grain, and a huge caravan of 500 wagons would be needed to move each shipment (Engles, 1978). The route runs through harsh country, particularly severe in drought conditions, and it is doubtful that the oxen would find enough browse along the route. Even if they could, the first caravan to pass might clean off the landscape around the route, leaving little browse for following caravans. Tarhuntassa cities along the way could not have provided feed. They would have been starving themselves.

Oxen are slow, and average progress of about ten miles per day is realistic. Such a caravan would take thirty-three days to reach Hattusa. A two-ox team would have required one hundred pounds of feed each day, and if the feed were to be taken out of the grain in the wagons, the entire load would be consumed in ten days. Nothing would reach Hattusa. Horse-drawn wagons could carry much less, and if the horses were fed from the load, they wouldn't go as far as the ox-wagons. Horses carrying packs on their backs would fare no better, nor would asses.

Similarly, human porters, if they could carry sixty-pound loads and still average twenty miles per day, would reach Hattusa in seventeen days. For such labor, 5,000 calories per day for each carrier is reasonable. But they would consume the grain in their load in perhaps twelve days. Whether ox, horse, or man, the story is the same. If the hard labor of transport is entirely fueled out of the transported grain stock, nothing would be left even before the caravan reached Hatti.

There also would have been a requirement for water. The caravan path was arid and there were few good streams. Where would the caravan get the large amount of drinking water required for men, oxen, or horses? If oxen or horses could have survived the trip, it is unlikely they could have repeated it. How could oxen or horses be provided in sufficient number to support new caravans week after week? Further, it is certain that there would have been grain losses by pilferage and sell-offs by dishonest officials and caravaneers. The entire undertaking would have been a logistics nightmare.

Hittites might have done better if they were able to bring in grain from the grainlands of the Crimea, across the Black Sea, to the north. These grainlands were suppliers to Athens in the Classical period, but there is no evidence that the Hittites were able to use that source. The Kaska stood across that northern land route.

The evidence of the Hittite letters shows, however, that grain was imported to Ura, and it must be believed that some got through to Hattusa. How this was accomplished is a mystery. Were the caravans able to diversify the routes sufficiently that oxen could find browse unconsumed by earlier caravans? Were the cities and towns of Tarhuntassa tasked to set up and maintain silages along the trails? Were cisterns set up at certain points, and streams dammed, to form a string of watering points? Archaeologists might look for evidence of trails, cisterns, and silages set up in those places and times. If those responsibilities fell on Tarhuntassa, the maintenance of these food routes may have been an additional reason for establishing the sub-kingdom of Tarhuntassa with Kurunta and his successors in charge.

If this was the situation in the Hittite land toward the end of the empire—internal dissension and deadly famine—then the Hittite Empire was a hollow shell in the final years. Outwardly, it may have appeared as the strong ruler in Anatolia. But inwardly, there would have been no strength. In those circumstances, the end would not have been the result of some inevitable destiny but would have been due to a fatal combination of conditions that could not be overcome.

How the End May Have Come

The end of Hattusa and the collapse of the Hittite Empire could not have been long after the end of Ugarit. It may have followed closely upon it. Political dissent and dissolution and the impact of destructive famine form the stark background.

In the foreground, there is a confrontation with an enemy, identity unknown. Concerning this confrontation, something can be inferred from the last Ugarit records, those found in the oven. There is an urgent message to Ammurapi, the last Ugarit king, from "My Majesty, your lord." From that, it is clear that the message is from the Great King of the Hittites. The damaged text, part of which was quoted earlier (RS-18.38), covers a strange mix of subjects. The message opens with the customary "With the My Majesty, all is well," but Ammurapi is not even accorded the customary good wishes which custom demands, and is berated for his failure to come to the Hittite court to do his obeisance as a vassal.

However, the message acknowledges that Ammurapi has sent food and supplies to the Hittites at great privation to himself. Most important, the damaged text contains words about an enemy, though the situation is not easily understood. It continues

> The enemy advances against me and there is no number....our number is....send whatever is available, look to it and send it to me.

The apparent reference to the number of the enemy must reflect a deep anxiety. Their number is large. Closely tied to this is the request for support. What is it that the Hittite king needs? Men? Chariotry? Food? Whatever it is, it is clear that the need is urgent. That aid is requested from Ugarit shows that the conflict is somewhere not very far away.

Along with this was another message, one of those last messages from the oven. It is regrettable that it is so severely damaged. Sent to the king of Ugarit by one of his officers, it says:

> From Shipibaal your servant. To the feet of my lord seven times seven from afar I fall. Your servant in Lawazanda [Lawazantiya] fortified his positions with the king. And behold, the king retreated, fled, and there made sacrifices….. (RS-18.40)

The king to whom this referred may have been the Great King, king of the Hittite Empire. The implication would be that the Great King fled and in desperation offered sacrifices. From where and from whom did he flee? The involvement of an Ugarit commander again suggests a southern location, and possibly this was a critical battle for Cilicia or the passes north.

That the Hittite king fled from or to Lawazantiya (it is not clear which is meant) represents a disaster. Lawazantiya was the birthplace of Queen Pudu-Hepa in a slightly earlier time. For Hittite military campaigns in the eastern part of the empire, it was an ideal logistical base and headquarters where the armies of Hatti, Tarhuntassa, and Kargamish could be brought together. From there, they could march to meet an enemy in the northeast, east, or south in the direction of Syria or Cilicia.

Shipibaal could not return home. Ugarit was destroyed while he was with the Hittites. If this message refers to the Hittite Great King, as is assumed here, he still lived at the time of the end of Ugarit.

Exactly what happened is not known and may forever remain unknown. However, certain possibilities can be seen, though these involve much guesswork. It is likely that drought had struck in several successive years. Imports of grain, which in the less severe years provided some relief, would now be all but useless. Not only the common people but the elite of Hatti society would have begun to believe that a god was angry. Why hadn't the prayers and sacrifices of the Great King of the Hittites assuaged this anger? The king was the chief priest of his realm and his prayers ought to be the most effective of all. It must be that the god was displeased with the king himself.

More than half the population of Hatti would have disappeared due to starvation, disease, or migration. Peasants who could do so would begin to leave the land. As the estates upon which the aristocracy depended for income withered, landed gentry and urban elites would begin to leave Hattusa and other Hittite cities of the homeland. Pleas from the king, in whom no great confidence resided in any case, would be ineffective. He had lost the mandate of the gods. In time, he too might have deserted the city, taking family, treasury, and the essential elements of the government with him. Had not King Muwatalli II (1295–1271 BC) before him removed himself and the government from Hattusa in favor of a new southern capital? This move would be no different.

Perhaps King Suppiluliuma attempted to reestablish the government in Lawazantiya. Here, political support could be expected since the Hittite royalty descended from Pudu-Hepa, who was born in that city. In the northern cities, there remained only meager garrisons and those who were too old, too sick, too poor to join the exiting stream. The Hittite king, though weakened, would have considered himself still in charge of a great empire. In this extremely vulnerable circumstance, some fatal missteps may have been made, it can be assumed, which lead to an irreversible collapse. The Hittites were at the end of their power.

It is likely that the Kaska in their eyries in the northern mountains heard about the catastrophe in Hatti, and knew also the weakness of the Hittite cities. Now they struck the weakened cities. Garrisons were driven out and those who remained were slaughtered. These cities of the eternal enemy were looted and torched. No enduring attempt was made to live in these cities, for no grain could be grown nor stock raised in the drought-parched land. Such may have been the fate of the once powerful Hittites.

Except for an occasional passing nomad group, the cities were unoccupied until a new people came as occupiers years later. None knew the original name of the city or the name of the people who once lived here.

The demise of Hatti left the Hittite empire without leadership. There were surviving kings of the Hittite royal line in Tarhuntassa and Kargamish. Why didn't one of these kings assume imperial power and exercise rule over the empire, or at least its few still living parts? There is no answer.

The end of centralized power was to have immediate consequences. Within a few years, Assyria would advance freely into the eastern reaches of the once Hittite empire. The seas between Anatolia, Cyprus, and Syria were freely open to the sea raiders. Cyprus would be affected and would descend into turmoil.

11

CYPRUS, DESTRUCTION AND RENEWAL

Hittite power had collapsed. Ugarit had been destroyed and the Ugarit fleet had presumably been captured by the Sea Peoples. As a consequence, there was now little to impede free movement of Sea Peoples on the seas around Cyprus. If it was a new homeland which they sought, the coast of Cilicia and Mukish offered possibilities and evidently had been tried. If a rich loot was the objective, Ugarit had been a plump and easy target. Cyprus might furnish both land and wealth, since there were ample grain-lands and rich cities. In such times, raiders might thrive, and a soldier might find employment amid the increasing chaos.

Many of the ancient cities of Cyprus have been excavated by archaeologists, at least in part, and the results clearly show that there was a major island-wide disruption seemingly at just the time when the Sea Peoples were abroad on the seas. Cities were abandoned or destroyed. Hardly a city was untouched. Some historians hold the Sea Peoples responsible since Ramesses III said of them, "No land could stand before their arms…" and listed Cyprus as one of their victims.

Other historians hold that there was a invasion of Greeks, perhaps fleeing the collapse which was taking place about that time in their homeland. Yet others see both factors at work—destruction caused by the Greeks, followed in short order by a second destruction due to the Sea Peoples. Still others reconcile those viewpoints. They hold that the Greeks were the Sea Peoples, or a major component of them.

That there are contradictory explanations for the catastrophe in Cyprus demonstrates the woefully inadequate knowledge concerning events of over 3,000 years ago. So far as historical reconstruction is concerned, the situation resembles that of Greece. The name of not one king of Greece of the Bronze Age is known from any contemporary record, and hardly any major event of the history of Greece in the Bronze Age is known. Nearly the same can be said of Cyprus. A very few specimens of writing from Cyprus exist, so that it is known that there was literacy, but no extensive archives of Cyprus have ever been found.

Though many historians believe that one or more invasions account for the destruction and abandonments, it is possible that these disturbances were not due to external factors. They may have been a consequence of conditions internal to Cyprus. In Cyprus, as may have been in Greece, strife between cities or classes might have been an important factor in the deterioration. Ethnic discord may also have played a role, for according to some evidence, there lived in Cyprus in those times two quite unrelated major ethnic groups, as will be reviewed in the next chapter.

Prosperity and Peace

Archaeologists call the period toward the end of the Bronze Age in Cyprus the Late Cypriote period. Late Cypriote II extended from about 1450 BC to about 1180 BC. The end of this period is defined by the widespread destruction and abandonments of cities. Dates are uncertain, and the date of the end of Late Cypriote II is particularly so. The year 1180 BC, given above, is hardly more than a guess.

Based on somewhat arbitrary dates, Late Cypriote II is divided into three subperiods:

Subperiod	Absolute Date
Late Cypriote IIA	1450–1375 BC
Late Cypriote IIB	1375–1300 BC
Late Cypriote IIC	1300–1180 BC

Late Cypriote II was followed by:

Late Cypriote IIIA	1180 BC to ?

Little is known of the cause of the destruction that marked the end of Late Cypriote II. The few Cypriote records of the Bronze Age that are known are in the Cypro-Minoan script, as yet undeciphered. No decipherment can be expected unless many more records in this script are discovered, or a "bilingual" is found, a Cypriote Rosetta stone. Not much should be expected of the Cypro-Minoan records even if some day they are deciphered. The much more extensive Hittite and Ugarit records deal largely with religious rites, mythology, law, commerce, and administration, and only a relatively few deal directly with historical matter. The existing Cypro-Minoan texts are likely to fall in those less informative categories. Something, however, is learned of Cyprus from records in other lands. Hittite, Ugaritic, and Egyptian records speak of Alasia or Alashia. The preponderance of the evidence indicates that Alasia was Cyprus, or a major kingdom of Cyprus. Archaeological excavations in Cyprus have also produced substantial information.

That information shows that toward the beginning of Late Cypriote IIB (now abbreviated to LC IIB), and thus almost two hundred years before these great disturbances,

Cyprus was growing in wealth. Lukka people of southern Anatolia seemed to have thought so, because they raided Cyprus annually. That prince of opportunists, Madduwatta (see Chapter 3), also may have thought so, for he and his newfound friend Attarissiyas raided Alasia taking off prisoners as they departed. The Hittite king Arnuwanda I (1370–1344 BC) must also have thought so, for he took Alasia under "protection" and ordered Madduwatta to return the prisoners, which he did. It appears that Cyprus was drawing increasing attention and was beginning to be an inviting target for raiders.

Archaeological work in the cities of Late Bronze Age Cyprus seem to confirm a progressive development of the economy, probably a consequence of increased trade. In the Amarna period (about 1350 BC), Cypriote copper was sought by the Egyptians and others. A good amount of pottery came to Cyprus from Greece. From Cyprus much of it was reshipped, sometimes together with Cypriote pottery, to cities in Syria and Canaan. So much Mycenaean pottery of this period has been recovered in Cyprus that some archaeologists believe that Greek potters had taken residence there.

In the years directly after 1300 BC, prosperity reached its highest level and trade continued to be a major contributor. The Peace of Kadesh provided Cyprus and the entire region with the security and stability that allowed international trade to thrive. More than anything else, for Cyprus copper was the basis of prosperity. In the Troodos Mountains in western Cyprus were some of the largest copper deposits known to the ancient world, and there is evidence in Cyprus of copper smelting (the process of extracting copper from its ore) as early as 2000 BC. Under the impact of increased demand for copper and benefiting from a location along a major sea lane of the ancient world, Cyprus of the Late Bronze Age seems to have entered into a boom economy.

The major copper-bearing mineral in Cyprus is chalcopyrite, a copper and iron sulfide. The golden glint of this mineral, or the blue, green, and rust-colored stains of weathered chalcopyrite, would draw the attention of early prospectors. The essential steps in producing copper included mining and concentration of the ore; roasting of the ore in an open fire or open furnace to covert the sulfide to oxide; reduction of the oxide in a high-temperature furnace to produce molten metal and slags; breakup of the cooled slags to release beads and stringers of metallic copper; remelting and casting of the copper into ingots. Roasting was probably carried out near the mines where there were open spaces and relatively few people. There is some evidence that roasting may have also been carried out within the city, though one might suppose that no city would tolerate within its walls the highly noxious fumes produced by roasting sulfide ores. In the cities would be the "value-added" operations of producing copper products, or bronze and bronze products.

Who owned these mines, regulated the production of copper and bronze, and directed the metals trade? If there were one king over all of Cyprus, it would be him. Evidence of the Amarna letters clearly shows that the king of Alasia controlled copper activities and controlled the overseas trade in copper as well. But there is no certainty that he was the only king in Cyprus. If Cyprus had been divided into separate kingdoms, likely the king of each would control mines in his territory. True private ownership of the mines, in which the king or kings had no stake, is unimaginable. The remains of copper or bronze casting operations and imported luxury goods have been found in several Cypriote cities, which indicates that these cities were in the metals trade. If there were several kingdoms and several kings in Cyprus, each controlling his own mining and copper production, was there competition for a limited and shrinking overseas market? If so, could conflict result?

The shipwreck off Ulu Burun mentioned in Chapter 6 provides an additional insight into the trade to which Cyprus owed its prosperity. The ship carried Cypriote copper and she may have been a Cypriote. Or she may have been from one of the cities of the Syria-Canaan coast, or from Greece. But the goods that she carried would have been typical of the sea trade of the eastern Mediterranean. In addition to copper, in the form of at least 354 ingots, there were ingots of tin, pellets of purple dye, purple glass and blue glass ingots (which could be used in furniture inlays or enamels), raw ivory from Syria or Egypt, a "china barrel" packed with Cypriote pottery, Canaanite jars, fine bronze swords and scrap bronze, a magnificent gold chalice, a folding writing tablet such as one may imagine Bellerophon carried (*Iliad*, Book 6), jewelry and scarabs, musical instruments, a bit of "fish-scale" armor. In addition, there were coriander and cumin, incense, wheat, barley, figs, and olives. Sea trade was essential to the economy of Cyprus.

While only limited parts of most Cypriote cities of the Late Bronze Age have been excavated, a picture of a now rather uniform Late Cypriote IIC culture emerges. Cities were enclosed with defensive walls of brick or stone. Within the city, buildings were also constructed of brick or stone, and in some cases they were extended structures internally partitioned, resulting in a rabbit warren of interconnected small rooms. There were also temples with their open courtyards. Temples and copper works were found close together, and the seemingly mysterious outcome of copper processing may have required supernatural oversight by one of the gods if it was to come out right.

Tombs were found within the cities and even beneath houses. Most were looted in a time before scientific archaeology, yet things have been discovered in them which suggest a high level of artistry. In tombs in the cities of Enkomi and Kition, there were carved ivories, gold jewelry, faience (glazed ceramic), bronze vases, vases of Egyptian alabaster, Egyptian scarabs, finely carved cylinder seals, Mycenaean pottery. Some of these objects may have been imported, and some may have been produced by foreign craftsmen resident in Cyprus.

Two finds deserve special mention because of artistic merit. From a tomb in the city of Enkomi, there is a remarkable silver bowl, possibly the finest work in silver surviving from the Bronze Age. It is a nearly hemispherical and has one wishbone-shaped handle near the top. Around the rim is a black band in which are set discs of metallic gold. Near the bottom is a design of arches executed in gold and outlined in black, and under each arch there is a rosette in gold and black. Gold had been applied by cutting away the silver and bonding gold in its place. Black was produced by recessing the silver and oxidizing the remaining silver surface (niello process). Around the bowl in the middle there are faces of bulls, facing outward. These are in silver, gold, and black, and each bull had been provided with different markings, giving each an individuality. Their horns are of gold and sweep grandly out and downward, forming a frame for each face. Between each face, there are medallions in gold and black.

Some suppose the bowl to be Greek. A Mycenaean sword or dagger of the earlier Shaft Grave period (before 1500 BC) is decorated with war scenes in gold and silver and with niello. The decorative motifs of the Cyprus bowl, however, of bulls and rosettes, were universally known at the time the bowl was made, as were the manufacturing techniques. Jewelry of niello, for example, was made in Syria as early as 1800 BC, centuries before the beginnings of Mycenaean Greece. The shape of the bowl, a shallow hemisphere with a wishbone handle near the top, closely duplicates a traditional Cypriote pottery called White Slip. The bowl is Cypriote, though the craftsman could have been a resident Syrian, Cretan, or Greek.

A remarkable rhyton (libation vessel) in faience was found in the city of Kition. This vessel is ice-cream-cone shaped and almost a foot tall and deeply glazed in light blue. The rim is dark blue and yellow. Directly below the rim various young animals, colored in yellow and red and outlined in black, gambol across the landscape. Farther down, raised bands of bright yellow and red encircle the vessel. Below that, there are two young bulls in yellow and outlined in black. A herdsman, red and outlined in black, tries to restrain one of the bulls by means of a rope. He wears a loincloth or kilt, and on his head a peaked cap with a string and tassels. Another herdsman chases the other bull. Flowers are sprinkled throughout the scene. Below this, the rhyton is finished in yellow spiral decorations. The entire vessel is a masterpiece of the ceramic art. The dress of the men is probably representative of what might be expected of working folk in Syria, southern Anatolia, and likely Cyprus itself. Egypt excelled at this type of ceramic, but rhytons of just this shape are typically Cretan. This rhyton may be the work of an Egyptian or Cretan craftsman resident in Cyprus. These objects reflect the wealth of the tomb owners and the skills of the artisans which wealth brought to Cyprus in LC IIC.

Signs of Trouble

Conditions in Cyprus began to deteriorate. Peace and prosperity seem to have been replaced by island-wide disturbances. Three important towns were abandoned. Kalavassos was located a short distance from the south coast, near copper mines (see Figure 11-1). After abandonment, fire brought down the walls of the town. Close by on the south coast was Maroni, the port city which dealt in copper coming through Kalavassos (names given here are of the nearest present-day town or city). Maroni, too, was suddenly abandoned. Far to the north, Toumba tou Skourou was abandoned at about the same time. On the evidence of pottery, these events took place toward the end of LC IIC.

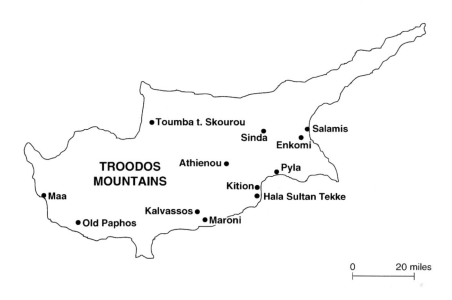

Figure 11-1. Sites of Cypriote cities of the Late Bronze Age. Names are post Bronze Age.

Also at about this time, it seems that something had gone wrong with international trade. There was a severe drop in the amount of pottery coming from the Greek mainland. Cypriote potters made up for the loss by producing imitations in the current Mycenaean style. Exports of pottery from Cyprus to Canaan also dropped off. Abandoned towns, a sharp decline in trade—these were clouds on the horizon. Or perhaps the storm had already arrived. The situation suggests several possibilities: a great natural disturbance; an international economic depression, perhaps worsened by the closing of the sea routes around Cyprus by the piratical activities of the Sea Peoples; or even the outbreak of war in Cyprus.

It was probably a few years before that Suppiluliuma II battled ships from Alasia. And it was near this time, probably, that Eshuwara, a Cypriote commander assigned to sea duty, wrote to the king of Ugarit to report the dereliction of the Ugarit fleet in what was probably an anti-Sea Peoples campaign. Something was definitely amiss in Cyprus and the vicinity.

The situation worsened. Archaeological evidence shows unequivocally that more cities of Cyprus were abandoned, and others destroyed, while a few new settlements were established. Some of the destroyed cities were rebuilt in following years on a more elaborate scale, but abandoned sites remained so. There was thus a reduction in the number of occupied cities in Cyprus, and possibly a reduction in population.

A few examples will illustrate the deterioration. On a peninsula on the west coast of Cyprus, a settlement was newly established, late in LC IIC according to Vassos Karageorghis, the principal excavator. The settlement was on a height below which were beaches where ships might be pulled up. Across the narrow neck of the peninsula, facing the mainland, a strong defensive wall was built. Maa, as this site is now known, seems a strange place for a town, out of the way, isolated. Why was a town established in this remote and inhospitable place on the west coast? Karageorghis (1990) suggests various possibilities. Invaders from Greece might have settled there. They might have selected this isolated location as a protection against attack from unwelcoming Cypriotes. He points out that a Greek settlement of later times on the coast of Sicily was located on a peninsula as a defense against the local population.

However, Karageorghis notes that the buildings, so far as can be judged from the remains, were typically Cypriote in design and construction. Therefore, it is just as reasonable to believe that Maa was established by Cypriotes as a military settlement from which to ward off enemy ships moving along the south coast toward the eastern Cypriote cities. Maa was destroyed at the beginning of LC IIIA, according to the excavator, and was reoccupied and rebuilt and then abandoned again in a few years—an indication of unstable conditions.

Near the southeast coast, on a rocky plateau about 190 feet above sea level, was the town of Pyla, established at the end of IIC or beginning of IIIA. The location could not have been chosen for practicality or convenience. Defense was a primary objective in picking this high site, as it had been for Maa. There was no drinkable water at the site, and water had to be brought from afar. Then Pyla was mysteriously abandoned. Before abandonment, a silversmith hid two silver ingots and silver scrap between two stone blocks. In a pit, a goldsmith buried unworked gold and finished gold jewelry. A coppersmith buried his tools, copper scrap, and parts of oxhide ingots. Perhaps these were the day-to-day safe deposit boxes of these artisans in those times, but more likely they were hasty concealments during an emergency. The situation is reminiscent of the last days of Ugarit in which, in one place, statues of the gods Baal or El were stashed away.

However, there is no sign of purposeful destruction or subsequent occupation at Pyla. It is a rare occurrence for people to depart while leaving behind such valuables. It is rare for precious metals to remain undisturbed over centuries and to be found by archaeologists, since metals were an objective of scavengers and site robbers in all ages.

Why the hasty and complete abandonment of the town without destruction or reoccupation? There is no sure answer.

Enkomi, one of the largest Bronze Age cities on the island of Cyprus, has been extensively excavated by several generations of archaeologists. Given the size of Enkomi and its location across a narrow sea from Ugarit, it is possible that Enkomi was Alasia or the capital of Alasia. Claude Schaeffer, one of the early excavators in Enkomi, was convinced of that but he was never able to prove it.

At the north end of the city, excavation has revealed temples, homes, tombs, and copper works. Toward the end of LC IIC, disaster struck. Walls collapsed, pottery crashed to the floor. In some areas, there is evidence of damage by fire, indicated by thick ashes and carbonized matter. Only about 15 percent of this ancient city has been excavated, and these remains may or may not be a fair representation of what happened throughout the entire city.

Reconstruction in Enkomi followed the disaster. The streets of the restored city followed an orderly plan. A new pottery seems to have appeared for the first time with the reconstruction. This pottery, called Mycenaean IIIC:1b, was based on newer Greek designs. In the rebuilt Enkomi there were impressive and imposing temples, private residences, and a structure known as Building 18, all made of ashlar masonry. As distinct from brick or roughly shaped stone, ashlar is characterized by carefully sculpted stone blocks with plane faces and squared corners. In Cyprus, much of the ashlar masonry had drafted margins, an indented rim around the outer face of each block, forming an attractive frame or border. An entire wall might be ashlar, or ashlar might be used only as decorative facing over an inner construction of irregular stone.

During the reconstruction, the city wall of Enkomi was improved and greatly strengthened—a defensive measure in anticipation of further attack which, according to the excavators, followed shortly after the first.

Investigations at Enkomi have produced some of the most interesting artistic finds. The silver bowl with bull faces, thought to be from LC IIC, the pre-destruction period, has already been described. Believed to be from LC IIIA, the reconstruction period, a mirror back of ivory shows a warrior in close combat with a griffin. Carved in fine detail, elaborately decorated, the Griffin Slayer as it is called, is an artistic treasure. Very similar to this is a second mirror back from another city in which a warrior fights a lion. This ivory is called the Lion Slayer. The most wonderful of the finds in ivory from Enkomi, however, is the Game Box which will be described in the next chapter.

From temples in Enkomi of the LC IIIA period, two small bronze statues are outstanding. One shows a warrior, slim in figure, with a helmet from which two horns protrude. In one hand, he holds a spear ready to strike, and with the other hand a circular shield is raised in defense. He stands on a miniature ox-hide ingot. The statue is referred to as the Ingot God or, from his pose, the Smiting God, Figure 12-1. It may have been offered in a religious rite, and may represent a god relating to copper-working. The second figure, again with a horned helmet, holds out one hand and holds the other against its chest. This is given the name Horned God.

Enkomi faced further troubles. After a few decades, Enkomi was a ghost town or nearly so, and all important activity shifted to the new site, known as Salamis.

Another town, Sinda, was inland of Enkomi in the direction of the mines, and probably served as a station in the processing and movement of copper to Enkomi. A very limited amount of excavation indicates destruction, with subsequent rebuilding. The destruction was a violent one with indications of fire. The town was reoccupied and then, apparently, destroyed again. The results of excavation at Sinda, taken together with findings in Enkomi, were very influential in shaping the opinion that there were two episodes of destruction in Cyprus. Mentioned earlier, a theory was proposed in which a first destruction was due to Greek invaders, the second to Sea Peoples. Such theories do not seem quite so convincing today.

Ancient Kition provides an additional illustration of radical change. Kition was located on a rise near a marsh which in ancient days may have been a bay, in which case Kition had direct access to the sea. It was one of the larger cities in Cyprus, with extensive copper workshops, temples, and tombs. Clear evidence of rebuilding is present, yet there is no clear evidence of destruction. Some of the new buildings were on a grand scale. Temple 1, as it is now called, measured close to 60 feet by 90 feet and contained handsome ashlar construction and a number of monumental columns. In the remains of the reconstructed buildings of Kition, Mycenaean III C:1b pottery has been found.

Only about 1 percent of Kition has been excavated, so findings to date may not be representative of the entire ancient city. Since ancient Kition lies beneath the present city of Larnica, further excavation possibilities are limited. Other Bronze Age cities of Cyprus, including Hala Sultan Tekke and Old Paphos, are important archaeologically, but have yielded little to further clarify events of the period of disruption.

These are examples showing that cities experienced abandonment or destruction. Most were rebuilt. Kition underwent rebuilding without evident destruction. Whatever the cause or causes, the peaceful and prosperous society of LC IIC had been profoundly shaken. Whoever the rebuilders were, it is obvious that they hoped to recapture the earlier prosperity. Copper processing facilities were restored, work in bronze surged, and pottery production increased in the newer Mycenaean Greek styles.

Date of Destruction and Rebuilding

When were the cities destroyed? When were the cities rebuilt? Evidence of destruction marks the end of LC IIC. The presence of Mycenaean IIIC:1b pottery and the use of ashlar masonry, have been assumed to mark the beginning of LC IIIA, the period of restoration. Neatly, it all seemed to have occurred at about the same time, datable to the same year or nearly so. In the light of present-day evidence, it uncertain that the period of disturbance was a short one, or that all towns and cities felt the shock at the nearly the same time, or were rebuilt at nearly the same time. The end of the largely peaceful and prosperous LC IIC period and the rebuilding which marks the start of LC IIIA could have been many years apart as Cypriotes waited for social and political stability to return. Chaos may have ruled in Cyprus over much of that period, giving little encouragement to restoration. The entire time of disturbance may have lasted a year, or as much as several decades. In that case, the transition from LC IIC to LC IIIA would have no narrowly specifiable date.

Where there are no records, pottery evidence is often relied upon to provide an approximate date. It has usually been assumed that the presence of the newer Greek pottery style marks the beginning of LC IIIA. That pottery is the so-called Mycenaean III C:1b. This designation is applied by archaeologists to pottery made locally in Cyprus with shape and painted decoration similar to certain pottery of LH IIIC style of the Greek mainland. It is, admittedly, a cumbersome term, but archaeologists have been unable to agree on another, simpler one. Several pottery shapes are included under this heading. One shape, the deep bowl or "skyphos" is particularly important to archaeologists, as it was the most often found of the new pottery in Cyprus. A skyphos (Figure 11-2), might be six inches or a bit more in height with two loop-shaped handles on opposite sides not far from the top. The most common decorations are flat spirals in dark paint. Near the rim and the bottom, there might be encircling bands. Bands might also be painted on the inside, and a single spiral on the inside bottom. All of these style elements were known from the past, but not put together in quite this way.

Mycenaean IIIC:1b pottery seemed characteristic of the rebuilding period and might serve to date that period. Dates are attached to it by matching the style (shape and decoration) to Greek mainland pottery whose dates are thought to be known, if only approximately. The American scholar Barbara Kling, who has studied the pottery extensively, judges that Mycenaean IIIC:1b was inspired by Greek mainland pottery called LH IIIC Early (Chapter 6), which began around 1190 BC, with an uncertainty of about ten years either way. The LH IIIC Early pottery phase may have ended by about 1165 BC, but there is great uncertainty in that date.

Did Mycenaean IIIC:1b derive from mainland styles toward the beginning of the LH IIIC Early style or toward its end? So far as present knowledge allows, there is a span of about twenty five years in which this may have occurred, which means that at present, Myceaean IIIC:1b cannot be dated any closer than this.

Kling (1987) notes that some Cypriote pottery of the LC IIC period, the time just before the destruction, is hardly distinguishable from Mycenaean IIIC:1b pottery. Perhaps it really was Mycaean IIIC:1b pottery. Further, Karageorghis maintains that at least some Mycenaean IIIC:1b pottery has been found in a pre-destruction context. If Mycenaean IIIC:1b was in use in Cyprus before the destruction, it cannot be used as a reliable indicator of the time of the destruction, or the rebuilding.

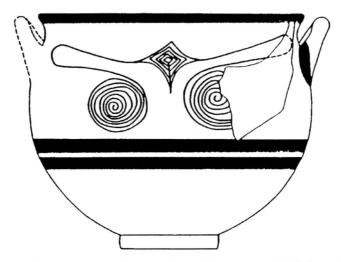

Figure 11-2. A bowl from Maa in western Cyprus, in the Mycenaean III C:1b style.

With such uncertainties, full reliance on pottery to provide a date for the destruction or reconstruction of cities in Cyprus is no longer justified. Perhaps the most that can be obtained from pottery is that these events may have occurred in a period between about 1190 BC and 1165 BC.

Evidence from Ugarit may help to clarify the date or dates. In a letter recovered from the oven in the ruins of Ugarit, there is a letter from Pgn who was mentioned in Chapter 9. It is clear that Pgn (the writing provides no vowels) was still in charge of affairs in his land, usually thought to be Cyprus/Alasia, shortly before Ugarit went up in flames. The end of Ugarit can be placed at 1193 BC or slightly after (see Chapter 9), so that Pgn still ruled at that time. Unfortunately, it is but a guess that Pgn was a king of Alasia. The letter from Pgn gives no hint of any trouble in his land except food shortages. This may mean that it was not Alasia where he ruled or, alternatively, that the most serious troubles for Alasia were yet ahead.

It must have been only a short time before the Pgn letter that the seven ships hauled up before Ugarit and disgorged the attackers who set fires in the city. The report of this event appears in a letter definitely addressed to the king of Alasia. From these letters, however, it appears that Alasia was still intact and functioning at the time of the destruction of Ugarit.

It is usually assumed that the wave of troubles in Cyprus had run its course by the time of the Medinet Habu inscriptions of Ramesses III, though there is no certainty of that. Those inscriptions may have been written as late as 1170 BC. It seems, then, that it was is in that troubled period, between 1193 BC and 1170 BC, that Hattusa fell, Ugarit was destroyed, and disaster ravaged Cyprus. These dates are consistent with dates provided by pottery evidence.

Is Cyprus Alasia?

In the year 1895, after reviewing the evidence then available, the scholar Max Muller declared that Alasia was Cyprus. In line with this view, the British historian H. R. Hall wrote in 1901 that Alasia was "a country which may be placed with great probability in Cyprus." It seems to be characteristic of efforts to reconstruct the history of the Bronze Age that conclusions seem to start with certainty and then gradually move toward uncertainty. That has been the fate of the "Alasia question." Today, approximately one hundred years after Muller and Hall wrote, it is less certain that the ancient name Alasia refers to Cyprus. If it is not Cyprus or part of Cyprus, what and where is it? Some not yet identified locality on the north Syrian or Cilician coasts, say some scholars. However, when the facts are assessed, a preponderance of the evidence continues to favor Cyprus.

There is no dispute on one matter: Alasia was by the sea. Alasia is known to have had ships in the sea trade. Hittites fought against ships from Alasia. The king of Ugarit asked the king of Alasia to warn him if he sees enemy ships, and that places Alasia not only by the sea but probably near Ugarit. In turn, that would mean that Alasia was either on Cyprus or on the mainland coast near Ugarit. Unfortunately, no Hittite, Ugaritic, or Egyptian writing gives directions to Alasia, or a precise location. Thus, other evidence must be sought.

The Land of Copper

From Babylon and Mari, ancient cities on the Euphrates River, archaeologists have recovered texts dating to about 1800–1700 BC which mention Alasia as the land of copper. Archaeology produces evidence of copper workings in Cyprus as early as that time or earlier.

That Alasia was a major trader in copper in the period of the Amarna letters, the decades around 1350 BC, is clearly shown in the letters themselves. Letter EA 33 (*El Amarna 33*) mentions two hundred talents of copper from Alasia to Egypt. In letter EA 34, the king of Alasia states that he has forwarded one hundred talents of copper to Egypt. In return, the king of Alasia says "let your messenger bring me, for presents, one bed-stead of ebony inlaid with gold, a chariot with gold, two horses" and a number of other items.

It appears that copper carried a high value. Letter EA 35 covers other matters on the mind of the king of Alasia. "I have sent five hundred talents of copper to you, as a present. Don't be upset that there is so little." In fact, this is a large shipment by the standards of those times when copper smelting was a small-scale, almost "cottage industry," activity.

The king of Alasia also writes of Nergal, a north Semitic god of death and the underworld (see Figure 16-3).

> In my land the hand of Nergal my lord has killed all the men of the land and so there is no one to produce copper....the hand of Nergal is upon my land and upon my house; my wife bore a son who is now dead..(*EA 35*)

That Nergal stalks the land suggests an epidemic or plague, striking at young and old. In return for copper, the king of Alasia now asks the king of Egypt for silver. There is also a request for oil and an ox. Other matters are brought to the attention of the Egyptians. Alasia had sent a shipment of wood to Egypt and had not yet been paid. "So, my brother, give me the worth of it." Further, a citizen of Alasia had died in Egypt. Please collect his possessions, the king of Alasia requests, and return them for the benefit of his son and widow. As a final note, "…the silver for which I asked, let my brother send it in great quantity."

It is clear that Alasia is a primary producer of copper, and not just a middleman or trans-shipper. "In my land the hand of Nergal, my lord, has killed all the men of the land and so there is no one to produce copper." That most likely means that Alasia had its own rich resources of copper, and that very likely indicates Cyprus.

Present knowledge is not perfect, however. The coasts of Syria and Cilicia have not been so thoroughly investigated by archaeologists as to rule out an undiscovered port city of the Bronze Age with significant nearby copper deposits. So long as that possibility remains, the fact that Cyprus was a copper producer and exporter is not conclusive evidence that Alasia was Cyprus. Other evidence is required.

The Land of Exile

Hittite records may provide indirect evidence of the location of Alasia. On several occasions, Hittite kings banished political enemies to Alasia. One such banishment occurred during the time of Arnuwanda I (1370–1355 BC) and another under Hattusili III (1264–1239 BC) who banished to Alasia the deposed Urhi-Tesub, the rightful king of the Hittites. In about 1300 BC, the king in Kargamish banished the sons of the queen of Ugarit. The sons had been caught in a conspiracy. They too were sent to Alasia.

Why Alasia? Why not any of the other lands or cities under Hittite control? There must have been something about Alasia itself which provided confinement, and this seems to indicate that Alasia is an island or part of an island. To the landlocked Hittites, Cyprus might seem as if surrounded by a vast moat so that escape would be very difficult. Of course, to those familiar with the sea, it would have been a highway not a barrier and, in fact, Urhi-Tesub escaped to Egypt. Still, it is difficult to see any advantage or purpose which an Alasia located on the Syrian or Cilician coast would have as a place for exiles.

"My Brother" in Egypt

In the El Amarna Letters, the king of Alasia addresses the king of Egypt as "My Brother." Wherever Alasia was located, it could not have been very big, or very powerful. That the king of Alasia should address the king of mighty Egypt as "brother" seems insolent. But it appears to be a style allowed to kings of small countries if they are independent—not subordinate to another king. During the political disturbances in Syria and Canaan in the time period of the Amarna letters, some small kings gained a temporary independence, and that circumstance might embolden one to talk of "brother." However, in the time of Hattusili III when the Hittites dominated Syria, there was no possibility of an independent king. Yet in a letter, Pudu-Hepa, wife of Hattusili, addressed the king of Alasia as "brother." Pudu-Hepa has arranged a marriage for this Alasia king and scolded him for quibbling over the bride price (and worst, she promises to visit him). Among small countries, only an island nation might have preserved some political independence, allowing its king to speak of brother or be addressed as "brother." That suggests that Alasia is Cyprus or part of it.

Battle at Sea

Hittite king Suppiluliuma II writes that he attacked ships from Alasia on the sea and burned them. Subsequently, he landed on Alasia shores and battled the enemy. There is no mainland locality in the Hittite sphere of interest that her armies could not reach by a land march. Why did the Hittites not attack this enemy by a land approach? It is true that a sea assault against a city on the mainland coast could offer tactical advantages, including surprise, put there is no information that the Hittites ever before or since landed troops from the sea in an attack of this sort. This suggests that Alasia could only be approached by sea. The circumstances strongly suggest that Alasia was an island, or part of an island, and Cyprus is the only island in the vicinity.

The Troubles of Rib-Hadda

In the time of the El Amarna letters, Rib-Hadda was king of the small country of Byblos, Figure 2-1, and was steadfastly loyal to Egypt. In return for loyalty, he expected Egyptian help in times of trouble. Now his land was under incessant attack, and in a number of letters he implored Egypt for help. But in that time, Akhenaton ruled in Egypt and political conditions in Syria and Canaan were largely ignored. An Amarna letter tells an interesting tale. This letter is from Rib-Hadda to the king of Egypt. In it, Aziru, king of Amurru, is mentioned. His main coastal city is north of Byblos. To the south of Byblos is Tyre, where King Yapah-Hadda rules. This letter from Rib-Hadda in Byblos to the king of Egypt states:

> May the Lady of Byblos grant power to the king my lord. I fall at the feet of my lord seven times and seven times. May the king my lord know that Aziru [of Amurru] is at war with me. He has seized twelve men of mine and the ransom is set at fifty shekels of silver. It was the men I sent to Sumur that he has seized….As Yapah-Hadda [of Tyre] is now on the side of Aziru against me, he has seized a ship of mine and has been going to sea to seize my ships. If you are unable to rescue me from my enemies, then send back word so that I know what action I am to take. …Look, I must keep writing like this to you… (EA 114)

The letter continues to describe the rapid deterioration of the situation and implores the Egyptians to help. Hostile forces of Amurru control the coast and the sea-lanes to the north of Byblos. Equally hostile forces of Tyre control the seas to the south. How did letter EA 114 get through to Egypt? Rib-Hadda provides an answer in the letter. "Ask Amanmassa if I did not send him from Alasia to you." Amanmassa was an Egyptian official returning to Egypt. That his route to Egypt was via Alasia is important for the Egyptian king to understand. It vividly demonstrates that Rib-Hadda is almost completely cut off from freedom of movement by sea. The only way to escape through enemy sea patrols to the north and south is to make for Alasia first. If Alasia were on the coast to the north or the south of Byblos, it is difficult to see how Amanmassa could reach it, or how this would facilitate his ultimate arrival in Egypt. But the island of Cyprus is almost due west of Byblos. Slipping out of the port of Byblos by night and making due west and then slightly north, Amanmassa could clear the enemy ships lurking along the coast and could reach Cyprus. From there, taking advantage of the prevailing wind, he could safely reach Egypt (Wachsmann, 1986). It is only if Alasia is on Cyprus that any sense can be made of the journey of Amanmassa.

Science Enters the Picture

To bypass the study of ancient texts and their ambiguities, and to come to some resolution of the "Alasia problem," an ingenious idea was proposed. Why not analyze the clay in Alasia tablets and determine if it matches the composition of clay from Cyprus? Clay deposits used in the present day in Cyprus might not be identical to those utilized over three thousand years ago. To overcome this difficulty, the chemical composition of the tablets would be compared to that of clay in Bronze Age pottery found in various Cypriote archaeological sites.

Representing the Alasia tablets were two from the British Museum which, although they had been purchased on the antiquities market in Cairo, were almost certainly from El Amarna. The tablet clays were compared to those of the ancient pottery in Cyprus, site by site. The basis of comparison was the relative content of eighteen chemical elements. Analysis showed that the tablet clays did not match pottery from Enkomi. Nor did it match pottery of Kition, nor pottery from a number of other Bronze Age sites on Cyprus. The pottery from only one site of those tested provided a partial match: Old Paphos in southwest Cyprus. Old Paphos is out of the way of the main cities of Bronze Age Cyprus and seems an unlikely location for Alasia, and it is difficult to know what to make of the test result.

Tests such as these have a peculiar property. If an exact match were found between the Amarna tablet clay and pottery clay from a Cypriote site, the result would almost certainly demonstrate that the site was the ancient Alasia. But the converse is not necessarily true. If a match is not found, it does not prove that the site was not Alasia. Too many factors interfere. It is possible that the Bronze Age potters used clay blends produced by mixing clays from different clay beds. Blends are used today to give the clay just those physical properties of plasticity, surface, color, stability that the potter requires. In recent times, backcountry potters in Cyprus have been observed to use blends, mixing clays from up to four different sources. If the clay used in the Bronze Age pottery was a blend and if the tablet clay was a different blend, or if it was taken from one of the unblended clay stocks, the chemical compositions of pottery and tablets would differ from one another. Also, certain dry fillers are often added to pottery clay, and if fillers differed between pottery and tablets, the chemical results again would be different.

In spite of the chemical test results, when all the evidence is taken together, it favors the location of Alasia on Cyprus. The name Alasia appears in different records over hundreds of years, and over this time Alasia may have been at one time most or all of the island, at other times less than the whole, perhaps only one city. Further, even if Alasia was less than the whole island, Hittites or Egyptians may have referred to it as if the whole of Cyprus, just as today, some use the term England when referring to the whole of Great Britain.

12
SEA PEOPLES AND CYPRUS

For decades, one theory has dominated scholarly thinking about the collapse of the Bronze Age. Invaders swept out of Europe and into Greece, destroying Mycenaean Greek civilization. A branch of the same invading horde thrust into Anatolia and destroyed the Hittites. Greeks and Anatolians were driven before them, or joining with them, in a human flood that spread southeast to Cyprus and ultimately to Egypt. Thus, the Greeks came to Cyprus as invaders, themselves victims of invasion. Conflict with the Cypriotes was inescapable. War and destruction resulted, ending Cypriote dominance on the island, establishing Greeks as the new rulers. Cyprus became Greek. It was the Greeks who rebuilt the cities of Cyprus in the LC IIIA period.

Implicit in the "Greek invasion" theory is the assumption that the abandonment and destruction in Cyprus which marked the end of Late Cypriote IIC was the result of war. But Claude Schaeffer, who excavated at Enkomi, disagreed with that conclusion. He maintained that the destruction, at least in Enkomi, was due to an earthquake. Schaeffer's views were not taken seriously by other experts, for he was beginning to believe and to write that earthquake accounted for the end of Ugarit and many other cities of the period. It was, according to him, a time of unusually frequent and intense earthquakes, presumably not observable in today's world.

Differences in interpretation of the evidence are understandable. In the excavated ruins of an ancient city, it is often hard to distinguish between the effects of war and the consequences of earthquake. All of the lands fringing the eastern Mediterranean—Greece, Anatolia, Cyprus, Syria, Canaan, Egypt—are and were subject to intense earthquakes. Both war and earthquake may bring walls down and cause fires in the ruins. Even stone buildings may have wooden beams which can burn.

What constitutes evidence of war? If the remains of siege engines or ramps against the outside of the city wall are found, it is certain proof of an attack on the city. In the absence of such direct and clear evidence, signs of war might include arrowheads and spear points in the streets, pieces of swords or armor, skeletons with unhealed wound marks. Strangely, little or no evidence of any of these things has been reported from any of the many excavations in the abandoned or destroyed cities of Cyprus.

While the evidence of war is absent, the view taken here is that war did occur and was responsible for some or most of the damage or abandonment observed in the remains of these cities. Support for this conclusion comes not from the direct evidence, which is lacking, but from the circumstances of the times. Before those circumstances are considered, it is necessary to deal further with the theory of a Greek invasion and conquest.

Theory and Evidence

Both legend and archaeological discoveries seemed to support the Greek invasion theory, so it is small wonder that archaeologists came to believe it. In the Classical period, the population of Cyprus was largely Greek and had been so for some time. When did Greeks arrive in Cyprus? Legends seemed to provide the answer. They relate that Greeks arrived under a variety of troubled circumstances arising from the aftermath of the Trojan War. Told and retold over centuries, these legends preserved perhaps only some small core of genuine history.

Agapenor was leader of the Greeks of Arcadia who fought at Troy. Arcadia was located in the mountains in the middle of the Peloponnese. As Arcadia was land-bound and had no ships of its own, *Iliad* tells that King Agamemnon lent the Arcadians the ships needed to take them to Troy. On his way home from the war, Agapenor and his men were swept up in a storm that brought them to Cyprus. There, they established (or perhaps reestablished or reoccupied) the city of Paphos. A contrary legend tells that King Kinyras was the founder of Paphos, but such confusion is typical of these legends. In yet another tale, Agapenor established a colony in Libya, as was mentioned in Chapter 8.

Unlike Agapenor, Teukros arrived home in Greece without difficulty after the War. Then he was banished by his father for not preventing the death of his brother. Teukros went to Cyprus, taking with him a number of captives from the Trojan War. He became king of Salamis, the successor city of Enkomi. In still another version of this very tangled tale, the Trojan captives were a people called Teukrians who came from the northwest coast of Anatolia near Troy, or from Troy itself. It is said that the Teukrians were descendants of a certain Teukros, who was not a Greek at all but an ancestor of the Trojan race. Evidently, the Teukros legend had an origin in two earlier stories which later became joined; one which deals with Teukros, a Greek hero of the Trojan War, the second with a people known as Teukrians whom Greeks knew to be native to Anatolia. Similarity of names may have resulted in a fusion of two legends.

Beyond the tales of Agapenor and Teukros, there are many other stories dealing with the foundations of Greek settlements in Cyprus. Civic pride required that a Greek colony claim a credible Trojan War hero as the founder. However shaky the stories, however twisted the details, when all are taken together they suggest a Greek migration to Cyprus approximately at the time of the Trojan War or shortly after.

What is known of Greek dialects appeared to support this view. It is known that the Greek dialect spoken in Cyprus in the Classical period was similar to that spoken in Arcadia in central Greece. In Classical times, Arcadia was surrounded by peoples who spoke the Dorian dialect, and that must have been true for many centuries. Presumably, it was the result of the Dorian invasion. Invading Dorians flowed around the high mountains of Arcadia but did not penetrate them. Scholars drew the seemingly logical conclusion: speakers of the Arcadian dialect migrated to Cyprus before the Dorian invasion had cut off their access to the sea.

Discoveries in the ruins of ancient Cypriote cities also seemed to support the Greek invasion theory. There were the destructions. And there was the Mycenaean IIIC:1b pottery, which seemed to appear suddenly and in profusion in the rebuilt cities. Surely, it was thought, this is evidence that Greeks had arrived in Cyprus in large numbers at the time of the destructions, and it was they who were responsible for the reconstruction. Then there was the orderly, well-planned new city layout observable in Enkomi. It was, no doubt, a reflection of the "logical" Greek mind. Ashlar masonry, with its neatly sculpted forms, was also thought a reflection of Greek rationality and aesthetics.

In Enkomi, in Tomb 18, the remains of a warrior were found together with bronze greaves (shin armor) and the newer type of sword. Bronze greaves were known from Greece. The famous "Warrior Vase" (Figure 7-1) found by Heinrich Schliemann in Mycenae seems to show warriors wearing greaves. Here in Tomb 18 must be the remains of a Greek warrior, one of the chieftains of the conquering invaders.

Legend, language, destruction, new Mycenaean pottery, orderly town plan and refined architecture of the restored cities, the warrior and his equipment, these must be evidence of a massive invasion and occupation by Greeks. As archaeological excavations in Cyprus continued, almost every new find began to be seen as evidence of the presence of Greeks, even when other explanations were just as logical, or more so.

As is often the case, early archaeological finds may lead to a theory that seems to explain the limited evidence. As time goes on, the theory begins to be accepted as fact and presented as fact as doubts and uncertainties are suppressed. Later, more evidence, or a reexamination of old evidence by new eyes, leads to doubt. As noted earlier, archaeology sometimes seems to move from certainty to uncertainty. The "fact" of the Greek conquest with destruction of Cypriote cities, once so certain, is now much less so.

Ashlar, once thought to have been used for the first time in the rebuilding of the cities is now known to have been used for important buildings in Cyprus before the period of destruction. Kition had ashlar in the foundations of a tower at the seaport entrance, datable to LC IIC. In Kalavassos, there was a building of impressive size and orderly design constructed of fine ashlar masonry. It was of pre-destruction times, the LC IIC period. Nearby Maroni had a smaller ashlar building. Thus, there was no need for Greeks to introduce ashlar to Cyprus. It was already known, and used, and if knowledge of ashlar techniques was not native to Cyprus, if outside inspiration was needed, it could be found a short distance across the sea in Ugarit. There, ashlar had been extensively used in palaces, residences, and tombs.

After the destruction, the rebuilt city of Enkomi was layed out with carefully placed streets and avenues on a rectangular grid. It is this orderliness in Enkomi which has been credited to the Greeks, presumably on the assumption that the Greeks possessed what others did not—a mental outlook given to order and logic. But Ora Negbi of Tel Aviv University (1986) makes a persuasive case that this rectangular grid plan already existed in Enkomi during LC IIC, before the destruction, and was simply followed again during reconstruction. There is no reason to attribute the grid plan to Greeks, particularly Greeks from the mainland, where there is hardly an example of such orderly town planning. If outside stimulus for such planning was needed, it could be found in Ibn Hani, the seaport of Ugarit, where an orderly grid layout existed. There was certainly close contact and relations between Cyprus and Ugarit as between two nearby Cypriote cities.

Buildings in Kalavassos are aligned closely with one another with an accuracy of five degrees. This too suggests that Kalavassos was built according to an orderly town plan well before the period of destruction.

The warrior in Tomb 18 with his arms and armor, including greaves, was one of several persons, male and female, interred in the tomb. With them were rich objects of gold, ivory, and pottery of Mycenaean IIIB style that was popular in Cyprus during LC IIC, before the destructions. By the pottery style, and the closing off of the tomb by construction of Building 18 during the renewal, the tomb is dated to the LC IIC period. Some believe that the interment could have taken place even after the destruction of the city but before the beginning of work on Building 18, or perhaps even after. A later date for his internment allows the warrior to be thought of as one of the Greek conquerors.

What is the evidence that he was Greek? It is largely the newer sword design and the greaves. Sword and greaves do not necessarily show that the owner was a Greek, however. A sword such as found in the tomb might easily arrive in Cyprus in trade or as a gift for a Cypriote king. In all ages, weapons, or the designs of them, move rapidly from place to place. No great number of Bronze Age greaves have been discovered, and about as many have been found in Cyprus as in Greece. Nearly as many greaves are illustrated in the art of Cyprus (the Smiting God) as in the art of Greece (on the Warrior Vase perhaps, and a stela with the same picture as on the vase). It is no more than a guess that greaves were something especially Greek in that period.

It is no more than a possibility that the warrior of Tomb 18 was Greek. It is more reasonable to believe that he was a Cypriote of high standing. "Where are the burials of the other warriors?" asks Vassos Karageorghis, a leading archaeologist in Cyprus. None have been found.

It is the Mycenaean IIIC:1b pottery which seems to be the most persuasive evidence of the presence of Greeks. Such pottery has been found in large quantity in the remains of the rebuilt cities, together with an ample amount of native Cypriote pottery. However, an invasion or a mass migration of Greeks was not required to bring Mycenaean IIIC:1b to Cyprus. Greek pottery had long been popular in Cyprus, and for that matter in Cilicia, Ugarit, and the cities of Syria and Canaan. Greek potters alone may have come to Cyprus. Escaping the poor conditions which had spread over the homeland, they may have been welcomed to the reconstructed Cypriote cities of LC IIIA, the post-destruction period. There, the skills which they brought might contribute to the hoped for renewed trade and prosperity.

That possibility is illustrated by events of a later time. In the Classical period Athenian potters, wishing to escape the hardships of the Peloponnesian War (431–404 BC), emigrated to southern Italy. There, they set up shop and produced "Athenian" pottery that flooded the markets of Italy and abroad. Archaeological excavation has shown that Athenian-style pottery appeared suddenly and in quantity in southern Italy. Except for the existence of historical records which prove otherwise, it might be thought from the archaeological evidence alone that a Greek invasion or conquest of southern Italy had taken place. There was no such conquest. Mycenaean IIIC:1b pottery in Cyprus might have no greater significance than this; an influx of Greek potters, escaping deteriorating conditions at home.

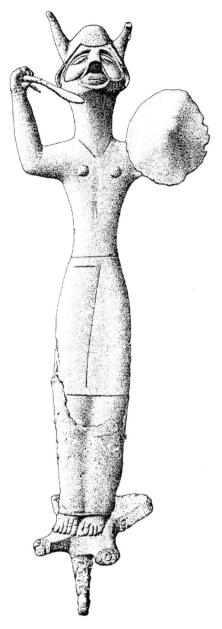

Figure 12-1. A small figure in bronze from Enkomi, Cyprus, called the Ingot God because he stands on an "ox-hide" ingot. Also called the Smiting God because of his belligerent stance.

Nor were Greek potters needed. To satisfy local demand, imitations of Mycenaean pottery were being produced in Cyprus during the LC IIC period in the Greek style current at that time. The later Mycenaean IIIC:1b pottery could easily have been made by Cypriote potters, inspired by glimpses of the latest styles and trends from the mainland and some of the islands. Native Cypriote potters were certainly capable of producing an authentic-looking "Greek" pot. In western Anatolia, in Miletus (Millawanda), archaeologists have discovered remains of a pottery factory, and it appears that this factory was manufacturing in both "Mycenaean" and also "Anatolian" styles. Evidently, production could be switched between Mycenaean and Anatolian depending on market requirements. It should be granted that many professional potters of the Late Bronze Age could produce in whatever style market conditions demanded.

There are many other finds in excavations which under the influence of the Greek invasion theory were interpreted as evidence of the presence of Greeks. One prominent archaeologist continually referred to a "megaron"—the traditional palace design of Greece—in a welter of rooms in the north part of the Enkomi excavation. Independent observers see no such megaron.

Others have attributed small bronze statues such as the Ingot God or Smiting God from Enkomi (Figure 12-1) to Greeks. He wears a helmet with horns and on one arm carries a round shield and in the other hand a raised spear. On his legs seem to be greaves. The horns, the round shield, greaves, all seem to make him Greek to those disposed to see Greek in the archaeological finds of this period. Horned helmets were known in Greece, it is true. But gods with horned helmets had long infested Syria and Anatolia, and many images are known. They are seen in seal engravings, sculpture, and in bronze statues with just this same Smiting God pose.

The Horned God from Enkomi was mentioned in the previous chapter. Some who study this statue see something Greek in his expression, which looks like that seen in Greek sculpture of the Archaic period that preceded the Classical period. But Archaic period sculptural style, or more exactly the strange smiling expression, may have originated in Cyprus. If so, the Horned God may be an early manifestation of the style, in which case there would be nothing Greek about the expression of the Horned God, except that the Greeks later copied it.

Such small bronze cast statues as the Smiting God and the Horned God are hardly known from Greece in any case. Taken in total, these bronze works show much more local characteristics than Greek attributes, and do little to demonstrate the presence of Greeks.

The negative evidence must also be considered. Important things that seem to characterize Greek life of the mainland haven't been found in the reconstructed cities of Cyprus. No confirmed megaron has been found. No tombs of the beehive type and no chamber tombs with a dromos (descending roadway) have been found datable to this time. These were the typical tombs of mainland Greece in the Late Bronze Age. No evidence of the use of Greek Linear B writing has yet been found in Cyprus. Nor have the remains of murals such as those in the palaces of Greece been found. A number of pottery types known from the mainland also are absent, or found in small quantities. There is, for example, little evidence among the pottery of found in the reconstruction of the kylix, the favored stemmed drinking cup of the mainland.

It is possible that some of these Greek features were characteristic of the elite or upper stratum of mainland Greek society, and that the invaders came from a lower level of society. Or the invaders may have been Greeks from Anatolia who perhaps had grown away from these "Greek" things. If the supposed invaders did not carry a recognizable Greek culture with them to Cyprus, how is the presence of Greeks in Cyprus to be recognized? There is no clear way. As a result, that Greeks from any social stratum or any geographic location came to Cyprus and conquered it is no more than a guess, lacking good evidence.

On the other hand, there is good evidence, not of an intruding foreign culture of any kind, but for cultural continuity in Cyprus. The culture of LC IIIA seems to be an outgrowth of the pre-destruction culture. Temples were rebuilt, more grandly than before, featuring ashlar masonry construction, as before. Such temples were unknown in mainland Greece in the Bronze Age. Temple builders in Cyprus embedded stone anchors in the walls or floors, just as in the temples of the pre-destruction period. These anchors must have had a religious significance, and that suggests that the rebuilders held the same religious beliefs as did those before destruction. Continued use of the earlier tombs suggests the same. The people of LC IIIA had no religious problems in the continuing use of LC IIC tombs.

In the new ashlar buildings of LC IIIA, some of the building blocks have architects' or masons' marks in the Cypro-Minoan script, the same writing system as was used in LC IIC. Cast bronze figures continued to display native Cypriote or Syrian themes. Most of the pottery found in the ruins of settlements remained Cypriote as before. These things too suggest ethnic continuity from LC IIC into LC IIIA. It is likely that both before and after the destruction, language, belief, dress, and in short the culture, remained much the same as before.

The Greek invasion theory is thus without reasonable demonstration let alone proof. It has become like the Cheshire Cat of *Alice in Wonderland*, which slowly faded to invisibility except that its smile remains. The assumed evidence for a Greek invasion has faded away, but the Greek invasion is still spoken of as an indisputable fact.

The Cypriotes

Fine ashlar temples and other buildings, renewed and expanded metal and pottery industries, workshops in ivory and gold, all the requirements of international trade were reestablished in Cyprus. The rebuilders were evidently a highly urban group. Only such people, or at least their leaders, would have understood all of the requirements of urban life and the needs of commercial cities. War must, in part, account for the disruptions in Cyprus. The rebuilders were certainly those who triumphed in the conflict, and material and cultural continuity indicates that they were the Cypriotes themselves, or people of nearly identical culture. Cypriotes may have defeated a massive invasion of foreigners, Greeks or Sea Peoples, vanquishing them so thoroughly that hardly a material trace is to be found of the invaders. But it is even more likely that the war was not fought against a mass of invaders but was fought among Cypriotes. It may have been a kind of civil war, and civil wars can be the most destructive, particularly if ethnic or class differences are involved.

Did such ethnic distinctions exist? Pottery evidence of about 1500 BC suggests that there were several distinctive cultures on the island. In the northwest, a pottery known as Base Ring, with its clearly defined circular bases was used, and in the northeast "panhandle" of the island a style known as Red on Black was dominant. In the east, people used White Painted pottery, and in the Troodos Mountains, White Slip pottery. White Slip favored hemispherical cups and bowls with wishbone-shaped handles. The form is reflected in the extraordinary silver bowl from Enkomi described in the Chapter 11. All the pottery was handmade, meaning that they were fashioned without the use of the potter's wheel. The significance of these distinctive pottery styles is that they may represent evidence of distinctive cultural zones in Cyprus, and possibly of distinctive ethnic and linguistic groups.

One part of the population may have been of Hurrian or Semitic descent. From the El Amarna archives of about 1350 BC, there is a letter in which the king of Alasia asked for the return of certain of his subjects who were detained in Egypt. Their names are given. The American scholar Michael Astour studied the names and concluded that one is Hurrian and the rest are North West Semitic (Astour, 1964). A tablet found in Ugarit and another from the inland Syrian city of Alalakh give the names of certain Alasia citizens. These names too are a mix of Hurrian and North West Semitic. Hurrian and North West Semitic names were common in Ugarit on the Syrian coast. Other evidence may point to a substantially Semitic and Hurrian population in Cyprus. An Alasia letter to Egypt mentions a god who has laid low the copper workers of Cyprus. The name of this god is given in symbols which ordinarily are translated as Nergal. An Ugarit letter dealing with a banishment of exiles to Cyprus mentions a goddess of Cyprus whose name, written in symbols, is usually translated as Ishtar. Both Nergal and Ishtar were worshiped in Syria, where Semitic-speaking people were numerous.

Already mentioned is one temple feature, stone anchors. Ship anchors of that time were large flat stones, roughly rectangular or elliptical in shape. A hole was driven through for an anchor rope and another hole took a wood stake that served as anchor flukes. These were crude, perhaps, but effective and were widely used in the Mediterranean in those times. Such stone anchors have been found embedded in the floors or walls of temples in Kition and Enkomi, and a very similar anchor is known from a temple in Ugarit. Thus, Temples in Cyprus and Ugarit were united by a similar religious expression.

Personal names, names of gods and religious ideas evident in the construction of temples suggest that people of similar culture or ethnicity lived in Cyprus and the Syrian coast opposite, where there were people of Hurrian and Semitic descent.

Tablets written in the Cypro-Minoan writing system provide hints of another ethnicity in Cyprus. The name "Cypro-Minoan" was given to the Cypriote script by Arthur Evans, the celebrated excavator of ancient Knossos in Crete. It was his assumption that the Cypriote script came from Crete. That has not been proven and is by no means certain. The Cypro-Minoan script first appeared in Cyprus before 1500 BC and continued in use, though strongly altered, into the Classical period. Not much in the way of lengthy text in Bronze Age Cypro-Minoan has been found, only a few incomplete tablets. In addition, there are a number of isolated Cypro-Minoan symbols on masonry, pottery, clay "marbles," bronze tools, and weapons. This may indicate that this script was widely used, even among ordinary people, and was not the sole property of professional scribes.

For purposes of decipherment, much more text than now exists is needed in order to determine patterns of word use, declensions, and the like. But even short of decipherment, there may be sufficient text to determine the language family to which Cypro-Minoan belongs. With this possibility in mind, J. C. Billigmeier undertook a scholarly experiment (Billigmeier, 1976). Both Linear B and the daughter script of Cypro-Minoan of the Classical period have been translated. The sound values of their symbols are known. Where the shape of a Bronze Age Cypro-Minoan symbol resembles that in Linear B, the sound of that Cypro-Minoan symbol is assumed to be identical to that from Linear B. Similarly, where a Bronze Age Cypro-Minoan symbol resembles that of the daughter writing system of the Classical period, the Classical period sound is assumed to apply to Bronze Age Cypro-Minoan symbol. Thus, a limited number of Cypro-Minoan sound values may be established.

Billigmeier examined a clay tablet known as Tablet 90, found in Enkomi (see Figure 12-2). Though broken and incomplete, the tablet contains the longest Cypro-Minoan text thus far discovered. This tablet had been discarded, apparently, and later set down to form part of the floor of a hearth. Though this hearth foundation was laid in LC IIIA, the tablet may date to the earlier LC IIC period, according to the excavators. Applying to Tablet 90 sounds values as described above, Billigmeier was able to determine the pronunciation of parts of words. Looking around the Eastern Mediterranean of the Bronze Age, he found that neither Semitic, nor Hurrian, nor Greek contained these sound groups. Only the Anatolian languages, Hittite and Luvian, provided a good match. If Billigmeier is right, the language of Tablet 90 is Hittite or the closely related Luvian. Luvian is the more likely, as the north coast of Cyprus lies but a short distance from the south coast of Anatolia where the Luvian language was at home. In Cyprus, the major concentration of speakers of Luvian may have been in the north, nearest Anatolia. The city of Enkomi lies toward the north and may have had a mixed population.

Figure 12-2. Tablet 90 from Enkomi, Cyprus, written in the Cypro-Minoan script.

It has been mentioned that Astour had found that Alasia personal names in an Amarna tablet were either Semitic or Hurrian. The Italian scholar Onofrio Corruba also studied those same tablets. He confirmed that certain names were Semitic or Hurrian, but also suggested that some were Anatolian (Corruba, 1968). Further, skulls found in Enkomi have been measured by anthropologists. The measurements suggest an Anatolian origin. Anthropology, linguistics, and personal names, point to an Anatolian origin of certain Cypriote populations.

Linguists believe that Cypro-Minoan symbols were used to write two different languages, and if one is Luvian, then it is reasonable to believe that the other was North West Semitic. A text written in Cypro-Minoan has been found in Ugarit itself, which may support this view. It is thus reasonable to think that there were at least two major ethnic groups in Cyprus at the end of the Bronze Age—one Semitic or Hurro-Semitic, the other Anatolian.

In addition, there may have been other ethnic groups in smaller numbers. Cyprus was located along a major sea-lane of the ancient world and was accessible from many directions. Some of these peoples may have been hidden away in remote places on the island, descendants of ancient migrations. Others may have arrived later, finding employment as craftsmen or mercenaries. In LC IIIA there may have been Cretans, Greeks, and Anatolians living on the island. Greeks may have been invited to establish pottery and weaving industries. Those of other nationalities may have set up shop in other crafts. Pottery survives the vicissitudes of time better than the remains of other crafts, and for that reason, pottery found in Cypriote archaeological sites may create a misleading impression of the presence of an overwhelming number of Greeks to the exclusion of others.

Signs of War

Much of the evidence of abandonment and destruction in Cyprus could be explained either by earthquake or by war. Circumstances of the times suggest that war played a role, though it may not be the entire explanation. Most important among those circumstances was the collapse of Hittite power. A Hittite presence had loomed over Cyprus and had been a fact of life for centuries, and at times Cyprus seems to have been some sort of a Hittite "protectorate." Hittites could be heavy-handed at times, as imperial people often are. Late in LC IIC (the exact date is unknown) a Hittite military force came ashore in Cyprus and laid hands on the king and his chief minister, "imposing tribute on the spot," a Hittite report says. This measure does not have the ring of a military conquest but of a bill-collecting visit, the result of tribute owed and not timely paid, and perhaps even resisted.

To the Cypriotes, the collapse of Hittite power might at first have seemed like a gift. But Hittite "protection" had been a real benefit. For centuries, Hittite military expeditions into western and southern Anatolia, aimed at establishing stability and order, had also tended to protect Cyprus from raids by lawless elements from those regions. Under Hittite direction, the seas to the north and east of Cyprus were policed with some success by ships from the port cities of Hittite vassals. The Peace of Kadesh between the Hittites and Egypt brought stability to Syria, and provided the tranquility throughout the region upon which the mercantile success of Cyprus depended. The prosperity of the LC IIC period in Cyprus would probably not have been possible without the Hittites. Now the Hittites were finished as a power, and with that came increasing instability.

Then Ugarit was destroyed. As a major hub of overland and sea trade routes, Ugarit was the indispensable trading partner of Cyprus, providing access to the raw materials and markets of the continental interior. The shock of the sudden end of the Hittites and Ugarit must have reverberated throughout Cyprus. And to add to the problem, the Sea Peoples were now in and around Cyprus. For that or other reasons, trade with Greece, Canaan, and Egypt had dropped to a trickle. The result may have been economic collapse in Cyprus.

Societies often have their internal cleavages, healed over so long as times are good or the ruler is strong, but liable to rupture if the situation reverses. If bitter war in Cyprus did not result from these disastrous changes, it is hard to see how it was avoided.

Sea Peoples in Cyprus

Long before the period of destruction, Madduwatta and Attarissiyas raided Cyprus from a base in western or southern Anatolia. It was an attack in the style of the later Sea Peoples, and can be seen as the earliest known manifestation of the activities of Sea Peoples. Only

Figure 12-3. Side of the ivory Game Box showing charioteer, hunter with bow, and helper on foot.

a few years later, attacks on Cyprus resumed. An El Amarna letter to Alasia tells of the situation. Lukka people had attacked Egyptian territory, the Egyptians charge, and people of Cyprus collaborated with the raiders. Concerned with this accusation, the king of Cyprus indignantly replied to Egypt:

> People of the land of Lukka year by year take a small city in my land.....If Cypriotes are with them, let me know and I will take appropriate action. (*EA 38*)

As far back as the Amarna period, Cyprus was attacked by Lukka, whose descendants were among the Sea Peoples who battled Merneptah years later. A tradition of raids and occupation in Cyprus was established early. At any time, internal weakness in Cyprus or international disorder might encourage further raids.

Then, in the time of the troubles at the end of the Bronze Age, a Hittite king was concerned about the "Shikala who live on ships." Ugarit was attacked from the sea and burned. Hittites engaged in a sea battle with ships from Cyprus followed by a fight ashore. It is certain that Sea Peoples were again roaming the seas around Cyprus, and were again ashore on Cyprus.

Figure 12-4. Drawing of the figure on the Game Box showing the headdress, with feathers around the top, and headband with circles or discs. Different from the drawing, the photo shows nearly complete circles in the headband.

Two finds in the city of Enkomi are particularly revealing of the presence of Sea Peoples. The first is a seal-stone, found in a context that indicates that it may have been of the LC IIC period. On the oval face is engraved the figure of a warrior. He is crouched behind his large circular shield, his sword thrust forward. On his head, he wears the unmistakable headdress of the Sea Peoples.

The second find is the "Game Box." The box is constructed of carved ivory panels and is 11.5 inches long, 3 inches wide, and 3.25 inches high. Two massive bulls resting decorate the narrow end panels. Hunting scenes are carved on the two long side panels. The top is marked for a board game and one end panel opens as a drawer to hold the game pieces. The game was played in ancient Mesopotamia, and in Egypt, where several very similar game boxes have been found. There, it was known as Senet.

Only one of the side panels of the box is reasonably well preserved and presents a hunting scene of vigorous action, Figure 12-3. In it, a chariot charges furiously. Bent over the reins, whip in hand, is the charioteer. The rider on the chariot has his bow fully flexed and is about to release an arrow toward the quarry. Front and back legs of the chariot horses are stretched out nearly horizontally, indicating unrestrained pursuit of the quarry, and a hunting dog is similarly in full pursuit. Fleeing before the hunters are a variety of animals. A bull has turned around, head lowered, making a stand.

A member of the hunting party is afoot near the chariot. He holds an axe, possibly to administer the coup de grace. He is bearded, and wears a kilt of the kind well known in representations of Syrians of this period. On his head, he wears the unmistakable headdress of the Sea Peoples, just as shown on the seal-stone. Elsewhere in the scene (and not shown in the figure), a second member of the hunting party is also one of the Sea Peoples, though that part of the panel is not well preserved.

There has been a good deal of discussion concerning the nationality of the carvers of this box. Stylistic comparisons have been made with ivory work of Greece, Ugarit and Egypt. The galloping animals with legs outstretched are similar to representations on a sword from the Shaft Graves at Mycenae of centuries earlier, but that manner of representation was widely known. A fine gold bowl from Ugarit shows a hunting scene much like that of the ivory Game Box, with chariot, hunter with bow flexed, and horses and quarry depicted in the same mad dash. Gold workers, ivory carvers, and other artisans shared design ideas with one another as do artists today, and did so between cities and countries, so that such representations were at home in Syria, Egypt, and probably in Cyprus. Ugarit exported raw elephant ivory to Cyprus. Blocks of unworked ivory have been found in Cyprus. It is certain that ivory carvers were resident there. There is no need to look past Cyprus for the origin of the Game Box.

The horses shown on the Game Box have neatly braided tails and are richly caparisoned, closely resembling illustrations of the horses of Ramesses II on the walls at Luxor temple, and the horses of Ramesses III at Medinet Habu temple. The rider with his bow is obviously a man of great status and wealth, probably a king. He is dressed in a thigh-length garment, overfolded in front, and belted at the waist. He has a full beard. His hair falls long over the back of his head, thick and straight, and is retained by a headband. His appearance is unlike anything illustrating Greeks, Cretans, Hittites, Egyptians, or Libyans of that period. On the other hand, he closely resembles one of the Syrian allies of the Hittites in an Egyptian illustration of Kadesh (Figure 2-3), and of Syrians in many other Egyptian illustrations. While no one knows how Cypriotes of the end of the Bronze Age looked and dressed, many must have looked like Syrians, to whom they may have been related. A bronze caldron stand found in Cyprus shows a figure who looks very nearly like the rider in the chariot in beard, hairstyle, headband, and dress. This strongly suggests that the chariot owner, the man with the bow, could be at home in Cyprus, and that the scene is set in Cyprus.

The seal-stone with the individual wearing the Sea Peoples headdress, the figures on the Game Box with the same headdress, were both found in Cyprus, and this makes it even more likely that they illustrate people in Cyprus. Two finds are not a large number, it is true, but no such clear and certain representations of Sea Peoples with such headgear have ever been found in Greece, Crete, western and central Anatolia of this period.

The Game Box was found in a tomb by an expedition in the late 1800s, more a treasure hunt than skillful archaeology. Documentation of the finds in the tomb is poor. As a result, information which might help in dating has been lost. Tomb finds are hard to date narrowly in any case, since tombs are reopened and additional interments made and gifts added over a number of years so that it is hard to know which artifacts go with which datable pottery. Some experts place the box in LC IIIA. It could have been made earlier, in LC IIC, since it is obviously precious and may have been an heirloom passed down over a few generations to this final interment.

Whichever the period of the carving of the box, it is a reasonable conclusion that the seal and the box demonstrate the presence of Sea Peoples in Cyprus at the close of the Bronze Age.

The hunting scene on the box is particularly important for what it appears to say of these individuals of the Sea Peoples and their relationship to one who is in power in Cyprus. In the chariot is a man of high estate, likely a king, possibly the king of Alasia. He is a man of wealth, as shown by the rich trappings of the horses. He is no man of a distant land, but in all likelihood a native son of Cyprus. With him are two of the Sea Peoples.

These are not enemies of the king but are his subordinates, part of his hunting party. Sea People have been noted in the role of fighters and destroyers. Here they are shown in a peaceful role. Their relationship with the king may even indicate that these particular Sea Peoples are native to Cyprus, owing allegiance to the king by reason of place of birth. Or, they may be mercenaries from some distant land. In this scene, they idle away at hunting along with the king. There is no war in which to fight at this moment.

War in Cyprus

Evidence which has been described shows that internal conditions in Cyprus had seriously deteriorated. Much resembles evidence of destruction or abandonment in Greece and, as is in Greece, a mixture of factors may have been involved. Even Plague cannot be ruled out. When Plague appears, it transcends borders and afflicts many lands at nearly the same time.

Strife or war in Cyprus must have been a leading factor. But strife between whom, and what war? A life-and-death clash of Greek against Cypriote in which the Greeks were victorious? As already noted, that is not supported by any overwhelming evidence. An invasion of peoples from western or southwestern Anatolia, or even from Cilicia are possibilities, but equally difficult to demonstrate. In any case, present evidence does not require a significant foreign invasion. Perhaps future archaeological research can say more.

Until new evidence is produced, attention has to be given to the evidence that the native culture was uninterrupted from LC IIC into LC IIIA. From that, it is reasonable to conclude that the rulers in the rebuilt Cyprus were Cypriotes, as before. That suggests that the conflict was internal, Cypriote against Cypriote. That conclusion does not mean that only Cypriotes were involved; and foreigners may have been drawn into the conflict. The precise cause of this conflict, who fought against whom, what foreign groups were involved, exactly when it started and ended, how it may have related to a possible natural catastrophe, including epidemic, are not known and may never be known. Rivalry between cities, economic and class conflict resulting from economic collapse, ethnic clashes resulting from both, and the presence of Sea Peoples on the island as a potentially disruptive element were probably all factors. They may have made war inevitable, and once started, difficult to stop. Since the events of these critical times in Cyprus are unknown, what happened can only be guessed, and the description below is entirely speculative.

Serious disturbances in Greece, difficulties among the Hittites, and chaotic rule in Egypt following the reign of Merneptah may have weakened the regional economy and reduced the demand for Cypriot copper and bronze. Trade would have been seriously affected, and disruptions by Sea Peoples of the sea-lanes may have further reduced the little trade that remained. These came at a particularly bad time for Kalavassos and Maroni, for the copper deposits that they controlled, and upon which their economy depended, was beginning to play out. A weak market could no longer justify the high cost of extracting the remaining ores. These cities could no longer compete with other Cypriote copper cities. Thus, the mines were closed. The king ordered abandonment and marched the population to remaining cities. (In India shortly after AD 1325, the raja of Delhi ordered all his subjects to abandon Delhi for a new and distant city which he built. Later, he marched them back.) Competition between cities for the limited remaining markets intensified and this led to clashes between cities.

It can be assumed that Hatti had used its power to prop up kings of its own liking in Cyprus. Now, with the Hittite collapse, that prop disappeared, and enemies of existing rule and some who were ambitious may have revolted. Clashes between ethnic elements broke out, and the situation was no longer controllable. It became civil war—bitter, destructive, enduring. Opposing leaders reached out for mercenaries. Sea People were welcomed. They were skilled fighters, and would be loyal so long as they were paid.

In a war largely of mercenary against mercenary, the side with the greater fiscal resources is likely to prevail. In time, the war in Cyprus burned itself out as resources were exhausted. Truce was reluctantly agreed upon among the factions, which became a peace, and one by one, cities began to rebuild and restore themselves. In some cities, wealth brought over earlier from Ugarit supported the rebuilding. Restoration meant the reestablishment and reinvigoration of industries that supported trade. Foreign craftsmen were invited to settle and to carry on their work. New pottery works were established. Put into production were copies of the most recent and fashionable pottery designs from Greece, the kind which home and overseas markets would welcome, just as they welcomed earlier Mycenaean pottery.

Support of the gods, lost during the conflict, was now urgently needed. There were new and enlarged temples. There were new and better copper and bronze facilities. Iron, a sometime byproduct of the smelting of copper-iron ores, was exploited in small amounts, a potential new product for overseas markets.

While Cypriotes and their culture dominated the rebuilding period, the island had become more than ever a checkerboard of ethnicities. Greeks lived in Cyprus, before and after the destruction. They may have been employed in the various crafts or as soldiers. But they were no majority, nor in control of Cyprus. There came a time, however, not long after the destruction and rebuilding, when Greeks did begin to come to Cyprus in large numbers.

With the rebuilding in Cyprus came renewed prosperity, at least for a time. But for many of the mercenaries there was unemployment. Meanwhile, ethnic movements were working themselves out in the hills of Canaan, while on the shores of Canaan, opportunities would develop for restless or unemployed Sea Peoples.

13

ISRAEL AND CANAAN

Events occurred in Canaan at the end of the Bronze Age which are unmentioned in surviving documents of the period, but which had immense implications for the future. It was then, according to archaeological evidence, that new settlements began in the highlands of Canaan that became the core of the nation of ancient Israel.

Israel was no more than a minor factor in the military, political, and economic life of the ancient world, and it would hardly be noted today if it were not for the profound religious experience of Israel as recorded in the Bible. The Hebrew Bible, which reports the life of Israel over more than one thousand years of its existence, today influences belief of Jew, Christian, and Muslim and thus a major portion of the present world population.

The biblical books of Exodus, Numbers, Deuteronomy, and Joshua tell of the entrance of the people of Israel into Canaan. No date is given in the Bible, but archaeological evidence and the weight of much scholarly opinion favors the end of the Bronze Age. The beginning of the settlement of Israel in Canaan would then relate to the other events that were taking place at that time, when the previously stable world of the Bronze Age was in the midst of profound change.

Scholars have labored to understand the circumstances of the origin of Israel. The use of the Bible to reconstruct the early history of Israel would seem to be a rational approach. However, for a number of reasons, many scholars reject much or all of the earlier books of the Bible as history and prefer to depend on the findings of archaeology. In what place and in which period of the archaeological record should evidence be sought? Most clues come from the Bible itself, and so the Bible cannot be set entirely aside, even by the most skeptical scholars.

Important for historic reconstruction is knowledge of the approximate date of the entry into Canaan. In the biblical account, the Exodus and then the entry into Canaan are separated by forty years or a little more—approximately one generation—so that if the time of the Exodus were known, the time of the arrival in Canaan would also be known.

The Bible (1 Kings 6:1), states that the Exodus occurred 480 years before the fourth year of Solomon's reign. The date of his reign is known with reasonable accuracy and a calculation from that would place the Exodus at about 1447 BC. Forty years later, or approximately 1407 BC, the tribes would be at the Jordan, looking across the river toward Jericho.

The account of the crossing into Canaan and the immediate fall of Jericho is well known. Archaeologists have found evidence that the city was destroyed. One archaeologist dates that destruction to about 1400 BC, in close agreement with the 1407 BC date. That date is debated among archaeologists, however, and dates more than a century earlier or later have been proposed. Thus, the date of the destruction of Jericho is not really known.

Evidence from Egypt, however, suggests another date for the Exodus. According to the biblical Book of Genesis, Joseph's family had been settled in Egypt in the land of Goshen, likely the Wadi Tumilat as it is known today, a fertile and well-watered valley on the eastern edge of the Nile Delta, Figure 13-1. After some generations, according to the Bible, descendants of Joseph and his brothers were put to forced labor on the Pharaoh's building projects. Exodus 1:11 tells that the Egyptians:

> ...set taskmasters over them to afflict them with their burdens. And they built for Pharaoh supply cities, Pithom and Raamses.

The name "Raamses" as given in the Bible is without doubt the same as "Ramesses" of Egyptian records. There were several Egyptian kings named Ramesses. Most famous was Ramesses II, the self-proclaimed hero of the Battle of Kadesh. In Egypt, Ramesses was an energetic builder, more so than other pharaohs of the Late Bronze Age. In the eastern Delta, at the present-day site of Kantir, where an ancient branch of the Nile once flowed, archaeologists have excavated an extensive field of ruins. It was a sleepy frontier town of the Late Bronze Age when Ramesses' father, Seti I, and his architects began to make plans for a vast palace and temple complex. Construction began under Seti, and Ramesses pressed the work forward with vigor. According to what has been found in the ruins, it seems that Ramesses wanted his name placed everywhere. This site is likely to have been the supply city "Raamses" of the Bible.

The other supply city, "Pithom," may be the Per-Atum or Pi-Atum mentioned in an Egyptian papyrus, Papyrus Anastasi IV. It was located, some archaeologists believe, at present-day Tell er-Rabata in the Wadi Tumilat. Unfortunately, the biblical text does not provide corroborative detail about Pithom and Raamses of the kind that might confirm the above identifications.

It was, presumably, from forced labor on the construction of these cities that the descendants of Jacob, Israelites as they now may be called, made their escape. A generation later would mark their arrival in Canaan. The construction activity in Egypt would likely have peaked in the earlier years of rule of Ramesses II, and thus in the decades immediately after 1279 BC.

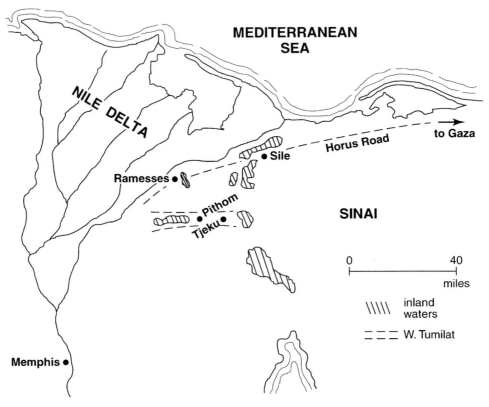

Figure 13-1. The Nile Delta, showing the biblical supply cities and the great highway.

An additional piece of Egyptian evidence of the Israelites in or near Canaan is quite striking, and does not depend upon the Bible except for the name "Israel" itself. In 1896, the Egyptologist Flinders Petrie investigated the funerary temple of Merneptah in Thebes. There, he found a free-standing black granite stone with inscriptions, now known as the Merneptah Stela, or the Israel Stela. It was set up some time after Merneptah's defeat of the Libyans and the Sea Peoples, and is given over to every sort of praise of this Pharaoh. After going on at great length on that subject, the inscription ends with:

> The princes are prostrate saying 'Shalom.'
> No one raises his head among the Nine Bows.
> Desolation is for Tehenu; Hatti is pacified.
> Plundered is Canaan with every evil.
> Carried off is Ashkelon; seized upon is Gezer;

Yenoam is made as that which does not exist.
Israel is laid waste, his seed is not.
Hurru is become a widow for Egypt.
All lands together, they are pacified.
Everyone who was restless has been bound.(*ANET*)

Figure 13-2. The name "Israel" (dark area) on the Merneptah Stela, written in Egyptian hieroglyphics from right to left. To the left, a seated figure with arm up and the three vertical dashes below are determinatives.

A restatement in more familiar terms would be: "The enemy princes are prostrate crying 'Mercy.' No one raises his head among the traditional enemies of Egypt. Libya has been desolated and the Hittites are at peace. Canaan has been plundered and plunged into hardship. The [city] of Ashkelon has been captured, and the [city] of Gezer has been seized. The [city] of Yenoam has been completely destroyed. The [people] of Israel have been wasted and left with no descendants. Canaan and Amurru are widowed because of Egypt. All lands are pacified, and all who were rebellious have been subdued."

Though the name "Israel" contains both "*l*" and "*r*" and though these are given by identical symbols in Egyptian hieroglyphic writing, scholars appear to be unanimous in agreeing that it is "Israel" which is spelled out by the hieroglyphs on the stela (see Figure 13-2).

This is the earliest surviving record of the name Israel, and the only known mention in Egyptian records. On the stela, "[city]" is represented by a special hieroglyphic symbol known as a "determinative," which is not intended to be pronounced but only to qualify or explain the associated word. The city determinative is represented by three hills and has the general meaning of an established and settled foreign city or country. In contrast, the word "Israel" is accompanied by the quite different determinative, "[people]," shown as a sitting man, a woman, a walking stick, and three dashes indicating a multitude. The meaning is that of a group not related to a definable homeland, and therefore an unsettled people.

The stela text above seems to refer to a military sweep through Canaan, in the style of campaigns boasted of by Merneptah's predecessors. Merneptah and his forces might have first attacked Ashkelon as it is nearest Egypt. The second objective would have been Gezer, Figure 13-3. Further north was Yenoam, the exact location of which is uncertain but which was likely near the Jordan River south of Lake Kinnereth (Sea of Galilee).

Israel is mentioned next. Israel, a people on the move, or recently arrived, would have been located at that time not far from Yenoam. As Yenoam was near the Jordan River, Israel could have been on either side of the Jordan River at that time, in Transjordan or in Canaan. The Merneptah Stela inscription is thus taken to show the presence of Israel in Canaan in the time of Merneptah, or if not yet in Canaan, in Transjordan (hereafter called Jordan). Whether this referred to all of the tribes of Israel or a part of them is taken up again in the next chapter. This military campaign, if it really took place, may have been during the kingship of Merneptah or during the long years in which he was a prince and a general in the army of his father, and thus from about 1240 to 1207 BC.

The dates implied by the building activity of Ramesses and by the Merneptah Stela are consistent with one another. They suggest the existence, and indeed the emergence (there is no earlier record of them), of a group known as Israel in the few decades before or after 1250 BC. This range of dates is also consistent with archaeological evidence of the beginning of new settlements in the hill country of Canaan in about that time. Remains of pottery found in those settlement sites provide a date in a rather broad range, perhaps 1250 to 1150 BC.

With the evidence of the first settlement of Israel in Canaan, some scholars define a new period, the Iron Age. No curtain suddenly closed on the Bronze Age and it is certain that no great increase in the use of iron marked the transition. In fact, there was not an immediate and profound change in the material culture of Canaan. Rather, the transition from Bronze Age to Iron Age had many manifestations, including introduction of several new peoples into the region and the collapse of old systems of rule, all of which were more significant than the slowly increasing use of iron.

In view of dating uncertainties for the end of the Bronze Age and the beginning of the Iron Age in Canaan, archaeologists often substitute a defined date for an actual date. For that purpose, the end of the Bronze Age and beginning of the Iron Age in Canaan is usually set at 1200 BC.

The Land of Canaan

For Egypt, Canaan was the stage upon which the last important conflict of the Bronze Age took place, to be described in Chapter 15. For Israel, it was the land of new settlement.

In the Late Bronze Age, there were Canaanite cities along the Mediterranean coast and inland, from Ugarit in the north to Gaza in the south. Based largely on records recovered at Ugarit which preserve the language of the north, and the Amarna archives which preserve personal names and some of the language of the south, it appears that variants of the North West Semitic language was spoken in the entire region. While the region was largely Canaanite in culture, the name "Canaan," will be used here in a narrower sense: to the land from Tyre to Gaza along the coast and inland to the waters of Lake Kinnereth, the river Jordan River, and the Dead Sea. This corresponds to most Biblical usage, and to that of the Egyptians who had major imperial interests there. The Bible refers to various peoples who inhabited this region, predominantly Canaanites and Amorites. It is likely that there was not much difference between these two. The term "Canaanite" was applied primarily to those who lived near the coast and toward the south, and "Amorite" to those inland and toward the north, toward Amurru, the land of Amorites.

The natural geography of Canaan is dominated by the Mediterranean Sea on the west, and the rift valley on the east in which are Lake Kinnereth, the Jordan river, and the Dead Sea. Parallel to these are low mountains or high hills. In the Late Bronze Age, woodlands covered the hills where rain was ample, or grasses where rain was sparse. The hill region just to the west of the River Jordan is known to archaeologists as the "Central Hill Country."

In southern Canaan, inland cities were few, reflecting the difficult conditions in that region. Today, desert or steppe lie to the south and southwest of Beersheba. This is the Negev, which merges southward with the Sinai. Rain is sometimes plentiful here but occurs in bursts and runs off quickly. It is possible that in the Late Bronze Age, conditions were not quite so harsh, but there is no certainty of that. A map of the locations of Canaanite cities is virtually a map of regions of available water and easily cultivated land. Natural geography was thus a key factor in determining where Canaanite populations were concentrated. Proximity to avenues of trade was an additional factor. Canaanite cities were at or near harbors or important overland trade routes.

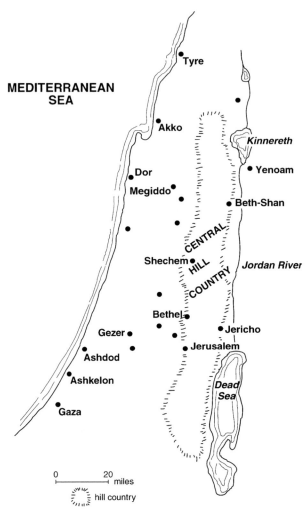

Figure 13-3. Cities of Canaan in the Late Bronze Age. The Central Hill Country and the inland south were thinly populated.

The most important route was the Horus road, also called the Way of the Sea, the ancient highway which led from the Nile Delta along the coast of Canaan and inland past Lake Kinnereth, with extensions north to Kadesh or Damascus. Farther north, additional extensions continued to Anatolia, Assyria, and Babylon. In Canaan, branch roads connected the highway with Jordan and possibly with Arabia.

In the Late Bronze Age, the cities of Canaan were subservient to Egypt, which dealt with the cities in a high-handed and imperial fashion. A strong light is cast on the relationship of Canaan (and Amurru) to Egypt in the Amarna period, the years around 1350 BC. The Amarna archive contained numerous tablets written in the Akkadian (Babylonian) cuneiform favored for diplomatic correspondence. These are mostly letters from kings of Canaan and Amurru representing about a dozen cities.

Figure 13-4. Once thought to be a Seti I or Ramesses II relief, now attributed to Merneptah, Egyptians storm a Canaanite city, probably Ashkelon. Canaanites are shown on battlements and wounded below. From the Karnak temple.

No such rich treasure of information has been found relating to other times in Canaan. The Amarna letters are practically the only direct testimony of the situation in Canaan in the Late Bronze Age, and much is made of them. The picture they paint is not a pretty one. The petty kings are servile to an amazing degree. One Canaanite king writes to pharaoh:

> Say to the king, my lord, my Sun, my god: message of Zitriyara, your servant, the dirt under your feet, the mire you tread on. I fall at the feet of the king, my lord, my Sun, my god, seven times and seven times, both on the stomach and on the back. (*EA 213*)

Apparently, such obsequious writings were not mere formalities of diplomatic address. They were reflected in actual behavior. A painting in an Egyptian tomb shows a delegation of Canaanites presenting themselves to an Egyptian official. One Canaanite is nearly prostrate on his stomach while another grovels on his back before the Egyptian official.

Figure 13-5. **A Canaanite king, right, brings in captives. On left, he is attended by the queen, a musician, and servants. From an ivory panel found in Megiddo.**

A perusal of the correspondence shows the little kings of Canaan (and Amurru) are at odds with one another. King accuses neighboring king of disloyalty to Egypt. The writer is the only loyal one, the only trustworthy one. He is threatened with attack from those others, those traitorous kings, those treacherous dogs. Will not Egypt support him by sending archers, and charioteers? The letters from Canaan and Amurru are a kaleidoscope of recriminations and mutual finger-pointing.

But help from Egypt rarely came. It was the time of Akhenaton, and Egyptians had problems at home. So long as tribute flowed to Egypt, there was no need to be drawn into these Canaanite squabbles. In any case, quarreling among Canaanite kings was useful to Egyptian imperial policy. There need be no worry about Canaanites uniting against Egypt. Small Egyptian garrison forces in certain cities would suffice.

The Peace of Kadesh gave Egypt recognized control in Canaan. Ramesses II took steps to put matters in Canaan on a more organized basis, one which would ensure greater benefits to Egypt. Archaeological finds in Canaan indicate an enlarged Egyptian government and military presence after Kadesh. That meant increased oppression and taxation. The wealth of Canaan, such as it was, was increasingly drained off to maintain an enlarged occupation army, to line the pockets of corrupt Egyptian officials in Canaan, and no doubt also to support Ramesses' spectacular building activities in Egypt. Those Canaanite kings and others of the privileged class who supported Egyptian interests might have prospered, but the land at large became increasingly destitute.

Following Merneptah, there was a period of weak rule, misrule, and even chaos in Egypt, and a near collapse of international trade related to the troubles in Greece, Anatolia, Cyprus, and Ugarit. It may have been in this period, when Egyptian attention again turned inward, that Israel was first able to establish itself in the hills of Canaan.

Evidence of the Beginning of Israel

Between Jerusalem and Lake Kinnereth is Samaria. The Bible refers to northern Samaria as Manasseh, and southern Samaria as Ephraim, the names of two Israelite tribes (Figure 13-6). This is part of the Central Hill Country referred to earlier, a region of great interest to archaeologists

One of the important investigative tools of archaeology is the regional survey, in which an extensive reconnaissance is carried out, often on foot and sometimes foot by foot. Archaeologists look for surface remains of ancient occupation. Ancient foundations or pottery remains may indicate a settlement, and the pottery helps to provide a date. The extent of the site and the food-producing capability of the surrounding land provide a basis upon which to estimate the number of people who might have lived there.

Surveys in both Manasseh and Ephraim carried out in the 1970s and 1980s have produced important evidence relating to the beginning of Israel—evidence independent of the biblical text yet consistent with it. These surveys show that a remarkable change had taken place there near the close of the Bronze Age. The regions of both Manasseh and Ephraim were sparsely populated, and Ephraim particularly so. Then, at the close of the Bronze Age and the beginning of the Iron Age, a flood of new settlements rather suddenly appeared. These settlements were small, many only a few acres, while others occupied perhaps a dozen acres. The numbers are revealing. In Manasseh, the survey found remains of thirty-nine sites of occupation dating to the close of the Bronze Age. In the Early Iron Age (approximately 1200–1000 BC), the number of sites had grown to 136. In Ephraim directly to the south, the facts are even more dramatic. The end of the Bronze Age is represented by about six known sites, while 100 Early Iron Age settlement sites have been found.

Such settlements, unwalled for the most part, might contain only a few houses that are likely to have been the residences of an extended family, the father and his married sons and their families. Larger clusters would be those of a clan. These houses, many of which were on hillsides, were rustic and simple in the extreme, the dwellings of farmers or flock-tenders living at a subsistence level.

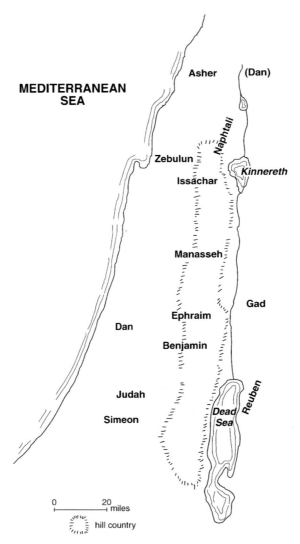

Figure 13-6. Approximate locations of the tribes of Israel. The tribe of Levi had no territory.

Largely of stone, houses contained several small rooms and one large area. Toward the center of this area, there was a row of pillars supporting either a second story or a partial roof over about half the space, thus forming a partly covered courtyard. Such houses are referred to by archaeologists as pillar houses, or three-room or four-room houses, depending on the floor plan. The design allowed flexibility in the use of space. The courtyard might enclose animals. It might be the center of domestic activities under the open sky, or of the variety of support activities required of self-reliant farmers.

The stony terrain of the hillsides was difficult from which to wrest a living, and many adaptations were required. In the rain-shadows of the east-facing slopes, settlers depended on dry farming of grain and sheep or goat keeping. In areas of more rain, olive trees and grapevines were planted. In many of the houses, deep pits were excavated below the floor where grain could be stored. Most settlements were at a distance from springs or streams. Access to water was thus a major problem. In order to store rain runoff, settlers excavated cisterns out of the hard limestone of the region. Where the limestone was porous, the inside surfaces were plastered to aid in water retention. Large clay jars known as collar-rim jars were also employed for water storage. Where it would help in improving land by retaining soil and water, terraces were built.

At one time, the pillared house, under-floor silos, plastered cisterns, collar-rim jars, were thought to be uniquely Israelite inventions and thus unique early Israelite ethnic markers. It is now known that isolated examples are found elsewhere so that these may not be ethnic markers but simply necessary inventions and adaptations to the difficult hill country environment. Still, where most or all are found together, they identify a new community, a new occupancy, formed at the end of the Bronze Age and the beginning of the Iron Age.

Judging by the archaeological remains, there were no significant class distinctions among the population of these settlements. There is no evidence of palaces, patrician or noble's houses, or grand temples. Sacred places were open-air platforms of simple construction. Only in the remains of Shiloh is there evidence of elaborate buildings and centralized storage that may indicate a religious center of importance. Testimony of the Bible and the findings of archaeology agree. These people were not peasants beholden to a lord. They held their small plots as free men in an essentially unstratified society. These settlements and their characteristics correspond well with the way of life described in the Books of Judges and First Samuel.

How is it known that the people of these early settlements were Israelites? In part, it is a matter of definition. It was only centuries later, in the time of David, that a political-geographical Israel can first be defined with confidence. The people of Manasseh, Ephraim and nearby Benjamin were at the core of that Israel. Archaeological evidence shows that pillared houses of Manasseh and Ephraim were used without interruption or foreign intrusion from the time of the earliest settlers until the time of David. As William Dever of Arizona University has argued, such continuity logically requires that the Manassites and Ephraimites of David's time were descendants of those early settlers in the Central Hill Country (Dever, 1997). Since those of David's time were certainly Israelites, those early settlers must have been too.

Biblical testimony confirms that Israel began in the Central Hill Country. Nearly all of the early history of Israel as reported in the Books of Numbers, Joshua, Judges, and First Samuel, took place in the tribal areas of Manasseh, Ephraim, or Benjamin. These are the so-called Rachel Tribes, Figure 14-1. In this region also were the early sanctuaries known from the Bible, including Gilgal, Shiloh, Shechem, and Bethel. It is clear that this area was the birthplace of Israel, and biblical testimony traces the people of the region back to the beginning of settlement.

At the time that intensive settlement began in Manasseh and Ephraim, or perhaps shortly before or shortly after, new settlements were also established to the north in Galilee and to the south in Judah. In Jordan also, a spurt of increased occupation is noted at the beginning of the Iron Age, including some evidence of collar-rim jars and pillared houses. Descendants of these populations, or portions of them, were also part of Israel of the time of David.

The occupants of those hundreds of sites which arose in the Central Hill Country toward the end of the Bronze Age and the beginning of the Iron Age would remain anonymous, like so many whose settlement remains have been found by archaeologists, were it not for the Bible. The Bible gives a name to the people and the place: Israel.

The Bible and the Entry into Canaan

The Bible tells of the Exodus, wanderings in the wilderness of Sinai, the northward movement of the people into Jordan, and the crossing of the Jordan River near Jericho. The story then tells of the conquest of Canaan under Joshua.

A vivid and dramatic account of a military conquest of Canaan emerges from the text. There is nothing impossible in migration, conquest, and occupation of a new land. Conquest is a common-place of history, and most of the nations of today stand on lands obtained, in part or in whole, by invasion or conquest by distant ancestors. A close reading of the biblical text, however, shows that there is hardly any uncontradicted claim of conquest and occupation of Canaanite cities. The earlier part of the Book of Joshua speaks of conquest. The Book of Judges and part of the Book of Joshua deny it. City after city are named for which it is said that the Canaanite inhabitants had not been driven out. In many cases, these are the very cities earlier said to have been conquered. The Canaanites are too strong, they cannot be defeated, they have "chariots of iron." Israelites, still rural and technically primitive, could not match the professional armies of the Canaanites—though a time would come when most of Canaan would be incorporated in David's kingdom. But that would be far in the future.

That the land was not really subdued by force as described early in the Book of Joshua is further recognized in theological terms. God guided and accompanied the Israelites out of Egypt, through the wilderness, and up to the Jordan River. But He would not cross over with them. He would not drive out the Canaanites. The occupation of Canaan was up to the Israelites themselves. It was also at the Jordan that the supply of manna ceased, another indication that the Israelite tribes were on their own.

Archaeologists have excavated extensively in the Late Bronze Age cities of Canaan and found evidence of destruction or abandonment. Various evidence, including pottery, reveals the approximate date of destruction. The dates are not as a whole consistent with closely spaced, lightning-fast attacks as told in the Book of Joshua. Indeed, evidence produced by archaeology shows the destruction or abandonment of these cities could not all have occurred in the lifetime of one man. There is no single period of large-scale destruction which can be attributed to an Israelite invasion. The present tendency among Bible scholars is to accept as more realistic the peaceful occupation implied in the books of Numbers and Judges rather than the rapid conquest presentation.

The conquest as represented in the early part of the Book of Joshua may in part reflect the expansive and imaginative use of prose, common in ancient times, which tends to greatly overstate and dramatize in order to make its point. Such writing is well known of the Bronze Age in the Near East and Egypt. It is only necessary to recall the conquest claims of Ramesses following Kadesh and of Tiglath-Pileser after the encounter with the Kaska.

Origin of the Bible

Archaeological evidence is solid in its testimony of the sudden and rapid increase in settlements and population in the Central Hill Country of Canaan. It is certain that this population was the foundation, or one of the foundations, of what would later be the nation of Israel under David. But what of the origin of these new peoples, new communities? In short, what is the origin of earliest Israel? The biblical account of the Exodus, wandering in the wilderness of Sinai, and occupation of Canaan may have first been committed to writing hundreds of years after the events which are described. How many hundreds of years is not known. Could the Bible writers have known anything of events that occurred hundreds of years before their own time? The circumstances in which the Bible came into existence bear directly on the degree to which the Bible may preserve historic memory.

The history of Israel provides the background and defines the periods to which it is necessary to refer (see Figure 13-7). As already noted, the period of initial settlement and subsequent population growth lasted from the end of the Bronze Age to close to the time of David, a period of about two centuries. Archaeologically, this is referred to as the Early Iron Age, or the Settlement Period. There seems to have been no centralized rule nor king among the Israelites in that period. According to the Bible, the first significant chieftain or king in Israel was Saul. He was succeeded by David. With David's reign, historic dates begin to become more certain; his rule is dated approximately 1010–970 BC.

Figure 13-7. Schematic history of Israel and the stages in the development of the early books of the Bible.

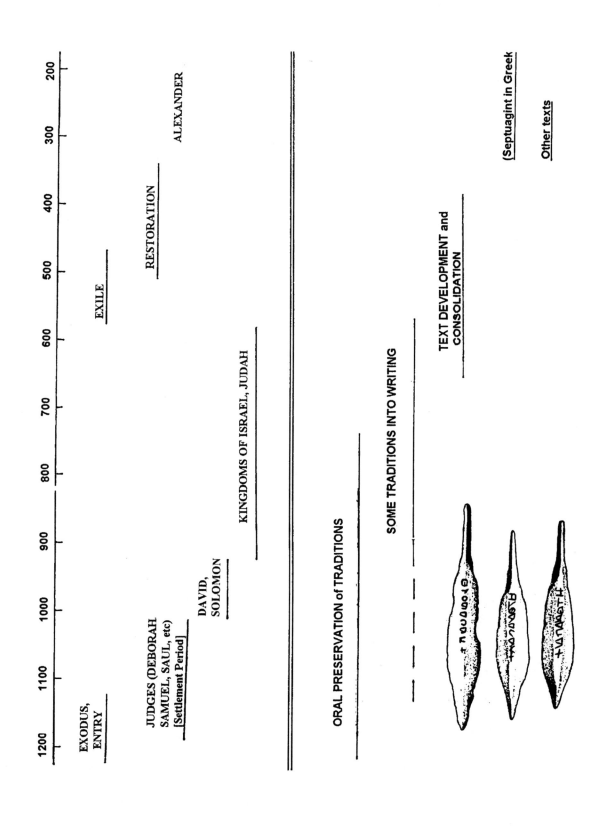

With the kingship of David, a period known as the Monarchy began and David and his descendants formed one of the longest royal dynasties known. After the death of David's son, Solomon, a dispute erupted between the leaders of the Israelite tribes in the north and Solomon's son in Jerusalem in the south. The result was an irreparable split in the kingdom in about 925 BC. Two kingdoms resulted. The southern kingdom was known as Judah, while the northern kingdom retained the name Israel. (After the rupture, only those who lived in the northern kingdom are properly referred to as Israelites, but for convenience, the term will be retained here for all of the biblical community, north or south.)

After Solomon's reign, militant Assyria began to extend its domination, sending military expeditions down the Mediterranean coast. In 722 BC Israel, the northern kingdom, was destroyed by the Assyrians, never to revive. In a short time Assyria was replaced by Babylonia as the dominant power in the East. Judah survived as a vassal state of Babylonia.

There was a revolt against Babylonian rule, and a Babylonian army came and destroyed Jerusalem in 586 BC. The leading elements of the Judean population were removed to Babylon while others fled to Egypt. Thus began the exile. Soon, the Persians crushed Babylonia and allowed the Judean exiles to return and rebuild Jerusalem in the decades before 500 BC. In the last, revolts against Roman domination resulted in the end of Judea and the dispersal of the people. All of these events influenced the Bible in a profound way.

The Hebrew Bible is a vast work, with different portions originating under different circumstances. It is the Books of Genesis, Exodus, Numbers, Joshua, and Deuteronomy that are of special interest here, since these tell of the beginning of Israel. These are referred to here as the "early books" since they relate to the earliest times and are placed at the beginning of the Bible. The circumstances in which these books were written, and the sources of the information which they contain, have been the subject of intense study and much controversy.

It is widely believed that during the exile in Babylon, or on the subsequent return to Jerusalem, these books were edited and arranged in something close to the form now known. This major undertaking would have responded to a need to find meaning and hope in past tragic events, and to develop identity and cohesion in the shattered Israelite community.

In Alexandria, Egypt, a translation of the Hebrew Bible into Greek was begun and was well advanced by 285 BC, during the reign of Ptolemy Philadelphus. A legend is associated with this undertaking. Ptolemy, wishing to enlarge his library of great books, sent to Jerusalem for seventy Jewish scholars. In Alexandria, the scholars were set to work on the translation. They labored for seventy days. From this, or from the seventy translators, there came the Latin name "Septuagint," meaning Seventy. The Septuagint text of the Bible is the earliest of which there is a continuous trace to present times. It was used by Jews and early Christians of the Greek world. Jews in Judea, Syria, and

Babylon are more likely to have relied on the proto-Masoretic text which was maintained in Hebrew.

The oldest Masoretic Bible that can be definitely identified goes back to about AD 800-900. Its earlier history is unknown, although Origen, an early Christian scholar working in about AD 285, made use of the Hebrew text of his time in order to correct the Septuagint. It is primarily on the Septuagint and the Masoretic that modern Bible translations are based.

The Earlier Sources

There is little reason to doubt a continuous transmission between the early books of the Bible, which were established during or after the exile, and those books as they are known today. Whether there was a continuous transmission of historic lore from the remote Settlement Period to the text of the exile or post-exile period is far more difficult to establish.

It is an inescapable conclusion, however, that the Bible text that was formalized in the exile or post-exile period was based on a number of earlier texts. As in a book of the present day, the Bible itself provides references. Among these are the "Book of the Covenant" or the "Book of the Laws of Moses," the "Book of the Wars of the Lord," the "Book of Jashar." Records or annals of the kings of Israel and Judah are also referenced in the Bible. These manuscripts are now entirely lost, and little is known of their contents or the time in which they were written. Other written sources were almost certainly used, though not explicitly mentioned in the Bible.

The Bible tells that in the time of King Josiah (640–609 BC), a manuscript was found during a repair of the Temple. Biblical scholars believe that this was the Book of Deuteronomy in some earlier version, or some part of it. The manuscript may have languished for unknown years in an ancient equivalent of a "genizah," an out-of-the-way storage space in which worn-out sacred scrolls were consigned to a peaceful retirement. Or, as many scholars assume, this early Deuteronomy may have been written during the reign of Josiah by a priest who wished to encourage a major religious reform which, in fact, King Josiah carried out. If there was such a writer, he was aware of the content of earlier sources, with little doubt including "J" and "E."

According to what is called the "Documentary Hypothesis," the books of Genesis through Numbers derive substantially from two earlier sources. One is referred to as the "J" source because of the frequent use of the name Jehovah. As now recognized, the name is more accurately given as Yahweh, but the "J" label is still retained. In most present English translations, "LORD" has replaced the name Yahweh. The "J" source is thought to have been maintained in Judah, the southern kingdom. A second is referred to as the "E" source, since it refers to God as El or Elohim. "E" is thought to have been initially maintained in Israel, the northern kingdom.

Bible scholars believe that they can identify those passages in the Bible which derive from "J" and those which derive from "E." To an extent, the content of the two sources run parallel to one another, relating much the same story. Both "E" and "J" tell of the Patriarchs, the descent into Egypt, the Exodus, the encounter with God in the Sinai. A still earlier source is thought to lie behind "J" and "E," a body of narrative and lore available to both. That early body of lore is no longer clearly evident in the present biblical text, though it has been given a label "G" for "Groundwork."

Moreover, according to the Documentary Hypothesis, a writer or group of writers labeled "D" was responsible for Deuteronomy, while the so-called "P" text supposedly derives from priestly groups that added the laws and rules of religious behavior, and some genealogies. Most supporters of the Documentary Hypothesis believe that the order of development was G, J, E, D, P. Some would place P before D.

On the basis of limited evidence and substantial intuition, some scholars place the development of the content of "J" in the time of David or Solomon, and thus between approximately 1000 and 900 BC, and the "E" source somewhat later. Many later dates have been proposed and the matter remains unresolved. It is likely that "J" and "E" both developed from aggregates of earlier stories, rolling snowballs of accumulating lore, including the "G" source already referred to. Further, there were probably several cycles of revision in which an early form of "J" or "E" (or both) received a story-teller's polish. Thus, it is likely that no single date can be attached to the time of writing of either "J" or "E" or the whole of the contents of either.

The "G" source, which may have consisted of songs and stories originating as early as the Settlement Period or even earlier, may have been maintained by oral means, by priestly or prophetic groups. Anthropologists have argued that, in societies in which lore is handed down orally, events that happen in the lifetime of the grandfather will be retained more or less correctly to the time of the grandson. After that, changes may seep in. That is a span of about one hundred years, but perhaps a somewhat longer time might be granted. The beginning of the Israelite settlement may be tentatively placed at a time close to 1200 BC. Could remnants of history from that time have been kept by oral means for several hundred years until its incorporation in "J" or "E"?

Perhaps oral means was supplemented by writing. The art of writing appears to have vanished in Greece and central and western Anatolia with the end of the Bronze Age. Cuneiform, a script favored by the kingly courts, faded away in Canaan with the end of the Bronze Age. But writing never entirely disappeared in Canaan. Archaeological evidence shows that alphabetic writing existed in Canaan in the Late Bronze Age and that it continued into the Iron Age. It is demonstrated by various discoveries: alphabetic graffiti at the copper mines at Timna in the Sinai of about 1400 BC; alphabetic markings on pottery in Canaan dating from the period 1200–1100 BC; writing on arrowheads in Canaan, 1100–1000 BC (see Figure 13-7, bottom). The significance of these alphabetic scratchings in a Semitic language is that they were the work of ordinary people, not professional scribes. Unlike cuneiform or hieroglyphic, alphabet symbols were few in number and simple in form, which could have made writing widely accessible to common people. There would have been no need to graduate from a scribal school. It would not have been hard for anyone, even a simple Israelite farmer, to master the two dozen easily drawn symbols of an early alphabet.

Among the scant remains of those times, no alphabetic text of great length has yet been found in Canaan. For that matter, very little Late Bronze Age cuneiform writing has been found either, though it is certain that Canaanite kings or administrators were prolific writers. The lack of examples of extended alphabetic texts does not disprove the existence of literacy. In the ruins of a village on the edge of the Central Hill Country, there has been found a student's alphabetic exercise of the Early Iron Age, scratched on a piece of pottery. The existence of that early alphabetic exercise is evidence of teaching, which suggests that there was some pool of people who could read and write. Surely, something more than a few scratchings were set down for some purpose and for some readership. Preservation of tradition and lore by priestly or prophetic groups might have been that purpose. It is possible that some of what later appeared in the Bible had been preserved in writing in primitive form from earliest times and constituted part of "G."

Though the Bible is largely a prose text, there are in it a few poetic segments referred to as "songs." The Song of the Sea and the Song of Deborah are particularly important. It is almost universally agreed among scholars that these were composed in a very early time and are preserved in the Bible in close to the early form. The first tells of the escape from Egypt. The second tells of Deborah, who rallies a number of Israelite tribes in a battle against a powerful Canaanite chariot force. The Canaanites are defeated. Israelite tribes that rallied to the cause are praised, and tribes that held back are condemned. The circumstance of a gathering of tribes for war could only have existed before the Monarchy in Israel, before David, and before the centralized government and professional army which he established.

The grammatical forms in the Song of Deborah testify that it is one of the most ancient texts in the Bible. Historic analysis, style, grammar, confirm that the Song of Deborah originated before the time of David, perhaps as early as 1100 BC. The Song of the Sea appears to be even earlier. Both songs derive, it appears, from the Settlement Period. While "J" and "E" are in prose, they may well have been in part reworked from earlier poetic forms, such as these songs, and may also preserve authentic memory of early events.

In view of the early date of the "songs," and the possible use of alphabetic writing, a continuous though imperfect chain of transmission of historic memory may have existed from the Settlement Period to the exile and thence to the present text. However, there is no certainty of that. In part because of this uncertainty, and doubts which exist in part for that reason concerning the biblical account of the origin of Israel, there have arisen a number of alternative theories, to be considered next.

14
ORIGIN OF THE PEOPLE OF ISRAEL

The biblical story is well known. The Israelites, descendants of Jacob, lived in Egypt. They were pressed into slavery by the Pharaoh. Following the Exodus and a period of wandering, they settled in Canaan. However, in our skeptical age, the biblical account has been largely rejected by historians. If it was not as the Bible says, how did Israel begin? Another explanation must be sought, and to that end scholars have labored for well over a century.

That lengthy effort has not been a resounding success. Though a variety of theories have been produced, they are less than satisfactory. The difficulty lies in the almost total absence of information beyond what is supplied in the Bible itself. While archaeology can test certain theories of origin or suggest others, in the absence of ancient contemporary texts, archaeology is limited in what it can say of historic events. It would take a substantial body of new discoveries to determine what happened in those times when Israel began, 3,200 or more years ago. Whether the result of such discoveries would support the essential elements of the biblical account or yield a new account entirely can only be guessed. The appeal of various theories is largely to logic, not to a substantial body of independent evidence which hardly exists. These theories are, however, quite interesting and suggest directions in which the historic picture may be sought.

Theory of Tribes

At the invitation of Joseph, his father, Jacob, and Jacob's other sons came into Egypt. In Egypt, descendants of the sons of Jacob increased in number. In time, they became the twelve tribes of Israel. Each tribe received its name from whichever son of Jacob was their ancestor. In the manner of the ancient East, Jacob had several wives, or a wife and concubines, and so his sons had different mothers. Accordingly, the tribes had different lines of descent.

It is an ancient idea that peoples, whether clans, tribes, or nations, are descended from a certain ancestor whose name is taken by the group. It was an idea or theory of great explanatory power, roughly equivalent to the present theory of evolution. It was supported by so much that was evident, for example, the known relationship of one group or clan to a neighboring one through a still-remembered common ancestor. This observation needed only to be generalized, and carried backward in time to arrive at a real or imagined common ancestor for whole nations or peoples.

It was not the Israelites alone who thought in this way. Greece of the Classical period contained speakers of several different dialects, including Ionians and Dorians. To the Greeks, these groups each descended from a common ancestor, Ion and Dorus respectively. That the Trojans descended from Tros and the Dardanians from Dardanus, according to Greek belief, has been mentioned in Chapter 5.

Given the legendary nature of such accounts, many biblical scholars assume that the origin of the tribes of Israel through the sons of Jacob is also no more than a legend. If the tribes of Israel were not related to one another by common descent, the tribes might have had different and distinctive origins. From that possibility, a number of theories of the beginnings of Israel in Canaan have been proposed. Such theories attempt to trace a separate history and origin for each of the tribes or groups of tribes. Each such theory may seem more or less plausible in itself but, unfortunately, one theory contradicts another, and none is capable of proof.

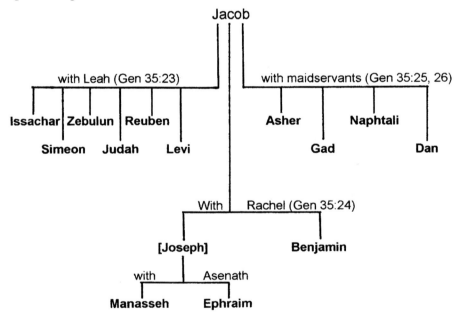

Figure 14-1. The tribes of Israel and their lines of descent according to the book of Genesis.

In one theory for example, only the "Rachel tribes" as they are called—Manasseh, Ephraim, and Benjamin—participated in the Exodus under the leadership of Moses (see

Figure 14-1). The other tribes were already settled in Canaan, according to this theory, and perhaps had never been in Egypt. In a contrary theory, this same "Rachel" group is said to have departed Egypt at an early date and settled in Canaan. Moses and Joshua, with the tribe of Levi, came about a century later. There are many such theories, many variations, for which some degree of support can be drawn from the Bible. It is all a matter of selecting certain words, phrases, or whole verses and endowing them with special meaning or disproportionate significance.

What should be gleaned from these theories is that the narrative of twelve tribes entering Jordan or Canaan as one may be legendary, a means to explain not only the origin of the tribes known later in Israel, but to explain also the closer relationship of certain tribes to certain others. In theological terms, furthermore, the descent of all Israel from Jacob would provide a conduit by which God's promise to Abraham, Isaac, and Jacob would flow to following generations of all of Israel.

If it was not twelve tribes that came through Jordan to Canaan, what is the "Israel" referred to in the Merneptah Stela? That Israel may have been one tribe only, or a small group of clans or tribes, later to be part of the larger twelve-tribe group. Which tribe or tribes these might have been is a matter of guesswork.

In view of the possibility of a diverse origin of clans or tribes of Israel, it is at least possible that some tribes began as "Hapiru," or as "Shasu," or as long-settled Canaanites, while others were of an origin which is now unknown and unknowable after the passage of more than three thousand years.

Shasu and Hapiru Theories

Egyptian records mention peoples referred to as Shasu. In the time of Merneptah, an Egyptian frontier official reported that Shasu had appeared with their herds at the border of Egypt, seeking refuge because of drought. A record of the later king, Ramesses III, boasts that he has "destroyed the...clans of the Shasu people and plundered their tent camps of people and possessions and cattle likewise." The cattle referred to were sheep or goats, for no other herd animals could survive on the resources of the desert and steppe of Sinai. It is clear that the Shasu were largely or entirely a pastoral people. Because they were tenders of flocks, as were at times the biblical Patriarchs, and because Shasu were present in the regions of Canaan where the Patriarchs are said to have traveled, or resided, scholars have wondered if certain Shasu were somehow the Israelites.

Egyptian temple reliefs profusely show Shasu, defeated by various Pharaohs in the triumphal manner required of Egyptian temple illustrations. According to the illustrations, Shasu sometimes wear a simple pointed kilt and no upper garment. Or they may wear a full robe. They are usually bearded, but the beard is less full than that shown of settled Canaanites or Syrians. Hair is swept back and contained in a cloth wrap, or hair and wrap together may be tucked in as a turban, Figure 14-2. As the Egyptian illustrations are of military encounters, Shasu are often shown with their weapons. These were the common weapons of antiquity—spear, bow, and sword. The swords shown are the curved variety, the scimitar favored by Egyptians.

The Egyptian word *Shasu* is not an ethnic designation but a term referring to those who led a largely transient and flock-tending way of life, largely free of Egyptian control. Shasu were not entirely wanderers, however. They had small settlements and camps. Nor were they entirely people of the near-desert or steppe but were in contact with urban life. In the encounter between Ramesses II and the Hittites at Kadesh, certain Shasu were allied with the Hittites, and an Egyptian relief shows Shasu on the battlements of Kadesh, Figure 2-3. Shasu also defended a city in Canaan against the Egyptians. There is no way of knowing whether these Shasu were mercenaries, or whether there were bonds of clan affiliation and obligation between the Shasu and the inhabitants of those cities.

Figure 14-2. Shasu captives, bound at the elbows or handcuffed. They wear two forms of headgear. This photograph shows the present appearance of the sculptural relief at Karnak temple.

Shasu are the focus of certain pastoral or nomadic theories of the origin of Israel. The name of Albrecht Alt is associated with one of these theories. His objective was to explain how a wandering pastoral people might have become settled Israelites. He assumed that there were certain Shasu groups wandering in the hill country of Canaan. They would have moved their flocks seasonally, to the high mountain slopes in summer, and then down into the valleys when the summer ended. In some of these valleys there were Canaanite villages. After the harvest, these Canaanites might allow the Shasu to browse their flocks in the stubble.

Flock keepers and villagers were thus in contact, which provided opportunities for trade. It is only possible to guess what may have been traded. The pastoralists might offer animals, wool and wool products, carved horn, milk products, or aromatic herbs gathered in the wilderness. From the village, Shasu would need grain, oil, wine, fruits, pottery, and other manufactured goods. These pastoralists, according to Alt, occasionally set in a small crop themselves in the unoccupied spaces of the valleys. In time, their stay in the valley became longer. Finally, the stay became essentially full time. Farming became the mainstay, though flocks were still kept. According to Alt, it was in this way that the first Israelite settlements began, and these particular Shasu were the first Israelites.

There is, in his theory, no really satisfactory explanation of why occupation of the land and settlement took place when it did, and why it proceeded so rapidly. The land had been thinly occupied and open to settlement for hundreds of years.

A second group of people of the Late Bronze Age has also drawn the intense interest of scholars. Among the letters found in the Amarna archives, there is one from Abdi-Hepa, king of Jerusalem, in which he complained of depredations by the Habiru, as the name seemed to be. In other Amarna letters, several of the little kings of Canaan and Amurru complained of groups designated as "SA.GAZ." SA.GAZ are cuneiform symbols which scholars began to recognize as equivalent to Habiru.

The resemblance of the name Habiru to "Hebrew" was immediately apparent. From the Amarna letters, it seems that Habiru were present in a number of places in Canaan. Further, records from the Euphrates cities of Nuzi and Mari, dated centuries earlier than the Amarna letters, mention Habiru. The Hittites had a contingent of them in their army. These place Habiru in the north, not far from Harran, the city from which Abraham is said to have begun his journey to Canaan. It was thus natural to see in the Habiru the earliest evidence of the Hebrews, first in the north in the vicinity of Harran, then later in the south, in Canaan. Habiru attacks on cities in Canaan, frequently mentioned in the Amarna letters, might have been the invasion of Canaan under Joshua as told in the Bible.

Linguists studied the name Habiru. In time, they concluded that the name was probably pronounced *Apiru*, not *Habiru* as had been thought earlier. With that, the similarity to the name Hebrew was lessened. And in any case, the name found in the Hebrew language text of the Bible is not "Hebrew," as in English translations, but "*ibri*," plural "*ibrim*." The match of *Apiru* to *ibri* or *ibrim* was not so compelling. The entire question of the linguistic relationship of the two names, Apiru and ibrim, has been a subject of extensive examination and intense debate. Results are contradictory and can be summarized by the opinions of two eminent scholars. Anson Rainey states in strongest certainty that there is no connection between the names "Apiru" and "ibrim" (Rainey, 1987). Manfred Weippert, states with equal confidence that the equation of "Hapiru" to "ibrim" is substantiated by linguistic proofs (Weippert, 1971). Thus, from the linguistic viewpoint, the matter is unresolved.

Who were the Apiru? Ancient records which refer to Apiru, or SA.GAZ, cover a period of over a thousand years. From these records, the meaning of the term can be understood, and relates to the nature of Bronze Age society. Apiru were people who, for various reasons, were disenfranchised and were forced to live on the fringes of society. These might include younger sons who did not inherit land, those forced off the land by debt, tax collectors, or drought, homicides who fled their homes for fear of blood revenge, war refugees, victims of political intrigues, or others torn from a fixed place in society. Such people were difficult to absorb back into social systems of the ancient world and they were often troublesome to the established order.

Apiru came from no one level of society. Even a king became an Apiru. Fleeing a palace coup in his home city of Alalakh in northern Syria, King Idrimi joined an Apiru group with which he lived for seven years.

How did such people survive? Any way they could. A record from the city of Nuzi tells that some Apiru accepted indentured servitude. Some Apiru were brigands. Judging by records over a wide span of time, a great many Apiru took up the military life. Apiru appear as soldiers under various kings over the centuries. It is likely that, in time, some Apiru organized under their own commanders. They became "Condotiere," military groups who hired out to the highest bidder, and who might also engage in military actions for their own benefit. By organizing into such groups, they were able to control their own destinies. Many centuries later, fleeing the wrath of King Saul, David with a band of discontented or exiled men took up the life of mercenaries and freebooters. These were, in effect, Apiru.

Opinion has sharply swung away from the view that the Apiru were the earliest Israelites, in part because "Apiru" was not an ethnic term nor were Apiru an ethnic group. Evidence of ethnic diversity among Apiru comes from early documents of the north Syrian cities. From Alalakh, there is a of list names of Apiru soldiers. Some of the names are Semitic, others are Hurrian. From the city of Tikunai between the Tigris and Euphrates, 438 names of Apiru are listed. Many of the names are Hurrian, some Semitic. Apiru of those regions seem to have had mixed origins and ethnicities. Still, an Apiru group could be ethnically uniform if they had originated in an ethnically uniform region. Such a group might travel far from their place of origin, in search of opportunity, military employment perhaps. It is often taken for granted that Israel originated in a single ethnic group. If it is required that early Israel be ethnically uniform, and yet distinct from the population in Canaan among whom they settled, Apiru arising from one such migrating Apiru group might fill the requirement.

Though scholars now dismiss the connection of the Apiru to the Israelites, it is possible that just such disenfranchised and unsettled groups might have settled in the Central Hill Country of Canaan once the opportunity presented itself.

The Apiru and Shasu theories attempt to relate the early Israelites to unsettled groups which are known from ancient records outside of the Bible. A Shasu or Apiru origin can neither be confirmed nor dismissed, and one or both may account, in part perhaps, for the origin of the Israelites.

Theory of Canaanite Origin

There are times when scholarship in any one subject of study appears to be exhausted. All that can be said seems to have been said, and all the possibilities explored, and whatever energy is left goes into narrower and narrower issues. Such seems to have been the case in studies of the origin of Israel when George Mendenhall introduced a new and quite distinctive theory (Mendenhall, 1962). In part, this theory was inspired by the conclusion that certain Apiru were "dropouts" from established society. For Mendenhall, the earliest Israelites were such disaffected or dropout Canaanites.

As this theory would have it, the Israelite invasion of Canaan was, in effect, an internal invasion, a movement of people from Canaanite cities or villages of the low lands into the Central Hill Country. These Canaanites had never been in Egypt or experienced the Exodus.

Mendenhall provides an intriguing motive that would account for this movement. It is obvious from the Amarna letters of about 1350 BC that the little kings of Canaan tried to outdo one another in currying favor with Egypt, best achieved by the timely turnover of an exorbitant tribute. Mendenhall assumes that the situation in approximately 1250 to 1200 BC was much the same, or even worse. To assemble this tribute, the common people were squeezed to an intolerable degree until they could stand it no longer. By ones and by twos, then by the dozens, they abandoned towns and cities and fled to the hills to establish a new life.

In the hills they encountered a few people with a new and strange ideology. They were believers in the god Yahweh. Belief in Yahweh had revolutionary implications. Unlike other gods, He did not favor earthly kings and had no high regard for them. It was He who set peoples in their lands, and the land was granted by Him and no other. It was therefore He who was the one true king to whom all loyalty was due. Canaanites had no choice of their earthly kings, but any could accept Yahweh voluntarily, and allegiance was rendered to

Him. Land was now understood as a gift not of the Canaanite king but of the new Lord, who did not demand tribute but obedience to a moral code. The Canaanite kings were owed nothing and, in fact, could be regarded as enemies. This new ideology was a magnet that rapidly drew many fresh adherents to the hill country, strengthening earliest Israel.

A closely related theory holds that the first Israelites were Canaanite peasants who revolted against the Canaanite kings. In an Amarna letter, King Rib Hadda of Byblos wrote to Egypt of his worries. His peasants will rise against him, they will strike him down. Revolt by peasants in those ancient times was possible, because Rib Hadda, who was there, said it was possible.

Certainly, there is much that can be considered evidence in favor of these theories. Hebrew and Canaanite seem to have been closely related languages. Further, in a number of passages of the Bible, the name of the ancient Canaanite god El was used as an alternative to the name Yahweh. English translations of the Bible usually substitute "God" for "El," thus El Olem, "the Everlasting God," and El Elyon, "God Most High." The name El is preserved in many Israelite personal names such as Samu*el*, Ezeki*el*, and Dani*el*, in place names such as Beth*el*, and seemingly even in the very name Isra*el* itself. In addition to El, the name of the detested Canaanite god Baal is found in a number of Israelite names. Such would be easily and directly understandable if Israelites were descendants of Canaanites.

Even the early modes of Israelite worship involving sacred stones, high places, and animal sacrifice may have been Canaanite. Much of the poetic language which describes the power and majesty of God, particularly well known from the psalms, may also have been Canaanite in origin.

Remains of hill country settlements that archaeologists have found are hardly rich in material remains, but fragments of domestic pottery have been found. This pottery is Canaanite, identical to that found in the remains of some Late Bronze Age Canaanite cities. On the basis of those material remains only, putting the Bible testimony aside, some archaeologists would not hesitate to identify the new Central Hill Country settlements as Canaanite. Thus, linguistic, cultic, and archaeological evidence seems to support the theory of Canaanite origin. However, as in other cases in which the evidence is very limited, significant weaknesses can be seen in the Canaanite Theory.

Surviving examples of the earliest Hebrew language are very few (the Songs, primarily) and come from a time a century or more after the beginning of the settlements. The few known scraps of the language of ancient Canaan are centuries older (the Amarna letters). It is thus impossible to be certain whether the Hebrew spoken by the settlers was close to Canaanite or a somewhat distant linguistic relative. No one doubts that Israelites arose from somewhere within the large region where North West Semitic languages were spoken, Figure 1-2. No matter where the place of origin of the Israelites, their speech would, for that reason, be at least somewhat similar to that of the Canaanites. Once Israelites and

Canaanites lived as neighbors, there would be further convergence in the manner or pattern of speech. Thus, the assumed close similarity of Hebrew to Canaanite does not necessarily show that early Israelites were Canaanites.

Texts found in Ugarit, and reports of the Phoenicians of a later age, confirm the importance of the god El among those two peoples who were closely related to the Canaanites. El is the Ancient One, remote and powerful, the father of Baal who is the more present and accessible god. It is certain that the people of Canaan were Baal-worshipers and probably El-worshipers as well. Had El not already been known to the earliest Israelites (in the Book of Genesis it is said that El was known to the Patriarchs) they would have learned of El as they lived among the Canaanites. As for the Canaanite modes of worship, these would either have been part of the common heritage of the western Semitic peoples or could have been quickly adopted by the Israelites from their new neighbors.

Pottery evidence is also equivocal. One does not have to be a Canaanite to use Canaanite pottery. Suppose that the Israelites entered Canaan from outside, perhaps as pastoralists, like the Shasu. Among such people, the amount of pottery carried about would not be great, and inevitably, some would be broken in normal use. Archaeologists know that broken pottery marks the location of nomad camps of the Bronze and Iron Ages in the Negev and southern Jordan. Broken pottery would need to be replaced, and that could be accomplished in the course of trade with village and town. That pottery would reflect the pottery traditions of those towns. If these pastoralists entered Canaan, it would have been Canaanite pottery that they would obtain. As they settled in Canaan, Canaanite pottery might have been obtained in that way for decades. As the settlers began to make their own pottery, the design would follow the already familiar Canaanite pattern. That the pottery of the early Israelite settlements was Canaanite does not demonstrate that the Israelites were Canaanites.

In broad terms, similarities noted between earliest Israelites and Canaanites can be accounted for either by common heritage, by trade, or by close contact and influence. The "Canaanite Theory" is not fully convincing, though it cannot be entirely dismissed.

Exodus

The Bible contains fragments or whole memories of the distant past of Israel. There are, however, no stories in the Bible which speak of persecution by Canaanite kings, withdrawal from their control, rebellion against them, or movement of the peoples to the hill country.

Nothing recalls the origin of Israel in Canaanite drop-outs or in peasant revolts. On the other hand, the ancient memory of persecution and subsequent flight from Egypt and then entry into Canaan permeates the biblical text from the Book of Exodus forward. Overwhelmingly, the Bible insists that Israel originated as a group that left Egypt, and that Yahweh was learned of (or recalled) in the Sinai. These were fundamental beliefs of Israel, and are evidently quite early in origin. This biblical testimony cannot be lightly dismissed. Unless a theory of origin explains these beliefs, it cannot be successful.

In the following, an account of the possible beginnings of Israel is offered in outline. It recognizes elements of the biblical account and also certain elements of the other theories which have been presented above. In view of the mountain of uncertainties, it is admittedly speculative.

In the background of the circumstances in which Israel first arose in Canaan, there were events of larger geographic scope. Whole peoples or nations were on the move, some scholars believe, not only Sea Peoples moving southward, by sea most likely, but also other peoples moving overland.

Shalmaneser I, king of Assyria (1274–1245 BC), reported that he fought against a horde of the "Ahlamu" in the vicinity of Harran along the upper Euphrates River in eastern Anatolia. These Ahlamu are a branch of the Arameans, it is believed. South of Harran, between the Mediterranean and the Euphrates, the city of Emar was destroyed in 1175 BC. A record in cuneiform recovered from the ruins of Emar states that the city was under siege by an "army of peoples," a "horde" as they might now be called. In a report of a few decades later, Assyrian king Tiglath-Pileser I (1116–1093 BC) stated that he crossed the Euphrates again and again to fight the Ahlamu. They seemed to have been on the move, these Ahlamu or Arameans, and a group of them were already in southern Syria in the time of that king.

It is suspected that peoples from central and western Anatolia were also on the move southward. Burials dating from the Late Bronze Age have been found in Canaan in which each body was interred in a large pottery jar, or two large jars mouth-to-mouth. This form of burial is known to have been practiced in central Anatolia of an earlier time. These movements are shadowy, indistinct in the records. Such movements would not have been the first of the southward migrations. Centuries earlier, Hurrians had come south from eastern Anatolia and left kings on the thrones of Amurru and Canaan.

What drove such migrations can only be guessed. Aramean movements, which originated in a region of frequent Hittite or Assyrian domination in eastern Anatolia, seem to have peaked at a time when the strength of the Assyrian and Hittite empires had begun to wane. The withdrawal of firm control by these previously domineering states might have enabled these folk movements to take place. Perhaps the famine that appears to have afflicted central Anatolia reached eastern Anatolia, Figure 10-2. The movements of peoples out of eastern Anatolia might have been driven by hunger.

The Bible tells that Abraham started his southward journey in Harran, a region where Arameans are believed to have been concentrated. His travel seems to correspond to the southward trajectory of the Arameans into southern Syria. Abraham went farther, according to the Bible, and settled in Canaan. Told in terms of the lives of a few individuals, the Patriarchs, these Biblical stories may reflect the southward movement of Arameans and others to Syria, Jordan, and Canaan.

It is known that at the end of the Bronze Age and the beginning of the Iron Age, new peoples had settled in a zone from southern Syria to the southern end of the Dead Sea. Tradition or language suggest a relationship of these peoples to one another, and to the Israelites also. Arameans who settled in Syria spoke a language that was related to Hebrew. On the eastern side of the Jordan River, Gadites and Ammonites settled. Gadites, according to the Bible, were part of the Israelite family of tribes. On the east of the Dead Sea were the Moabites, speaking a language close to Hebrew. To the south of them were Edomites, recognized in the Bible as distant kin of the Israelites.

Returning to the biblical story, Jacob, grandson of Abraham, went still farther south with his sons, to Egypt. That Semites entered Egypt and resided in the eastern delta is beyond dispute. An Egyptian official, stationed at the frontier near Pi-Atum, prepared a report. He wrote:

> We have finished letting the Shasu tribes of Edom pass the Fortress of Merneptah (life, prosperity, health!) which is in Tjeku to the pools of Per-Atum…to keep them alive and to keep their cattle alive through the great ka of Pharaoh (life, prosperity, health!) the good Sun of every land…(*Papyrus Anastasi VI*)

Though those mentioned in the papyrus were not specifically Jacob and his family, the resemblance to the account from the Book of Genesis is striking.

> …the famine was over all the face of the earth…..So they took their livestock …and went to Egypt, Jacob and all his descendents with him….Then Joseph went and told Pharaoh, and said, 'My father and my brothers, their flocks and their herds, and all that they possess, have come from the land of Canaan; and indeed they are in the land of Goshen… (Gen. 41:56, 46:6, 47:1)

Movement of Semites into Egypt, and presumably out of Egypt as well, are known to have occurred over many centuries.

In Egypt, arriving groups were probably assigned certain tracts or districts in the Wadi Tumilat which, as noted in the previous chapter, was probably the "Land of Goshen" of the Bible. Here, they were able to maintain their herds and preserve their language and customs. When Seti and Ramesses launched their building campaigns nearby, it would have been natural for them to draft these pastoralists for labor as Pharaohs had similarly conscripted Egyptian fellahin (peasants). This was "corvee," required labor on public works or royal projects, largely during the slack of the agricultural season. It was an age-old and presumably accepted duty for the fellahin. By such means were the pyramids built more than a thousand years before. To the pastoralists, however, free spirits used to their own work rhythms, draft into corvee would have been a shock, the slavery and oppression of Pharaoh.

That a number of these corvee tried to escape forced labor is likely, and it is also likely that some succeeded. They and their families made their departure and, as Pharaoh's strong force pursued, something may have happened which allowed the pastoralists to escape destruction or further enslavement, something which created an indelible memory of a supernatural intervention. The Bible tells of the destruction of Pharaoh's forces:

> Pharaoh's chariots and his army He cast into the Sea; his chosen captains are also drowned in the Reed Sea…For the horses of Pharaoh went with his chariots and his horsemen into the sea, and the LORD brought back the waters of the sea upon them…(Exod. 15:4, 19)

This surviving fragment of a very early poem or song, the Song of the Sea, as it is called, was undoubtedly part of a larger story, the entirety of which is no longer preserved in its original ancient poetic form. The song may have been composed sufficiently close to the time of the event as to contain an authentic memory.

The prose narrative of the escape from Egypt as now appears in the Bible is likely to be a composition of a much later date, an elaboration which drew upon earlier sources. It is said that six hundred thousand men plus women and children and a mixed multitude left Egypt—a number which the natural resources of the Sinai could not possibly support. The later writer of the narrative must have understood that. The text states that another supernatural intervention was required, the divine provision of water and manna.

Large numbers such as appear in many ancient texts, thousands and millions, seem to be figurative language, lacking the quantitative meaning which one would insist upon today. In the story of the Exodus there is a battle, not by the Israelites but by God on their behalf, against Pharaoh and Pharaoh's forces and gods. In orally preserved tradition, it is around battles that legendary heroic figures gather and the number of participants grows, sometimes to astonishing proportions. Recall the unrealistically large numbers of Greeks who were said to have gone to Troy, and the impossibly large number of Serbians said to have been at the Battle of Kosovo (Chapter 4). The number of Israelites who escaped Egypt can only be guessed, and may have been only a thousand or so. Even with such small numbers, survival in the harsh conditions of the Sinai would have been difficult and would require detailed local knowledge.

According to the Bible, Moses fled Egypt to the Sinai, where he came to the camp of Jethro, a Midianite, a priest, and a keeper of flocks. Jethro and his kinsmen would have been Shasu in the eyes of the Egyptians. Moses tended Jethro's flocks in the Sinai, and married Jethro's daughter. He would have gained some practical knowledge of conditions in the region. The Bible also says that Hobab, a Midianite, accompanied the Israelites as a guide. In any case, those who escaped Egypt would have included many who remembered the essential geography of the Sinai, and further, they would have encountered one band of Shasu or another who might advise them of the location of pastures and springs.

The Bible tells that it was while Moses was with Jethro's flocks that God spoke to Moses and revealed his unique identity and his name, "Yahweh." It was then that God instructed Moses to return to Egypt to confront Pharaoh and to bring out the people. After his encounters with Pharaoh, and following the Exodus, Moses met again with Jethro, Jethro the priest. A priest of what god? The Bible does not say. When Jethro heard of the great deeds which God had done in Egypt, Jethro the priest presided over a sacrifice of thanksgiving, to Yahweh it is said. According to what is called the Midianite or Kenite Hypothesis (Jethro is identified as a Midianite, or alternatively as a Kenite), Yahweh had long been worshiped by the Midianites or Kenites of the Sinai. It might be said that those who escaped Egypt and camped with the Midianites recognized in this Midianite god the same One who saved them from the Egyptians.

Scholars have combed the surviving records of Egypt, Canaan, and elsewhere in a search for the origin of the worship of Yahweh. It was not in Egypt, or among the settled Canaanites. There seems to be no early trace, no clue in the records, with but one exception. In remote Nubia, there are two Egyptian temples, one built by Amenhotep III (1386–1349 BC) and the other by Ramesses II (1279–1212 BC). On the walls of these temples appear nearly identical lists relating to Shasu peoples. One list mentions the "Shasu of Seir." Seir is the region of the Sinai south of the Dead Sea, and it is no surprise that the Egyptians encountered Shasu in that region. But another reference is to the "Shasu of Yahweh." This seems to be the oldest known reference to the sacred name.

According to the grammatical relationship of the words, "Shasu of Yahweh" refers to a place, in effect a settlement or camp of certain Shasu. Some scholars deduce that it was in the Sinai. Whatever the location, this list from the Egyptian temples appears to tie Shasu together with Yahweh at a time which, if the approximate dating of the Exodus in the previous chapter is right, was a hundred or more years before the Exodus.

This ancient relationship of Yahweh to certain Shasu, presumably of the Sinai, gives support to the Midianite-Kenite Hypothesis. It also gives support to the tradition of the Bible that Israelites had been present in the Sinai and learned of Yahweh in the Sinai (or there regained knowledge of Yahweh after a lapse of contact, since the "J" source asserts that Yahweh was known from primeval times).

> O Yahweh, when you can out of Seir
> When you marched from Edom's land
> > Earth quaked
> > With thunder the skies rained
> > With thunder the clouds rained water
> Mountains shook
> > Before Yahweh, the One of Sinai. (Judges 5:4)

This from the Song of Deborah, a very early text, and it recalls that Yahweh was learned of in the south, in Sinai, or in Seir or Edom in the northern Sinai. It appears to confirm that it was people who came up from the south, from Sinai or through Sinai, who brought the knowledge of Yahweh into Canaan.

Ramesses II sent a military force into Seir and Ramesses III brags of raiding Shasu camps, and there were probably other such attacks on these pastoral peoples for which no records remain. The raids may have sent a stream of Shasu fleeing northward. Shasu people who recognized Yahweh might have supplied a stream of believers to Canaan over some decades, swelling the ranks of the initial Israelite settlers in the Central Hill Country.

Archaeological evidence of the new settlements in the Central Hill Country of Canaan and Jordan was described in the previous chapter. A. Zertal, an Israeli archaeologist, was responsible for the ground survey in the geographic region of Manasseh. In settlement sites, he found various pottery for which he was able to establish relative dates. That dated earliest was found at those settlements closest to the Jordan river. Settlements farther westward, away from the Jordan River, used this early pottery but also a significant amount of pottery of a later style (Zertal, 1991, 1998). A logical conclusion to be drawn is that the more westerly settlements were established later than those nearer the Jordan River. In turn, this suggests a movement of people from east to west, in accordance with the biblical account of the crossing of the Jordan and entry into Canaan.

The scenario outlined above seems plausible. It seems hard to otherwise account for the persistence of the Exodus story in Israelite tradition, and to account also for the source of the belief in Yahweh.

The City of Shechem

In Canaan, the new arrivals would have encountered a sparsely settled region of a few villages and towns, and also the ancient strong-walled city of Shechem. In about 1350 BC, Shechem was ruled by Labayu, "the Lion," who was much complained of by other Canaanite kings. With the help of Apiru, Labayu and his sons attacked other Canaanite cities toward the coast and threatened Jerusalem to the south. Over this, Abdi-Hepa of

Jerusalem had been particularly outraged. In a letter to Egypt, he accuses Labayu of "...giving the land of Shechem to the Apiru" (EA 289). It seems likely that Labayu made a grant of land to the Apiru in return for military services. It would have been a little over a century later that the Israelite settlement sites began in Canaan. Nearer the time of settlement, Seti I (1291–1279 BC) clashed with Apiru about twenty five miles north of Shechem. Were descendants of these Apiru still present, still known as Apiru, when the Israelite settlement began? It is possible that certain Apiru were among the settlers in the hills and may have been among the foundation peoples of Israel.

That Apiru, presumably long present in Canaan, may have been part of the foundation of Israel seems to challenge a fundamental view expressed in the Bible. That view is that all Israel was descended from Jacob, and that all had shared in the Egyptian experience. Though it is the dominant view, it is by no means the only view for which support can be found in the Bible. It is told that the Israelites left Egypt accompanied by a "mixed multitude" (Exodus 12:38, Numbers 11:4). This certainly refers to people who were not considered to be descendants of Jacob. The mixed multitude was with the Israelites in the wilderness migration. There is no indication in the Bible that this multitude ever departed to the left or to the right nor did anything but enter Canaan with the Israelites. It seems that the Israelites entered Canaan along with these others, former corvee laborers like themselves perhaps. The Bible thus acknowledges the mixed nature of the group that entered Canaan.

In Canaan, one can learn from the Bible, fusion took place with the resident population, both at the individual and the group level.

> The children of Israel dwelt among the Canaanites, the Hittites, the Amorites, the Perizzites, the Hivites, and the Jebusites...and they took their daughters to be their wives, and gave their daughters to their sons... (Judges 3:6)

Speaking of Jerusalem, the prophet Ezekiel said:

> ...your birth and your nativity are from the land of Canaan; your father was an Amorite and your mother a Hittite. (Ezekiel 16:3)

"Strangers" stood before the Ark of the Covenant along with Israelites, and this reference to strangers likely means those who were not descended of Jacob (Joshua 8:33). Joseph, Moses, David, Solomon, to name a few, had non-Jacobite wives. One of the most memorable stories of the Bible tells of Ruth, a Moabite woman who lost her first husband and in time married Boaz, an Israelite. It seems that there were no religious bars to intermarriage and acceptance of strangers in those early times, and in the nature of things, in Canaan, intermarriage must have taken place extensively.

More interesting than the fusion at the level of individuals is the possibility that whole groups, later to be counted among the twelve tribes of Israel, originated outside of the initial Israelite community. These groups had not necessarily been in Egypt, nor were they, even in theory, descendants of Jacob. Shechem was a Canaanite city, referred to in the Amarna letters as "Shakmu." Yet Shechemites are listed among the clans of the tribe of Manasseh (Joshua 17:2). This seems to show that the people of the Canaanite city had been accepted into the Manasseh tribe. Caleb, the devoted lieutenant of Moses, was a Kenizzite. These were kin to Edomites (Genesis 36:9,11), peoples of the Sinai, Shasu as the Egyptians might have called them, with no evident descent from Jacob. Later the Calebites are listed as part of the tribe of Judah (Joshua 15:13). Calebites had been brought into the tribe, it seems, though they were originally outsiders.

That tribes can absorb outsiders, individuals or groups, is no surprise. Tribes are often open societies, able to admit those who are prepared to live by its rules and accept its values and beliefs. In a much later time, Edomites (Idumaeans) converted to Judaism. They became among the most fervent of believers, and there appears to have been no bar to their acceptance in the community of Yahweh and Israel.

If the Shechemites, Calebites, Edomites were admitted to the community of Israel, then it is equally possible that one or several of the twelve tribes or clans of Israel were originally outside groups. The tribe of Dan may provide a specific example, Chapter 16. Such tribes would have their own earlier histories, no longer preserved.

Through intermarriage and absorption, a new community was created, and resulted in a merger of ancient lore, ancestral tales, and modes of worship. Traditions and beliefs of later Israel would, according to this view, owe as much to those others as to those who experienced the Exodus and the wandering in the Sinai.

Earliest in the forging of this new ethnicity, and most important for the formation of tradition and belief, were the peoples in the Central Hill Country in the vicinity of Shechem. The ancient city of Shechem seems to have played a major but still poorly understood role in the fusion, but it may have been particularly influential in aspects of belief and forms of worship.

Within this walled city, excavators have found the remains of a formidable building which may have been a temple. The Bible (Judges 9:4, 46) speaks of a temple at Shechem, the temple of Baal Berith or El Berith, the latter meaning "El, God of the Covenant." Much biblical tradition centers on Shechem and the nearby hilltop holy sites of Ebal and Gerizim. It was in the vicinity of Shechem, possibly, that the identification or fusion of El with Yahweh took place. In this fusion, Yahweh belief exercised the leading role. How this came to be is mysterious in view of what must have been the small size of the newly arrived group from the Sinai. Religious fervor of the new arrivals must have played a part. Polytheists, as were the Canaanites, would have had no great problem in the acceptance of yet another god, Yahweh. It was helpful that many of the attributes of El were similar to those of Yahweh, allowing both Canaanites and the new arrivals to see them as one and the same.

The designation "El, God of Israel" was given to an altar by Jacob at Shechem (Genesis 33:20). Later, an alter at Mount Ebal overlooking Shechem was dedicated to "Yahweh, God of Israel" (Joshua 8:30). The identity in form of these two titles may not be a coincidence but a recognition of the identification of El with Yahweh.

It was to Shechem, according to tradition, that Joshua called together the leaders of the tribes (Joshua 24). He recalled for them the Israelite sacred experience. He called upon them to choose: their old gods or Yahweh. Here they renewed the pledge to the Covenant. This biblical story may encapsulate the complex fusion of peoples that would later constitute historic Israel. Acceptance of Yahweh as the primary god, then the sole God of Israel, and acceptance of the Exodus experience as the shared heritage of all would have been only a matter of time.

The role of Shechem ceased after approximately 1125 BC when, according to the archaeological evidence, the city was destroyed. It was revived, and later became the capital of the newly established northern kingdom.

Limitations imposed by the terrain in the Central Hill Country required dispersion of population. Most settlements consisted of only a few houses. Against the organized and strong forces of the Canaanites, these small settlements could not be defended by their own resources. The futility of individual defense is reflected in the fact that there was not even an attempt to put up defensive walls around most settlements. Only in Shechem, perhaps, were there strong walls available to the Israelites, and this only on the assumption that the Shechemites were in treaty or covenant relationship with settlers and would allow them shelter. With the possible exception of Shechem, the answer to the security needs of widespread settlements would have been a militia, drawn from all sufficiently nearby clans or tribes. A unifying ideology would provide the necessary bond to bring clans or tribes to their duty. The continuing survival of earliest Israel may be accounted for by this bond, a bond to one another and to Yahweh through the Covenant.

As early as the time of the composition of the Song of Deborah, a league of tribes already existed, already referred to as Israel, already recognized as the people of Yahweh, functioning together under military necessity. Descendants of these people would be the core of the state of ancient Israel under Saul, David, Solomon—a state which was to be forged on the iron anvil of the Philistines.

15

LAST ATTACK OF THE SEA PEOPLES

Following the death of Merneptah in 1202 BC, Egypt entered a difficult and chaotic period. No more were there boasts of conquests, as Merneptah had boasted of defeating the Libyans and destroying Israel. Now, ruler succeeded ruler in rapid and confused succession. Seti II, son of Merneptah, ruled for six years and was followed by his son, Siptah. Twosert, Siptah's mother, ruled in her own name for a time. Then there was Amenmesse. His place in the sequence of these rulers is uncertain. What is certain however, is that after Amenmesse the line of kings which included Seti I, Ramesses II, and Merneptah came to an end when Setnakht succeeded to the throne. He ruled a scant two years, but with him a new dynasty began.

A papyrus was written under the direction of Setnakht's grandson. This papyrus—Papyrus Harris as it is called—looked back at that troubled period.

> Egypt was adrift and every man was thrown out of his right. There was no leader for years…Egypt was ruled by chiefs and town rulers. Men killed both the high and the low. This was followed by empty years when Irsu the Syrian was with them as chief. He subjugated the whole land. He together with his companions plundered the land, treated the gods as if mere men and no offerings were made in the temples. (*Papyrus Harris*)

This disturbed period, from the death of Merneptah to the time of Setnakht, lasted approximately twenty years during which there was at times misrule or no rule. It may have been then, when Egypt looked inward, that Israel was able to gain a stable footing in the hills of Canaan. It may also have been then that a new generation of Sea Peoples raided along the eastern coast of the Mediterranean as far south as the shores of Canaan. In time, Egypt or Egyptian-controlled territory would experience an invasion by Sea Peoples. From the viewpoint of today, that invasion was one of the most dramatic events of the Late Bronze Age. It may have seemed equally dramatic to those Egyptians who lived through it.

Almost all that is known of the Sea Peoples invasion comes from a remarkably well-preserved Egyptian temple constructed by Pharaoh Ramesses III. This Ramesses was the son of Setnakht. His name may have suggested to him that he was destined to walk in the footsteps of the great Ramesses II, and it is certain that Egypt required such a strong hand. Ramesses III (1182–1151 BC) was a builder, though not on the grand scale of the earlier Ramesses. On the west bank of the Nile opposite Luxor (ancient Thebes), Ramesses III built a temple, which is known by the name of the present-day village where it is located, Medinet Habu. The interior and exterior wall surfaces of this still magnificent structure are a storybook of the deeds of this Pharaoh. In pictures and prose, they tell of a tidal wave of invaders which threatened to engulf Egypt and which Ramesses III claimed to have totally defeated.

But before these Sea Peoples arrived, there were other problems for Ramesses. The Libyans were once more troubling the western Delta. Though a generation earlier Merneptah had defeated the Libyans, he had not finished them. The Libyan conflict of the fifth year of Ramesses III was set off by a political miscalculation by the Egyptians, a match thrown into dry tinder. For some time, sons of kings or chiefs of subordinated peoples were brought to Egypt, where they would receive the benefits of a "civilized" Egyptian upbringing. They would, presumably, return home "Egyptianized," with a pro-Egyptian political outlook. With a dangerous insensitivity to Libyan tribal politics, the Egyptians attempted to impose one such princeling on the Libyans as their king, and that provoked war.

The clash is pictured in a large sculptural relief on the outside north wall of the Medinet Habu temple, and is accompanied by a lengthy text. A town in the northwestern part of the Nile Delta seems to have been the focus of the battle. A number of Libyan tribes had come together for the battle, including Libu and Meshwesh, peoples who had fought against Merneptah. The inscriptions tell that the Libyans suffered a terrible defeat and a vast slaughter. A thousand prisoners were taken, and there were 3,000 each of severed phalli and hands.

In the eleventh year of Ramesses III, the war with the Libyans flared again. A text on the temple wall suggests the arrogance of the Libyans. "We will settle in Egypt. So spoke they with one accord and continually entered the boundaries of Egypt." Many prisoners and over 42,000 cattle were taken as the Libyans suffered another resounding defeat. Mesher, the son of the Libyan chief, was captured. The chief, Keper, went to the Egyptians to beg for his son's release. There was no mercy here as Homer says there was at Troy, when Priam begged Achilles for the release of the body of his son Hector. Keper was seized and chained to the Pharaoh's horse team. There was no end to Pharaoh's triumphs. Yet the Libyans remained, and over time they gained an increasing grip on part of the Nile Delta.

War with the Sea Peoples

It was in the eighth year of the kingship of Ramesses III, 1174 BC, that two great battles with the Sea Peoples were said to have taken place. When had these Sea Peoples arrived in the region? After Merneptah, there is no mention of Sea Peoples in known Egyptian records, giving the impression that the new invaders came suddenly, out of nowhere, "a bolt from the blue." But during the chaotic years, no Pharaoh produced great monuments in which the presence of Sea Peoples would have been recorded. In a sculptural relief at Medinet Habu, a few Sea Peoples fighters are shown scattered among the Egyptian forces that fought against the Libyans as early as the fifth year of the king's reign, 1177 BC. Most scholars believe that these Sea Peoples are out of place in this relief and that they were "borrowed" from the year eight conflict and inserted into the illustration of the war of year five. However, it is reasonable to believe that Sea Peoples had come to the region in small but increasing numbers over some time, and that they were available to the Egyptians as mercenaries for Ramesses' first Libyan war. If Sea Peoples had already arrived in the region, if their numbers were increasing, it might have been viewed as threatening by the Egyptians. The great "battles" against the Sea Peoples, so vividly described on the wall of the temple at Medinet Habu, may reflect not only an attack by Sea Peoples on Egypt or Egyptian interests, but preemptive attacks by the Egyptians on the Sea Peoples.

Nearly all that is known of the situation comes from texts and illustrations on the temple walls. Much about Sea Peoples war would be clearer if the purpose of the extensive sculptural reliefs and inscriptions at Medinet Habu were to provide a historical record. In fact, that was not their purpose at all. The purpose was, rather, to support the political and religious ideology of Egypt. The ideology included a belief in the dominance of the Egyptian gods in the natural and supernatural worlds, the centrality of Egypt in worldly affairs, and the invincibility of the kings of Egypt. In support of this ideology, the walls of the Medinet Habu temple are largely given over to laudation of the Egyptian king. Ramesses is the:

> "Mighty Bull…Strong-Armed…Slayer of Tehenu [Libyans]." "[Foreign] chiefs come with fearful step to crave the breath of life" from him. The name of Ramesses is "…a flame, the terror of him is in the [foreign] countries." He is the "valiant warrior…taking captive every land" and he is "without equal, smiting millions alone by himself." He is also "like the lion with deep roar upon the mountain tops whose terror is feared from afar…taking away the breath from the countries by the heat of his body." Moreover "The countries come, bowing down to the fame of his majesty, with their tribute…upon their backs" and "the messengers of every land come, their hearts fluttering, so transposed that their hearts are no longer in their bodies." "He rages like a hawk among the birds and doves; valiant upon the

battlefield, fighting hand-to-hand upon his feet, seizing the chiefs with his two hands, even this King Ramesses III." And he concedes that "…my hand is equal to my courage following my valor…I am the strong and valiant one, my designs come to pass without fail." (Historical Records)

Most of the texts on the temple walls are of this sort, and the sculptural reliefs are, like the texts, largely dedicated to scenes of the conquering might of the Pharaoh. Perhaps in this still early stage of the intellectual development of humankind, sympathetic magic was believed in. Constant repetition in words and images of the might of Pharaoh would insure that it was so and would ever be so. Considering the purpose of the inscriptions and illustrations, objective reporting or historic content is not to be expected and such as appears is incidental, meager. For that reason, sound historic conclusions cannot be derived by excessive reliance on specific details given in these wall texts or reliefs. Still, text and illustrations provide information—almost the only information—of the fateful conflict with the Sea Peoples.

This information is veiled in a certain diffuseness, a vagueness of detail concerning events and places. But it is certain that Sea Peoples alone were involved, no Libyans as in the attack on Merneptah. Two battles are illustrated in the sculptural reliefs. From the order of the reliefs along the wall, it appears that the "Land Battle" occurred first.

The Land Battle

The Land Battle pictorial relief on the outside face of the north wall measures about forty feet wide. Close to thirty-two centuries have passed since artists applied themselves to the task of creating this great wall illustration. Before completion, minor mistakes in the relief were corrected with plaster and then all was richly overpainted, which made every detail distinct and clear. Plaster and paint has since eroded away, although it still remains on some scenes on the inside walls of the temple. The Land Battle scene as it now appears is cluttered and visually overloaded, and is somewhat difficult to follow without the resolution of detail which paint once provided.

Certainly Pharaoh stands out clearly. He is positioned on the right side of the Land Battle illustration, larger than life. He launches his arrows effortlessly upon the enemy. His figure is a nearly exact duplicate of that of Ramesses II in a Kadesh relief at Luxor temple, just across the Nile river, and with which the Medinet Habu artists were surely familiar. The rest of the Land Battle scene depicts the utter chaos of battle, Figure 15-1. Sea Peoples and Egyptians are locked in close combat. Sea Peoples posture with their javelins, while clusters of Egyptians and loyal Sherdan armed with swords oppose them. Scattered everywhere, disposed at every angle, are bodies of the injured or dead. These are Sea Peoples, for none

Figure 15-1. A part of the Land Battle relief. Evident are the wagons of the Sea Peoples. A door had later been cut through the wall, blank area bottom center.

of the Egyptian forces suffer a wound. Most of the fallen Sea Peoples are impaled with arrows, and in the illustration only Ramesses is shown using the bow. The vast slaughter must be his work alone. These are conventions of Egyptian battle illustrations and have all been presented before. What is strikingly new in these illustrations, however, are two elements seen here for the first time in Egyptian art.

The first new feature is the appearance of the Sea People themselves. Each warrior wears a "feathered" headdress, Figure 15-3. The traditional foes of Egypt—Nubians, Libyans, Canaanites, and Syrians—had been shown in Egyptian illustrations since a thousand years before. In the Land Battle scene, that strange headdress seems to identify an entirely new foe. The texts inform that they are different, for the most part, from those Sea Peoples who, a generation earlier, attacked Egypt along with the Libyans. No one knows what those earlier Sea Peoples looked like, since there are no surviving illustrations of those who fought Merneptah. Now, in these sculptural reliefs of the war of Ramesses' eighth year, Sea Peoples are vividly illustrated.

The Sea Peoples fought largely on foot, but a few had chariots. Egypt's enemies of the past are occasionally shown with chariots, so that chariots in the hands of the enemy were not a new thing in Egyptian battle illustrations. The second new feature, however, are not chariots but wagons that accompany the Sea Peoples. These are crude affairs of stakes and wicker with a pair of crude wooden disc wheels, and they carry women and children. Boys are illustrated as men in miniature. They wear miniature feather headgear, like that of their elders. Women have long hair held by headbands. Women and children are caught in the midst of this battle, and the illustration shows that Egyptian forces do not hesitate to attack them.

At Medinet Habu, the names of these Sea Peoples groups are given in hieroglyphics. These contain no vowels, and the vowels and their placements are mostly a matter of guesswork. Scholars are usually content to place a neutral "e" sound between consonants of the hieroglyphic writing, to allow the names to be pronounced. With this augmentation of the hieroglyphics, the invaders were the *Peleset*, *Tjeker*, *Shekelesh*, *Weshesh*, and also the *Danuna*. Of these, only the Shekelesh have been mentioned before. From the frequency with which they are mentioned, it is clear that the Peleset are the most numerous among this new wave of Sea Peoples, and their leading element.

More will be said in following chapters about the origin or identity of these Sea Peoples. For the present, it is important to identify the Peleset, the P-L-S-T of the hieroglyphics. Scholars are unanimous in this. The Peleset are the Philistines. In the texts and illustrations at Medinet Habu, they make their first appearance in history.

The Sea Battle

To the left of the Land Battle scene is a hunting scene without historical significance. Ramesses kills a lion. Further left is the Sea Battle scene. The presence of the hunting scene between the Land and Sea Battles suggests a delay between the first and the second battle, but how long the delay may have been is not known.

The Sea Battle sculptural relief on the north wall of the temple is about 55 feet wide and, like the Land Battle relief, was originally augmented with plaster and paint. Here, represented in a compressed composition at which the Egyptians were very skilled was a clash which occurred on the water somewhere near shore.

This is, by any measure, the most remarkable and novel large-scale sculptural relief produced by the Egyptians in the Late Bronze Age. In contrast to the design of the Land Battle scene, which lacks focus and clarity, the Sea Battle scene shows a high degree of structure and order. On the right stands the Pharaoh—as in the Land Battle illustration gigantic in stature—launching shafts at the enemy from his unerring bow. Stretching across the bottom of the illustration are Egyptian soldiers, marching off with Sea Peoples prisoners. On the left is the battle on the water, and it is to this that all eyes are drawn.

Here there is a clash among ships. All ships are shown broadside, which enabled the master designer of the scene to avoid problems of perspective while still enabling him to maximize the number of ships and the number of men shown (Figure 15-2). So well is the composition carried out that it is hardly noticed that ships, men, and river mouth or harbor are represented at different scales.

Ships are arranged in three rows, one above the other. In each row there are three ships. Three along the left and one on the lower right are manned by Egyptians, and the rest are those of the Sea Peoples. While the general appearance of the Egyptian ships are like those seen in illustrations of an earlier time, a feature of the Sea Peoples' ships has not been seen before: the vertical stem and stern posts topped with "bird" heads. Two of these Sea Peoples ships are manned by warriors who wear the same feathered headgear as shown in the Land Battle relief, and two others by those in horned helmets. While these helmets lack the knob characteristic of the Sherdan helmet (see Figure 16-5), these men are most likely Sherdan, free Sherdan who don't owe obedience to Pharaoh.

Figure 15-2. Part of the Sea Battle relief. Egyptian ships are shown on the left, and one at the lower right. The remaining ships are those of the Sea Peoples. Below, Sea Peoples prisoners are marched off.

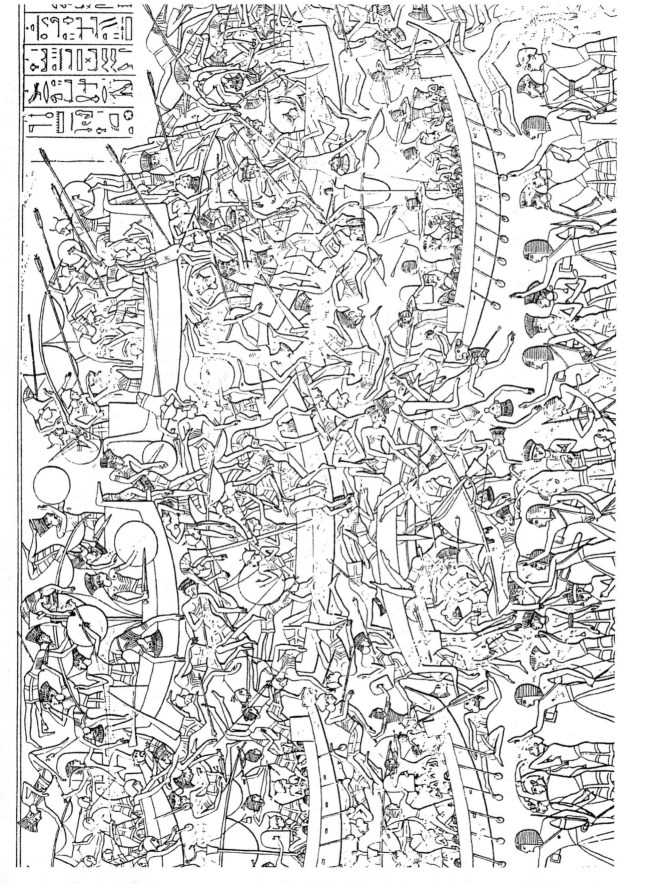

Relying, perhaps, on their hand-to-hand combat superiority, the Sea Peoples came armed only with close-combat weapons—dirk swords and a few lances—and that was a fatal mistake. The Egyptian forces, on the other hand, had not only close-combat weapons but stand-off weapons as well, their bows. With these, they had reaped havoc on the Sea Peoples in their ships before they could close with the Egyptians.

The scene shows a fierce melee of close combat. Egyptian boats have their oars out so that they are able to maneuver, but in the Sea Peoples boats, oars are shipped. They are unable to maneuver. They have been caught by surprise, it seems. From a crow's nest on an Egyptian ship, a slinger rains missiles down on the Sea Peoples. A grappling hook has been swung out from an Egyptian ship and lands on a Sea Peoples ship. The ship is hauled close and a Sea Peoples fighter is dispatched with a lance. Another Sea Peoples ship is dismasted, a third capsized. Sea Peoples are in disarray, drowned, dead. The water is filled with them. Those still living are fished out, to be sent to shore to join the line of captives. The Sea Battle is shown as a clear Egyptian victory. The inscription states:

> As for the countries who came from the land in isles in the midst of the sea, as they were coming forward toward Egypt, their hearts relying on their hands, a net was prepared for them…
>
> …..
>
> I caused the Nile mouth [?] to be prepared like a strong wall with warships, galleys, and coasters equipped, for they were manned completely from bow to stern with valiant worriers with their weapons. (*Historical Records*)

It seems that the Egyptians were, as they claimed, "prepared." They had achieved tactical surprise, and appear to have sprung some sort of trap. Perhaps the Sea Peoples had approached, dropped anchor and shipped oars, unaware of the presence of Egyptian forces nearby. The circumstances are murky. But the Sea Peoples are dealt a resounding defeat, it is said, just as they were defeated on land.

> As for those who came forward together on the sea, the full flame was in front of them at the Nile mouths [?], while a stockade of lances surrounded them on the shore…[they were] prostrated on the beach, slain, and made into heaps…Their ships and their goods were as if fallen into the water. (*Historical Records*)

That is how the story is told and illustrated by the Egyptians. The Sea Peoples left no records that might say otherwise. The Sea Peoples prisoners would work the royal farms and temple estates. Some would serve in the Egyptian army and are shown as part of the Egyptian forces attacking Libyans in the year eleven battle.

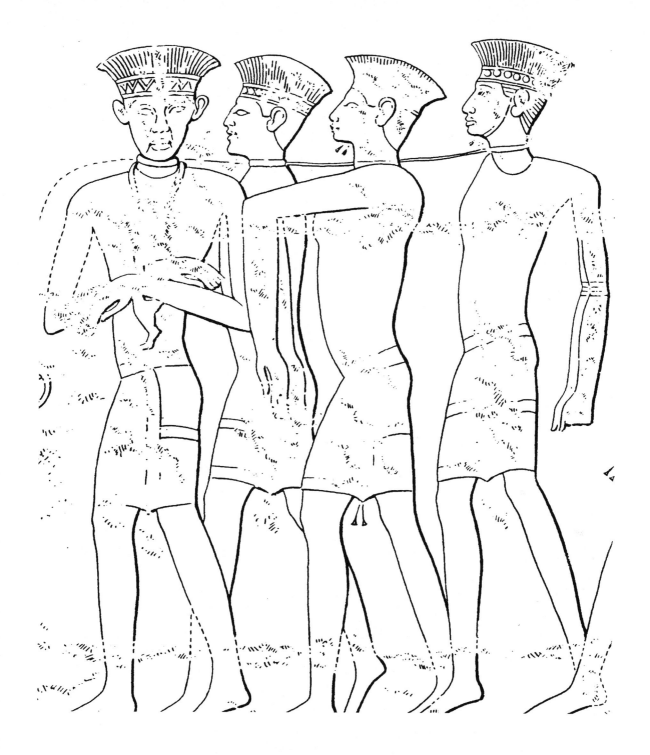

Figure 15-3. Sea Peoples as prisoners, a detail from the Sea Battle scene.

The Loss of Canaan

In spite of the extensive illustrations and texts at Medinet Habu, and a substantial amount of ink expended by scholars, most of the circumstances of the conflict with the Sea Peoples remains baffling. Only one thing is certain. In a major historic reverse for Egypt, Egypt lost control of the coast of Canaan to the Sea Peoples. The battles with the Sea Peoples which are described on the wall of Medinet Habu are certainly related to the circumstances of that loss. How they are related is not known and must be inferred. The relationship of the Land to the Sea Battle and of either to the loss of coastal Canaan also remains a mystery.

Did Sea Peoples attempt an invasion, a landing at the mouth of the Nile? Were the Land and Sea Battles two aspects of one fight for control of the entrance to the Nile? Surprisingly, there is nothing in the text or illustrations to show that either battle took place in Egypt. The term "Nile mouth" which appears in the translations is largely a guess. The Egyptian hieroglyph does not represent a name, "Nile" or otherwise. It is, rather, a term which could mean harbor, river mouth, estuary, or bay. It is entirely possible that the Sea Battle did not take place at a Nile mouth but in one of the harbors of the coast of Canaan. However, the fact that the Egyptians were able to mobilize troops and a variety of ships and spring a trap suggests that the Sea Battle in fact did take place near Egypt, at a Nile mouth, perhaps the mouth of the eastern or Pelusiac branch. An attempt of the Sea Peoples to enter the Pelusiac branch of the Nile would threaten the city of Ramesses, Figure 13-1, the great Egyptian capital of the northeast, and would have provoked a massive Egyptian response.

The Land Battle may have been a quite separate affair, fought to contain an attempted or already successful Sea Peoples invasion of Canaan. Portions of the Medinet Habu text rather clearly show that the locale of the Land Battle was northward, in the direction of Canaan, and probably in Canaan itself. "His majesty sets out for Zahi…..to crush every enemy…" says an inscription referring to the Land Battle. Ramesses states "I organized my frontier in Zahi. I prepared before [the Sea Peoples] the princes, the garrison commanders, the Mariannu…"

Zahi is an Egyptian term designating Canaan or the coast of Canaan, perhaps including the coast as far north as Amurru. Thus, the text makes it clear that the Land Battle did not take place in Egypt but north of it. "I slay those who violate my frontier…" declares Ramesses. That cannot refer to the inner Egyptian frontier which was at Sile. Nor could it refer to distant Amurru (Figure 2-1), since no Egyptian king since Ramesses II maintained a frontier that far north. In these inscriptions, Zahi must refer to Canaan. The Land Battle took place in Canaan, and probably near the coast.

Evidence and logic suggest that the Land Battle was fought for control of the coastal towns or cities of Canaan which were under attack or which possibly had already been seized by the Sea Peoples. For the Egyptians, all of Canaan was at risk, and ultimately Egypt itself. "They were coming forward toward Egypt" says the Medinet Habu text, "their hearts relying on their hands." Sound military considerations would require that the Egyptians engage the enemy on land northward, in Zahi, in Canaan, before they advanced farther south and attacked Egypt directly. That objective was accomplished. An advance into Egypt was prevented.

How and when did the Sea Peoples gain control of the coast? Many years ago, the renowned historian Gaston Maspero offered his view (Maspero, 1910). In later years, that view was taken up and elaborated by the American scholar William Albright, the German scholar Albrecht Alt, and others. The broadest representation of the theory depends on two separate Egyptian texts. The first speaks of a battle in Amurru.

> A camp was set up in one place in Amurru. They [the Sea Peoples] desolated its peoples and its land was like that which had never come into being. *(Historical Records)*

The second relates that the prisoners were assigned to strongholds, or garrisons.

> I…brought them [Sea Peoples] as captives to Egypt like the sands of the shore. I settled them in strongholds, bound in my name. Numerous were their classes like hundred-thousands. *(Papyrus Harris)*

According to this theory, in response to the threat of the Sea Peoples, Ramesses III mobilized his army and marched north to Amurru. There, he attacked the main camp of the Sea Peoples, engaged them in decisive battle and defeated them and so forestalled their further advance to the south. Many prisoners were taken. Subsequently, some of these prisoners were formed by the Egyptians into military units and sent to man garrisons of the Egyptian empire in Canaan. These were the "strongholds" referred to above. What happened after the placement of Sea Peoples in garrisons in Canaan the theory does not answer. Perhaps they revolted, seized control, or for some reason the Egyptians simply handed over the keys and departed.

This theory explains a good deal, yet it is unconvincing. The monumental inscriptions and reliefs at Medinet Habu tell of more than battles or wars with Libyans or Sea Peoples. They also tell of a battle in distant Amurru. But in the inscriptions which deal with the Amurru, there is no mention or illustration of Sea Peoples. Many historians believe that this "Amurru War" of Ramesses III never took place. It is not historical. It was "borrowed" from earlier Pharaohs, to fill out some wall space, and to round out and inflate Ramesses' accomplishments. Thus, there is good reason to doubt that the Egyptians under Ramesses III ever fought in Amurru, or took Sea Peoples prisoners there.

The garrison portion of the theory also is questionable. "I settled them in strongholds," but where were those strongholds? Years earlier, when Ramesses II settled the Sherdan who he had captured, it was in Egypt and well inland, well away from vital strategic points, and certainly well away from the sea where they might establish contact with their free Sherdan brethren.

From Sile in Egypt, through Gaza and then close by Ashkelon and Ashdod, passed the great highway called the Horus Road. It was the vital Egyptian land link to the rest of the world. It is doubtful that the Egyptians would place armed Sea Peoples, Philistines, in just those cities which were near this vital road, the jugular of the Egyptian empire, cities near the sea where Philistines might make contact with their free kinsmen and make common cause with them.

It is much more likely that the Sea Peoples came to Canaan as invaders. It has sometimes been assumed that they arrived overland, in a massive migration, through Syria and into Canaan, past the Egyptian fortresses of Megiddo and Beth Shan. That possibility is intimately connected to the theory that the Sea Peoples were elements of a vast southward movement of peoples out of Anatolia, or even Europe. Women and children in wagons in the Land Battle scene are taken to support this view. In these wagons are the families of the Sea Peoples, arriving in Amurru or Canaan, it is assumed, after a long and grueling land trek from Anatolia.

However, there is little objective support for any theory of a vast migration and an overland trek of Sea Peoples. It is a more reasonable assumption that these Sea Peoples, men whose immediate predecessors harried the coasts of southern Anatolia, Cyprus, and Ugarit from the sea, arrived in Canaan by sea. Their initial occupation of only those Canaanite cities nearest the sea speaks clearly of an invasion from the sea. Surely, they came to Canaan uninvited, as raiders, making the most of their opportunities in disturbed times.

Sea Peoples may have arrived in the region in small numbers even before the reign of Ramesses III, for the inscriptions suggest that some Sea Peoples had already settled before the battles. "The Philistines were anxious, hidden in their towns…" reports an inscription at Medinet Habu, which appears to indicate that the Philistine enemy was already in possession of one or more cities or towns, most likely in Canaan. Those in wagons may have been families formed in Canaan, moving in an attempted expansion out of their initial enclaves in Canaan, perhaps even thinking to reach Egypt.

Date of the Sea Peoples in Canaan

If the date of the beginning of Sea Peoples occupation in Canaan were known, the events of those times would be much clearer. It is usually assumed that it began during the reign of Ramesses III, but there is no certainty of that. There is an Egyptian document of a somewhat later time, a geographic text referred to as the Onomasticon of Amenope. It contains references to various cities in the Egyptian sphere of interest. In the Onomasticon, Sherdan, Tjeker, and Philistines are mentioned in conjunction with the Canaanite coastal cities of Ashkelon, Ashdod, and Gaza. This almost certainly means that these Sea Peoples were already in those cities and in control of those cities when the Onomasticon was written, around 1100 BC.

A second Egyptian document, the Tale of Wen Amon, dates to a few years later. Wen Amon was an Egyptian official who traveled by sea to the port city of Byblos (Figure 2-1), in order to arrange for the shipment of timber to Egypt. Wen Amon reported that Tjeker were in control of Dor, a city on the coast of Canaan south of Byblos. Thus, Tjeker were also comfortably at home on the coast in the time of Wen Amon, around 1075 BC.

The Onomasticon and the Wen Amon story were not official Egyptian documents. The writers apparently felt no need to maintain the myth of invincible Egypt and invincible Pharaoh, if such was still even believed. The presence of Sea Peoples in what for centuries had been Egyptian-controlled territory is mentioned without apparent embarrassment, without concern for loss of face. By 1100 BC, the presence of Sea Peoples in Canaan was an accepted fact, and they may have been in control there for decades.

Excavation in Israel has produced substantial evidence of the Philistines in coastal cities and archaeologists have sought evidence of the date of their arrival. The Bible tells that the centers of Philistine power were five cities of the coastal plain—Ashdod, Ashkelon, Gaza, Gath, Ekron (Josh. 13:3)—referred to collectively as the "Pentapolis." Archaeology confirms that three of these were occupied by Sea Peoples, presumably Philistines (insufficient archaeological work has been done in Gaza and Gath), and adds a somewhat later sixth city, Tel Qasile, located in present-day Tel Aviv. Archaeology also confirms a Sea Peoples presence at Dor, presumably Tjeker as mentioned by Wen Amon. It is also possible that Akko, Figure 13-3, was a Sherdan town.

Almost all ancient cities experienced episodes of destruction, the result of war, natural calamity, or even leveling due to planned civic renewal. The remains of ancient cities often form a mound consisting of layers, one above the other—the result of new construction over the collapsed or leveled remains of the old. A long-lived city will contain many such layers, or strata. As they dig deeper into the remains of such a city, archaeologists may find evidence of earlier and earlier occupation, layer by layer.

Such a pattern is shown in the remains of Ashdod, one of the cities of the Pentapolis. Evidence from the lowest and thus earliest stratum shows that the city was founded in the Middle Bronze Age. Higher in the mound, and significantly later, is a layer designated by excavators as Stratum XIV. This stratum contains the remains of the last purely Canaanite occupation of Ashdod. Directly above this lies evidence of destruction with thick piles of ash and rubble in some places, showing that the occupation experienced a violent interruption. Rebuilding and reoccupation took place over remains of this destruction, and the evidence of this reoccupation is referred to as Stratum XIII. Compared to the Canaanite layer, there are some changes in buildings, new internal walls with changes in the use of space. Based on evidence of destruction and the presence in Stratum XIII of alien pottery, this stratum is believed to mark the arrival of the Sea Peoples, the Philistines.

Pottery, as noted in earlier chapters, is commonly found in excavations and can be important in establishing dates or the cultural background of those who fabricate it. At Ashdod, a trove of pottery was found in one room of Stratum XIII, twenty-seven pots of various shapes, neatly laid out on the floor and nearly intact. This room was probably part of a potters workshop. Some of the pottery was utilitarian ware and in the Canaanite design tradition. But there were also pots which very closely resemble Late Helladic IIIC pottery of Greece and Mycenaean IIIC1:b pottery from Cyprus, Figure 11-2. As with the similar pottery of Cyprus, this pottery was painted in a single color, black or dark reddish brown. Among archaeologists working in Israel, this pottery is referred to as "Monochrome." Chemical analysis confirms that these pots were made from local clays in Ashdod and were not imports.

A following phase of occupation shows evidence of significant and widespread changes in the town plan and is referred to as Stratum XII. New walls and major new construction are evident. Canaanite pottery continued to be used, and some Monochrome ware was also still in use, but in this stratum a new pottery appears. It is characterized by a luxuriant painted decoration. Horizontal bands and vertical dividers mark out panels. Within the panels is a varied and dense ornamentation. A common motif is a large goose-like bird which usually looks backward over its shoulder. Fish are sometimes shown. Inanimate decorations include flat spirals, concentric half-circles, diamonds, chevrons, and abstract lotus flowers. The use of two colors, black and red, adds to the exuberance of the decoration and gives this pottery the name "Bichrome." As with Monochrome, many of the shapes and decorative elements reflect those of pottery from Greece or Cyprus. Bichrome pottery, however, reflects a new tradition, no longer completely and slavishly dependent on Greek or Cypriote designs.

Archaeological work shows that Ashkelon and Ekron experienced much the same sequence of events as did Ashdod: destruction followed by rebuilding in which Monochrome pottery appeared along with Canaanite pottery, which in turn was followed by a phase in which Bichrome appeared. Most likely, if they were extensively excavated, Gaza and Gath would reflect the same sequence.

That the shapes and painted designs of Monochrome pottery looks to Greece or Cyprus for inspiration strongly colors discussion of the origin of the Philistines. It inevitably suggests that the Philistines came from Greece, or elsewhere nearby. That conclusion may not stand the test of the evidence, however, as will be discussed in following chapters.

There are two approaches which have been attempted to closely date the arrival of the Philistines in Canaan. In the first, it is accepted that the presence of Monochrome pottery marks their arrival. The date of the earliest manufacture or use of the Monochrome pottery in Canaan is sought. In the second approach, it is assumed that, with the arrival of the Philistines, Egyptian control of the coast ended and the Egyptians departed. Here, the date of the end of an Egyptian presence in Canaan is sought.

Monochrome pottery carries no date. It can only be dated by close association with some datable object. In practice, this usually means an Egyptian object. There are many problems with dating by association, however. The close association of the pottery or pottery fragment with the Egyptian object may be illusory, a result, for example, of accidental mixing which may have brought them together. There are also problems of a more fundamental sort. Egyptian objects usually lack specific year dates. They may at most bear the name of a Pharaoh. Ramesses III ruled for decades, and an object with his name cannot be dated more closely then that. Since an Egyptian object, with rare exceptions, cannot be dated narrowly, it cannot be used to narrowly date a piece of pottery with which it is found. Further, the lifetime of manufacture or use of Monochrome is unknown. Monochrome may have been fashionable and in use for many years. A specimen of Monochrome pottery need not have come from the beginning of Philistine occupation but from years after. For those reasons, Monochrome cannot be dated more closely than a few decades, and cannot be used to closely date the arrival of the Philistines.

The end of the Egyptian rule is marked by only few archaeological remains in Canaan, in part the consequence of a reduced Egyptian presence and a resultant reduction in Egyptian objects. The Canaanite city of Beth Shan near the Jordan River was under Egyptian military and political control toward the end of the Bronze Age. A statue of Ramesses III has been found in Beth Shan as well as a scarab of his son and successor Ramesses IV (1151–1145 BC). An inscription with the name of the Egyptian in command at Beth Shan in the time of Ramesses III has also been found. In the nearby town of Delhamiya, a stone fragment bearing the name of Ramesses IV was found. These finds suggest that Beth Shan still was in the hands of the Egyptians in the time of Ramesses III, and probably in the time of Ramesses IV.

That Egyptians continued to control Canaan, or at least inland Canaan, through the reign of Ramesses IV appears to be supported by other finds. An ivory pen case bearing the name of Ramesses III was found in the ruins of the city of Megiddo west of Beth Shan. A copper statue base was also found at Megiddo bearing the name of Ramesses VI (1141–1133 BC). At Lachish, closer to what would become the zone of Philistine occupation, a Bronze plaque with the name of Ramesses III was found in a metal scrap pile. A scarab with his name was also found in Lachish.

South of Gaza are the remains of Canaanite towns on the edge of the Sinai. In Tel Sera, one of the few objects bearing a date was found, a fragment of a bowl inscribed with the words "in the 22 year of…" The king's name is missing, but the inscription is understood by most scholars to refer to the 22 year of Ramesses III, the year 1160 BC. In various other southern towns, scarabs of Ramesses III, IV, and possibly Ramesses X have been found.

In Ashdod, a scarab with the name of Ramesses III has been found, and nothing more of him. There is nothing of his direct successors in Ashdod. Possibly, these results are due to chance which governs archaeological discovery. Negative evidence is not the most dependable. But taken as it is, the evidence suggests that, sometime in the reign of Ramesses III (1182–1151 BC) or shortly after, the south coast of Canaan was no longer under full Egyptian control. Some or all had already been lost to the Sea Peoples. The larger picture suggests that there was a continued Egyptian presence in much of inland Canaan during the time of Ramesses III and probably into that of Ramesses IV, followed in a few years by a withdrawal of the Egyptian army and administration to bases in the Sinai.

The arrival of the Sea Peoples in Canaan and the collapse of Egyptian rule are additional markers of the end of the Bronze Age and beginning of the Iron Age in Canaan.

It is only from this time—the time in which the Philistines arrived—that southwestern Canaan can properly be called Palestine, a term later applied to much of Canaan by the Assyrians, then by the Greeks and Romans, a usage which was current into modern times.

Beginning of Egyptian Decline

With the complete and thorough defeat of the Sea Peoples by Ramesses III—that is what the Egyptians claimed—the matter seemingly ended as suddenly as it had begun. It may have been a disturbing experience, but a mere incident in the divinely predetermined order of things. Before time, the gods of Egypt had appointed Pharaoh as the inevitable victor. The cosmic order remained intact. Egypt remained the central kingdom, and Pharaoh the all powerful sovereign of all lands. It was a reassuring message. But it is doubtful that it was widely believed.

Egyptian prestige and self-confidence must have been dealt a serious blow by the arrival of the Sea Peoples. For hundreds of years, Canaan had been in the grasp of Egypt. Egyptian armies moved at will, imposed kings of their choosing, extracted taxes in silver, gold, and products of the land. The wealth of the land was stripped for the sake of Egypt. Now suddenly, in the time of Ramesses III or close to it, Egyptian control along the south coast of Canaan ceased, never to be renewed. The Egyptians attempted to make the best of the situation, no doubt. Recognizing the inevitable, they probably negotiated with the Philistines. The Philistines may have agreed to pay the Egyptians a token tribute. This would enable the Egyptians to maintain that the Philistines were their vassals, and that the Philistines were in Canaan with Egyptian permission. For the Philistines, there would be recognition and legitimacy. They would be the legitimate successors of the previous Canaanite kings.

For a time, Egypt may have maintained contact with the northern lands through a precarious path squeezed between the Sea Peoples on the coast to the west and the Israelites in the hills to the east. In time, it must have become clear to the Egyptians that there was little hope of regaining control of the lost parts of Canaan. Furthermore, in the north, Hittite Anatolia was gone and trade routes in the north, to Assyria and Babylon, were no longer secure. They had become the haunts of Arameans and other lawless elements. Contact with the northern countries had been effectively severed. There was little justification for maintaining a fragile and costly Egyptian presence as far north as Megiddo and Beth Shan. A trickle of trade from across the Jordan River could not justify it. The Egyptians cut their losses and withdrew from Canaan.

These events may have contributed to the decay that began to take hold in Egypt. In the Valley of the Kings in western Thebes, a large force of craftsmen had been employed on a permanent basis in the work of tomb and temple building. In the twenty-ninth year of Ramesses III, wages of the workers fell in arrears. Month after month, pay was delayed or only partly given, or skipped outright. These workers were no mere peasants who might be intimidated by authority, but literate scribes, skilled craftsmen—artisans who knew their rights. They were used to dealing with authority and knew the avenues of power. Groups of these workers entered temple gates and sat, the first known sit-down strike in history. A delegation took the problem to temple priests and some further pay was extracted. Yet it is clear that the fault was not with the temples but elsewhere.

The mayor of Thebes, the police chief, various temple authorities, were in a panic as these workers threatened to take the problem to the Pharaoh. The cause of the problem is not now known. It may have been local, or it might have been the result of a severe problem in the national economy resulting, perhaps, from the expenses of maintaining a presence in Canaan and the loss of the revenues from Canaan.

Matters got worse. A conspiracy of breathtaking audacity was hatched against the life of the Pharaoh. The instigator was a secondary wife of the king, and her goal was to place her son on the throne, but the conspiracy was widespread. Other royal wives, key officials of the palace, army officers, some from as far away as Nubia were brought into the plot. Wives of palace officials were accused of running messages between conspirators in the palace and those outside. A revolution was to be stirred up, presumably to take place at the time of the palace coup. Black magic was attempted against the Pharaoh, it was said, and wax images made for that purpose.

The plot was exposed, and special courts convened to try the accused. Death penalties were handed out to most of them, and they were allowed to commit suicide then and there. In the midst of the trials, it was discovered that certain judges were secretly cavorting with certain of the accused women. These judges were brought to justice and condemned to have noses or ears cut off.

Whether the accusations were justified, or whether the accused were themselves victims of a conspiracy or even of the paranoia of an aging Pharaoh is impossible to say. If there was such a conspiracy, it suggests a deep degeneration in public morals and a collapse of the great national myth of the authority of Pharaoh, to which the loss of Canaan to the Sea Peoples must have contributed. Egypt had begun a slide into an abyss.

The Sea Peoples occupied but a small bit of Canaan. A short distance to the east were the Israelites, themselves occupying only a small territory. In time, Philistine expansion and military pressure forced the Israelites to accept a king over themselves. From that followed David and his dynasty, the primacy of the city of Jerusalem, and a theology centered on Jerusalem and the house of David. That theology became an indispensable foundation of Jewish and then Christian belief, with incalculable significance in history.

16
HOMELAND OF THE INVADERS

Where did the invaders who fought Ramesses come from? The Sea Peoples themselves do not tell. No authentic writing of the Sea Peoples has ever been found. The Egyptian texts say that they came from the north. In the north were disturbances which threatened the cosmic order. "Now the northern countries which are in their isles [or shores] were agitated in their bodies"—according to the usual translation. Perhaps the older translation by Maspero gives a better sense of the intended meaning: "The islands [or shores] quivered, and had vomited forth their people at once." The texts also say that the Sea Peoples came from the "middle of the sea," but that may indicate no more than the obvious: they came in ships.

What is meant by "northern countries?" What is meant by "islands" or "shores" (the Egyptian word has both meanings)? By the time of Ramesses III, the center of Sea Peoples' activity appears to have been in and around Cyprus and the Syrian and Anatolian coasts nearby. These are directly north of Egypt. The Game Box and seal from Cyprus with images of Sea Peoples certainly suggest their presence in Cyprus (Chapter 12). Cyprus or the nearby coasts must have been the launching point for the raids on Egypt and Egyptian-controlled Canaan. Yet the Egyptian texts at Medinet Habu do not name Cyprus as the place from which the Sea Peoples came, nor did they name any other specific place. It could not have been due to ignorance of geography. The Egyptians knew of Cyprus and seem to have also known the names of Cypriote cities. But they also knew the names of the cities in Canaan which Sea Peoples had attacked, and did not name those either. Such details apparently did not serve the purposes of the Medinet Habu inscriptions, which was to satisfy ideological, not historical or geographical aims.

After the abandonments and destructions in Cyprus had run their course, the leadership of Cyprus undertook an extensive and costly program of renewal. He or they encouraged the expansion of industry and looked forward to renewed trade and prosperity. Trade with Egypt would have been vital, and leaders in Cyprus would hardly have wanted an attack on

Egypt or Canaan to be launched from their shores. But they may have wanted restless and quarrelsome Sea Peoples even less, and may have turned a blind eye to their aggressive preparations and departure. On the other hand, an attack launched from the shores opposite Cyprus would have been facilitated by the collapse of Hittite control in Anatolia or Syria.

The Confederates

The relationship between the Sea Peoples groups whom Ramesses encountered is uncertain—a mystery which Egyptian texts and reliefs do little to clarify. Egyptian texts at Medinet Habu speak of an alliance or confederation of peoples:

> Their confederation consisted of the Peleset [Philistines], Tjeker, Shekelesh, Danuna, and Weshesh, lands united. They laid their hands upon the lands to the very circuit of the earth, their hearts confident and trusting. 'Our plans will succeed!'

Thus, the texts present the various confederate peoples as different from one another. Each is given a distinctive group name, and the Egyptian texts persistently maintained that distinction. Accepting the viewpoint of the texts, it must be allowed that the various Sea Peoples groups could have had different origins. They may have come together for the first time in Cyprus or the vicinity, under the pressure of circumstances in disturbed times. In contrast, so far as can be judged from the illustrations of the Sea and Land Battles, the Sea Peoples are indistinguishable from one another. The only exception is the Sherdan. Except for them, all wear feather headdresses. That suggests two possibilities. The first is that those shown with feather headdresses were ethnically identical, though perhaps from different towns or villages. It should be remembered that in ancient times, neighboring groups, even those sharing language and culture, would identify themselves by different names according to their towns of origin. The second possibility is that only one Sea Peoples group wore the feather headdress and the Egyptians used them as a model for all. In that case, the most numerous or powerful group would be the logical model: the Philistines.

As for their ultimate place of origin, there is no shortage of theories. Cyprus itself might have been the native home of some of them. The oldest specific account of the origin of the Philistines, the chief group among the Sea Peoples, is contained in the Bible, which affirms that they came from Caphtor. Among scholars today, Caphtor is usually thought to be Crete, but it is an uncertain matter (Chapter 17).

Most archaeologists who have worked at Sea Peoples archaeological sites in Israel maintain that Greece was the homeland of the Philistines, and possibly of their various confederates. Some speak more broadly of the "Aegean region" rather than Greece specifically. The primary reason for either is the presence of "Greek" pottery in the Philistine archaeological sites. The pottery is, of course, the Monochrome and Bichrome pottery.

Some scholars believe that the homeland of some or all of the Sea Peoples was in "Europe"—Europe north of Greece. The region near the eastern side of the Adriatic Sea, in Roman times called Illyria, is a favored focal point of that theory.

There are other theories. The region around Sicily and Sardinia has been suggested. Western Anatolia has its adherents. That there are still so many possibilities after years of investigation shows that no one theory is supported by convincing evidence. Perhaps the search, particularly for the Philistines, has been in the wrong direction. Many scholars, believing that the irruption of the Sea Peoples was part of the "great migrations" out of Europe, have overlooked the possibility of a homeland closer to the scene of action, closer to the eastern Mediterranean coast.

Below, the origin of those Sea Peoples whom Ramesses III encountered will be examined further. Because of their leading role in events, the Philistines will be considered separately, in the following chapter. The Sherdan are clearly distinct from the others. It seems to be Sherdan who are vividly pictured in the Sea Battle relief, wearing horned helmets. Though they are not named among the enemy in the Medinet Habu texts, Papyrus Harris so names them, and their origin is considered first.

The Sherdan

Rib Hadda of Byblos provides the earliest mention of the Sherdan. In a letter to the Egyptians dating to about 1350 BC, he mentions an attempt on his life by a Sherdan man. In another letter to Egypt, he notes that passing nomads killed some of his Sherdan and took others to Egypt as slaves. These letters maintain a tone of familiarity about the Sherdan, as if they are a people well known to everyone. Even at that time, it appears, the Sherdan were nothing new to the world. In a tablet from Ugarit of about a century later, Sherdan are again mentioned. The king of Ugarit has taken back some land which he had granted to a Sherdan. In Byblos and Ugarit, it seems that the Sherdan were a minor group within a larger population and, in Ugarit at least, were dedicated to military duties.

It is clear that Sherdan were already familiar to the Egyptians at the time that Sherdan attacked Egypt from the sea in the reign of Ramesses II. It is not known where those Sherdan came from, whether from some coastal city or some distant homeland.

Once in the hands of Ramesses II, Sherdan were pressed into military service. They excelled at close combat and were given the dangerous assignments. Sherdan were an important part of the Egyptian army in the Kadesh campaign, Figure 16-1. There were, of course, still Sherdan who were free and owed no obedience to Egypt. They were among those who participated with the Libyans against Merneptah. In the Sea Peoples campaigns of Ramesses III, Sherdan fought on both sides it seems, free Sherdan against the Egyptians in the Sea Battle, and loyal Sherdan who were in the Egyptian forces in the Land Battle, Figure 16-2.

Ramesses III boasted that he had restored order and peace to Egypt. Women could go about where they want unmolested, he said, and Sherdan could lie about on their backs with nothing to do. He refers, of course, to loyal Sherdan, now long settled in Egypt. After Ramesses III, little or nothing more is heard of the Sherdan. According to a papyrus of the time of Ramesses V (1145–1141 BC), Sherden held land near the Fayum oasis and had since taken Egyptian names. In the tomb of Ramesses IX (1126–1108 BC) there is an illustration of a warrior with horns on the head and with a short sword in hand. This may be a last illustration of a Sherdan. Free Sherdan may have settled on the Canaanite coast, at Akko, according to the belief of some scholars, at the time of the settlement of the other Sea Peoples.

Figure 16-1. Sherdan in the Egyptian army of Ramesses II at Kadesh (top). In another campaign of Ramesses II, Sherdan along with Egyptians storm the city of Tunip in Syria (bottom). Note difference in the swords in the two illustrations.

In the illustrations of Kadesh and the Land Battle, Sherdan are shown with their round shields and dirk swords, meaning swords with straight edges converging to the point, a sharp, acute triangle of deadly bronze. This sword was their characteristic weapon. Illustrations give no dimensions but the length of the sword can be judged by comparison to the length of the arm. According to an illustration of the Kadesh battle at the Luxor Temple in central Egypt, the Sherdan sword is short, about a forearm in length. In an illustration of the same battle at Abu Simbel in southern Egypt, Sherdan swords are longer than the fully extended arm. Such an inconsistency provides additional testimony, if any is needed, that Egyptian reliefs—and texts, for that matter—cannot be counted as a fully reliable source of information.

Figure 16-2a. In a detail from the Land Battle relief, Sherdan fight against the Sea Peoples.

As is evident from almost all illustrations of them, the most striking characteristic of the Sherdan was their helmet. Mounted on the helmet were two bulls horns and, quite strangely, a large round ball or knob on a stalk. Some paint remains on sculptural reliefs that are inside the temple at Medinet Habu, and a Sherdan helmet shown there is painted in yellow-brown, which probably represents bronze. In addition, those who are presumably Sherdan in the Sea Battle relief wear body armor of some sort, shown as bands across the chest, side, and around the back.

If the place of origin of this military equipment could be identified, it might indicate the homeland of the Sherdan. First, there is the shield. Some scholars see something characteristically Greek about the round shield. Logically, if the round shield is to be used to identify the user as Greek, it must be shown that it was commonly used by Greeks, and that no other peoples used that shield. On various fragments of Greek pottery, there are illustrations of shields that were current among Greek fighting men at the end of the Bronze Age. Judging from these, there was no uniformity in the Greek equipment. Greeks used the round shield, the elliptical shield with a bottom cutout, the elliptical shield with side cutouts, and the rectangular shield with side cutouts. That variety does not suggest that there was something particularly Greek in the use of the round shield. The end of the Bronze Age was uncommonly troubled, and it seems that all lands were armed for war. What was the shield favored among fighting men of Arzawa, Seha River Land, Cilicia? From those lands, no illustrations of shields are known. On an ivory mirror handle from Cyprus, a fighting man is shown with a large round shield. Is he a Cypriote? Egyptian illustrations show Hittites and their allies with either rectangular or elliptical shields with side cutouts. Given the incomplete information, there is no basis for concluding that the round shield was uniquely Greek. In any case, fighting men could copy the arms of others, or acquire arms and armor from others by trade, or as a result of conquest, and they might use whatever was superior that came into their hands.

A good deal has been said by scholars about the new "slashing sword" design which came out of Europe toward the end of the Bronze Age. Some insist that the slashing sword accounts for the supposed military superiority of the assumed European invaders (if there were such invaders). But such swords were not the swords used by the Sherdan. A slash with the edge of the Sherdan dirk sword against an unprotected arm or neck would be deadly enough—no slashing sword from Europe was needed. In illustrations of the Kadesh battle of Ramesses II and a Libyan campaign of Ramesses III, with traditional dirk swords Sherden go about methodically slashing off hands of the enemy dead.

Sherdan swords seem to have been identical to Hittite swords and were a common design long known in the East. The use of this sword does not give support to the view that Sherdan came out of Greece, or Europe north of Greece.

Banded armor, worn by Sherdan in the Sea Battle scene, is old in the East and in Egypt. A decorated box was found in the tomb of Egyptian king Tut (1334–1325 BC). A painting on the box shows Tut attacking enemies who wear banded armor and who brandish dirk swords. Those bands are painted white, which suggests that they represent linen wraps. On an inside wall of the Medinet Habu temple, an illustration of Ramesses III is preserved with color intact. His chest is crossed with brightly colored bands to which fish-scale armor is attached, and thus it may have been of the band armor of the Sherdan. (Fish-scale armor consists of small metal plates sown closely spaced on an underlying fabric.) As with the dirk sword, fish-scale armor is rather old in the East, and may have initially been a Hurrian development. Fish-scale was found in the Ulu Burun shipwreck as part of the cargo of trade goods, indicating that at the end of the Bronze Age such armor was universally available, and cannot be related to a single homeland.

Figure 16-2 b. In a detail from the Sea Battle relief, Sherdan in their ships fight against the Egyptians.

In *Iliad,* Homer speaks of horned helmets worn by the Greeks. In this, certainly, his information of Mycenaean times is accurate. The Warrior Vase, found in the ruins of Mycenae, bears the best illustration of Greek fighting men of the end of the Bronze Age. They wear horned helmets, Figure 7-1. In Cyprus, bronze images known as the Smiting God (Figure 12-1) and the Horned God wear helmets with horns. There are many such examples. Bull horns were a too obvious symbol of masculine power, too suggestive to ignore, liable to be mounted on helmets in many lands. The god Nergal of Ugarit wears a helmet with horns, Figure 16-3. Judging from what is seen on much small art, including seals, Syria and Anatolia had more than a fair share of male gods wearing horned helmets. Usually gods are shown wearing the same cloths and using the same weapons and armor which men use, though of course for gods it is of "upscale" quality. These god-images strongly suggest that some fighting men of Syria or Anatolia used horned helmets. A Russian scholar reports that horned helmets were worn in the Bronze Age in the Caucuses mountains of the Black Sea coast. It is certain that the horned helmet was not unique to any one land.

The Sherdan came in ships which are well illustrated in the Sea Battle relief. The design of these ships has drawn attention, because it is thought to be unusual and may point to a homeland. More will be said about these ships in the next chapter since, if the Medinet Habu illustrations are taken to be reliable, Philistines and Sherdan came in identical ships.

It is also possible that the name of a people points to a place of origin. Near the west coast of Anatolia, there is a mountain known to the Greeks of the Classical period as Mount Sardene. The origin of the name is a mystery. In early Greek, there was a *"sh"* sound which later fell out of use, replaced by the *"s"* sound, so that Sardene may earlier have been *Shardene*. Not far from Mount Sardene was the city of Sardis or Sardies. In Classical times that city was a center of gold mining, which made one king of legend "as rich as Croesus." A town of modest size existed here in the Bronze Age. The location is in what was Luvian-speaking country, in the region which was either Arzawa or Seha River Land in the Late Bronze Age.

It has been suggested that the name Sardis derives from a theoretical Luvian name *Swardant* (Szemerenyi, 1987). Allowing for the fluidity which frequently exists between the *"s"* and *"sh"* sounds, the pronunciation might have been *Shwardant. This name, and the later name Sardene or *Shardene, may tie the region to the Sherdan. This evidence is not robust, however, and the origin of Sherdan in western Anatolia is by no means certain.

For some time, it has been apparent that the island of Sardinia may derive its name from the Sherdan. A number of small bronze figures with horned helmets and round shields have been discovered in Sardinia. These may be representations of gods, akin to the Smiting God from Cyprus. In Cyprus, such images were probably assigned the job of blessing the smelting of copper or casting of bronze. Sardinia was the other great copper production center of the Mediterranean, and perhaps Cypriote metalworkers went to Sardinia and brought their god-images with them. But if these little statues are not gods but representations of men, then they may represent Sherdan, which they certainly resemble. It has not been possible to determine the time period of these Sardinian bronze figures, but they are usually thought to date to the Iron Age.

Figure 16-3. A god from Ugarit, in a "smiting" stance, usually thought to be Nergal. However, since he carries a lightning bolt and he is shown as god of the storm, he may be Baal.

Phoenicians are known to have come to Sardinia in the Iron Age. A Phoenician inscription on what is called the "Nora Stone" is dated, somewhat uncertainly, to the 900-800 BC period. The inscription reports Sherdan on the island. In Phoenician alphabetic writing as in the closely related Hebrew, vowels were not represented and the name is given as "*Shrdn*." A few miles to the north of Sardinia, in the southern part of Corsica nearest

Sardinia, large stone statues of warriors have been found. One warrior wears a helmet shaped like those of the Sherdan in the Sea Battle illustration, and on either side of this helmet there are holes in which bulls horns surely once had been placed. He carries a short sword. Another of these statues shows marks around the chest indicating banded armor amazingly like the Sherdan armor in the Sea Battle relief.

Taken together, the name of Sardinia, the presence of "Shrdn," the little bronze statues, and the statues in Corsica who look like Sherdan, seems to be compelling evidence that Sherdan were in Sardinia and Corsica. Since there is no archaeological evidence of Sherdan in these islands which can be confidently dated to the Bronze Age, the islands are likely to have been a destination for Sherdan after the calamities of the Bronze Age rather than a place of origin.

As is quite evident, the most distinctive feature of the Sherdan is their horned helmet with top knob, and that may provide a significant clue of their origin. Horns of themselves do not suggest any one place, but the horned helmet with a ball-like knob is unusual and may indicate a particular region. Certain cylinder seals of the Late Bronze Age have been found in Cyprus and Ugarit which show gods or supernatural beings wearing horned helmets with a large ball or knob at the top. A similar seal stone was found in the ancient Greek city of Thebes, part of an ancient collectors trove of Near Eastern seals (Figure 16-4). In that seal stone, showing a winged god or spirit, the knob is appears to be mounted atop a short stalk. That seal stone very likely came from either Cyprus or northern Syria.

Figure 16-4. From a seal stone, a god wears a helmet with horns and a knob at the top. Found in Thebes, Greece, but originating in Cyprus or Ugarit.

Near Maltai on the upper Tigris River is a large sculptural relief on the side of a cliff. It shows a procession of gods. The gods wear cylindrical hats, and on the top of each is a knob or ball on a stalk. From Babylon, a plaque shows several deities whose helmets are topped with ball knobs. On an unusual seal stone, there is a procession, and one individual in the procession wears a Sherdan helmet. The seal had been purchased from an antiquities dealer in southern Anatolia, and its specific place of origin is therefore uncertain, but elements of the seal design assure an Anatolian origin.

Though some of these helmets and hats are shaped differently than those of the Sherdan, there is still likely to be a linkage. The knob, which serves no practical purpose in a warrior's helmet, may be a religious symbol. It may unite the Sherdan with certain gods of the East, the gods shown on the seal stones and sculptural reliefs. The Sherdan may not have been an ethnic group in the usual sense, but a religious fraternity or warrior brotherhood, like the Knights Templars of the Crusades, dedicated to a particular god. That god would have been resident in Cyprus, Syria, or eastern Anatolia, which could mean that the Sherdan came from that region of overlapping Semitic and Hurrian culture.

Other evidence favors this "eastern" origin of the Sherdan. The dirk sword such as the Sherdan used is illustrated in cylinder seals of the East centuries before the first encounter of the Sherdan with Egypt, and was among the arms of the Hittites, Figure 3-3. What is known of the swords of Greece or Illyria does not suggest that they favored that sword. The dirk sword indicates the East, the Semitic and Hurrian regions, as possible places of origin of the Sherdan.

Sherdan personal names may support that origin. The father of the Sherdan of the Ugarit tablet mentioned earlier bears a Semitic name: Mut-Baal. The image of the captured Sherdan chief, Figure 16-5, closely resembles that of Semites as the Egyptians habitually portrayed them, and that also suggests that Sherdan were native to the East with its ancient Semitic population.

The Tjeker

After the Philistines and Sherdan, it appears that the Tjeker loomed largest in the thoughts of the Egyptians. "Give us the breath of our nostrils" cry out Tjeker captives before Pharaoh, but so do they all. An individual identified as a Tjeker chief is illustrated in a Medinet Habu relief, Figure 16-5. He is bearded and wears a strange cap. In a different sculptural relief, a group of prisoners, all bearded wearing what appear to be just such caps, are presented to the Egyptian gods, Figure 16-6. Who knows what their fate will be? The sculpted outline of their caps is rather strange, since it is virtually the same as that of the feather headdress shown elsewhere. Is it possible that these caps were originally represented as feather headgear, in which feathers were painted in but not sculpted? Paint might have weathered away. That is not likely, however, since other fine sculpted and painted detail in the same illustration are still intact, and so it is very doubtful that feathers were ever intended. These are caps that the prisoners wear, and they were probably Tjeker, like the captive Tjeker chief.

Figure 16-5. Shown as captives, a Tjeker chief on the left, a Sherdan chief on the right. From Medinet Habu.

In addition to the usual difficulties in tracing the origin of any of the Sea Peoples where there is often little to rely on but the name, the Egyptian hieroglyphic texts present an additional difficulty. Because of the uncertainties in the sound values of some hieroglyphs, these people may not have been called Tjeker at all.

The name in the Medinet Habu texts consists of three hieroglyphic consonants, usually rendered as Tj-K-R. The first symbol, represented here by "Tj," may have had the sound "ch" as in the word *ch*eckers. But it is also possible that the hieroglyph intended a "ts" sound as in the familiar Japanese word *ts*unami. Or it may have been an "s" or even a "z" sound. With these possibilities, the consonant sound may have been Ch-K-R, Ts-K-R, S-K-R, or Z-K-R.

The third consonant is represented here as "R" but the Egyptians used the same hieroglyphic symbol for the "l" sound. This adds Ch-K-L, Ts-K-L, S-K-L, Z-K-L as possibilities. When the uncertainties of the vowels and their placements are added, the list of possible pronunciations becomes daunting. Indeed, many different renderings of the name have been used in modern writings. *Tjeker* and *Sikil* seem to be the most widely favored, for reasons which are not very solid but relate to certain assumptions about the identity of these people.

The spelling "Tjeker" has been favored because it has often been linked to the Teukrians mentioned in Chapter 12. According to Greek legend, these were an Anatolian people who, as a consequence of the Trojan War, came to Cyprus. The legend is vague and muddled, but it might represent a memory of some part of a movement of the Sea Peoples. The linkage of Tjeker to Teukrians is hardly more than a guess, however.

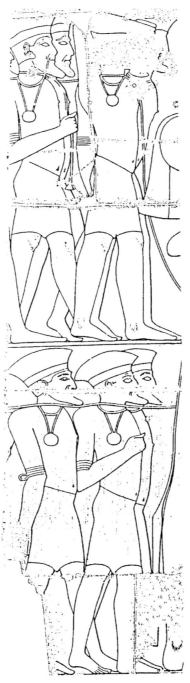

Figure 16-6. Two rows of captive Sea Peoples. Based on resemblance to the Tjeker chief, previous figure, these may be Tjeker. Note that they are bearded and wear medallions. From Medinet Habu.

Alternatively, the spelling "Sikil" has been favored by those who see a linkage with the Sikils, a people of Sicily. The Greek historian Thucydides (460-400 BC) reported that, in the distant past, Sikils lived in Italy and then crossed over to Sicily. The name Sicily may have came from the name of these people. Whether the Sikils of Sicily whom Thucydides mentioned were Sea Peoples of the Medinet Habu inscription depends in part on the pronunciation intended in the Egyptian inscriptions.

The assumption that the one of the Sea Peoples—the Sikils—had been in Sicily provides the foundation of a theory of Sea Peoples movements. Virgil, the Roman poet, reported that the Etruscans fled the ruin of the Trojan War and came to Italy. As it appears possible that Sherdan came to Sardinia and Corsica in close to that same time, a kind of "Tyrrhenian Sea Theory" has evolved (Figure 1-1). According to this theory, a loosely coordinated movement of various peoples took place from western Anatolia to the shores around the Tyrrhenian Sea. Their names became attached to those lands—Sardinia, Sicily, and Tuscany after the Etruscans. This would have been a final destination of some of the Sea Peoples. That theory has been run in reverse. The shores of the Tyrrhenian Sea may have been the original homeland of the Sea Peoples, or some of them. They need only have put their ships in the open sea, and the prevailing currents would have wafted them to Egypt and Canaan. These are intriguing possibilities, difficult to prove or disprove.

The pronunciations "Tjeker" and "Sikil" cannot both be right. It must be one or the other, or possibly one of the other pronunciations that have been mentioned. If either Sikil or Tjeker is rejected, the related theory collapses. How to choose?

Chapter 9 tells of attacks of piratical peoples who harried the north Syrian coast around Ugarit. One such attack drew the attention of the king in Kargamish. The king wrote to Ugarit, "send me Lunadushu." Lunadushu, a citizen of Ugarit, apparently, had been with certain Sea Peoples and could provide information about them. The king's scribe wrote the message in cuneiform, which gave vowel sounds and which distinguishes "*r*" and "*l.*" According to the message, these sea raiders are the "Shikala" or similar. The name strongly suggests either of two Sea Peoples, the Shekelesh or the Sikils. Which is it? The Israeli scholar Anson Rainey has shown that for the first character the scribe intended an "*s*" and not "*sh*" sound (Rainey, 1982). The pronunciation would have been "*Sikalayu*," according to Rainey, which favors "Sikil." But the sibilant sounds "*s*" and "*sh*" are notoriously slippery. The scribe in Kargamish lived far from Ugarit and the coast. Did he hear the name correctly? If the Sea Peoples with whom Lunadushu spent a holiday were *Shikalayu*, perhaps they were the Shekelesh. Thus, there is no certainty that Sikils were referred to, and no confirmation here of the name Sikil. The American scholar William Albright has studied the writing of foreign names as written by the Egyptians, and concludes that the name of the Sea Peoples who accompanied the Philistines was pronounced "Tsikel" or the like (Albright, 1934). If so, there is probably no relationship to Sicily. The linguistic arguments, as so often before, are contradictory and inconclusive.

Perhaps the Egyptians preserve a hint of the origin of this group. In an Egyptian inscription on the Karnak temple of Thutmose III (1504-1450 BC), a place-name appears in hieroglyphics. It is read as Tjeker (or is it Sikil, or Tsikel?). The place was located in northern Syria. Is northern Syria the homeland of the Tjeker/Sikil/Tsikel? An eminent Egyptologist declared that the place-name cannot be related to the name of one of the Sea Peoples. The similarity in names is a coincidence, in his view, since the Tjeker/Sikils could not have come from northern Syria. Why? Because that Egyptologist was convinced that the Sea Peoples came from Europe.

In a relief at Medinet Habu, round medallions are strung around the necks of the Tjeker/Sikils, Figure 16-6. In Egyptian illustrations, such medallions are reserved for Semitic people. From archaeological information, such medallions are known to have been worn as far north as Anatolia, and appears on a wall painting from the palace at Mari near the Euphrates River. Certainly, this suggests that Tjeker/Sikils may have come from the East, from somewhere in the region between the Mediterranean and the Euphrates, of which Syria is part.

The Danuna

"Breath, breath!" plead the captive Danuna, as do the other captive Sea Peoples. The hieroglyphic text gives several different spellings, and there is the usual problem of vowels, but *Danuna* seems to be the favored translation. The name, rendered this way, strongly suggests a connection to the Danaans of Homer. In the works of Homer, the name Danaan is used interchangeably with Achaean and Argive, all three meaning Greeks. In *Iliad*, Achaean is used 605 times, Argive 176 times, and Danaan 146 times. *Odyssey* reflects a similar ratio. That assumed identity of Danuna with Danaans has been another prop in the theory of the Greek origin of the Sea Peoples. The likelihood is somewhat reduced, however, when it is recognized that in the Greek of Homer, the name is *Danaoi*, with one less "n." Still, the possibility that they are the same people is not thereby totally eliminated.

It is too much to expect that things would be so simple. Over a century before the irruption of these Sea Peoples, the Egyptians had asked Abi-Milki, king of Tyre, what he had heard of developments along the north coast. Abi-Milki was glad to report what had come to his ear. In one of the Amarna letters he wrote "The king of Danuna is dead and his brother has become king in his place and his land is quiet." He also reported about other places, including Ugarit. From the order in which cities were discussed, it is evident that Danuna lies north of Ugarit. It is very likely that the Danuna to which Abi-Milki referred is the Adana or Adaniya of Hittite references, Figure 9-2.

Adana was already an ancient city in about 1500 BC, when it was mentioned in Hittite records. And it was still in existence in after 800 BC, when it was mentioned in the inscription of Azitawadda. That inscription was discovered at Karatepe, not far from Adana. The inscription was written in two languages as described in Chapter 9. The Luvian version of the inscription refers to the king of "*Adanawa*," which is the exact Luvian equivalent of the Hittite *Adaniya*, and the present-day place name Adana. In the Semitic script version of the same inscription, which is without vowels, the king is described in terms of the people whom he rules. He is the king of the *Dynnm*. The final "*m*" merely indicates the plural, from which it seems rather clear that the people mentioned were the Danuna. That king ruled the Danuna, and the inscription was found close by Adana.

All this is disturbing to scholars, since two possible places of origin—Greece and Anatolia—seem equally plausible. Naturally, there has been an attempt to unite these peoples. Perhaps, during the supposed Sea People migrations, Greek Danaans came to eastern Cilicia and settled, giving the region and its peoples their name. But that cannot be, since it is certain that the city of Adana and the Danuna people were in place hundreds of years earlier. Greek legend may allow the opposite possibility, that the ancestors of the Danaans came to Greece from the region of Syria, the northern part of which adjoins Adana. Whatever were the facts, they are now completely lost in the fog that envelops that distant past.

Evidence suggests that the Philistines, Sherdan, and Tjeker/Sikils may each have seized their own piece of territory on the coast of Canaan, Figure 16-7. All the invaders are accounted for on the map but the Danuna (and the Weshesh, of whom nothing at all is known). On that map, one significant stretch of coast is without a Sea Peoples occupation, the region between the Tjeker/Sikils at Dor toward the north and the Philistines in the south.

The Israeli archaeologist Yigal Yadin had a suggestion. He observed that, according to the Bible, the Israelite tribe of Dan initially lived in that territory before migrating to the northeastern corner of Canaan (Figure 13-6). Yadin also showed that the tribe of Dan has an unnatural fit among the tribes of Israel. In contrast to the other tribes, the Bible gives no genealogy which might account for the origin of the tribe of Dan, and no explanation for their presence on the coast. As for the theoretical ancestor of the tribe, it is said, according to one translation, that "Dan shall judge his people *as one* of the tribes of Israel" (Gen. 49:16). It may mean "Dan shall judge his people *as if* they are one of the tribes of Israel," as if to suggest that Dan was not originally or fully one of those tribes.

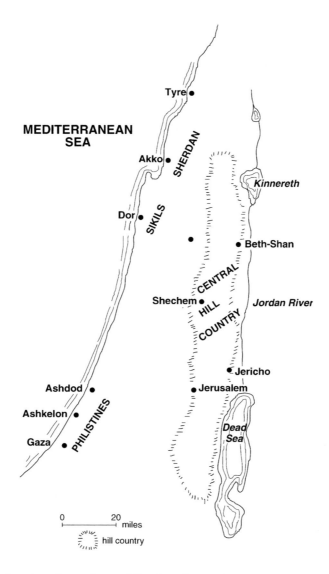

Figure 16-7. Canaan, showing the regions of Sea Peoples settlement along the coast.

The hero of the tribe of Dan is Sampson. His deeds are out of character for an Israelite champion, given over as they are to mischief and licentiousness. He and his fellow Danites are close to the Philistines, not only geographically, but in almost all of their dealings. His wife is a Philistine, and his girlfriend, Delilah, is either a Philistine or has very close ties to them. Of this tribe, Deborah asks, "And Dan, why did he remain in ships?" from which it appears that the tribe may have been a seafaring group.

From these considerations, it is fair to suggest that the Danites were not an original or early tribe among the Israelites, but were incorporated into Israel at some later time. Their earlier location on or near the coast, between the Sikils and Philistines, suggests that the Danites of the Bible may have been the Danuna of the Sea Peoples. The Danites may have been forced away from the coast by rival Philistines, and migrated north. Because of these pressures, they may have sought security by joining the Israelite confederation of tribes. Acceptance of Yahweh would have been a requirement. If they had not yet accepted Yahweh while they were on the coast, they soon adapted to the need in a very rough and ready way. During their migration to the north of Canaan, they kidnapped a Levite priest and idols (Judges 18) and took them along with them and installed priest and idols in their new northern settlement.

17
ORIGIN OF THE PHILISTINES

More than three thousand years have passed since the time of the Sea Peoples. Until the archaeological discoveries of recent centuries, particularly the inscriptions and illustrations on the walls of the temple at Medinet Habu, the Sea Peoples had been thoroughly forgotten, all but one group. That group was, of course, the Philistines, remembered largely through the Bible. Many of the most dramatic stories in the Bible involve the Philistines: the adventures of Samson, the capture of the Ark of the Covenant, David's fight with Goliath, David's service with the Philistines, the death of Saul following his defeat by the Philistines. It is no wonder that much effort has gone into the search for the origin of the Philistines.

The Bible affirms, and archaeology confirms, the Philistines were not a native people of Canaan. The Septuagint, the Greek translation of the Bible, uses the term "Stranger" in place of "Philistine" as if to emphasize that point. The arrival of the Philistines in Canaan may have been a living historical memory at the time that the relevant parts of the Bible was written, but there is no certainty of that. Even if it was not, Israelite contact with the Philistines was too extensive, too enduring, for Israelites to have been mistaken in this matter. The Israelites could not have failed to notice the differences between Philistines and themselves, or between Philistines and Canaanites. The Bible and the Medinet Habu inscriptions agree: the Philistines were aliens in the region.

Where did the Philistines come from? The search for origin has occupied nearly two centuries of modern scholarship, yet has not achieved clear success. The search may seem unnecessary to those who believe that the answer is already given in the Bible.

> Are you different from the Cushites to me, Children of Israel? says the Lord. Did I not bring Israel out of the land of Egypt? And the Philistines from Caphtor and the Arameans from Kir? (*Amos 9:7*)

Thus from the prophet Amos, who emphasizes the lordship of Yahweh over all peoples, not Israel alone. Deuteronomy states:

> As for the Avim who dwelt in villages as far as Gaza, it was the Caphtorites who came from Caphtor who destroyed them and settles instead of them. (*Deut. 2:23*)

Gaza was a coastal city taken by the invading Philistines, and this passage rather clearly ties "Caphtor" to them.

All would seem settled. The Philistines came from Caphtor, and the biblical Table of Nations (Gen. 10:14) further affirms it. But where is Caphtor? Most scholars today take it as certain that Caphtor is Crete. For now, it is enough to say that the certainty may be misplaced. It is based on not one but a string of assumptions. If any of these assumptions are wrong, the conclusion fails, and these assumptions are shaky. Archaeologists have found little or nothing in Crete which clearly relates to the Sea Peoples, and in particular to the Philistines. The Septuagint translators worked at a time when much ancient knowledge still existed, more than two thousand years closer than we to the time of the arrival of the Philistines. Apparently, the translators believed that Caphtor was in Anatolia.

More will be said about Caphtor at the end of the chapter. As with other Sea Peoples, a number of alternatives have been advocated as the homeland of the Philistines.

Greece

That the Philistines came from Greece is a view that enjoys strong support today. More than anything else, it is the Monochrome pottery from Philistine sites in Israel which seems to point to Greece as the land of origin. Bichrome pottery which followed Monochrome continued to be inspired by the shapes and painted themes of Mycenaean pottery, though it incorporated Canaanite and Egyptian design elements as well.

Along with pottery, other evidence of Greek culture has been found in Philistine sites. Outstanding among these is Ashdoda. Ashdoda is a small ceramic figure of a seated goddess found in Stratum XII in Ashdod. Her face and neck are ingeniously molded to the back of her seat or throne, which is thus simultaneously torso and throne. Her face and head resemble those of small pottery figurines of Greece, as do some elements of her painted body decoration. Hearths furnish another example. Round hearths formed on the floor as a circle of stones have been found in some Philistine sites. Though smaller, they are reminiscent of the great round hearths found in the megarons of Pylos and Mycenae in Greece.

It would be quite natural to assume that such things point to the presence of Greeks in Ashdod or other Pentapolis cities, and from that to conclude that the Philistines came from Greece. That conclusion would seem to fit with a belief concerning the unfolding of historic events. It had been assumed that Cyprus had been overwhelmed by Greeks from the Greek mainland shortly before the arrival of Philistines in Canaan. The sequence and the path of the invaders was clear: first Greece, then Cyprus, then Canaan and Egypt. It was also assumed that the Medinet Habu texts named Greeks, the Danaans, as one of the invading peoples. Thus, the conclusion that the Philistines came from Greece seemed to fit archaeologically verified historic circumstances.

However, as noted in Chapter 12, there is now reason to doubt that Greeks came to Cyprus in any great numbers close to the time of the attack on Canaan and Egypt, and there is also reason to doubt that Danuna were the Danaans of Greece. As a prop for the "Greek Theory" of Philistine origin, those assumptions are not valid. That leaves the archaeological evidence, which requires a closer examination.

Small clay images of seated deities, such as Ashdoda, are known not only from Greece but from Cyprus. Cyprus was culturally connected to the nearby Syrian mainland and clay images of seated goddesses were common there. As an example, at Chagar Bazar on the upper Euphrates River, small seated goddesses in clay have been discovered. These date well earlier than the Greek images. The faces of these goddesses are shaped like Ashdodas, and like Ashdoda, the bodies are painted with decorative patterns. Also earlier than Ashdoda are female figurines with painted stripes from Byblos, a city a few days' sail to the north of Ashdod. Are not these more likely the ancestors of Ashdoda than idols from far-off Greece? Circular hearths were not limited to Greece alone. They have been found in archaeological investigations in Troy and Beycesultan in Anatolia. A circle of stones to contain a domestic fire is too obvious a configuration to be confined to Greece, and may have been in use in many places in Anatolia or northern Syria subject to the cold blasts of winter.

The strongest argument for a Greek origin is furnished by Monochrome pottery. Yet paradoxically, it is also the weakest. Archaeologists often voice a caution that is often ignored: pots do not equal people. Monochrome pottery of Greek inspiration in Philistine sites does not necessarily mean that the Philistines came from Greece. There are a number of ways in which pottery in the "Greek" style could have become popular in the Philistine cities, and the similar situation in Cyprus may be recalled (Chapter 12). In the Philistine sites, there is no evidence of a Greek palace or megaron, wall paintings, tombs, arms or armor, Linear B writing, seal stones, or Greek ivory work. Nor is there the full variety of pottery shapes and designs that were popular in the Greek homeland. The repertoire of the Mycenaean style pottery, particularly in the Monochrome stratum, is strangely limited.

Among excavations of Philistine sites, those at Tell Qasile under the direction of Israeli archaeologist Ami Mazar, and Ashdod under the direction of Israeli archaeologist Moshe Dothan, are particularly thorough and well documented. Qasile is a later settlement and less informative of the first Philistine occupation, so Ashdod will be emphasized. The Greek inspiration of Monochrome pottery found at Ashdod has already been mentioned. In the earliest stratum in which it is found—the first stratum of Philistine occupation—it stands nearly alone as evidence of Greeks. The evidence of a somewhat increasing number objects of supposed Greek inspiration which has been found above the Monochrome stratum, and therefore later, does not necessarily reinforce the evidence from the Monochrome stratum. The date of Stratum XII, with its Bichrome pottery and a few other more or less Greek objects, is unknown and may have followed Monochrome Stratum XIII only after decades had passed. In that time, fashions from a place in which Greek culture was present could have indirectly influenced the production of material things in Ashdod and elsewhere in coastal Canaan. That source of influence could have been Cyprus where, in this later time, Greek craftsmen may have begun to increasingly concentrate. Thus, later influences or fashions evident in the Philistine sites do not necessarily cast light on the origin of the first Philistine occupiers.

It is important to recognize that the origin of the initial Philistine material culture in Canaan, with its mix of Greek and non-Greek elements, need not be the same as the origin of the Philistines themselves. If the Philistines had been in Cyprus (the Game Box should be recalled), it would not be surprising if they adopted the Cypriote fondness for Mycenaean pottery, or saw in it a marketable item, useful in their new settlements in Canaan.

The situation of the Philistines newly arrived in Canaan should also be considered. There is no evidence that Philistines came to Canaan in large numbers. They were likely a minority, surrounded by a sea of Canaanites, for there is no reason to believe that the Canaanites were massively expelled from their cities. In that circumstance, perhaps the Philistines thought it necessary to encourage immigration from outside of Canaan to their newly acquired territory. They would want to build up a population of peoples kindred to themselves, or if not kindred, at least non-Canaanite. Such people would have no ties of loyalty to Canaanites and their allegiance would be entirely to the Philistines. By that means, Philistines might assure their own survival and control. Such a precaution might have been farsighted. Once settled in Canaan, the Tjeker/Sikils and Sherden quickly disappeared as distinctive peoples, swallowed up in the local populations. In coming years, the Philistines themselves would become substantially Semitic in culture.

The Philistines seized power in the Canaanite cities, and with power goes a desire for wealth. In Canaan, which has few natural resources, wealth could best be obtained through trade. Immigrants with talents in the crafts, who might help the Philistine economy, might have been welcomed. Greek potters and Greek weavers could have been among the earliest of these, possibly coming by way of Cyprus after taking silent leave of their masters on the Greek mainland. With wars, destruction of cities, collapse of regional economies, many people were on the move, looking for a stable footing. Coastal Canaan had just been occupied by the Philistines. In those circumstances, Canaan could not be counted as an ethnically sealed region, closed to continuing new arrivals, and Greeks and others may have found a welcome and an opportunity there. Thus, through inspiration developed in Cyprus, by contributions of Greek craft specialists who may have come to Canaan, "Greek" traits may have found their way into the Philistine material culture. What has been said in Chapter 12, about Greek potters in Italy in the Classical period, should be recalled. The presence of Greek pottery does not mean a Greek invasion, or even a substantial migration.

Figure 17-1. A captive Philistine chief. This is the only case in which an individual illustrated at Medinet Habu is explicitly named as a Philistine. The name appears in hieroglyphics top, right, left column.

Much evidence not only fails to support the Greek theory of Philistine origin but actually opposes it. There seem to be no memory or legend among the Greeks of a Greek group called Philistines, or Peleset, or the like. Nor is there any evidence of their confederates, the Sherden, Shekelesh, or Tjeker/Sikils. Only for the Danuna could there be a match, highly unlikely though that may be. Greek legends recall a migration and occupation of Cyprus, and there is no doubt that it occurred, but so far as a Greek occupation of the coast of Canaan is concerned, the Greeks seem to have no memory, no legend of such an event. Greek scholars of the Classical period, ever willing and able to demonstrate an early Greek presence at so many places overseas, seem to have had nothing to say of an early Greek settlement in Canaan and, as required, a heroic leader of such a settlement.

Philistines and their weapons do not resemble what little is known of the appearance or arms of Greeks. In Enkomi, Cyprus, a tomb was found in which were remains of a warrior, (Chapter 12). Some scholars have insisted that he was a Greek, since he was interred with a slashing sword and greaves (knee and shin guards). The disconnect of this "Greek" with the Sea Peoples or Philistines at Medinet Habu is immediately apparent. They use no slashing sword and wore no greaves. They wore banded armor and brandished dirk swords, which have no clear connection with Greece. Similarly, the warriors on the Warrior Vase found at Mycenae (Figure 7-1), the best available illustration of Greek fighting men of the end of the Bronze Age, do not at all resemble the Philistines of the Sea Battle or Land Battle illustrations.

The characteristic feathered headdress of the Philistines is unlike anything known from Greece warrior culture. It is decidedly "un-Greek." Figure 17-1 shows a Philistine leader as a captive. He is bearded and wears a peculiar cap, presumably part of his "civilian" clothes. His beard is commonplace, and there is nothing about his cap, nothing about his appearance, to suggest Greece.

At Medinet Habu, the ships in which the Sea Peoples came are shown in considerable detail. To some observers, they suggest a Greek ship design. However, there is a serious problem with the use of the ship illustrations as evidence. The problem begins with the depiction of the Egyptian ships. The Medinet Habu text clearly says the Egyptian war fleet was made up of three kinds of ships:

> I caused the Nile mouth [?] to be prepared like a strong wall with warships, galleys, and coasters, equipped, for they were manned completely from bow to stern with valiant warriors. (*Historical Records*)

It is clear from this text that a variety of ships was employed by the Egyptians. Yet the illustration shows the Egyptian ships as identical. This strongly suggests that the illustration of Egyptian ships at Medinet Habu is not an accurate representation, and that must also raise suspicion about the illustration of the Sea Peoples ships. As with the Egyptian ships, all of the Sea Peoples ships are shown exactly alike. Did various Philistines, Danuna, Sherdan, or others all came in identical ships? It is suspicious, and leads to a question. Just what information did the Egyptian artists have concerning the appearance of the Sea Peoples ships?

Possibly, a combat artist accompanied the Egyptian forces during the Sea Battle. It is more likely, however, that no drawings were made at the battle scene. There is no evidence that Egyptians attached war artists to their armies, and there is some evidence against it. After the Ramesses II military expedition to Kadesh, illustrations of the Kadesh battle were set up at several places in Egypt. Two of the best preserved are at Thebes and Abu Simbel. The Kadesh fortress, a distinctive architectural feature, is quite different in the two illustrations. This strongly suggests that no artist accompanied that carefully organized, long planned, and well-supported military expedition. The seemingly more hastily prepared Sea Peoples campaign of Ramesses III would have done no better justice to the artistic record.

In all likelihood, there was no authentic drawing or model of Sea Peoples ships for the artists who worked at Medinet Habu, who would then have needed to use their imaginations. The yard arms, sails, brailes, crows nests, castles or cabins, and general shape of the hulls are identical, Egyptian and Sea Peoples, and that suggests the artificial or contrived nature of the ship illustrations. Sea Peoples ships are shown without oars, and that is a point of distinction, but here the artist may only have attempted to illustrate that the Sea Peoples were caught with oars shipped, caught by surprise. It is certain that ships of that time, with the possible exception of the largest merchant ships, were fitted with oars for control of the ship close to shore.

It is primarily at the front and rear that there is a striking difference between the Sea Peoples and Egyptian ships. Unlike the Egyptian, the stem and stern posts of the Sea Peoples ships are vertical. That is an uncommon configuration, but there are precedents in Egyptian art. A tomb of Iniwia shows three ships in a harbor (Wachsmann, 1997). Men who certainly look like Egyptians are moving a cargo of Canaanite containers. The stem and stern posts of those ships are vertical, and virtually identical to those shown for Sea Peoples ships at Medinet Habu. Similar ships frequenting Egyptian waters must have contributed to the illustrations of Sea Peoples ships.

The prow of the Egyptian ships shown at Medinet Habu supports a figurehead of a lion, and in his mouth the head of a Syrian, an obvious emblem of Egyptian triumphalism. Egyptian artists needed a similar symbol for the Sea Peoples ships which would identify them as alien, exotic, and thus the bird heads (if that is what they are) atop stem and stern posts. The heads may even represent those of a serpent rather than a bird, since the ancients often represented serpents as beaked. What really was intended cannot be known for certain. Only the Egyptian illustration exists, and not any archaeological remains of the Sea Peoples ships.

A Greek pottery fragment from Tiryns shows a ship with what could be duck or serpent heads at front and rear. The necks, however, are highly curved like a swan's, and thus unlike the Egyptian illustration. Another pottery fragment from the Aegean island of Skyros shows a boat with an animal head of some kind at one end. The creature has ears, however. These pottery fragments are given a LH IIIC date. As evidence of Sea Peoples origin in Greece or vicinity, they would be far more convincing if they were earlier. An earlier date would demonstrate that such ship figures, and the people who displayed them, were long at home in Greece. From whatever place the Sea Peoples came, once the Sea Peoples were in the eastern Mediterranean, it would be no surprise if their ships also swarmed into the Aegean where they might make an impression on Greek pottery painters. Because of the late date of the pottery and the uncertainty of what is represented in the painting, these pottery illustrations are not evidence of a Greek origin of the ships or the Philistines.

In any case, it would not be enough to demonstrate that ships of design similar to Sea Peoples ships may have been used in Greece. As has been said of shields, it would also be necessary to show that such ships were not used by others—not by Anatolians, Cypriotes, or Syrians. In fact, that cannot be done. The information which is available concerning Late Bronze Age ships falls far short of that need. There exists only a few Greek pottery fragments and Cretan seal stones of the Late Bronze Age which show ships, very crudely and imperfectly illustrated, and a few clay models of ships, or rock drawings of ships, from Cyprus and Syria. There is virtually nothing known of ships from the west or south coast of Anatolia, the Black Sea, Italy, Sardinia, Sicily or the Adriatic Sea of this period.

In summary, it appears certain that, except for those design features fore and aft, all of the Egyptian and Sea Peoples ships were drawn from the same artist's pattern. It is very illogical to assume that the artists portrayed Egyptian ships according to a Sea Peoples ship design. As the Sea Peoples ships were probably unfamiliar to the artists, it is likely that familiar ships were the primary model. The design which the artists followed was probably a synthesis, based on known Egyptian, Canaanite, or Syrian seagoing ships. The ship illustrations do not support a Greek origin of the Sea Peoples or their leading group, the Philistines.

The cloths of the Sea Peoples or Philistines are no more informative. The "kilt" which all Sea Peoples wear in the illustrations seems to have been a hot climate work garment of the East and of Egypt, worn by desert Shasu, Syrian sailors, and even Egyptians in the Sea Battle scene.

As shown in the Sea Battle relief, Philistine shields and swords are identical to those of the Sherdan. These have no clearly identifiable homeland. Philistines wore the same wrap armor as the Sherdan. So far as is known, this armor began in the East, and was worn by Shasu and by other foes of the Egyptians as early as the time of King Tut (1325 BC). Metal fish-scale may have been sown on the fabric of wrap armor. Though fish-scale armor may have originated among the Hurrians, by the end of the Bronze Age, fish-scale armor was widely available, and its use reveals nothing of origin of the wearers.

When one looks at the illustrations of the Sea Peoples or Philistines at Medinet Habu, or their ships, and compares them with illustrations of Greek fighting men, or Greek men in hunting parties, or Greek ships, as shown on Greek seal stones, gold rings, wall paintings, and pottery, there is no resemblance.

Illyria

The name "Philistine," by which these people are now known, or "Palestine" as their former territory in Canaan was called, are late terms applied by the Greeks of the Classical period. Herodotus wrote of "Syrians of Palestine" and said that part of the coast "is known by the name of Palestine." These names probably came to the Greeks from the Assyrians, who referred to the territory of Piliste or Palastu.

The earliest record of the name of these people appears in the texts on the temple walls at Medinet Habu. In Egyptian hieroglyphs, the name is P-L-S-T, which leaves it to the reader to supply the vowels. As memory of the invaders was still fresh when the temple at Medinet Habu was built, there was no problem of pronunciation for Egyptians. Today, however, the original pronunciation is no longer known. There is no lack of opinions. *Pelesti*, *Pulasati*, *Pelesata*, *Pelsata*, *Palaste*, are among the ways which different scholars propose. The Israelites knew the invaders well, perhaps as early as the Egyptians, and the Bible gives the name as *Pelishti*, but vowels were supplied to the biblical text late and does not necessarily reflect knowledge of the original pronunciation. One prominent scholar says "the Hebrew biblical term…presupposes an original *Plast*." Another scholar gives *Palaisti*, as the original form of the name. Yet another states "…possibly the original pronunciation was *Phirisite*…" The Assyrian pronunciations are also of late date. These proposed pronunciations have been reviewed, because the "Illyrian Theory" depends much upon the name.

Along the Strymon River north of Greece, there was in the Classical period a people known as the *Palaistinos*, a name with a perfect match for "Palestinian" in its Greek spelling. In Epirus on the Adriatic coast north of Greece there was a place named *Palaeste* in the Classical period. That name too is striking in the similarity to the name Palestine. The Strymon River and Palaeste were in what can be considered part of Illyria, a region along and inland from the east coast of the Adriatic Sea. As the name suggests, the Illyrian Theory maintains that Philistines came from that region.

In *Iliad*, Homer speaks of the *Pelasgians*. Some scholars have attempted to link the Pelasgians to the Philistines. Greeks, according to one view, could not pronounce the original name of the Philistines, saying instead "Pelasgian." *Iliad* says that the Pelasgians were allies of Troy, and one group of them lived in Thrace, northeast of Greece. Those Pelasgians might have been the ancestors of the Palaistinos of the Classical period, who lived along the Strymon River, in the vicinity of Thrace. In *Odyssey*, Homer also tells of Pelasgians in Crete.

These facts or fancies can be assembled into an interesting scenario. In this scenario, the original home of the Pelasgians or Philistines would have been in the mountains or valleys northwest or northeast of Greece. They would have migrated south, overrunning and fatally damaging Mycenaean Greek civilization. Shortly after, many would have gone farther south to Crete. There, some settled, later to be recognized by the poet-singers, including Homer, as Pelasgians of Crete. In time, opportunities developed which would draw them farther south where, after encounters with the Egyptians, they settled on the coast of Canaan. In their short sojourns in Greece and Crete, they developed a taste for Greek culture and brought Greek craftsmen with them to Canaan. The Palaistinos north of Greece in the Classical period would have been descendants of those who did not join the southward movement.

The weakest link in this scenario is the assumption that the Pelasgians were the Philistines. There is no evidence to support it. Whether or not the Pelasgians were the Philistines, however, or had anything to do with the disturbances at the end of the Bronze Age, it is still possible that the Philistines came from a homeland in Illyria. In favor of it may be the bird or serpent heads that, in the Medinet Habu reliefs, decorate stem and stern posts of the ships. Similar heads have been noted in small objects of various sorts which archaeologists have found in Illyria or the overlapping Urn Field region of the Balkans. Some of these objects look like ships, with curved swan's necks and heads at either end. If such objects were models of ships, if they were known to have existed in those regions before the Sea Peoples arrived in Canaan, it might suggest a movement from the earlier place to the later, from Illyria to Canaan. Unfortunately, the date of these objects has never been settled, and there is no convincing reason to believe that they date to the time of the Bronze Age disruptions or earlier.

Illyria or the Urn Field region is thought to be an early home of both the slashing sword and Coarse Ware pottery. It might be expected that some evidence of these would appear in Canaan or Egypt, brought by the Philistines. Yet the slashing sword of Europe is not the Philistine sword shown in illustrations at Medinet Habu. Coarse Ware is unknown or hardly known from archaeological sites in Canaan or Egypt. There is thus little or no direct archaeological evidence to support the Illyrian Theory.

That leaves the names—Palaeste and Palaistinos—as evidence. These are known only from late, in the Classical period, and there is no way of knowing if there were such a place and such a people in Illyria in the Bronze Age. For the second name, it is certain that the ending "-*inos*" did not appear in the original name of the Philistines. If Palaistinos from Illyria were the invaders of Canaan and Egypt, the Egyptians should have written about the P-L-S-T-N rather than the P-L-S-T. But they did not. That a people who lived north of

Greece had a name identical to that by which the Greeks called the dwellers on the coast of Canaan now looses significance, since neither was the orginal name of those who attacked Egypt. It is likely that the Greeks of the Classical period (or somewhat before), noting the resemblance of the name Palastu used by the Assyrians to the name of the people who lived to the north of Greece, decided that these were the same people. They applied the name Palaistinos to those in Canaan.

The Illyrian origin of the Philistines is no more than a possibility. Certain theories of Sea Peoples and Philistine origin, whether in Illyria or Greece, have been influenced by the conviction that Sea Peoples came from Europe. Such views have roots in the late nineteenth and early twentieth century, and were due to scholars, most of whom were Europeans, who lived at a time when Europe seemed destined to subdue and rule in Asia and Africa. It was consistent with the atmosphere of those times that scholars found it credible that vigorous Europeans of the Bronze Age might thrust to the south and east and conquer the supposedly effete peoples of Egypt and the Near East.

Through a good part of the twentieth century, race was much on peoples' minds, including the minds of scholars, some of whom thought that they could recognize race by physical appearance. One scholar declared that he could see by their faces that the Philistines illustrated at Medinet Habu were "Europeans." Readers may judge for themselves, Figure 15-3.

Western Anatolia

A linkage or relationship of some sort between the Sea Peoples who fought Ramesses III and those who attacked Merneptah is usually taken for granted. The conflicts came within a generation of one another in those same disturbed times. Two groups, it seems, Shekelesh and Sherdan, fought in both conflicts, and possibly the Tursha also. As it is likely that most of the Sea Peoples who joined the Libyans against Merneptah came from western or southern Anatolia, so might have the later Sea Peoples, including the Philistines.

Legend tells that Mopsus brought a mix of Greeks and people from the west coast of Anatolia to the vicinity of Adana in southeast Anatolia. Afterward, he or they went south and attacked the Canaanite city of Ashkelon. Does this legend preserve a memory of the Bronze Age, of raids of western Anatolians against the cities of the Canaanite coast? Were these Anatolians the Philistines? Xanthus, a historian of the Classical period who lived in western Anatolia, claimed that the Philistines originated there. Did Xanthus really know, or was he influenced by some version of the Mopsus legend? Neither the Mopsus legend or the Xanthus story are satisfactory evidence of a Philistine origin.

Hittite records might say something of the Philistines. In the records which relate to western Anatolia, there appears to be no mention which might relate to "Philistine" in any of its forms. That does not entirely dispose of a possible origin of the Philistines in western Anatolia, however. Hittite records of them may not have survived, or the Hittites could have known them by a different name. Dardanians furnish an example. The Egyptian account of the Battle of Kadesh lists Dardanians (Dardany) among the Hittite allies. Certainly the Hittites knew these people. Yet Dardanians are not mentioned in any known Hittite record.

Knowledge of the early Philistine language is limited to a very few words, mostly extracted from the Bible. Any noun in the Bible which is not Semitic, and which occurs in a story relating to the Philistines, has been assumed to have come from the Philistines. These words have been scrutinized for indications of relationship to a known ancient language, and thus to a homeland. Of these, the word *seranim* and the names *Goliath* and *Akish* (or *Akis* or *Achish*) have been tied to western Anatolia. In the Bible, seranim (the "-*im*" ending provides the plural) is the term which designates the lords or rulers of the five Philistine cities. It appears in the Bible only in that context, and it is reasonable to believe that it is a Philistine term of early date. A Hittite word *tarwanis* has been suggested as the source. Or a word in the Luvian language has been postulated, *tsarn*. According to this, the word *tsarn was carried to Canaan where it became *seran*, and later it was adopted by Greeks of the Anatolian coast as *turannos,* tyrant. These are, of course, speculations.

Goliath was the Philistine champion whom David slew. It has been suggested that the original form of his name was *Golyat*, or *Golyatte*, similar in ending to that of certain Luvian personal names. Examples of such names include Maddu*watta* of Chapter 3 and Azita*wadda* of Chapter 9. Obviously, because of assumptions which have been made about the original form of the name Goliath, these name relationships too are speculations.

When David incurred the wrath of Saul, he and his band of loyal supporters fled and took up employment with Akish, the Philistine seran, or lord, of the city of Gath. The name has suggested an interesting relationship. Aeneas was a Trojan prince, according to *Iliad,* and the name of his father was *Anchises*. Was this name related to Akish or Achish? If so, the place of origin of the name Akish could have been the northwest coast of Anatolia. There are other possible links to the name Akish, however, to be discussed later.

All of these possible connections with western Anatolia involve special assumptions. When all of the evidence for a Philistine origin in western Anatolia are taken together, they seem to be rather weak.

The evidence for a Philistine origin in Greece, Illyria, or western Anatolia has been reviewed, and Caphtor will be considered at the end of the chapter. None of these solutions are supported by convincing evidence. The effect in particular of the tenacious belief in a European origin, or even a western Anatolian origin, takes a toll because it has discouraged a search elsewhere for the homeland of the Philistines. What might such a search show? It might show that the Philistines came from the East, perhaps from somewhere in eastern

Anatolia or northern Syria, a rugged region of many tribes. The evidence for a Philistine origin in the East is no weaker, and may perhaps be stronger, than that for the localities already considered.

Lands to the East

For close to two centuries, visitors to the temple at Medinet Habu have been struck by the appearance of the Sea Peoples, and nothing about them is more striking than their feather headdress or headgear. It is likely that, as the most numerous of the Sea Peoples and the most troublesome to the Egyptians, it was the Philistines who are illustrated at Medinet Habu and who wore the feathered headdress. If other Sea Peoples were close kin of the Philistines, they also may have worn this headdress.

For over a thousand years, Egyptian artists had portrayed the foreigners whom they had encountered: Libyans; Nubians; Semites including Syrians, Canaanites, and Shasu; Hittites from the remote north; and various other peoples. The Egyptians had an obvious interest in ethnic characteristics, and these the Egyptian artist attempted to portray. The Philistines with their strange headgear seem to have been something entirely new to the Egyptian temple artists. That headgear may provide the most distinctive and specific clue to Philistine origin.

What was the purpose of those feathers around the head? It gave no protection in combat. It served no practical purpose. Likely, the purpose was not in the world of the practical but of the symbolic or magical. The feather headgear may have symbolized a particular tribe or people. Or it may have been the emblem of a warrior guild or a religious fraternity, the equivalent of the Sherdan knobbed helmet. Weapons, shields, ships, pottery may be exchanged among peoples, or their designs adopted, and are not reliable markers of ethnic identity. There is something very personal, however, about a tribe or group symbol, and it is not likely to be quickly taken by others.

Unlike the illustration of Sea People ships, whose authenticity is open to doubt, the illustrations of this headgear must be authentic. There is little reason to doubt that the illustrations were taken from actual examples. Fighting men of all times have taken war trophies. The feathered headgear of the Philistines might have been brought home by Egyptian veterans. Further, if Medinet Habu illustrations are to be believed, Sea Peoples were allowed to keep their headgear even as they were marched off as prisoners, and later when they fought in the ranks of the Egyptian army against the Libyans. There must have been many examples of the feathered gear in Egypt following the battles, and these could have served as models for the illustrations. The Game Box and seal stone from Cyprus, which show just such feather headgear, confirm the authenticity of the Egyptian illustrations.

The Philistine headgear included a ring of feathers, but it was more than that. The feathers were mounted around a helmet, probably of metal, which provided protection for the head and the back of the neck. Feathers were retained in a headband which was decorated by disks, triangles, or vertical bars. A retaining strap tied beneath the chin held the headgear in place. Thus, the headgear consisted of two components, a helmet for practical protection and a feathered crown as a symbolic element.

The feather headdress may have been a new thing to the Egyptians, but it was not new in the ancient world. A number of representations of the feather headdress or crown exist on seal stones, monuments, and pottery, perhaps sufficient to establish a geographic and temporal pattern. These representations are described in detail in the Appendix.

As the Appendix shows, early representations of the feather headgear or feather crown appear in the earliest home of civilization, Mesopotamia, the land between and around the Tigris and Euphrates Rivers. A very early representation appears in an illustration from Urkish, a Hurrian city on the upper Euphrates. A number of representations have been found in the vicinity of the ancient cities of Ur and Uruk along the lower Euphrates. In those illustrations, the headgear is worn by gods, warriors, or heroic figures of legend. These demonstrate the existence of a feathered headdress tradition in the vicinity of the Tigris and Euphrates in the 3000-2000 BC period. The feather headgear representation was still alive in Mesopotamian tradition many centuries later and was shown on Babylon (Kassite) stone boundary markers and major sculptural reliefs of the Assyrians.

After 2000 BC, there were further appearances of the feather headdress in the mountainous northern extensions of the Tigris and Euphrates. From that region, fewer representations of the feather headgear are known than from lower Mesopotamia. Two reasons may account for this. First, cities in the northern region of the two rivers were less extensive, developed, or rich than those in lower Mesopotamia so that fewer works of art or craft of every sort were produced. Second, since the region was less developed, archaeological investigation has been less extensive. Hittites and Assyrians mounted military expeditions into the mountains and valleys of the upper Tigris and Euphrates, and their records testify to the presence of a number of different peoples. To what extent these peoples were related to one another isn't known. What is known is that perhaps as early as 2000 BC, Hurrians began to expand into the entire region, and elements of Hurrian culture were superimposed over, or blended with, earlier cultures of the various peoples.

Somewhat later than 2000 BC is the palace of Mari on the Euphrates. The walls were decorated with murals. In one appears a sphinx with a human head on the body of a winged lion. The head wears the feather headdress.

Molded in relief to the side of a cup found in Beth Shan, Israel, is a figure who appears to wear a feather headdress. The cup is slightly earlier than 1250 BC. Of about the same date is a Chariot Vase found in Ugarit with figures which seem to wear the feather headdress. The Beth Shan and Ugarit illustrations may represent the earliest appearance of the feather headdress along or close to the Mediterranean coast. This was followed in short order by the appearance in Cyprus and Egypt of men who wore the feather headdress and who fought the Egyptians.

Greece and Crete have been extensively excavated. There seems to be no evidence of the feathered headdress in these regions earlier than the first appearance of the Philistines on the Cypriote Game Box or seal stone. The absence cannot be due to insufficient excavation, which suggests that the wearers of the feather headgear were not native to those lands.

From Sardinia or Carthage in the central Mediterranean, objects have been found bearing representations of the Phoenician god Melqart. He wears what is very clearly the feather headdress. A seal from Cyprus contains an identical image and may have come from a Phoenician settlement there. "Phoenicia" refers to the coast from Byblos to Tyre during the Iron Age. Some archaeologists believe that this section of coast experienced an influx of Sea Peoples in the period of the disturbances. Presumably these Sea Peoples merged with the resident population of Canaanite culture. Possibly, these Sea Peoples brought the feather head gear representation with them to Phoenicia. Feather headdress representations seem to have moved westward with the Phoenician expansion from the eastern coast of the Mediterranean after 1000 BC, and there is no evidence of the feather headdress of clearly earlier date in the central Mediterranean.

The appearance of the feather headdress in the archaeological evidence shows a pattern, a spread from east to west. The home of the feather headdress must be sought in the East, and probably in the northern mountainous region of the upper Tigris or Euphrates Rivers. The region includes eastern Anatolia, northern Syria and northern Iraq. The ancient home of the Philistines may lie in that region.

Something is known of names of peoples and cities of that region from Hittite and Assyrian records. There does not seem to be a name, it is granted, either of place or peoples in these records which corresponds to Egyptian P-L-S-T or the various vocalizations which have been suggested. There were, however, interesting place name elements in the region. In northern Anatolia were the *Pala* people and in eastern Anatolia there were places named *Pala, Paliya,* and *Palas*. There were a number of Bronze Age cities or towns with names ending in *-asta, -ashta, -asata*. These suggest that there could have been a place or people named, approximately, **Pala-aste,* in which the name has not survived in the records.

Philistine personal names suggest the same region. Akish, the Philistine seran, or lord, of Gath, has been mentioned. In the cuneiform writing of the city of Nuzi near the Tigris River, a city under Hurrian cultural influence, the personal name *Aki-ia-ash* appears. From the city of Ebla located between Ugarit and the Euphrates River, there is the name *A-ga-ish*. Nearby was the city of Alalakh. Records of that city contain a name *Ak-ki*. Personal names can have great persistence over centuries. When it is recognized that pronunciations may shift somewhat over time, and that the writing systems of those times did not represent sounds identically or perfectly, these examples are quite close to *Akish* of the Bible. How much more reasonable it is to see in these names the prototype of the biblical name Akish than to believe that Akish is related to Anchises, the legendary and distant father of Aeneas of the Trojan War.

A source of the strength of David was his loyal mercenarily brigades. One brigade was lead by *Ittai*, a man from the Philistine city of Gath. The name is perhaps not Semitic and is assumed to have been Philistine. From the city of Nuzi again, there are personal names *It-hi*-Tesub and *Itti*-Sharri. From Alalakh, there is *It-ti-ia*. These cities were under Hurrian influence, and the names are probably Hurrian.

Centuries after David, the Assyrians marched into Canaan. Assyrian records report the names of kings in Philistia of that time. Though it is by no means certain, some of these names may be authentic Philistine names. Among these is the name *Padi*. Similar names, *Pa-a-ta* and *Pad-da-ti-s,* are known to have been used during the Bronze Age in eastern Cilicia, at the western edge of the Hurrian region. From Nuzi there is the name *Pu-ud-du*. Either of these may reflect a kinship with the name Padi.

Before the "home" of an object or design can be determined, it is first necessary to map or catalog all localities in which something similar has been found. The bird or serpent head of the Sea Peoples ships merits a similar effort. That is not done here and it will suffice to show that this image or representation was known in the East and frequently appeared on seals showing the Sun-God at the helm of his supernatural ship. As with cloths, weapons, and other features of these supernatural scenes, what the gods used often reflects what men used, and so it may be with certain features of the ships, particularity the bird or serpent head, Figure 17-2. From the East, that design element could have been carried westward to the Mediterranean by peoples from the Mesopotamian region.

The various threads can now be brought together. As noted earlier, the Tjeker/Sikils may have come from the vicinity of a town in northern Syria mentioned in an Egyptian inscription. Danuna were very likely to have been people of the city or vicinity of Adana in Cilicia, on the western fringe of that same area. That suggests that the lead element of these Sea Peoples, the Philistines, also come from that region.

That region is also the early home of the feather headdress, worn by the Philistines and perhaps others. It also may be the home of the personal names discussed above. The dirk sword which the Sea Peoples employed and the body armor which they wore (if it employed fish-scale), were also at home in that region.

The religion of the Philistines must also be considered. According to the Bible, they worshiped Dagon and Ashtaroth. Those were gods of the Canaanites of the coast and other Semitic peoples inland. It is usually thought that either the Philistines adopted these Canaanite gods once they settled in Canaan, or that the Bible writers used the names of

Canaanite gods in place of those of obscure Philistine gods. Either way, it would mean that Dagon and Ashtaroth were not gods authentic to the Philistines, and cannot be used to trace the Philistines. It may be more reasonable, however, to accept that Dagon and Ashtaroth were authentic Philistine deities. That conclusion would place the Philistine homeland in or close to the Semitic sphere of culture and possibly in the same Eastern region as has been discussed.

Figure 17-2. From two seals from Mesopotamia, the Sun God at the helm of his supernatural ship.

The Medinet Habu texts which discuss the Sea Peoples occasionally mention "Asiatics." For the Egyptians, Asiatics were those from a broad geographical area from Canaan to the Euphrates. Why this mention when speaking of Sea Peoples? Reference to Asiatics would be very much out of place if the Sea Peoples came from Illyria, Greece, Crete, or western

Anatolia. Those puzzling comments about Asiatics have been taken to be mere rhetoric, a wave of the hand in the direction in which earlier Pharaohs had fought enemies. Now, however, word of the defeat of Asiatics by Ramesses would no longer be puzzling. It would make sense if the Philistines and some other Sea Peoples came from the region here called the East.

Those Philistines who troubled the Egyptians may have been a small but war-like group or warrior fraternity. Perhaps they were a mercenary force in the employ of the Hittites, or Ugarit, or Cyprus. They may have been cut off from their homeland by the calamity of those times, deprived of both employer and a way home, much as were certain Greeks of the Classical period of whom Xenophon wrote in his great work *Anabasis*. Those Greeks had taken service as a mercenarily brigade in the employ of the brother of the king of Persia. Their employer was killed in battle, and the Greeks were left isolated and cut off, a thousand miles from home.

Medinet Habu provides hints of such circumstances. In the Land Battle illustration, Sea Peoples are shown, not as a disorderly mob as Libyans or Shasu are traditionally portrayed, but in units of three or four, in orderly combat formations, suggesting that they may have been professional soldiers. A rather obscure portion of the Medinet Habu text is now clearer. In it, the term *tyr* is used, which is thought to mean professional soldier or mercenary. Referring to the Sea Peoples, the text says "They were cut off from their land, coming, their spirits broken. They were *tyr* warriors on land; others were on the sea."

The homeland of the Philistines may have been somewhere in the East, with Cilicia to the Euphrates as a possible focal area.

It is hard to say if the origin of the Philistines will ever be known with certainty. The problem is not only the insufficiency of concrete evidence but the easy cultural adaptability of mankind. Philistines could adopt things originated by others: gods, weapons, ships, pottery, language. What trait is left which would be distinctly and authentically theirs? Perhaps only the feather headgear. If an early Philistine archive could be found, if such ever existed, something might be learned. If an authentic Philistine skeleton were to be found from which DNA could be extracted, something might be learned. Both are very unlikely to happen.

Where Is Biblical Caphtor?

The Bible reports that the Philistines came from Caphtor. The Bible does not say where Caphtor may be. Most knowledge of the ancient world has been lost, and so the identification or location of Caphtor has had to be resurrected. In what may be a rush to judgment, scholars today declare that Caphtor was Crete, and they do so with the same confidence with which in earlier years they placed Caphtor elsewhere.

In the time of David, about 1000 BC, much that was authentically Philistine would have still existed. Two presumably non-Israelite groups, the *Cherethites* and the *Pelethites*, were part of David's private army. A good deal is made of those names. The apparent similarity of the names "Chereth" and "Crete" is taken to mean that Cherethites were Cretans. It is further supposed that Pelethite is a synonym for Philistine. Then, since Cherethites and Pelethites are often mentioned together in the Bible (and in later years occupied neighboring territories), it is also assumed that Philistines and Cherethites were related or even identical. Then the conclusion is reached that, since the Cherethites are from Crete, so must be the Philistines. Thus, Philistines=Pelethites=Cherethites=Crete. It is not so much a logical equation as a string of suppositions. Little in this is convincing.

The Bible mentions both Cherethites and Pelethites, and consistently gives them separate names, so that one may suppose that they, or the writers of the Bible, thought it important to distinguish between them. Thus, even if Pelethites were Philistines, there is no basis for assuming that Pelethites came from the same homeland as did the Cherethites. In any case, there is no evidence that Pelethites were Philistines, and no evidence that Crete was the home of the Cherethites. It is difficult to see why the Bible would employ two different terms, "Cherethite" and "Caphtorite" in order to refer to people of Crete. It is more reasonable that one or the other name, or even both, have nothing to do with Crete. Further, there is no independent evidence that the island now known as Crete bore that name at the end of the Bronze Age or the Early Iron Age. The chain of reasoning is weak at every link.

There are various references to a land called Kaptara in ancient Assyrian writings, and that may be identical to biblical Caphtor. Those Assyrian writings offer little help about the location of Kaptara, however. One of those texts mentions that Kaptara was reached by ship, as the island of Crete must be, but in ancient days the sea was also the best and fastest way from one place to another on the mainland coast, so that the reference to ships does not require that Kaptara be an island.

In the absence of further information, scholars turn to Egyptian texts. In the period around 1500 BC, the Egyptians referred to a place called "Keftiu." Scholars assume that Keftiu is Caphtor. There is no satisfactory explanation of the fact that Caphtor ends with "r" which is missing in the Egyptian name, Keftiu. Nor is there a shred of independent evidence that Caphtor and Keftiu are the same. Still, it is useful to see where Keftiu may be located. That location also is usually taken to be Crete.

Keftiu

On the west bank of the Nile opposite Thebes, a number of men of high rank in the political and social life of Egypt had tombs built for themselves, not as elaborate as those of the Pharaohs, yet containing fascinating painted illustrations accompanied by texts.

Several of these tomb texts and illustrations have been called upon to demonstrate that Keftiu is Crete. Indeed, the paintings and inscriptions in these tombs have been the main support for that identification.

In the tomb of an Egyptian official, Menkheperre-Seneb, a line of foreigners is shown, bearing gifts to Egypt. Egyptians liked to think of such gifts as tribute. All the world was subject to Egypt. In fact, such gifts were in part "bakshish," needed to open bureaucratic doors, and also gifts given in full expectation of things in return. In this tomb, the gift-bearers include one man who is labeled "the Chief of Keftiu." He is shown on his knees, forehead to the ground, groveling abjectly before an Egyptian official. Where is the homeland of this visitor? Is this Keftiu chief from Crete? Thanks to the remarkable archaeological discoveries in Knossos in Crete, a good deal is known of the appearance of Cretans of that time. The illustration of this "Chief of Keftiu" is not well preserved, but to the extent that it is clear, he does not resemble illustrations of people of Crete. He seems closer to Egyptian illustrations of certain Syrians. This tomb picture was copied and slightly modified for use in the tomb of Sebekhotep. That painting is better preserved, and shows the man to be a Syrian. If he was indeed from Keftiu, it would seem to place Keftiu in Syria.

An illustration in the tomb of Ireni shows a man identified as a Keftian. He wears a gown open in front and tied across the shoulder. On his head he wears a skull cap, and the hair in a typically Syrian coiffure but with braided forelocks. He resembles a Libyan as illustrated in color tiles recovered from the temple of Medinet Habu, and if not an Libyan, than a Syrian.

In the tomb of Amenemhab, a line of gift bearers is shown. They are referred to in the text as "from Keftiu, Mannas, all lands united." In appearance these men are Syrians. Mannas is believed to be in northern Syria.

In these three tombs in which men of "Keftiu" are said to be shown, none of them seem to be Cretans. They seem to be from Syria.

In the tomb of Amenuser, the usual lines of gift bearers is shown. Based on the wavy locks down the back of one individual, the open kilt, bare chest, the bull head object which he offers, he could be a Cretan. All that is said of his origin is "spoils which the might of His Majesty brought back from the lands in the north of Asia and the Islands in the Midst of the Sea." The term Keftiu is not used. There is no testimony here that this man, who has the appearance of a Cretan, is from Keftiu.

In the tomb of Senenmut, some figures are shown who resemble Cretans. One carries a near exact replica of the wonderfully wrought Vapheio Cup with its depiction of the faces of bulls. The cup was found in Greece, but might have been made in Crete. These men are not said to be from Keftiu. In neither of these two cases, in which the men resembled Cretans, did the tomb designers call them Keftiu.

Several other tombs show foreign visitors of a somewhat Cretan look. Perhaps the most interesting is the tomb of Rekhmire. Little more than an adit in the hillside, open and affording little protection against the elements or nearby villagers, the illustrations in the tomb remain intact. In the antechamber, five rows of tribute bears are shown, a variety of ethnic types, and they bear a marvelous variety of gifts. Of these, the men in the second row are significant. "Coming in peace by the chiefs of Keftiu and the islands in the midst of the sea" says the caption. Each man wears a kilt and sandals but is bare from the waist up. These kilts are not those well known from Crete and are closer to Syrian kilts. Their hair is formed in long locks down the back, such as seen in some illustration of Cretans, but long locks are shown in illustrations of some Hittites and Syrians. Note the god from Ugarit in Syria, Figure 16-3. These visitors bring an interesting variety of goods most of which are not particularly Cretan: a tusk of ivory, large necklaces, elaborate vases of various designs, copper ox-hide ingots, cone-shaped rhytons, a dirk sword. Tusks suggest Syria where elephants still lived, copper ox-hide ingots suggest the copper centers of Cyprus, and a faience rhyton from Cyprus has been mentioned in Chapter 11. Design elements of the vases are known from Syria. As for the caption, "Coming in peace by the chiefs of Keftiu and the islands in the midst of the sea," as the expression stands grammatically "Keftiu" and "islands" are parallel and are therefore different from one another, so that this seems to deny that Keftiu is an island. Thus, the people and the goods shown are not clearly Cretan nor necessarily from Keftiu.

There is no doubt that at the time these tombs were built, largely between 1500 and 1450 BC, a major trade contact had been established between Egypt and the North, quite possibly including Crete, and gifts were probably exchanged. Also, a land named Keftiu was known to the Egyptians. Yet in those tombs that clearly claim to show a man of Keftiu, it is not a Cretan who is illustrated. And when those who may be Cretans are illustrated, they are not called people of Keftiu. Thus, the tomb paintings fail to show that Keftiu was Crete.

In the south of Egypt, at Kom el Hatan, Amenhotep III (1504–1450 BC) had a temple constructed. Some statue bases survive, and sculpted in a horizontal row on them are a series of place-names. On one base, a vertical dividing line is engraved. Written to the left of that divider are twelve place-names. These are located in Crete and Greece and include the names Amnisos, Knossos, Mycenae. The first two names have been discussed in Chapter 8. To the right of the divider, only two names appear, Keftiu and Tinay. For those who insist that Keftiu is Crete, these names to the right of the divider are "headings" for all the list of names to the left. That would seem to place Keftiu with Greece or Crete. And what of Tinay? A somewhat forced explanation is that it might stand for the Greek Danaoi, the Danaans. More reasonable, however, is that the short list to the right of the divider has nothing to do with that on the left. Keftiu would not relate to Greece or Crete. Tinay could as easily refer to Danuna of Adana as Danaans of Greece. That might place Keftiu somewhere in the vicinity of Adana, in eastern Anatolia.

A final note on Keftiu deals with a student's writing board found in Egypt. It contains a scribal exercise titled "To make names in Keftiu." The exercise required that several Keftiu names be written in hieroglyphics. The renowned American scholar William Albright (Albright, 1934) determined the sounds to be assigned to certain hieroglyphs representing foreign names, and another American scholar, Michael Astour, studied the origin of the names on the writing board (Astour, 1964). He found that six names were Hurrian, six more were Semitic, and two may have been Hurrian or Semitic. While the language of Crete before the arrival of the Greeks is not known, there is not the slightest evidence to show that Crete had a substantial Hurrian or Semitic population. This would seem to place Keftiu where there were population elements of Hurrian and Semitic descent—Cyprus, Syria or eastern Anatolia.

That covers substantially the arguments that Caphtor was Keftiu or that either was Crete. There seems to be little or nothing to support such conclusions. In ancient times when there were no printed maps which might help to stabilize place names, a name applied to a remote locality might over centuries drift and be applied later to a different locality. It is reasonable to say that the locations of Keftiu, and Caphtor of the Bible, remain a mystery.

18
Aftermath

A panorama of events, evidence, theories have been presented. The close of the Bronze Age, from the last years of its integrity and strength to its end in weakness and social or political collapse, has been traced. Since these events of the distant past first came to the attention of historians, largely in the 19th and early 20th centuries, there have been reoccurring questions. What was the cause of the calamity, or at least far-reaching changes? The barbarian invasion theory, advocated by many scholars over many years, has emerged as the global answer. It appears to supply both initial cause and universal explanation.

However, it should now be clear that the barbarian invasion theory is unsupported by concrete evidence. There is no doubt that people, "barbarians" or otherwise, were on the move, and some were probably responsible for disruptions and attacks on cities. But it is reasonable to believe that they were victims of circumstances themselves and not the initial cause or main agent of disruption. If the breakdown of the established order was not due to barbarian invasion or mass migrations, what was the underlying cause? Unfortunately, much that happened more than three thousand years ago is irretrievably lost in the deep shadows of time. Any explanation must, therefor, be largely conjectural.

It is only an impression that the author can offer. It is likely that events started in the northern tier of lands—Greece and Anatolia. Famine, or famine and the plague together, seem best to account for the facts as they are known from Greece. In Anatolia, there is good reason to believe that famine occurred at close to the same time as in Greece, whether or not with epidemic.

Crop failure due to drought was probably responsible for the famine. Crop failure was no new thing to the ancients. They made allowances for it, or tried to. There was a safety net of sorts—stored grain both private and royal. Thoroughly in keeping with patterns of the Bronze Age was Joseph's seven years of stored grain in Egypt. But Greece and Anatolia were no Egypt, with its boundless crops in good times. It must be assumed that adverse climatic conditions arose in Greece and Anatolia that were so prolonged and severe that the safety net failed, and failed quickly for the many people who lived on marginal lands. With the onset of famine, epidemic might follow, as it has often in history, adding greatly to the disruption of society. Rule was brittle, and must have given way before the challenge presented by a hostile nature. In the northern tier of lands, the result was abandonment of villages and societal breakdown, and a wave of disorder rolled southward toward the middle tier of lands—Cyprus, Ugarit and northern Syria.

The disorder consisted of no single thing. It included refugees on the move, opportunistic adventurers, piratical raiders. But it also included disrupted trade routes and failed overseas markets. The result was not only widespread lawlessness but a general economic collapse which today might be called a great depression.

In the southern tier—Canaan and Egypt—Egyptian weakness was evident early, in the chaotic rule following the death of Merneptah. Egypt was ill-prepared when the troubles that had roiled in the north rolled further south. It is likely that, Viking-like, adventurers began to raid the Canaanite coast shortly after the death of Merneptah and began to establish a footing on the shores of Canaan. Ramesses III attempted to reverse these events, ultimately without success. The Canaanite population made room for Israelites and Sea Peoples, primarily Philistines, and Egypt retreated from her empire of centuries and slipped into centuries of slumber. From Greece to Egypt, the old order had been severely damaged or had collapsed.

The entire regression appears to reflect two factors. The first was a serious natural calamity that struck the northern tier of lands, creating a profound social disorder. Had that not happened, if it could have been dealt with, the Bronze Age system might have continued as it was for a considerable time. The second factor was an underlying fragility of rule, and weakness in the social structure, which would not have been fatal in the absence of a great stress. Evidently, leadership in Greece, Anatolia, Cyprus, and Egypt did not or could not respond in a clear and determined way to famine, roving bands, and piratical raiders. A response to the economic collapse was even more beyond their reach. Certainly they had no knowledge of macroeconomics, no means to coordinate economic policy between lands, no way to reverse the downward economic spiral.

The fragile and disunited states could not stand the combined effect of natural disaster and internal weakness or misrule, and an economic situation beyond experience. The resulting dislocations and regressions marked the end of the Bronze Age.

The Result

The crisis in the civilized world had transformed society and profoundly affected political structures and relationships. However, it did not impact each land in the same way. Each was affected according to its previous circumstances. None of the previous "great powers" survived as such, and in some lands, the old political or social structures vanished without a trace. In many places, new peoples occupied the land, entering not so much by military strength as by lack of resistance in what had become weakened and depopulated areas. These new occupiers merged in greater or lesser degree with resident populations. In time, new nations or states emerged. These developments are largely shrouded in historic silence, due in part to the collapse of rule and the resulting disappearance of official writing. Much of what is known of this period is the work of writers of many centuries later, and there is no certainty of the reliability of their reports.

Greece

In Greece, Linear B records were no longer kept after the disasters that occurred toward the end of LH IIIB (for convenience, now taken to be 1190 BC), and this seems to signal the end of the palace-centered management of the economy which had functioned for centuries. If the palace ceased to manage the economy, it is safe to say that the palace no longer ruled. After the widespread abandonment and destruction, society struggled to right itself. In the greatly damaged citadel of Mycenae, a feeble attempt at reconstruction took place, and with it a revival in skilled pottery work. That was the so-called Close Style with its intricate baroque designs, and the Granary Style with a certain simple elegance. Then, following some further damage in the citadel, the resurgence lost its drive. In Tiryns, the citadel was all but abandoned after 1190 BC, and life only resumed to a degree in an expanded lower town. Throughout much of Greece, revival was fitful, uneven, and short. Greece began to sink irreversibly into a profound depression that lasted for centuries.

It was perhaps around 1100 BC that significant migrations from the Greek mainland began to take place, primarily to the islands and shores of Anatolia, where Greeks had been in the Late Bronze Age, and to Cyprus. It was also near this time, most likely, that the Dorians came into the Peloponnese. In view of the near collapse of population in Greece, their arrival may have been largely unopposed.

Nothing is known of Greece in the long-lasting dark period that followed from any contemporary record, and the land was so impoverished, so lacking in material possessions, that archaeologists have found little which would illuminate those times. Great buildings were not built, and houses were of the simplest sort, hardly more than huts. Frescos were not painted, gemstones or ivory were not carved, bronze became scare and was replaced in part by iron. Pottery design and execution degenerated, though in Athens, which was perhaps less affected by the collapse, new designs were pioneered. There was no writing, even in the alphabetic script which came into Greece later.

An infrequent trade still existed in this period. Objects from oversees, evidence of trade, are scarce in the archaeological record, though Athenian pottery of the period has been found in Cyprus. Somewhat later, there was a short but lucrative trade between Euboea on east of the Greek mainland and the Syrian coast, but it did not relieve the general gloom in the rest of Greece. Other than some pottery, it is difficult to see what Greece might have had in those times that others might want. The number of settlements of that period which archaeologists have found number little more than a few dozen, in contrast to the five hundred known settlements in Late-Helladic IIIB around 1300-1190 BC. All aspects of high culture were gone. It is a question whether what remained can still be considered civilization, so severe seems the regression.

No special time span can be allocated to this regressive period, but widespread signs of some recovery are evident by 900–800 BC.

However terrible the times, and severe the depopulation of mainland Greece, certain core elements of Bronze Age Greek culture were preserved largely by overseas Greeks. These were language; names of many of the gods; memories of the Bronze Age; mythology; poet-singers' work which would later form the basis of Homer's work; and likely much more which cannot now be identified.

As Greece began to emerge from this decline, Athens and the Ionian-speaking cities of Anatolia seem to have led the way. Homer lived at some time near the beginning of recovery, and the Phoenician alphabet began to be adopted among Greek-speaking people.

Objects found in graves show that trade with the Syrian coast had picked up, and near 750 BC a Greek trading post was established at Al Mina at the mouth of the Orontes River, in what in the Bronze Age was Mukish. In following years, Greeks appear as mercenaries in the East and in the navy of Pharaoh Necho in Egypt, which may indicate that once again population growth and population pressure were developing in Greece.

By 500 BC, Persian ruled most of the civilized world. Greek cities in Anatolia were under the rule of the Persians. Athens, expressing a kinship with the Ionian Greek cities of western Anatolia, encouraged a revolt. The revolt failed. Irritated by Athenian meddling, the Persians attempted a punitive raid against Athens. Landing at Marathon across a narrow peninsula from Athens, the Persian force was defeated on the beach by the Athenians. The Persians then organized a massive invasion of Greece. In 480 BC, they reached Thermopylae where they were delayed by the resolute Spartans. They reached Athens shortly after, and burned the city. However, in a battle at sea just beyond Athenian shores, the Persian fleet was defeated and much of the Persian force withdrew. In a decisive land battle the next year, Persia was defeated. This spelled the end of the direct Persian threat to mainland Greece.

The victory over this great superpower led to a burst of self-confidence and optimism in Athens which played a catalytic role in the blossoming of the Classical period, the most accomplished period of Greek civilization.

Anatolia

After the destruction of Hattusa, settled life did not return to that location for a substantial time, and when it did, the occupants seemed to have no relationship to the Hittites. There is no evidence of continuity of civilization in what was Hatti, the Hittite homeland, in the decades after the destruction.

Isolated fragments of what had been the Hittite empire did survive for a time. Far to the east of Hatti, Kargamish and some of the territory that it controlled remained relatively intact. Kings claiming descent from the Hittite Great King Suppiluliuma continued to rule. Through certain inscriptions, scholars have traced this line of kings into the 1100–1000 BC period. Kings in Malatya were a branch of this ruling family. Similarly, a line of kings of Hittite origin continued in Tarhuntassa. Scholars have also traced those kings through a number of generations.

It may be wondered why the last legitimate king in Hattusa—whether king Arnuwanda or a descendant—did not move to Kargamish or Tarhuntassa and reassert centralized control of all that remained of the once Hittite empire. It may be wondered why the king of Kargamish or the king of Tarhuntassa did not do so. So far as can be determined from the evidence, none did.

These lands, Kargamish and Tarhuntassa, can hardly be considered to be Hittite states, however. It is uncertain that the people of Tarhuntassa were ethnically Hittite and it is certain that most of the subjects of the kings in Kargamish and Malatya were not Hittite. Those kings, no doubt, held to the memory of the Hittite empire, and held tenaciously to their pedigrees, for these things gave them legitimacy. But Kargamish and Tarhuntassa were no more Hittite than England was German when Hanovarian (German) kings were placed on the throne of England.

In marked contrast to the late Hittite great power, these states were of little consequence. When Assyrian king Tiglath-Pileser I campaigned in the north around 1100 BC, he easily defeated troops of Malatya (Milid) and extracted tribute from the king of Kargamish. Much later, in 858 BC, Assyrian king Shalmaneser III swept across much of central Anatolia, and met no resistance from any great power. He mentions no state or king of Tarhuntassa.

With Assyrian penetration into Anatolia, some written history of Anatolia begins to appear once more. The Assyrian records of Tiglath-Pileser I and later kings note a number of kingdoms throughout the region. Most of these are powers of a very local sort and no more. However, around 900 BC, Urartu (Ararat) emerged in eastern Anatolia in the vicinity of Lake Van and began to form a rather powerful kingdom. They spoke a language distantly related to Hurrian. In the west at about the same time, the Phrygians were bestirring themselves and were shortly to become the dominant group in western Anatolia.

As discussed earlier, an invasion of Phrygians, or vaguely of others, had been proposed as the cause of the Hittite collapse, entirely without proof. But a Cimmerian invasion of Anatolia shortly after 700 BC is certain. They struck east and toppled Urartu, then turned west and did the same for the Phrygians. They also raided the Greek cities on the west coast.

Among the peoples that lived in the highlands east of Mesopotamia were Medes and Persians. In about 612 BC, Assyria was destroyed and shortly Persians brought what was the Assyrian empire under their control. Soon Anatolia as far as the west coast became part of the Persian Empire.

Cyprus

At first, Cyprus recovered rapidly from the catastrophe. With the restoration of cities and the expansion of industry in the period called LC IIIA, a limited prosperity had returned. Egyptian and Cretan objects are noted in the archaeological remains of the rebuilt cities. These indicate either trade with Egypt and Crete, or the presence in Cyprus of foreign craftsmen, also an indicator of ongoing trade. For reasons that are not entirely clear, this success did not last. It appears that within a few generations—even before 1100 BC—a new general collapse set in. Of the cities of Cyprus that appeared to thrive at the beginning of LC IIIA, only two significant cities remained, Kition and Old Paphos. That reduction suggests a collapse of population in the island.

The foundation of some new cities beginning in about that time may indicate the arrival of a new ethnic group. That the old cemeteries were no longer used and that new burial customs were established is even more suggestive of a new ethnic presence. In place of the customary Cypriote tombs, there were chamber tombs with dromos (descending entranceways)—characteristically Greek tombs. In one tomb in Old Paphos, three bronze spits were found, each with writing in the Cypro-Minoan script. These were translated (something is known of the sounds of those Cypro-Minoan symbols), and one spit proved to record the name "Opheltas," a Greek name. This is taken to indicate that the Greeks had come, at last, in substantial numbers. They came to a land that was largely depopulated, and there would have been little need to fight for possession.

The legends of the Greeks pertaining to the founding of cities in Cyprus, supposedly by veterans of the Trojan War, may really refer to this period.

Phoenicians also came to Cyprus, and Kition became their main city. Assyrian king Assurnasirpal (883-859 BC) and his armies reached the Mediterranean coast and with that began a period in which Assyria was a dominating force in the entire region. It was a new era of the superpower through much of the Near East, not known since the end of the Bronze Age. With the passage of centuries, Assyrian kings had lost none of their talent for grandiose prose. Assyrian king Sennacherib (705-681 BC) bragged of his pursuit of the king of Sidon, "my terrifying splendor overcame him and from Tyre he fled to Cyprus." Assyrian king Esarhaddon set up a monument in about 672 BC which named the Cypriote kings who paid him tribute. These included Greek names, and possibly one or more Phoenician names. Unless king "Pgn" (Chapter 9) was from Cyprus—as is sometimes thought—the names that Esarhaddon wrote are the first of Cypriote kings which are known to history.

Nearly two centuries later, in the war between Athens and the Persian empire of which Cyprus was then a part, Cyprus furnished 150 ships in support of the Persians.

The Syrian Coast

On the north coast, Ugarit remained unoccupied for centuries, though the port town of Ibn Hani was quickly reoccupied by at least a few people who used IIIC: 1b-style pottery. To some archaeologists, that demonstrates that the occupiers were Sea Peoples. Such conclusions drawn from pottery, it now should be clear, have been overworked.

The situation on the central coast following the great disturbances is known to some degree, thanks to the trip report of Wen Amon which dates to about 1075 BC. Wen Amon was an official in the temple of the god Amon at Thebes, and was sent on a mission to Byblos to obtain timber, the legendary "cedars of Lebanon." The Wen Amon report is the only known documentation of conditions on the coast in the years after the raids of the Sea Peoples. His report shows that a high degree of normality had been restored, and that normality may have already existed for several decades. If the arrival of the Sea Peoples had made the seas unsafe for trade, if as some believe, they had invaded or destroyed cities along the entire east coast of the Mediterranean, by the time of Wen Amon, all that was in the past. A substantial sea trade existed. Egypt alone had dozens of ships from the Syrian coastal ports under charter. How many other ships of the coastal cities were on the seas can only be guessed. Even Cyprus, at that time in the midst of severe dislocations, had many ships at sea, as one may judge from the Wen Amon report.

The vigorous maritime activities of the coastal cites can be recognized as the beginning of a vast expansion from the central coast of Syria—that of the Phoenicians in following centuries. By about 900 BC, Phoenicians were in Sardinia, probably dealing in copper. In time, the Phoenicians established Carthage on the African coast, a military power which would invade Europe and challenge Rome itself. This was part of the most remarkable expansion in the history of the Canaanite people and culture.

After the collapse of Assyria, Phoenicia along with the rest of the cities of the coast, was incorporated into the Persian empire.

Israel and Philistia

Following the Philistine occupation of cities of coastal Canaan, pottery, metal working and textile manufacturing were rather quickly established in an effort at industrialization, just as in Cyprus during the LC IIIA period. Trade was the objective, and it is likely that Philistine ships were prominent in the coastal trade along with ships of Dor, Tyre, Sidon, Byblos, and Cyprus.

The Philistines also looked inland, at the overland trade routes crossing the Jordan River, and there, they inevitably clashed with the Israelite tribes of the Central Hill Country. The Bible speaks of years of dominance of the Israelites by the Philistines. At a time shortly before 1000 BC, Saul fought them in a series of battles, sometimes successfully, but in a battle at Mount Gilboa, Saul and his sons were killed. Their bodies were hung on the walls at Beth Shan, which may indicate that the Philistines then controlled that strategic inland city. With the rise of David, the Philistine expansion was stopped and rolled back, and thereafter the Philistines appear to have resigned themselves to their positions along the coast.

For a number of years, Assyria terrorized the city-states of Syria and Canaan, and placed them under tribute. The small states of Syria and Canaan struggled against Assyrian domination as best they could. Tiglath-Pileser III (744–727 BC) put the Philistine cities under tribute and turned Gaza into an Assyrian military and commercial base. With Egyptian encouragement, King Hosea of Israel resisted the Assyrians. Galilee had already been seized by Assyria, and the Assyrians put Israel (the northern kingdom) under attack. Assyrian king Sargon ended Israel in 722 BC. He claimed to have deported over 27,000 people to Assyria and incorporated the captured chariot force of Israel into his own army. In Israel, he resettled populations taken from other areas, including Arab groups.

A successor, Esarhaddon (680–669 BC), wishing to send a message to the defiant, put a subject king from a town near Egypt in a cage, and paraded him about the Assyrian capital. The head of the king of Sidon was also prominently displayed in Assyria. Then, in a bold stroke, Esarhaddon invaded Egypt itself and reached Memphis, near present-day Cairo.

Assyria itself began to face difficulties: a persistent revolt in Babylon, and barbarians in the north—Scythians, Cimmerians and Medes, kin of Persians. Babylonian king Nabopolassar in alliance with the Medes invaded and destroyed the Assyrian capital. The Assyrian empire was no more.

Babylon took over what had been the Assyrian empire. Judah, the southern kingdom, submitted to the Babylonians. Then Judah revolted with terrible consequences. Jerusalem was captured, the Temple and other buildings were burned. Leaders were slaughtered and many more sent into exile.

In 539 BC, the Persians conquered Babylon and assumed control of what had been the Assyrian empire. Jewish exiles were allowed to return home, and many elected to do so.

Under a directive of the king of Persia, the temple was restored and Nehemiah rebuilt the walls of Jerusalem.

Egypt

After the death of Ramesses III, a string of weak kings followed. It was early in this period that Egyptian forces and administration withdrew entirely from Canaan to garrison towns in the northern Sinai.

With great audacity and meeting with little opposition, in the time of Ramesses IX (1126–1108 BC) or Ramesses X (1108–1098 BC), bands of Libyans raided western Thebes, putting tomb workers to flight. The Egyptian governor of Nubia was asked to come north to Thebes to restore order, which he did, but he attempted to seize power and in turn had to be driven out by force. Egypt was in a state of internal disintegration. It was an opportunity for the ambitious. General Herihor imposed himself as ruler in south Egypt, and declared himself priest of Amon at Thebes as well. Smendes played a similar role in the north, and Ramesses XI (1098–1070 BC) became a mere figurehead. It was Herihor who sent Wen Amon on his mission, and Smendes who reviewed and approved it. On the death of Ramesses XI, Smendes was recognized as Pharaoh. Egypt was sundered. Egypt was no longer influential on the international scene, though, according to the Wen Amon report, it was still a factor in international trade.

For centuries, Egypt attempted to control the Libyans, fought Libyans, sent them off as slaves to work the farms, impressed them into army ranks. Over the years, professional soldiers of Libyan descent assumed increasing position and influence in the army. Toward the year 945 BC, what would have been unthinkable earlier happened. A Libyan, a Meshwesh, seized the throne in Egypt. Sheshonk was now Pharaoh. In the Bible, he was known as Shishak. He sought to bolster his position by uttering the boasts and adopting the ambitions of Pharaohs of the distant past. One of his first acts was a raid into Judah and Israel. All of the riches of Solomon's temple fell into the hands of Sheshonk.

The Libyan dynasty reunited the north and the south, but Egypt was no match to the power of Assyria. Egypt did what it could to oppose Assyrian expansion by encouraging others to resist, but the forward movement of Assyria was unrelenting.

Egypt was rent by further internal decay, revolt, and confusion. Nubian forces under Piyi (747–716 BC) came up from the south and entered Thebes, and in short order, Nubians dominated much of Egypt. Piyi's successors became Pharaohs, or rather, among the Pharaohs, for there were now several rulers in Egypt at the same time.

In response to what he took to be provocations, Assyrian king Esarhaddon invaded Egypt as far as Memphis, and in 664 BC, Assurbanipal sacked Egyptian Thebes. With the capture of the Assyrian capital by the Medes and Babylonians, Assyria was finished, and Egyptians were then able to exert more influence in nearby countries. Pharaoh Necho developed a navy, employing Greeks for that purpose, and encouraged Zedekiah in Jerusalem to revolt against the new rulers, the Babylonians, resulting in the destruction of Jerusalem.

Persia took over what had been the Assyrian and Babylonian Empires, and in 525 BC, Egypt was taken by the Persians. Now, close to seven hundred years after the end of the Bronze Age, Persia ruled all of the lands discussed earlier, with the exception of mainland Greece which had nearly fallen under Persian rule as well.

Appendix
The Philistine Feathered Headdress

The origin of the Sea Peoples, and particularly Philistines, is one of the great mysteries of the Bronze Age. There are very few clues to their place of origin or homeland, and among these clues, their headdress may be the most important.

That the upright elements of the headdress of the Philistines shown at Medinet Habu represent feathers is suggested by three lines of evidence. First, while in most of the reliefs at Medinet Habu the headdress seems to be rigid and flat across the top, and in that way unlike feathers, a careful examination shows that some of the sculptural reliefs render them somewhat curved, with each element tapered to a pointed tip, as might be expected of feathers. Second, there is no doubt that the Medinet Habu headdress is the same as that shown on the Game Box and the seal stone from Cyprus. An examination of those illustrations shows, convincingly, that they illustrate feathers. Third, there is ample precedent for a feathered headdress in the ancient world of the Bronze Age.

As the feathered headdress was long known before the irruption of the Sea Peoples, a search for the traditional home of the feathered headdress may indicate the origin of Philistines. No writing from the Bronze Age discusses such headdresses, and all information comes from illustrations. These are primarily seal stone engravings or impressions, wall paintings or reliefs, and pottery paintings.

Certain illustrations that definitely show feathers on the head must be excluded, since they clearly do not relate to the present subject. Thus excluded are single or double feathers such as sometimes worn by Libyans or Nubians, and feather headgear worn by goddesses, or by the dwarf Egyptian god Bes. The image of a feathered figure on the Phaistos Disk (a disk of clay discovered in Crete from about 1500 BC upon which are stamped various images) is also rejected. It shows feathers running across the top of the head, front to back, rather than around the head. The craftsman who made the stamps could easily have represented feathers around the head if that was what he wished to show.

Certain seals or seal impressions may show a crown which should not be mistaken for a feather headdress. The crown has ancient roots in the East and its origin is unknown. If the feathered headdress began as some early, even Neolithic symbol, the crown may represent a later abstract representation of that symbol in metal. In that case, even ancient images of crowns may be relevant here, as they may help to indicate the region in which the feather headdress was at home.

A large number of Bronze Age seal stones or clay impressions of seals exist, and these represent an important repository of Bronze Age art. Most seals were cylindric (roller) seals, while a few are stamp seals. Cylindric seals may be about two inches in length and frequently enough no more than one inch. Engraved on these small cylinders are images of men, gods, beasts, demons, and monsters. While many are crudely engraved, some are masterpieces in miniature, a triumph of almost microscopic art. Because of the limitations of size and of tools, these images often are not highly detailed, and sometimes it requires judgment that feathers are represented. Most representations seem beyond dispute, however.

The precise design of the headdress is not necessarily identical from place to place, or in different times, just as American Indian feather headdresses were not identical. Though it is possible that the Bronze Age feather headdress derives, ultimately, from a common root, the design was expressed differently in different places or times. The representation does not always have to be incorporated into a military helmet as at Medinet Habu or on the Game Box.

The period in which various seals was made is often uncertain, but experts have made their judgments, represented here as time ranges, in centuries in most cases. Examples of feathered headdress representations are discussed below, in approximate chronological order. Many representations show a complex scene based on a mythological theme. Only the relevant part of such illustrations are shown here in most cases.

1. Figure A is drawn from the impression of a seal stone, stylistically from the ancient city of Ur in Mesopotamia, dating from around 2500 BC. The figure wears what is rather clearly a feather headdress. He holds a standard with what may be a religious symbol.

2. Urkesh is the earliest known capital of the Hurrians. An impression of a seal belonging to King Tupkish of Urkesh shows an individual standing next to the king. That individual wears an unmistakable feathered headdress. The seal (not shown here) is dated to about 2500 BC.

3. From Ur, a panel inlaid with shell and lapis lazuli is dated to about 2500 BC. It is referred to as the Ur Standard (not shown here). It shows a number of men and pack animals in a procession following a battle. Two of the men carry on their shoulders

large sacks of what is probably grain. They may be captives, carrying war loot for the victors, and they wear headdresses with a number of upward projections. These projections are slightly curved toward the rear and rounded at the ends and strongly resemble Figure B. they probably represent feathers.

4. A seal stone impression from Mesopotamia, Figure B, of the same period and probably from Ur, shows a hero who wrestles with a stag. He wears a headdress virtually identical to that of the captives on the Ur Standard.

5. Figure C is drawn from a seal impression from Ur of the same period. It shows a hero among assorted supernatural figures and animals. He dispatches a lion with a thrust of his sword. On his head is a headdress identical to that of Figure B and the Ur Standard.

    It has been suggested that these upright projections referred to here and in 3, 4, and 6 are not part of a headdress but hair, a hairdo of some sort. In Figure C, the seal engraver seems to show that a strap comes down from the headdress and goes under the chin. It can have no other purpose but to hold a headdress in place, and not a hair set.

6. From a door seal impression from Susa, Iran, a hero dispatches a lion, Figure D. He wears a headgear similar to the previous and that of the Ur standard. A headband with a projection alone the back of the neck suggests (as in 5 above) that a headdress is shown, not a hairdo.

7. From Shuba near Ur, dated to the Early Dynastic Period and thus before 2100 BC, Figure E is from a hero and lion scene. On the hero's head are a number of tall curved tapered projections. The engraver seems to have intended feathers.

8. Figure F is from a seal which is much worn and which was in any case no great work of art. In the full seal, two captives are illustrated, their arms tie behind them. In this crude engraving, triangles are shown on the heads of the captives, but not on the heads of the victors (only one captive is shown here), and this may have been intended to represent the feathered headdress. The seal is from Uruk, not far from Ur. The period is about 2200 BC.

9. Moving from seal stones, the smallest of ancient artworks, the next illustration is from a large sculptural relief found at Sulaimaniyah in the mountains east of Kirkuk near the Tigris River. Annubanini, king of the Lullubi, is shown with his war prisoners. He stands with one foot on the stomach of a prone captive while his deity holds another prisoner by a leash. Below is a row of captives with hands tied. The lead captive, figure G, wears what is clearly a feathered headdress. The period is estimated as about 2100 BC.

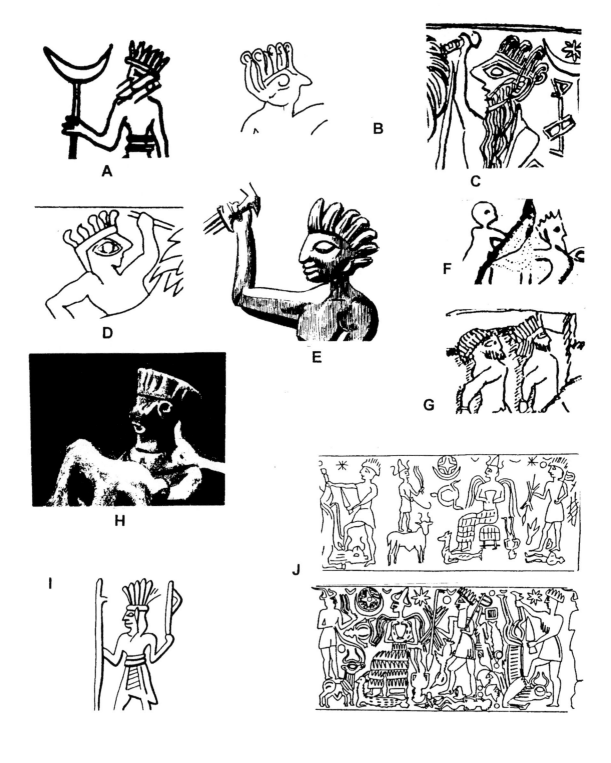

Appendix

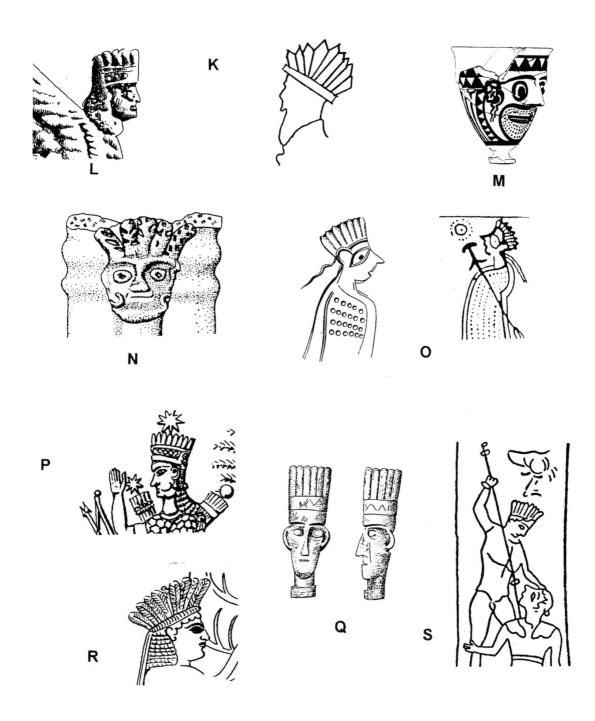

10. There are a large number of seal stones (not shown here) from upper and lower Mesopotamia in which the hero wears a headdress with upright projections. As the seal craftsmen have shown them, these projections are hardly spaced apart, and the top of the whole cluster is flat. They closely resemble Figure H. A feathered headdress may have been intended, or a crown. As noted earlier, the crown may be a representation in metal of the feathered headdress.

11. In Figure H, a chariot and driver are modeled in clay. It is from northern Syria, perhaps near the Habur River, and the period is thought to lie between 2400 and 1800 BC. The charioteer wears what appears to be a feathered headdress.

12. From the Syrian coast and inland to the upper Euphrates have come a number of small bronze figures that show rather clearly a feather headdress. Some appear only as a tiara across the front of the head, but others go completely around. Most of these figures have been looted from their original sites, so that precise places of origin and time periods cannot be pinpointed, but a span of 2000-1500 BC is likely.

13. Returning to seals, Figure I is a drawing of a sea impression. A warrior carries a battle-axe in one hand and a spear or standard in the other. More clearly than some of images, this shows that he wears a feather headdress. The time period is estimated as 2000-1500 BC. It is from the East but the specific location is unknown.

14. Figures J (top and bottom) were transcribed from the same Syro-Hittite seal stone by two different artists. (The two illustrations start at different places around the cylinder.) The top drawing appears to be based on the deepest point of each cut of the engraving, the bottom on the wide top of each cut. The seal is most likely from the upper Euphrates region. The hero has dispatched a bull with a dirk sword. He is represented again holding a spear and a battle-axe. On his head are shown upright projections, triangular in shape per one of the drawings. That these are not hair but a head dress is indicated by the overhang, and it is quite possible that feathers are intended. Similar representations are found on a number of seals of the period.

15. In the city of Mari on the Euphrates, excavators have uncovered a palace dating to shortly before 1700 BC. On the interior walls murals had been painted, one of which shows a mythological figure in full color with the body of a lion, eagles wings, and a human head—a sphinx. On the head is an unmistakable crown of feathers, Figure K, each painted in a different color. That these are feathers is confirmed by the fact that they are identically drawn and colored on the wing (not shown here) where they are certainly feathers.

16. That sphinx can be compared to another on a roller seal from Mesopotamia of nearly the same period, Figure L. Note that the headband is decorated with disks or

circles, just as on many of the feathered headgear illustrated at Medinet Habu, or as worn by the figure on the Game Box from Cyprus.

17. A problematical representation appears on an unusual cup, dated to 1500 BC, from Tell Brak on the upper Euphrates. The outside of the cup has been shaped and painted in the representation of a man's head, Figure **M**. He wears a headdress as demonstrated by the presence of a chin strap and vertical straps at the back. The rim of the cup is painted to represent the headdress, with triangles in a double row across the back and single row at the front. Some who have studied this unusual cup believe that these triangles are representations of feathers. Or, the lower row may represent the headband portion of the headdress since at Medinet Habu some headbands are shown decorated with triangles or zigzags. In seal stones, which were engraved with crude tools and which allow little room for detail, triangles may in some cases have been the best that some craftsmen could do to represent feathers. On the cup, however, which provides adequate room, something closer to the appearance of feathers should be expected if those were intended. This cup may show an early representation of the Tjeker/Sikil cap, Figure 16-6, rather than a feather headdress.

18. A head molded in clay, Figure **N**, appears on the side of a cup or cylinder from an Egyptian temple in Beth Shan in inland Canaan. On the head is what appears to be a crown of feathers. Dated to 1300-1250 BC, this is the earliest known representation of the feather crown in the Canaan-Egypt region, and predates the Medinet Habu reliefs by about a century.

19. Vase figures painted on Mycenaean style pottery are invariably sketchy and cartoon-like, probably with the intention of providing a lighthearted touch. As a result, details are not clearly and accurately represented. One such painting appears on a vase fragment found in the ruins of Ugarit. Several men are shown standing by their chariot. These men are warriors, judging by their swords. They wear Syrian robes, and on their head what may be the feathered headdress. Figure **O** (left) is from an artist's copy of the painting. In a different copy of this same vase by another artist, Figure **O** (right), the projections at the top are less tall, more triangular. From these copies, it isn't clear what the ancient vase painter intended. Most but not all vases in this "Chariot Vase" style were made in Greece for the export market. This vase was likely to have been made between 1300 and 1200 BC. Most were destined for Cyprus, some for Ugarit. It isn't certain whether the painting represents a Greek scene or a scene tailored to the tastes of the Cyprus or Ugarit markets. It appears that nothing which can confidently called a feathered headdress scene is known from Greece. Ugarit was in close and continuous contact

with the region to the east, the likely home region of the feather headgear, so that this chariot vase may represent a scene familiar to the people of Ugarit. If it is indeed the feathered headdress which is represented, this would be the earliest representation in the Cyprus-Ugarit region. These warriors are shown in a tranquil scene, and they do not represent persons threatening to vase buyers in Ugarit. These warriors may be native to Ugarit, or supportive mercenary soldiers.

20. A number of Babylonian boundary stones and seal stones show a warrior with a cylindric cap topped by what seem to be feathers, Figure **P**. In this illustration, the headband is decorated with disks or circles, like the headbands of the Sea Peoples at Medinet Habu. These are from the Kassite Period, broadly between 1550 and 1150 BC. These feathers are short in some cases, and presumably now only symbolic representations of an earlier feather headdress tradition, perhaps descended from those of Ur centuries before.

21. The Sea Peoples with their feather headdresses, as shown on the Game Box, Cypriote seal stone, and at the Egyptian temple at Medinet Habu, appeared between approximately 1200 and 1150 BC. Certain pottery pieces from the Aegean (not shown here) depict ships with men who have protrusions from their heads that are sometimes taken to be feathers. However, these images are so extraordinarily poorly drawn as to be impossible to interpret with confidence.

22. A small bronze figure from Sardinia, dated to about 800 BC, wears a feathered headdress, Figure **Q**. (This drawing is not quit accurate to the bronze, however, as the upright elements of the headdress actually flare outward somewhat at the top, and are thus more like feathers.) The headband is decorated with triangles, as are some at Medinet Habu.

23. An Assyrian wall relief from the time of Assyrian king Assurbanipal (about 650 BC) shows a procession of men, one of whom wears what is clearly a feathered headdress, Figure **R**. Whoever he may be, wherever he may have come from, his headgear seems to represent a continuation of the already ancient Mesopotamian feathered headdress tradition.

24. On a bronze razor, Figure **S**, from either Sardinia or Carthage, and dated to approximately 600 BC, there is a figure skewering a victim. The feather headgear is clear.

25. An identical image (not shown here) is displayed by a seal stone from Cyprus, presumably of similar date. In the period of these images, 800-600 BC, Sardinia, Carthage, and Cyprus had a significant Phoenician population, and images with the feathered headdress may represent the Phoenician god Melqart. Broadly speaking, Phoenicians are descendants of peoples from the coast from Byblos to

Tyre. They are thus latter day Canaanites, possibly with some Sea Peoples in their background.

26. Herodotus tells of the various military contingents that supported the Persian king in his war against the Athenians. Among those were the Lycians from the southwest coast of Anatolia. According to Herodotus, "their headdress [was] a hat encircled with plumes." These Lycians of Classical times lived in what was Lukka land a millennium earlier. Lycians may have been descendants of the Lukka. No illustration of the ancient Lukka is known, and whether the Lukka of the Late Bronze Age wore a feathered headdress is probably now impossible to know.

In summary, the feather headdress appears to have originated in the East, in Mesopotamia Figure T, where representations were both early and persistent over many centuries. Earliest examples are 1 and 2, in lower and upper Mesopotamia, and numerous other examples cluster around these. All earlier examples are found to the east of the dotted line marked 1200 BC. Those to the west of the dotted line 1100BC are later, and are dated after the invasion of the eastern Mediterranean by the Sea Peoples. They suggest that the homeland of the feathered headdress and those who wore it was in the East. It would be a reasonable guess that those who participated in the attacks on Canaan and Egypt came from the upper Mesopotamian region, a source of unrest and migrations over many centuries.

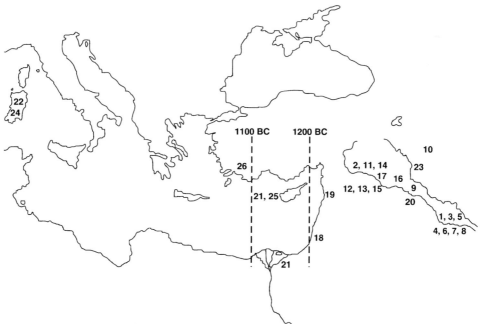

Figure T. Location of the feather headdress representations discussed in the appendix.

Quotations and Illustrations

Hesiod: *Hesiod-The Homeric Hymns and Homerica.* 1920. Harvard University Press.

Kadesh: *The Kadesh inscriptions* by Sir Allen Gardiner. 1960. With the generous permission of the Griffith Institute, the Ashmolean Museum, Oxford.

Geography: *Geography of the Hittite Empire* by John Garstang and Oliver Gurney. 1959. Published by the British Institute of Archaeology at Ankara. With the generous permission of Professor Oliver Gurney.

Madduwatta: *Madduwatta* by Albrecht Goetze. Mitteilungen der vorderasiatisch-agyptische Gesellschaft. Heft 1. 1927.

ANET: *Ancient Near Eastern Texts Relating to the Old Testament* by James B. Pritchard. Copyright 1950, 1955, 1969, 1978 by Princeton University Press. With the generous permission of Princeton University Press.

Deeds: *Deeds of Suppiluliuma as told by his son, Mursili II* by Hans Guterbock. Journal of Cuneiform Studies 10, 1956

Chrestomathy: *A Hittite Chrestomathy.* by Sturtevant, E. H. and Bechtel, G. 1935. Linguistic Society of America.

Aid to the Hittites: *Merneptah's aid to the Hittites* by G. A. Wainwright. Journal of Egyptian Archaeology. 46, 1960. With the generous permission of the Committee of the Egyptian Exploration Society.

Iliad: (except for the quote from Book 20) from *The Iliad* by Homer. Translated by Robert Fagles with introduction and notes by Bernard Knox.

Copyright 1990. By permission of Viking Penguin, a division of Penguin Putnam Inc.

Icelandic Sagas: *Icelandic Sagas, Eddas, and Art*. 1982. With the generous permission of the Pierpont Morgan Library.

Singer: A *Singer of Tales* by Albert B. Lord. Copyright 1960 by the President and Fellows of Harvard College, 1988 by Albert Bates Lord. With the generous permission of Harvard University Press.

Kissuwatna: *Kizzuwatna and the problem of Hittite geography* by A. Goetze. 1940. Yale University Press.

The Hittites: *The Hittites* by Oliver Gurney. Copyright by Oliver Gurney 1952, 1954, 1981, 1990. With the generous permission of Penguin Books Ltd.

Economic Development: *The Economic Development of Medieval Europe* by R. H. Bautier. Copyright 1971. With the generous permission of Thames and Hudson, London.

Medieval Centuries: *The Medieval Centuries* by Denys Hay. 1953. Methuen.

Egyptian Ancient Records: *Ancient Records of Egypt. Vol. 3.* by J. H. Breasted. 1906. University of Chicago Press.

Napoleon: *The Age of Napoleon* by J. C. Herold. 1963. Heritage Publishing Co.

Odyssey: (except for quote from Book 8) from *The Odyssey of Homer* by Ennis Rees. 1991. With the generous permission of Prentice-Hall, Upper Saddle River, NJ.

Archaologische Situation: *Die archaologische situation in kleinasien um 1200 v. Chr. und wahrend der nachfolgenden vier jahrhunderte* by Kurt Bittel [in] *Griechenland die Agais und Die Levante Wahrend der "Dark Ages."* 1983. Sigrid Deger-Jalkotzy, editor.

Ancient Records of Assyria: *Ancient Records of Assyria and Babylonia* by D. D. Luckenbill. 1926. University of Chicago Press.

Cyprus Reconsidered: *The Hittite conquest of Cyprus reconsidered* by H. G. Guterbock. Journal of Near Eastern Studies 26, 1967.

RS 16-420 and RS 16-379: New *evidence on the last days of Ugarit* by M. C. Astour. American Journal of Archaeology 79. 1965.

RSL-1: *Mission de Ras Shamra-Ugaritica V.*

RS 20.238, RS 20.18: *Mission de Ras Shamra: Archeologic de Ras Shamra-Tomb XVI. Ugaritica* by J. Nougayrol. 1968. Paul Geuthner.

Bo 2810: *Hungerjahre in Hatti* by H. Klengel. 1974. Altorientalische Forschungen. Akademie Verlag.

RS-18.38, RS-18.40: *Mission de Ras Shamra-Tomb XI. Palas d' Ugarit 60, 63.* C. A. Shaeffer, 1965. Library Klincksieck. Paris.

EA 114, EA 38, EA 35, EA 213: *The Amarna Letters* Edited and translated by William Moran. 1992. With permission of Johns Hopkins Press.

Papyrus Harris: *The rise of the twentieth dynasty: Sethnakhte* by R. O. Faulkner. 1975. Cambridge Ancient History. Cambridge University Press.

Historical Records: *Historical Records of Ramses III. The Texts in Medinet Habu volumes I and II.* Edgerton, W. F. and Wilson, J. A. 1936. The Oriental Institute, Univesity of Chicago. With permission of the University of Chicago Press.

Figures 2-2, 2-3, 3-3, 4-1, 13-4: *Atlas zur Altaegyptischen Kulturgeschichte zweiter Teil* by Walter Wreszinski, 1988. With the generous permission of Editions Slatkine, Geneve, Suisse.

Figure 3-4: Biblical Archaeologist, March, 1986. With the generous permission of the American Schools of Oriental Research.

Figures 3-5, 4-2, 16-4: By Patricia McCart-Malloy With generous permission of the artist.

Figure 5-2 By Loyd K. Townsend. With the generous permission and help of Elizabeth Townsend.

Figure 6-2: *Art in Primitive Greece* by G. Perrot and G. Chipiez. 1894. A. C. Armstrong and Son.

Figure 6-3: *The Plyos Tablets: Texts of the Inscriptions Found in 1939-1954* by E. Bennett. 1955. With the generous permission of Princeton University Press

Figures 8-2, 8-4, 15-1, 15-2, 15-3, 16-2,16-5, 16-6,17-1: *Medinet Habu—Early Historical Records of Ramses III*. 1930. Courtesy of the Oriental Institute, of the University of Chicago.

Figure 10-1: *Mission de Ras Shamra. Tome XI—Palais Royal d'Ugarit*.

Figure 11-2: *Excavations at Maa-Palaeokastro, 1979-1982*. With the generous permission of the Department of Antiquities, Nicosia, Republic of Cyprus.

Figure 12-1, 16-3: *Prehistorische Bronzefunde* by H. Seden. 1980. With the generous permission of Verlag C. H. Beck, Munchen.

Figure 12-2: By E. Masson in *Enkomi Excavations-vol II*. by P. Dikaios. 1969.

Figure 12-3: With permission of the British Museum. British Museum Photographic Services.

Figure 12-4: Journal of Egyptian Archaeology volume 47. With the generous permission of the Committee of the Egyptian Exploration Society.

Figure 13-5: *The Megiddo Ivories* by G. Load. 1939. Courtesy of the Oriental Institute of the University of Chicago.

Figure A: From Buchanan, *Early Near Eastern Seals in the Yale Babylonian Collection*. Yale University Press.

Figure B: Drawn from a photograph in *Ancient Near Eastern Seals* by E. W. Forte. 1976.

Figure C: From *Archaic Seal Impressions* by L. Legrain. 1936. University of Pennsylvania.

Figure D and Figure J (lower): *Cylinder Seals: A Documentary Essay on the Art and Religion of the Ancient Near East* by H. Frankfort. 1939. MacMillan.

Figure E: By Patricia McCart-Malloy, from a photograph in H. Frankfort (above).

Figure F: *Siegelabrollungen Aus den Archaischen Bauschichten in Uruk-Warka* by M. Brandes. 1979. With the generous permission of Franz Steiner Verlag. Stuttgart, Germany.

Figure H: By Patricia McCart-Malloy, from a photograph provided by the Milwaukee Public Museum.

Figure I: *Prehistorische Bronzefunde* by H. Seden. 1980. With the generous permission of Verlag C. H. Beck, Munchen.

Figure J (upper): *La Glyptique Syro-Hittite* by G. Continau, 1922. (lower). From H. Frankfort (see Frankfort above).

Figure K: Drawn from a photograph in *Studia Marianna* by A. Perrot. 1950. Brill.

Figure L: *Catalogue des Cylindres Orientaux*. 1910. C.. Delaporte.

Figure M:. *Excavations at Brak and Chagar Bazar, Syria* by M.E.L. Mallowan. Iraq 9, 1947. With the generous permission of the British School of Archaeology in Iraq.

Figure N: *The Late Bronze Age Garrison at Beth Shan: A Study of Levels VII and VIII. Vol. II,* 1993. University of Pennsylvania.

Figure P: Barrelet, M-T, *Les Deesses Armees et Ailees* by M-T Barrelet. Syria 32, 1955.

Figure O and Figure Q: *Homerische Helm* by J. Borchhardt. 1972. Verlag Philipp v. Zubern.

Figure R: *Le dans l' art de la Mesopotamie ancienne* by M. Rutten. Syria 22, 1941.

Figure S: *Melqart* by R. Dussard. Syria 25, 1946-48.

Cover (top figure): (see Figure 5-2 above).

Cover (bottom figure): *Tomb of Thoutmoses IV* by A. Constable. 1904.

Maps prepared from the author's drafts by MATRIX, York, Pennsylvania.

Photographs other than 12-3 from the author's collection.

Bibliography and References

(Partial list of books and papers which were consulted in the preparation of this work)

Abbreviations: symposia, collected papers.

AANE=Anatolia and the Ancient Near East: Studies in Honor of Tarhisin Ozgug. 1989.
ABI=Archaeology and Biblical Interpretation. {Ed.] Bartlett, J. R. 1997. Routledge.
Age Hom.=Ages of Homer. B. J. Carter et. al. [Ed.] 1995
AIA3=Anatolian Iron Ages 3: Proceedings of the 3rd. Anatolian Iron Ages Colloqium at Van. British Institute of Archaeology at Ankara. 1994.
AIR=Ancient Israelite Religion: Essays in Honor of Frank Moore Cross. [Ed.] Miller, P. D., Hanson, P. D., McBride, S. 1987. Fortress.
AISCOO=Acts of the International Archaeological Symposium: Cyprus Between Orient and Occident. [Ed.]Karageorghis, V. 1986.
AISMEM=Acts of the International Symposium: Mycenaeans in the Eastern Mediterranean. 1973.
AJS=Archaeology of Jordan and Other Studies. [Ed.] E. Geraty et. al. 1986.
AMCIM=Atti e Memorie del 1 Congresso Internationale di Micenologie Roma 27 Oct 1967.
AS=Atlante Storico Del Vicino Oriente Antico. Universita Degli Studi di Roma.
ASAA=Annuario della Scuola Archeologica di Atene
ASAE=Annales du Service des Antiquites de l'Egypt.
As. Af.=Asian Affairs
ASHG=Anatolian Studies Presented to Hans Gustav Guterbock on the Occasion of his 65th Birthday
   [Ed.] Bittel, K. et al. 1974. Nederlands Historisch-Arch. Inst.
ASHL=The Archaeology of Society in the Holy Land [Ed.] Levy, T. E. 1995. Facts on File.
ASICAP=Acta of the 2nd. International Colloquium on Aegean Prehistory

Asp. Art=Aspects of Art and Iconography. Anatolia and its Neighbors. Studies in Honor of Nimet Ozguc. [Ed.] M. Mellink, et. al.1993

ASOR=American Schools of Oriental Research

ASWR=Anatolian Studies Presented to William Ramsey. 1923.

BAM=Bronze Age Migrations in the Aegean. [Ed.] Crossland, R. A. and Birchall. 1974. Noyes Press.

BARIS=BAR International Series. Oxford.

BIA=British Institute of Archaeology: Ankara

BAT/84=Biblical Archaeology Today 1984: Proceedings of the International Congress on Biblical Archaeology. [Ed.] Amitai, J. Israel Exploration Society. 1985.

BAT/90 Biblical Archaeology Today 1990: (above) [Ed.] Biran, A. and Aviram, J. 1993.

CAH=Cambridge Ancient History. Cambridge University Press. 1975.

CAH26=Cambridge Ancient History. Cambridge University Press. 1926.

CBOO=Acts of the International Archaaeological Symposium "Cyprus Between Orientand and Occident." [Ed.] Karageorghis, V. 1986.

CCLP=Climate Change in Late Prehistory. [Ed.] Harding, A. 1982. Edinburgh University Press

CC:RPR=Cypriote Ceramics: Reading the Prehistoric Record. [Ed.] Barlow, J. A., Bolger, D.C.,
   Kling, B. 1991.

CEDE=The Civilizatios of the Aegean and their Diffusion in Cyprus and the Eastern Mediterranian, 2000-600[Ed.]. Karageorghis, V. 1989.

CY=The Crisis Years: The 12th Century B.C. [Ed.]. Ward, W. A. and Joukowsky, M. S. 1989. Kendall/Hunt Publishing.

C-11-C.=Proceedings of the International Symposium "Cyprus in the 11th Century." 1994.

EAASS=Esays on Ancient Anatolian and Syrian Studies in th 2nd. millennium B.C. [Ed.] Prince T. Mikasa. 1991.

EAL=Egypt, the Aegean, and the Levant. [ed.] Davis, W. V and Schofield, L. 1995. British Museum Press.

EEM=Early Edom and Moab: The Beginning of the Iron Age in Southern Jordan [Ed.] Bienkowski, P. 1992. J. R. Collins Publications

EHNG=Essays in Honor of Nelson Gluck. 1970. [Ed.] Sanders, J. A.

EMC=Acta of the International Archaeoogical Symposium: Early Metallurgy in Cyprus, 4000-500 BC.

EOTHR=Essays on Old Testament History and Religion.

ESC=Early Society in Cyprus [Ed.] Peltenburg, E. 1989.

FNTM=From Nomadism to Monarchy. [Ed.] Finkelstein, I. And Na'aman, N. Israel Exploration Society. 1994.

FSA=Festschrift fur S. Alp. [Ed.] Otten, H. 1992

FSF=Festschrift Johannes Friedrich. 1959. Carl Winter.

GE=Gordion Excavations (final reports). [Ed.] Kohler, E. L. University Museum, University of Pennsylvania

GDA=Griechenland die Agais und Die Levante Wahrend der "Dark Ages." [Ed.] Sigrid Deger-Jalkotzy. 1983.

ICAP=International Colloquium on Aegean Prehistory. 1987.

KAV=Schrifften des Deutschen Archaologen-Verbandes IX. Kolloquium zur Agaischen Vorgeschichte.

LI=Land of Israel: Cross-roads of Civilizations. 1985. [Ed.] Lipinski, E. U. Peeters.

LMAOS=Liverpool Monographs in Archaeaology and Oriental Studies. Aris and Phillips.

MEM.=Acts of the International Symposium : The Mycenaeans in the E. Mediterranian. 1973. Department of Cyprus

MPT=Mediterranean Peoples in Transition. [Ed.] Gitin, S. Mazar, A. Stern, E. Israel ExplorationSociety 1998.

Op. Ath. =Opuscula Atheniensia

PAPS=Proceedings of the American Philosophical Society.

PU=Palais d'Ugarit

PAP=Prehistory and protohistory. [Ed.] Christopoulos, G. A. 1974. Ekdotike Athenon.

PAPS=Proceedings of the American Philosophical Society

PGP=Problems in Greek Prehistory. 1986. [Ed.] Wardle, K. A. and French, E. B. Bristol Classical Press.

POTT=People of Old Testament Times. [Ed.] Wiseman, D. j. 1973

PT=Palestine in Transition. [Ed.] Freedman, D. N. and Graf, N. 1983. ASOR.

PTRS.=Philosophical Transactions of the Royal Society, London.

P-8th-ICMS=Tractata Mycenaea: Proceedings of the 8th International Colloquium on Mycenaean Studies.1987.

RADC=Report of the Department of Antiqities, Cyprus.

REI=Recent Excavations in Israel: Annual of the American School of Oriental Research (v.49) [Ed.}Dever, W. and Gitin, S. 1989.

RPIMC=The Role of the Phoenicians in the Interaction of Mediterranean Civilizations. [Ed.] Ward, W. 1968

SC75A=Symposium Celebrating the Seventy-Fifth Anniversary of the Founding of the American SchoolsOrientl Research. [Ed.] Cross, F. M.
SDAG=Symposium on the Dark Ages in Greece. Arcaeologicl Institute of America. 1977.
SHAJ=Studies in the History and Archaeology of Jordan III. [Ed.] Hadadi, A. 1987.
SHBL=Studies in Honor of Benno Landsberger on his seventy-fifth birthday. 1965.
SHGH=Studies in Honor of George R. Hughes. [1977]. Oriental Institute #39. University of Chicago.
SHTJ=Studies in Honor of Tom B. Jones. 1979. Verlag Butzon and Bercker Kevelaer.
SMCG=Studies in Mycenaean and Classical Greek presented to John Chadwick. [Ed.] Killen, J. T., Melena, J. L., Olivier, J. P. 1987.
TMCC=Third Millennium BC Climate Change and World Collapse. [Ed.] Dalfes, H. N., Kukla, G., Weiss, H. 1977. Springer/NATO
TTW=Troy and the Trojan War [Ed.] Mellink, M. J. 1986.
TWHC=The Trojan War, Its Historicity and Cantext. 1981. [Ed.] Foshall, L. and Davies, J. K. Bristol Press
UF=Ugarit Forschungen. Verlag Butzon & Bercker Kevlaer
WHJP=World History of the Jewish People.
WWC=When Worlds Collide. The Indo-Europeans and the Pre-Indo-Europeans. 1990. Karoma Publishers

Abbreviations: journals and periodicals

AA=Archaologischer Anzeiger.
AJA=American Journal of Archaeology
Anat.=Anatolica
Anat. St.=Anatolian Studies
Ant.=Antiquity
Arch.=Archaeology
B.=Biblical Archaeologist
BAR.=Biblical Archaeology Review.
BASOR=Bulletin of the American Schools of Oriental Research.
Ber=Berytus
BSA=Annual of the British School at Athens
CBQ=Catholic Biblical Quarterly. Catholic Biblical Association of America
CC=Climate Change
EI=Eretz Israel
Exp.=Expedition

Gl.=Glotta
Heth.=Hethitica
Hesp.=Hesperia. American School of Clasical Studies at Athens
Hist.=Historia
IEJ=Israel Exporation Journal
IJNA=International Journal of Nautical Archaeology and Underwater Exploration.
Ir.=Iraq
JAOS=Journal of the American Oriental Society
JARCE=Journal of th American Research Center in Egypt.
JBL=Journal of Biblical Literature
JCS=Journal of Cunieform Studies
JEA=Journal of Egyptian Archaeology
JESHO=Journal of the Economic and Social History of th Orient.
JFA=Journal of Field Archaeology
JHS=Journal of Hellenic Studies. Society for the Promotion of Hellenic Studies
JMA=Journal of Mediteranean Archaeology.
JNES=Journal of the Near Eastern Society
JPS=Journal of the Prehistorical Society
JSOT=Journal for the Study of the Old Testement. Sheffield Academic Press
Kl.=Klio
L and E=Libya and Egypt. [Ed.] Leahy, A. 1990.
Lv.=Levant
Min=Minos. Universidad Salamanca
Or.=Orientalia. Pontifical Biblical Institute
Ox. Jr. Arch.=Oxford Journal of Archaeology
Pal.=Palaeohistoria
PEQ=Palistine Exploration Quarterly
PZ=Praehistorische Zeitschrift
Qed.=Qedem (Israel Exploration Society)
Sc.=Science
SIMA=Studies in Mediterranean Archaeology
SJOT=Scandinavian Journal of the Old Testament
SMEA=Studi Micenei ed Egio-Anatolici
SCO=Studi Classic Orientali
St. Tr.=Studia Troica. Verlag Phillip v. Zabern.
St. Stor. =Studi di Storia e di Filologia Anatolica
Sy=Syria
TA=Tel Aviv

VT=Vetus Testamentum. International Organization for the Study of the Old Testament. Brill

ZA=Zeitschrift fur Assyriologie

Abbreviations of contents keys

A=aftermath
Ah. =Ahhiyawa
Ar=archaeological finds
Ch.=chronology, dating
E=ethnicity
H=history
Hu=Hurrians
G=general
Ge=geography
K=Keftiu
L=language, scripts, names
O=oral tradition, legend
P=Phrygians
S=Shasu

Hittites, Luvians, Anatolia

Astour, C. M. 1965. New evidence of the last days of Ugarit. [H, Ch.]. AJA 69: 253-259.

Bartl, K. 1995. Some remarks on early iron Age in eastern Anatolia. Anat. 21: 205-212.

Beal, R. 1983. Studies in Hittite history.[H, Ch.]. JCS 35: 122-126.

Beal, R. 1986. The history of Kizzuwatna and the Sunassura treaty. [H, Ch.]. Or. 55: 424-445.

Beal, R. H. 1988. [Review of] Macqueen, J. G. The Hittites. JNES 47:292-294.

Beal, R. H. 1992. Organisation of the Hittite militry. Carl Winter.

Beal, R. H. 1992. The location of Cilician Ura. Anat. St. 42: 65-73.

Beckman, G. 1996. Hittite diplomatic texts. [Ed.] Hoffner, H. [G., H.]. Scholars Press.

Billigmeier, J. C. 1970. An inquiry into the non-Greek names on the Linear B tablets from Knossos and their relationship to the languages of Asia Minor. Min. X: 177-184.

Bittel, K. 1970. Hattusha: The capital of the Hittites. Oxford University Press.

Bittel, K. 1976. The great temple of Hattusha-Bogazkoy. AJA 80:66-73.

Bittel, K. 1983. Die archaologische situation in kleinasien um 1200 v. Chr. und wahrend der nachfolgenden vier jahrhunderte {in] Griechenland, die Agais und levante in den "Dark Ages:" [H, A].GDA P. 25-65.

Benzi, M. 1986. Rhodes in the LH IIIC period. [A, H]. [in] Problems of Greek prehistory. [Ed.] French, E. B. and Wardle, K. A.

Bryce, T. R. 1974. Some geographical and political aspects of Mursilis' Arzawan campaign. Anat. St. 24 : 103-117.

Bryce, T. R. 1977. Ahhiyawa and Troy-A case of mistaken identity? Hist. 26:24-32.

Bryce, T. R. 1985. A reinterpretation of the Milawata Letter in the light of the new join piece. Anat. St. 35:13-23.

Bryce, T. R. 1986. The boundaries of Hatti and Hittite border policy. TA 13: 85-102.

Bryce, T. R. 1986. The Lycians in literary and epigraphic sources. [L, A] Museum Tusculanum Press

Bryce, T. R. 1989. Ahhiyawans and Mycenaeans: Anatolian viewpoint. [Ak.]. OJA 8/3:297-310.

Bryce, 1989. The nature of Mycenaean involvement in western Anatolia. Hist. 38:1-21.

Bryce, T. R.1992. Lukka revisited. [H, L, Ch]. JNES 51: 121-130.

Buchanan, B. 1967. Five Hittite hieroglyphic seals. JCS 21:18-23.

Burney, C. 1989. Hurrians and Indo-europeans: the ethnic context of the early trans-caucasian culture. [H]. AANE. p45-51.

Carrington, P. 1977 The heroic age of Phrygia in ancient literature and art. Anat. St.117-126

Cornelius, F. 1962. Zum Ahhijawaa-problem. [Ah.]. Hist. 11: 112-123.

Cornelius, F. 1973. Geschichte der Hithiter. [G, H, Ge, L]. Darmstadt.

DeVries, K. 1990. The Gordion excavation seasons of 1969-1973 and subseguent research. AJA 94: 371-407.

Diakonoff, I. M. 1985. Phrygian. Caravan Books.

Diamant, S, and Rutter, J. 1963. Horned objects in Anatolia and the Near East and possible connections with the Minoan "Horns of Consecration." Anat. St. 19:147-179.

Djahukian, G. B. 1990. Did Armenians live in Asia Minor before the twelfth century B.C.? WWC: 25F.

Engels, D. W. 1978. Alexander the Great and the logistics of the Macedonian army. University of California Press.

Ertekin, A. and Ediz, I. 1993. The unique sword from Bogazkoy/Hattusa. [H] Asp. Art.719-725.

Finkelberg, M. 1988. From Ahhiyawa to *Axaioi*. [Ah.]. Gl. LXVI band 3-4:127-134.

Forlanini, M. 1985. Remarques geographiques sur les textes Cappadociens. Heth: VI: 45-67.

Franken, H. J. 1961. The excavations at Deir 'Alla in Jordan. [Ex., H, Ch. l] VT. XI/4:361-379.

French, D. H. 1967. Prehistoric sites in northwest Anatolia:The Iznik area. Anat. St. 17:49-101.

Freu, J. 1987. Problems de chronologie et de geographie Hittites Madduwatta et les debuts de l'empire. Heth. VIII:123-175.

Freu, J. 1988. La tablette RS 86.2230 et la phase finale du royaume d'Ugarit. [Ch.] Syr. LXV:395-398.

Friedrich, J. 1957. Extinct languages. Dorset Press.

Gardiner, A. 1960. The kadesh inscriptios. Griffith Institute, Ashmolean Museum.

Garstang, J. 1943. Hittite military roads. AJA 47:35f.

Garstang, J. and Gurney, O. R. 1959. The geography of the Hittite empire. [G., E., H.]. British Institute of Archaeology at Ankara.

Gates, M-H. 1994. Archaeology in Turkey: Kas-Uluburun. [Ar.]. AJA 98:259-260.

Gates, M-H. 1995. Archaeologyin Turkey. Anat. St.:207-255.

Gates, M-H. 1997. Archaeology in Turkey. AJA 101:241-243

Gelb, I. J. 1944.*Hurrians and Subarians.* [G, L] U.C.

Goetze, A. 1940. Kizzuwanta and the problem of Hittite geography. [Ge, H, L] Yale University Press.

Goetze, A. 1962. Cilicians. [L, E]. JCS 16:48-58.

Goetze, A. 1975. The struggle for the domination of Syria (1400-1300 B.C.) CAH:1-21.

Goetze, A. 1975. Anatolia from Shuppiluliumah to the Egyptian war of Muwatallish. CAH: 117-130.

Goetze, A. 1975. The Hittites and Syria (1300-1200 B.C.). CAH:252-273.

Goetze, A. 1975. The struggle for the domination of Syria (1400-1300 B.C.) CAH:121.

Gorny, R. L. 1989. Environment, archaeology, and history in Hittite Anatolia. BA J/S:78-96

Gunter, A. C. 1991. The Bronze Age. Final reports III. GE.

Gurney, O. R. 1990. The Hittites. Penguin Books Ltd.

Gurney, O. R. 1992. Hittite geography: Thirty years after. [in] Hittite and other Anatolians and Near Eastern studies in honour of Sedet Alp.

Guterbock, H. G. 1954. Carchemish. JNES 13:102-114.

Guterbock, H.G. 1956. Deeds of Suppiluliuma as told by his son, Mursili II. [H]. JCS 10

Guterbock, H. G. 1957. Toward a definition of the term Hittite. [L]. Oriens 10:233-239.

Gutterbock, H. G. 1961. The north-central area of Hittite Anatolia. JNES 20:96f.

Guterbock, H. G. 1967. The Hittite conquest of Cyprus reconsidered. [H,Ge]. JNES 26/6:73-81.

Guterbock, H. G. 1983. The Hittites and the Aegean world: The Ahhiyawa problem reconsidered. [Ak.] AJA 87:133-138.

Guterbock, H. G. 1984. Hittites and Akhaeans: A new look. [Ak., H]. PAPS. 128:114-122.

Guterbock, H. C. 1986. Troy in the Hittite texts? Wilusa, Ahhiyawa, and Hittite history. TTW:33-44.

Guterbock, H. G. 1989. Survival of the Hittite Dynasty. [H, Ch.] CY:53-55.

Guterbock, H. G. 1992. A new look at one Ahhiyawa text. [Ak.]. FSA: 241-243.

Hanfmann, G. M. 1948. Archaeology in Homeric Asia Minor. AJA 52: 135-155.

Hansen, O. 1994. A Mycenaean sword from Bogazkoy-Hattusa found in 1991. BSA 89:213-215.

Hansen, O. 1994. Reflections on the Bronze Age topography of NW Anatolia. Anat. 20:227-231.

Hawkins, J. D. 1974. Assyrians and Hittites. Ir. 36:67f.

Hawkins, J. D.1988. Kuzi-Tesub and the "Great Kings" of Karkamish. [A]. Anat. St. 99-108

Hawkins, D. 1992. The inscriptions of the Kizildag and the Karadag in the light of the Yarlurt inscription. [A]. FSA:259-275.

Hawkins, J. D. 1993. The historical significance of the Karahoyuk (Elbistan) stela. Asp. Art. 273-279.

Hawkins, J. D. 1994. The end of the Bronze Age in Anatolia: New light from recent discoveries. AIA3 p. 91-93.

Heinhold-Kramer. 1977. Arzawa Untersuchung. Carl Winter.

Heinhold-Kramer, S. 1983. Untersuchungen Piyamaradu. Or. 52:81-97.

Helk, W. W. 1963. Urhi-Tesup im Agypten. JCS 17: 87f.

Henrickson, R. C. 1994. Continuity and discontinuity in the ceramic tradition of Gordion during the Iron Age. AIA3: 95-130

Hoffner, H. 1968. A Hittite text in epic style about merchants. JCS 22:34-45.

Hoffner, H. 1969. [review of] Studia Mycenaea: Proceedings of the Mycenaean symposium, Brno. 1966. [Ed.] Bartonek, A. [Ak.]. AJA 73:474-475.

Hoffner, H. A. 1980. Histories and historians of the ancient Near East: The Hittites. Or.49: 283-332.

Hoffner, H. A. 1989. The last days of Khattusha. [H, Ch.] CY:46-52.

van der Hout., T. P. J. 1989. A chronology of the Tarhuntassa-treaties. JCS 41/1: 100-114.

Houwink ten Cate, P. 1974. Records of the early Hittite empire: Historical considerations. ASHG: 57F.

Houwink ten Cate, P. 1974. The early and late phases of Urhi-Tesub's career. ASHG:123-150.

Houwink ten Cate, H. P 1974. Cantact between the Aegean region and Anatolia in the second millenium. [L, Ar, Ah.] BAM141-167.

Houwink ten Cate. P. 1992. The bronze tablet of Tudhaliyas IV. [H,Ge]. p. 233-270.

Huxley, G. L. 1960. Achaeans and Hittites. Oxford University Press.

Iakovides, S. 1973. Rhodes and Ahhijawa. MEM:189-192.

Jewell, E. R. 1974. The archaeology and history of western Anatolia during the second millenium B.C. Thesis: University of Pennsylvania.

Jones, R. E. and Mee, C. 1978. Spectrographic analyses of Mycenaean pottery from Ialysos on Rhodes: results and implications. [H, E, Ch.] JFA V.5:461-470

Kammenhuber, A. 1988. On Hittites, Mitanni-Hurrians, Indo-Aryans, and horse tablets in the IInd millennium B.C. [E,L]. [in] Essays on Anatolian studies in the second millenium B.C. [Ed] Prince T. Mikasu. Harrassowitz.

Klengel, H. 1974. "Hungerjahre" in Hatti. [in] Altorientalische Forschungen I. Akademie Verlag.

Kosak, S. 1981. Western neighbors of the Hittites. [Ah.]. WI 15:12-16.

Lehmann, J. 1997. The Hittites-People of a thousand gods. Viking.

Lemaire, A. 1993. Ougarit, Oura et la Cilicie vers la fin du XIIIe av. J.C. [H, Ch.] U.F. 25:227-236.

Liverani, M. 1986. Anatolia: L' Impero Hittita. [Ge.]. AS Fascicolo 4/3.

Liverani, M. 1990. Prestige and interest: International relations in the N. E. 1600-1100 BC. Sargon.

Lloyd, S. 1954. Mound surveys Ant. 28/112:214f.

Lloyd, S. 1956. Early Anatolia. [G]. Penguin Books.

Luckenbill, D.D. 1986. Ancient records of Assyria and Babylonian histories. [H, Ch.]. Histories and Mysteries of Man

Macqueen, J. G. 1968. Geography and history in western Asia Minor in the second millennium B.C. Anat. St. 18:169-186.

Macqueen, J. G. 1986. The hittites and their contemporaries in Asia Minor. [E, H, Ch., Ge. G]. Thames and Hudson

Maisels, C. K. 1990. The emergence of civilization. Routledge

Mallory, J. P. 1989. In search of th Indo-Europeans. Thames and Hudson

McMahon, G. 1989. The history of the Hittites. BA J/S:62-77.

Mee, C. B. 1978. Aeagean trade and settlement in Anatolia in the second millennium B.C. Anat. St. 28:121-156.

Mellaart, J. 1978. The archaeology of ancient Turkey. Rowman and Littlefield.

Mellaart, J. 1993. The present state of "Hitite geography." Asp. Art. 415-421.

Mellink, M. J.1956. A Hittite cemetary at Gordion. [Ar.]. University Museum (Philadelphia).

Mellink, M. J. 1974. Archaeology in Asia Minor. AJA 78:105-130.

Mellink, M. J. 1983. Archaeological comments on Ahhiyawa-Achaians in western Anatolia. [Ah.]. AJA 87: 138-141.

Mellink, M. J. 1992. Archaeology in Asia Minor. AJA 96:119-150.

Mellink, M. J. 1992. Ortakoy-Corum. [Ar.]. AJA 96: 130

Mellink, M. a. 1992. Kaman-Kalehoyuk. [Ar. P.]. AJA 96 130.

Mellink, M. J. 1993. Bogazkoy/Bogazkoy Assuwa booty/Kaman-Kalehoyuk AJA 97: 111-114.

Mellink, M. J. 1995. Kaman-Kalehoyuk. [Ar., Ch. P]. AJA 99:219.

Merrilles, R. 1986. Political conditions in the eastern Mediterranean during the Late Bronze Age. BA March p. 42-51.

Mora, C. 1992. Regarding some inscriptions of post-Hittite kings and "Great Kings." FSA;385-390.

Muhly, J. D. 1974. Hittites and Achaeans: Ahhijawa redomitus. [Ah.]. Hist. 23:129-145.

Muscarella, O. W. 1995. The iron age background to the formation of the Phrygian state. [P] BASOR 299/300. 91-101

Neve, P. J. 1989/1990. Bogazkoy-Hattusha. [Ar.]. Anat. 16:7-14

Orthmann, W. 1984. Keramik aus den altesten schichten von Buyukale. Bogazkoy VI:9-64.

Otten, H. 1983. Die letzte phase des Heethitischen grossreiches nach den texten. GDA

Ozdogan, M. 1987. Taslicabayir. A Late Bronze Age burial mound in eastern Thrace. [Ar. Ch.]. Anat. 14: 5-18.

Ozguc, T. 1980. Excavations at the Hittite site, Masat Hoyuk: Palace, archives, Mycenaean pottery. [Ar. Ch]. AJA 84:305-309.

Page, D. L. 1963. History and the Homeric Iliad. University of California Press.

Pritchard, J. B. 1978. Ancient near eastern texts relating to th Old Testament. Priceton University P.

Renfrew, C. 1989. The origins of the Indo-European Languages. [L]. Scientific American. Oct. 1989.

Rowton, M. B. 1959. Background of the treaty between Ramesses II and Hattusilis III. JCS 13: 1-11.

Runciman, S. 1962. A history of the crucades. Ch. III. Cambridge University Press.

Sams, K. 1989. Western Anatolia. [H, Ch.] CY:56-60.

Sams, K. S. 1994. the early Phrygian pottery. Final Reports III. GE

Sayce, A. H. 1923. The early geography of south-eastern Asia Minor. JHS 43:44f.

Seeher, J. 1998. Die ausgrabungen in Bogazkoy-Hattusa 1997: Getreidesilos und stutzmauer auf dem unteren plateau. AA: 229-231.

Sevin, V. 1991. The early Iron Age in the Elazic region and the problem of the Mushkians. Anat. St.87-97.

Singer, I. 1985. The battle of Nihriya and the end of the Hittite empire. [H, Ch.].TA75:100-123.

Singer, i. 1983. Western Anatolia in the thirteenth century B.C. according to Hittite sources. [H, Ch. Ak]. Anat. St. 33: 205-217.

Singer, I. 1987. Dating the end of the Hittite empire. Heth. 8: 413-421.

Singer, I. 1996. Great kings of Tathuntassa. [H] SMEA:63f.

Steiner, G. 1989. "Schiffe von Ahhijawa' oder "Kriegsschiffe von Amurru" in Sauskamuwa-Vertrag? [H, G]. U.F. Band 21. p.393-411.

Sturtevant, E. H. and Bechtel, G. 1935. A hittite crestomathy. [H]. Linguistic society of America.

Tritsch, F. J. 1967. Bellerophon's letter. AMCIM:1123-1130.

Unal, A. 1989. The power of narration in Hittite literature. BA J/S:130-145.

Unal, A. 1991. Two peoples on both sides of the Aeagean sea: Did the Achaeans and the Hittites know each other? EAASS

Vermeule, E. T. 1983. Response to Hans Guterbock. [Ah.]. AJA 87:141-143.

Voigt, M. M. 1994. Excavations at Gordion 1988-89: The Yassihoyuk statigraphic sequence. AIA3: 265f.

Wainwright, G. A. 1959. The Teresh, the Etruscans and Asia minor. Anat. St. 9: 197-213.

Wainwright, G. A. 1960. Merneptah's aid to the Hittites. J.E.A. 46:24-28.

Warren, P. and Hankey, V. 1989. Aegean Bronze Age chronology. [Ch.]. Bristol Classics Press.

Wilhelm, G. 1989. The Hurrians. [E., H., Ch., L.] Aris and Phillips

Yakar, J. 1992. Beyond the eastern borders of the Hittite empire: An archaeological assessment. FSA:507-514.

Yakar, J. 1976. Hitite involvement in western Anatolia. BIA 26:117-128.

Yon, M. 1989. The end of the kingdom of Ugarit. [Ch. H.]. CY:111-122.

Zaccagnini, C. 1988. A note on hittite international relations at thetime of Tudhaliya IV. [H]. p. 295f.

—1994. Complete retrograde glossary of the Hittite language. [L]. Nederlands Historisch-Archaeologisch Inst.

Homer, Troy

Albright, W. F. 1950. Some oriental glosses on the homeric problem. [E, L]. AJA 50:162-176.

Aldrich, K. 1975. The library of Greek mythology by Apollodorus. Coronado Press.

Alexander, C. 1996. Troy's prodigious ruin.Natural History 4/96: 42-51.

Allen, T. W. Homer. 1969. The origins and the transmission. [O]. Oxford Press

Blegen, C. W. 1937. Excavations at Troy, 1936. AJA 41:17-51.

Blegen, C. W. 1939 Excavations at Troy, 1938.. [Ar. Ch.]. AJA 43:204-228.

Blegen C. W. 1939. Excavations at Troy. [Ar. Ch.]. AJA 43:204f.

Blegen, C. W. 1995. Troy and the Trojans. Barnes and Noble.

Blegen, C. W. 1950-1958. Troy: Excavations conducted by the University of Cincinnati 1932-1938. [Ar, Ch. G.]. Princeton University Press.

Bloedow, E. 1988. The Trojan War ad Late Helladic IIIC. [H, Ch]. PZ 63:23-52.

Burkert, W. 1995. Lydia between east and west or how to date the Trojan War. [O] Age Hom.p.139-148.

Carpenter, R. 1956. Folk tale, fiction and saga in the Homeric epics. [O]. Univ. of California Press

Caskey, J. L. 1948. Notes on Trojan chronology. AJA 52: 119-122.

Cowen, R. C. 1998. The trojan horse just might have been an earthquake.[O]. Christian Sc. Monitor. Jan 6.

Dictionary of the Middle Ages. 1982. (Atlakvida, Atmal, Morovingians, Nibelungleid) [O]. Scribners and Sons.

Davies, J. K. 1981. The reliability of the oral tradition. [O]. TWHC:87-110.

Easton, D. F. 1981. Hittite history and the Trojan War. TWHC:23-44.

Easton, D. 1985. Has the Trojan War been found? Ant. LIX: 188-196.

Evelyn-White, H. G. 1959. Hesiod. The homeric hymns and homerica. Harvard University Press.

Fagles, R. 1990. Homer. The Iliad. Penquin Classics

Finley, M. i. 1964. The Trojan War. JHS LXXXIV:1-9.

Foley, J. M. 1988. The theory of oral composition. [O]. Indiana Univ. Press.

Fowler, H. N. 1928. A history of ancient Greek literature. MacMillan.

Hadas, M. 1950. A history of Greek Literature. Columbia University Press

Hainsworth, J. B. 1981. The fallibility of an oral heroic tradition. [O.].TWHC:111-136.

Hanfmann, G. M. 1948. Archaeology in Homeric Asia Minor. [AR.] AJA 52: 135-155.

Harvey, P. 1940 The Oxford companion to classical literature. Clarendon Press.

Hawkins, J. D. and Easton, D. F. 1996. A hieroglyphic seal from Troia. [Ar. e]. St. Tr. 6: 111-118.

Hiller, S. 1991. Two Trojan Wars? On the destructions of Troy VIh and VIIa. [H, Ch.]. St. Tr. Band 1. 145-154.

Jablonka, P, Heike, K., Riehl, S. 1994. Datierung. [Ch.]. St. Tr. 4:64-68.

Kirk, G. S. 1975. The Homeric poems as history. CAH: 820-850.

Korfmann, M. 1976. Late Bronze Age, Middle Bronze Age Troia VI-Late Troia VII. St. Tr.6-7.

Korfmann, M. 1986. Besik Tepe: New evidence for the period of the Trojan Sixth and seventh settlements [in] TTW:17-28.

Korfmann, M. 1995. Ausgrabungen-Abstract: 1. Early to Late Bronze Age. St. Tr. p.3.

Korfmann, M. 1995. Ausgrabungen unmittelbar ausserhalb der burg und akropolis von Troia/Ilion=prahistorische unterstadt von Troia VI/VII und stadtgebiet von Ilion.[H, Ch.]. St.Tr. Band 6:33-39.

Korfmann, M. 1996. Ausgrabungen-Abstract: 2. Late Bronze Age, Middle Bronze Age Troia VI-Late Troia VII St. Tr. P.6-7.

Korfmann, M. 1997. Ausgrabungen-Abstract: B. Excavations. Middle and Late Bronze Age, Troia VI-viii p. 9-10.

Lang, A. 1970. Homer and the epic. [O]. AMS Press.

Lattimore, R. 1951. The Iliad of Homer. University of Chicago Press

Leaf, W. 1915. Homer and history. [O]. McMillan and Co.

Lord, A. B. 1964. The singer of tales. [O]. Harvard University Press

Lorimer, H. L. 1950. Homer and the monuments. [O., C., G.]. Macmillan.

Luce, J. V. 1984. The Homeric topography of the Trojan plain reconsidered. {O, Ge] Ox. Jour. Arch.

Mellaart, J. 1981. Troy VIIA in an Anatolian perspective. TWHC:63-82.

Mellink, M. J. 1984. Besiktepe. [Ar. Ch.]. AJA 88: 446.

Millard, A. R. 1981. Events at the end of the Late Bronze Age in the Near East. [G]. TWHC:1-16.

Murray, G. 1934. The rise of the Greek epic. Clarondon Press.

Mylonas, G. E. 1964. Priam's Troy and the date of its fall. [Ch.]. Hesp. 33:352-380.

Nilsson, M. P. 1968. Homer and Mycenae. Cooper Square Publishers.

Nylander, C. 1963. The fall of Troy. Ant. 37:6-11.

Ottaway, J. H. 1991. New assault on Troy. Arch. S/O: 55-59.

Ozdogan, M. 1987. Taslicabayir. A Late Bronze Age burial mound in eastern Thrace. [Ar. Ch.]. Anat. 14: 5-18.

Page, D. L. 1959. History and the Homeric Iliad. University of California Press.

Rapp, G. 1982. Earthquakes in the Troad. Troy, the archaeological geology:43-58.

Rees, E. 1991. The Odyssey of Homer. MacMillan

Rose, B. 1994, 1998, 1999. Friends of Troy Newsletter.

Sayce, A. H. 1923. The languages of Asia Minor. ASWR: 391-397.

Schliemann, H. 1875. Troy and its remains. Arno Press.

Schliemann, H. 1884. Troy: Results of the latest researches and discoveries on the site of Homer's Troy. Arno Press

Sevinc, N. 1992. Troia. A Turizm Yayinlari Ltd.

Schuchardt, C. 1979. Schliemann's discoveries of the ancient world. Avenel Books.

Sherratt, E. S. 1990. Reading the text: archaeology and the Homeric question. [O]. Ant. 64:807-24.

Simpson, H. and Lazenby, J. F. 1970. The Catalog of Ships in Homer's Iliad. [O, Ex.] Clarendon Press.

Sperling, J. 1991. The last phase of Troy VI and Mycenaean expansion. St. Tr. Band 1: 155-158.

Subotic, D. 1932. Yugoslav popular ballads. [O]. Cambridge Press

Traill, D. 1997. Schliemann of Troy. St. Martin's Press.

Tritsch, F. J. 1967. Bellerophon's letter. AMCIM:1123-1130.

Van der Valk, M. 1963. Researches on the text and scholia of Iliad. [O]. E. J. Brill

Vermeule, E. D. T. 1986. Priam's castle blazing. A thousand years of Trojan memories. TTW:77-92.

Vervenne, M. Hebrew SALIS-Ugarit TLT. UF 19: 355ff.

Warren, P. and Hankey, V. 1989. Aegean Bronze Age chronology. [Ch.]. Bristol Classics Press.

Watkins, C. 1986. The language of the Trojans. TTW: 45-62.

West, M. L. 1988. The rise of the Greek epic. [O]. JHS 108:151-172.

—Icelandic sagas, Eddas, and art. Pierpont Morgan Library.

—Archaeological map of Troy. Arkeolojik Haritasi.

Greece, Mycenaeans

Astrom, P. 1987. A Late Helladic IIIB2 deposit from the acropolis of Midea. [Ar.] KAV 152-154

Astrom, P. 1987. Demakopoulou, K., Walberg, G. 1990. Excavations in Midea. [Ar.] Op. Ath. 9-23.

Bartonek, A. 1974. The place of the Dorians in the Late Helladic world. BAM

Bautier, R. H. 1971. The economic development of medeival Europe. Harcourt Brace.

Bennett, E. 1955. The Pylos tablets. Princeton University Press.

Betancourt, P. 1976. The end of the Greek Bronze Age. Ant. 50:40-47.

Blegen, C. W. 1963. Troy and the Trojans. Praeger.

Blegen, C. W., Kourouniotis, K. 1939. Excavations at Pylos. [Ar., Ch.] AJA 43:569-576.

Blegen, C. W. 1957. The Palace of Nestor: Excavations of 1956. [Ar. Ch.] AJA 61:130-135 and plates 39-46.

Blegen, C. W. 1960. The Palace of Nestor: Excavations of 1959. [Ar., Ch.]. AJA 64:153-160 and plates 39-48.

Bloedow, E. 1988. The Trojan War ad Late Helladic IIIC. [H, Ch]. PZ 63:23-52.

Boardman, J. 1964. The overseas Greeks. Penguin.

Bouzek, J. 1974. Archaeology of the Late Bronze Age and early Iron Age. Bronze Age Greece and the Balkans: problems of migrations. BAM:169-177.

Bouzek, J.. 1997. Greece, Anatolia, and Europe: Cultural interrelations during the Early Iron age. [G]. Paul Astoms F.

Bouzek, J. 1994. Late Bronze Age Greece and the Balkans: A review of the present picture. BSA 89:217-234.

Broneer, O. 1939. Mycenaean fountain on the Acropolos. [Ar., Ch.]. Hesp. 8

Broneer, O. 1966. The cyclopean wall on the isthmus of Corinth. [Ar., Ch.] Hesp. 35:346-362.

Broneer, O. 1968. The cyclopean wall on the isthmus of Corinth, Addendum. [Ar. Ch.] Hesp. 37: 25-35

Buck, R. J. 1969. The Mycenaean time of troubles. Hist. 18:276-298.

Burn, A. R. 1968. Minoans, Philistines, and Greeks. Dawsons of Pall Mall.

Carpenter, R. 1968. Discontinuity in Greek civilization. W. W. Norton and Co.

Catling, H. W. and Catling, E. A. 1981. 'Barbarian' pottery from the Mycenaean settlement at the Menelaion, Sparta. BSA 76:71-82 and plates 5-8.

Chadwick, J. 1958. The decipherment of Linear B. Random House.

Chadwick, J. 1976. The mycenaean world. Cambridge University Press.

Chadwick, J. 1987. The muster of the Pylian fleet. P-8th-ICMS. 75-84.

Chimes, K. M. T. 1949. Ancient Sparta [Ch.]. Manchester University Press.

Cline, E. H. 1991. Of shoes and ships and sealing wax. Exp. 33/3: 54f.

Diamant, S. 1975. [review of] Bronze age migrations in the Aegean: Archaeological and linguistic problems in Greek prehistory. AJA 79:287-289.

Daniel, J. F., Broneer, O., Wade-Gery, H. T. The Setting [by] Daniel, J. F. 1948. The Dorian invasion. [O]. AJA 52:107-110.

Deger-Jalkotzy, S. 1977. Fremde zuwanderer im spatmykenischen Griechland. [E, H]. Osterreichischen Akademe der Wissenschaften.

Deger-Jalkotzy, S. 1983. Das problem der "Handmade burnished ware" von Myk. IIIC. [H,E]. G.D.A. p. 161-178.

Deger-Jalkotzy, S. 1994. The post-palatial period of Greece: An Aegean prelude to the 11th century B.C. in Cyprus. [Ch. H.]. C-11-C:11-30.

Desborough, V. R. d'A. 1964. The last Mycenaeans and their successors. [H., Ch., Ar.]. Clarendon Press.

Desborough, V. R. d'A. 1972. The Greek Dark Ages. St. Martin's Press.

Desborough, V. R. d'A. 1975. The end of the Mycenaean civilization and the dark age: The archaeological background. [A]. CAH: 658-676.

DeVries, K. 1990. The Gordion excavation seasons of 1969-1973 and subseguent research. [A]. AJA 94: 371-406.

Dickinson, O. T. P. K. 1977. Origins of Mycenaean civilization. P. Astrom's Forlag.

Drews, R. The end of the Bronze Age. Priceton Univ. Press

Fine, J. V. A. 1983. The Greeks: A critical history. Harvard Univerity Press.

Finley, M. I. 1970. Early Greece: The Bronze and Archaic Ages. W. W. Norton.

Foltiny, S. 1964. Flange-hilted cutting swords of bronze in central Europe, northeast Italy, and Greece. AJA 68:247f.

Forsdyke, J. 1957. Greece before Homer. [Ch.]. W. W. Norton.

Franken, H. J. 1961. The excavations at Deir 'Alla in Jordan. [Ex., H, Ch. 1] VT XI/4:361-379.

French, E. B. 1969. The first phase of LH IIIC. [Ar., Ch.]. AA: 133-136.

French, E. and Rutter, J. 1977. The handmade burnished ware of the Late Helladic period. AJA 81:111-112.

French, E. 1987 [draft]. Using pottery for chronology. [Ch.]. ICAP.

French, E. 1998. The ups and downs of Mycenae: 1250-1150 BCE. MPT:2-5

Furumark, A. 1941. The Mycenaean pottery: Analysis and classification. Royal Academy of Letters, History, and Antiquities [Sweden].

Gallant, T. W. 1991. Risk and survival in Greece. Stanford University Press

Gimbutas, M. 1965. Bronze Age cultures in central and eastern Europe. [Ar.] Mouton.

Greenhalgh, P. A. L. 1978. How the mighty have fallen. Acta Classica. Proceedings of the Clasical Association of South Africa. A. A. Balkema.

Grote, G. 1872. History of Greece. Ch. XIX [Ch.].

Hallager, B. P. 1985. Crete and Italy in the Late Bronze Age III period. AJA 89: 293-305.

Hammond, N. G. L. 1967. Epirus. Oxford Press.

Hammond, N. G. L. 1971. Dating some burials in tumuli in south Albania. [Ar., Ch.]. BSA 66: 229f.

Hammond, N. G. L. 1975. The end of Mycenaean civilization: The literary tradition for migrations. CAH: 678-712.

Hankey, V. 1952. Late Helladic tombs at Khalkis. [Ar.]. BSA:49-96 and plates 15-25.

Harding, A. F. 1884. The Mycenaeans and Europe. Academic Press.

Hay, D. 1964. The medieval centuries. [H]. Harper.

Heurtley, W. A. and Hutchinson. 1925-1926. Excavations at Vardroftsa. [Ar.]. BSA 27: 1-66.

Heurtley, W. A. 1926 A W. A prehistoric site in western Macedonia and the Dorian invasion. BSA 28: 158-194.

Higgins, R. 1981. Minoan and Mycenaean art. Thames and Hudson.

Holloway, R. R. 1989. Italy and the central Mediterranean in the crisis years. CY:40-45.

Hooker, J. T. 1976. Mycenaean Greece. Routledge and Kegan Paul.

Hooker, J. T. 1976. Mycenaean Greece. [G]. Routleedge & Kegan Paul

Hooker, J. 1982. The end of Pylos and the Linear B evidence. [H,L]. SMEA 23:209-217

Hurwit, J. M. 1989. The art and culture of earlyGreece, 1100-480 B.C. Cornell University Press.

Iakovides, S. 1974. The centuries of Achaian soveignty. [H, G.]. PAP:268-300.

Iakovides, S. 1974. Building and Architecture, 14th to 11th century B.C. PAP:310-337.

Iakovidis, S. 1979. The chronology of LH IIIC. AJA 83: 454-462.

Iakovides, S. E. 1979. Mycenae-Epidaurus. Ekdotike Athenon S. A.

Iakovides, S. 1980. Excavations of the necropolis of Perati. [Ch.] Occasional Papers of the Institute of Archaeology, University of California.

Iakovides, S. 1986. Destruction horizons at Late Bronze Age Mycenae. Philia Epi eis G. E. Mylonas vol. A: 233-260.

Iakovides, S. 1990. The impact of trade disruption on the Mycenaean economy in the 13th-12th centuries B.C.E. BAT/90: 307f.

Immerwahr, S. A. 1960. Mycenaean trade and colonization. Arch. 13/1:4-13.

Johnson, G. 1972. A Mycenaean hegemony? University of Pennsylvania thesis.

Kemenczei, T. 1984. Die Spatbronzezeit nordostungarns. [Ar.] Akademiai Kiado.

Kilian, K. 1986. Mycenaeans up to date: Trends and changes in recent research [in] Problems in Greek Prehistory. [Ed.] French, E. B and Wardle, K. A. P. 115-152. Bristol Classical Press

Korkuti, M Vehdbanimi prehistorik Trenit. Iliria studime Dhe materiale archeologjike 1.

Lattimore, R. 1965. The Odyssey of Homer. Harper and Row.

Leonard, A. 1986. Problems inherent in dating Mycenaean/Syro-Plaestinian synchronisms. PGP: 319f.

Lewartowski, K. 1989. The decline of the Mycenaean civilization. [Ar, G]. Polska Akademia.

Matz, F. 1962. The art of Crete and early Greece. Crown Publishers.

Montjoy, P. A. 1986. Mycenaean decorated pottery: A guide to identification. [Cr.]. Paul Astroms F.

Mountjoy, P. A. 1993. Mycenaean pottery: An introduction. Oxford.

Muhly, J. D. 1989. the crisis years in the Mediterranean World: Transition or cultural disintegration. [H, Ch.] C.Y.

Mylonas, G. E. 1964. Priam's Troy and the date of its fall. [Ch.]. Hesp. 33:352-380.

Mylonas, G. E. 1974. The gold age of Myceae: Historical background/Early Myceaean times. [H. G] PAP:242-249.

Negbi, O. 1988. Levantine elemets in the sacred architecture of the Aegean in the close of the Bronze Age. BSA 83:339-357.

Palmer, L. R. 1963. The interpretation of Mycenaean texts. Oxford Press.

Perrot, g. and Chipiez, G. Art in primative Greece.

Platon, N. E. 1974. The origin of Mycenaean power. [H, G]. PAP: 250-267.

Platon, N. E. 1974. Writing during the late Mycenaean period. PAP:302-306.

Rees, I. 1991. The Odyssey of Homer. Macmillan Publishing Company.

Renfrew, C. 1978. The Mycenaean sanctuary at Phylokopi. Ant. LII:7-15.

Rutter, J. B. 1975. Ceramic evidence for northern invaders in southern Greece at beginning of the Late Helladic IIIC period. AJA 79: 17-32.

Rutter, J. B. 1976. "Non-Mycenaean" pottery: A reply to Gisela Walberg. AJA 80:187-188.

Rutter, J. B. 1977. Late Heladic III C pottery and some historic implications [H, Ch.]. SDAG:1-20.

Rutter, J. 1977. [review of] Tiryns, Forschungen und berichte. Muller, K. et al. AJA 81:392-394.

Rutter, J. 1989. Cutural novelties in the post-palatial Aegean World: Indices of vitality or decline? CY:61-78.

Samuel, A. E. 1966. The Mycenaeans in history [H]. Prentice-Hall.

Sanders, N. 1964. The last Mycenaeans and the European Late Bronze Age. Ant. 38:258-262

Sanders, N. 1983. North and south at the end of the Mycenaean age: Aspects of an old problem. [G]. Ox. Jr. Arch. 2(1):43-68.

Schuchardt, C. 1979. Schliemann's discoveries of the ancient world. Avenel Books.

Shelmerdine, C. W. 1987. Industrial activities at Pylos. P-8th-ICMS:333-342.

Shelmerdine, C. W. 1997. Review of prehistory: The palatial Bronze Age. [H, Ch.] AJA 101:537-585.

Shelmerdine, C. W. 1987.Architectural change and economic decline at Pylos. SMCG: 557-568

Sherratt, E. S. 1980. Regional variation in the pottery of Late Helladic IIIB: BSA 75. 175-202 plus plates.

Smith, T. R. 1987. Mycenaean trade and interaction in the west central Mediterranean 1600-1000 BC. BAR International Series 371.

Snodgrass, A. M. 1967. Arms and armour of the Greeks. Cornell University Press.

Snodgrass 1971. The Dark Ages: An archaeological survey of the 11th. to the 8th. centuries BC. [A]. Edinburgh University Press.

Stiros, S. and Jones, R. E. [Ed.] 1996. Archaeoseismology. BSA Occasional Paper 7.

Stubbings, F. H. 1975. The recession of Mycenaean civilization. CAH: 338-358.

Taylor, Lord W. 1970. New light o Mycenaean religion. Ant. XLIV:270-280.

Taylor, Lord W. 1971. The house of idols, Mycenae, and its chronological implications. [G, Ch.]. AJA 75: 266-268.

Taylor, Lord W. 1983. The Mycenaeans. Thames and Hudson

Thomas, C. G. 1970. A Mycenaean hegemony? A reconsideration. JHS 90

Thomas, C. G. `976. The nature of Mycenaean kingship. SMEA 17:93-116.

Thomas, C.G. 1978. A Dorian invasion? [H,O] SMEA. p. 77-87.

Thomas, C.G. 1984. Mycenaean Law in its oral Content. [O]. SMEA

Tomlinson, R. A. 1972. Argos and the Argolid. Cornell University Press.

Tigyey, I. 1974. Messenia and the catastrophe at the end of the Late Helladic IIIB. BAM: 227-239.

Tucker, w. 1967. A note on the interpretation of Mycenaean sibilants. [L]. AJA 71:179-181.

Vagnetti, L. 1998. Variety and function of the Aegean derivable pottery in the central

Ventris, M. and Chadwick, J. 1973. Documents in Mycenaean Greek. Cambridge University Press.

Vermeule, E. T. The fall of the Mycenaean empire. [H, G]. Arch. 13/1:66-75.

Vermeule, E. 1972. Greece in th Bronze Age. University of Chicago Press.

Vermeule, E. T. 1960. The Mycenaeans in Achaia. [Ar.] AJA 64:1-21 and plates 1-6.

Vermeule, E. T. and Karageorghis, V. 1982. Mycenaean Pictoral Vase Painting.

Vermeule, E. T. 1986. Priam's castle blazing. A thousand years of Trojan memories. TTW:77-92.

Wace, M. A. and Thompson, B. A. 1912. Prehistoric Thessaly. Cambridge Pres.s

Wace, A. J. B. 1957. Mycenae 1939-1956: Part V. The chronology of Late Helladic IIIB. [Ch.]. BSA 52: 220-223.

Wace, A. J. B. and Blegen, C. 1939. Pottery as evidence for trade in the Aegean Bronze Age. Klio 32:131-147.

Walberg, G. 1976. Northern intruders in Myc. IIIC? AJA 80:186-187.

Wardle, K. A. 1981. Well built Mycenae. Aris and Phillips.

Wardle, K. A. 1980. Excavations at Assiros 1975-9. BSA 229f.

Wardle, K. A. 1973. A group of Late Helladic IIIB 2 pottery from within the citadel at Mycenae 'the Causeway Deposit. [Ar., Ch.]. BSA 68:297f. and plates 57-62.

Warren, P. 1989. The Aegean cililizations. [H, E, G]. Peter Bedrick Books.

Warren, P. and Hankey, V. 1899. Aegean Bronze Age chronology. [Ch.]. Bristol Classics Press.

Weisshaar, H-J. 1991. Ausgrabungen in Tiryns 1978-1979. AA.

Wells, P. S. 1989. Crisis years? The 12th century B.C. in central and southeastern Europe. CY:31-39.

—1972. The Minnesota Messenia expedition. [Ed.] McDonald, W. A. and Rapp, G. R. Jr.

Winter, F. A. 1977. An historically derived model for the Dorian invasion. SDAG:60-76.

Cyprus, Ugarit

Allen, S. H. 1989. Rare Trojan wares in Cyprus. [Ar., E]. RDAC. p. 83-87.

Allen, S. H. 1991. Late Bronze Age Grey Wares in Cyprus. [C, H]. CC:RPR

Artzy, M. Perlman, I, and Asaro, F. 1976. Alasiya of the Amarna letters. JNES 35:171f.

Aravantinos, V. l. 1989. Agracultural production and subsistence economy in Cyprus during the Late Cypriot II period. CEDE: 57-65.

Asaro, F. and Perlman, I. 1973. Provenience studies of Mycenaean Pottery employing neutron activaton analysis. [C]. AISMEM p. 213-214

Astrom, L. and Astrom, P. 1972. The Swedish Cyprus expedition: Vol. IV Part 1D. [Ex. H. c. Ch.]. The Swedish Cyprus Expedition.

Astrom, P. 1973. Comments on the corpus of Mycenaean pottery in Cyprus. MEM: 122-127.

Astrom, P. 1990. Late Cypriot Bronze Age pottery in Palestine. BAT: 307-313.

Astrom, P. 1998. Continuity or discontinuity: Indigenous and foreign elements in Cyprus around 1200 BCE. [H., E] MPt:80-86.

Astour, M. C. 1965. Hellenosemitica [H, L, E, G]. Brill

Astour, C.M. 1964. Second Millenium B.C. Cypriot and Cretan onomastica reconsidered. [L,E]. JAOS

Astour, C. M. 1965. New evidence of the last days of Ugarit. [H, Ch.]. AJA 69:253-259.

Bass, G. F. 1986. A Bronze Age shipwreck at Ulu Burun (Kas): 1984 campaign. [Ch. H.]. AJA 90:269296.

Bass, G. 1987. Oldest known shipwreck reveals splendors of the Bronze Age.

National Geographic 172/6: 693-733.

Bass, G. F., Pulak, C., Collon, D., and Weinstein, J. 1989. The Bronze Age shipwreck at Ulu Burun: 1986 campaign. [Ch. H.]. AJA 93: 1-29.

Bikai, P. 1984. the Phoenicians and Cyprus. [h,Ch.]. PISC11C. p. 31-36.

Billigmeier, J. C. 1976. Toward the decipherment of Cypro-Minoan. [L. E]. AJA 80.

Bouni, A. et al. 1979. Rapport preliminaire sur la troisieme campagne de fouilles (1977) a Ibn Hani. Syr. 56: 217-287.

Bouzek, J.. 1997. Greece, Anatolia, and Europe: Cultural interrelations during the Early Iron age. [G]. Paul Astoms Forlag.

Brugsch-Bey. 1881. Egypt under the Pharaohs VII Ch. XV. John Murray.

Buchholz, H-G. and Karageorghis, V. 1973. Prehistoric Greece and Cyprus. Phaidon.

Buchholz, H-G. 1974. Grey Trojan ware in Cyprus and northern Syria. BAM:179-187.

Burdajewicz, M. 1990. Aegean Sea Peoples and religeous archeatecture. BAR International Series 588. Oxford Press.

Cadogan, G.1991. Cypriot Bronze Age pottery and the Aegean. [C, Ch.] CC:RPR. p. 169-172

Catling, H. W. 1962. Patterns of settlement in Bronze Age Cyprus. [H, Ch.] Op. Ath. IV: 129-169.

Catling, H. W. 1955. A Bronze Age greave from a 13th century B.C. tomb at Enkomi. [C, E, Ch.].

Op. Ath. 2.

Catling, H. W. 1956. Bronze cut and thrust swords in the eastern Mediterranean. J.P.S. V. 22:118-125.

Catling, H. W. 1964. Cypriot bronze in the Mycenaean world. Oxford University Press.

Catling, H. 1973. The Achaean settlement of Cyprus. [E, Ch. H] MEM.34-39.

Catling, H. W. 1975. Cyprus in the Late BronzeAge. CAH: 188-217.

Catling, H. W. 1986. Cypriot bronze work—East or West? p. CBOO: 91-103

Caubet, A. 1989. Reoccupation of the Syrian coast after the destruction of the "Crisis Years." CY:123-131.

Cook, v. 1988. Cyprus and the outside world during the transition from the Bronze Age to the Iron Age. Op. Ath. XVII 3. P. 13-31.

Cook, V. 1991. Bronze Age ashlar construction in Cyprus. [C]. RADC 93-97.

Corruba, O. 1968. Contributo alla storia di cipro II millennio. [L, E]. 7:5-29.

Deger-Jalkotzy, S. 1994. The post-palatial period of Greece: An Aegean prelude to the 11th century B.C. in Cyprus. [Ch. H.]. C-11-C:11-30.

Deger-Jalkotzy, S. 1998. The Last Mycenaeans and their Successors updated. [H.]. MPT:114-128.

Dikaios, P. 1953. A second enscribed tablet from Enkomi. Ant. 27/105:233-237.

Dikaios, P. 1971. Enkomi excavations 1948-1958. [G, Ge., C, Eth., Ch.]. Verlag P. v. Zabern.

Doumas, C. G. 1998. Aegeans in the Levant: Myth and reality. [O.]. MPT:129-139.

Freu, J. 1988. La tablette RS 86.2230 et la phase finale du royaume d'Ugarit. [H, Ch. Syria. LXV. 395-398

Furumark, A. 1965. The excavations at Sinda. [Ex., Ch., H]. Op. Ath. VI p. 99f.

Gale, H. Noel, and Stos-Gale, Zofia A. 1982. Bronze Age copper sources in the Mediterranean: a new approach. [C]. Sc. v. 216 2 April. p. 11-19.

Gittlen, B. M. 1981. The cultural and chronological implications of the Cypro-Palestinian trade during the Late Bronze Age. BASOR241:49-59.

Gjerstad, E. 1944. The colonization of Cyprus in Greek legend. [O.]. Opuscula Archaeologia 3:107-123.

Georgiou, H. 1979. Relations between Cyprus and the Near East in the middle of the Late Bronze Age. [H, Ch.]. Lv. II

Guterbock, H. G. 1967. The Hittite conquest of Cyprus reconsidered. [H,Ge]. JNES 26/6:73-81.

Hayward, L. G. 1990. The origin of raw elephant ivory used in Greece and the Aegean during the Late Bronze Age. Ant. 64:103-109

Helbing, L, 1979. Alasia according to other written sources than the Amarna letters sent from Alasia [in] Alasia problems. [ed.] P. Astrom

Holmes. Y. L. 1971. The location of Alashiya. [E, G]. JAOS. 91.3. p. 426-429.

Hood, S. 1973. Mycenaean settlement in Cyprus and the coming of the Greeks. [E, H]. M.E.M: 40-50.

Hult, G. 1983. Bronze Age ashlar masonry in the eastern Mediterranean. [C. Ch.] Astroms Verlag.

Iakovides, S. 1990. The impact of trade disruption on the Mycenaean economy in the 13th-12th centuries B.C.E. BAT/90.

Iacovou, M. 1984. The topography of eleventh century B.C Cyprus. C-11-C. 149-162.

Iakovou, M. 1989. Society and settlements in Late Cypriot III. ESC: 52-59.

Iacovou, M. 1994. The topology of elevnth century B.C. Cyprus. C-11-C:149-165.

Jones, R. E. 1986. Greek and Cypriote pottery. [C. Ch.] British School at Athens. p. 314 ff.

Karageorghis, V and Demas, M.1981. Excavations at Kition IV. [Ex., C, Ch.] Dept. of Antiquities-Cyprus.

Karageorghis, V and Demas. 1985. Excavations at Kition. V. [Ex., C, Ch.]

Karageorghis, V. 1969. The ancient civilization of Cyprus. [H, E, G]. Cowles Education Corp.

Karageorhis, V. and Muhly, J. D. 1984. Cyprus at the close of the Bronze Age. [G, E, C, Ar.]. Leventis Foundation. Zavallis Press.

Karageorghis, V. 1976. Kition. [G, H. C, Ch]. Thames and Hudson.

Karageorghis, V. 1986. 'Barbarian' ware in Cyprus. [E, C. Ch.]. CBOO. p. 246-264.

Karageorghis, V. 1989. The crisis years in cyprus. [H, Ch.] C.Y.

Karageorghis, V. 1990. The end of the Late Bronze Age in Cyprus. [Ar.]. Pierides Foundation.

Karageorghis, V. 1994. The prehistory of ethnogenesis. [E,H]. C-11-C. p.1-7.

Kling, B. 1982. Excavations at Maaa-Palaeokastro, 1979-1982. [C]. RDAC.

Kling, B. 1984. Mycenaean IIIC:1b pottery in Cyprus: Principal characteristics and historical context. [Ar., Ch.]. [reprint from] Cyprus at the close of the Bronze Age.

Kling, B. 1986. Comments on the Mycenaean IIIC:1b pottery from Kition areas I and II. Kition V. The prephoenician levels.

Kling, B. 1987a. Mycenaean IIIC:1b and related pottery in Cyprus. Dissertation. University of Pennsylvania

Kling, B. 1987b. Pottery classification and relaltive chronology of the LC IIC-IIIA periods. [C, Ch.] [in] Western Cyprus connections. [Ed.}Rupp, D. W. SIMA LXXVII

Kling, B. 1989. Mycenaean IIIC:1b and related pottery in Cyprus. [C. Ch.]. SIMA LXXVII.

Kling, B. 1991. A terminology for the matte-painted, wheelmade pottery of the Late Cypriot IIC-IIIA. [C, Ch. E]. CC:BOO. p. 181-184.

Knudtzon, J. A. 1915. Die El-Amarna-Tafeln. Hinrichs.

Lehmann, G. A. 1979. Die Sikalaju-ein neues zeugnis zu den "seevolker"-heerfahrten im spaten 13. jh. v. Chr. (RS 34.129). [H]. U.F. band 11.

Lemaire, A. 1993. Ougarit, Oura et la Cilicie vers la fin du XIIIe av. J.C. [H, Ch.] U.F. 25:227-236.

Linder, E. 1970. the maritime texts of Ugarit. [H, G, E]. Dissertation: Brandis Univ.

Masson, E. 1978. The origin of the classical Cypriote script. [L]. AIAS.

Masson, E. 1986. Les ecritures Chypro-Minoennes. [E,L]. 1986. AIS

Meier, E. G. 1973. Evidence for Mycenaean settlement at Old Paphos. [E, H]. M.E.M: 68-78.

Maier, F. 1986. Kinyras and Agapenor. [O]. AISCOO: 311-320.

Mercer, S. A. B. 1939. The Tell El-Amarna tablets. Macmillan.

Merrillees, R. S. 1971. The early history of the Late Cypriote I. Lv. v. 3

Merrillees, R. S. 1975. Problems in Cypriote history. [H, E, C]. Archaeology in Cyprus

Robertson, N [Ed]. Noyes Press.

Merrillees, R. S. 1975. Reflections on the Late Bronze Age in Cyprus. [G, H, Ch.] Op. Ath. VI

Merrillees, R. S. 1987. Alashia revisited. [L, Ge]. Paris.

Merrilles, R.S. 1989. The crisis years, A rejoiner. C.Y.

Merrillees, R. S. 1992. The absolute chronology of the Bronze Age in Cyprus:a revision. [Ch.]. BASOR 288:47-53.

Montjoy, P. A. 1986. Mycenaean decorated pottery: A guide to identification. [Cr.]. Paul Astroms .

Moran, W. L. 1992. The Amarna Letters. Johns Hopkins Press.

Muhly, J. D. 1980. Bronze figures and Near Eastern metalwork. IEJ 30/3:148-161.

Muhly, J. D. 1982. The nature of trade in the LBA eastern Mediterranean: The orgnization of the metals' trade and the role of Cyprus. EMC:251-269

Muhly, J. D. 1983. Lead isotope analysis and the kingdom of Alashiya. [Ge] RADC.

Muhly, J. D. 1984. The role of the Sea Peoples in Cyprus during the LC III period [in] Cyprus at the close of the Late Bronze Age [Ed.] Karageorghis, V.

Muhly, J. D. 1989. The crisis years in the Mediterranian world: Transition or cultural disintegration? CY:10-26.

Negbi, O. 1976. Canaanite gods in metal. An archaeological study of ancient Syrio-Palestinian figures. Publications of the Institute of Archaeology 5. Tel Aviv.

Negbi, O. 1982. Evidence for early Phoenician communities on ther eastern Mediteranean islands. Lev. 14:179-182.

Negbi, O. 1986. The climax of urban development in Bronze Age Cyprus. [Ex., H]. RADC:97-120.

Negbi, O. 1988. Levantine elements in the sacred architecture of the Aegean in
the close of the Bronze Age. BSA 83:339-357.

Negbi, O. 1992. Early Phoenician presene in the Mediterranean islands: A reappraisal. AJA 96:599f.

Negbi, O. 1998. Reflections on the ethnicity of Cyprus in the eleventh centurty BCE [H., E.]. MPR:87f.

Ormerod, H. A. Piracy in the ancient world: An essay in Mediteranean history. Argonaut inc.

Pilides, D. 1991. Handmade burnished wares of the Late Bronze Age: Toward a clearer classification system. [C, Ch.]. CC:RPR p. 139-149.

Sasson, J. M. 1966. Canaanite maritime involvement in the second millenium B.C. JAOS 86: 126-138.

Schaeffer, C. F. A. 1948. Enkomi. [Ex., C, Ch]. AJA 52: 156-177+plates.

Schaeffer, C. F. A. 1952. Enkomi-Alasia, Nouvelles missions en Chypre 1946-1950.

Schaeffer, C. F. A. 1952. Enkomi-Alasia. [G, H, C]. Librarie C. Klincksieck.

Schaeffer, C. F. A. 1955. A Bronze Age sword from Ugarit with cartouche of Mineptah (Ras Shamra, Syria). Ant. 29/16: 226-229.

Schaeffer, C. F. A. 1983. Last days of Ugarit. [H, Ch.] B.A.R. sept/oct. p. 74-75.

Seeden, H. 1980. The standing armed figurines in theLevant. Prahistorische Bronzefunde Ab. 1 band 1. C. H. Beck'sche Verlagsbuchhandlung

Sherratt, S. 1990 a. Palaepaphos-Teratsoudhia tomb 105 chamber B: Myc. IIIC:1' sherds [C, Ch.] [in] Tombs at Palaepaphos. [C]. Karageorghis, V. [Ed.] p.108-121

Sherratt, S. 1990 b. Note on two pots from Palaepahpos-Elliomylia tomb 119. [C. Ch.][in] Tombs at Palaepaphos. Karageorghis, V. [ed.] p. 156-163.

Sherratt, S. E. 1991. Cypriote pottery of the Aegean type in LC II-III:Problems of clasification, chronology, and interpretation. [Ch.]. CC:RPR:185-198.

Sherratt, S. 1992. Cypriot pottery of Aegean type in LC II-III: Problems of clasifiction,chronology, and interpretation [in] CC:RPR. p.185-198..

Sherratt, S. 1994. Commerce, iron and ideology: Metallurgical innovation in the 12th-11th century Cyprus. [A]. C-11-C. p.59-106.

Sigrist, M. 1990. Emar. BAT 1990. [H]. p. 508-517.

Snodgrass, A. M. 1994. Gains, losses, and survivals: What we can infer for the eleventh century B.C. C-11-C. 167-173.

Sjoqvist, E. 1940. Problems of the Late Cypriote Bronze Age.

Stech, T. 1982. Urban metallurgy in Late Bronze Age Cyprus. [C]. EMC:105-113.

Steel, L. 1993. Establishment of the city kingdoms in Iron Age Cyprus: An archaeological commentary. RADC 147-154.

Stiros, S. and Jones, R. E. [Ed.] 1996. Archaeoseismology. BSA Occasional Paper 7.

Stubbings, F.1973. Mycenaean pottery in Cyprus. [C]. AISMEM p. 207-212

Taylor, J. P. 1956. Late Cypriot III. PEQ:22-39.

Taylor, J. P. 1957. Myrtou-Pigadhes. The sanctuary. [Ex.]. p. 103-112. Ashmolean Museum.

Vagnetti, L. 1986. Cypriot elements beyond the Aegean in the Bronze Age. CBOO:201-216.

Vermeule, E. and Wolsky, F. 1978. New Aegean relations with Cyprus: The Minoan and Mycenaean pottery from Toumba tou Skourou., Morphou. PAPS:112/5:294-327.

Wachsmann, S. 1986. Is Cyprus Alashiya? [Ge]. B.A. Mar. 1986:37-40.

Wachsmann, S. 1997. Seagoing ships and seamanship in the Bronze Age Lv. [G, E] Texas A&M Press.

Wainwright, G. A. 1914. Alashia=Alasa; and Asy. [Ge]. Kl. 14:1-15.

Warren, P. and Hankey, V. 1899. Aegean Bronze Age chronology. [Ch.]. Bristol Classics Press.

Webster, T. B. L. 1964. From Mycenae to Homer. Methuen.

Yener, K. A, Ozbal, H. 1987. Tin in the Turkish Taurus mountains: The Bolkardag mining district. Ant. 61:220-226.

Yon, M. 1989. The end of the kingdom of Ugarit. [Ch. H.]. CY:111-122.

Israel, Canaan

Aharoni, Y. 1967. The land of the Bible: A historic geography. Westminster.

Aharoni, Y. 1970. New aspects of the Israelite occupation in the north. EHNG p. 254-267.

Ahlstrom, G. W. 1993. The history of Ancient Palestine. Fortress Press.

Ahlstrom, G. W. Merneptah's Israel. [H, O]. JNES 44/1: 59-61.

Albright, W. F. 1927. The names "Israel" and "Judah" [L,O]. JBL 46: 151-185.

Albright, W. F. 1935. Archaeology and the date of the Hebrew conquest of Palestine. [H, O, Ch.]. BASOR 58: 10-18.

Albright, W. F. 1936. The Song of Deborah in the light of archeaeology. BASOR 62:26-31.

Albright, W. F. 1939. The Israelite conquest of Canaan in the light of archaeology. [H, O, Ch.]. BASOR 74:11-23.

Albright, W. F. 1949. The archaeology of Palestine. Penguin.

Albright, W. F. 1952. The smaller Beth-Shan stele of Sethos (1309-1290 B.C.). [E, H, G]. BASOR 125: 24-32.

Albright, W. F. 1959. Dunand's new Byblos volume:A Lycian at the Byblian court. [H, Ch.] BASOR 155: 31-34.

Albright, W. F. 1975. The Amarna letters from Palestine. CAH: 98-117.

Albright, W. F. 1975. Syria, the Philistines, and Phoenicia. CAH: 507-536.

Aldred, C. 1975. The Amarna period and the end of the Eighteenth Dynasty. CAH: 49-98.

Alt, A. 1967. The settlement of Israel in Palestine. EOTHR:135-169.

Anderson, G. W. 1950. Some aspects of theUppsala school of Old Testiment study. HTR XLIII/4: 239f.

Astour, M. C. 1979. Yahweh in Egyptian topographic lists. [in] Festschrift Elmar Edel. p. 17-31.Bamberg.

Axelsson, L. E. 1987. The Lord rose up from Seir. Almqvist & Wiksell International.

Baly, D. 1963. Geographical companion to the Bible. McGraw-Hill.

Bartlett, J. R. 1989. Edom and the Edomites. [E, Ch, G]. JSOT Press.

Bartlett, J. R. 1992. Biblical sources for the Early Iron Age in Edom. EEM: 13-21.

.Bienkowski, P. 1989. Prosperity and decline in LBA Canaan: A reply to Liebowitz and Knapp. BASOR 275:59-61.

Bienkowski, P. 1992. The beginning of the Iron Age in southern Jordan [in] EEM:1-13

Bietak, M. 1986. Avaris and Piramesse: Archaeological exploration in the eastern Nile delta. British Academy.

Bietak, M. 1987. Comments on "Exodus." [in] Egypt, Israel, Sinai. Rainey, A. [Ed.]. Tel Aviv University

Bimson, J. J. 1987. Redating the Exodus. [H, Ch. O]. BAR S/O: 40f.

Brandl, B. 1986-1987. Two scarabs and a trapezoidal seal from mount Ebal. TA 13-14:166-172.

Brinkman, J. A. 1968. Political history of post Kassite Babylonia. Pontifical Institute.

Bright, J. 1956. Early Israel in recent history writing: A study in method. SCM Press.

Bright, J. 1981. A history of Israel. [H., O]. Westminster.

Bunimovitz, S. and Yasur-Landau, A. 1996. Philistine and Israelite pottery: a comparitive approach to the question of pots and people. TA 23

Bunimovitz, S. 1990. Problems in the "ethnic" identification of Philistine material culture. TA 17/2: 210-222.

Bunimovitz, S. 1995: On the edge of empires-Late Bronze Age (1500-1200BCE). ASHL: 320-332.

Burney, C. F. 1917. Israel's settlement in Canaan. The Biblical tradition and historical background.

[A, H]. Oxford University Press.

Burney, C. F. 1970. The Book of Judges. KTAV Publishing. House.

Callaway, J. A. 1984. [response]. BAT/85: 72-78.

Cambell, E. F. 1991. Shechem II. Scholars Press.

Chaney, M. L. 1983. Ancient Palestinian peasant movements and the formation of premonarchic Israel. PT:39-89.

Childs, B. S. 1970. The Reed Sea tradition. VT 20/4:406-418.

Clements, R. E. 1968. Baal-berith of Shechem. JSS 13: 21-32.

Clements, R. E. 1977. [review of] Rendtorff, Das uberlieferungeschichtliche problem des Pentateuch. JSOT 3: 46-56.

Coats, G. W. 1979. The sea tradition in the wilderness theme. JSOT 12:2-8.

Cornfeld, G. 1976. Archaeology of the Bible: Book by book. Harper and Row.

Cross, F. M. 1973. Canaanite myth and Hebrew epic: essays in the history of religion of Israel. Harvard Univ. Press

Cross, F. M. 1955. The Song of Miriam. [O, Ch. H]. JNES 14:237f.

Cross, F. M. 1979. Early aphabetic scripts.[in] SC75A p.97-111.

Cross, F M, 1980. Newly found inscriptions in Old Canaanite and Early Phoenician scripts. [L]. BASOR 238: 1-20.

Cross, F. M. 1980. New found inscriptions in old Canaanite and early Phoenician scripts. [L]. BASOR 238:1-20.

Cross, F. M. 1990. Newly discovered inscribed arrowheads of the 11th century B.C.E. BAT/90533-542.

Cross, F. M. 1993. Canaanite myth and Hebrew epic. Essays in the history of the religion of Israel. Harvard University Press.

Darnell, J. C. and Jasnow, R. 1993. On the Moabite inscriptions of Ramesses II at Luxor temple. JNES 52: 263-274.

Demsky, A. 1977. A proto-Canaanite Abecedary from the period of the Judges and its impications for the history of the alphbet. BASOR

Deutsch, R. and Heltzer, M. 1997. 'Abday on eleventh-century B.C.E. arrowheads. IEJ 47:111-112.

Dearman, J. A. 1992. Settlement patterns and the beginning of the Iron Age in Moab. EEM:65-77.

Demsky, A. 1986. The 'Izbwet Sartah ostracon ten years later. [L]. BARIS 299:186-197.

Dever, W. G. 1987. The contribution of archaeology to the study of Canaanite and early Israelite religion. AIR:209-248

Dever, W. G. 1990. Recent archaeological discoveries and biblical research. [H, O]. University of Washington Press.

Dever, W. G. 1991. Archaeological data on the Israelite settlement: A review of two recent works. BASOR 284: 77-90

Dever, W. G. 1992. How to tell a Canaanite from an Israelite [E, H]. [in] The rise of ancient Israel [ed.]. Shanks, H. Biblical Archaeology Society.

Dever, W. G. Ceramics, ethnicity, and the question of Israel's origins. BA 58/4: 200-213.

Dever, W. 1996. [review] History of Israelite Religion in the Old Testament Period by R. Albertz. BASOR 301:83-90.

Dever, W. G. 1997. Archaeology and the emergence of early Israel {E. H.] ABI: 20f.

Dever, W. G. 1998. Israelite origins and the "nomadic ideal:" Can archaeology seperate fact from fiction? MPT:197-219.

Dornemann, R. H. 1983. The archaeology of Transjordan in the Bronze and Iron Ages. Milwaukee Public Museum

Dothan, T. 1989. The arrival of the Sea Peoples: Cultural diversity in the Early Iron Age in Canaan. REI p. 1-22.

Dothan, T. and Gitin, S. 1990. Ekron of the Philistines. BAR J/F: 20f.

Eissfeldt, O. 1965. The Old Testament. An introduction. Harper and Row.

Finkelstein, I. 1985. [response] BAT/85: 80-83.

Finkelstein, I. 1986. 'Izbet Sarah. [Ar.] BAR International Series 299. Oxford Press.

Finkelstein, I. 1988. The archaeology of the Israelite settlement. [Ar. Ch. H]. Israel Exploration Society.

Finkelstein, I. 1990. The emergence of early Israel: Anthropology, environment and archaeology.

[H. O. Ch.]. JAOS 110.4:677-686.

Finkelstein, I. 1995. The great transformation: The 'conquest' of the highlands frontiers and the rise of the territorial states. ASHL:349-365.

Fox, E. 1995. Five books of Moses. Schocken Bible v. I.

Franken, H. J. 1961. The excavations at Deir 'Alla in Jordan. [Ex., H, Ch. l] VT XI/4:361-379.

Friedman, R. E. 1989. Who wrote the Bible? Harper.

Fritz, V. 1981. The Israelite "conquest" in the light of recent excavations at Khirbet el-Meshash.

[Ar. O]. BASOR 241 :61f.

Fritz, V. 1987. Conquest or settlement? [H, Ch., O, S]. BA June. 84-100.

Gal, Z. 1982. The settlement of Issachar: Some new observations. TA 9:79-86.

Gal, Z. 1988. The Late Bronze Age in Galilee: A reassessment. BASOR 272:79-83.

Garsiel, M and Finkelstein, I. 1978. The westward expansion of the house of Joseph in the light of the 'Izbet Sartah excavations. [Ex., H]. TA 5:192-198.

Gardiner, A. 1961 Egypt of the Pharaohs. Oxford Press.

Gerleman, G. 1951. The song of Deborah in the light of stylistics. [O, H, Ch]. VT 1:168-180.

de Geus, C. H. J. 1976. The tribes of Israel. [H, O]. Van Gorcum.

Gibson, J. C. L. 1962. Light from Mari on the Patriarchs. [Ar., O]. JSS 7: 44ff.

Giten, S. and Dothan, T. 1993. Tel Miqne-Ekron. ASOR Letters 43/3:5

Goetze, A. 1940. The city of Khalbe and the Khapiru people. [E] BASOR 79:32-34.

Gorg, M. 1979. Tuthmosis III und die ssw region. JNES 38/3:199-202.

Gottwald, N. K. 1979. The tribes of Israel: A sociology of the religion of liberated Israel, 1250-1050 B.C.E. Orbis.

Gray, J. 1953. The god YW in the religion of Canaan. JNES 12.

Greenberg, M. 1970. Hab/piru and Hebrews. [E]. WHJP p. !88-200. Rutgers Univesity Press

Gunneweg, G., Dothan, T., Perlman, I., Giten, S. 1986. On the origin of pottery from Tel Miqne-Ekron. [Ar.]. BASOR 269: 3-16.

Halpern, B. 1983. The emergence of Israel in Canaan. SBL [Ed.] Crenshaw, J. L. [O, L, E, H] Scholars Press.

Halpern, B. 1992. The Exodus from Egypt: Myth or reality? The rise of ancient Israel [Ed.] Shanks, H. Biblical Archaeology Society.

Hart, S. 1992. Iron Age settlement in the Land of Edom. EEM:93-112.

Hauser, A. j. 1978. Israel's conquest of Palestine. JSOT 7: 2-20.

Herr, L. G. 1998. Tell el-'Umayri and the Madaba plains region during the Late Bronze-Iron Age I transition. [E., H.]. MPT:238-264.

Hess, B. Animal use at Tel Miqne-Ekron in the Bronze Age and Iron Age. BASOR 269:17-27.

Hess, R. S. 1991. The divine name Yahweh in Late Bronze Age Sources? U.F. 23:181-188.

Hess, R. S. 1993. Early Israel in Canaan:a survey of recent evidnce and interpretations. [H, E, O,Ch]. PEQ 125:125-142.

Holladay, J. S. 1995. The kingdoms of Israel and Judah: Political and economic centralization in the Iron IIA-B (ca. 1000-750 BCE). [Ar., H]. ASHL: 368f.

Hopkins, D. C. 1993. Pastoralists in Late Bronze Age Palestine: Which way did they go. BA 56:4, p.200-211.

Isserlin, B. S. J. 1983. The Israelite conquest of Canaan: A comparative review of the arguments applicable. [H, O]. PEQ 115:85-94.

Janzen, J. G. 1994. The "wandering Aramean" reconsidered. VT 44:359f.

Kempinski, A. 1979. Hitites in the bible. BAR Sept/Oct. p. 21-45.

Kempinski, A. 1986. Joshua's alter-An Iron Age I watchtower. [Ar. O]. BAR J/F: 42-53.

Kenyon, K. M. 1957. Digging up Jericho. Ernest Benn.

Kitchen,K. A. 1964. Asiatic wars of Ramesses II. [G, O, H] JEA 50. p.

Kitchen, K. A. 1992. The Exodus [in] Anchor Bible Dictionary [ed.] Friedman, D. N. Doubleday.

Kitchen, K. A. 1992. The Egyptian evidence on ancient Jordan. EEM: 21-35.

Knauf, E. A. 1984. Yahweh. V.T. 34: 467-471.

Kochavi, M. 1984. The Israelite settlement in Canaan in the light of archaeological surveys. [H, Ch.]. BAT/85:54-60.

Krecher, J. 1990. The Ebla tablets and their possible significance for biblical studies. [L]. BAT 1990.

Lemaire, A. 1973. Asriel, SR'L, Israel et l'origine de la confederation Israelite. VT 23:239-234.

Lemche, N. P. 1978. [review of] Sichim. Eine archaologische und religionsgeschichteliche studie [by] Jaros, K.

Lemche, N. P. 1985. Early Israel: Anthropological and historic studies. Brill.

Leonard, A. 1989. Archaeological sources for the history of Palesine: The Late Bronze Age. BA 52/1:4f.

Lewy, J. 1939. Habiru and Hebrews [in] Hebrew Union College Annual. V. 14. p. 587-623

London, G. 1989. A comparison of two contemporaneous lifestyles of the late second millennium B.C. BASOR 273: 37-55.

Loud, G. 1939. Megiddo Ivories. University of Chicago Press.

MacDonald, B. 1982. The Wadi el-Hasa survey 1979 and previous archaeological work in southern Jordan. BASOR 245:35-53.

MacDonald, B. 1992. Evidence from the Wadi-Hasa and southern Ghors and northern Arabah archaeological surveys. EEM:113-143.

Marks, E. 1967. Bedouin of the Negev. [G]. Praeger.

Mayes, A. D. H. 1976. Israel in the pre-monarchy period. VT 23: 151-170.

Mayes, A. D. H. 1989. The battle against Sisera. VT 19/3: 353-357.

Mayes, A. D. 1999. Deuteronomic ideaology. JSOT 82: 57-82.

Mazar, A. 1982. The 'Bull Site.' An Iron Age open cult place. BASOR 247: 27-42..

Mazar, A. 1985. The Israelite settlement in Canaan in the light of archaeological excavations. BAT/85:61f.

Mazar, A. 1985. The emergence of the Philistine material culture. IEJ 35:95-107.

Mazar, A. 1992. Archaeology of the land of th Bible. 10,000-586 B.C.E. Doubleday.

Mazar, B. 1969. The historical background of the Book of Genesis. [H, O]. JNES 28/2: 73-83.

Mazar, B. 1981. The early Israelite settlement in the Hill County. [H, Ch.]. BASOR 241:7585.

Mazar, B. 1971. The Exodus and the conquest. [H, O]. WHJP Ch. 4.

McCarter, P. K. 1987. Aspects of the religion of the Israelite monarchy: Biblical and epigraphic data. AIR: 137-155.

McGovern, P. E. 1978. Central Transjordan in the Late Bronze and Early Iron Ages: An alternative hypothesis of socio-economic transformation and collapse. SHAJ p. 267273.

Meek, T. J. 1936. Hebrew origins: The Haskell lectures. [E]. Harper Brothers.

Mendenhall, G. E. 1962. The Hebrew conquest of Palestine. BA 25/3:66-87.

Mendenhall, G. E. 1973. The tenth generation: The origin s of biblical tradition [E] Johns Hopkins University Press.

Millard, A. R. 1985. An assessment of the evidence for writing in ancient Israel. BAT/85: 301f.

Miller, J. M. 1992. Early monarchy in Moab? [E, Ch.]. EEM:77-92.

Miller, J. M. and Hayes, J. H. 1986. A history of ancient Israel and Judah. Westminster Press

Moran, W. L. 1992. The Amarna Letters. Johns Hopkins Press.

Moor, J. C. 1990. The rise of Yahwism. Biliotheca Ephemeridum Theologicarum Lovaniensium. XCI. Leuven University Press.

Moor, J. C. 1993. The twelve tribes in the Song of Deborah. VT XLIII: 483-493.

Na'aman, N. 1977. Yeno'am. TA 4:168-177.

Nielsen, E. 1955. Shechem: A traditio-historical investigation G. E. C. Gad.

Noth, M. 1958. The history of Israel. [H, O, Ch.]. Harper and Brothers.

Oren, E. 1982. Ziklag: A biblical city on the edge of the Negev. BA 45:155-166.

Parker, S. T. 1987. Peasants, pastoralists and Pax Romana: A different view. BASOR 265:35f.

Pope, M. N. 1955. El in Ugarit texts. Brill.

Rainey, A. 1987 [review of] Habiru-Hebraer, Eine sozio-linguistiche studie uber die herkunst des gentiliziums ibri vom apellativeum habiru [by] Loretz, O. JAOS 107.3: 539-541.

Rainey, A. F. 1989. Biblical archaeology yesterday (and today). [H, E, Ch.] BASOR 273:87-96

Rainey, A. F. 1991. Can you name the panel with the Israelite? [E, H]. BAR N/D: 54-60, 93. Frank Yurco's response, p. 61.

Rainey, A. 1995. [review of] In search of ancient Israel [by] Davis, P. R. JAOS 115.1: 100-104.

Redford, D. B. An Egyptological perspective on the Exodus narative. EIS p. 137-171.

Redford, D. B. 1985. The relations between Egypt andIsrael from El-Amarna to the Babylonian conquest. BAT/84: 192f.

Redford, D. 1986. The Ashkelon relief at Karnak and the Israel Stela. IEJ 36: 188-200.

Redford, D. 1990. Egypt and Canaan in the New Kingdom [in] Beer-Shiva v. IV.[E, H, Ch]

[Ed.] Ahituv, S. Ben-Gurion University Press.

Rendtorff, R. 1977. The 'Yahwist' as theologian? The dilema of Pentateuchal criticism. JSOT 3: 2-9.

Rendsburg, G. A. 1992. The date of the Exodus and the conquest/settlement: The case for the 1100s. [H, Ch. O]. VT XLII/4:510-527.

Robertson, D. A. 1972. Linguistic evidence in dating the early Hebrew poetry. [L, Ch.]. SBL p. 1-6 and 138-156.

Rowley, H. H. 1948. From Joseph to Joshua. [H, O, Ch.]. Oxford University Press.

Rowton, M. B. 1953. The problem of Exodus. PEQ. Jan-April p. 46-60.

Rowton, M. 1974. Enclosed nomadism. JESHO: 17/1: 1-30.

Rowton, M. B. 1976. Dimorphic structures and the problem of the Apiru-Ibrim. [E]. JNES 35/1:13-20

Rowton M. B. 1965. The topological factor in the Hapiru problem. SHBL: 375-387.

Rozelaar, M. 1952. Song of the Sea. [O, H. Ch.]. VT 2:221-228.

Sader, H. 1989. The 12th century in Syria: The problem of the rise of the Aramaeans. [H, Ch.] CY.

Sauer, J. 1985. Amon, Moab, and Edom [with discussion]. BAT/85:206-232.

Sauer, J. A. 1986. Transjordan in the Bronze and Iron Ages: a critique of Glueck's synthesis. BASOR 263:1-20.

Schloen, J. D. 1993. Caravans, Kenites, and casus belli: Enmity and alliance in the Song of Deborah. [Ch. H]. CBQ 55/18: 18-38.

Shanks, H. 1981. The Exodus and the crossing of the Red Sea, according to Hans Goedicke. [Ch. O]. BAR S/O: 42f.

Shiloh, Y. 1970. The four room house: Its situation and function in the Isrealite city. IEJ 20: 180-190.

Sigrist, M. 1990. Emar. BAT 1990. [H]. p. 508-517.

Singer, 1988. Mereneptah's campaign to Canaan and the Egyptian occupation of the southern coastal plain of Palestine in the Ramesside period. BASOR 269:1-10.

Smith, G. A. 1966. The historical geography of the Holy Land. Harper Torchbooks.

Soggin, J. A. 1981. Judges-a commentary. Westminster Press. van der Steen, E. J. 1996. The east Jordan valley in the Late Bronze and Early Iron Ages. [E., Ch., H,]. BASOR 302: 51-74.

Speiser, E. A. 1933. Ethnic movements. [E]. Furst Co.

Speiser, E. A. 1951. A note on alphabetic origins. [L]. BASOR 121: 17-21.

Stager, L. E. 1985 [response] BAT/85: 83-87.

Stager, L. E. 1985. The archaeology of the family in ancient Israel. BASOR 260:1-35

Stager, L. E. 1985. Merneptah, Israel, and the Sea Peoples: New light on an old relief. EI 18: 56f.

Stager, L. 1989. The Song of Deborah: Why some tribes answered the call and others did not. [H, Ch., O]. BAR J/F: 51f.

Stiebing, W H. 1985. Should the Exodus and the settlement be redated? [H, Ch.}. BAR J/A:58f.

Stiebing, W. h. 1989. Out of the desert? Archaeology and the Exodus/conquest narrative. Prometheus.

Strange, J. 1987. The transition from the Bronze Age to the Iron Age in the Eastern Mediterranean and the emergence of the Israelite state. SJOT 1:120.

Tigay, J. H. 1987. Israelite religion: The onomastic and epigraphic evidence. AIR:157-194.

Toombs, L. E. 1976. The stratification of Tell Balatah (Shechem). BASOR 223: 5759.

Uphill, E. P. 1968 Pithom and Raamses: Their location and significance. JNES 27: 291f.

Uphill, E. P. 1984. The temples of Ramesses. Aris and Phillips.

Van Seters, J. 1972. The terms "Amorite" and "Hittite" in the Old Testament. VT 22:4f.

de Vaux, R. 1987. The early history of Israel. Westminster.

Warner, S. M. 1978. The dating of the period of the Judges. VT 28 Fasc 4: 455-463.

Watts, J. D. W. 1957. The Song of the Sea. [O, H, Ch.]. VT 7: 371-380.

Weinfeld, M. 1987. The tribal league at Sinai. AIR:303-314.

Weippert, M. 1971. The settlement of the Israelite tribes in Palestine: A critical survey of recent debate. SCM Press.

Weippert, H. 1988. Palastina in vorhellenistischer zeit. C. H. Beck'sche Verlagbuchhandlung.

Wiseman, D. J. 1973. Peoples of Old Testament times. Oxfrd Clarendon.

Wood, B. 1990. Did the Israelites conquer Jericho? A new look at the archaeological evidence. [H, Ch.] BAR M/A: 45ff.

Wright, G. E. 1946. The literary and historical problem of Joshua and Judges 1. [H, O]. JNES 5/2: 105f.

Wright, G. E. 1957. Biblical archaeology. Westminster. Gerald Duckworth.

Wright, G. E. 1965. Shechem: The biography of a biblical city. Gerald Duckworth.

Young, I. 1992. The style of the Gezer calender and some "archaic biblical Hebrew" passages.VT XLII/3:362-390.

Yurco, F. 1990. 3,200 year old picture of Israelites found in Egypt. BAR S/O. 20f.

Zertal, A. 1986/7. Cultic site on mount Ebal. [Ar. O]. TA 13-14:105-165.

Zertal, A. 1986. How can Kempinski be so wrong? BAR J/F p. 43f.

Zertal, A. 1991. Following the pottery trail-Israel enters Canaan. [H., E]. BAR 17/5: 28-47.

Zertal, A. 1991. Using pottery forms and width stratigraphy to trace population movements. BAR S/O: 39-42.

Zertal, A. 1998. The Iron Age I culture in the Hill-Country of Canaan-A Manassite perspective. MPT:238-250.

Zertal, A. 1991. The treck of the tribes as they settled in Canaan. BAR S/O: 48ff.

—1975. The Song of Deborah and Baraq. Anchor Bible. [Ed.] Boling, R. G. Doubleday.

Sea Peoples, Philistines

Albright, W. F. 1975. Syria, the Philistines, and Phoenicia. CAH: 507-536.

Alexoiu, S. Minoan civilization. Spyros Alexiou sons.

Amlet, P. 1961. Le glyptique Mesopotamienne. Cntr National la Researche scientifique.

Artzy, M. 1987. On boats and Sea Peoples. BASOR 266: 75-84.

Astour, M. 1963. Place-names from the kigdom of Alalah. [L, E] JNES 22: 236-241.

Astour, M. C. 1965. Hellenosemitica [H, L, E, G]. Brill

Astour, M. C. 1966. Aegean place-names in an Egyptian inscription. [L, E, Ge] AJA 70:313-317.

Balensi, J. 1985. Revising Tell Abu Hawam. BASOR 257:65-74.

Barnett, R. D. 1975. The Sea Peoples. CAH:359-380.

Bass, G. 1972. History of Seafaring. Walker.

Beyer, D.1993. Quelques scaux-cylindres Syrio-Hittites inedits ou peu connus. [E]. Asp. Art.

Bezold, C. 1926. Babylonisch-Assyrischees Glossar. [L]. Carl Winter's University

Bietak, M. 1993. The Sea Peoples and the end of the Egyptian administration in Canaan. BAT/90:292-306.

Black, J. and Green, A. & Rickards, T. Gods, demons, and symbols of ancient Mesopotamia. University of Texas, Austin

Bonfante. G. 1946. Who were the Philistines? [E]. AJA 50. p. 251-262.

Boskovic, D. Quelques observations sur le char cultuel de Dupljaja. Archaeologia MCMLIX.

Brondsted, J. 1967. The vikings. Penguin Books.

Brug, J. F. 1985. A literary and archaeological study of the Philistines. BAR International Series 265.

Bunimovitz, S. 1990. Problems in the "ethnic" identification of the Phiistine material culture. TA 17: 210-222.

Bunimovitz, S. and Yasur-Landau, A. 1996. Philistine and Israelite pottery: a comparitive approach to the question of pots and people. TA 23

Buccellati, G. and Kelly-Buccellati, M. 1997. Urkish: The first Hurrian capital.

Casson, L. 1958. The ancient mariners. Minerva Press.

Cline, E. 1987. Amenhotep III and the Aegean: A reassessment of Egypto-Aegean relations in the 14th. century BC. Or. 56:1-36.

Daressey, G. M. 1911. Plaquettes emaillees de Medinet-Habou. ASAE Tome XI.

Dothan, M. 1979. Ashdod at the end of the Late Bronze Age and the beginning of the Iron Age [Ar., Ch.]. SC75A. p. 125-134.

Dothan, M. 1989. Archaeological evidence for movements of the early Sea Peoples in Canaan. AASOR. 49:59-70.

Dothan, M and Porath, Y. 1993. Ashdod V. Excavation of Area G. Forth and sixth season of excavations 1968-1970. Israel Antiquities Authority.

Dothan, M. 1993. Ethnicity and archaeology:Some observations on the Sea Peoples. BAT/90: 53f.

Dothan, T. 1973. Anthropoid clay coffins from a Late Bronze Age cemetery near Deir el-Balah. IEJ 23: 129-146.

Dothan, T. 1982. The Philistines and their material culture. Yale Univ. Pres.

Dothan, T. Lost outpost of ancient Egypt. National Geographic 162: 739-769.

Dothan, T. 1985. Miqne. LI: 67-75.

Dothan, T. 1985. The Philistines reconsidered. BAT/84: 165-176.

Dothan, T. and M. 1992. People of the Sea. The search for the Philistines. Macmillan

Dothan, T. 1990. Ekron of the Philistines Part 1. Where they came from, how they settled down and the place they worshipped in. BAR !^/1:26-36.

Edel, E. 1966. Die ortsnamenlisten aus dem totentempel Amenophis III. [K]. P. Hanstein Verlag.

Finkelstein, I 1995. The date of the settlement of the Philistines in Canaan. [Ch., H]. TA 22: 213-239.

Finkelstein, I. 1998. Philistine chronology: High, middle or low? [Ch.]. MPT:140-147.

Finkelstein, J. J. and Greenberg, M. 1967. Oriental and Biblical studies: Collected work of E. A. Speiser. [E, O, Ch.] University of Pennsylvania.

Franfort, H. 1939. Cylinder seals. [E, C]. Macmillan.

Gardiner, A. H. 1947. Ancient Egyptian onomastica. {L. E., G.]. Oxford Univ. Press.

Gelb, I. J. 1944. Hurrians and Subarians. [E, Ch.] U.C.

Gitin, S, and Dothan, T. 1997. A royal dedicatory inscription from Ekon. [L, E] IEJ 47/1-2:1-16

Goetze, A. 1959. Hurrian place names in -s(s)e. FSF.

Goldwasser, O, 1982. The Lachish hieratic bowl once again. [Ch.]. TA 9:137-138.

Hall, H. R. 1926. The Keftians, Philistines, and other peoples of the Levant: CAH26, VII Chapter XII.

Hammond, N. G. L. 1967. Epirus. Oxford Press.

Hankey, V. 1966.Late Mycenaean pottery at Beth-Shan. [Ar., Ch.]. AJA 70:169-171
Hankey, V. 1974. Turmoil in the Near East, c. 1200 B.C. As. Af. 61/5: 51-59.

L'Heureux, C. E. 1976. The yelide harapa-a cultic association of warriors. BASOR 221:83-85.

Higgins, R. 1985. Minoan and Mycenaean art. Thames and Hudson.

Holloway, R. R. 1989. Italy and the central Mediterranean in the crisis years. CY:40-45.

Ilievski, H. R. 1972. A note on the suffix -s/s/os in the Lineir B texts. [L]. A S I C A. P: 99-103.

Jones, F. W. and McGovern, P. E. 1993. Late Bronze Age Egyptian garrison at Beth Shan: A study of levels VII and VIII. University of Pennsylvania.

Kitchen, K. A. 1965. Theban topographical lists, old and new. Or. 34: 1-9

Kitchen, K. A. 1973. The Philistines. [E, H, O]. POTT. p. 53-78.

Knudson, J. A. 1915. Die El-Amarna-tafeln. Hinrichs

Krebernik, M. V. 1988. Personenname der Ebla-texte. [L]. Dietrich-Reimer Verlag

Lacheman, E. R. 1941. Nuzi geographical names. [L, E]. BASOR 81: 10-15.

Landstrom, B. 1970. Ships of the Pharaohs. Doubleday.

Lehmann, G. A. 1979. Die Sikalaju-ein neues zeugnis zu den "seevolker"-heerfahrten im spaten 13. jh. v. Chr. (RS 34.129). [H]. U.F. band 11:481-494.

Leonard, A. 1989. Archaeological sources for the history of Palesine: The Late Bronze Age. BA 52/1:4f.

Lipinski, E. 1885. Aramaic-Akkadian archives from the Gozan-Harran area. [L]. BAT/85:340-348.

Lochner-Huttenbach, F. 1960. Die Pelasger. Gerold and Co.

Macalister, R. A. 1914. The Philistines, their history and civilization. Oxford university Press

Mallowan, M. E. L., 1936. Excavations at Tall Chagar Bazar. [Ex.]. Oxford University Press

Margalith, O. 1994. The Sea Peoples in the Bible. [O, L]. Harrassowitz Verlag.

Maspero, G. 1910. The struggle of the nations: Egypt, Syria, and Assyria. Society for the Promotion of Christian Knowledge.

Maxwell-Hyslop, R1946. Daggers and swords in western Asia. Iraq p. 1f.

Mazar, A. 1980. Excavations at Tell Qasile I. Qed. 12

Mazar, A. 1985. Excavations at Tell Qasile. Part 2. Institute for Archaeology. Hebrew University.

Mazar, A. 1985. The emergence of the Philistine material culture. [C, E, Ch.]. IEJ 35:95—107.

McClellan, T. L. 1979. Chronology of the "Philistine" burials at Tell el-Far'ah (south). [Ch.]. JFA 6: 57-77.

Mendenhall, G. E. 1973. The tenth generation: The "Sea-Peoples" in Palestine. Johns Hopkins University Press.

Mendenhall, G. E. 1986. Cultural history of the Philistine problem [H,O]. AJA:533-546.

Meyer, E. 1928. Geschichte des altertums. J. G. Cotta'sche buchhandlung

Muhly, J. D. [book review of] The Philistines and their material culture, by T. Dothan. AJA 87 p. 559f.

Muhly, J. D. 1982. The nature of trade in the LBA eastern Mediterranean: The orgnization of the metals' trade and the role of Cyprus. [K]. EMC:251-269

Munro, J. A. R. 1934. Pelasgians and Ionians. JHS 54: 109f.

Negbi, O. 1976. Canaanite gods in metal. An archaeological study of ancient Syrio-Palestinian figures. Publications of the Institute of Archaeology 5. Tel Aviv.

Negbi, O. 1991. Were there Sea Peoples in the Jordan Valley at the transition from Bronze Age to the Iron Age? TA 18: 205-243.

Nibbi, A. 1975. Sea Peoples in Egypt. Noyes Press.

Nibbi, A. 1974. The identification of the Sea Peoples. BAM: 203-207.

Niemeier, W-D. 1998. The Mycenaeans in western Anatolia and th problem of the origin of the Sea Peoples. MPT:17-65.

Oren, E. D. 1973. The northern cemetary at Beth Shean. Brill.

Parola, S. 1970. Neo-Assyrian toponyms. [L]. Verlag Butzon und Bercker Kevelaer.

Parrot, A. 1950. Studia Mariana. E. J. Brill.

Pendlebury, J. D. S. 1965. The archaeology of Crete. W. W. Norton.

Prichard, J. B. 1943. Palestinian figures in relation to certain goddesses known through literature. University of Pennsylvania.

Pritchard, J. 1968. New evidence on the role of the Sea Peoples in Canaan at the beginning of the Iron Age. RPIMC. p. 99-112.

Raban, A. 1991. The Philistines in the western Jezreel valley. BASOR 284:17-28.

Raban, A. and Stieglitz, R. R. 1991. The Sea Peoples contributions to civilization. BAR N/D:34ff.

Rabinovich, A. 1996. Tell it in Ekron. Jerusalem Post Intenational Edition Oct 12:19-21.

Redford, D. B. 1983. [review of] Helck, Die Beziehungen Agyptens und vorderasiens zur Agais.[H,E]. JAOS 103: p481-483

Rees, E. 1991. The Odyssey of Homer. Macmillan.

Riss, P.J. 1973. The Mycenaean expansion in the light of the Danish excavations at Hama and Sukas.[E]. P.198-206. AISMEM

Rowe, A. 1940. The four Canaanite temples of Beth-Shan. vol. II part I. University of Pennsylvania.

Sales, J. F. La necropole "K" de Byblos. Pl. 29.

Sanders, N. K. 1978. The Sea Peoples: Warriors of the Ancient Mediterranean 1250-1150 B.C. [G]. Thames and Hudson

Sapir, E. 1936. Hebrew 'argaz. A Philistine word. JAOS 56: 272-283.

Sasson, J. 1979. Hurrian personal names in the Rimah archives. [L]. Assur 2/2: 37-68.

Sasson, V. 1998. The inscription of Achish, governor of Eqron. and Philistine dialect, cult, and culture. [L]. UF 29:627640.

Schachermeyr. F. 1984. Seevolkerangriff auf Griechenland [in] Griechische Frugeschichte. Osterreichischen Akadamie der Wisenschaften.

Schaden, O. J. 1979. Some observations on the Sea Peoples. SHTJ: 143-155.

Singer, I. 1985. The beginning of Philistine settlement in Canaan and the northern boundary of Philistia. TA 12:109-122.

Singer, I. 1988. Mereneptah's campaign to Canaan and the Egyptian occupation of the southern coastal plain of Palestine in the Ramesside period. BASOR 269:1-10.

Singer, I. 1994. Egyptians, Cananites, and Philistines in the period of the emergence of Israel. FNTM.

Singer, I. 1988. The origin of the Sea peoples and their settlement on the coast of Canaan. {E, L, H]. [in] Society and Economy in the Eastern Mediterranean. p.239-250.

Speiser, E. A. 1950. On some articles of armor and their names. [L, E]. JAOS. 70: p. 47-49.

Stager, L. 1991. When did the Philistines arrive in Canaan? Multiple clues help solve the mystery. BAR M/A. p. 32-43.

Stager, L. A. 1991. When Canaanites and Philistines ruled Ashkelon. BAR 17/2: 24-43.

Stager, L. E. 1995. The impact of the Sea Peoples in Canaan (1185-1050 BCE). ASHL:331-587.

Stern, E. 1994. A Phoenician-Cypriote votive scapula from Tel Dor: A maritime scene. IEJ 44/1-2f.

Stiebring, W. H. 1970. Another look at the origins of the Philistine tombs at Tell el-Far'ah. AJA 74/3:139-143.

Strange, J. 1980. Acta theologica Danica: Vol XIV: Caphtor/Keftiu. E. J. Brill.

Strobel, A 1976. Der spatbronzezeitlische Seevolkersturm. Walter de Gruyter.

Stubbings, F.1973. Mycenaean pottery in Cyprus. [C]. AISMEM p. 207-212

Szemernyi, O. 1988. Hounded out of Academe: The sad fate of a genius [in] Studi di storia e di filolaogia anatolica. [L]. Imparati.

Tubb, J. N. 1995. An Aegean presence in Egypto-Canaan. AEL: 136-145.

Vandersleyen, C. 1985. Le dossier Egyptien des Philistines [in] Land of Israel: Crosseroads of civilization [Ed.] Lipinski, E.

Wachsmann, S. 1981. The ships of the Sea Peoples. IJNA 10/3: 187-220.

Wachsmann, S. 1982. The ships of the Sea Peoples (IJNA, 10.3): additional notes. IJNA 11/4: 197-304.

Wachsmann, S. 1987. Aegeans in the Theban tombs. Leuven.

Wachsmann, S. 1987. Aegeans in Thebean tombs. Egyptian artistic conventions which influence the scenes veracity. Uitgeverij Peeters.

Wachsmann, S. 1997. Seagoing ships and seamanship in the Bronze Age Levant. [G, E] Texas A&M Press.

Waelkens, M. 1995. Rise and fall of Sagalassos. Arch. M/J p. 28-34.

Wainwright, G. A. 1939. Some Sea-Peoples and others in the Hittite archives. JEA 25:148-153.

Wainwright, G. A. 1959. The Teresh, the Etruscans and Asia minor. Anat. St. 9: 197-213.

Wainwright, G. A. 1959. Same early Philistine history. VT 9.

Wainwright, G. A. 1961. Some sea peoples. [G]. JEA 47: p.71-90.

Wainwright, G. A. 1963. A Teucrian in Salamis in Cyprus. JHS 83:146-152.

Waldbaum, J. C. 1966. Philistine tombs and their Aegean prototypes. AJA 70:331-340.

Warren, P. and Hankey, V. 1899. Aegean Bronze Age chronology. [Ch.]. Bristol Classics Press.

Wells, P. S. 1989. Crisis years? The 12th century B.C. in central and southeastern Europe. CY:31-39.

Westerberg, K. 1983. Cypriot ships of the Bronze Age. Astrom.

White, D. 1990. Provisional evidence for the seasonal occupation of the Marsa Matruh area by Late Bronze Age Libyans. [H, Ch.]. L and E. 1-14.

Wilhelm, G. 1989. The Hurrians. [E., H., Ch., L.] Aris and Phillips

Willetts, R. F. 1976. The civilization of ancient Crete. Barnes and Noble.

Wreszinski, W. 1988. Atla zur Altaegyptischen kulturegeschichte. Editions Slatkine.

Wood, B. G. 1991. The Philistines enter Canaan. [E, H, Ch.]. BAR Nov/Dec.

Wright, E. G. 1959. Philistine coffins and mercinaries. [H,E]. BA 3: p. 54-66.

Young, G. D. [Ed.].1992. Mari in retrospect. [L]. Eisenbrauns.

—*1975*. Coo-scavi e scoperte nel "Serraglio" e in locality minori (*1935-1943*). [E]. ASAA

—1994. Complete retrograde glossary of the Hittite language. [L]. Nederlands Historisch-Archaeologisch Inst.

Egypt

Aldred, C. 1975. The Amarna period and the end of the Eighteenth Dynasty. CAH 49-98.

Astour, M. C. 1966. Aegean place-names in an Egyptian inscription. [L, E, Ge] AJA 70:313-317.

Albright, W. F. 1934. The vocalization of the Egyptian syllabic orthography. [L]. American Oriental Society.

Albrght, W. F. 1952. The smaller Beth-Shan stela of Sethos I (1309-1290 B.C.) BASOR 125: 24-32

Albright, W. F. 1975. The Amarna letters from Palestine. CAH: 98-117.

Bierbrier, M. L. 1975. The late New Kingdom in Egypt. [Ch.]. LMAOS.

Bietak, M. 1986. Avaris and Piramesse: Archaeological exploration in the eastern Nile delta. British Academy.

Bietak, M. 1990. The Sea Peoples and the end of the Egyptian Administration in Canaan.[H]. BAT/90.292-306.

Breasted, J. H. 1906. Ancient Records of Egypt. Vol. 3. [H].University of Chicago.

Burn, A. R. 1968. Minoans, Philistines, and Greeks. Dawsons of Pall Mall.

Cerny, J. 1975. Egypt: From the death of Ramesses III to the end of the Twenty-First Dynasty. CAH: 600-643.

Cifola, B. 1991. The terminology of Ramses III"s historical records with a formal analysis of the war scenes. Or. 60: 9-57.

Clayton, P. A. 1994. Chronicle of the pharaohs: The reign-by-reign record of the rulers and dynasties of ancient Egypt. Thames and Hudson.

Edgerton, W. F. 1951. The strikes in Ramses III's twenty-ninth year. JNES X/3: 137-145.

Edgerton, W. F. and Wilson, J. A. 1936. Historical records of Ramses III. The texts in Medinet Habu volumes I and II. [H]. U.C.

Faulkner, R. O. 1975. Egypt: From the inception of the Nineteenth Dynasty to the death of Ramesses III. CAH: 217-251.

Gardiner, A. 1960. The Kadesh inscriptions. Griffith Institute, Oxford.

Gardiner, A. 1961 Egypt of the Pharaohs. Oxford University Press.

Gardiner, A. H. 1968. Ancient Egyptian onomastica. [H, L, E, Ge]. Oxford University Press

Goedicke, H. 1985. Perspectives on the Battle of Kadesh: A reassessment. Halgo.

Grandet, P. 1994. Le Papyrus Harris.

Grimal, N. 1992. A history of ancient Egypt. Blackwell.

Herold, J. C. 1963. The age of Napoleon. [H]. Heritage Publishing Co.

Iskander, Z. and Badawy, A. 1954. Brief history of ancient Egypt. Urwand Fils.

Kitchen, K. A. 1983. Pharaoh triumphant: The life and times of Ramesses II. Aris and Philips.

Kitchen, K. A. 1990. The arrival of the Libyans in Late New Kingdom Egypt. [H, Ch.]. L and E. 15-27.

Leonard, A. 1989. The Late BronzeAge. BA March: 4-39.

Lesko, L. H. 1989. Egypt in the 12th Century B.C. [H]. C.Y.

Maspero, G. 1903. History of Egypt, vol V. Grolier.

Maspero, G. 1910. The struggle of the nations: Egypt, Syria, and Assyria. Society for the Promotion of Christian Knowledge.

Moret, A. 1927. The Nile and Egyptian civilization. A. Knopf.

Muhly, J. D. 1991. Egypt, the Aegean, and Late Bronze Age chronology in the eastern Mediterranean: A review article. JMA 4/2:235-247

Murnane, W. J. 1985. The road to Kadesh. Oriental Institute, University of Chicago.

O'Connor, D. 1990. The nature of Tjemhu (Libyan) society in the late New Kingdom. L and E. 29-113.

Nelson, H. H. 1943. The naval battle pictured at Medinet Habu. JNES 2: 40-55.

Romer, J. 1984.Valley of the kings. Henry Holt.

Rowton, M. B. 1959. The background of the treaty between Ramesses II and Hattusilis III. JCS 13:1-11.

Schaden, O. J. 1979. Some observations on the Sea Peoples. SHTJ: 143-155.

Schulman, A. R. 1987. The great historical inscription of Merneptah at Karnak: a partial reappraisal. JARCE XXIV. p. 21-34.

Siliotti, A. 1997. Guide to the valley of the kings. Barnes and Noble Books.

Singer, 1988. Mereneptah's campaign to Canaan and the Egyptian occupation of the southern coastal plain of Palestine in the Ramesside period. BASOR 269:1-10.

Stieglitz, R. S. 1991. The city of Amurru. JNES 50/1: 45-48.

Vermeule, E. T. and Karageorghis, V. 1982. Mycenaean pictorial vase painting. Harvard University Press.

Wachsmann, S. 1997. Seagoing ships and Seamanship in the Bronze Age Levant. Texas A&M Press

Wainwright, G. A. 1960. Merneptah's aid to the Hittites. J.E.A. 46:24-28.

Wainwright, G. A. 1962. The Meshwesh. [H]. JEA 48: 89-99.

Ward, W. A. 1992. The present status of Egyptian chronology. BASOR 288:53-64.

Wente, E. F. 1963. Shekelesh or Shasu? JNES 22: 167-172.

Wente, E. F. and Van Siclen, C. 1977. A chronology of the New Kingdom. SHGH: 217f.

Weigall, A. E. P. 1910. A guide to the antiquities od upper Egypt. Macmillan.

Weinstein, J. M. 1981. The Egyptian empire in Palestine: a reassessment. [H, Ch.] BASOR 241:1-28.

Weinstein, J. 1989. The collapse of the Egyptian Empire in the southern Levant. [H, Ch.] CY:142-150.

Weinstein, J. M. 1998. Egyptin relations with the eastern Mediterranean world at the end of the second milennium BCE. MPT:188-196.

White, D. 1990. Provisional evidence for the seasonal occupation of the Marsa Matruh area by Late Bronze Age Libyans. [H, Ch.]. Land E. 1-14.

Wilson, J. A. 1927/8. Medinet Habu studies. Oriental institute, University of Chicago

Wilson, J. A. 1951. The burden of Egypt-An interpretation of ancient Egyptian culture. University of Chicago Press.

Famine, Plague, Climate

Baillie, M. G. L. 1995. A slice through time. B.T. Batsford.

Bintliff, J. L. 1982. Climate change, archaeology, and quartenary science in the eastern Mediterranean region. CCLP.

Brinkman, J. A. 1984. Settlement surveys and documentary evidence: regional variation and secular trend in mesopotamian demography. JNES 43.

Broshi, M. 1990. Methodology of population estimates:the Roman-Byzantine period as a case study. BAT/90 420-425.

Bryson, R. A., Lamb, H.H., Donley, D.L. 1974. Drought and the decline of Mycenae. Ant 48:46-53.

deCastro, J. 1952 The geography of hunger. Little, Brown and Company.

Conrad, L. I. 1984. The biblical tradition for the plague of the Philistines. JAOS 104.2. p. 281-287.

Deaux, G. 1969. The Black Death. Weybright and Talley.

Erinc, S. 1950. Climatic types and the variation of moisture regions in Turkey. American Geographical Society 40:224-235.

Gallant, T. W. 1991. Risk and survival in Greece. Stanford University Press

Garnsey, P. 1988. Famine and food supply in the Graeco-Roman world. Cambridge.

Garnsey, P., Morris, I. 1989. Risk and the polis: the evolution of institutionalized responses to food supply problems in the ancient Greek state [in] Bad year economics. p.98-105. Cambridge University Press.

GISP volcani markers.ftp:/ftp.ngdc.noaa.gov/paleo/icecore/greenland/summit/gisp/gisp2

Helck, W. W. 1963. Urhi-Tehub in Agypten. JCS 17.

Herlihy, D. 1997 The Black Death and the transformation of the West. Harvard University Press.

Issar, A. S. Climate change and the history of the Middle East. American Scientist. 83:350-355.

Kay, P. A. 1981. Estimation of Tigris-Euphrates streamflow from regionl paleoenvironmental proxy data. C.C. 3. 251-263.

Klengel, H. 1974. "Hungerjahre" in Hatti. [in] Altorientalische Forschungen I. Akademie Verlag.

Kuniholm, P. I., Striker, C. L. 1987. Dendrochronological investigations in the Aegean and neighboring regions, 1983-1986. JFA 14:385f.

Kuniholm, P. I. 1990. Archaeological evidence and non-evidence for climate change. PTRS. A 330:247-257.

Kuniholm, P. I., Kromer, B. Manning, S. W. et al. 1996. Ananatolian tree rings and the absolute chronology of the eastern Mediterranian, 2220-718 BC. Nature 381:780-82.

Livadas, G. C. 1972. Evaporation in Tessaloniki-Greece. Meteorological Inst. Univ. Thessaloniki

Manning, S. 1991. Response to Muhly on problems of chronology in the Aegean Late Bronze Age. JMA 4/2:249-262.

Manning, S. W., Weninger, B. 1992. A light in the dark: archaeological wiggle matching and the absolute chronology of the close of the Aegean Late Bronze Age. Ant. 66: 636-663.

Manning, S. W. 1997. Cultural change in the Aegean c. 2200 BC. TMCC:149-173.

McEvedy, C. and Jones, R. 1978. Atlas of world population history. Facts on File.

McNeill, W. H. 1976.Plagues and peoples. History Book Club.

Muhly, J. D. 1991. Egypt, the Aegean, and Late Bronze Age chronology in the eastern Mediterranean: A review article. JMA 4/2:235-247.

Neumann, J. and Parpola, S. 1987. Climate change and the eleventh-tenth century eclipse of Assyria and Babylonia. JNES 46:161-182.

Pearson, G and Stuiver, M. 1993. High-precision bidecadal calibration of the radiocarbon time scale 500-2500 BC. Radiocarbon v. 35 p. 25-33.

Sasson, J. M. 1966. Canaanite maritime involvement in the second millenium B.C. JAOS 86: 126-138.

Singer, I. 1983. Tukuhlini and Haya. Tel Aviv 10.

Southern, J. R. 1995. The GISP ice core rcord of volcanism since 7000 B.C. Science. 267:256-257.

Van Zeist, W. 1968. Studies of modern and holocene pollen precipitation in southeastern Turkey. Pal. 14. 19-41.

Wainwright, G. A. 1960. Merneptahs aid to the Hittites. JEA 46. 24-28.

Weiss, B. 1982. The decline of Late Bronze Age civilization as a possible response to climate change.

C. C. 4:173-199.

Wright, H. E 1968. Climatic change in Mycenaean Greece. Ant. XLII:123-127.

Zieger, P. 1969. The Black Death. The John day Company.

INDEX

A

Abdi-Hepa, 265, 274
Abi-Milki, 311
Abraham, 263, 265, 271
Abu Simbel, 53, 301, 321
Achaeans, 15, 57-58, 61, 76, 90-92, 101, 158, 372-374
Adana, Adaniya, 162, 312, 336
Adriatic Sea, 129, 131-132, 299, 322-323
Aegean Sea, 33, 92, 169, 384
Aeneas, 326, 330
Agamemnon, 15, 62, 72, 76-77, 86, 101-102, 108, 113-116, 135, 137, 142, 221
Agapenor, 160, 221-222, 387
Ahhiyawa, 40, 45, 47-49, 54-60, 89, 91, 100, 102, 104, 114-115, 158, 368-371
Akhenaton, 22-23, 165, 217, 248
Akkadian, 14, 246
Akko, 291, 300
Akwash, 147-148, 151, 158-159
Alaksandus, 48-49, 87-89, 156
Alaksandus treaty, 87, 89
Alasia, 39-40, 184, 187, 205-206, 209, 211, 214-219, 228, 230, 234, 236, 386
Albright, W., 289, 336
Alt, Albrecht, 264-265, 289

Amarna letters, 206, 215, 217, 248, 265, 267-268, 276, 311, 359, 383, 386-387, 390, 395, 405
Ammurapi, 171, 187, 201
Amnisos, 155, 335
Amurru, 23, 27, 30, 43, 59, 91, 218, 243-246, 248, 265, 270, 288-290, 374, 406
Anatolia, 3-5, 7, 10, 13-14, 17-21, 25, 33-37, 42-43, 47, 51, 54-56, 59-61, 64, 70, 78-79, 88-90, 92, 97, 99, 102-105, 109, 114, 133-134, 152, 154-157, 160, 162-165, 170, 172-177, 179-184, 186, 188-193, 197-199, 201, 203, 206, 208, 220-222, 226-227, 230-232, 236-237, 246, 249, 258, 270, 290, 295, 298-299, 304, 307, 310-312, 316-317, 322, 325-327, 329, 332, 336-342, 355, 363-364, 368-375, 378, 384, 402
Anitta, 7, 9, 17, 20
Ankhesenamun, 44
Apasas, 35-36, 47, 60
Apiru, 265-267, 274-275
Apollo, 75, 104, 142-143
Arameans, 190, 270-271, 295, 315
Arcadia, 221-222
Argives, 57
Argos, 137, 382
Arinna, 41

409

Arnuwanda I, 37, 41, 175, 177, 206, 216
Arnuwanda III, 57, 192
Arzawa, 20, 31, 33-39, 42, 45-48, 55, 106, 156-157, 161, 169, 172, 179-180, 183, 191, 197, 302, 304, 371
Ashdod, 25, 290-292, 294, 316-318, 399
Ashkelon, 25, 242-244, 247, 290-292, 325, 396, 403
ashlar masonry, 211, 222-223, 227, 386
Ashtaroth, 330-331
Asmunikal, 42
Assyria, 10, 43, 49, 51-52, 56-57, 59, 73, 91-92, 174, 178, 186, 190, 193-194, 203, 246, 256, 270, 295, 342-345, 358, 372, 401, 406, 408
Astour, M., 230, 336
Athens, 3, 71, 108, 113, 120-123, 126, 128, 132, 137, 140, 200, 339-340, 343, 366-367, 386
Athribis stela, 150-151
Atlakvida, 68, 375
Atli, 68
Atpas, 55, 90
Attarissiyas, 37-40, 59, 103, 183-184, 206, 232
Attila, 68-69, 82
Aulis, 91-92
Avdo Mededovic, 67
Aziru, 218
Azitawadda, 184, 312, 326

B

Babylon, 7, 10, 20-21, 83, 215, 246, 256-257, 295, 306, 328, 344
Babylonia, 49, 186, 256, 358, 391, 408
barbarians, 14, 122, 127-129, 131, 133-134, 136, 337, 344

Battle of Kadesh, 5, 8, 33, 48-49, 51-52, 156, 163, 241, 326, 405
Benteshina, 23, 25
Beth Shan, 25, 290, 293-295, 328-329, 344, 353, 361, 401
Berbers, 167
Besik Bay, 93
Bethel, 252, 268
Beya, 118-119, 171
Bible, 8, 17-18, 62, 240-242, 245, 249, 251-254, 256-259, 261, 263, 265, 267-273, 275-276, 291, 298, 312, 314-315, 323, 326, 330, 332-333, 336, 344-345, 389-391, 393-395, 398, 401
Bichrome, 292-293, 299, 316, 318
Billigmeier, J. C., 229, 368, 384
Bittel, K., 169, 178
Blegen, Carl, 94, 97, 99, 123
Boar's tusk helmet, 80
Boeotia, 126
Boghazkoy, 17
Bosnia, 67
Breasted, C., 151
Bronze Age, 20, 24, 26, 28, 30, 32-36, 38, 40, 42, 44, 46, 48, 50, 52, 54, 56-58, 60, 62-66, 68-76, 78-82, 84-86, 88-96, 98, 100-106, 108-110, 112, 114-118, 120-124, 126, 128, 130-132, 134, 136-146, 148, 150, 152-162, 164-166, 168-170, 172, 174-176, 178, 180-184, 186, 188, 190-192, 194, 196-200, 202, 204-212, 214-216, 218-220, 222, 224, 226-232, 234, 236, 238, 240-242, 244-246, 248-254, 256, 258-260, 262, 264-266, 268, 270-272, 274, 276, 278, 280, 282, 284, 286, 288, 290, 292-

294, 296, 298, 300, 302-304, 306, 308, 310, 312, 314, 316, 318, 320, 322, 324-326, 328-330, 332-334, 336-340, 342, 344, 346-348, 350, 352, 354-355, 358, 360-362, 364, 366, 368, 370-374, 376-394, 396-402, 404, 406, 408, 410, 412, 414, 416, 418, 420
Brunhilde, 68-69
Bubonic Plague, 141, 143
Byblos, 218, 291, 317

C

Calchas, 183
Caleb, 276
Canaan, 3, 8, 18-19, 21-23, 25, 33, 99, 146, 184, 206, 209, 217-218, 220, 224, 232, 239-249, 251-253, 257-259, 261-265, 267-271, 273-275, 278, 288-291, 293-298, 310, 312-315, 317-320, 323-326, 330-331, 338, 344-345, 353, 355, 389-400, 402-406
Canaanites, 245, 247-248, 252-253, 259, 263-265, 267-269, 273, 275-277, 283, 315, 318, 327, 330, 355, 403
Canaanite Theory, 268-269
Caphtor, 298, 315-316, 326, 332-333, 336, 403
Catalog of Ships, 72, 82, 100, 377
Caucasian languages, 19
Celts, 133-134
Central Hill Country, 245-246, 249, 251-253, 259, 267-268, 274, 276-277, 344
chariotry, 26-27, 29-30, 46, 48, 53, 74-76, 149, 201

Cherethites, 333
Cilicia, 83, 180-184, 202, 204, 216, 224, 237, 302, 312, 330, 332
Cimmerians, 344
Classical period, 9-10, 14, 34-35, 57, 62, 65, 69, 71, 85-87, 96, 133-135, 156-157, 161-162, 170, 183, 200, 221-222, 224, 226, 229, 262, 304, 319-320, 323-325, 332, 340
Coarse Ware, 127-129, 132-133, 136, 176, 324
Colophon, 60, 183
Copper, 1, 3, 9, 114, 150, 153, 186, 193, 206-207, 209-212, 215-216, 228, 237-238, 259, 294, 304, 335, 343, 385
Corinth, 126, 131, 378
Corvee labor, 272
Crete, 3, 11, 15, 88, 109, 113, 128, 153, 155, 158-159, 167, 183, 186, 229, 236, 298, 316, 324, 329, 331-336, 342, 347, 380-381, 402, 404
Cuneiform, 7, 14, 17-18, 37, 52-53, 56, 58, 171, 196, 246, 258-259, 265, 270, 310, 329, 357
Cypria, 91-92, 96, 102
Cypro-Minoan, 205, 227, 229-231, 342, 384
Cyprus, 3, 8, 19-20, 39-40, 64, 80, 99, 113-114, 128, 137, 153, 156, 160, 169, 180-181, 184-190, 193, 203-232, 234-239, 249, 290, 292-293, 297-298, 302, 304, 306-308, 316-320, 322, 327, 329, 332, 335-336, 338-339, 342-344, 347, 353-354, 359-360, 363-365, 371, 379, 383-389, 402-404
Cyprus collapse, date, 212-215
Cyrenaica, 165

D

Dagon, 330-331
Dan, 25, 276, 312-313
Danaans, 57, 143, 311-312, 317, 335-336
Danuna, 311-314
Dardanelles, 92, 106
Dardanians, 89, 105-106, 262, 326
Dardanus, 262
dating, 80, 99, 117, 119-120, 123, 126, 156, 182, 196, 215, 236, 245, 249, 259, 270, 273, 293, 299, 348, 352, 368, 374, 380-381, 396, 398
David, 8, 251-254, 256, 258-259, 266, 275, 277, 296, 315, 326, 330, 333, 344
Deborah, 259, 274, 277, 313, 390, 393, 396-398
Demodocus, 63-64
destruction, 17-18, 45, 71, 86-87, 91-92, 96-103, 105, 108, 116, 119-123, 126-128, 130-133, 138, 144, 149, 162, 169-170, 172, 176, 178-180, 182, 187, 189, 191, 204-205, 207, 209-215, 217, 219-220, 222-223, 227, 231-232, 237-238, 241, 253, 272, 291-292, 318, 339, 341, 346, 380, 385
determinative, 244
Deuteronomy, 240, 256-258, 316
Dever, W., 251, 365, 392
Dionysus, hymn, 161
Documentary Hypothesis, 257-258
Dodona, 128, 136
Dothan, Moshe, 317
Dor, 291, 312, 344, 403
Dorian, 64, 85-86, 135-136, 222, 379-380, 382-383
Dorians, 64, 85, 135-136, 142, 222, 262, 339, 378
Dorpfeld, W., 93-94

E

Edom, 13, 271, 274, 364, 390, 393, 397
Edomites, 271, 276, 390
Egypt, 2-11, 15, 19-25, 27-30, 35-36, 42-44, 48-50, 52-53, 71, 83, 99, 101, 113, 141, 146-147, 149-165, 167-169, 171, 177, 180, 186, 189, 193-195, 197-199, 207-208, 215-218, 220, 228, 232, 234-235, 237, 241, 243-246, 248-249, 253, 256, 258-259, 261, 263, 267-268, 270-273, 275-276, 278-280, 283, 286, 288-291, 294-301, 303, 307, 310, 315, 317, 321-322, 324-325, 327, 329, 333-338, 340, 342-346, 355, 358, 363-364, 367, 384, 390, 393, 396, 398, 400-402, 404-406, 408
Ekron, 291-292, 392, 400, 402
Ekwesh, 158
Elazig, 178
El-names, 210, 268-269, 276-277
Emar, 270, 388, 397
Enkomi, 207, 211-212, 219-223, 225-226, 228-230, 235, 320, 360, 384-385, 388
Ephesus, 35-36, 47, 60
Epirus, 323, 380, 400
Ephraim, 249, 251-252, 262
Eshuwara, 188-189, 209
Eskisehir, 197
ethnic landscape, 10
Etzel, 68
Euboea, 128, 340
Ewir-Sharruma, 185

Exodus, 8, 240-241, 252-253, 256, 258, 261-262, 267, 269-270, 272-277, 390, 393-397

F

famine, 137, 139-145, 154-155, 163-165, 186, 194-198, 201, 270-271, 337-338, 407
feather headdress, 283, 298, 307, 327-330, 348, 352-355
Forrer, E., 58, 87, 104, 158
Fraktin, 170, 173

G

Galatians, 133
Galilee, 25, 244, 252, 344, 393
Game Box, 211, 232, 234-236, 297, 318, 327, 329, 347-348, 353-354
Gath, 291, 293, 326, 329-330
Gaza, 25, 245, 290-291, 293-294, 316, 344
Gelidonya shipwreck, 114
Genesis, 241, 256-257, 262, 269, 271, 276-277, 395
Gerizim, 276
Gezer, 242-244, 398
Gilgal, 252
Gla, 123
Goldman, H., 182
Goliath, 315, 326
Gordion, 172-174, 176, 179, 365, 369, 371, 373-374, 379
Goshen, 241, 271
Grain shipments, 199-201
Grave Circle, 112, 115, 122

Greece, 2-3, 8-11, 15-17, 19, 35, 57, 59-60, 62-64, 67, 70, 76, 82, 85-87, 91, 100-101, 103-104, 106, 108, 113-118, 120-121, 126-141, 143-145, 155, 167, 176, 186, 194, 204-208, 210, 220-222, 224, 226-227, 232, 235-238, 249, 258, 262, 292-293, 298-299, 302, 306-307, 312, 316-317, 320, 322-326, 329, 331, 334-340, 346, 353, 360, 366, 378-381, 383-385, 407-408
Greeks, 5, 15, 17, 19-20, 35, 37, 40, 42, 45, 48, 54-55, 57-58, 60-62, 65, 70-72, 74, 83-84, 88-92, 96-107, 109, 115, 131, 133-137, 143, 156-160, 165, 172-173, 176, 179, 182-184, 204, 220-224, 226-228, 231, 236-238, 262, 272, 294, 302, 304, 311, 316-320, 323, 325-326, 332, 336, 339-340, 342, 346, 378-379, 382, 386, 405
Gunnarr, 68-69
Gunther, 68-69
Gurney, O., 34
Gutterbock, H., 184, 371

H

Habiru, 265, 394, 396
Hakpis, 41-42, 50
Hala Sultan Tekke, 212
Halys River, 17, 51, 178
Handmade Ware, 127, 176, 191
Harran, 265, 270-271
Hatti, 25-27, 38-39, 41-43, 45-49, 51, 53-56, 89-90, 163, 169-171, 177-180, 195-197, 199-200, 202-203, 238, 242, 341, 359, 369, 372, 407

Hattusa, 17, 20, 23, 25, 33, 36-43, 48-53, 60, 89, 92, 125, 169-171, 174, 176-180, 184, 193-195, 197, 199-202, 215, 341, 370

Hattusili III, 49-52, 100, 192, 170, 216-217

headdress, 234-236, 283, 298, 307, 320, 327-330, 347-349, 352-355

Hebrew, 13, 265-268, 305

Hector, 66, 76-78, 83, 96-97, 106, 279

Herihor, 345

Herodotus, 10, 66, 86, 135, 161, 323, 355

hieroglyphic writing, 31, 155, 244, 283

Hissarlik hill, 92-93

Hittite, 5-8, 17-31, 33-51, 53-60, 73, 75, 77-78, 87-92, 98, 100, 102-107, 113, 115, 156-158, 160-164, 169-206, 215-217, 230-232, 234, 238, 270, 275, 295, 298, 302, 311-312, 325-326, 329, 341-342, 357-359, 368-375, 385, 398, 404

Hittite collapse date, 170-171

Hittites, 5-6, 8, 11, 13, 17-18, 20-21, 23, 25-31, 33-39, 41-43, 45-49, 51-61, 73, 77-78, 87-92, 98, 100, 104, 107-108, 114-115, 152, 156-157, 163-164, 169-180, 182, 185, 187-188, 190-194, 196-197, 200-203, 215-217, 219-220, 231-232, 234, 236-237, 243, 264-265, 275, 302, 307, 326-328, 332, 335, 341, 357-358, 368-374, 406, 408

Homer, 4-5, 8, 15, 17, 19, 42, 57-58, 61-75, 77, 79-83, 85, 87, 92, 99-102, 110, 158, 161, 180, 279, 304, 311, 323-324, 340, 357-358, 363, 375-377, 379, 381, 389, 402

Horites, 18

Horned God, 212, 226, 304

Horus Road, 246, 290

hunger, 38, 192, 194-195, 198, 270, 407

Hurrians, 8, 13, 36, 228, 230, 266, 328

I

Iasos, 60

Ibrahim Pasha, 83

ibrim, 265-266

Iliad, 8, 19, 42, 57-58, 62-67, 69-85, 87-89, 91-93, 96-106, 108, 114-116, 123, 131, 137, 142-143, 156, 158-159, 172, 175, 179, 207, 221, 304, 311, 323, 326, 357, 373, 375-377

Ilios, 87, 89, 96, 102, 104-105

Illyria, 299, 307, 323-326, 331

Illyrian Theory, 323-324

Indian names, 19

Indictment of Madduwatta, 37, 40, 183

Indo-European languages, 15, 17-19, 374

Iolkos, 108, 123, 126, 132, 137

Iron Age, 1, 8-9, 64, 74, 76, 85, 141, 244-245, 249, 251-252, 254, 258-259, 271, 294, 305, 329, 333, 364, 368, 371, 373-374, 378, 384-385, 389-390, 392-395, 397-399, 402

iron, 1-2, 8-10, 64-65, 73-74, 76, 85, 136, 141, 206, 238, 244-245, 249, 251-252, 254, 258-259, 269, 271, 277, 294, 305, 329, 333, 339, 363-364, 368, 371, 373-374, 378, 384-385, 388-390, 392-395, 397-399, 402

Israel, 8, 164, 240-245, 247, 249-254, 256-271, 273, 275-278, 291-292, 298, 312-313, 315-316, 328, 344-345, 364-367, 389-399, 403

Israel stela, 164, 242, 396

J

Jacob, 241, 261-263, 271, 275-277
Jashar, 257
Jericho, 241, 252, 394, 398
Jerusalem, 9, 18, 249, 256, 265, 274-275, 296, 344-346, 402
Jethro, 273
Jones, William, 16
Jordan, 19, 25, 118, 241, 244-246, 252-253, 263, 269, 271, 274, 293, 295, 344, 363-364, 366, 370, 379, 390, 393-395, 397, 402
Joseph, 241, 261, 271, 275, 337, 393, 396
Joshua, 240, 252-253, 256, 263, 265, 275-277, 394, 396, 398
Josiah, 257
Judah, 252, 256-257, 276, 344-345, 389, 394-395
Judea, 256
Judges, 65, 213, 251-253, 274-276, 296, 314, 391-392, 398

K

Kadesh, 5, 8, 13, 21-31, 33, 43, 48-53, 75, 105, 146, 156, 163, 169, 178, 206, 232, 236, 241, 246, 248-249, 253, 264, 281, 299-302, 321, 326, 357, 370, 405-406
Kantir, 23, 241
Kalavassos, 208-209, 223, 238
Karageorghis, Vassos, 210, 224
Karatepe, 184, 312
Kargamish, 21, 31, 43-46, 170-171, 177-180, 186-187, 190, 194, 198, 202-203, 216, 310, 341
Karnak, 43, 52-53, 147, 149-153, 158, 163, 247, 264, 311, 396, 406
Kaska people, 33, 40-42, 50, 170, 177-179
Kaska Theory, 178
Kayseri, 178, 197
Keftiu, 333-336, 368, 403
Kenites, 273, 397
Kenizzites, 276
Keper, 279
Khufu, 7, 167
Kinnereth, 245, 249
Kisnapili, 38
Kition, 207-208, 212, 219, 223, 229, 342, 386
Kling, B., 213, 364, 386-387
Knossos, 15, 20, 88, 113, 155, 183, 229, 334-335, 368
Konya, 197
Korfmann, M., 94
Kosovo, 82, 272
Kukunnis, 88
Kupanta-Runta, 38
Kurunta, 51, 170, 192-194, 201
Kutmuhi, 174

L

Labayu, 274-275
Land Battle, 186, 281-284, 288-290, 300-301, 320, 332, 340
Laomedon, 97-98, 105
Lawazanda, 202
Lawazantiya, 50-51, 202-203
Lazpas, 35, 48, 90, 104
Lefkandi, 128

Lesbos, 35, 48, 90, 104, 161
Libyans, 12, 15, 146-147, 149-154, 156, 163, 165-168, 180, 182, 236, 242, 278-281, 283, 286, 289, 299, 325, 327, 332, 345, 347, 404-406
Libu, 147, 149, 165, 167, 279
Linear A, 15
Linear B, 15, 17-18, 57, 64, 66, 78-79, 87-88, 108-109, 113, 115, 117, 121, 123-124, 138, 183, 226, 229, 317, 339, 368, 378, 380
Luka, 147-148, 151, 155-156
Lukka, 31, 33-34, 37-38, 40, 46-47, 54-56, 114, 156-157, 159-160, 163-164, 188, 191, 198, 206, 234, 355, 369
Lunadushu, 187, 310
Luvian, 18, 35, 88, 106-107, 156-157, 184, 230-231, 304, 312, 326
Luvian language, 35, 106, 157, 230, 326
Luxor, 28-29, 44, 53, 147, 236, 279, 281, 301, 391
Lycaonia, 157
Lycia, 34, 114, 156-157, 159
Lycians, 156, 159, 355, 369
Lydia, 34, 157, 161, 375

M

Maa, 210, 214
Macedonia, 128, 380
Madduwatta, 37-41, 47, 59, 179, 183-184, 206, 232, 326, 357, 370
Malatya, 170, 341
Manapa-Tarhunda, 89-91, 98, 104
Manasseh, 249, 251-252, 262, 274, 276
Mari, 215, 265, 311, 328, 352, 393, 404
Marsa Matruh, 153, 404, 406
Masat, 170, 173, 373
Masoretic text, 257
Maspero, Gaston, 168, 289, 297
Mazar, A., 317
Medinet Habu, 161, 166, 169, 171, 180-181, 215, 236, 279-281, 283, 288-290, 297-299, 302-304, 307-311, 315, 317, 319-321, 323-325, 327, 331-332, 334, 347-348, 353-354, 359-360, 405-407
Megaron, 109-110, 112, 123, 226, 317
Megiddo, 25, 248, 290, 294-295, 360, 395
Mendenhall, G., 267
Menelaion, 123, 127, 378
Menelaus, 104, 106, 113, 115, 123
Merneptah, 146-147, 149-155, 159, 163-165, 180, 182, 186-187, 193, 195, 234, 237, 242-244, 247, 249, 263, 271, 278-281, 283, 299, 325, 338, 357, 374, 389, 397, 406
Merneptah stela, 164, 242-244, 263
Meryey, 147, 149-151, 153-154
Mesher, 279
Meshwesh, 147, 150, 153, 165, 167, 279, 345, 406
Mesopotamia, 3-7, 10, 14, 20, 235, 328, 331, 342, 348-349, 352, 355, 399
Midianites, 273
Midea, 123, 130, 378
migrations, 16, 79, 134, 172, 231, 270, 299, 312, 337, 339, 355, 364, 378-380
Milawata, 35, 369
Millawanda, 35, 37, 45, 48-49, 54-56, 59, 90, 92, 164, 226
Miletus, 35-36, 45, 60, 90, 226
Mira, 48
Mita, 175-176
Mitanni, 8, 18, 20, 22, 42-43, 51, 73, 169

Moab, 364, 392, 395, 397
Monochrome, 292-293, 299, 316-318
Mopsus, 182-184, 325
Mukish, 43, 180, 185-186, 195, 204, 340
Mumin Vlahovljak, 67
Mursili II, 23, 27, 45, 49, 89, 357, 371
Musgebi, 60
Mushki people, 174-176
Muwatalli II, 48, 177, 202
Mycenae, 15, 19, 60, 62, 80-81, 108, 110, 112-116, 121-123, 126-127, 130-131, 137-138, 222, 235, 304, 316, 320, 335, 339, 377, 379-380, 382-383, 389, 407
Mycenaean, 15, 17, 19, 37, 40, 45, 48, 54, 56, 58-62, 64-65, 69, 78-79, 85-86, 99, 108-109, 112-121, 123, 125-130, 132, 134-137, 139, 141, 143-144, 172, 182, 206-209, 211-214, 220, 222-226, 238, 292, 304, 316-318, 324, 353, 365-366, 369, 371-373, 377-387, 389, 400, 402-403, 406, 408
Mycenaeans, 8, 15, 65, 76, 78, 80, 114, 117, 127, 131, 135-136, 363, 365, 369, 379-383, 385, 402
Mysia, 34
Mysians, 175, 179

N

Narmer, 7, 9, 20
Negbi, O., 223, 381, 388, 402
Neolithic Period, 2-3, 9, 128
Nergal, 216, 228, 304-305
Nerik, 41-42, 50
Nestor's cup, 81-82
Nibelunglied, 68
niello, 208

Nile River, 14, 281
Niwall, 39
Nora Stone, 305
North West Semitic, 13-14, 228, 231, 245, 268
Nubia, 147-149, 154, 273, 295, 345
Nuzi, 265-266, 329-330, 401

O

O'Carolan, 70
Odyssey, 8, 57-58, 62-71, 78-79, 85-87, 92, 96, 101-102, 110, 123, 155, 158-159, 172, 311, 324, 358, 377, 381, 402
Old Paphos, 212, 219, 342, 387
Onomasticon, 291
oral transmission, 63, 72, 86, 135
Orchomenos, 108, 123, 126
Orontes River, 25, 28, 185, 340

P

Palaic language, 10, 18
Pamphylia, 181, 183
Paphos, 212, 219, 221, 342, 387
Papyrus Anastasi, 241, 271
Papyrus Harris, 278, 289, 299, 359, 405
Parry, M., 66-68
Parsons, James, 16
Patroclus, 73, 76-78
Pelasgians, 323-324, 402
Peleset, 283, 298, 319
Pelethites, 333
Peloponnese, 64, 108, 115, 123, 125, 128, 131, 134-136, 140, 142, 221, 339
Perati, 128, 380
Persian empire, 342-343
Petrie, Flinders, 242

Pgn, 189, 214, 343

Phaistos, 347

Philistine, 290-291, 293-294, 296, 299, 313, 315-320, 322-333, 344, 347, 391, 395, 399-404

Philistines, 277, 283, 290-295, 298-299, 304, 307, 310, 312-327, 329-333, 335, 338, 344, 347, 378, 390, 392, 398-405, 407

Phrygians, 172-176, 179, 191, 341-342, 368

Phrygian Theory, 172-174, 178

Pisidia, 157

Pithom, 241, 397

Pitkhana, 7, 9, 17

Piyama-Radu, 54-55, 59-60, 90-91, 106, 156, 179, 184, 371

Plague, 5, 137, 141-144, 194, 216, 237, 337, 407

Poseidon, 98, 103, 105

pottery, 2-3, 17, 19, 60, 93, 96-97, 99-100, 106, 110, 113, 115-121, 123, 125-129, 132-133, 136, 153, 172-176, 181-182, 206-209, 211-215, 218-219, 222-229, 231, 236, 238, 244, 249, 253, 259, 265, 268-270, 274, 292-293, 299, 302, 316-319, 321-324, 327-328, 332, 339-340, 343-344, 347, 353-354, 372-374, 378-379, 381-384, 386-389, 391, 393, 398-400, 403

Priam, 62, 87-88, 92-93, 98, 103, 105-107, 172, 279, 377, 381, 383

Pudu-Hepa, 6, 18, 50-53, 182, 195, 202-203, 217

Pylos, 15, 62, 87, 108, 112-113, 115, 123-126, 131-132, 134, 316, 378, 380, 382

R

Rachel tribes, 252, 262

Rainey, A., 266

Ramesses II, 5, 23, 30, 146, 152, 157, 163, 165, 195, 236, 241-242, 247-248, 264, 273-274, 278-279, 281, 288, 290, 299-300, 302, 321, 374, 391, 394, 405-406

Ramesses III, 151, 165, 169, 171, 204, 215, 236, 263, 274, 279-281, 289-291, 293-295, 297, 299-300, 302-303, 321, 325, 338, 345, 405

Ramesses IV, 293-294

Ramesses VI, 294

Ramesses IX, 300, 345

Ramesses X, 294, 345

Ras Ibn Hani, 2233, 343

Rekhmire, 335

Rib Hadda, 268, 299

Roland, 79, 83

S

Sagalassos, 160, 404

Salamis, 212, 221, 404

Samaria, 249

Samos, 60, 86

Samuha, 42, 50, 178

Sangarius River, 172

Sardinia, 299, 304-306, 310, 322, 329, 343, 354

Sardis, 304

Sargon, 7, 13, 344, 372

Saul, 254, 266, 277, 315, 326, 344

Schaeffer, Claude, 189, 211

Schliemann, Heinrich, 15, 81, 92, 112-113, 222

Scorpion, 7, 9
Scythians, 344
Sea Battle, 184-185, 190, 234, 284, 286-288, 299-300, 302-304, 306, 320-322
Sea Peoples, 8, 32, 146-159, 161-165, 167, 172, 180-191, 193, 198, 204, 209, 212, 220-221, 223, 225, 227-229, 231-232, 234-239, 242, 270, 278-284, 286-301, 308-316, 320-325, 327, 329-332, 338, 343, 347, 354-355, 384, 387, 392, 397-406
Sea Peoples in Canaan, date, 291-294
Seha River Land, 34, 47-48, 54-57, 89-91, 104, 106, 161, 164, 179, 193, 197, 302, 304
Seir, 273-274, 390
Semites, 11, 14, 271, 228, 230, 307, 327
Semitic languages, 13-14, 268
Septuagint text, 256, 315-316
Serbia, 82
Seti I, 23, 165, 241, 247, 275, 278
Seti II, 118, 278
Setnakht, 278-279
Seventh City, 98, 100, 103
Shasu people, 263, 265, 271, 273, 274
Shechem, 252, 274-277, 391, 396-398
Shekelesh, 147-148, 151, 159-160, 187, 191, 283, 298, 310, 319, 325, 406
Sherdan, 24, 31, 147-148, 281, 284, 290-291, 298-308, 310, 312, 320, 322, 325, 327
Shikila, 187, 190, 234
Shiloh, 251-252, 397
Shipibaal, 202
Shishak, 345
Shubarti, 177
Sicily, 113, 210, 299, 310-311, 322
Sikils, 187, 310-312, 314, 318-319, 330

Sile, 288, 290
Sinai, 245, 252-253, 258-259, 263, 270, 272-274, 276, 294, 345, 390, 398
Sinda, 212, 385
Siptah, 278
Sixth City, 7, 96-98, 100, 291
Siyanta River, 39
Skyros, 321
Slavs, 133-134
Smailagic' Meho, 68
Smiting God, 211, 224-226, 304
Solomon, 241, 256, 258, 275, 277, 345
Song of Deborah, 259, 268, 274, 277
Song of the Sea, 259, 268, 272
Sparta, 85-86, 103-104, 123, 127, 378-379
Strymon River, 323-324
Sumur, 218
Suppiluliuma I, 42-45, 170-171, 178
Suppiluliuma II, 57, 169, 171, 184, 192, 194, 209, 217

T

Tarhuntassa, 50-51, 170, 192, 194, 197, 199-203, 341
Tarsa, 162
Tarsus, 162-163, 170, 182
Taruisa, 105, 160
Tawagalawa letter, 54, 59, 90, 106
Tehenu, 242, 280
Tell er-Rabata, 241
Tell Qasile, 317, 401
Tenedos, 142
Teuthrania, 91
Teukrians, 221-222, 308-309
Teukros, 161, 221-222

Thebes, 15, 22-23, 108, 115, 123, 137, 147-148, 242, 279, 295, 306, 321, 333, 343, 345
Theogony, 161
theophoric names, 4
Theory of Tribes, 261
Thrace, 323-324, 373, 377
Thucydides, 10, 135, 161, 310
Tiglath-Pileser I, 174-175, 270, 341
Timur, 130-131, 134
Tiryns, 108, 115, 122-123, 126-128, 130-131, 137, 159, 321, 339, 382-383
Tjeker, 283, 291, 298, 307-312, 318-319, 330, 353
Tjeku, 271
Tomb 18, 222-224
Toumba tou Skourou, 209, 389
tribes, 25, 33, 130, 241, 244, 249-250, 252-253, 256, 259, 261-263, 271, 276-277, 279, 312, 314, 327, 344, 393, 396-398
Trojan cycle, 69, 96, 100, 180
Trojan War, 8, 20, 62-63, 69, 71-72, 79-80, 82-83, 85-89, 91-92, 94-95, 97-98, 100, 102-103, 105, 114, 127, 133, 135, 137, 158-160, 172, 183, 221-222, 308, 310, 330, 342, 366, 375, 378
Tros, 105, 262
Trojans, 20, 74, 76, 89, 92, 96, 101, 104-107, 160-161, 262, 375, 377-378
Troy, 7, 15, 17, 20, 35-36, 42, 62-67, 69-73, 75-79, 81-107, 115, 119-120, 123, 125, 128, 131, 152, 156, 160, 172, 175-176, 179-180, 183, 221, 272, 279, 317, 323, 366, 371, 375-378, 381
Tudhaliya II, 37, 41, 59, 102, 104, 156, 177

Tudhaliya IV, 56, 59, 91, 100, 157, 164, 177, 184, 192-193, 375
Tukulti-Ninurta, 174
Tunip, 300
Turkey, 10, 67, 83, 114, 196-199, 370, 373, 407-408
Tursha, 147-148, 151, 155, 160-162, 182, 325
Tushratta, 19, 73
Tutankhamon, 6, 23, 44, 73, 303
Twosert, 118-119, 278
Tyre, 189, 218, 245, 311, 329, 343-344, 355
Tyrrhenian Sea Theory, 310

U

Ugarit, 11, 20, 31, 43, 118, 132, 157, 170-171, 180, 185-190, 194-196, 198-199, 201-202, 204-205, 209-211, 214-216, 220, 223-224, 228-229, 231-232, 234-235, 238, 245, 249, 269, 290, 299, 304-307, 310-311, 328-329, 332, 335, 338, 343, 353-354, 359-360, 365-366, 368, 370, 375, 383-385, 387-389, 396
Uhha-Ziti, 45-48, 60, 156, 179
Ulu Burun shipwreck, 207, 303
Ur, 7, 328, 348-349, 354
Ura, 51, 157, 186, 195, 199-200, 368
Urhi-Tesub, 18, 49-51, 54, 89-91, 192, 216-217, 372
Urkesh, 348
Ur-Nammu, 6
Urumi, 177, 179

V, W

Ventris, Michael, 15
Wachsmann, S., 389, 403-404, 406
Wadi Tumilat, 241, 271
Walmu, 56-57, 98, 100
Warrior Vase, 80, 112, 138, 222, 224, 304, 320
Wassukkanni, 42-43
Weippert, Manfred, 266
Wen Amon, 291, 343, 345
Weshesh, 283, 298, 312
Wilios, 87, 104
Wilusa, 34, 48-49, 54-57, 87-91, 104-105, 172, 193, 197, 371
writing, 3, 7-10, 14-15, 17-18, 31, 56-58, 60, 63-64, 66-68, 70-71, 78, 86-87, 126, 128, 154-155, 160, 172, 178, 188, 204, 207, 214-215, 218, 226-227, 229, 244, 253, 258-260, 283, 297, 305, 310, 317, 329-330, 336, 339, 342, 347, 381, 391, 395

X, Y, Z

Xanthus, 161, 325
Xenophon, 332
Yadin, Y., 312
Yahweh, 257, 267-268, 270, 273-274, 276-277, 314, 316, 390, 394
Yenoam, 243-244
Zahi, 288-289
Zannanza, 44
Zertal, A., 274
Zippasla, 37-38
Zitriyara, 248

0-595-13664-8

Printed in the United States
40911LVS00003B